# The
# STREAM
# TONE

## *The Future of*
## *Personal Computing?*

4MSG♥

# COLOPHON

*The small print*

**TITLE:** The STREAM TONE: The Future of Personal Computing? **AUTHOR:** T. Gilling **WEBSITE:** www.TheStreamTone.com **ISBN-13:** 978-1-78462-081-3 (paperback) 978-1-78462-086-8 (hardback) **COPYRIGHT:** Copyright © 2014 T. Gilling. All rights reserved. No part of this publication may be copied, displayed, distributed, modified, reproduced, stored in a retrieval system, used, or transmitted in any form by any means electronic, mechanical, photocopying, recording, or otherwise without the prior written permission of the author. **PUBLISHER:** Matador, Troubador Publishing Limited, 9 Priory Business Park, Wistow Road, Kibworth Beauchamp, Leicestershire, LE8 0RX, United Kingdom. Telephone: (+44) 116 279 2299 Fax: (+44) 116 279 2277 Email: books@troubador.co.uk Website: www.troubador.co.uk/matador **LIMITATIONS:** This book documents the author's personal understanding of a wide range of third-party concepts, entities, ideas, laws, methods, practices, processes, products, regulations, services, techniques, technologies, thinking, and tools; collectively referred to as the Subjects in the following text. The principle source of information on the Subjects was the World Wide Web (Web). Some of this information was obtained from publicly accessible information sources that were specifically designed to advertise or explain the Subjects, and some was obtained from other publicly accessible information sources, such as academic research paper repositories, government Web sites, news Web sites, regulatory Web sites, Web logs, and the Wikipedia Web site. Some of these sources have been recorded within this book, in the form of links to further reading materials, and others have not. Many Web-based information sources change rapidly and it may be necessary to use the Wayback Machine of the Internet Archive with a search date prior to the publication date of this book in order to find the exact same information on the Subjects as that which was used in the preparation of this book. Information obtained from the Web is often contradictory, inaccurate, open to subjective interpretation, and unverifiable. Consequently, the author's understanding of the Subjects, as documented in this book, may be incorrect or incomplete. Upon a number of occasions the author has made reasonable assumptions relating to the Subjects, and such assumptions have not been explicitly noted. The accuracy of information presented in this book must, therefore, be verified in other information sources before it is used. This book also contains speculation based on the author's personal understanding of the Subjects in respect of a theoretical concept, created by the author, known as the Stream Tone. The Subjects were selected based on their apparent ability to support a speculative exploration of this concept, and the author does not endorse or recommend any of the Subjects beyond this particular use. The author has not received any type of compensation from any of the Subjects in return for including the Subjects within this book. The author has, in the past, made use of products and services provided by some of the Subjects, and which the author is likely to make use of again, in the future, on a non-preferential basis. The author is not an official spokesperson for any of the Subjects. The author has attempted to describe the Subjects accurately, fairly, positively, and respectfully. In general, Subject descriptions are minimal and are focused on aspects that appear to support an exploration of the Stream Tone concept. Subject descriptions vary in detail and structure from Subject to Subject. The objective of this book is to provoke thoughtful consideration of the Stream Tone concept, and to catalyse community-based development activities associated with this concept. Any implementation of the Stream Tone may substantially differ from the version of the Stream Tone described within this book. No guarantees are implied or offered that any of the benefits attributed to the Stream Tone within this book can actually be realised. **DISCLAIMER:** No warranty is given by the author or publisher of this publication as to the accuracy or completeness of the information contained herein and neither the author nor the publisher shall be liable or responsible for any damage or loss whatsoever arising by virtue of such information or any advice or instructions contained within this publication or by any of the aforementioned. **INTELLECTUAL PROPERTY MARKS:** All intellectual property marks, including certification marks, registered names, service marks, trade marks, trade names, etc., referenced within this publication are the property of their respective owners. **EDITING:** United Kingdom English spelling and the Oxford Comma grammatical convention have been applied throughout this book, except for quoted third-party materials and uniform resource identifiers which are presented verbatim. **ERRATA:** Any errata relating to this book will be published on the www.TheStreamTone.com Web site, at the sole discretion of the author. Readers are encouraged to check regularly for errata.

*British Library Cataloguing in Publication Data: A catalogue record for this book is available from the British Library.*

# DEDICATION

*With thanks*

The person that I am today, the person that has written this book, has been, to a very large extent, created by some of the many people that have touched my life. People that have loved me, educated me, believed in me, supported me, and at one time or another that have shown me endless patience and understanding. What I am today is because of you. I am immensely grateful. At a personal level, this book is dedicated to you. Thank you.

A.J.C., D.H.E., F.S.C., G.R.C., I.F.C., J.R.G., L.M.C., M.T.C.Y., M.S.G., N.P.C., S.S., W.M.C.

Few inventions in the modern world are wholly unique. Mankind rarely starts with a totally clean slate when a new device or concept is required. New inventions are nearly always based on existing technologies to some greater or lesser degree. Since the printed word allowed descendants to learn from their forebears we have built on that which went before. We learn from the past. We take the best and make it better. We discard that which we do not need. Long has it been thus. We all now stand on the shoulders of giants.[1] Everything we are, and everything we will be, we owe to those that went before us. This book, and the ideas contained within it, could not exist if it were not for all the people that have directly and indirectly invented the modern world in which we all now live. This book builds on many of their ideas and inventions and it is only right and proper to both acknowledge that fact and to offer thanks for their invaluable contributions. At a professional level, this book is dedicated to all those that have helped to invent our most wonderful modern world and by so doing have given us the platform and tools to build an even better future. Thank you.

---

[1] Some of the earliest references to building upon the work of others can be found in the following texts: "Jacula Prudentum", published in 1651 by George Herbert; "Letter to Robert Hooke", written in 1676 by Isaac Newton; "The Anatomy of Melancholy", published in 1621 by Robert Burton; "The Friend", published in 1828 by Samuel Taylor Coleridge.

# CONTENTS

*Stock-in-trade*

# 0   PROLOGUE

*A dream of Elysium*[2]

a)   This book is based on my observations of the technology world, made over many years. It discusses how certain technologies could be combined to yield a world changing result, and why current trends in both society and technology may allow that to happen far sooner than you might have thought possible.

b)   I have no special inside knowledge that what I am suggesting will actually come to pass, I am simply reading between the lines, putting two and two together, and coming up with what I think is a logical conclusion. It's all an educated guess, really. Of course history may well conspire against me on this matter, in which case my prognostications will simply serve as a sad reminder of opportunities missed and the world will probably be a poorer place for that.

c)   We already live in a science fiction world. Young people that have grown up with computers in their lives, right from the beginning, probably do not realise just how fantastic the world has become. Older folks, that experienced the world before computers, and the arrival of the Internet and the Web, know different. We truly appreciate the impacts, both good and bad, and we can see the bigger picture of how the world has changed, and continues to change.

d)   I have recently seen that certain key building blocks are now available, which could be aggregated in a particular way to give a unique result. In fact, from a certain perspective, the technology that I envision already exists, in various nascent forms, and can be experienced today; it is just a mouse-click away. However, what exists today is but a small taste of the full solution. With a bit more effort and refinement it can be real. It is so very close.

e)   Why do we need this new thing? Because the constant change that we have experienced over the last thirty or so years, the change that we pay for in terms of both time and money again and again and again has to stop, or, at the very least, markedly slow down. We need a period of quiescence and stability in which logical consolidation and refinement can start to take place. Not technological stagnation; simply a change of focus such that progress can still be made, possibly at an even more accelerated rate, but in a way that does not unnecessarily inconvenience, or burden, each and every user of that technology.

f)   The irony, that to stop the constant change that we have all been experiencing will need one more change, is not lost on me. It is also not lost on me that our modern technology-oriented world is a bit like a giant ocean-going super-tanker; it does not stop or alter course easily. So, even if my foretelling is deemed to have merit and make good sense in theory, the world may be so set on its current technological heading that it just sails on by, leaving my utopian vision undiscovered and unexplored; like a tropical island paradise tantalisingly glimpsed on the horizon that will never be a port of call. I am, however, cautiously optimistic; the signs are, in many ways, quite favourable. This book might be

---

[2] *Not the 2013 film but the true utopia; the place of ideal happiness and trouble-free life.*

the blueprint for a better future, or it might just be a strange new form of science fiction; only the future knows.

# 0.1    AUDIENCE

*Suitable for everyone*

a)    This book has an easy-going style that does not assume that the reader is some sort of egg head or rocket scientist. It should, therefore, be suitable for almost anyone that has an interest in what might come next in the world of personal computing. Most of the subject matter is explained in enough detail that even a technical novice should be able to understand what is being discussed. Of course, some of the subjects touched upon in this book are actually pretty complex but the reader really does not need to understand any of that complexity in order to enjoy this book. For readers that wish to better understand some of the more complex subjects, references to supporting materials have been provided.

# 0.2    INCEPTION

*From a tiny acorn ...*

a)    At one point in the 1956 MGM film, "Forbidden Planet", Dr Edward Morbius takes Commander John J. Adams and Lieutenant "Doc" Ostrow on a tour of the Great Machine of the Krell; a vast cube-shaped underground complex, 20 miles on a side, that was powered by thousands of nuclear reactors, and which was buried deep within the planet known as Altair IV. The Great Machine was capable of making thoughts real, by creating matter from energy. It was the last great achievement of the Krell, who were then apparently destroyed by their own subconscious thoughts,[3] which had been made real by their incredible new invention. It is a sad and cautionary tale, to be sure, and one that we would do well to heed as we race ever quicker towards our own technological utopia; the Singularity.[4] I have always been impressed by that machine; not by the fact that it ended up inadvertently destroying its creators, but by its shear size and ability. Whilst I fully appreciate that this is merely a film that I am talking about, I still wonder how any civilization might get to the point where it can build a machine that is 8,000 cubic miles in size, and, more importantly, why don't we have one? It looked very useful, even if that particular one was, in the end, rather dangerous.

b)    I had not thought about that film for many years, and it was not until I recently completed some professional studies that I was somehow reminded of it again. The studies focused, in some detail, on computer data centres. The data centres that I read about reminded me of the Great Machine; but they were of course so much smaller, had much less electricity

---

[3] *It was theorised by Sigmund Freud that the Id, Ego, and Super-Ego were functions of the mind. The Id was thought to be the source of bodily desires, impulses, needs, and wants, particularly those relating to aggression and sex. So whilst most people might have the outward appearance of being well-balanced and civilised, inside they were a seething mass of dark emotion, and which, in the case of the Krell, the Great Machine let loose upon their world, causing them to perish in a single terrible night. {Dramatic electronic tonalities play. Fade to black.}*
[4] *The hypothetical point when artificial intelligence becomes greater than human intelligence, beyond which human history becomes highly unpredictable.*

arcing over head, and were sadly unable to realise human thought. Nevertheless, it was still possible to see their potential for greatness, how they could evolve, grow, and improve to become so much more than they are today. How they could become our own Great Machines of tomorrow. I did not dwell on the matter long; it was just a brief consideration of the funny way that life could potentially imitate art. Sometime later, I started to read about the technology of Web-based gaming services that worked by streaming computer games over the Internet. These services ran games on powerful computer servers housed in remotely-located data centres, which then sent the game audio and video to a distant game player. The player only needed a good Internet connection and a relatively low-performance personal computing device in order to access computationally-demanding three-dimensional photorealistic games, because all the hard work had already been done in the data centre. It made me realise that the data centre was becoming the very best place to run almost all digital services, even highly demanding ones like computer games, and that devices to access such services could become very simple and cheap. It was a personal epiphany, my "Aha!" moment, when everything finally became clear, when I truly grasped what now seems so obvious. The way that we did personal computing could change. Should change. Must change. Not just for the sake of yet another change in our perpetually changing world but because it could potentially bring real benefit to everyone, everywhere. Of course, I was not the first to have such a realisation; in fact, many multi-million dollar businesses are already based on similar ideas, so in many ways I was just catching up. Still, it affected me profoundly, as personal epiphanies tend to do. So much so, in fact, that I decided to write this book. I felt that something was still missing from all the Web-based personal computing solutions that currently existed, and I had an idea what that might be. That is what this book is about, the missing stuff, the conceptual and technological glue that would unite what we have today, and turn it into the personal computing paradigm of tomorrow.

c)  So, how do we get to the point where we can have an 8,000 cubic mile-sized data centre? Well, I strongly suspect that it is not going to be by everyone on the planet having their own little pocket-sized computer. It is going to happen by consolidating all of our data processing resources into giant, super-efficient, data centres that use techniques such as broad network access, on-demand self-service, measured service, multi-tenancy, rapid elasticity, and resource pooling to intelligently and cost-effectively meet all of our personal computing needs. Such concentrated data processing power can either serve up a lot of Web pages, as it mainly does today, or perhaps it can do something really exciting tomorrow, like make our thoughts real, although with hopefully much less subconsciously-induced self-destruction. Of course I am being somewhat facetious[5] here, but I am sure you get the point. To put it all very simply, big machines can do big things, when required. Little machines, even if you have a lot of them all linked together, just can't compete; the network eventually gets in the way, adds overhead, and dilutes the potential. So we need to start moving away from our current world of individual personal computing devices if we are ever going to get to a point where we can build our own Great Machine.

d)  Of course the idea behind the Stream Tone is not about building a Great Machine per se, even though that would be very cool, and probably very useful. It is actually about creating a personal computing future based wholly on data streaming. The Stream Tone concept is based on the simple and straightforward idea that the modern data centre can

---

[5] *Playfully jocular or humorous.*

stream, on-demand, all the digital content and services that we require over the Internet, and that a device to access such streams can be very, very simple, and very, very affordable. The Stream Tone can deliver many benefits, and if one should just happen to be a Great Machine at some point in the future, then all well and good. However, for the here and now, the focus of the Stream Tone is much more sensible and realistic; building a better and more affordable approach to personal computing through the use of data streaming technologies.

# 0.3    NOMENCLATURE

*What's in a name?*

a)   It might seem a little bit weird but sometimes new things do not need a name. This is especially true when the new thing is just a simple variant of something that already exists and already has a unique name of its own. For example, if you invented something that looked like a pink crocodile you could simply refer to it as the Pink Crocodile. You are not required by some mysterious law of the universe to give it its own unique name like a Pinkodile or a Crocopink. Well, not unless you work in some sort of madly-stereotypical marketing department.

b)   Sometimes new things can simply be identified by referencing their various attributes, such as their behaviour, colour, components, construction, function, material, shape, state, or use. Such as an airtight, durable, and lightweight spherically-shaped rubber bladder that can be filled with pressurised air through a self-sealing valve until it is taut, at which point it can then be used for individual play or team-oriented sports. However, when you plan to refer to that new thing innumerable times in a book, it is probably best to give it a nice catchy little name, like a football.[6] It just makes life so much simpler for author and reader alike. So, given that the concept discussed in this book really has way too many attributes to repeatedly list in such a manner it was decided that it should be given a name of its own; the Stream Tone.

c)   The Stream Tone name is based on a commonly used telecommunications term; the Dial Tone. In simple terms, the Dial Tone is the low-frequency noise that you hear when you pick up an old-fashioned telephone handset; it indicates that the handset is correctly connected to a telephony infrastructure, and is ready and able to make a telephone call.

d)   Another term that was also based on the Dial Tone concept is the Web Tone. The Web Tone is a telecommunications signal that provides immediate and continuous access to the Internet when it is connected to a suitable interface device. Today, the term has generally fallen into disuse.

e)   The Stream Tone will use a type of digital telecommunications known as data streaming, where data is sent continuously and a receiving device is able to immediately process that data and present it to a user with almost no delay. The Stream Tone will be a communications protocol that provides access to new and existing Web-based content and services via the Internet. The Stream Tone will enable the creation of a whole new

---

[6] *For those divided by the common language of English, also known as a soccer ball.*

technology ecosystem.

f) Given its nature and purpose, the Stream Tone name seems apt, easily explainable, easily understandable, and is, most importantly, memorable.

# 0.4  ASSUMPTION

*Making a donkey...*

a) Every prediction contains certain assumptions; such as that an envisioned product will be wanted, that it can actually be built, or that it is in some discernible way going to be much better than the established norm. The Stream Tone is no different, but in amongst its many assumptions is a single big one:

b) *That wired and wireless telecommunications will become highly affordable, high bandwidth, low latency, highly reliable, and ubiquitously available.*

c) In a version of the future where we never leave home, our current wired connectivity solutions would probably be enough to support all the needs of the Stream Tone. However, in a future that is much like today where we actually leave our homes, and go mobile, the Stream Tone will need all aspects of the global wireless telecommunications infrastructure, not just bandwidth, to move to the next level, and provide one, two, or even three orders of magnitude more than it does today. Without this, the Stream Tone can still be created, it can still be useful, and it will still move personal computing forward, probably in hugely helpful ways, but it will fall short of its full, world-changing, potential.

d) Current trends in a range of technological areas suggest that we are indeed moving in the right direction, so that the Stream Tone, in all its glory, will soon be possible. However, one area in particular that causes real concern, and may potentially slow the pace of Stream Tone progress, is the capabilities of wireless telecommunications, primarily in terms of their ubiquitous availability. Being able to have constant access to the Stream Tone in all situations and from all locations is going to be highly challenging. Whole new approaches to wireless telecommunications will probably need to be developed in order to ensure that whether a user is on land, at sea, or in the air that the Stream Tone can always be accessed without interruption. Today, there are many situations and locations in which wireless telecommunications will simply just not work, unless locale-specific telecommunications infrastructure has been installed. So whilst such problems are quite common and are generally not insurmountable, solving them on a large scale has, to date, often been prohibitively expensive. It is for this simple reason that Internet and telephony services will not always work when you travel through underground rail systems or by aeroplane; the necessary infrastructure required for constant connectivity has simply not been installed because it is just too costly. The Stream Tone has to work in all situations, and from all locations, if it is to successfully compete with, and eventually replace, current, locally-based, personal computing technology. It must successfully overcome these and other challenges if it is to stand any chance of becoming real, and it must do so in a highly cost-effective manner. If it cannot do this then it will never be able to achieve its full potential, deliver its many benefits, and change the world.

e) To a lesser extent, another problem, that currently affects both wired and wireless telecommunications, is that of data caps; limits on the quantity of digital data that can be sent or received by a user. Such caps are often imposed by an Internet service provider (ISP) as part of a strategy to better manage finite telecommunications resources. The services that will be delivered using the Stream Tone communications protocol will eventually need far more data than is currently being made available by even today's most generous ISP. However, as telecommunications infrastructures mature, some of the current capacity limitations are expected to be greatly reduced or completely removed. Data may still be capped in the future but it will be at such a high level that it will be more than sufficient for an average user to access all required content and services when using Stream Tone-based technologies.

f)    So, the vision of the future, presented in the following pages of this book, is going to be based on one really big assumption, that whatever the Stream Tone needs from telecommunications it will get... eventually.

# 0.5    ANSWERS

*Start by asking the right questions*

a)    This book does not have all the answers. In fact, it does not have even half the answers, or even half the questions. This book describes an alternative approach to personal computing in the broadest of strokes but, as the saying goes, the Devil is in the detail, and there will be a lot of detail in the Stream Tone. Detail that has not yet even been considered, let alone defined, or documented.

b)    The Stream Tone will require the creation of a whole new technology ecosystem, a highly complex task that will require the input of many, many, clever people. It is such people that will ultimately make the detailed decisions about what the Stream Tone is and how it will work. The Stream Tone will definitely not be the product of just one person, such as the author of this book. The Stream Tone will, hopefully, be developed as a free and open-source initiative that, by definition, will be based on the consensus of its many contributors, both individuals and large organisations. So whilst this book attempts to answer many questions, it is really only scratching the surface, and will probably raise just as many new questions as it gives answers. In terms of understanding the Stream Tone, this book is really just the start of that process.

# 0.6    MOVING TARGETS

*Bernie, the bolt!*

a)    Writing any book, but particularly a book that discusses modern technology, can take a long time, during which the technologies under discussion often have the most troublesome habit of changing, generally in very strange and highly unpredictable ways. Ensuring that a book captures a reasonably accurate snapshot of the latest technologies can, therefore, be incredibly difficult, and typically involves a fair amount of time-consuming iteration and probably an equal amount of good old-fashioned luck.

b)    However, whilst it is possible to win many battles on this front, the war is invariably lost, simply because the pace of modern technological change is just so fantastically fast. Cognitive enhancers, such as caffeine, can definitely help, but they are sadly not the panacea you might imagine them to be. So, the goal of being spot-on-target for each and every subject discussed remains annoyingly elusive.

c)    This book discusses a wide range of technologies, and, whilst every reasonable attempt has been made to capture the ethereal essence of their most current incarnation, it is highly likely that, in the end, some of those technologies will probably have been superseded, possibly several times over, by the time it is finally published. Such is the anachronistic nature of books. Perhaps, looking at this matter from the glass-is-half-full perspective, it will give this particular publication an exciting retro-futuristic slant; something that is apparently all the rage these days.

# 0.7    TO ARMS

*Do your part; join up today!*

a)    Earlier in this Prologue I suggested that this book might be a blueprint for the future, however, upon reflection I think that that might be overstating things somewhat; it might be just a bit too bold. This book contains some high-level ideas for a possible future, and as with any vision of the future, it has just as much chance of coming true as anything else that you could imagine about tomorrow or the day after.

b)    This book is not a peer-reviewed academic research paper, and although it does contain some references to other related works, they have simply been provided as an aid to further reading around a subject rather than to conclusively prove I did all my homework on that subject. It is neither a requirements document nor a design document; although it does contain a large number of requirements and design-like statements, which could easily confuse you into thinking that the Stream Tone is much more than it actually is. At best, it is a high-level discussion document. An attempt to capture an idea in some breadth and depth and put it down on paper so that others can start to understand and consider it, and then determine for themselves whether any part of it has any merit. It puts some speculative flesh on some speculative bones in order to conduct a thorough examination of just what sort of a beast the Stream Tone could potentially be. It is something to whet the appetite. An unfiltered brain-dump. A straw man. A thought experiment. A grey-matter stimulant. A conversation starter. A cat amongst the pigeons. A beginning. What it most definitely is not, is any sort of endpoint.

c)    Perhaps what this book might actually be is a call to arms. A polite, and hopefully persuasive, rallying cry to those that can see the benefits of the vision that is contained within this book, to become a part of it, and to help make it a reality.

d)    Making the Stream Tone a reality does not need a revolution, just steady, directed evolution from where we are today to where we want to be tomorrow. It needs a well-considered nudge or two, at just the right time, in just the right place, to get things moving in the right direction, followed by a few more to keep it firmly on track. It all sounds pretty easy when put in such terms, but it probably won't be.

e)    Maybe you can help with that. Maybe you are an expert that understands some of the fine detail that will need to be considered before the Stream Tone can emerge. Maybe you are a philanthropist that wants to invest in a better future for everyone, everywhere, or maybe you are a business that wants to get in on the ground floor of the next big thing! It does not matter; all are welcome! So, come one, come all, there is room enough for everyone; just remember to play nice.

f) It is said that vision without execution is hallucination.[7] So, if you do have something to contribute, please do, your efforts may be more important than you could ever imagine, and you will also help to confirm that I am not completely off my trolley. The only rule that really needs to be imposed on any such contributions is that the Stream Tone is meant to be a free and open-source initiative. It is not intended that it will be based on patents that will restrict its use or availability to a rich or privileged few. The Stream Tone is for everyone, and that needs to be baked in, right from the very start. That is why it is being mentioned here, at the beginning of this book. For sure, there will be commercial opportunities along the way but they should be incidental to the Stream Tone's story and not its central theme. As can be seen today, the delivery of content and services from Web-based sources provides more than ample opportunity for profit, but the technology underlying the delivery mechanism, provided by the Stream Tone, is not for profit. The Stream Tone is a chance to re-invent personal computing for the twenty-first century and beyond. To bring something new and useful to the world. You... could be a part of that. Please help, if you can.

# 0.8   NAYSAYERS

*Change-averse*

a) Nobody likes change. We say we do. We may even believe that we do, but deep, deep, down, if we are really honest, we really don't. We like the way things currently work. We like the status quo. It makes us feel comfortable. Puts us at our ease. Like the fictional Rip Van Winkle[8] who accidentally slept through the American Revolutionary War after helping the ghostly English mariner, Henry Hudson, carry his otherworldly-moonshine up a mountain to his silent, nine-pin playing, crewmates, we do not want to wake up one day and discover that the world we once knew and loved has mysteriously vanished. Too much change all at once can be very alienating, and we really do not like to be alienated, it makes us feel lost, stressed, and uncomfortable. We like to feel warm and fuzzy about change. Upbeat. We want change to be good for us, like winning the lottery, not bad, like crashing a car. Most of us actually want to be able to accept change and not refuse it. So, if we must be subjected to change, then we want it to be slow and incremental; so that we can understand the how and the why of that change, and ensure that the familiarities of the past are always kept close to hand. Of course, as Rip Van Winkle discovered to his dismay, some changes are simply thrust upon us whether we like them or not.

b) The Stream Tone will change the way personal computing is performed, and is the sort of change that will potentially impact a lot of people; hopefully in some very positive ways. Nevertheless, even though the Stream Tone will be able to deliver a personal computing

---

[7] *Apocryphally attributed to Thomas Alva Edison, 1847 - 1931, inventor, scientist, and businessman, probably because it's the pithy sort of thing he was noted for saying. Edison is considered to be one of history's most prolific inventors, with 1,093 patents to his name. One of his most notable inventions was a practical electric light bulb.*
[8] *A short story contained within "The Sketch Book of Geoffrey Crayon, Gent", a collection of essays and short stories published serially by Washington Irving between 1819 and 1820.*

experience that is very similar, if not identical, to current personal computing solutions, the differences, however small, will still be very obvious to many people.

c)   Some of those people will like the Stream Tone. They will like it simply because it is new and different. Some will like it for technical reasons and others for purely aesthetic reasons. Some other people, however, will really not like it at all, and will probably be quite demonstrative and vocal in their disapproval. They will say that we do not have the technology to make it work. That it will be expensive, and we cannot afford it. That we do not need it, want it, trust it, like it, or believe in it. Some will say that it is based on the wrong sort of thinking, and is a huge technological step backwards. Whilst others will just say "No!" and shake their heads as if they were admonishing a foolishly deluded child. Such detractors will say a whole lot of things; some of which will be really quite insightful and convincing, and quite possibly even true. However, behind most of this negativity is the simple fact that people really don't like change, even change for the better, and this sort of reaction is to be expected.

d)   Perhaps this particular change will be greeted like a visiting ogre; by an angry mob armed with pitchforks and torches. In our modern commerce-oriented world that angry mob is very likely to be comprised of many business entities that are heavily invested in the status quo, and that have their own agendas in play. Such businesses exist to make a profit, and know how to turn any change to their advantage. What upsets them is change that is not on their terms, on their schedule, or to their immediate benefit. If the Stream Tone can profitably fit in with their plans for the future, then it will most probably be eagerly embraced. If not, then it will be vigorously resisted, possibly forever, or maybe just until they are ready to change direction. At which point, they will herald the Stream Tone as the greatest thing, ever! Their previous, negative, comments on the subject dismissed as mere misunderstandings of a subtle yet strangely complex viewpoint that is no longer relevant. Ah! Such is the fickle and multi-faced world of business.

e)   So, regardless of what you may have heard in the past, or will hear in the future, to the contrary, the Stream Tone concept is actually a very good idea, with many merits, and is based on some sound thinking, as documented in this book. A full implementation will probably not be quick or easy, but it is possible, and it is worthwhile. Try to keep an open mind as you gather enough facts to make your own informed decisions on the subject, and be able to determine for yourself whether the naysayers are afraid of the Stream Tone just because it represents a change to a familiar and comfortable way of doing things or that they are just trying to protect their current vested interests, albeit temporarily.

# 0.9    ACRONYMS

*Jargon abbreviated*

a)   This book introduces a number of new terms, which have been listed, along with their acronyms, below:

| | |
|---|---|
| CRPC | Comprehensive Remote Personal Computing |
| STAD | Stream Tone Access Device |
| STADE | Stream Tone Access Device Emulator |
| STAPI | Stream Tone Application Programming Interface |
| STC | Stream Tone Community |

| | |
|---|---|
| STCF | Stream Tone Community Forum |
| STCM | Stream Tone Certification Mark |
| STF | Stream Tone Foundation |
| STFL | Stream Tone Function Library |
| STGI | Stream Tone Graphics Interface |
| STI | Stream Tone Indicator |
| STIC | Stream Tone Image Cache |
| STIC-ID | Stream Tone Image Cache Identifier |
| STSDK | Stream Tone Software Development Kit |
| STSI | Stream Tone Service Infrastructure |
| STSP | Stream Tone Service Portal |
| STSS | Stream Tone Security Service |
| STTI | Stream Tone Telecommunications Infrastructure |
| STTP | Stream Tone Transfer Protocol |
| STTP-CODEC | Stream Tone Transfer Protocol Codec |
| STTPD | Stream Tone Transfer Protocol Decoder |
| STTPE | Stream Tone Transfer Protocol Encoder |
| STWB | Stream Tone Web Browse |

# 1    INTRODUCTION

*Our technology is not yet magic; for in the history of such things we are nowhere near the end, in fact, we are not even at the end of the beginning*[9]

a)    Have you ever looked at your latest personal computing device and wondered what comes next? For as surely as night follows day, something better will soon be along to replace it; because even the most advanced piece of modern technology is pretty much obsolete the moment it is conceived, let alone built. Of course, it will be useful and cherished for a while, but ultimately it represents just the briefest of waypoints on the endless path of progress.

b)    Over recent years, personal computing devices have become a lot more powerful and a lot smaller. Some have even become battery powered and wirelessly connected. Advancements that have, collectively, allowed us to leave our homes and offices, and compute on the move, from almost anywhere and at almost any time. These are bold steps forward, to be sure, but the capabilities that can be built directly into our individual personal computing devices, particularly the data processing capabilities built into highly portable devices, will always be finite, and the users of such devices will always push those capabilities to the very limit, no matter how much those capabilities grow over time. What happens when we reach such a limit and there is no more? We will obviously want more. We will probably need more. But, there will be no more. We will have hit a technological brick wall. In a world that has grown accustomed to continuous technological growth the consequences of hitting such a wall will be that progress is slowed, or even halted, in a whole range of different fields that have become highly dependent on the ever increasing capabilities of our personal computing devices. The fact that we know, in advance, that such limits most probably exist raises the very real question of whether or not our current technological goals will always be able to take mankind where it really needs to go in the future. We will always want more, that is a certainty, but what if we want, or even need, our personal computing technology to take us somewhere different, new, and unlimited. What then?

c)    Perhaps we need to adopt some new goals before we start to hit the limits of our current personal computing technologies. Goals that will let us achieve more than we ever thought possible, wherever we are, whatever we are doing, and not just individually but collectively as well. What if our personal computing devices worked in a fundamentally different way? What if personal computing could be redesigned to support both accelerated advancement and technological stability at the same time? What if the connectivity of our personal computing devices became more important than their built-in capabilities? What if instead of a future where everyone carries a supercomputer in their pocket, we simply carry a connection to a computing service that is inherently capable of meeting all our digital needs forever. Such an approach would be even better than each of us having our very own supercomputer because when we weren't using it, somebody else could. Wouldn't that be a much more efficient, equitable, and sensible approach to personal computing? It could help take computing, and mankind along with it, into a new and exciting world of unimagined possibilities, where science fiction finally starts to

---

[9] *Based on two famous quotes; the third of Arthur C. Clarke's Three Laws, which states that "Any sufficiently advanced technology is indistinguishable from magic", and the famous "The End of the Beginning" speech made by Sir Winston Churchill on 10th November 1942 at the Lord Mayor's Luncheon, Mansion House, London.*

become science fact.

d) A world where your next personal computing device is the last one that you would ever need to buy. Where you would never need to worry about operating systems, software patches, or viruses. Where you always had enough processing power, memory, storage, and top-of-the-line graphics. Where you could access all of the very best software applications, regardless of their platform. Where you had a constant connection to all of your favourite digital services, and your battery lasted for days, perhaps even weeks, of full-on use. Sounds good, doesn't it? Well, this is the world of the Stream Tone. A world that does not exist in some far off future; this could be, figuratively speaking, our world a mere five minutes from now. All that is needed to make it a reality is the creative convergence of certain technologies that are already available and in use today.

# 1.1    WHAT IS THE STREAM TONE?

*The what*

a) The Stream Tone is a concept that is based on the technology of data streaming, also known as bit-streaming or pixel-streaming, and it will be the next step in the evolution of personal computing. Data streaming is not a new technology, it has been around in one form, or another, for many, many years. In fact, radio is a data streaming technology, and so is television. There are also many modern Web-based services that are based on data streaming technologies. Data streaming, is a client-server technology, where data is continuously transmitted from a server to a simple client, of generally singular function, in the same way that the old mainframe computers transmitted alpha-numeric data to their dumb access terminals. Today, cloud computing-based data streaming supports a very wide range of fully-interactive Web-based services, such as computer-aided design, computer gaming, data processing and storage, language translation, music on demand, navigation, office productivity, remote computer desktops, social networking, telephony, video conferencing, video on demand, and voice-controlled information search, to name but a few. The Stream Tone will support all these things, and much, much more.

b) The Stream Tone will enable Comprehensive Remote Personal Computing (CRPC), which is a Web-oriented approach to personal computing in which local personal computing functionality, previously provided by technologies such as operating systems and software applications, is either migrated in toto onto the Web or replaced with equivalent Web-based services that are then remotely accessed over the Internet. CRPC will even replace existing Web-based services that are currently accessed using a local Web browser, with remotely-sourced Web browsing services. CRPC is comprehensive because it will replace not just some but all of such functionality, and also because it will be a remote personal computing solution that is suitable for use by everyone, everywhere, including the billions of people that have not yet been able to fully embrace the Internet, personal computing, and Web. The Stream Tone will move remote personal computing from the niche to the mainstream.

c) The Stream Tone will be a stream of streams, in the same way that the Internet is a network of networks. The Stream Tone will represent both a sage step backwards, a return to the simplicities of the past, and a bold step forward, into an even more rapidly evolving and complex future. In many ways the Stream Tone will be nothing that has not been seen before, but, in other ways, it will be unique, and it will change the world. No single technology will enable the Stream Tone. It will be an aggregate of many, many, different technologies, each contributing a small but vital part to a whole that is so much more than just the sum of those individual parts. When considered from a certain perspective the Stream Tone will be incredibly simple, straightforward, and maybe even elegant, but the aggregated technologies behind it will have a very real complexity; just like all the other systems that currently power the Internet and the Web.

d) The Stream Tone will be an adaptive, bi-directional, intelligent, low-latency, real-time, secure, data streaming communications protocol designed to support the use of CRPC services accessed via computer networks, such as the Internet. The Stream Tone communications protocol will be the heart of a technology ecosystem that will also include an access device, service infrastructure, and telecommunications infrastructure.

e) The communications protocol of the Stream Tone will be known as the Stream Tone Transfer Protocol (STTP), the access device of the Stream Tone will be known as the Stream Tone Access Device (STAD), the service infrastructure of the Stream Tone will be known as the Stream Tone Service Infrastructure (STSI), the telecommunications infrastructure of the Stream Tone will be known as the Stream Tone Telecommunications Infrastructure (STTI), and, collectively, these elements will be known as the Stream Tone Technology Ecosystem (STTE). The Stream Tone will also be a generic term that can be used, depending on context, interchangeably with STTE and STTP.

f) The Stream Tone will be used to deliver Web-based digital content and services that will then be accessed using a hardware-based thin client that is conceptually similar to a dumb computer terminal. The access device will have a fixed functionality, and will be non-programmable. The access device will wholly rely on remotely-sourced services for the provision of user-oriented functionality.

g) The Stream Tone will be used to access all existing Web-based digital content and services, as well as new content and services that will be specifically created for use with Stream Tone-based technologies. Functionality that was previously provided by local personal computing devices, such as application software and desktop operating systems, will be migrated onto the Web, into data centres, and accessed remotely. The Stream Tone will rely on cloud computing-based service infrastructures that are able to provide affordable, low-latency, reliable Web-based services through the efficient and effective use of data centre resources. The Stream Tone will be compatible with current and next generation service infrastructures. The hardware and software used by such service infrastructures may need to be optimised in order to support the operational characteristics required to provide Stream Tone-based services.

h) The Stream Tone will be designed for use on packet-switched computer networks, such as the Internet, and will be dependent on third-party telecommunications infrastructures that are able to provide highly affordable, high bandwidth, low latency, highly reliable, and ubiquitously available Internet connectivity. The Stream Tone will be compatible with current and next generation telecommunications infrastructures. The hardware and software used by such telecommunications infrastructures may need to be optimised in order to support the operational characteristics required to deliver Stream Tone-based services.

i)　The diagram[10] presented in Figure 1 shows a simplified and stylised view of the key entities, and the interactions between those entities, that the Stream Tone will support. A user will interact with a STAD. The STAD will use a STTI to communicate with a STSI using the STTP. A STSI will use a STTI to communicate with a STAD using the STTP. The STSI can also use a STTI to access the Web via the Internet. A STSI is actually a part of, or a subset of, the Web and a STTI is actually a part of, or a subset of, the Internet, even though they have been presented as distinct entities on this diagram.

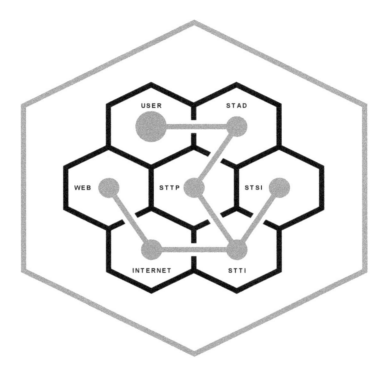

*Figure 1: The Stream Tone*

# 1.2　WHY IS IT NEEDED?

*The why*

a)　Is the Stream Tone needed just because personal computing may be heading towards some sort of technological brick wall, as was suggested at the start of this chapter? Perhaps in part, but mainly it is because personal computing is continually subject to change. This is, of course, a rather strange thing to suggest because change is, on the

---

[10] Artwork

whole, a very good thing. Change represents advancement, evolution, improvement, replacement, and succession. Change is about fixing things that are broken. Change is about discovery. Change is a stimulant. Change is interesting. Change is what colours our lives. Change is what makes tomorrow different from today. Change is what allows us to make the world a better place. Change, however, often comes with a price, and the continuous fast-paced change that is a mark of our technologically-oriented modern world means that we pay that price, in a whole variety of ways, again and again and again, at what seems to be an ever quickening pace. Change has, in many instances, become both inconvenient and costly. The Stream Tone is a way to reduce some of the cost and to limit some of the inconvenience of change as it relates to personal computing.

b) In terms of personal computing, change can bring new communications technologies, devices, operating systems, peripherals, software applications, and Web-based services. Some of these changes will be available free-of-charge, but many will not. One thing, in particular, that is rarely available for free is your personal computing device, which can be a real problem if it needs to be replaced on a regular basis because of obsolescence, whether real or imagined. Most personal computing devices can easily last for a decade, or more, if they are well maintained, yet, few are actively used for such a duration. In general, personal computing devices become obsolete very quickly, often within a few short years. In fact in many developed countries, the rapid obsolescence of modern personal computing devices, such as smart-phones and tablet computers, has become widely accepted as simply the price that must be paid for technological advancement in our continually modernising world. Even the most sophisticated and capable devices are now considered to be largely disposable, little more than the casual consumables of a modern life. There are many reasons for this obsolescence, but all are due to some form of change. Sometimes it is due to new software applications or operating systems that will not run optimally, or are not available for use, on a current device. Sometimes it is due to the emergence of a new device form factor that enables personal computing to take place in unusual circumstances or locations that are not supported by a current device. Sometimes it is due to the fact that a current device does not support a new type of communications technology, malware defence, peripheral, or Web-based service and cannot be easily or cost-effectively upgraded to do so. In fact, on many occasions the reasons for obsolescence are incredibly trivial, such as an existing device being the wrong colour, shape, size, or weight. On other occasions, incredible though it may seem, obsolescence seems to have been purposefully engineered directly into devices through the use of poor product designs that, for instance, do not support even the most basic repairs, and the use of construction materials that seem destined to fail in some way just after a device's warranty period comes to an end, with the result that it seems to be far more cost effective to simply buy a more modern replacement than to attempt any sort of fix, even when the underlying fault is relatively minor and the device is still largely functional. Of course, it is always possible to make-do with an older device, to run previous generation software applications and operating systems, to forego the latest capabilities, and to ignore minor functional failures, but few people do. Most people want to ride on, or, at the very least, near technology's leading edge. They want, and in many cases need, to be able to use all the latest technological capabilities, not just because of the increasingly important role that all forms of personal computing play within modern business and personal life, but also because such capabilities are no longer seen as optional but as non-negotiable necessities of the progressive modern lifestyle to which most people now aspire. The problem is that staying on, or even close to, that leading edge comes with a price, a price that many people simply cannot afford, especially when it is a price that must be paid on an increasingly regular basis.

c)  For some people, especially those in developing countries, purchasing a personal computing device is a big decision, as it represents the expenditure of a significant portion of annual household income. It is a purchase that cannot be regularly repeated just because something new has come along, technological fashion trends have changed, or a device has broken. There just isn't the money. Ideally, for such people, personal computing devices would remain functional and relevant for many, many years; unfortunately, obsolescence, brought about by the rapid pace of technological change, fickle personal tastes, poor design, and even peer pressure, makes that very unlikely. Also, some lower-cost devices, that are available in developing countries, are just not built to last, or be repaired. Some are constructed from low-grade materials that will quickly degrade, and eventually cause a device to fail long before the end of its expected life. This means that another device will need to be purchased, within a year or two, if it can be afforded. Of course, the cost of many new personal computing devices, particularly smart-phones and tablet computers, have become much lower recently, and can therefore be afforded by many more people, particularly those in developing countries. Nevertheless, the speed at which such devices become obsolete and need to be replaced is a problem that affects everyone, everywhere, rich and poor alike, and whilst the rich can easily afford to regularly upgrade their devices, the poor cannot. This continuous upgrade cycle potentially excludes, or delays, the less affluent members of global society from participating in some of the newest and most important aspects of the modern world. This is, of course, wholly understandable given the nature of global wealth distribution and the rapid pace of technological change, but it is very far from fair. It is also highly nonsensical from the perspective of an efficient and effective use of the natural resources required to produce such devices, something that really should not be the norm in what is supposed to be the enlightened twenty-first century. We should know better. In fact, we already do know better, we just need to start putting what we know into practice.

d)  The Stream Tone will enable a much fairer and more cost-effective approach to personal computing through the use of a highly-affordable, long-lasting, thin client access device, and a new data-streaming communications protocol, which will be used to access a comprehensive range of Web-based content and services. The Stream Tone will be able to converge all of today's various data streams into a single stream, a stream of streams, that is capable of serving the personal computing needs of a whole planet, and, by so doing, usher in a period of accelerated advancement and technological stability. The simultaneous achievement of both accelerated advancement and technological stability is somewhat contradictory and highly counter-intuitive. However, it is the very real product of decoupling the development of Web-based services from the development and maintenance of the device used to access those services. The device that will be used to access Stream Tone-based services will have a completely fixed functionality, just like a non-programmable, dumb, computer terminal, ensuring that all service development will be limited to only the computer servers and data centres that are used to provide those services. This access device will never become obsolete, subject to attack by malware, or require regular maintenance; primarily because it will not contain an operating system or support the direct execution of software applications. It will also be completely immune to the adverse effects of any technological brick wall that may arise in the future, such as the ending of Moore's Law. It will be a purely hardware-based technology that will have the singular purpose of presenting audio-visual data sent from a wide range of Web-based sources. The access device will be useful and relevant as long as it continues to function, and will only need replacing when it is completely unrepairable. The fixed functional design of the access device will enable the use of highly cost-effective manufacturing processes that will ensure that the access device will be affordable by everyone, everywhere. The Stream Tone will allow personal computing to finally become reliable, simple, stable, and affordable by all. The cloud computing-based systems that will stream the Web-based content and services will be able to change as much, and as quickly, as required, both in terms of hardware and software, as long as the final result is a Stream Tone-compliant data stream everything will just continue to work. The Stream Tone will be an accelerator for technological advancement, and the factors that used to constrain progress, such as the need to upgrade or replace aspects on the client-side to match changes on the server-side, will be permanently removed. Of course, the concept of decoupling the development of a client from the development of a server in this way is not new, and its benefits are well understood. Over the years it has allowed the installation of a new mainframe computer without replacing the dumb terminals used to access it, the music from a new radio station to be received on an old radio receiver set, the latest movie broadcast on a new television channel to be watched on your current television, and new or improved Web sites to be viewed through an existing Web browser. Historically, if every server-side change had required a corresponding change in the client that accesses it, the world would be nowhere near as advanced as it now is. Thankfully the world is not like that. Still, it could be better. Being able to independently change Web-based services is not new, nor is being able to use a fixed and unchanging client, what is new, and this is what the Stream Tone provides, is being able to finally do these things together on a global scale to deliver a greatly improved personal computing experience in a way that can benefit everyone, everywhere.

e) The technological and societal move from localised personal computing to remote personal computing is already well under way. At this point in time, this move is really more of a general trend that is characterised by various interested parties, such as Web-based service providers, personal computing device manufacturers, software developers, and telecommunications operators, that have already built a wide range of proprietary remote personal computing solutions for use in their own market verticals, rather than a tangibly cohesive cross-party movement that is working towards a definitive common goal. In simple terms, many of these interested parties are big businesses that see remote personal computing as a prize that they must win and commercially control, and if they cannot control it all then they will seek to control an integral part of it. Consequently, these parties are not working together quite as much as they could or should. Another reason for the lack of cooperation between these parties is also probably due to the absence of any kind of formal framework for Comprehensive Remote Personal Computing (CRPC), or its equivalent, that would potentially be able to unify the efforts of the current participants. Nevertheless, the move to CRPC is largely inevitable, primarily because the promised cost and convenience benefits are just too great to ignore, and also because many of the foundational technologies that will be able to enable CRPC, such as cloud computing-based service infrastructures, computer hardware, operating systems, software applications, and telecommunications infrastructures, are rapidly maturing, becoming both cheaper and much more practical. Probably the most important of these technologies are those relating to telecommunications infrastructures, which are rapidly reaching the point at which they will be able to provide the highly affordable, high bandwidth, low latency, highly reliable, ubiquitously available Internet connectivity that CRPC will require. CRPC will allow personal computing to be conducted from anywhere, and at any time, using a very simple, and very low-cost, access device. The Web-based services upon which CRPC will depend will be affordable and robust, and the user will be insulated from the consequent cost and inconvenience when such services are inevitably changed. In many ways, the move towards CRPC is a natural progression that is being

17

driven by the maturation of the Internet and the Web, which has lead to the emergence of a very wide range of increasingly capable Web-based services. In fact, everything that the Stream Tone hopes to be may just naturally arise from this very progression, without any real effort on anyone's part. It could, quite literally, just pop into existence tomorrow. For this reason alone, it might seem that an initiative like the Stream Tone would therefore be wholly unnecessary, and all we need to do is just sit back, take it easy, and wait for it appear. Unfortunately, there can be no certainty that this will actually occur, and such wishful thinking is unlikely to deliver what is exactly needed from such an important new technology. Therefore, the transition to CRPC will need to be carefully handled, and the Stream Tone initiative will be the conscious effort to formally plan for, and manage, that transition. The Stream Tone will, as a consequence, also provide a much needed framework for CRPC. A framework that will be able to focus the collective efforts of all interested parties on the common goal of moving personal computing technology to its next logical phase. Thereby ensuring that by the time that the next generation of service and telecommunications infrastructures become available the Stream Tone will be ready to make good use of them.

f)   Many different technologies for delivering digital content and services over the Internet already exist. Some of these technologies are proprietary, encumbered by patents, and require the payment of licensing and royalty fees, and some are available on a free and open-source basis. As the Stream Tone is envisioned as a very low-cost technology, that will be affordable by everyone, everywhere, it will therefore be based on free and open-source concepts and technologies. The Stream Tone will not be controlled by the usual players, such as multinational for-profit organisations. Put simply, the future of personal computing needs to rest firmly within the hands of the many and not just the few, because the Stream Tone will be far too important a technology to allow it to be financially exploited and monopolised as so many other important modern technologies already are. The Stream Tone will therefore be the purposeful and specific development of the definitive CRPC solution, based on existing free and open-source concepts and technologies.

g)   In simple terms, many of the existing technologies that could potentially be used to build the Stream Tone are either very good at handling the transmission of fast-changing visual data or slow-changing visual data over computer networks, such as the Internet, but are generally not so good at handling both types of data. Technologies that are optimised for fast-changing visual data are typically used for the transmission of content such as movies and computer games. Technologies that are optimised for slow-changing visual data are used for the transmission of content such as the graphical user-interfaces of desktop operating systems and software applications. Both types of visual data are compressed using lossy compression algorithms that consequently cause a reduction of visual quality to some degree. Fast-changing visual data is generally compressed more than slow-changing visual data, with the result that fast-changing visual data generally has a lower visual quality than slow-changing visual data. For fast-changing visual data the reduction in visual quality is hardly noticeable, or problematic, because of the rapid rate of visual change; with one video frame replacing the previous frame after a small fraction of a second, far faster than the time in which the human eye can typically perceive the reduction. If the same amount of compression was applied to slow-changing visual data the reduction in visual quality would be very noticeable and would, most likely, adversely impact the usability of the services that it was used to access. For this reason, slow-changing visual data employs less data compression than is typically used for handling fast-changing visual data. If fast-changing visual data was transmitted using a technology optimised for slow-changing visual data then unacceptably slow video-frame refresh rates would most likely be obtained. Any technology designed to support CRPC will need to be able to efficiently and effectively handle both types of visual data. Therefore, the Stream Tone will adopt a hybrid approach, applying the most appropriate level of compression based on the type of visual data that is being communicated.

h) Software-based systems, even after many years of development, can still contain many coding errors, and can fail in highly unpredictable ways when operated in circumstances that were unforeseen when the software was originally designed, or when the operational environment is changed, such as when an operating system, software application, or software-stack is periodically updated. Any personal computing device based on such a system can become very unreliable and consequently in need of continuous maintenance. As a general rule, the more complex the software environment the less reliable it will be. Conversely, the simpler the software environment, the greater the chance that it will be more reliable, because simpler software is easier to design, implement, test, deploy, and maintain. The functionality provided by simple software can often be implemented in hardware, allowing for the creation of highly reliable, maintenance-free, devices. Hardware-based devices can also offer greatly increased performance and power efficiency compared to their software-based counterparts. This is one of the reasons why the devices that will be used to access the digital content and services communicated using the STTP will be purely hardware-based. Unfortunately, many of the technologies that could potentially be used to build the Stream Tone are software-based, and rely on a complex ecosystem of operating systems, software applications, and software stacks, in order to function. Few of these technologies are ready for hardware-only implementation. This is why the Stream Tone's communications protocol and the functionalities of the Stream Tone's access devices will be specifically designed for hardware-only implementation.

i) Moving forward, the capabilities of global telecommunications infrastructure is very likely going to become far more important than the capabilities of individual personal computing devices, which are, in may ways, already good enough for most tasks. The Stream Tone will help to focus attention on the key aspects of the global telecommunications infrastructure that will need to be improved, such as affordability, availability, bandwidth, latency, and reliability, in order to support CRPC. So, even though telecommunications infrastructures will naturally mature and improve, the Stream Tone will help ensure that such maturation and improvement will eventually yield a telecommunications environment that is well suited to all aspects of CRPC.

j) The most important feature of the Stream Tone will be its ability to protect a user's personal data. If users cannot completely trust that their data will always be safe when using Stream Tone-based technologies then the Stream Tone will never be adopted and its full potential will never be realised. Of course, there will be many situations relating to CRPC in which the protection of personal data will be beyond the control of the Stream Tone. At its heart the Stream Tone is simply a communications protocol, and CRPC extends far beyond the sending and receiving of data into areas where the Stream Tone will naturally have much less influence. The Stream Tone will also be a technology ecosystem, but its ability to directly influence things even within that ecosystem, such as service and telecommunications infrastructures, will, most probably, be very limited at best. However, to the extent that is practical, both from a technological perspective as well from a cost perspective, the Stream Tone will therefore be specifically designed to protect all personal data, whether at rest, in motion, or in use, when such data is within its sphere of control. The protection of personal data will be built into the Stream Tone from its very inception, and it will not be an afterthought that is bolted on at the end.

# 1.3 HOW WILL IT BE BUILT?

*The how*

a) Comprehensive Remote Personal Computing (CRPC), as enabled by the Stream Tone, is the delivery of all required personal computing functionality, over the Internet, from remotely-located sources. CRPC will depend on a number of technologies, provided by the Stream Tone, in order to deliver that functionality, including an access device, communications protocol, service infrastructure, and telecommunications infrastructure.

b) The access device will need to be able to support the presentation of, and user interaction with, all required CRPC content and services. The access device will need to be affordable, durable, and simple. A wide range of personal computing devices already exist, including desktop computers, laptop computers, smart-phones, and tablet computers. The Stream Tone will build upon the technologies used by such devices in order to provide an affordable, durable, and simple access device that is suitable for CRPC.

c) The communications protocol will need to be able to support the transmission of all required CRPC content and services. The protocol will need to be optimised for low-latency operation over computer networks, such as the Internet, in order to support the use of interactive, real-time, services. A wide range of secure communications protocols already exist, many of which are suitable for use on packet-switched computer networks, such as the Internet, and are able to support the interactive, real-time, operation that will be required by CRPC. The Stream Tone will build upon such protocols in order to provide a secure low-latency data transport solution that is suitable for CRPC.

d) The service infrastructure will need to be able to provide all the digital content and services required for CRPC. The content and services will be created on computer servers housed within remotely-located data centres. All data centre resources will need to be used highly efficiently and highly effectively if remote personal computing services are to become a viable low-cost alternative to local personal computing. Cloud computing is a rapidly maturing approach for using data centre resources efficiently and effectively. The Stream Tone will leverage such cloud computing-based technologies in order to provide a complete range of viable low-cost CRPC services.

e) The telecommunications infrastructure will need to be able to support the delivery of all CRPC data. This infrastructure will need to be able to provide Internet connectivity that is highly affordable, high bandwidth, low latency, highly reliable, and ubiquitously available. Telecommunications technologies are available in two main forms; wired and wireless. Many wired telecommunications technologies are already capable of supporting CRPC from fixed locations, such as the home and office. Wireless telecommunications technologies that are capable of supporting CRPC also exist, but are not yet ubiquitously available. Many currently deployed wireless telecommunications systems are not yet able to meet all the operational requirements for CRPC. The Stream Tone will leverage current and future wired telecommunications infrastructures, and next-generation wireless telecommunications infrastructures, in order to provide a highly affordable, high bandwidth, low latency, highly reliable, and ubiquitously available Internet connectivity solution that is suitable for CRPC.

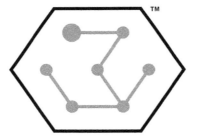

# 2 THE PAST

*Everything old is new again*

a)  The Stream Tone will be, in many ways, a new and different technology, but it will also be one that is built on a number of well established concepts. In fact some of the thinking behind the Stream Tone dates from a time before programmable digital computers had even been invented. So, before exploring what will hopefully be the future of personal computing, it may be useful to briefly revisit a little of its past in order to better understand some of its foundations.

## 2.1 PAUL OTLET

*Retro-futurism*

a)  Paul Marie Ghislain Otlet (1868-1944) was a Belgian lawyer that went on to become a bibliographic scientist and author, who is currently considered to be the father of Information Science. In 1934, Otlet published "Traité de Documentation: Le livre sur le livre, théorie et pratique" (Treatise on Documentation: The book about the book, theory and practice), which described how information should be classified and indexed. Also included in this book were some visionary ideas on how information could be accessed in the future. Otlet's vision of the future would eventually be known as the Televised Book, which was a system that consisted of a television-based viewing screen and a telephone connected to an information repository, termed the Radiated Library. Users would use the telephone to request information from a librarian, who would then use a video camera to send the requested information via television signals to the user's viewing screen. It is now considered that Otlet's writings were prescient of the World Wide Web.

## 2.2 PERSONAL COMPUTING[11]

*In the beginning...*

a)  When I first started to learn about computers, in the United Kingdom (UK), at the start of the 1980s, affordable personal computers for home use were still very much in their infancy. Of course, personal computers had been generally available since the mid-1970s, mainly in the United States of America, but they were rather expensive, often required self-assembly, and really had not yet caught on culturally in a big way in the UK. They were something that white-coated scientists used. They were seen with their many blinking lights in films and on television. They were not yet a part of normal daily life, and they were definitely not something you had at home. Cultural awareness of what a computer was, and what it could do, was, however, steadily growing. So when personal computers did eventually become more widely available, and much more affordable, at the start of the 1980s, there was a ready and eager mass market for them.

---

[11] *This section is not intended to be a complete and detailed history of personal computing; just the author's briefly described personal recollections of some key parts of that history.*

b)   Those early personal computers were very different to the desktops, laptops, smart-phones, and tablets that we have today. Back then, personal computers came in many different models, each with its own unique internal architecture, operating system, physical appearance, programming languages, and storage technology. Few of the different personal computers were compatible with other models; each was largely an island unto itself. They were incredibly slow compared to modern machines, with their primitive eight-bit central processing units running at speeds of between one and four megahertz. They possessed only tiny amounts of random-access memory, sometimes as little as one kilobyte, and those that boasted more often topped out at a mere 64 kilobytes. None had hard disk drive-based storage, which would not become practical or affordable enough for home use until the end of the 1980s. Some machines used eight-inch diameter floppy disks for storage, whilst the cheaper entry-level models used audio-cassette tapes. The primary input device was the keyboard; the computer mouse had not yet been adopted, even though it was patented as early as 1970. There was no windows, icons, menus, and pointer-style graphical user-interface, just a simple alphanumeric display. Most personal computers could only display a dozen or so colours, and some even needed to be connected to the family television because they had no screen of their own. Sharing anything digitally was quite challenging, as the Internet was still being invented, so even if you were lucky enough to own a modem there were relatively few people to communicate with; although, around this time, bulletin boards and telecomputing services were starting to appear. Nevertheless, for most people, certainly in the UK, personal computing at this time was pretty much an individual pursuit, a hobby.

c)   In many ways, a lot of those first personal computers were just expensive toys, but toys that seemed to herald the arrival of the science fiction future that we had imagined only a few years earlier. We had grown up believing that by the year 2000 mankind would be exploring the stars, living on the moon, and travelling to work by jet-pack. The arrival of personal computers just made sense; it was simply the first part of our long-promised future finally arriving. If you hadn't believed in those stories of man's inevitable conquest of the cosmos before personal computers arrived on the scene, then you surely did after. At the time it all seemed so natural, as only a few years earlier affordable electronic calculators and digital wristwatches had started to appear. Personal computers were just the next step in what promised to be a long line of revolutionary technology that was designed to improve every aspect of our lives. As a certain pointy-eared alien frequently seen on television liked to observe, it was just logical. However, as we now look back, it is possible to see just how revolutionary this time actually was. It was like living through the industrial revolution, but without the wanton destruction of weaving machines by rioting Luddites.[12] It was my generation's great leap forward.

d)   Those early machines were the very first taste of computing by the masses, and a lot of people from my generation started their computing careers on such machines. The machines were in many ways very simplistic in their design, limited in their capabilities, and pretty much did nothing out of the box. They needed to be programmed in order to bring them to life, so you tended to focus on learning their programming languages, and because their random-access memory was so limited, the design of efficient and effective

---

[12] *Named after Ned Ludd; an English labourer who allegedly destroyed two stocking frames, which were a type of mechanical knitting machine that was used in the textiles industry, around the year 1779. When English textile artisans started to destructively protest against the use of labour saving machinery between 1811 and 1817 they adopted a fictional General Ludd or King Ludd as their leader, and were consequently known as the Luddites.*

algorithms. It was all quite challenging, but people rose to that challenge, taught themselves, had a lot of fun, and really started to master this new technology. However, as familiarity, interest, and understanding grew, the failings and limitations of this nascent technology became apparent, and very soon everyone wanted their personal computer to do more; they wanted it to be, not just fun and interesting, but useful as well.

e) On the other side of the fence, in the world of business, the grass was most definitely greener, and far more mature. Business computing was already well established, based primarily on a centralised model of a powerful mainframe computer connected, via serial communications, to dumb access terminals. Mainframe computers were so named because they required a main framework of dedicated infrastructure that provided specialised air conditioning, electrical power, heating, and ventilation in order to operate. The mainframe computer had arisen in the late 1950s, and was a pre-eminent form factor for business computing until the mid-1980s, when smaller computers started to find useful business roles. Mainframe computers were designed for reliable transaction processing applications, such as airline reservations, banking, and inventory control. They were particularly well suited to running database applications but could also be used for many other things, including nuclear research and weather prediction. In the late 1960s, mainframe computers were used to pioneer the concept of virtualisation; a computing technique which permits a single machine to simultaneously host, or run, multiple operating systems.

f) The mainframe computer could have also been a good solution for bringing computing out of the office and into the homes of ordinary people. Unfortunately, the telecommunications infrastructure of the 1980s was really not up to such a task, and a typical business mainframe computer was extremely expensive and unlikely to be shared with anyone outside the company that owned it, so the mainframe computer remained a tool for academia and big business. Home computing would need to rely on a different approach; a distributed model, based on individually owned personal computers. Of course, some personal computers were used in business around this time, but their adoption was initially quite modest. They were typically reserved for use by a limited number of professionals that could justify the significant capital expenditure involved in the purchase of a business-grade personal computer. A mainframe computer could easily serve a whole business but a personal computer might only serve one person, so even back in those days cost/benefit was a very real consideration.

g) Within a large organisation, everyone could, theoretically, have access to the wonders of computing through their very own dumb terminal; either a teleprinter machine, or if you were very lucky via a video terminal. To be fair, the electromechanical teleprinters were largely on their way out by this time, being replaced by solid-state video terminals. However, due to their somewhat robust construction there were still quite a few teleprinters left over from the 1970s, and they were still in common use. The user-interface on these terminals was incredibly primitive compared to modern displays. A teleprinter was like a typewriter, and one of its key advantages was that it kept a printed record, on a continuous flow of fan-fold paper, of all user-input and mainframe computer output. A video terminal had a keyboard and a cathode-ray tube-based monochrome display screen that was capable of displaying 80 columns by 24 lines of alphanumeric characters, or, if you were particularly fortunate, 132 columns by 24 lines. Video terminals did not keep a permanent record of input and output, and were, therefore, often used in conjunction with a separate, departmental, printer that was also connected to the mainframe computer. In many respects, the video terminals were very similar to the technology used in the first personal computers that people were starting to buy for home use, except that the video terminals could not be reprogrammed by their users and they were built to fulfil a single specific task; to interact with a centralised computer system via serial communications links. They were not called dumb for nothing; user-input was not processed by the terminals, it was sent directly to the mainframe, one typed character at a time, and processed there. Output from the mainframe computer, to these terminals, was limited to alphanumeric characters and simple screen, or printer, formatting commands.

h) Computing within the business setting often worked well, as it was centrally maintained by skilled professionals, and tended to focus on a relatively small number of well-understood, business-critical, software applications. If the mainframe computer and its applications were working as intended, then most user problems could easily be resolved. In simple terms, you could either see the mainframe login prompt or you couldn't; if there was no connectivity between the mainframe and a dumb terminal the problem was generally fixed by swapping out defective dumb terminals, or replacing the serial communications cables that connected them to the mainframe computer. Fixing user problems in such an environment was typically quick and straightforward, and the impact of a problem was often limited to a single user. However, if the mainframe computer stopped working then quite a lot of people might have to stop work. The impact of such a failure was varied, depending on how integral mainframe computer operation was to the business. When used in a support role the impact might be quite limited as productive work could continue whilst the mainframe computer was repaired. When wholly relied upon for line-of-business operations, such as in the banking sector, any disruption would have been highly problematic. Where mainframe computer use was considered mission-critical, a systems architecture of instantly available back-up systems was used to avoid completely, or at the very least minimise, any unplanned downtime.

i) Outside of the computer room, computer use was pretty straightforward. Most users were simply business professionals that used mainframe computer services as part of their jobs. How the mainframe computer did what it did was a mystery that a typical user just did not need to understand. In fact, most users did not need to become computer experts in any way. They were trained in the use of the mainframe computer's applications so that they could do their jobs, and nothing more. They did not need to troubleshoot problems, patch software, install new operating system releases, or worry about viruses. Their main interface was their dumb terminal, and it really was just a simple tool of work. However, from a user's point of view, the dumb terminal-based interface was rather boring and typically only permitted the execution of a limited range of approved applications. Task execution was often prioritised, with less important jobs being queued behind, or slowed by, higher priority jobs, which meant that some users could not always progress swiftly in their work whilst, for example, the monthly payroll job was executing. It became apparent that whilst the mainframe computer was really good for some things, like running the company's accounting or stock-keeping systems, other smaller tasks might be better handled by a less powerful device, such as a personal computer, that could potentially deliver results far more quickly, regardless of the mainframe computer's workload.

j) The desire to move away from the centralised computing model, exemplified by the mainframe computer, to a more independent, distributed, approach, eventually lead to the creation of the standardised personal computer that we know today. International Business Machines Corporation launched a personal computer[13] in 1981 that would influence and standardise the design of personal computers for the next thirty-five years. Initially designed as a versatile personal computer for business it was quite rapidly accepted into the home as well, because people wanted to be able to use the same computer system at home as they did at work. This convergence of home and work computing into a single standardised solution was incredibly popular and lead to the manufacture of personal computers in vast numbers. By the start of the 1990s, economies of scale, associated with manufacturing a standardised unit in large volumes, helped to reduce costs, ensuring that these standardised personal computers became easily affordable by many ordinary people.

k)    From the early 1980s onwards, mainframe computer use steadily reduced, and personal computer use increased substantially. Mainframe computers did not go away completely; in fact they are still manufactured today, although in relatively small numbers. Some of their descendants became today's computer servers, which are now accessed by powerful personal computer-based clients, instead of by dumb terminals. Such servers still run a lot of the critical line-of-business applications, but the personal computer is used to enable nearly all other business activities.

l)    Over time, personal computers became more capable but also more complicated. Users that wanted a simple tool for work, or a device for fun, found themselves becoming self-taught computer experts; some people loved this and others were simply frustrated and annoyed. Personal computers became part of everyday life, a big part. Personal computer technology continued to evolve and many people, outside the Information Technology profession, quietly struggled to keep up with the latest operating system release, new must-have peripheral, or to protect themselves from the latest virus or Web-based scam. There was almost universal acknowledgement of the many benefits that the personal computer had brought to the world, but at the same time a lot of people were getting tired of the continual change that was occurring, and the need for their co-opted involvement in supporting those changes. It was realised that whilst change is often good, continual change can be tiring, and a lot of people were starting to wonder if there was not a better way to do things. By the end of the first decade of the twenty-first century, the processing power of a typical personal computer had increased by more than a hundred thousand fold[14] since the early 1980s, but it was not a hundred thousand times easier to use, maintain, or benefit from.

m)    In the world of computer games, a greatly simplified approach to computing had evolved in parallel to the rise of the personal computer; in the form of consoles dedicated to the singular task of entertainment. These games consoles were a tool for fun, and were completely locked-down in terms of their configuration and expandability. Even though these consoles were fully-fledged personal computers, albeit ones dedicated to a specific task, their form factor was quite unlike their counterparts; they did not have keyboards, just game control pads, they were much smaller, and they used the family television as a

---

[13] *The IBM PC Model 5150 was the first in a long line of, what would become known as, IBM-compatible personal computers.*
[14] *For example: In 1981 the Commodore Vic-20 personal computer with a MOS Technology 6502 microprocessor running at 1 megahertz had a performance of 0.5 million instructions per second (non-Dhrystone) whilst in 2010 an IBM-compatible personal computer with an AMD Phenom II X6 1100T microprocessor running at 3.3 gigahertz had a performance of 78,440 million instructions per second (Dhrystone), which in simple terms represents a more than 150,000 fold performance improvement. Real-world performance differences between these two microprocessors are probably even greater.*

display because they had no screen of their own, just like some the first personal computers for home use back in the early 1980s. Many people really appreciated the simplicity and reliability of the gaming console approach of turn it on, use it, turn it off, and that it just worked, each time, every time. Eventually the game consoles gained access to Web-based content, and facilitated Web-based social interactions within the global gaming community, and, in so doing, became a little more like a typical personal computer that could already do these types of things. The emergence of similar functionality between the games console and the personal computer again raised, in the minds of average folk, the question of why personal computers could sometimes be so complex and troublesome when the average games console often was not. Obviously, this was primarily because the games consoles had a much narrower functional remit than a typical personal computer, but in the eyes of many users the two devices were both just computers, one of which was generally far less troublesome than the other.

n)   During the time that personal computers and games consoles were becoming an established part of modern life, mobile-phones had also risen in popularity to become an affordable and indispensable communication tool for the masses. The convenience of owning such a device was so compelling that it was rapidly adopted on a global scale. In fact, such was the popularity of the mobile-phone that many traditional public telephone boxes were decommissioned because they had fallen into almost complete disuse, and many people terminated their landline-based home telephone subscriptions. The first mobile-phones provided just the basics of voice calls and text messaging, but over time they were substantially enhanced, adding many extra features, including access to Web-based data services. These enhanced phones became known as feature-phones. Eventually the feature-phone evolved into the even more powerful and sophisticated smart-phone.

o)   Smart-phones, like their feature-phone forbears, were, in many ways, just small personal computers. With their relatively large, high-resolution, touch-sensitive, colour screens, audio systems, compasses, gyroscopes, long-life batteries, video cameras, and wireless communications, they were truly science fiction made real. In fact, the smart-phone was such a capable device that for some users it quickly supplanted their use of their existing personal computer, as it permitted something that the more traditional devices had always struggled with, true mobile computing.

p)   From the smart-phone rose another portable device known as the tablet computer; this was essentially a very large smart-phone that did not, typically, support the telephony features associated with its smaller brethren. Tablet computers had been created many times in the past, when alternative personal computing form factors were being explored, but they had always failed to achieve widespread acceptance. However, this most recent attempt, essentially based on the underpinnings of the smart-phone, did succeed.

q)   One of the key features of smart-phones and tablet computers was that, like their simpler mobile-phone forebears, they just worked; you turned them on, they did their job, and the user really did not have to very much of anything to manage or maintain them. Unlike a more traditional personal computer, the application software and operating systems that ran on these devices were much more tightly controlled. Software developers often worked closely with the hardware manufacturers and telecommunications companies to push out new versions of operating systems to specific models using well-tested procedures that greatly minimised problems. Application software was largely supplied from curated stores that ensured that such software was virus free and conformed to acceptable behaviours. The application stores also permitted users to publish feedback on the functionality and performance of the applications, allowing other users to make informed decisions about whether a particular piece of software was good or bad before they installed it; an approach that really helped users avoid poor quality or troublesome software. Whilst such approaches were not new, collectively they helped make the smart-phone and tablet computer experience far superior to the more traditional personal computing experience, which because of its greater complexity made the life of the average user much less straightforward. By 2010, smart-phones and tablet computers already had the processing power of a personal computer dating from the year 2000, and many people started to realistically consider that their old style personal computer was finally going to be replaced with one of these new, reliable, and simple tools. However, whilst the new smart-phones and tablet computers seemed on the surface to be well qualified to take over the reins from the traditional personal computer, many users quickly learned that they were not yet wholly up to the job, and required, what seemed to be, a never ending list of new features and functionality to be added in order to be really useful. This meant that until these new devices were actually able to provide all needed functionality they would be largely relegated to the role of content consumption, while the bulk of content creation remained firmly in the domain of the traditional personal computer. The continual demand for smart-phones and tablet computers to be able to do more, has resulted in each new generation of such devices offering faster processing, faster graphics, more memory, better screens, better connectivity, and better battery life, which was all tied together by more capable and more sophisticated software. Improvements which were all necessary to provide even more complex and demanding functionalities, such as content creation. The danger now is that these devices may soon start to travel the exact same path as was previously trodden by traditional personal computers, and become overly complex and consequently much less reliable.

r)   At the same time as all the aforementioned personal computing devices were evolving, the Internet was rapidly maturing. The Internet is a worldwide network of networks that permits the global sharing of all types of digital information, and which has become an integral part of both business and personal life for a significant proportion of the world's population, particularly in more-developed countries. The Internet originated out of research conducted in the 1960s into how to build robust, fault-tolerant, distributed, computer networks. The Internet now provides access to a wide range of digital content and services, including the inter-linked documents of the World Wide Web (Web) and the global email system.

s)   Many of the services available from the Internet originate from computer servers; the modern day descendants of the old mainframe computers. An individual computer server might have a processing capability similar to a modern day desktop computer, but is physically much smaller, being of a simplified and modular design that is more suited to the computer racks within which it is typically installed. Computer servers deliver a wide range of digital content and services, via the Internet, to personal computer client devices, such as desktop computers, laptop computers, smart-phones, and tablet computers. Increasingly, the application software that used to be executed locally on a personal computing device is now executed on these remote computer servers and the results are then sent back to the personal computing device, or stored, somewhere on the Web, ready for later retrieval. These computer servers are housed in data centres that are located all around the world. A typical data centre can house thousands of servers, which collectively are incredibly powerful.

t)   Harnessing the collective processing power of multiple computers has been an on-going challenge ever since they started to be mass produced. Many different approaches have been tried over the years, but none were considered perfect, each having its own strengths and weaknesses. In the past, a typical computer server ran a single operating system that supported the execution of a single application, or application suite, which in turn provided a particular service to users located anywhere in the world, via the Internet. That computer server may have been overworked, or underutilised, depending on the level of demand for the service that it was providing. An overworked computer server might not provide the expected quality of service, and an underutilised computer server could be wasting a valuable resource that could theoretically be better deployed elsewhere. Ensuring that a computer server was being used optimally, that it was being fully utilised, but not overworked was difficult, as dynamically scaling workloads or reassigning tasks to more appropriate computer servers was in practice quite difficult. Optimal use was not impossible but it was often challenging and imperfect, especially when trying to meet the largely unpredictable demands of remote Web users. A new technique was developed, or rather reinvented, called virtualisation, which permitted a computer server to run more than one instance of an operating system. This technique was actually pioneered on the old mainframe computers during the late 1960s, but which had not been pursued on a large scale in the context of computer servers and personal computers until relatively recently. An operating system that is run in this way is known as a virtual machine. Being able to run more than one virtual machine on a single computer server allows a potentially underutilised computer server to become fully utilised. As this virtualisation technology matured, it become possible to provision virtual machines dynamically; allocating and de-allocating resources based on service demand. Eventually whole data centres adopted the virtualisation approach, and services could be assigned to any virtual machine within a particular data centre, or group of geographically-distant data centres. The dynamic use of virtualisation, coupled with a number of other techniques, to provide Web-based services eventually became known as cloud computing, or, more generically, the cloud.

u) Many businesses that previously managed their own in-house data centres then started to move their operations onto cloud computing-based services because they offered a scalable solution that could more easily and cost-effectively meet their changing needs, including a way to handle peak demand without having to invest in solutions that might spend most of the time sitting idle, waiting for the next peak. Cloud computing has permitted many businesses to swap capital expenditure, on systems, for operational expenditure, on services.

v) As the many technologies used for personal computing have evolved and improved over the last thirty-five years, so too have the many technologies that personal computing devices use to communicate. At the start of the 1980s, dumb terminals could communicate with a mainframe computer at bandwidths of 19,200 bits per second (bps). Today, a typical personal computing device can communicate over a wired local area network at bandwidths of up to 1,000,000,000 bps, whilst in some academic or business settings bandwidths of up to 100,000,000,000 bps are possible. At the start of the 1980s, the first personal computing devices, designed for home use, could be paired with modems that allowed remotely-located digital services to be accessed using the wired public telephone system at bandwidths of up to 1,200 bps. Wireless data communications did not become generally available until the late 1990s, when bandwidths of up to 115,000 bps became available via mobile communications services. Today, optical fibre-based Internet links support wired bandwidths of up to 2,000,000,000 bps, and the latest generation of mobile data communications can support wireless bandwidths of up to 450,000,000 bps. Other types of wireless communications, principally designed for short-range use inside the home or office, can even support bandwidths of up to 7,000,000,000 bps. The Internet is a network of networks, the principle links of which, known colloquially as the Internet backbone, communicate using optical fibre-based telecommunications infrastructures that can support bandwidths of 1,000,000,000,000 bps, or more, per link. The increase in data communications bandwidths over the last thirty-five years was largely due to continual incremental improvements in the many underlying technologies used to provide those communications. However, one particularly significant improvement was the sea change from copper wire-based telecommunications to optical fibre-based telecommunications, a change that significantly increased bandwidths and transmission range, reduced signal degradation, and for certain types of installation greatly reduced cost. Optical fibre-based telecommunications, along with other telecommunications technologies, such as communications satellites, have also helped to bring the Internet and Web to nearly every corner of the globe. Regulatory changes have also played a significant role, particularly in terms of the rapid growth of wireless communications, which was partly enabled by the reassignment of certain frequencies in national radio spectrums from analogue-based uses to digital communications services. The availability of these very substantial wired and wireless telecommunications bandwidths has enabled the development of many significant Web-based services, such as those that are able to provide real-time interactivity and high-resolution video, which are now fundamentally changing how personal computing solutions are designed, implemented, and used.

# 2.3 LESSONS FROM THE PAST

*Wisdom of our forefathers*

a)  Paul Otlet suggested a system built from, what we would consider today to be, some fairly simple components; telephone, television, video camera, and a well-stocked library, staffed by librarians. Of course, back in 1934 the television would have been considered one of the most advanced technological achievements of the modern world. Nevertheless, the television, is, by today's standards, a relatively simple device of singular purpose that cannot fulfil any useful function unless it is in receipt of its enabling service; a broadcast television signal. By using a telephone to request information, from a librarian, almost any sort of visually-oriented data could be viewed on a television. With a big enough library, and a veritable army of librarians, it would have been quite possible to provide access to almost all the world's published information. Adding in support for audio, as Otlet also suggested, would have yielded a system capable of supporting audio-visual learning, entertainment, and work on a global scale. It would have undoubtedly changed the world, and in fact when it was finally invented, albeit in a vastly different form, as the World Wide Web, it did just that. Otlet envisioned a system that would have tremendous value and usefulness, and which could now be built from some of today's simplest technologies. With his forward thinking, Otlet showed how a potentially world-changing result does not necessarily have to be complex in its construction or use, and that a large, centralised, resource could, in theory, be successfully shared between many distant users equipped with only the basic technologies of television and telephone.

b)  The world of computing had moved from a, generally efficient, centralised model, to a, much less efficient, distributed one. The centralised model is exemplified by the single mainframe computer, connected to many simple access terminals, which allowed it to be simultaneously shared between multiple users. The distributed model is exemplified by many individuals each having their own personal computer. Over recent years, computing has partially returned to the more centralised mode of operation due to numerous practical advancements in computer networking, telecommunication infrastructures, and the emergence of many popular Web-based services. However, a full return would, most likely, be dependent on all commonly required personal computing services becoming available from centralised Web-based sources, and the traditional personal computing device, currently used to access such services, being replaced by something much simpler. Personal computing services continue to steadily move onto the Web, and so will, in the fullness of time, most probably, be able to provide all the functionality currently available from a standalone personal computer. Unfortunately, the primary device used to access such Web-based services continues to be the traditional personal computer, even though a much simpler technology would suffice. This is partly due to the fact that people seem to have grown somewhat accustomed to having a highly-capable and fully-independent personal computing resource of their very own. The problem with this situation is that a traditional personal computer is very unlikely to be used optimally when used to receive remotely-sourced services, because it is generally far more powerful than is actually necessary for such a basic task. Not using a personal computing device in an optimal manner is a grossly inefficient and unjustifiable use of the resources needed to build and run it. Also, because a personal computer often belongs to an individual, when it is idle it typically cannot be reused for other tasks by someone else. In comparison, the cloud computing-based servers that are used to provide many Web-based services are rarely idle and are always used efficiently when they are used, and if a particular service is no longer needed its resources are immediately reused for something else that will benefit other users. Therefore, it would probably be much better if all personal computing activities were moved onto cloud computing-based services, and accessed using a device that was far simpler than a traditional personal computer. Successfully achieving both of these goals would permit personal computing to return to its much more efficient, highly centralised, roots.

c) Throughout the history of personal computing, whether in the home or in the office, there have been a number of occasions when the underlying technology has been noticeably more reliable and trouble-free, and other occasions when it has been less reliable and more problematic. It has arguably been at its most reliable when personal computing devices were technologically, or functionally, straightforward and simple, as in the case of the dumb terminal, the games console, and the mobile-phone, and at its least reliable when computing devices have been more complex, as in the case of the modern personal computer. Of course, reliability is a relative term, and many complex technologies are, in isolation, quite reliable, it is only when they are compared to other simpler technologies that a noticeable difference starts to become apparent. The more complex technologies typically delivered wide-ranging, standalone, capabilities, whilst the less complex ones were often dependent on external services or were only required to provide a narrow range of functionalities. The simpler technologies often required no maintenance, being of a fixed functionality, and were therefore much less susceptible to mistakes made by their users. More complex technologies often needed to be maintained, either by skilled technology professionals or by users who were required to informally develop the appropriate skills for such a task. It has to be remembered that whilst there are currently a lot of technology professionals in the world, there are many more people that do not possess an advanced level of technological understanding, but who, nevertheless, still need to use personal computing devices for work and pleasure on a regular basis. Users, being human, regularly make mistakes, especially when they are not trained technology professionals, so it is no wonder that any complex, user-supported, technology is going to be much less reliable than a technology that is inherently simpler, and does not require any maintenance at all. Therefore, in an ideal world, devices, such as personal computers, should preferably be of a highly simplified design that does not need any maintenance, so that they will be, on the whole, much more reliable and less problematic. Simpler technologies should also be much more affordable.

d)  A very large part of what is now possible in terms of personal computing is due as much to the capabilities of the latest personal computing devices as to the capabilities of the latest telecommunications infrastructures that are used to connect them, both of which have substantially evolved and improved over the years. Back in the 1980s, when the mainframe computer could have, theoretically, been used to bring computing to the masses, it was, in part, prevented by the inadequate telecommunications infrastructures of the day. Today, delivering alpha-numeric characters to millions of dumb terminals at 19,200 bits per second using modern telecommunications infrastructures would actually be incredibly easy. Over the last thirty-five years, since the start of the 1980s, wired digital communications bandwidths have increased by six orders of magnitude, or more than a million fold, whilst over the last fifteen years, since the end of the 1990s, wireless digital communications bandwidths have increased by three orders of magnitude, or more than a thousand fold. Increases which are now sufficient for both wired and wireless data communications to support the delivery of a very wide range of digital services, including those that require real-time interactivity, and high-resolution video. The telecommunications infrastructures that provide that bandwidth are expected to continue evolving and improving in the future, just as they have over the last few decades. So, any Web-based service that requires more bandwidth than is currently available will probably not have to wait very long, if the past growth in bandwidth can be taken as any indicator of the future, which it probably can. Therefore, a personal computing future that is wholly-based on the delivery of digital content and services over the Internet would now appear to be a very realistic possibility.

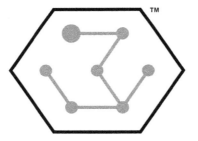

# 3    THE PRESENT

*The foundation of all our tomorrows*

a)    The Stream Tone will be a product of the present; it will be based on the knowledge, skills, techniques, technologies, thinking, and tools of today. This chapter considers some of the potential building blocks that could be used to create the Stream Tone, and some of the precursors that suggest that aspects of the Stream Tone may already exist today.

## 3.1    BUILDING BLOCKS

*No need to start from scratch!*

a)    If you were an engineer tasked with creating the Stream Tone, as envisioned today, the following Stream Tone building blocks might be the knowledge, skills, techniques, technologies, and thinking that you would first select for inclusion in your toolbox. Of course, choosing the right set of tools for this particular job would be largely impossible as the Stream Tone has not yet been fully defined. So all you could really do at this stage would be to select tools that appeared useful, or that might help you to better understand what the Stream Tone actually is or could be. The Stream Tone building blocks are where the Stream Tone starts to become more than just an idea. They mark the point at which the Stream Tone starts to be definitively defined, as the sum of its potential parts, the point at which the Stream starts to enter reality.

b)    Some of the Stream Tone building blocks, described in this section, are mature technologies that could readily be used to enable the creation of the Stream Tone, whilst others are just promising ideas, things that might be useful later on, and which, it would therefore, be wise to keep an eye on in the interim. Some of the building blocks are current **Web-based Services** that appear to be favourably shifting societal sentiment towards a future in which personal computing can be wholly-based on remotely-sourced services. Some of the building blocks will be required to create the foundational infrastructure of the Stream Tone, some will be required to create the many intermediates that will be needed on the Stream Tone's journey from inception to reality, and some will be required to bring the Stream Tone to full maturity. Consequently, there are quite a lot of them.

c)    Even though the list of building blocks provided in this section appears to be quite substantial, it should not be considered exhaustive or definitive, simply representative. The building blocks were subjectively selected on the basis that they appear to have the potential to contribute, in some way, towards the creation of the Stream Tone, as currently envisioned. The building blocks have been provided to demonstrate that the Stream Tone could, theoretically, be built from a wide range of current knowledge, skills, techniques, technologies, and thinking, and that, even at this very early stage, the Stream Tone is hopefully much less science fiction, and more science fact.

d)    Collectively, the Stream Tone building blocks define the physical and intellectual environment, the primordial soup, as it were, from which the Stream Tone will eventually emerge, and by better understanding the ingredients in that soup it is possible to better understand the Stream Tone. The building blocks will also provide a useful starting point for discussions that will better define what the Stream Tone should, or could, be. Such discussions may also help to identify the most efficient and effective approach for building and deploying the Stream Tone quickly and cheaply. In an ideal world, the Stream Tone would be wholly created from existing knowledge, skills, techniques, technologies, and thinking. Understanding whether that ideal is possible will depend on both a better definition of what the Stream Tone is, and what potential building blocks are actually going to be available. Of course, at this stage, the Stream Tone building blocks are just a bunch of raw ingredients that have yet to be combined in any particularly tasty way.

# 3.1.1    ACCELEROMETER

a)  **WHAT IS IT?** An accelerometer is a device that can detect the magnitude and direction of proper acceleration. Many modern portable personal computing devices, such as **Smart-Phones** and **Tablet Computers**, contain a multi-axis accelerometer that can be used to detect the orientation of the device. There are many different types of accelerometer, but the type most commonly found in portable electronic devices is a micro-machined accelerometer.

b)  **HOW COULD IT HELP?** Accelerometer technologies, used in many modern personal computing devices, are well understood and mature. Stream Tone Access Devices are intended to be direct replacements for all current personal computing devices, including **Smart-Phones** and **Tablet Computers**, and will therefore need to include Accelerometer technologies in order to be able to deliver functionality comparable to current personal computing devices.

c)  **FURTHER READING**
Accelerometer: *https://en.wikipedia.org/wiki/Accelerometer*

# 3.1.2    AERIAL PLATFORM NETWORK

a)  **WHAT IS IT?** An Aerial Platform Network (APN) is a type of telecommunications infrastructure that is based on aerial platforms (APs), such as airplanes, airships, or balloons, which is able to provide telecommunications services to a large geographic area. Typically, an APN maintains a communications link with an established telecommunications infrastructure, such as a terrestrial telecommunications network, which is then shared with telecommunications devices located within the geographic area below the AP. The geographic area that a particular AP is able to serve is directly proportional to the altitude at which the AP operates. In simple terms, the higher the altitude the greater the geographic area, the lower the altitude the smaller the geographic area. Different types of AP are able to operate at different altitudes, with certain types of aircraft-based APs being able to consistently operate at altitudes of 20 kilometres (km) or more and balloon-based APs at altitudes of up to 40 km. Consequently, APNs are also known as high-altitude platforms. Aircraft-based and airship-based APs are required to maintain their position within the geographic area that they are designed to serve, by following a repetitive flight path. Balloon-based APs are either tethered to the ground, or allowed to float free, circumnavigating the globe by riding the jet streams found near the troposphere. APNs are able to provide a wide range of wireless telecommunications services, including second-generation mobile communications (2G), third-generation mobile communications (3G), and *Wi-Fi*. In the future, it is also expected that APNs will be able to offer access to *Fourth-Generation Mobile Communications* (4G) as well. APNs offer many advantages, especially when compared to other types of telecommunications infrastructure. Compared to a *Communications Satellite*, a typical AP that is used as part of an APN is far cheaper to deploy and operate, and can be more easily returned to the ground for maintenance and upgrade. Compared to a terrestrial telecommunications infrastructure, an APN can be more cheaply, easily, and rapidly deployed to highly remote or physically challenging geographies. APNs can be particularly useful when used as a temporary replacement for telecommunications infrastructures that have failed due to a natural disaster. APNs have been previously used by the military to provide ad hoc battlefield communications. APNs are now actively being explored as a way to cost-effectively bring *Internet* connectivity to remote geographies that are not currently supported by more traditional telecommunications infrastructures. Being able to provide cost-effective *Internet* connectivity to such geographies will help to bring the *Web* to the next billion people. Two particular technologies that are being explored in this respect are the use of solar-powered electric unmanned aerial vehicles, also known as drones, and free-flying high-altitude balloons.

b) **HOW COULD IT HELP?** The Stream Tone needs both wired and wireless telecommunications that are highly affordable, high bandwidth, low latency, highly reliable, and ubiquitously available. Telecommunications technologies, such as APNs, can help to ensure that Stream Tone Transfer Protocol-based services will be accessible from even the most remote and challenging geographies, with sufficient bandwidth, low latency, and at an affordable price.

c) **FURTHER READING**
2G: *https://en.wikipedia.org/wiki/2G*
3G: *https://en.wikipedia.org/wiki/3G*
4G: *https://en.wikipedia.org/wiki/4G*
Airship: *https://en.wikipedia.org/wiki/Airship*
Broadband Communications From Aerial Platform Networks:
*http://www.researchgate.net/publication/215650814_broadband_communications_from_a
erial_platform_networks/file/79e41510815e28b01b.pdf*
CAPANINA.Org: *http://www.capanina.org/*
Communications Satellite: *https://en.wikipedia.org/wiki/Communications_satellite*
Electric Aircraft: *https://en.wikipedia.org/wiki/Electric_aircraft*
High-Altitude Balloon: *https://en.wikipedia.org/wiki/High-altitude_balloon*
High-Altitude Platform: *https://en.wikipedia.org/wiki/High-altitude_platform*
Internet: *https://en.wikipedia.org/wiki/Internet*
Jet Stream: *https://en.wikipedia.org/wiki/Jet_stream*
Telecommunications Network:
*https://en.wikipedia.org/wiki/Telecommunications_network*
Unmanned Aerial Vehicle: *https://en.wikipedia.org/wiki/Unmanned_aerial_vehicle*
Wi-Fi: *https://en.wikipedia.org/wiki/Wi-Fi*

# 3.1.3 AMBIENT LIGHT SENSOR

a) **WHAT IS IT?** An Ambient Light Sensor (ALS) is a device for measuring light levels in a given locale. Most ALSs are based on photodiodes, photoresistors, or phototransistors.

Many modern, battery-powered, portable, personal computing devices use ALSs to dynamically alter the light output of their display screens, based on local lighting conditions. When ambient light levels are high the screen needs to generate more light, and when light levels are low the screen's output can be reduced. Actively controlling the light output of a display screen in this way can often lead to substantial power savings, helping to extend the battery life of many portable personal computing devices. ALSs can also be used for *Visible Light Communication*.

b) **HOW COULD IT HELP?** Whilst some Stream Tone Access Devices (STADs) will be powered by a direct connection to mains electricity, most will be portable devices that rely on battery power. ALSs, as used in many modern personal computing devices, are well understood, mature, and can be used to efficiently manage the power used by STADs with a portable form factor.

c) **FURTHER READING**
Ambient Light Sensor: *http://ambient-light-sensor.software.informer.com/wiki/*
Photodetector: *https://en.wikipedia.org/wiki/Photodetector*
Photodiode: *https://en.wikipedia.org/wiki/Photodiode*
Photoresistor: *https://en.wikipedia.org/wiki/Photoresistor*
Visible Light Communication: *https://en.wikipedia.org/wiki/Visible_light_communication*

# 3.1.4 ANAMORPHIC STRETCH TRANSFORM

a) **WHAT IS IT?** The Anamorphic Stretch Transform (AST) is a physics-based mathematical transform that can be used for the acquisition and *Compression* of analogue and digital data, which was developed by the Henry Samueli School of Engineering and Applied Science, University of California, Los Angeles. The AST works by self-adaptively stretching and warping data in such a manner that after it is then downsampled the quantity of data is reduced without loss of pertinent data. When used in analogue applications, the AST allows signals to be captured and digitised faster than the operational speed of the sensor and the digitiser would normally allow, and to minimise the quantity of data generated in the process. The AST can be used for lossy digital image *Compression*, either as a standalone algorithm or combined with existing image *Compression* algorithms, and can offer a significant improvement in terms of *Compression* ratio and image quality compared to existing image *Compression* algorithms, such as Joint Photographic Experts Group (JPEG) or JPEG 2000. AST-based image *Compression* has not yet entered mainstream use.

b) **HOW COULD IT HELP?** The Stream Tone Transfer Protocol (STTP) will be used to communicate digital content and services over the *Internet* from the *Web* to a Stream Tone Access Device, and to send user-input back. The efficiency with which the STTP will be able to communicate such content and services will, in part, depend on the use of lossy and lossless data *Compression* algorithms that are optimised for compressing the different types of data that comprise such content and services. An AST-based *Compression* algorithm might be suitable for compressing static image data that will be communicated using the STTP.

c) **FURTHER READING**

Anamorphic Stretch Transform:
*https://en.wikipedia.org/wiki/Anamorphic_stretch_transform*
Anamorphic Transformation And Its Application To Time-Bandwidth Compression:
*http://arxiv.org/abs/1307.0137*
Data Compression: *https://en.wikipedia.org/wiki/Data_compression*
Discrete Anamorphic Transform For Image Compression:
*http://ieeexplore.ieee.org/stamp/stamp.jsp?arnumber=06804641*
Image Compression Using The Anamorphic Stretch Transform:
*http://ieeexplore.ieee.org/xpl/login.jsp?tp=&arnumber=6781885&url=http%3A%2F%2*
*Fieeexplore.ieee.org%2Fxpls%2Fabs_all.jsp%3Farnumber%3D6781885*
JPEG: *https://en.wikipedia.org/wiki/JPEG*
JPEG 2000: *https://en.wikipedia.org/wiki/JPEG_2000*
Lossy Compression: *https://en.wikipedia.org/wiki/Lossy_compression*
The Anamorphic Stretch Transform - Putting The Squeeze On "Big Data":
*http://www.osa-*
*opn.org/home/articles/volume_25/february_2014/features/the_anamorphic_stretch_transf*
*orm_putting_the_squee/#.U6aKlFFSisp*

# 3.1.5 APPLICATION PROGRAMMING INTERFACE

a) **WHAT IS IT?** An Application Programming Interface (API) is a specification and a method for interacting with software-based functionality. An API can be used for programmatic access to a wide variety of functionality, such as routines held within a software development library, application services, and **Web-based Services**. API specifications can be defined using more than one computer language in order to provide compatibility with a wide range of software-based systems. **Web**-based APIs are typically defined using **HyperText Transfer Protocol**, Extensible Markup Language (XML), and JavaScript Object Notation (JSON), and often use Representational State Transfer-style communications. **Web**-based APIs provide access to functionality for blogging, enterprise, email, **File Hosting**, financial, games, government, **Internet**, mapping, medical, messaging, music, news, office, payment, photo, search, security, shopping, social, storage, telephony, tools, transportation, travel, utility, video, and weather. **Web**-based APIs permit functionality from different providers to be selectively combined to create new composite services, known as mash-ups. For example, some **Web Desktop** providers use APIs to integrate functionality from other **Web-based Services** into their **Web Desktop** service in order to create a **Web Desktop** service with features comparable to a local desktop operating system, but without the need to create all such functionality themselves. **Web**-based APIs are helping to create a new and better version of the **Web**, an evolved **Web**, which is increasingly built from reusable **Web**-based components, accessed via API.

b) **HOW COULD IT HELP?** **Web**-based APIs can be used to create digital services that are greater than the sum of their individual parts. All of the services that will be communicated using the Stream Tone Transfer Protocol (STTP) will be **Web**-based. Digital service providers will need to make extensive use of **Web**-based APIs in order to create all the STTP-based services that will be required to support Comprehensive Remote Personal Computing. Being able to leverage a wide range of existing **Web**-based functionalities can reduce development costs, which will help to keep STTP-based services affordable.

c) **FURTHER READING**
Application Programming Interface:
*https://en.wikipedia.org/wiki/Application_programming_interface*
HyperText Transfer Protocol: *https://en.wikipedia.org/wiki/Hypertext_Transfer_Protocol*
JSON: *https://en.wikipedia.org/wiki/JSON*
Mash-Up (Web Application Hybrid): *https://en.wikipedia.org/wiki/Mash-up_%28web_application_hybrid%29*
Representational State Transfer:
*https://en.wikipedia.org/wiki/Representational_state_transfer*
World Wide Web: *https://en.wikipedia.org/wiki/World_Wide_Web*
XML: *https://en.wikipedia.org/wiki/XML*

# 3.1.6 APPLICATION-SPECIFIC INTEGRATED CIRCUIT

a) **WHAT IS IT?** An Application-Specific Integrated Circuit (ASIC) is an integrated circuit that has been customised to meet a particular need. Modern ASICs can contain microprocessors and memory blocks, and can be used to build a *System on a Chip*. ASICS cannot be reprogrammed after they have been manufactured, unlike *Field-Programmable Gate Arrays* (FPGAs). The creation of an ASIC often incurs substantial non-recurring engineering (NRE) costs, compared to an FPGA alternative. ASICs are physically smaller than a functionally comparable FPGA, are of a higher performance, and require less power. ASICs are ideally suited to high volume production, where functionality will not be subject to change. Ignoring the initial NRE cost of developing a new ASIC, the on-going component cost will typically be much less than a comparable FPGA-based solution.

b) **HOW COULD IT HELP?** The first Stream Tone Access Device (STAD) hardware is likely to be based on FPGA components, as these will support the many functional changes that will most likely be required by a rapidly evolving new technology, such as the Stream Tone. However, once the functional requirements for a STAD have been finalised it will be possible to design a fully-custom ASIC that will be cheaper, faster, and physically smaller than the FPGA initially used. The move from FPGA to ASIC will reduce the cost of a STAD, making it much more affordable, which will, in turn, spur accelerated adoption of the Stream Tone.

c) **FURTHER READING**
Application-Specific Integrated Circuit: *https://en.wikipedia.org/wiki/Application-specific_integrated_circuit*
Field-Programmable Gate Array: *https://en.wikipedia.org/wiki/Field-programmable_gate_array*
Microprocessor: *https://en.wikipedia.org/wiki/Microprocessor*
Non-Recurring Engineering: *https://en.wikipedia.org/wiki/Non-recurring_engineering*
System On A Chip: *https://en.wikipedia.org/wiki/System_on_a_chip*

# 3.1.7 APPLICATION STORE

a) **WHAT IS IT?** An application store is a curated, **Web**-based, digital, distribution service for software applications. A typical application store can often contain hundreds of thousands of software applications. Application stores provide a search engine that permits a user to identify application software based on a wide range of search criteria. Application stores generally limit their offerings to software applications that are intended to be run on a particular type of computing hardware or on a particular type of operating system. The software applications provided by application stores are typically inspected, either manually or programmatically, by the operators of those stores to ensure that they are virus free and behave in an acceptable manner. Application stores often support a feedback mechanism that allows users to publish comments on the fitness for purpose, performance, and quality of the applications offered, which can help other users avoid poor quality applications. The software application installation process is usually highly simplified, and can be easily used by users with only the most basic information technology skills. Application stores have become the principle mechanism for distributing software applications to **Smart-Phones** and **Tablet Computers**.

b) **HOW COULD IT HELP?** Before dedicated Stream Tone Access Devices (STADs) are created it is most likely that Stream Tone Transfer Protocol (STTP)-based services will be accessed using software that emulates a STAD, and which will be run on an existing personal computing device. Application stores could be used to distribute a Stream Tone Access Device Emulator (STADE) software application, permitting STTP-based functionality to be accessed from the current generation of personal computing devices. The simplified installation process offered by most application stores will help remove barriers, such as the need for advanced information technology skills, which might otherwise slow the rate of STADE adoption.

c) **FURTHER READING**
Application Software: *https://en.wikipedia.org/wiki/Application_software*
Application Store: *https://en.wikipedia.org/wiki/Application_store*
Computer Virus: *https://en.wikipedia.org/wiki/Computer_virus*
Information Technology: *https://en.wikipedia.org/wiki/Information_technology*

# 3.1.8 APPLICATION STREAMING

a) **WHAT IS IT?** Application streaming is the on-demand delivery of a software application over a computer network, such as the **Internet**, one portion at a time. Streamed applications have the advantage that they do not need to be installed or maintained on the user's personal computing device. Streamed applications are delivered from a remotely-located application server to a user's personal computer via a computer network connection, using secure **Web** protocols, such as Transport Layer Security. Maintenance of the streamed applications is centralised onto the application server. Application streaming technology can use **Digital Rights Management** to protect intellectual property rights. Licenses for the software applications being streamed can be effectively managed on the application server. Only the portions of the software application that are needed for the application to start executing or containing required user functionality are initially delivered. Remaining portions of the software application may be delivered in the background or when required. Delivered applications, whether in full or in part, may be

41

cached locally on the user's personal computing device, to facilitate faster application start-up on subsequent use. Cached software applications are able to execute even if there is no network connection to the application server. Software applications that have not been cached are not available unless the network connection to the application server is working. Some application streaming services try to predict what portion of a software application will be required next, and will then pre-load that portion before the user requests it. Application streaming is often combined with **Cloud Computing**-based application virtualisation technologies, which are used to create an appropriate execution environment for the streamed software application without the need to install the software application locally on the executing computing device. Application virtualisation executes the streamed software application in a secure, isolated, execution environment, known as a sandbox that helps protect the local personal computing device. When the software application is terminated by the user, it can be completely removed from the user's personal computing device.

b) **HOW COULD IT HELP?** Application streaming demonstrates the viability of delivering personal computing functionalities over a computer network, such as the **Internet**. The Stream Tone Transfer Protocol (STTP) will be used to communicate a wide range of personal computing functionalities that will be provided by **Cloud Computing**-based Stream Tone Service Infrastructures and delivered by Stream Tone Telecommunications Infrastructures. If application streaming is considered acceptable to the average user then STTP-based services should also be acceptable, as both technologies are able to deliver personal computing functionalities from a remote source, albeit in very different ways.

c) **FURTHER READING**
Application Software: *https://en.wikipedia.org/wiki/Application_software*
Application Streaming: *https://en.wikipedia.org/wiki/Application_streaming*
Cloud Computing: *https://en.wikipedia.org/wiki/Cloud_computing*
Computer Network: *https://en.wikipedia.org/wiki/Computer_network*
Digital Rights Management: *https://en.wikipedia.org/wiki/Digital_rights_management*
Intellectual Property: *https://en.wikipedia.org/wiki/Intellectual_property*
Internet: *https://en.wikipedia.org/wiki/Internet*
Sandbox (Computer Security):
*https://en.wikipedia.org/wiki/Sandbox_%28computer_security%29*
Server (Computing): *https://en.wikipedia.org/wiki/Server_%28computing%29*
Transport Layer Security: *https://en.wikipedia.org/wiki/Transport_Layer_Security*
Virtualization: *https://en.wikipedia.org/wiki/Virtualization*

# 3.1.9 ARM VERSION 8

a) **WHAT IS IT?** ARM Version 8 (ARMv8) is a low-cost, power-efficient, **Reduced Instruction Set Computing** (RISC) architecture that supports both 32-bit and 64-bit instructions, developed by ARM Holdings plc. ARM-based microprocessors are widely used in many modern electronic devices, such as calculators, cameras, disk players, entertainment systems, laptop computers, music players navigation devices, network equipment, photocopiers, printers, security systems, set-top boxes, **Smart-Phones**, smart meters, speakers, storage devices, **Tablet Computers**, telephones, televisions, toys, video conferencing systems, and video surveillance systems. Computer servers used in commercial **Data Centres** generally need to be able to access more than 4 gigabytes of random-access memory, which is the limit of 32-bit microprocessor architectures. As the

ARMv8 architecture supports 48-bit memory addressing it is considered suitable for use in **Data Centre** servers, such as those that are used to power many **Cloud Computing**-based services. ARMv8 supports single instruction multiple data (SIMD) functionality which provides acceleration for many media and signal-processing applications. The ARMv8 architecture supports hardware-based **Encryption** and decryption, an important feature that is required to help protect personal data at rest, in transit, and in use, especially within multi-tenant, **Cloud Computing**-based, virtualised environments. ARMv8 also includes hardware support for virtualisation. The ARMv8 architecture can be used to build a **System on a Chip**, which can contain multiple microprocessor cores. Computer servers built using ARMv8-based microprocessors are power-efficient and can help to reduce **Data Centre** operating costs.

b) **HOW COULD IT HELP?** The ARMv8 microprocessor architecture brings cost-effective and power-efficient RISC technology to **Cloud-Computing**-based **Data Centres**. **Cloud Computing**-based servers will, in the future, be responsible for generating all Stream Tone Transfer Protocol (STTP)-based services. Modern RISC-based architectures, such as ARMv8, can help **Cloud Computing**-based **Data Centres** deliver affordable STTP-based content and services.

c) **FURTHER READING**
32-Bit: *https://en.wikipedia.org/wiki/32-bit*
64-Bit Computing: *https://en.wikipedia.org/wiki/64-bit_computing*
ARM Architecture: *https://en.wikipedia.org/wiki/Arm_architecture*
ARMv8 Architecture: *http://www.arm.com/products/processors/armv8-architecture.php*
Cloud Computing: *https://en.wikipedia.org/wiki/Cloud_computing*
Data Center: *https://en.wikipedia.org/wiki/Data_center*
Microprocessor: *https://en.wikipedia.org/wiki/Microprocessor*
Random-Access Memory: *https://en.wikipedia.org/wiki/Random-access_memory*
Server (Computing): *https://en.wikipedia.org/wiki/Server_%28computing%29*
SIMD: *https://en.wikipedia.org/wiki/SIMD*
Virtualization: *https://en.wikipedia.org/wiki/Virtualization*

# 3.1.10 ASYMMETRIC MULTILEVEL OUTPHASING

a) **WHAT IS IT?** Asymmetric Multilevel Outphasing (AMO) is a radio frequency (RF) power amplifier (PA) architecture, which is more efficient than that used by traditional PAs, such as those based on linear amplification using non-linear components technology. RF PAs convert low-power RF signals into high-power RF signals suitable for driving the antenna of a radio transmitter, and can typically be found in telecommunications base-stations, also known as cell sites, and mobile communications devices, such as **Smart-Phones**. Traditional RF PAs are generally quite inefficient, and a lot of power is often wasted as heat. When a traditional RF PA is used in a base-station, active cooling is often required to remove the waste heat, and when used in a portable communications device, active RF communications will be a significant drain on power, reducing the time interval between battery charges. Traditional RF PAs are typically tuned for specific RF applications, such as third-generation mobile communications (3G) or **Wi-Fi**. Communications devices that need to support multiple RF applications need multiple, discrete, RF PA components, which can take up valuable space, particularly within highly

43

portable communications devices, such as **Smart-Phones**. The reason that traditional RF PAs are inefficient is that they must support two modes of operation; standby mode and signal output mode. In signal output mode, an RF signal is transmitted, and the RF PA operates at high power. In standby mode, no RF signal is transmitted, and the RF PAs reduces power usage. RF PAs often need to switch between these modes at a very fast rate. However, if the difference between standby power and signal output power is too great, the switch from low power to high power can cause the RF output signal to become distorted, particularly at the high radio frequencies used by modern wireless telecommunications. The traditional solution to this problem has been to set the standby power level quite high, so that its difference with the power level of signal output mode is not too great; an approach that is very power inefficient. AMO-based RF PAs are able to dynamically determine the optimal power requirements in all situations, both standby and signal output, without degrading even high-frequency signals. AMO-based RF PAs are expected to be approximately twice as power-efficient as traditional RF PAs. AMO-based RF PAs are just starting to be commercialised, but it is hoped that they will see widespread deployment in the near future. One the first uses for AMO-based RF PAs will be in telecommunications base-stations, where significant savings in the power used for RF signal generation, as well as active cooling, are expected. In particular, base-stations located in remote geographies that are often powered by diesel generators are likely to find AMO-based RF PA technology highly beneficial. Eventually, it is hoped that a single generic AMO-based RF PA component will be developed that can handle multiple RF applications, and which can be used to replace the multiple RF PA components currently used in many current portable communications devices. It is expected that portable communications devices that used AMO-based RF PAs will have significantly reduced power usage when actively using RF communications, which will help to increase the time interval between battery charges. AMO-based RF PAs are expected to lead to significant savings in capital expenditure for telecommunications base-station infrastructure, as well as on-going operational expenditure.

b) **HOW COULD IT HELP?** The Stream Tone needs both wired and wireless telecommunications that are highly affordable, high bandwidth, low latency, highly reliable, and ubiquitously available. It is hoped that modern telecommunications technologies, such as AMO-based RF PAs, will help to ensure that the Stream Tone will be ubiquitously available, with sufficient bandwidth, at an affordable price. Out of all the components typically found in a modern portable electronic device, the power consumed by RF communications is often one of the highest. Whilst some Stream Tone Access Devices will be powered by a direct connection to mains electricity, most will be portable devices that rely on battery power. AMO-based RF PA technology can be used to reduce the power used by a STAD and greatly increase the time interval between battery charges.

c) **FURTHER READING**

3G: *https://en.wikipedia.org/wiki/3G*
Asymmetric Multilevel Outphasing Architecture For Multi-Standard Transmitters:
*http://www-mtl.mit.edu/~jldawson/Dawson_digest2009.pdf*
Base Station: *https://en.wikipedia.org/wiki/Base_station*
Cell Site: *https://en.wikipedia.org/wiki/Cell_site*
Efficiency Breakthrough Promises Smartphones That Use Half The Power:
*http://www.technologyreview.com/news/506491/efficiency-breakthrough-promises-smartphones-that-use-half-the-power/*
Eta Devices, Inc.: *http://etadevices.com/*
Radio Frequency: *https://en.wikipedia.org/wiki/Radio_frequency*

RF Power Amplifier: *https://en.wikipedia.org/wiki/RF_power_amplifier*

# 3.1.11 AUTOSTEREOSCOPIC DISPLAY TECHNOLOGY

a) **WHAT IS IT?** Autostereoscopic Display Technology (ASDT) is able to present stereoscopic images that offer the illusion of three-dimensional (3D) depth without the use of specialised viewing equipment, such as eyeglasses. A common approach typically involves the use of a parallax barrier or lenticular lens, both of which overlay a standard display screen. The overlay directs a different image to each eye, when viewed from a particular position. The different images are then recombined by the viewer's brain creating an effective illusion of depth within the viewed image. ASDT can also be used to display more normal, two-dimensional (2D), imagery, if required.

b) **HOW COULD IT HELP?** Adding a parallax barrier or a lenticular lens overlay to a Stream Tone Access Device (STAD) display screen would permit the viewing of either 2D or 3D imagery. Alternative STAD form factors, such as augmented reality eyeglasses, will be able to inherently support 3D imagery without the use of overlays.

c) **FURTHER READING**
Augmented Reality: *https://en.wikipedia.org/wiki/Augmented_reality*
Autostereoscopy: *https://en.wikipedia.org/wiki/Autostereoscopy*

# 3.1.12 BACKWARD INCOMPATIBILITY

a) **WHAT IS IT?** Backward Incompatibility (BI) is a clean-slate design approach that consciously avoids support for previous generation features, functions, or technologies when designing a new product. A backwardly incompatible design approach potentially allows for product simplification because it does not need to support or incorporate elements from previous designs. Many new products are inherently backward incompatible simply because they embody radical new designs and are fundamentally incapable of providing compatibility with anything that has gone before. Products with an obvious lineage often seek to provide a level of Backward Compatibility (BC) in order to maintain a familiar interface or support the use of previous generation services. BC allows a product to seamlessly evolve from one version into the next without negating familiarity or investment in previous features or functionality, until its users are ready to do so. Abandoning BC can therefore present many challenges. Supporting BC can be expensive both in terms of design and implementation effort and costs. A product based on a BI approach can therefore be designed more easily, faster, and at a lower cost. The cost reductions associated with BI can be passed on to the consumer in terms of lower prices and a greatly simplified product. Another compatibility approach, that complements BI, is Forward Compatibility (FC), which is a design approach that seeks to ensure that the design of a new product or service is based on an extensible platform that can be easily modified to support a wide range of new features and functions in the future. An example of a product class that has recently adopted an element of BI is the laptop computer which no longer includes an optical disk drive because of the increased use of computer network-based downloads and solid-state memory cards. An example of a product class that currently requires BC is the modern ***Smart-Phone*** which typically contains several radio frequency chipsets in order to support the older generations of mobile communications standards that are still in global use. In the future, **Smart-Phones** may adopt a more BI design approach and will only support the most recent mobile communications standards in order to reduce costs. BI can be considered to be a form of accelerated obsolescence, in which currently common features and functionalities that will eventually no longer be affordable, practical, or required are simply removed earlier than might have occurred naturally.

b) **HOW COULD IT HELP?** The Stream Tone Access Device (STAD) needs to be a very affordable electronic device for accessing digital content and services communicated using the Stream Tone Transfer Protocol. In many ways, the STAD will be a wholly unique device that will be designed to fulfil a very particular set of tasks. However, the STAD, in all its various forms, will also be designed to replace all current personal computing devices and some degree of BC is likely to be necessary in order for the STAD to fit into the current world of personal computing. Nevertheless, the exclusion of certain functionalities, interfaces, and technologies will definitely be possible. Design approaches, such as BI, and FC, will be able to help to ensure that a STAD will be perfectly designed to fulfil its current and future roles, with minimal concessions to the past. The simpler the STAD is, the less it should cost, which is something that will ultimately benefit everyone.

c) **FURTHER READING**
Backward Compatibility: *https://en.wikipedia.org/wiki/Backward_compatibility*
Forward Compatibility: *https://en.wikipedia.org/wiki/Forward_compatibility*
Laptop: *https://en.wikipedia.org/wiki/Laptop*
Obsolescence: *https://en.wikipedia.org/wiki/Obsolescence*
Product Design: *https://en.wikipedia.org/wiki/Product_design*
Radio Frequency: *https://en.wikipedia.org/wiki/Radio_frequency*

# 3.1.13   BAROMETER

a) **WHAT IS IT?** A barometer is a device that measures atmospheric pressure, which can be used to determine altitude. Many modern, portable, personal computing devices include a **Global Positioning System** (GPS) receiver, which is very good at determining longitudinal and latitudinal position but which can sometimes struggle to quickly determine an accurate altitude, hence many such devices also include a barometer to assist in this process. The barometer included in such devices is typically based on a digital pressure-sensing transducer. Accurate location information can also be used for a wide range of sophisticated navigational and positional applications.

b) **HOW COULD IT HELP?** The accuracy and performance of modern navigational technologies, such as GPS, can be greatly enhanced through the use of complementary devices such as barometers. Stream Tone Access Devices are intended to be direct replacements for all current personal computing devices, including **Smart-Phones** and **Tablet Computers**, and will therefore need to include highly accurate navigational technologies, such as barometer-augmented GPS, in order to be able to deliver functionality comparable to current personal computing devices.

c) **FURTHER READING**
Barometer: *https://en.wikipedia.org/wiki/Barometer*

Global Positioning System: *https://en.wikipedia.org/wiki/Global_Positioning_System*

# 3.1.14    BLUETOOTH

a) **WHAT IS IT?** Bluetooth is an evolving, short-range, wireless communications technology. It uses a packet-based protocol based on frequency-hopping spread-spectrum technologies. Bluetooth is designed to be small form-factor, low power, low cost, and secure. It was originally designed as a wireless replacement for network cabling within business. Bluetooth can have a range of up to 100 metres, dependent on the nature of the physical environment that it is used within, and the class of device used. It can typically transmit data at up to 3 megabits per second, although much faster speeds are possible when it is coupled with other wireless technologies, as in the case of Bluetooth 3.0+HS. Bluetooth is a communications technology commonly featured in many modern personal computing devices, such as desktop computers, laptop computers, **Smart-Phones**, and **Tablet Computers**, where it provides access to a very wide range of electronic devices and computing peripherals. The Bluetooth Special Interest Group is responsible for the on-going development of the Bluetooth specification, management of the fee-based device qualification program, and protection of the Bluetooth trademarks. Bluetooth is built from a number of patented technologies, and licenses for its use are available, free-of-charge, only for qualified devices, so whilst the Bluetooth protocol is open, it is generally considered, for all practical purposes, to be a proprietary technology.

b) **HOW COULD IT HELP?** Short-range communications technology, suitable for inclusion in mobile personal computing devices, is well understood and mature. Stream Tone Access Devices are intended to be direct replacements for all current personal computing devices, including **Smart-Phones** and **Tablet Computers**, and will therefore need to include short-range communications technologies, such as Bluetooth, in order to be able to offer functionality comparable to today's mobile personal computing devices.

c) **FURTHER READING**
Bluetooth: *https://en.wikipedia.org/wiki/Bluetooth*
Bluetooth Special Interest Group: *https://www.bluetooth.org/en-us*
Wireless: *https://en.wikipedia.org/wiki/Wireless*

# 3.1.15    BROWSER-BASED OPERATING SYSTEM

a) **WHAT IS IT?** A Browser-Based Operating System (BBOS) is an operating system designed to run a single application, a **Web Browser**. Having to only support a single application permits the operating system to be greatly simplified, a process than improves reliability, and greatly reduces hardware requirements. A BBOS will run on relatively basic, and therefore cheap, personal computing hardware. Most personal computing activities are delivered by **Web-based Services** via the **Internet**. As most user-data is stored on the **Web**, local storage requirements are minimal.

b) **HOW COULD IT HELP?** The existence of BBOSs demonstrates the viability of personal computing devices that have little inherent ability and which totally rely on **Web-based Services** in order to be useful. The Stream Tone Access Device is a simple device for accessing digital content and services communicated using the Stream Tone Transfer Protocol, and which has no processing ability of its own.

c) **FURTHER READING**
Chrome OS:
*https://www.google.com/intl/en/chrome/browser/?hl=en&brand=CHMA&utm_campaign =en&utm_source=en-ha-sea-sg-bk&utm_medium=ha*
Chrome OS: *https://en.wikipedia.org/wiki/Chrome_os*
Cloud Computing: *https://en.wikipedia.org/wiki/Cloud_computing*
Firefox OS: *https://www.mozilla.org/en-US/firefox/os/*
Firefox OS: *https://en.wikipedia.org/wiki/Firefox_OS*
Internet: *https://en.wikipedia.org/wiki/Internet*
Operating System: *https://en.wikipedia.org/wiki/Operating_system*
Web Browser: *https://en.wikipedia.org/wiki/Web_browser*

# 3.1.16   CAPACITIVE SENSING

a) **WHAT IS IT?** Capacitive Sensing (CS) is a technology based on capacitive coupling, which is an electrical effect that can be used to detect the close proximity of anything that is conductive or has a different dielectric than air. Capacitance is an electrical phenomenon whereby a system, generally of two conducting elements that are separated by a non-conducting medium, is able to store an electrical charge. Such a system is generally referred to as a capacitor. As the human body is a good electrical conductor, CS can be used to detect human touch. In which case, a part of the human body, such as a hand, forms one of the two electrically conducting elements in a CS system, and the non-conducting medium is generally air. The other electrically conducting element is part of the touch-sensing mechanism. CS technology can be used as the basis for a human interface device (HID), such as the touch-sensitive display screens that are commonly found on many modern portable personal computing devices. The touch-sensitive surface generally consists of an insulator coated with a conductor, such as indium tin oxide. Touch-sensitive display screens typically have a glass insulator and a transparent conductor that sit on the topmost layer of the display screen so as not to obscure the screen output. The conductor is used to create an electrostatic field of known capacitance, which is distorted when it is touched, leading to a measurable change in capacitance. Control electronics then detect the change in capacitance and can determine where the touch occurred. When coupled with appropriate software, CS can be used as an alternative input technology to the traditional computer keyboard and mouse. Projected capacitive touch (PCT) is a type of CS technology that uses two separate grids of electrodes, one horizontally aligned and the other vertically aligned, to greatly enhance the accuracy of touch detection. An advanced type of PCT technology, known as mutual capacitance (MC), places a capacitor at the intersection of each grid row and column, and permits multiple touches to be simultaneously detected. MC sensors are used to build the multi-touch-sensitive display screens found on many modern personal computing devices, such as *Smart-Phones* and *Tablet Computers*.

b) **HOW COULD IT HELP?** CS technologies, as used in the multi-touch-sensitive display screens of many modern personal computing devices, are well understood and mature. Stream Tone Access Devices are intended to be direct replacements for all current personal computing devices, including *Smart-Phones* and *Tablet Computers*, and will therefore need to include modern HID technologies, such as CS, in order to be able to deliver functionality comparable to current personal computing devices.

c) **FURTHER READING**
Capacitive Sensing: *https://en.wikipedia.org/wiki/Capacitive_sensing*
Human Interface Device: *https://en.wikipedia.org/wiki/Human_interface_device*

# 3.1.17    CERTIFICATION MARK

a) **WHAT IS IT?** A Certification Mark (CM) is type of officially registered intellectual property mark, the use of which is controlled by its registered owner. A CM can only be applied to a product, or associated with a service, that has successfully met standards defined by the registered owner. The exact definition of a CM tends to vary country by country. Listed below are a number of brief definitions; the first is from the International Trademark Association, the second is from Singapore, the third is from the United Kingdom, the fourth is from the United States of America, and the fifth is from the World Intellectual Property Organisation. The International Trademark Association states that *"A certification mark certifies the nature or origin of the goods or services to which it has been applied. This includes, for example, region or location or origin, materials of construction, method or mode of manufacture or provision, quality assurance, accuracy of the goods or services or any definable characteristic of the goods or services. It can also certify manufacture or provision of services by members of a union or other organization to certain standards".* The Intellectual Property Office of Singapore states that *"This mark is granted to people who wish to certify the characteristics of a particular goods or service. The certification can relate to the origin, material or mode of manufacture of the goods, or the performance, quality or accuracy of a service. By applying for a certification mark, goods and services are easily distinguishable from other non-certified goods or services on the market. For example, if your product is organic, you may be in a position to use a certified organic mark on your packaging".* The Intellectual Property Office, the official government body responsible for granting intellectual property rights in the United Kingdom, states that *"A certification mark is a mark indicating that the goods and services in connection with which it is used are certified by the proprietor of the mark in respect of origin, material, mode of manufacture of goods or performance of services, quality, accuracy or other characteristics".* The United States Patent and Trademark Office states that *"A certification mark is any word, phrase, symbol or design, or a combination thereof owned by one party who certifies the goods and services of others when they meet certain standards. The owner of the mark exercises control over the use of the mark; however, because the sole purpose of a certification mark is to indicate that certain standards have been met, use of the mark is by others".* The World Intellectual Property Organisation states that *"Certification marks are usually given for compliance with defined standards, but are not confined to any membership. They may be used by anyone who can certify that the products involved meet certain established standards".*

b) **HOW COULD IT HELP?** The design, construction, and operation of many aspects of the Stream Tone Technology Ecosystem (STTE) will rest in the hands of many different parties over which the Stream Tone will probably have very little control. A CM could be used to ensure that products and services associated with the STTE meet the minimum performance requirements for a good user-experience.

c) **FURTHER READING**

Certification Mark: *https://en.wikipedia.org/wiki/Certification_mark*
Intellectual Property Office (United Kingdom) - Chapter 4 Certification And Collective
Trademarks: *https://ipo.gov.uk//tmmanual-chap4-certcoll.pdf*
Intellectual Property Office Of Singapore - What Is A Trademark?:
*http://www.ipos.gov.sg/AboutIP/TypesofIPWhatisIntellectualProperty/Whatisatrademark.*
*aspx*
International Trademark Association - Certification Marks:
*http://www.inta.org/TrademarkBasics/FactSheets/Pages/CertificationMarks.aspx*
United States Patent And Trademark Office - What Is A Certification Mark?:
*http://www.uspto.gov/faq/trademarks.jsp#_Toc275426676*
World Intellectual Property Organisation - Certification Marks:
*http://www.wipo.int/sme/en/ip_business/collective_marks/certification_marks.htm*

# 3.1.18   CHACHA20-POLY1305

a) **WHAT IS IT?** ChaCha20-Poly1305 is a new Transport Layer Security (TLS) cipher suite
that can be used to secure digital communications over packet-switched computer
networks, such as the *Internet*. The ChaCha20-Poly1305 cipher suite is comprised of the
ChaCha20 symmetric *Encryption* algorithm and the Poly1305 message authentication
code algorithm. The ChaCha20-Poly1305 cipher suite is algorithmically well suited to use
on *Reduced Instruction Set Computing*-based microprocessors that are commonly found
in mobile personal computing devices, such as *Smart-Phones* and *Tablet Computers*.
Testing on such devices has confirmed that the ChaCha20-Poly1305 cipher suite is
approximately three times faster than the Advanced *Encryption* Standard-Galois/Counter
Mode cipher suite, another well-regarded TLS cipher suite. ChaCha20-Poly1305 is a
supported cipher suite of OpenBSD Secure Shell (OpenSSH). Google, Inc., has added
support for the ChaCha20-Poly1305 cipher suite to its popular Chrome *Web Browser* and
to most of its *Web* properties, such as Gmail.

b) **HOW COULD IT HELP?** The Stream Tone Transfer Protocol (STTP) will be used to
securely communicate digital content and services across the *Internet*. New cipher suites,
such as ChaCha20-Poly1305 could allow a Stream Tone Access Device with a RISC-
based microprocessor to communicate efficiently and securely across the *Internet* using
the STTP.

c) **FURTHER READING**
A State-Of-The-Art Message Authentication Code: *http://cr.yp.to/mac.html*
Advanced Encryption Standard:
*https://en.wikipedia.org/wiki/Advanced_Encryption_Standard*
ChaCha20-Poly1305: *http://www.openbsd.org/cgi-*
*bin/cvsweb/src/usr.bin/ssh/PROTOCOL.chacha20poly1305?rev=HEAD;content-*
*type=text%2Fplain*
Cipher Suite: *https://en.wikipedia.org/wiki/Cipher_suite*
Computer Network: *https://en.wikipedia.org/wiki/Computer_network*
Encryption: *https://en.wikipedia.org/wiki/Encryption*
Galois/Counter Mode: *https://en.wikipedia.org/wiki/Galois/Counter_Mode*
Internet: *https://en.wikipedia.org/wiki/Internet*
OpenSSH: *https://en.wikipedia.org/wiki/Openssh*
Reduced Instruction Set Computing:
*https://en.wikipedia.org/wiki/Reduced_instruction_set_computing*

Speeding Up And Strengthening HTTPS Connections for Chrome On Android: *http://googleonlinesecurity.blogspot.com/2014/04/speeding-up-and-strengthening-https.html*
The ChaCha Family Of Stream Ciphers: *http://cr.yp.to/chacha.html*
Transport Layer Security: *https://en.wikipedia.org/wiki/Transport_Layer_Security*
World Wide Web: *https://en.wikipedia.org/wiki/World_Wide_Web*

# 3.1.19   CLOUD COMPUTING

a)   **WHAT IS IT?** Cloud Computing[15] (CC) is responsible for the creation and delivery of the ever increasing amorphous mass of *Web-based Services* that we are rapidly accepting as the new way to communicate, compute, do business, learn, and share over the *Internet*. CC-based service delivery is currently divided into three models; infrastructure-as-a-service (IAAS), platform-as-a-service (PAAS), and software-as-a-service (SAAS): IAAS typically allows the consumer to configure a customised service delivery and development environment, using capabilities such as networks, processing, storage, and other fundamental resources supplied by the IAAS provider. The consumer can then deploy into the customised environment application software and operating systems designed to deliver their services. PAAS typically provides a provisioned environment, that includes data processing, development tools, networking, operating system, software stacks, and storage, within which services can be built by the consumer. The control of the underlying infrastructure of networks, operating systems, servers, and storage is managed by the PAAS provider. SAAS typically permits the consumer to use the SAAS provider's software applications. The consumer does not manage or control the underlying infrastructure. Limited user-specific software application configuration settings may be managed by the consumer. All the CC models have some common characteristics; broad network access, measured service, on-demand self-service, rapid elasticity, and resource pooling. Broad network access: Consumer services are accessed via standard networking mechanisms from a wide range of devices, or other CC-based services. Measured service: Resource usage is monitored, controlled, and reported by metering, which permits the automatic control and optimisation of resources. On-demand self-service: The consumer can self-provision service resources without directly involving the staff of the service provider. Rapid elasticity: Capabilities can be provisioned based on real-time demand, expanding or contracting based on the dynamics of the moment. Resource pooling: The resources of the CC provider are pooled, and dynamically assigned and re-assigned, typically, based on the simultaneous demand of multiple consumers. Provider resources can often be sourced from anywhere from within the provider's operation; without the knowledge, or control, of the consumer. CC models can be deployed in four distinct ways; as a public cloud, private cloud, community cloud, or hybrid cloud. Public cloud: Services are available to the general public or large industry groups. Owned by the organisation selling the services. Private cloud: Services are for the sole benefit of a single organisation. It may be managed by the organisation or a third party. Infrastructure may be within the organisation or off-site. Community cloud: Services are shared by multiple organisations with common interests. Infrastructure may be managed by the organisations or a third party. Infrastructure may be on-premise or off. Hybrid cloud: Comprised of a combination of, two or more, CC deployment approaches (public, private,

---

[15] *Use of the 'Cloud Computing' term within this book typically refers to a public cloud type of deployment that has been used to provide Web-based digital content or services that are then communicated over the Internet.*

community), bound together with proprietary, or standardised, technologies that permit application and data portability.

b) **HOW COULD IT HELP?** In the future, CC will be responsible for generating all Stream Tone Transfer Protocol (STTP)-based services. CC-based techniques, such as resource pooling and rapid elasticity, will help to ensure that all available computing resources are used optimally to deliver STTP-based services that are affordable, efficient, effective, and ubiquitously available.

c) **FURTHER READING**
Cloud Computing: *http://searchcloudcomputing.techtarget.com/definition/cloud-computing*
Cloud Computing: *https://en.wikipedia.org/wiki/Cloud_computing*
Cloud Computing - Benefits, Risks and Recommendations for Information Security: *http://www.enisa.europa.eu/activities/risk-management/files/deliverables/cloud-computing-risk-assessment/at_download/fullReport*
Computer Data Storage: *https://en.wikipedia.org/wiki/Computer_data_storage*
Computer Network: *https://en.wikipedia.org/wiki/Computer_network*
Security Guidance for Critical Areas of Focus in Cloud Computing v3.0: *https://cloudsecurityalliance.org/guidance/csaguide.v3.0.pdf*
Server (Computing): *https://en.wikipedia.org/wiki/Server_%28computing%29*
Utility Computing: *https://en.wikipedia.org/wiki/Utility_computing*
What is Cloud Computing?: *https://www.youtube.com/watch?v=ae_DKNwK_ms&fmt=22*

# 3.1.20   CODED TRANSMISSION CONTROL PROTOCOL

a) **WHAT IS IT?** Coded Transmission Control Protocol (Coded TCP) is an approach for improving the resiliency of Transmission Control Protocol (TCP)-based wireless networks that works by minimising the potentially debilitating effects of packet loss. Coded TCP greatly reduces the likelihood that packets will be lost, avoiding the need to resend such missing packets, or that the TCP congestion control mechanism will be activated. The TCP is a core protocol of the ***Internet Protocol*** (IP) suite, and is designed to provide the reliable and ordered delivery of data from an application running on one computer to an application running on another computer across a computer network, such as the ***Internet***. The IP is responsible for relaying data packets across the network. The TCP is the interface between the application layer and the IP layer in the networking protocol stack. The TCP was originally designed for use on wired networks, where the loss of data, transmitted as network data packets, is typically quite rare. TCP interprets packet loss as a sign of network congestion and responds by effectively slowing the rate of data exchange so that all current users have a fair opportunity to communicate and any lost packets can be resent with a high probability that they will be delivered. In a wired network environment, this type of congestion control works well because it really is most likely caused by too much network traffic, but on TCP-based wireless networks this type of behaviour is unhelpful, potentially making a bad situation even worse. Packet loss on a wireless TCP-based network is very common, and is typically caused by the movement of the user, often at high-speed in a car or train, within built-up urban environments, rather than network congestion. Even relatively low levels, of a few percent, of persistent or regular packet loss can cause the TCP congestion control mechanism to activate, which can cause the useful throughput of wireless networks to become significantly reduced. The TCP congestion control mechanism temporarily prevents the efficient use of a wireless network's available capacity, and in environments that are prone to packet loss, useful wireless network throughput can become almost permanently reduced. Coded TCP is a new network layer, located between the TCP layer and the IP layer that modifies the behaviour of data transfer operations between those layers. The traditional control flows of TCP are unaffected, and pass through the Coded TCP layer unaltered. The IP layer is unaffected by the operation of Coded TCP and requires no modification. Software applications using a Coded TCP-based wireless network do not require modification as the application layer interface to the original TCP layer is not altered in any way. The Coded TCP layer must be present in the both the sender and receiver protocol stacks. The Coded TCP layer takes packets of data that are queued ready for transmission at the TCP layer and creates new coded packets. Each coded packet contains a random linear combination of data obtained from multiple queued packets, along with extra copies of parts of that data to provide a degree of redundancy. Should a coded packet become lost in transit, Coded TCP is able to reconstruct the missing data using the redundant copies of that data held within other coded packets. Coded TCP is able to effectively and efficiently handle random packet loss, ensuring that the TCP congestion control mechanism is far less likely to be activated. Coded TCP can transform wireless networks that have become almost unusable, due to packet-loss induced congestion control, into ones that can provide useful throughput at close to theoretical limits, taking into account that some degree of data redundancy is now involved. Should a Coded TCP-based wireless network sustain very high, non-random, packet loss, beyond that which can be handled by its coded packet mechanism, then the original TCP congestion control mechanism is still available. Coded TCP is just starting to be commercialised, and it is hoped that it will see widespread deployment over the coming years.

b) **HOW COULD IT HELP?** The Stream Tone needs both wired and wireless telecommunications that are highly affordable, high bandwidth, low latency, highly reliable, and ubiquitously available. It is hoped that modern telecommunications technologies, such as Coded TCP, will help to ensure that Stream Tone Transfer Protocol-based services will be ubiquitously available, with sufficient bandwidth, and at an affordable price.

c) **FURTHER READING**
A Bandwidth Breakthrough: *http://www.technologyreview.com/news/429722/a-bandwidth-breakthrough/*
Code On Technologies: *http://www.codeontechnologies.com/*
Internet Protocol: *https://en.wikipedia.org/wiki/Internet_Protocol*
Internet Protocol Suite: *https://en.wikipedia.org/wiki/Internet_protocol_suite*
Modeling Network Coded TCP Throughput - A Simple Model And Its Validation: *http://www.mit.edu/~medard/papers2011/Modeling%20Network%20Coded%20TCP.pdf*
Network Coding Meets TCP - Theory and Implementation: *http://home.iitj.ac.in/~ramana/tcp-ncd.pdf*
Transmission Control Protocol: *https://en.wikipedia.org/wiki/Transmission_Control_Protocol*

# 3.1.21   COGNITIVE RADIO

a) **WHAT IS IT?** Cognitive Radio (CR) is a dynamic radio frequency spectrum management technology that can automatically adjust its transmission and reception parameters so that wireless communications can make more efficient use of the spectrum available in a particular locale. CR works, in part, by sensing nearby spectrum use in real-time and altering its own transmissions so that they do not interfere. One of the key enabling technologies of CR is *Software-Defined Radio*. CR may become a key part of *Fifth-Generation Mobile Communications* (5G) standards.

b) **HOW COULD IT HELP?** The Stream Tone needs both wired and wireless telecommunications that are highly affordable, high bandwidth, low latency, highly reliable, and ubiquitously available. CR technology can make better use of available wireless spectrum, helping to ensure that Stream Tone Transfer Protocol-based services will be ubiquitously available, with sufficient bandwidth, at an affordable price.

c) **FURTHER READING**
5G: *https://en.wikipedia.org/wiki/5G*
Cognitive Radio: *http://searchnetworking.techtarget.com/definition/cognitive-radio*
Cognitive Radio: *https://en.wikipedia.org/wiki/Cognitive_radio*
Cognitive Radio Information Center: *http://grouper.ieee.org/groups/dyspan/crinfo/*
Software-Defined Radio: *https://en.wikipedia.org/wiki/Software-defined_radio*
Spectrum Management: *https://en.wikipedia.org/wiki/Spectrum_management*
Spectrum Sensing in Cognitive Radio:
*http://www.stanford.edu/~nayaks/reportsFolder/cognitiveRadio.pdf*

# 3.1.22   COMMUNICATIONS SATELLITE

a) **WHAT IS IT?** A Communications Satellite (COMSAT) is a space-based radio frequency (RF) telecommunications platform, in orbit around a planet, such as the Earth. COMSATs are able to provide telecommunications services to a wide range of geographies. COMSATs are often used to reach geographies that are not currently well served by terrestrial communications infrastructures or by *Submarine Communication Cables*. COMSAT-based telecommunications are also a key technology for accessing the *Internet* from aeroplanes and ships. Each COMSAT has a particular orbital trajectory that is designed to support telecommunications within a specific geography. Providing continuous telecommunications services may require the use of multiple COMSATs that are configured as a constellation, which ensures that at least one COMSAT is always within range of the supported geography. COMSATs are typically able to provide both bidirectional telecommunications services, such as *Internet* access, telephony, and video conferencing, as well as unidirectional services such as television broadcasts. COMSATs can either communicate directly with end-user communication devices or indirectly, via intermediary infrastructure, such as a ground-station, that then redistributes COMSAT-based services using more traditional terrestrial telecommunications infrastructure. COMSAT-based communications suffer from high latencies, due to the significant distance signals need to travel from the ground to orbit and back again, which makes it unsuitable for certain types of highly-interactive services. Some newer COMSATs, such as Hylas 2 and Intelsat 19, are optimised for broadband *Internet* services. One of the intended uses of Intelsat 19 will be to provide *Internet* access to aeroplanes and ships in Pacific Ocean regions, whilst Hylas 2 will help to expand broadband *Internet* use in Africa. COMSAT-based telecommunications are expected to be a key enabling technology for cost-effectively bringing the *Internet* to many developing nations. When used as a replacement for digital terrestrial television broadcasting, COMSAT-based television broadcasting may be able to free up radio spectrum that can then be used for mobile telecommunications.

b) **HOW COULD IT HELP?** The Stream Tone needs both wired and wireless telecommunications that are highly affordable, high bandwidth, low latency, highly reliable, and ubiquitously available. COMSATs can help ensure that Stream Tone Transfer Protocol-based services will be ubiquitously available, with sufficient bandwidth, at an affordable price.

c) **FURTHER READING**
Communications Satellite: *https://en.wikipedia.org/wiki/Communications_satellite*
Digital Terrestrial Television: *https://en.wikipedia.org/wiki/Digital_terrestrial_television*
Internet: *https://en.wikipedia.org/wiki/Internet*
Radio Frequency: *https://en.wikipedia.org/wiki/Radio_frequency*
Satellite Communication - An Introduction:
*http://www.mu.ac.in/myweb_test/Satelight%20Comm..pdf*
Spectrum Management: *https://en.wikipedia.org/wiki/Spectrum_management*

# 3.1.23   COMPRESSION

a) **WHAT IS IT?** Compression is the process by which a quantity of digital data, measured in bits, is reduced, or encoded, to a smaller quantity of bits, such that an acceptable version of the original data can be extracted, or decompressed, at a later date. The process of compression can be used to reduce the quantity of bits that is required to communicate, or store, a wide range of digital data, including audio, image, text, unstructured, and video data. There are two types of compression; lossless and lossy. Lossless compression works by identifying and eliminating statistical redundancy from a digital data set; a process that ensures that the original data set can always be perfectly recovered. Lossy compression works by permanently removing unnecessary data from the original data set; a process that only permits an acceptable but imperfect version of the original data set to be recovered. The compression of digital data is often achieved using a software-based implementation of a compression algorithm. Some compression algorithms are also suitable for hardware-only implementation using *Application-Specific Integrated Circuit* or *Field-Programmable Gate Array* technologies, and are consequently able to operate with higher performance and lower power consumption than an equivalent software-based implementation. Some compression algorithms are more efficient at compressing certain types of data. Also, some types of data contain greater levels of redundancy and can therefore be more easily and quickly compressed. Most compression algorithms exhibit a direct relationship between compression efficiency and the time taken to complete a compression, such that the greater the compression efficiency the longer the time that the compression operation will take to complete. Compression is a key enabling technology of many modern industries. The process of compression has greatly reduced the quantity of digital content and service data that needs to be communicated over the *Internet*, or processed and stored on the *Web*. Without compression, many modern technologies would be commercially and technically impractical, including the digital distribution of application software, high definition (HD) television broadcasts, and the storage of HD movies and music on removable storage media.

b) **HOW COULD IT HELP?** The Stream Tone Transfer Protocol (STTP) will be used to deliver digital content and services over computer networks, such as the *Internet*. Without the use of compression algorithms the quantity of data that would need to be communicated within a given period of time in order to support many STTP-based services would simply be too large. Consequently, many services, particularly those that are highly interactive in nature, would not be able to work as required. The STTP will therefore need to fully support the use of compression technologies in order to be able to effectively and efficiently communicate all required digital content and services over the *Internet*.

c) **FURTHER READING**
Algorithm: *https://en.wikipedia.org/wiki/Algorithm*
Application Software: *https://en.wikipedia.org/wiki/Application_software*
Application-Specific Integrated Circuit: *https://en.wikipedia.org/wiki/Application-specific_integrated_circuit*
Computer Network: *https://en.wikipedia.org/wiki/Computer_network*
Data Compression: *https://en.wikipedia.org/wiki/Data_compression*
Data Storage Device: *https://en.wikipedia.org/wiki/Data_storage_device*
Field-Programmable Gate Array: *https://en.wikipedia.org/wiki/Field-programmable_gate_array*
High-Definition Television: *https://en.wikipedia.org/wiki/High-definition_television*
Internet: *https://en.wikipedia.org/wiki/Internet*
Lossless Compression: *https://en.wikipedia.org/wiki/Lossless_compression*
Lossy Compression: *https://en.wikipedia.org/wiki/Lossy_compression*
Optical Disc: *https://en.wikipedia.org/wiki/Optical_disc*
Redundancy (Information Theory):
*https://en.wikipedia.org/wiki/Redundancy_%28information_theory%29*
World Wide Web: *https://en.wikipedia.org/wiki/World_Wide_Web*

# 3.1.24   CONTENT DELIVERY NETWORK

a) **WHAT IS IT?** A Content Delivery Network (CDN) is a system of high-availability, high-performance, geographically distributed data servers that are used to optimally deliver on-demand, third-party, content and services via the *Internet*. A significant amount of modern content delivery is repetitive, with the same set of data being sent again and again. CDNs are able to store such data in close geographic proximity to end-users, ensuring that content can be delivered faster and with less latency. Data that has been stored within a CDN no longer needs to be repetitively sent from its original source, which reduces the outgoing communications bandwidth requirements, and therefore the operating costs, for the original data provider. CDN services are often hosted within the *Data Centres* of *Internet* service providers and telecommunications service providers. Such *Data Centres* are typically geographically dispersed, and are located in close geographic proximity to large population centres. Some CDNs contain thousands of distribution points, and are able to dynamically load-balance by intelligently sharing content delivery across those points. Most CDNs are commercial operations that sell their services on the basis that it is generally cheaper and simpler to use an externally-based CDN service than to build and run internally-based CDN solutions that are capable of meeting peak demands but which may not always be fully utilised. CDN infrastructure is compatible with *Dynamic Adaptive Streaming over HTTP* (DASH), which is a data streaming approach that ensures smooth and uninterrupted multimedia delivery via the *Internet*. DASH uses multiple, pre-prepared, data files, each of which is suitable for transmission at a different bit-rate, and which can be stored within a CDN. A large proportion of all modern *Web*-based content is delivered via CDNs.

b) **HOW COULD IT HELP?** The Stream Tone needs both wired and wireless telecommunications that are highly affordable, high bandwidth, low latency, highly reliable, and ubiquitously available. Content distribution technologies, such as CDNs, can help the Stream Tone to cost-effectively deliver digital content and services at a high bandwidth and with a low latency into all required geographies.

c) **FURTHER READING**
Content Delivery Network: *https://en.wikipedia.org/wiki/Content_delivery_network*
Dynamic Adaptive Streaming Over HTTP:
*https://en.wikipedia.org/wiki/Dynamic_Adaptive_Streaming_over_HTTP*
Internet Service Provider: *https://en.wikipedia.org/wiki/Internet_service_provider*
Load Balancing (Computing):
*https://en.wikipedia.org/wiki/Load_balancing_%28computing%29*
Server (Computing): *https://en.wikipedia.org/wiki/Server_%28computing%29*
Telecommunications Service Provider:
*https://en.wikipedia.org/wiki/Telecommunications_service_provider*

# 3.1.25 DAALA

a) **WHAT IS IT?** Daala is the current working name for a royalty-free open-source lossy video *Compression* algorithm that is being designed by the Xiph open-source community to offer better visual quality, and be less computationally demanding, than both the High Efficiency Video Coding/*H.265* and the *VP9* video *Compression* standards. Daala will use a lapped transform in order to reduce the *Compression* artefacts caused by the use of the discrete cosine transform that is commonly used in other lossy video *Compression* algorithms. Daala will be suitable for encoding a wide range of video resolutions, including ultra high definition video, and for streaming video data over computer networks, such as the *Internet*.

b) **HOW COULD IT HELP?** The Stream Tone is a data streaming technology designed to deliver audio and video over the *Internet* from the *Web* to a Stream Tone Access Device, and to send user-input back. Daala will be a new, open-source, royalty-free, highly-efficient, video *Compression* technology that could potentially form a fundamental part of the Stream Tone Transfer Protocol; providing the technology to both encode and decode Stream Tone video data.

c) **FURTHER READING**
Computer Network: *https://en.wikipedia.org/wiki/Computer_network*
Daala: *https://en.wikipedia.org/wiki/Daala*
Data Compression: *https://en.wikipedia.org/wiki/Data_compression*
Discrete Cosine Transform: *https://en.wikipedia.org/wiki/Discrete_cosine_transform*
Free And Open-Source Software: *https://en.wikipedia.org/wiki/Free_and_open-source_software*
High-Definition Video: *https://en.wikipedia.org/wiki/High-definition_video*
High Efficiency Video Coding:
*https://en.wikipedia.org/wiki/High_Efficiency_Video_Coding*
Internet: *https://en.wikipedia.org/wiki/Internet*
Lapped Transform: *https://en.wikipedia.org/wiki/Lapped_transform*

Lossy Compression: *https://en.wikipedia.org/wiki/Lossy_compression*
Royalties: *https://en.wikipedia.org/wiki/Royalties*
Streaming Media: *https://en.wikipedia.org/wiki/Streaming_media*
VP9: *https://en.wikipedia.org/wiki/VP9*
World Wide Web: *https://en.wikipedia.org/wiki/World_Wide_Web*

# 3.1.26　DATA CENTRE

a)　**WHAT IS IT?** A Data Centre (DC) is a centralised computing infrastructure that contains data processing, networking, and storage systems, which can be used to provide **Web-based Services**. **Cloud Computing**-based DCs provide most of the digital content and services that underpin the modern **Web**. DCs can range in size from a room to a whole custom-built building. The principle resource of a DC is a computer server, which is mounted, along with many other servers, in computer cabinets. Large DCs can house hundreds of thousands of servers, which permits the use of advanced techniques and technologies that would be impractical or too expensive to implement on smaller scales. Some DCs are very efficient in their use of electrical power, and have a low power-usage-effectiveness (PUE) rating. PUE is a standard metric for describing the amount of power used by a whole DC against the amount of power used for just the data processing resources within that DC. The lower the PUE the better, indicating that the majority of power is used for data processing, not auxiliary services. The power used by a large DC can be substantial, such as tens of megawatts. Reducing DC power usage is important because most power used by DCs is generated from non-renewable sources, such as coal, gas, and oil, which emit greenhouse gases when they are burned to generate electricity. Some DCs are able to use power obtained from renewable sources, such as biomass, geothermal, hydro-electric, ocean currents, solar, or wind, that create much lower levels of greenhouse gas emissions. The servers within a DC can generate a lot of heat, which can affect their performance, and must be constantly cooled in order to work optimally and reliably. One strategy to reduce power usage is to locate the DC in a cold geography or near a cold water supply, which allows cold air or cold water to be used for passive cooling. Passive cooling systems use much less energy than active cooling systems. DCs are optimised to achieve the best data processing efficiencies per unit of power used. The servers used in a typical DC are far more power efficient than most of the personal computing devices that are typically used in the home or office. The microprocessor and other resources, such as memory and storage, within a server can be dynamically deployed based on demand, ensuring that such resources are only used when they are actually needed. Furthermore, in order to reduce the inefficient use of any individual server, the technique of virtualisation is employed. Server power usage is not wholly dependent on the amount of work done by its microprocessor, with a lightly worked server using almost as much power as a fully worked one. An individual server that is worked to its maximum capacity will therefore deliver more work per unit of power consumed than a server that is under utilised. Virtualisation permits multiple, isolated operating systems to be run, or hosted, simultaneously on a computer server that has sufficient capacity to handle such a workload. Each operating system instance, known as a **Virtual Machine**, is able to run its own software applications. A single server, with a modern microprocessor, is able to run many **Virtual Machines**, ensuring that the server can be used to its full computational potential, with the result that data processing per unit of power consumed can be maximised. Typically, user-data, held within a DC, is highly secure, protected from both digital and physical attack, as well as accidental loss. Digital access is controlled by network firewalls and granular resource access rights. Physical access to a DC is restricted to authorised personnel only. Data is encrypted in transit and at rest, and is regularly backed-up. Server failures, whether due to hardware or software faults, can be quickly resolved by simply redeploying affected services to alternate *Virtual Machines* within the current DC or a completely different DC connected by a wide area network. Services delivered from a DC are highly reliable, as the infrastructure and operational activities of the DC are designed for almost constant availability. Some DCs can achieve 99.995 percent uptime, which equates to only 26.28 minutes of downtime over the course of a full calendar year. In order to ensure that all DC operations are highly reliable, key infrastructure systems are duplicated. Redundancy ensures that multiple independent systems are employed for cooling, data processing, data storage, electrical power, *Internet* connectivity, and networking. The failure of any one system automatically triggers a switch over to a fully working alternative. In addition to having multiple power feeds into a DC, diesel-powered electric generators, or their equivalents, are on constant standby, should all external power sources fail. Comprehensive fire suppression systems are also available. Sending data from a DC to a distant user is not instantaneous, it takes time, and the longer the distance, the longer it takes to arrive at its destination. Also, when sending data over a long distance, it must be routed over the various networks that make up the *Internet*, and as the data moves, from one network to another, delays are added by the telecommunications systems forwarding the data. The time that requested data takes to arrive with a user is known as latency, with a low latency being better than a high latency. Interactive *Web-based Services*, such as streamed games, telephony, or video conferencing, need requested data to be sent very quickly, with minimal delay. Transmitting data at a fast rate can help to minimise latency but it is largely unavoidable over long distances, given the composite nature of the *Internet*, and the fact that the speed of data transmission is ultimately limited by physics. The need for low-latency services often dictates that DCs are located in close geographic proximity to their users, thereby ensuring that data will not need to travel over many different networks, or over long distances, before it reaches its final destination. Many business services are now being moved off-site, into *Cloud Computing*-based DCs. Many software applications that previously ran on a local personal computing device are also being moved into the *Cloud Computing*-based DCs. New DCs are constantly under construction all around the world, and many are located near population centres in order to minimise communications latencies.

b) **HOW COULD IT HELP?** DCs provide the digital content and services that now underpin most of the *Web*. For a very wide range of applications the most cost-effective, power-efficient, reliable, and secure place to create, share, and store digital content and services is a *Cloud Computing*-based DC. The content and services that will be communicated using the Stream Tone Transfer Protocol (STTP) will also be created by *Cloud Computing*-based DCs, and, in all likelihood, by the very same DCs that are in use today. The Stream Tone will not change digital content or services, simply deliver them in a new way. A DC tasked with providing STTP-based services will be little different from a traditional DC. Of course it may contain some new hardware and software, but in all other ways it will remain largely unchanged. The Stream Tone allows personal computing to be centralised into the DC. DCs are typically designed to operate in environmentally acceptable ways, and are able to use power very efficiently, which can help to keep unwanted greenhouse gas emissions to a minimum. The Stream Tone needs both wired and wireless telecommunications that are highly affordable, high bandwidth, low latency, highly reliable, and ubiquitously available. DCs are specifically engineered for constant operational availability, ensuring that content and service delivery can always be relied upon. DCs are often constructed near to their users in order to minimise data communication latencies. DCs can leverage economies of scale and use cost-efficient technologies, such as virtualisation, that can help to ensure that digital content and services communicated using the STTP will be highly affordable. DCs also commonly implement best of breed security measures, such as **Encryption** and **Multi-Factor Authentication**, in order to strongly protect user-data.

c) **FURTHER READING**
Application Software: *https://en.wikipedia.org/wiki/Application_software*
Cloud Computing: *https://en.wikipedia.org/wiki/Cloud_computing*
Data Center: *https://en.wikipedia.org/wiki/Data_centre*
Power Usage Effectiveness: *https://en.wikipedia.org/wiki/Power_usage_effectiveness*
Server (Computing): *https://en.wikipedia.org/wiki/Server_%28computing%29*
Virtualization: *https://en.wikipedia.org/wiki/Virtualization*
Wide Area Network: *https://en.wikipedia.org/wiki/Wide_area_network*
World Wide Web: *https://en.wikipedia.org/wiki/World_Wide_Web*

# 3.1.27   DIGITAL RIGHTS MANAGEMENT

a) **WHAT IS IT?** Digital Rights Management (DRM) is a wide range of evolving access control technologies designed to limit the use of digital content and devices after they have been sold. DRM is used by copyright holders, hardware manufacturers, individuals, and publishers to protect copyrighted content from unauthorised copying, conversion to other formats, or being accessed by unapproved software or hardware. DRM protections usually rely on the use of **Encryption**; requiring that copyrighted content be encrypted in a particular way, such that only approved software or hardware is then able to decrypt it. Some other types of DRM require that a user be continuously connected to DRM validation servers via the **Internet**. DRM is an imperfect solution as it can, on occasion, prevent legitimate owners of protected content from using that content in ways that are perfectly legal but unforeseen when that content was originally protected using a particular type of DRM technology. DRM is considered to be highly controversial by many people, with some calling it malicious and immoral.

b) **HOW COULD IT HELP?** DRM can help to protect intellectual property. The Stream Tone Transfer Protocol is a secure communications protocol that may need to support a range of DRM technologies in order to communicate all required types of digital content and services.

c) **FURTHER READING**
Copyright: *https://en.wikipedia.org/wiki/Copyright*
Digital Rights Management: *https://en.wikipedia.org/wiki/Digital_rights_management*
Encryption: *https://en.wikipedia.org/wiki/Encryption*
Intellectual Property: *https://en.wikipedia.org/wiki/Intellectual_property*

# 3.1.28   DISTRIBUTED-INPUT-DISTRIBUTED-OUTPUT

a) **WHAT IS IT?** Distributed-Input-Distributed-Output (DIDO) is a mobile telecommunications technology that is based on the principle of constructively interfering radio frequency (RF) signals. Currently, in simple terms, mobile telecommunications infrastructures are engineered to ensure that each mobile communications device, such as a **Smart-Phone** or **Tablet Computer**, will only communicate with one mobile communications base-station, or cell-site, at a time. That base-station should be the base-station that provides the strongest, and therefore the clearest, RF signal. The base-station that provides the strongest RF signal is, under normal circumstances, likely to be the base-station that is physically located closest to the mobile communications device. Any RF signals coming from other mobile communications base-stations are generally much weaker, and can, consequently, be ignored. However, if a mobile communications device does receive RF signals from more than one base-station at the same time then those signals will very likely destructively interfere and the quality of the communications link between that device and its closest base-station will be degraded. If the interfering RF signals are strong enough then the communications link between the mobile communications device and its closest base-station may fail completely. The maximum strength of the RF signals broadcast by each base-station are, therefore, purposely limited so that they do not, under normal circumstances, interfere with the operation of any nearby base-stations. The need to limit the strength of such RF signals in order to avoid destructive interference greatly reduces the range over which the mobile communications services provided by each base-station are able to operate. The total bandwidth of a mobile communications base-station is shared between all the simultaneous users of that base-station. Fewer users per base-station will result in a more bandwidth per user, and more users per base-station will result in less bandwidth per user. This characteristic can be a significant problem in highly-populated mobile communications environments, such as airports, city centres, shopping malls, and sports venues. In contrast, a mobile telecommunications infrastructure based on DIDO communications technology uses multiple mobile communications base-stations to communicate with each mobile communications device. The mobile communications device simultaneously receives a RF signal from each of those base-stations, which will then constructively interfere in a small spatial region that is centred on the device's antenna and by so doing provide that device with a very strong, full-bandwidth, mobile communications link. DIDO base-stations are much cheaper, simpler, and smaller than a traditional mobile communications base-stations because all of the computationally demanding signal processing needed to support DIDO-based communications is handled centrally, in a **Cloud Computing**-based **Data Centre** that is connected to the base-stations using **Radio over Fibre** technology. As the radio signals transmitted using DIDO communications technology are designed to constructively interfere, those signals can be much stronger than those transmitted by other types of mobile communications technology, which, as mentioned earlier, are purposely weakened to avoid destructive interference. Accordingly, DIDO-based telecommunications are able to operate over much a greater range and serve a much greater geographic area. The RF signal, or waveform, that is transmitted through each base-station, is processed, or encoded, in such a way that it will only be coherent, or useable, by the mobile communications device that it is intended for, when it is successfully recombined, through the process of constructive interference, with all the other RF signals intended for that device. The **Data Centre** uses **Software-Defined Radio** technologies to simulate different communications standards, such as **Fourth-Generation Mobile Communications** (4G) and **Wi-Fi**. Consequently, the receiving device does not need to apply any corresponding processing to decode the RF signal, as the final, received, RF signal is exactly the same as a RF signal sent from a non-DIDO-based mobile communications service. In order to correctly process the multiple RF signals ready for receipt by a particular mobile communications device, the **Data Centre** needs to understand which base-stations that device is currently able to communicate with, as well as various characteristics of the device's communications link to each of those base-stations. As the mobile communications device is physically moved within the geography served by the DIDO base-stations the **Data Centre** will alter the processing of the multiple RF signals, and which base-stations are actually used to communicate with that device, in order to ensure that the mobile communications device is always connected to a strong, full-bandwidth communication link. As the spatial region in which the multiple RF signals constructively interfere is physically very small, a DIDO-based communications service will be able to support a very large number of simultaneous users that are located in very close geographic proximity to each other, without any significant reduction in service quality. Each user will always receive a strong signal and a full-bandwidth link to the **Internet**, regardless of how many other active users are nearby. Additionally, since DIDO communications technology is able to use RF signal interference constructively, the interference mitigation technologies built into many types of current mobile communications technologies that add significant operational overhead and degrade overall performance, will no longer be needed, with the result that mobile communications will be able to operate with much less latency. When a mobile communications device is the source of a communication, rather than a recipient, its data is broadcast by RF signal as per normal but instead of that RF signal being received by just a single mobile communications base-station that RF signal is received by multiple base-stations. The received RF signals are then sent to the **Data Centre** where they are computationally recombined and the original communication data is reconstructed. DIDO communications technology allows mobile communications service providers to use their existing licensed radio spectrum substantially more efficiently and effectively, and to deliver a consistently high quality of service to significantly more simultaneous users. Consequently, DIDO-based mobile communications services should be much more affordable than current non-DIDO-based mobile communications services. DIDO communications technology is compatible with current-generation mobile and wireless communications standards, current licensed mobile communications radio spectrum, unlicensed wireless communications radio spectrum, and many current-generation mobile communications devices. DIDO communications technology can be used both indoors and outdoors, and does not require any hardware or software changes to be made to compatible mobile communications devices. DIDO communications technology is able to work alongside existing communications technologies, such as 4G and **Wi-Fi**, allowing, for example, a congested city centre to be switched to a 4G version of DIDO communications technology whilst the more sparsely populated suburbs of the city can remain on a non-DIDO version of 4G, and the same mobile communication device would be work correctly in both areas. DIDO communications technology is technically capable of replacing two commonly used wired **Internet** connectivity solutions; namely coaxial cable-based broadband and digital subscriber line-based broadband. DIDO is a very new communications technology that is just starting to be piloted, and is expected to become more widely available in the very near future, particularly in a number of highly-populated urban environments. If DIDO communications technology is able to successfully move from the research laboratory into the real-world, and work at commercially viable scales, then it could potentially deliver **Fifth-Generation Mobile Communications** (5G)-like capabilities many years earlier than was ever thought possible.

b) **HOW COULD IT HELP?** The Stream Tone needs both wired and wireless telecommunications that are highly affordable, high bandwidth, low latency, highly reliable, and ubiquitously available, and DIDO communications technology may be able to offer the Stream Tone all of this in the very near future.

c) **FURTHER READING**
4G: *https://en.wikipedia.org/wiki/4G*
5G: *https://en.wikipedia.org/wiki/5G*
Artemis Networks: *http://www.artemis.com/*
Base Station: *https://en.wikipedia.org/wiki/Base_station*
Cable Internet Access: *https://en.wikipedia.org/wiki/Cable_Internet_access*
Cell Site: *https://en.wikipedia.org/wiki/Cell_site*
Cloud Computing: *https://en.wikipedia.org/wiki/Cloud_computing*
Data Center: *https://en.wikipedia.org/wiki/Data_center*
Digital Subscriber Line: *https://en.wikipedia.org/wiki/Digital_subscriber_line*
Distributed-Input-Distributed-Output Wireless Technology - A New Approach to Multiuser Wireless: *http://www.rearden.com/DIDO/DIDO_White_Paper_110727.pdf*
Interference (Wave Propagation):
*https://en.wikipedia.org/wiki/Interference_%28wave_propagation%29*
Internet: *https://en.wikipedia.org/wiki/Internet*
Radio Spectrum: *https://en.wikipedia.org/wiki/Radio_spectrum*
Software-Defined Radio: *https://en.wikipedia.org/wiki/Software-defined_radio*
Spectrum Management: *https://en.wikipedia.org/wiki/Spectrum_management*
Telecommunications Network:
*https://en.wikipedia.org/wiki/Telecommunications_network*
Wi-Fi: *https://en.wikipedia.org/wiki/Wi-Fi*

# 3.1.29 DYNAMIC ADAPTIVE STREAMING OVER HTTP

a) **WHAT IS IT?** Dynamic Adaptive Streaming over HTTP (DASH) is a near-real-time multimedia data transmission technology that is able to adapt to prevailing computer network conditions. DASH uses the *HyperText Transfer Protocol* (HTTP) for data communications. DASH is particularly well suited to the on-demand transmission of audio and video data. DASH is compatible with most multimedia data formats. DASH also supports *Digital Rights Management*. DASH is an international standard, ISO/IEC 23009-1:2012, which was developed by the Moving Picture Experts Group (MPEG), and for this reason it is also known as MPEG-DASH. DASH sends multimedia data that has been requested by a software-based DASH client application from standard HTTP servers via the *Internet*. The client application has an awareness of current network conditions, determined by monitoring incoming data, and is able to use that information to intelligently request that future data be sent to it at the most appropriate bit-rate for the prevailing conditions. If network conditions are good then the client will request that data be sent to it at a high bit-rate, and if they are bad, at lower bit-rates. The data to be communicated via DASH can be prepared in advance or generated in real-time. When the data is prepared in advance, multiple versions of the data, each suitable for transmission at a different bit-rate are created and stored ready for later use. The data is typically split into short files, each representing a short time period, such as a few seconds, of a film or music track. The advance conversion of multimedia data into different bit-rates data files can significantly reduce on-going data processing requirements for commonly communicated multimedia data sets, such as films and music. The DASH client requests a specific data file, representing the next required portion of the data, at the most appropriate bit-rate, so that it can ensure a smooth and uninterrupted multimedia playback. If network conditions subsequently change then the DASH client can dynamically adapt by requesting higher or lower bit-rate data. The approach that DASH takes to streaming ensures that multimedia delivered via the *Internet* always plays smoothly, even though its quality may be temporarily degraded to some degree; a behaviour that is considered very acceptable to most users. Without DASH, multimedia delivered from the *Internet* will often halt temporarily as it waits for enough fixed bit-rate data to be received, so that the presentation can continue. One of the key benefits of the DASH approach is its relative simplicity, in that the HTTP servers do not need to do anything complex, such as dynamic real-time encoding, they just need to serve pre-prepared data files requested by the DASH client. DASH is compatible with *Content Delivery Network*s (CDNs), which can cache the various bit-rate data files in close geographic proximity to their end-users. DASH can use multiple sources, HTTP servers and/or CDNs, to deliver a single multimedia presentation, an approach that can be used to implement a form of load-balancing. The multiple data files used by the DASH approach can also be used to provide video from alternative viewing angles or to support the insertion of advertising. DASH is a relatively new standard that is expected to become widely adopted by many *Web*-based multimedia delivery services in the future.

b)  **HOW COULD IT HELP?** The DASH approach to data transmission over the *Internet* can ensure that multimedia presentations playback smoothly, with little or no interruption. The Stream Tone Transfer Protocol will be used to deliver multimedia content and could adopt approaches, such as those used by DASH, to ensure acceptable performance under a wide range of network conditions.

c)  **FURTHER READING**
Computer Network: *https://en.wikipedia.org/wiki/Computer_network*
Content Delivery Network: *https://en.wikipedia.org/wiki/Content_delivery_network*
Digital Rights Management: *https://en.wikipedia.org/wiki/Digital_rights_management*
Dynamic Adaptive Streaming Over HTTP:
*https://en.wikipedia.org/wiki/Dynamic_Adaptive_Streaming_over_HTTP*
Dynamic Adaptive Streaming over HTTP - Design Principles and Standards:
*http://www.w3.org/2010/11/web-and-tv/papers/webtv2_submission_64.pdf*
HyperText Transfer Protocol: *https://en.wikipedia.org/wiki/Hypertext_Transfer_Protocol*
Internet: *https://en.wikipedia.org/wiki/Internet*
Load Balancing (Computing):
*https://en.wikipedia.org/wiki/Load_balancing_%28computing%29*
Moving Picture Experts Group:
*https://en.wikipedia.org/wiki/Moving_Picture_Experts_Group*

# 3.1.30   ELECTRICALLY POWERED SPACECRAFT PROPULSION

a)  **WHAT IS IT?** Electrically Powered Spacecraft Propulsion (EPSP), or electric propulsion (EP), is an electrically-powered, energy-efficient, spacecraft propulsion technology that can typically be operated for extended time periods. EP systems are also known as ion drives, ion thrusters, or plasma drives. EP systems work by efficiently using electricity to accelerate a propellant to a very high velocity, thereby creating thrust. The thrust generated by an EP system is actually incredibly small, compared to a chemical rocket, and would not be capable of launching a spacecraft from the surface of the Earth into orbit. EP systems are best suited to use in the low-gravity vacuum-based environment of space. EP systems can be operated for very long time periods, such as hours, days, weeks, months, or even years, and can slowly but efficiently accelerate spacecraft to velocities far greater than comparable chemically-based propulsion systems are able to cost-effectively achieve. EP systems are ideally suited to manoeuvring **Communications Satellites** (COMSATs), or propelling interplanetary space probes. There are three main EP technologies; electromagnetic, electrostatic, and electrothermal. The most commonly deployed EP system is electrostatic, of which there are three main designs; gridded-electrostatic, Hall-effect, and field-emission electric propulsion (FEEP). Gridded-electrostatic and Hall-effect ion thrusters use xenon gas as a propellant, whilst FEEP uses a liquid metal such as caesium, indium, or mercury. COMSATs in low earth orbit are subject to atmospheric drag, which can cause them to drift away from their required orbital positions. EP systems can be continuously operated to keep a COMSAT in its correct position. A typical EP system has far less weight than a comparable chemically-based propulsion system, because EP is able to use its propellant much more efficiently, and so needs much less of it. Therefore, a COMSAT with EP will be lighter than a COMSAT with chemical thrusters. A lighter COMSAT will require less rocket fuel to put it into orbit, making the launch cheaper. Alternatively, the weight saved by using an EP system could be used for extra features such as more telecommunications transponders or bigger solar sails. Having more transponders would increase the COMSAT's ability to deliver high-bandwidth **Internet** access, telephony, and video-conferencing. Having bigger solar sails would allow the COMSAT to be able to transmit a stronger communications signal over a greater geographical area. The weight saved could also be used to hold more propellant for the EP system, ensuring that the COMSAT can stay in the correct orbital position for many years, greatly extending the working life of the COMSAT.

b) **HOW COULD IT HELP?** The Stream Tone needs both wired and wireless telecommunications that are highly affordable, high bandwidth, low latency, highly reliable, and ubiquitously available. COMSATs with EP systems can help ensure that Stream Tone Transfer Protocol-based services will be ubiquitously available, with sufficient bandwidth, at an affordable price.

c) **FURTHER READING**
Communications Satellite: *https://en.wikipedia.org/wiki/Communications_satellite*
Electrically Powered Spacecraft Propulsion:
*https://en.wikipedia.org/wiki/Electrically_powered_spacecraft_propulsion*
Low Earth Orbit: *https://en.wikipedia.org/wiki/Low_Earth_orbit*

# 3.1.31   ELECTRONIC PAPER

a) **WHAT IS IT?** Electronic Paper (EP) is a display technology designed to mimic the appearance of ink on paper. EP displays a stable image that does not need to be constantly refreshed and because such displays reflect light, just like a normal sheet of paper, and are, therefore, generally considered to be more comfortable to read than a conventional display. An EP display can be easily viewed in direct sunlight, unlike many other display technologies. When viewed under adequate ambient lighting conditions no additional lighting is needed. EP displays consume very little power and are therefore ideally suited to certain mobile applications such as e-book readers. Initially, EP was only able to display static black and white images but full colour video displays are now possible.

b) **HOW COULD IT HELP?** One of the expected features of portable Stream Tone Access Devices (STADs) is that they will have a very long lasting battery, and in order to meet that expectation the device will need to use power very efficiently. EP displays could potentially help to minimise STAD power consumption, and being daylight readable would also be well suited to regular outdoor use, as might be required in certain developing countries.

c) **FURTHER READING**
Electronic Paper: *https://en.wikipedia.org/wiki/Electronic_paper*
Electronic Paper Display: *http://whatis.techtarget.com/definition/electronic-paper-display-EPD*
Plastic Logic Ltd.: *http://www.plasticlogic.com/*

# 3.1.32 ELECTRONIC PRODUCT ENVIRONMENTAL ASSESSMENT TOOL

a) **WHAT IS IT?** The Electronic Product Environmental Assessment Tool (EPEAT) is a registry designed to support the purchasing of environmentally friendly electronic products. The registry lists products that meet the bronze, silver, or gold EPEAT rating. The registry contains ratings for computer displays, desktop computers, imaging equipment, laptop computers, notebook computers, photocopiers, printers, televisions, **Thin Clients**, and workstation computers. Computer servers and mobile devices are expected to be included into the registry in the future. The EPEAT rating system measures products against required and optional criteria. In order for a product to be added to the EPEAT registry it must meet all of the required criteria. The product is then assessed against the optional criteria, which determines whether it gets a bronze, silver, or gold EPEAT rating. The EPEAT assessment categories include the reduction or elimination of environmentally sensitive materials, material selection, design for end of life, product longevity or life extension, energy conservation, end-of-life management, corporate performance, and packaging. Products are registered by their manufacturers, who must produce and maintain evidence to support the rating they have assigned to their products. EPEAT uses a process of independent verification to ensure that registered products actually comply with all the criteria required for their declared rating level. The verification exercises are randomly scheduled, and unannounced, and any non-conformance is publicly reported. The EPEAT system is considered to be an effective and efficient solution for encouraging a shift towards the creation and use of more environmentally sustainable electronic products, a shift that is needed to help preserve the Earth's delicate ecosystems. EPEAT rated products are now the only acceptable choice for many environmentally aware governments and organisations.

b) **HOW COULD IT HELP?** Stream Tone Access Devices (STADs) are expected to be produced by the billion and it will be critically important that they are created, function, and are disposed of in a manner that is environmentally acceptable. STADs should be designed, right from the very start, to comply with the EPEAT gold rating.

c) **FURTHER READING**
Electronic Product Environmental Assessment Tool: *http://www.epeat.net/*

Electronic Product Environmental Assessment Tool:
*https://en.wikipedia.org/wiki/Electronic_Product_Environmental_Assessment_Tool*

# 3.1.33   ENCRYPTION

a)   **WHAT IS IT?** In simple terms, encryption is the process of converting plaintext, such as messages or information, into a data format that is unreadable by human or computer, known as cyphertext, using an encryption algorithm. The encryption algorithm requires the use of an encryption key in order to create the cyphertext. The process of converting cyphertext back into plaintext is known as decryption. Decryption requires the use of a decryption key. Some types of encryption algorithm use symmetric key schemes in which the encryption key and the decryption key are the same. Other types of encryption algorithms use asymmetric key schemes, in which the encryption key and decryption key are different. Public-key encryption uses an asymmetric key scheme in which the encryption key is published, and the decryption key is unpublished or kept secret. The published encryption key is known as the public key and the unpublished decryption key is known as the private key. Data can be encrypted by anyone using the public key and then sent to the owner of that public key, who will then use their private key to decrypt the data. The public and private keys are mathematically linked. It is computationally easy to generate a public-key pair and to use those keys to encrypt and decrypt data, but it is computationally impractical to generate a private key from just a public key. Consequently, data encrypted with a public key is rendered safe and protected since it can only be decrypted using its corresponding private key, and not by a brute force attack. Different encryption algorithms offer different degrees of protection. For example, the Advanced Encryption Standard algorithm, which was published in 2001, has been mathematically proven to be more secure than the Data Encryption Standard algorithm, which was published in 1977. Longer encryption keys, measured in bits, offer greater protection than shorter encryption keys. For example, a 256-bit key provides more protection than a 128-bit key when used by the same encryption algorithm. Encryption can be used to protect personal and intellectual property data whilst it is at rest in a data store, in transit across a computer network, and in use within a random-access memory or on a microprocessor. Today, public-key encryption is the principle mechanism for securing data that is communicated across the *Internet*, processed by a *Cloud Computing*-based service, or stored on the *Web*.

b)   **HOW COULD IT HELP?** The ultimate success of the Stream Tone will depend as much on its ability to support Comprehensive Remote Personal Computing as it will on its ability to protect personal and intellectual property data. The Stream Tone Transfer Protocol (STTP) will be a secure data streaming communications protocol that will need to use encryption in order to protect personal and intellectual property data when it is communicated over the *Internet* to a Stream Tone Access Device. The STTP will therefore need to be based on communications protocols that support very strong encryption in order to be able to guarantee the secure communication of all such data.

c)   **FURTHER READING**
Advanced Encryption Standard:
*https://en.wikipedia.org/wiki/Advanced_Encryption_Standard*
Cloud Computing: *https://en.wikipedia.org/wiki/Cloud_computing*
Computer Network: *https://en.wikipedia.org/wiki/Computer_network*
Cyphertext: *https://en.wikipedia.org/wiki/Ciphertext*

Data Encryption Standard: *https://en.wikipedia.org/wiki/Data_Encryption_Standard*
Data Store: *https://en.wikipedia.org/wiki/Data_store*
Encryption: *https://en.wikipedia.org/wiki/Encryption*
Internet: *https://en.wikipedia.org/wiki/Internet*
Microprocessor: *https://en.wikipedia.org/wiki/Microprocessor*
Plaintext: *https://en.wikipedia.org/wiki/Plaintext*
Public-Key Cryptography: *https://en.wikipedia.org/wiki/Public-key_cryptography*
Random-Access Memory: *https://en.wikipedia.org/wiki/Random-access_memory*
World Wide Web: *https://en.wikipedia.org/wiki/World_Wide_Web*

# 3.1.34   ENERGY STAR

a) **WHAT IS IT?** Energy Star is an internationally adopted programme designed to promote energy efficient consumer products. It is a joint program of the U.S. Department of Energy and the U.S. Environmental Protection Agency (EPA). Energy Star is based on a labelling system designed to help consumers more easily identify products that are more environmentally acceptable, and more cost effective, due to their more efficient use of energy. Energy Star certified products operate more efficiently compared to the minimum acceptable efficiency standards for such products defined by the U.S. government. Energy Star standards are applicable to a very wide range of products, which can be categorised as follows; appliances, battery chargers, building products, commercial and industrial buildings, commercial food service equipment, computers, electronics, heating and cooling, lighting and fans, new homes, and plumbing. All products labelled as Energy Star compliant must be third-party certified by EPA-recognised laboratories. The Energy Star standards are revised regularly to reflect the latest norms for energy efficient products. It is believed that the widespread adoption of Energy Star-compliant products has significantly reduced the worldwide consumption of energy, along with a corresponding reduction in greenhouse gas emissions, and operational costs.

b) **HOW COULD IT HELP?** Stream Tone Access Devices (STADs) are expected to be used by the billion and it will therefore be critically important that they operate in an energy efficient manner. STADs should be designed, right from the very start, to comply with the latest applicable Energy Star certification requirements.

c) **FURTHER READING**
Energy Star: *https://www.energystar.gov/*
Energy Star: *https://en.wikipedia.org/wiki/Energy_Star*
United States Environmental Protection Agency:
*https://en.wikipedia.org/wiki/United_States_Environmental_Protection_Agency*

# 3.1.35   ERROR-CORRECTING CODE MEMORY

a) **WHAT IS IT?** Error-Correcting Code Memory (ECCM) is a data storage technology that can detect and correct data corruption. Data corruption occurs when a single bit, or multiple bits, of data unexpectedly flip to an opposite state; from a one to a zero, or from a zero to a one. Dynamic random-access memory (DRAM) that is used for applications which cannot tolerate data corruption often uses ECCM technology. There are a number of causes for data corruption, such as background radiation from, for example, neutron particles generated by cosmic ray collisions, electrical or magnetic interference, heat, and manufacturing defects. ECCM is often used in mission critical systems, such as computer servers and spacecraft control systems. ECCM typically works by using extra data bits to store parity information for a small block of data, usually a 64-bit word in modern computers. If a single bit is determined to be wrong, it can be automatically corrected. If two bits are determined to be wrong, this can usually be reported but not automatically corrected. Understanding when a piece of data is corrupt allows a suitably programmed computer system to ignore, or re-compute, a result. Computer systems featuring ECCM are more reliable than systems without this technology, and are therefore much less likely to crash or present incorrect results.

b) **HOW COULD IT HELP?** All aspects of Stream Tone Technology Ecosystem (STTE) need to be highly reliable. ECCM is a mature and well understood technology that could be used, at appropriate points, throughout the STTE to ensure that its operation will be highly reliable.

c) **FURTHER READING**
Dynamic Random-Access Memory: *https://en.wikipedia.org/wiki/Dynamic_random-access_memory*
ECC Memory: *https://en.wikipedia.org/wiki/ECC_memory*

# 3.1.36 FAIR, REASONABLE, AND NON-DISCRIMINATORY LICENSING

a) **WHAT IS IT?** Fair, Reasonable, And Non-Discriminatory (FRAND) licensing is a legal obligation that can be used to ensure that patented technology can be openly shared with anyone that wishes to use it based on non-onerous terms and conditions. FRAND licensing is often used by standard-setting organisations to ensure that the licensing of patented technology included in a standard, generally referred to as a standard essential patent, cannot be abused by the patent holder. Standards help to ensure industry-wide hardware and software compatibility and interoperability. Patented technology is often included in a standard because such technology has become widely used, or an alternative non-patented solution simply does not exist. Patented technology that is included in a standard is offered by the patent holder on the understanding that FRAND licensing will be required. The fair commitment of FRAND licensing defines that the terms of the license are not anti-competitive or unlawful. For example, FRAND licensing cannot be used to force the purchase of other unwanted licenses or to enforce reciprocal licensing agreements onto the licensee to the benefit of the licensor. The reasonable commitment of FRAND licensing defines that licensing rates will be reasonable, even if multiple different licenses are used in aggregate. FRAND licensing rates cannot make any industry uncompetitive. The non-discriminatory commitment of FRAND licensing defines that the licensing terms and rates are the same for all licensees, regardless of any differences that may exist between licensees, such as one licensee being a direct competitor to the licensor, when another one is not. License variation based on unit volume or the creditworthiness of the licensee is generally permitted. Many patented technologies used in isolation, and in aggregate, have become essential parts of modern life. FRAND licensing helps to ensure that many of these essential technologies are available to everyone that needs them under fair, reasonable, and non-discriminatory terms.

b) **HOW COULD IT HELP?** The Stream Tone will be a complex content and service delivery system built from a wide range of hardware and software-based technologies. Some of those technologies will be new, whilst others will undoubtedly be pre-existing. If the Stream Tone needs to include patented technologies, because they are simply the best, or only, solution available, then it will need to rely on FRAND licensing to help ensure that patent holders do not impose unfair, unreasonable, or discriminatory licensing terms, which could ultimately make the Stream Tone unaffordable or restrict its availability.

c) **FURTHER READING**
Essential Patent: *https://en.wikipedia.org/wiki/Essential_patent*
Patent: *https://en.wikipedia.org/wiki/Patent*
Reasonable and Non-Discriminatory Licensing:
*https://en.wikipedia.org/wiki/Reasonable_and_non-discriminatory_licensing*

# 3.1.37 FIELD-PROGRAMMABLE GATE ARRAY

a) **WHAT IS IT?** A Field-Programmable Gate Array (FPGA) is an integrated circuit that can be configured to meet a customer's specific functional requirements after it has left the factory where it was manufactured and entered the field. FPGAs contain logic blocks that can be reconfigured using programmable interconnects to provide a very wide range of functionality. Some FPGAs contain embedded microprocessors and related peripherals which together can form the basis of a complete *System on a Chip*. A standard FPGA part can be used for many different purposes, and can be reprogrammed many times. Use of standardised and readily available FPGA parts can often help to significantly speed up product development by helping to reduce time to market. Alternative technologies, such as *Application-Specific Integrated Circuits* (ASICs), typically require a larger amount of non-recurring engineering than FPGAs. As a component, FPGAs are generally considered to be more expensive than ASICs, which can provide similar functionality but are not reprogrammable. FPGAs may have lower performance, use more power, and be physically bigger than a fully-optimised ASIC of identical functionality. FPGAs are considered an ideal solution for prototypes, low-volume production runs, and situations were the functionality required from the integrated circuit has not been finalised or may be subject to further refinement.

b) **HOW COULD IT HELP?** As Stream Tone Access Devices (STADs) start to emerge it may be beneficial to initially base them on a FPGA architecture until all required STAD functionality has been agreed, debugged, and matured; something that could take several years. It should also be noted that, even though a STAD is not meant to be updated, it may be possible to introduce new functionality, such as more efficient communications protocols, or fix minor problems simply by reprogramming its FPGA.

c) **FURTHER READING**
Application-Specific Integrated Circuit: *https://en.wikipedia.org/wiki/Application-specific_integrated_circuit*
Field-Programmable Gate Array: *https://en.wikipedia.org/wiki/Field-programmable_gate_array*
Microprocessor: *https://en.wikipedia.org/wiki/Microprocessor*

Non-Recurring Engineering: *https://en.wikipedia.org/wiki/Non-recurring_engineering*
System On A Chip: *https://en.wikipedia.org/wiki/System_on_a_chip*
What is FPGA?: *http://www.fpgacenter.com/fpga/index.php*

## 3.1.38    FIFTH-GENERATION MOBILE COMMUNICATIONS

a)   **WHAT IS IT?** Fifth-Generation Mobile Communications (5G) could be implemented around 2020, and will build upon the legacy of *Fourth-Generation Mobile Communications* (4G). However, unless significant and commercially viable advancements in the underlying technology of mobile telecommunications occurs in the relatively near future it is unlikely that 5G will be able to deliver any more bandwidth than what is currently expected from the final version of 4G, which is approximately 1 gigabit per second (Gbps). 5G may therefore deliver other benefits instead, such as lower latency, improved service coverage, better service reliability, increased battery life for mobile devices using such services, or greatly reduced traffic fees due to a corresponding reduction in service infrastructure and operational costs. Of course, research into higher mobile bandwidths is still on-going, and it is hoped that by the time that 5G is finally launched that bandwidths of 10 Gbps, or more, will be possible and commercially viable.

b)   **HOW COULD IT HELP?** The Stream Tone needs both wired and wireless telecommunications that are highly affordable, high bandwidth, low latency, highly reliable, and ubiquitously available. Some of these requirements will be met by the final versions of 4G but some may have to wait for the arrival of 5G. So, whilst the Stream Tone, in its ultimate form, may require the use of telecommunications technologies that do not exist today, it is most likely that such technologies will come to exist in the very near future.

c)   **FURTHER READING**
4G: *https://en.wikipedia.org/wiki/4G*
5G: *https://en.wikipedia.org/wiki/5G*

## 3.1.39    FILE HOSTING SERVICE

a)   **WHAT IS IT?** A File Hosting Service (FHS) is a centralised, *Web*-based, data file storage service that is accessed via a computer network, such as the *Internet*. The service can be used by businesses or individuals. Almost any type of file can be uploaded, stored, or downloaded. Files can be added, replaced, or deleted. Stored files can generally be accessed from any *Internet*-enabled personal computing device, located anywhere in the world. Some FHSs are able to transmit a stored file as a video or audio data stream. Hosted files can either be privately or publicly available, with private files being password protected. FHSs take great care to secure the files they host, using *Encryption* to protect such files at rest and in transit. FHSs often provide an *Application Programming Interface* that can be used to allow a user to access their stored data files from within other *Web-based Services*.

b)   **HOW COULD IT HELP?** The Stream Tone Access Device will be totally reliant upon Stream Tone Transfer Protocol (STTP)-based services, because it has little built-in data processing or storage capabilities of its own. Being able to effectively and efficiently share user-data between different STTP-based services, either directly or through the use of intermediaries, such as FHSs, will be a key enabling technology for the Stream Tone.

c) **FURTHER READING**
Application Programming Interface:
*https://en.wikipedia.org/wiki/Application_programming_interface*
Data File: *https://en.wikipedia.org/wiki/Data_file*
Encryption: *https://en.wikipedia.org/wiki/Encryption*
File Hosting Service: *https://en.wikipedia.org/wiki/File_hosting_service*
Internet: *https://en.wikipedia.org/wiki/Internet*
Streaming Media: *https://en.wikipedia.org/wiki/Streaming_media*

# 3.1.40 FOUNDATION

a) **WHAT IS IT?** A foundation is a legal categorisation of non-profit organisation (NPO) that uses surplus revenues to support its own charitable purposes rather than distributing them as dividends or profit. NPOs have boards, or controlling members, but no shareholders. Some NPOs have paid staff, whilst others rely on unpaid volunteers. A NPO my hold assets in its own name for purposes defined in its constitutive documents. The administration and operation of a NPO are carried out in accordance with its articles of association or statutes. The laws governing foundations vary by legal jurisdiction. Foundations typically have philanthropic goals designed to serve the common good or public interest. Some foundations exist to support free and open-source development communities.

b) **HOW COULD IT HELP?** The Stream Tone will be a free and open-source initiative, it will not be created by big-business, and it will require funding, leadership, and legal support just like any other modern organisation. A foundation designed to support the Stream Tone would be able to provide such support to the free and open-source communities that will be responsible for the Streams Tone's creation, deployment, and maturation.

c) **FURTHER READING**
Charitable Organization: *https://en.wikipedia.org/wiki/Charitable_organization*
Foundation (Non-Profit): *https://en.wikipedia.org/wiki/Foundation_%28nonprofit%29*
Free And Open-Source Software: *https://en.wikipedia.org/wiki/Free_and_open-source_software*
Nonprofit Organizations: *https://en.wikipedia.org/wiki/Nonprofit_organizations*
Philanthropy: *https://en.wikipedia.org/wiki/Philanthropy*
Shareholder: *https://en.wikipedia.org/wiki/Shareholder*

# 3.1.41 FOURTH-GENERATION MOBILE COMMUNICATIONS

a) **WHAT IS IT?** Fourth-Generation Mobile Communications (4G) are intended to support mobile, ultra-broadband, *Internet* access to services such as three-dimensional television, high definition mobile television, *Internet Protocol*-based telephony, *Web*-based gaming, and video conferencing. 4G does not support traditional circuit-switched telephony as used by previous generations, as it is a pure ***Internet Protocol***-based technology. The fourth generation of mobile communications standards was ratified in 2011; the first generation was introduced in 1981, the second in 1992, and the third in 2001. Implementations of 4G-like services have been available since 2006, although they did not meet all aspects of the 4G standard that was eventually ratified in 2011. Primarily, the early implementations did not meet the International Mobile Telecommunications-Advanced (IMT-Advanced) peak-bandwidth requirement of 100 megabits per second (Mbps) for high-mobility communications access, such as from users located in moving cars and trains, and 1,000 Mbps for low-mobility communications access, such as from pedestrians and stationary users. New and upgraded mobile communications implementations that are able to fully meet the final ratified 4G standard are expected to appear as early 2017.

b) **HOW COULD IT HELP?** The Stream Tone needs both wired and wireless telecommunications that are highly affordable, high bandwidth, low latency, highly reliable, and ubiquitously available. Some of these requirements will most likely be met by 4G implementations in the very near future. Others, such as affordability and ubiquity, may take a little longer.

c) **FURTHER READING**
4G: *https://en.wikipedia.org/wiki/4G*
4G - 4th Generation Mobile Communication Networks:
*http://services.eng.uts.edu.au/~kumbes/ra/4G/4g02a.html*
IMT-Advanced: *https://en.wikipedia.org/wiki/IMT_Advanced*
Internet Protocol: *https://en.wikipedia.org/wiki/Internet_Protocol*

# 3.1.42 FREE AND OPEN-SOURCE SOFTWARE

a) **WHAT IS IT?** Free and Open-Source Software (FOSS) refers to two similar concepts; free software and open-source software. The terms 'free software' and 'open-source software' are often used interchangeably, but they are in fact based on two different software distribution strategies. The FOSS term is typically used to minimise confusion, when referring to a piece of software, in the circumstance where the difference in meaning is largely unimportant. When a piece of software is identified as being FOSS, it is predominantly being labelled as software that is unrestricted in terms of a user's right to change, copy, improve, study, and use it. In comparison, proprietary or non-FOSS software often comes with many restrictions and fees. Free software is software that is based on certain freedoms, such as the freedom to change, copy, distribute, improve, run, and study such software. Free software may be distributed free-of-charge or for a fee. Open-source software is software which has made its source code freely available to any interested party, such that its source code can be can be copied, modified, and redistributed without requiring the payment of fees or royalties. Software licenses are used to enforce FOSS terms and conditions. When FOSS is redistributed, in either its original or modified form, the terms and conditions originally associated with that software are required by its license to be passed on to the next user unchanged. For example, FOSS developed under the GNU General Public License must comply with the requirement that further developments and applications are also distributed under the same licence, ensuring that improvements are shared with everyone. FOSS can be created by any individual, group, or entity; all that is required is that the software be distributed with a FOSS compliant license agreement. Many FOSS projects rely on communities of unpaid volunteer contributors for their development, but some are created by commercial entities. The creation of FOSS is driven by the need to solve a particular problem, and a desire to make the world a better place for everyone, rather than for commercial reasons. The FOSS approach is able to remove many of the financial and legal barriers that might otherwise prevent a particular piece of software becoming widely adopted. Of course, the success of any given piece of software rests purely on its own merits, and in this respect FOSS is no different. FOSS that is considered to be particularly useful can rapidly be adopted on a global scale. FOSS-based solutions often become de facto standards for implementing a particular functionality. Many of the technologies that help power the ***Internet*** and the ***Web*** are based on such FOSS principles. The FOSS approach can also be applied to hardware-based solutions, as hardware designs are often released as software-based blueprints.

b)   **HOW COULD IT HELP?** Creating the Stream Tone will undoubtedly be a challenging, complex, and multi-faceted undertaking, and it will be critically important to ensure that barriers to its development and deployment are minimised wherever possible. FOSS-based approaches can help develop the many technologies of the Stream Tone in a manner that is collaborative, cost-effective, innovative, non-bureaucratic, participative, royalty-free, transparent, and understandable. The Stream Tone is intended to benefit everyone, everywhere, and a FOSS-based approach will help to ensure that the adoption of the Stream Tone is not limited by its affordability, availability, or usefulness.

c)   **FURTHER READING**
Free And Open-Source Software: *https://en.wikipedia.org/wiki/Free_and_open-source_software*
Free Software: *https://en.wikipedia.org/wiki/Free_software*
Free Software Definition: *https://en.wikipedia.org/wiki/Free_Software_Definition*
Free Software Foundation: *https://en.wikipedia.org/wiki/Free_Software_Foundation*
GNU General Public License:
*https://en.wikipedia.org/wiki/GNU_General_Public_License*
Internet: *https://en.wikipedia.org/wiki/Internet*
Open Source Initiative: *https://en.wikipedia.org/wiki/Open_Source_Initiative*
Open-Source Software: *https://en.wikipedia.org/wiki/Open_source_software*
Royalties: *https://en.wikipedia.org/wiki/Royalties*
Software License: *https://en.wikipedia.org/wiki/Software_license*
Source Code: *https://en.wikipedia.org/wiki/Source_code*
World Wide Web: *https://en.wikipedia.org/wiki/World_Wide_Web*

# 3.1.43   FREE LOSSLESS AUDIO CODEC

a)   **WHAT IS IT?** The Free Lossless Audio Codec (FLAC) is a ***Free and Open-Source Software***-based lossless audio ***Compression*** algorithm that allows audio data to be encoded and then decoded without any loss of data. Audio sources encoded using the FLAC are usually reduced to 50 or 60 percent of their original size. The FLAC is one of the most popular lossless audio ***Compression*** algorithms currently available, and is supported by a large number of commercial audio equipment manufacturers

b) **HOW COULD IT HELP?** The Stream Tone is a data streaming technology designed to deliver audio and video over the ***Internet*** from the ***Web*** to a Stream Tone Access Device, and to send user-input back. The FLAC is an open-source, royalty free, audio ***Compression*** algorithm that could potentially form a fundamental part of the Stream Tone Transfer Protocol; providing the technology to encode and decode Stream Tone audio data without any loss of audio quality.

c) **FURTHER READING**
Data Compression: *https://en.wikipedia.org/wiki/Data_compression*
FLAC: *https://en.wikipedia.org/wiki/FLAC*
Free And Open-Source Software: *https://en.wikipedia.org/wiki/Free_and_open-source_software*
Lossless Compression: *https://en.wikipedia.org/wiki/Lossless_Compression*
Royalties: *https://en.wikipedia.org/wiki/Royalties*
Streaming Media: *https://en.wikipedia.org/wiki/Streaming_media*
World Wide Web: *https://en.wikipedia.org/wiki/World_Wide_Web*

# 3.1.44    FREEMIUM

a) **WHAT IS IT?** Freemium is a type of business model where a product or service, with reduced features or usability, is provided free-of-charge, whilst a more advanced, or premium, version of the same product or service, with more features or enhanced usability, is also available, for a fee. Freemium is a portmanteau of the words 'free' and 'premium'. The freemium business model is often applied to digital products and services. The products and services that are provided for free are restricted in some respect, such as by having reduced capacity, connectivity, content, duration, functionality, portability, support, or useability. Some freemium products and services are unrestricted initially but become restricted after a set time period has elapsed or after a set number of uses have occurred, and then require that a fee be paid in order to return the product or service to its unrestricted state. Of course, if the restricted version is still acceptable then a fee need not be paid. The freemium business model has been particularly successful when applied to computer games, where it is often referred to as free-to-play, as it allows a user to experience a game without having to buy it. If the game is found to be acceptable then the user may decide to purchase the premium version. The premium version of the game might then provide more game levels, unlimited gameplay, different characters, better equipment, more powerful transportation, or more interesting activities. Some games offer additional content that can be purchased from within the game, which can then be used to obtain an enhanced game experience. Purchasable in-game content can include such things as armour, buildings, clothing, cosmetics, currency, engines, food, furniture, gadgets, information, magic spells, maps, music, pets, potions, tools, tyres, weapons, or vehicles. Premium in-game abilities can also be purchased, including increased accuracy, healing, magic, skill, speed, stamina, and strength, or the power of flight, invincibility, invisibility, and night vision. The purchase of premium content or a premium version is always optional, and often unnecessary as most freemium products and services, even in their free form, are still very useful and enjoyable. Nevertheless, the premium versions do offer advantages that some users are willing to pay for. The provision of products and services free-of-charge, under the freemium business model, are funded by the sales of the premium versions of those same products and services. The freemium business model is only viable if such sales are sufficient to cover the development and operating costs of both the free and premium versions. The ultimate purpose of the freemium business model is to encourage users to purchase premium products and services. The freemium business model is also a marketing technique, a variant of the loss-leader concept, in which products or services are sold at, or below, cost in order to win market share, which will then be exploited in the future. In the case of the freemium model the loss is represented by the products and services that are provided free-of-charge, and which will hopefully lead to premium sales in the future. The modern world offers a very wide range of products and services, unfortunately, choosing the best one can often be an expensive process, as each product or service must first be purchased before it can be evaluated. The freemium business model removes the need for such upfront costs, allowing products and services to be evaluated before they are purchased. The try-before-you-buy aspect of the freemium business model can also be used to introduce new products and services into virgin markets. Often, customers in such markets will not purchase a new or unfamiliar type of product or service until they have directly experienced its benefits, especially if it seems expensive. The freemium business model allows new products and services to be experienced by a potential customer on a free-of-charge basis. Such an approach has successfully been used to introduce *Internet* services to mobile-phone users in a number of developing countries. The freemium business model has become an established approach for many modern businesses, and has proven to be particularly effective for marketing digital products and services that are delivered over the *Internet*. Businesses that offer their products and services under the freemium business model are often at a significant competitive advantage over those that do not.

b) **HOW COULD IT HELP?** The freemium business model effectively allows a wide range of products and services to be tested, albeit in some reduced capacity, before they are bought. The freemium business model can also be used to introduce new products and services into virgin markets. As is the case with many current *Web-based Services*, not all Stream Tone Transfer Protocol (STTP)-based services will be free. In fact, given that the Stream Tone pushes all data processing off of the client device and into the *Data Centre* means that there will be some very real costs involved in providing certain types of digital content and services that will then be communicated using the STTP. Some of these costs might be recoverable using creative business models, such as freemium. The freemium business model could also be used to introduce new STTP-based services; an approach that could greatly speed the adoption of Stream Tone-based technologies.

c) **FURTHER READING**
Business Model: *https://en.wikipedia.org/wiki/Business_model*
Free - The Future of a Radical Price:
*https://en.wikipedia.org/wiki/Free:_the_future_of_a_radical_price*
Free-To-Play: *https://en.wikipedia.org/wiki/Free-to-play*
Freemium: *https://en.wikipedia.org/wiki/Freemium*
What is Freemium?: *http://www.freemium.org/what-is-freemium-2/*

# 3.1.45    G.993.5

a) **WHAT IS IT?** G.993.5 is a far-end crosstalk-cancellation technology standard published by the International Telecommunication Union Telecommunication Standardization Sector (ITU-T). The technology behind G.993.5 is often referred to as copper vectoring by the communications-industry press. The G.993.5 standard is also informally known as G.Vector. G.993.5 is designed to work in conjunction with Very-High-Bit-Rate Digital

Subscriber Line version 2 (VDSL2), protocol standard ITU-T G.993.2, a copper wire-based broadband communications technology. VDSL2 is commonly used to deliver data over the 'last mile', from a broadband distribution point to the end user. The distribution point typically has an *Optical Fibre*-based connection to the *Internet*. VDSL2 provides moderately high-bandwidth data communications without the high costs associated with installing an *Optical Fibre* link to each user. VDSL2 has a theoretical maximum bandwidth, at source, of approximately 250 megabits per second (Mbps), which can be reduced, mainly due to crosstalk, down to 100 Mbps at a distance of 0.5 kilometres (km), and 50 Mbps at a distance of 1 km. Degradation over distances greater than 1 km are less severe. Many customers using VDSL2 are located at a distance of 1 km, or more, from a distribution point, which limits their available bandwidth to a maximum of 50 Mbps. The paired copper wires that are used to deliver VDSL2 are not run in isolation; they are normally part of a multi-wire communications cable. The crosstalk that degrades the performance of VDSL2-based communications is caused by electromagnetic interference between all the wires in a cable. G.993.5 technology is able to detect the crosstalk occurring on multiple wires and cancel most of it out. Even though G.993.5 requires the use of a fairly powerful computer in order to cancel the crosstalk on a typical 48-wire cable, the cost of G.993.5 is still less than the cost of installing *Optical Fibre* links to each user. G.993.5 can be used to greatly reduce VDSL2 crosstalk and thereby increase communications bandwidth, providing an average customer, at a distance of approximately one km from a distribution point, with up to 100 Mbps bandwidth. VDSL2-based communications using G.993.5 technology can be further enhanced by using multi-pair-bonding, ITU-T standard G.998.x, to provide bandwidths of up to 300 Mbps over the same distance. Higher bandwidths, of up to 1,000 Mbps, will be possible for customers located much closer to a distribution point. It is estimated that, worldwide, there are hundreds of millions of users that still rely on copper wire for their *Internet* connectivity, some of which will be upgraded to *Optical Fibre* links in the near future, but many will not, particularly those based in more rural locations. Technologies such as G.993.5 can help to significantly increase communications bandwidths over existing copper-wire-based communications infrastructure, and do so at a much lower cost than *Optical Fibre*.

b)   **HOW COULD IT HELP?** The Stream Tone needs both wired and wireless telecommunications that are highly affordable, high bandwidth, low latency, highly reliable, and ubiquitously available. Bandwidth boosting technologies, such as G.993.5, could be used to cost-effectively communicate digital content and services using the Stream Tone Transfer Protocol.

c)   **FURTHER READING**
G.993.2 - Very High Speed Digital Subscriber Line Transceivers 2 (VDSL2):
*https://www.itu.int/rec/dologin_pub.asp?lang=e&id=T-REC-G.993.2-201112-I!!PDF-E&type=items*
G.993.5 - Self-FEXT Cancellation (Vectoring) For Use With VDSL2 Transceivers:
*https://www.itu.int/rec/dologin_pub.asp?lang=e&id=T-REC-G.993.5-201004-I!!PDF-E&type=items*
G.998.1 - ATM-Based Multi-Pair Bonding:
*https://www.itu.int/rec/dologin_pub.asp?lang=e&id=T-REC-G.998.1-200501-I!!PDF-E&type=items*
G.998.2 - Ethernet-Based Multi-Pair Bonding:
*https://www.itu.int/rec/dologin_pub.asp?lang=e&id=T-REC-G.998.2-200501-I!!PDF-E&type=items*

G.998.3 - Multi-Pair Bonding Using Time-Division Inverse Multiplexing:
*https://www.itu.int/rec/dologin_pub.asp?lang=e&id=T-REC-G.998.3-200501-I!!PDF-E&type=items*
Internet: *https://en.wikipedia.org/wiki/Internet*
Very-High-Bit-Rate Digital Subscriber Line: *https://en.wikipedia.org/wiki/Very-high-bit-rate_digital_subscriber_line*
Very-High-Bit-Rate Digital Subscriber Line 2: *https://en.wikipedia.org/wiki/Very-high-bit-rate_digital_subscriber_line_2*

# 3.1.46 GLOBAL POSITIONING SYSTEM

a) **WHAT IS IT?** The Global Positioning System (GPS) is an American satellite-based navigation system that provides a worldwide real-time geographic location service. A GPS receiver requires an unobstructed line of sight to four or more satellites in order to work. The GPS service is available to anyone possessing a GPS receiver. Most modern mobile personal computing devices, such as **Smart-Phones** and **Tablet Computers**, contain a GPS receiver in order to provide a wide range of sophisticated location and navigation-based services. Support for the Russian Globalnaya Navigatsionnaya Sputnikovaya Sistema (GLONASS) and the Chinese BeiDou Navigation System is also starting to be common in such devices. In the future, these devices are also likely to support the European Union's Galileo global navigation satellite system, the Indian Regional Navigational Satellite System, and Japan's Quasi-Zenith Satellite System.

b) **HOW COULD IT HELP?** Navigation technologies, such as GPS, are well understood and mature. Stream Tone Access Devices are intended to be direct replacements for all current personal computing devices, including **Smart-Phones** and **Tablet Computers**, and will therefore need to include navigational technologies, such as GPS, in order to be able to deliver functionality comparable to current personal computing devices.

c) **FURTHER READING**
BeiDou Navigation Satellite System:
*https://en.wikipedia.org/wiki/BeiDou_Navigation_Satellite_System*
Galileo (Satellite Navigation):
*https://en.wikipedia.org/wiki/Galileo_%28satellite_navigation%29*
Global Positioning System: *https://en.wikipedia.org/wiki/Global_Positioning_System*
GLONASS: *https://en.wikipedia.org/wiki/GLONASS*
Indian Regional Navigation Satellite System:
*https://en.wikipedia.org/wiki/Indian_Regional_Navigation_Satellite_System*
Quasi-Zenith Satellite System: *https://en.wikipedia.org/wiki/Quasi-Zenith_Satellite_System*
Satellite Navigation: *https://en.wikipedia.org/wiki/Satellite_navigation*

# 3.1.47 GNU/LINUX

a) **WHAT IS IT?** GNU/Linux is, according to Richard Stallman and others, the full and proper name for the **Linux** operating system. GNU is the name of a set of UNIX-compatible user-space tools and libraries. **Linux** is the name of the operating system's kernel. The GNU/Linux operating system is comprised of GNU, **Linux**, and many other, equally important and fundamentally necessary, components.

b) **HOW COULD IT HELP?** Please see the section on **Linux** for details.

c) **FURTHER READING**
GNU: *https://en.wikipedia.org/wiki/GNU*
GNU/Linux Naming Controversy:
*https://en.wikipedia.org/wiki/GNU/Linux_naming_controversy*
GNU Operating System: *https://www.gnu.org/*
Richard Stallman: *https://en.wikipedia.org/wiki/Richard_Stallman*

# 3.1.48    GYROSCOPE

a) **WHAT IS IT?** A gyroscope is a device, based on the principles of angular momentum, for either maintaining orientation or measuring orientation. Many modern portable personal computing devices contain a gyroscope that is used to determine their orientation. Such devices typically contain a microelectromechanical system gyroscope.

b) **HOW COULD IT HELP?** Gyroscopes are a well understood and mature technology that can be used to determine the orientation of portable electronic devices. Stream Tone Access Devices are intended to be direct replacements for all current personal computing devices, including **Smart-Phones** and **Tablet Computers**, and will therefore need to include an orientation technology, such as a gyroscope, in order to be able to deliver functionality comparable to current personal computing devices.

c) **FURTHER READING**
Gyroscope: *https://en.wikipedia.org/wiki/Gyroscope*
Microelectromechanical Systems:
*https://en.wikipedia.org/wiki/Microelectromechanical_systems*

# 3.1.49    H.264

a) **WHAT IS IT?** H.264, or MPEG-4 Part 10, is an advanced, lossy, video **Compression** standard commonly used for the recording, **Compression**, and distribution of high definition video. H.264 is still evolving, with new feature sets, known as profiles, being regularly added to address specific applications. H.264 is a versatile standard that was designed to provide good video quality in a wide variety of situations; it can handle both low and high video resolutions in two and three dimensions, it can be used for video storage on media such as DVDs, it is suitable for multi-media telephony, and it can be communicated, at low or high bit-rates, over packet-switched networks such as the **Internet**, and broadcast by coaxial cable and **Communications Satellite**. Most famously, H.264 is one of the mandatory video **Compression** standards used by Blu-ray Disk players. Over recent years, H.264 has become commonly used for streaming video from the **Internet**, and is supported by many **Web Browsers**, running on many different operating systems. In countries where software patents are legal, commercial users and vendors of products that encode and decode H.264 video are currently required to pay license fees. In 2013, Cisco Systems, Inc., an international manufacturer of networking equipment, announced that it would release its own implementation of the H.264

algorithm as an open-source binary and pay all associated licensing fees, thereby making the H.264 algorithm freely available for everyone to use. It is expected that one of the first beneficiaries of the new open-source binary will be the **Web Real-Time Communication** project, which is developing an **Application Programming Interface** for real-time communication over the **Internet**.

b) **HOW COULD IT HELP?** The Stream Tone is a data streaming technology designed to deliver audio and video over the **Internet** from the **Web** to a Stream Tone Access Device, and to send user-input back. H.264 is a flexible, mature, and widely-used video **Compression** standard that could potentially form a fundamental part of the Stream Tone Transfer Protocol; providing the technology to encode and decode Stream Tone video data. However, the fact that its use currently requires the payment of patent licensing fees makes it less attractive when compared to other video **Compression** technologies that are clearly unencumbered by patents. In the future, it is hoped that the involvement of Cisco Systems, Inc., will help to ensure that the cost of licensing H.264 will no longer be an issue.

c) **FURTHER READING**
Application Programming Interface:
*https://en.wikipedia.org/wiki/Application_programming_interface*
Blu-ray Disc: *https://en.wikipedia.org/wiki/Blu-ray_Disc*
Blu-ray Disc Association: *http://www.blu-raydisc.com/en/*
Communications Satellite: *https://en.wikipedia.org/wiki/Communications_satellite*
Computer Network: *https://en.wikipedia.org/wiki/Computer_network*
Data Compression: *https://en.wikipedia.org/wiki/Data_compression*
H.264 - Advanced Video Coding For Generic Audiovisual Services:
*https://www.itu.int/rec/dologin_pub.asp?lang=e&id=T-REC-H.264-201304-I!!PDF-E&type=items*
H.264/MPEG-4 AVC: *https://en.wikipedia.org/wiki/H.264/MPEG-4_AVC*
High-Definition Video: *https://en.wikipedia.org/wiki/High-definition_video*
Internet: *https://en.wikipedia.org/wiki/Internet*
Lossy Compression: *https://en.wikipedia.org/wiki/Lossy_compression*
Open-Sourced H.264 Removes Barriers To WebRTC:
*http://blogs.cisco.com/collaboration/open-source-h-264-removes-barriers-webrtc/*
OpenH264: *http://www.openh264.org/*
Patent: *https://en.wikipedia.org/wiki/Patent*
Web Browser: *https://en.wikipedia.org/wiki/Web_browser*
WebRTC: *https://en.wikipedia.org/wiki/WebRTC*
World Wide Web: *https://en.wikipedia.org/wiki/World_Wide_Web*

# 3.1.50    H.265

a) **WHAT IS IT?** H.265 is a new, advanced, lossy, video **Compression** standard for the recording, **Compression**, and distribution of high definition and ultra high definition video. H.265 is the successor to the **H.264** Advanced Video **Compression** standard. H.265 is also known as the High Efficiency Video Coding standard. The H.265 video standard offers twice the **Compression** ratio of **H.264**-based video encoding. H.265 video requires only half the data bit-rate to deliver a video of similar size and quality to one encoded by **H.264**. H.265 can support video with resolutions up to 8192 pixels by 4320 pixels. H.265 can also be used to compress still images. Encoding and decoding H.265 video is computationally intensive, and requires the use of hardware-based codecs or powerful generic microprocessors. The H.265 standard supports the use of parallel processing, which can be used to reduce the time taken to encode or decode a video. Like *H.264*, H.265 is also encumbered by patents.

b) **HOW COULD IT HELP?** The Stream Tone is a data streaming technology designed to deliver audio and video over the *Internet* from the *Web* to a Stream Tone Access Device, and to send user-input back. H.265 is a new, efficient, video *Compression* standard that could potentially form a fundamental part of the Stream Tone Transfer Protocol; providing the technology to encode and decode Stream Tone video data. Being twice as efficient as its predecessor, H.265 encoded video would reduce network bandwidth requirements by half. H.265 encoding would also help to reduce video data transmission costs. However, the fact that H.265 is a patented technology makes it less attractive when compared to other video *Compression* technologies that are clearly unencumbered by patents.

c) **FURTHER READING**
Codec: *https://en.wikipedia.org/wiki/Codec*
Data Compression: *https://en.wikipedia.org/wiki/Data_compression*
H.264/MPEG-4 AVC: *https://en.wikipedia.org/wiki/H.264/MPEG-4_AVC*
H.265 - High Efficiency Video Coding:
*https://www.itu.int/rec/dologin_pub.asp?lang=e&id=T-REC-H.265-201304-I!!PDF-E&type=items*
High Efficiency Video Coding:
*https://en.wikipedia.org/wiki/High_Efficiency_Video_Coding*
High Efficiency Video Coding Tiers And Levels:
*https://en.wikipedia.org/wiki/High_Efficiency_Video_Coding_tiers_and_levels*
Lossy Compression: *https://en.wikipedia.org/wiki/Lossy_compression*
Microprocessor: *https://en.wikipedia.org/wiki/Microprocessor*
Patent: *https://en.wikipedia.org/wiki/Patent*
Ultra High Definition Television:
*https://en.wikipedia.org/wiki/Ultra_high_definition_television*
World Wide Web: *https://en.wikipedia.org/wiki/World_Wide_Web*

# 3.1.51    HARD DISK DRIVE

a) **WHAT IS IT?** A Hard Disk Drive (HDD) is a device for the non-volatile storage, and random retrieval, of digital data. HDDs consist of one or more rigid platters, or hard disks, which are rapidly rotated. The platters are usually made from aluminium alloy, ceramic, or glass. Data is stored by magnetising the microscopic regions, known as magnetic domains, of a thin film of ferromagnetic material; typically a cobalt-based alloy that coats each platter. Each domain is able to store one bit of binary data; a one or a zero. Data is read from, or written to, a domain by a combined read/write head, which flies over the platter, on a cushion of air created by aerodynamic effects. When writing data the write-head sets the magnetic orientation of the domain based on whether the data is a one or a zero. When reading data the read-head detects the magnetic orientation of the domain and is able to determine whether the data stored is a one or a zero. HDDs have been a key enabling technology in the history of computing, and can be found in a wide range of devices, including desktop computers, laptop computers, and computer servers. HDDs are starting to be replaced by smaller and faster *Solid-State Drives* (SSDs) for many applications, particularly in mobile personal computing devices, such as **Smart-Phones** and **Tablet Computers**. HDDs are roughly tens times cheaper than a similar capacity SSD. HDDs continue to be an important technology in enterprise-scale operations, such as in **Cloud Computing**-based **Data Centres** that are used to provide **Web**-based content and services. Current HDDs are based on a technology known as perpendicular magnetic recording (PMR), which will most likely reach its storage density limit, estimated to be an areal density of approximately one terabyte per square inch, sometime in the very near future. Replacement HDD technologies, such as bit patterned magnetic recording, heat assisted magnetic recording, microwave assisted magnetic recording, shingled magnetic recording, and two-dimensional magnetic recording, are already being researched and will ensure that HDDs continue to remain a viable storage technology for the foreseeable future. In the short-term, PMR technology will most likely get a boost from helium gas, which will be used to replace the air inside the HDD, and can greatly reduce air turbulence caused by the rotating platters inside the HDD. Helium can help to reduce power consumption, heat, and cost per gigabyte, whilst increasing storage capacity and performance. Helium-filled HDDs are primarily designed for enterprise applications. Another technology that may potentially help to extend the life of the HDD is based on block copolymers which can be made to quickly self-organise over a pre-etched surface to form isolated magnetic domains that are several times smaller than current HDD domains. Block copolymers could, theoretically, increase HDD areal density by up to five fold.

b) **HOW COULD IT HELP?** Stream Tone Transfer Protocol (STTP)-based services are intended to be affordable by all. HDDs are able to cost-effectively store digital information. HDD technology continues to evolve, and is expected to remain a viable data storage medium for the foreseeable future. The Stream Tone Service Infrastructures that will be used to provide STTP-based services will need to make use of cost-effective data storage technologies, such as HDDs, in order to ensure that such services will be affordable.

c) **FURTHER READING**
Data Centre: *https://en.wikipedia.org/wiki/Data_centre*
Hard Disk Drive: *https://en.wikipedia.org/wiki/Hard_disk_drive*
Heat-Assisted Magnetic Recording: *https://en.wikipedia.org/wiki/Heat-assisted_magnetic_recording*
Heat-Assisted Magnetic Recording: *http://nanomag.ucsd.edu/wp-content/uploads/2011/12/Kryder-review1.pdf*
HGST Announces Radically New, Helium-Filled Hard Disk Drive Platform: *http://www.hgst.com/press-room/press-releases/hgst-announces-radically-new-helium-filled-hard-disk-drive-platform*
Microwave Assisted Magnetic Recording For 2Tb/Sqin: *http://ieeetmc.com/r6/scv/mag/MtgSum/Meeting2012_09_Presentation.pdf*
New Paradigms In Magnetic Recording: *http://suessco.com/fileadmin/user_upload/Western_digital.pdf*
Patterned Media: *https://en.wikipedia.org/wiki/Patterned_media*
Shingled Magnetic Recording and Two-Dimensional Magnetic Recording: *http://www.ewh.ieee.org/r6/scv/mag/MtgSum/Meeting2010_10_Presentation.pdf*
Solid-State Drive: *https://en.wikipedia.org/wiki/Solid-state_drive*
World Wide Web: *https://en.wikipedia.org/wiki/World_Wide_Web*

# 3.1.52　HETEROGENEOUS COMPUTING

a)　**WHAT IS IT?** Heterogeneous Computing (HC) is a systems architecture approach that is based on the use of different computational units. For particular workloads, HC systems can be more efficient than homogeneous systems. HC systems are often technically complex as they need to include interfaces between the different computational units. Each computational unit in a HC system is designed to fulfil one particular task, or class of tasks. The functionality of some HC units is fixed, but most can be re-programmed if required. Some HC systems contain HC units with different instruction set architectures, which can greatly increase the complexity and cost of software development for such systems. HC units are often able to execute their allotted tasks faster, and/or use less power, than a general-purpose microprocessor. Some HC units are preferable simply because they are cheaper than homogeneous alternatives. Individual HC units can take a number of different forms, including a distinct computer system, a distinct microprocessor, a distinct functional part of a *System on a Chip* (SOC), an *Application-Specific Integrated Circuit*, or a *Field-Programmable Gate Array*, to name just a handful of possibilities. HC units can be combined in many different ways, using many different types of interface or manufacturing techniques, to produce a useful computational system in which the individual computational parts have been optimised for speed of execution, power consumption, and/or cost. Many modern HC solutions are based on highly customised SOCs. The individual functional units within a SOC are known as semiconductor intellectual property (IP) cores. Many different types of IP core are available, each dedicated to a different task, such as audio processing, cryptography, data-bus management, data storage, graphics processing, interface management, memory management, networking, signal processing, real-time control, and video processing. General-purpose microprocessor IP cores are also available, if required. The different IP cores are generally able to operate independently, allowing a SOC to execute many different tasks in parallel. Some SOCs can contain multiple instances of the same IP core, which are then used to process a particular task very quickly by simultaneously executing a small portion of the task on each core. For example, the graphics engine within a modern SOC often contains hundreds of identical IP cores dedicated to the creation of sophisticated photorealistic three-dimensional computer graphics, with each core simultaneously contributing a small portion of the larger final result. HC solutions allow tasks to be assigned to the most appropriate computational unit, ensuring that results are delivered quickly, whilst power consumption is keep to the absolute minimum required to get the job done. In certain circumstances, the performance improvements and power savings offered by HC can be highly significant. Many battery-powered portable devices rely on HC, in the form of SOCs. Without HC, such devices would not be as functionally rich, and nor would their batteries last as long. Some of the latest supercomputers are based on HC architectures, which typically combine general-purpose microprocessors with general-purpose graphics processing units. Similar architectures are also being adopted in the *Data Centre* in order to save power and reduce operating costs. Many different types of *Cloud Computing*-based services, such as computer-aided design and computer gaming, rely on systems based on HC architectures. HC is promoted by the Heterogeneous System Architecture (HSA) Foundation, which was founded in 2012 as a non-profit consortium for academia, independent software vendors, operating system vendors, original equipment manufacturers, SOC vendors, and SOC IP vendors. The goal of the HSA Foundation is to enable the advancement, industry specification, and promotion of heterogeneous systems architecture, and to support the market introduction of HSA-enabled software solutions and platforms. The HSA Foundation is also interested in making HSA-based parallel computing solutions easier to program. There are a number of HC development platforms currently available, including Compute Unified Device Architecture (CUDA) and Open Computing Language (OpenCL). CUDA is a proprietary platform created by Nvidia Corporation, a manufacturer of graphics processing units and SOCs. CUDA is currently only available for Nvidia hardware. OpenCL is an open and royalty free platform created by the Khronos Group, a non-profit member-funded industry consortium. OpenCL is compatible with the data processing solutions available from a wide range of manufacturers, including Advanced Micro Devices, Inc., Altera Corporation, ARM Holdings plc, Intel Corporation, Nvidia Corporation, Samsung Group, and Vivante Corporation.

b) **HOW COULD IT HELP?** The Stream Tone Access Device will have a HC-based architecture, in the form of a custom SOC with many application-specific IP cores, so that nearly all of its operation will be hardware-based. HC could also help to reduce the operating costs of the *Cloud Computing*-based Stream Tone Service Infrastructures that will be used to provide the digital content and services, which will then be communicated using the Stream Tone Transfer Protocol (STTP). The Stream Tone allows all personal computing to be moved onto STTP-based services and a wide variety of approaches, including HC-based architectures, will be needed in order to make such a transition affordable and practical.

c) **FURTHER READING**
Cloud Computing: *https://en.wikipedia.org/wiki/Cloud_computing*
CUDA: *https://en.wikipedia.org/wiki/CUDA*
General-Purpose Computing On Graphics Processing Units:
*https://en.wikipedia.org/wiki/General-purpose_computing_on_graphics_processing_units*
Graphics Processing Unit: *https://en.wikipedia.org/wiki/Graphics_processing_unit*
Heterogeneous Computing: *https://en.wikipedia.org/wiki/Heterogeneous_computing*
HSA Foundation: *http://hsafoundation.com/*
Instruction Set: *https://en.wikipedia.org/wiki/Instruction_set*
Khronos Group: *http://www.khronos.org/*
Khronos Group: *https://en.wikipedia.org/wiki/Khronos_Group*
Microprocessor: *https://en.wikipedia.org/wiki/Microprocessor*
OpenCL: *https://en.wikipedia.org/wiki/OpenCL*
Semiconductor Intellectual Property Core:
*https://en.wikipedia.org/wiki/Semiconductor_intellectual_property_core*
System On A Chip: *https://en.wikipedia.org/wiki/System_on_a_chip*
Systems Architecture: *https://en.wikipedia.org/wiki/Systems_architecture*

# 3.1.53   HOSTED DESKTOP

a) **WHAT IS IT?** A hosted desktop, or hosted virtual desktop, is an instance of a desktop operating system that is provided as a service from a remote *Cloud Computing*-based *Data Centre*. Hosted desktops can be delivered by local area network, wide area network, or the *Internet*. Hosted desktop services are also referred to as desktop-as-a-service and virtual desktop infrastructure. Hosted desktops are part of a client-server architecture. Access to the remote desktop operating system generally requires the use of a relatively simple client computing device capable running *Web Browser*-based application software. The client computer communicates with a computer server using a data streaming communications protocol that is optimised for the real-time control and display of a remote desktop, such as the *Free and Open-Source Software*-based *Remote*

*FrameBuffer* (RFB) protocol, or one of the many proprietary protocols that also exist. Communication between the client and the server is generally limited to display updates sent from the server to the client, and keyboard or mouse input sent from the client to the server. All computing resources, including data storage, reside within the server. Hosted desktop technology permits the use of a much simpler client computing device compared to what would be required to run the desktop operating system locally. Hosted desktop services move most support activity away from the end-user device, and onto a *Data Centre*-based computer server.

b)   **HOW COULD IT HELP?** Hosted desktops demonstrate the viability of delivering a complete personal computing experience as a *Web-based Service*. It is expected that the Stream Tone Transfer Protocol (STTP) will be used to communicate a wide range of digital services, including hosted desktop services. The STTP could be based on some of the technologies and tools currently used to deliver hosted desktops.

c)   **FURTHER READING**
Client-Server Model: *https://en.wikipedia.org/wiki/Client%E2%80%93server_model*
Cloud Computing: *https://en.wikipedia.org/wiki/Cloud_computing*
Data Centre: *https://en.wikipedia.org/wiki/Data_centre*
Desktop Virtualization: *https://en.wikipedia.org/wiki/Desktop_virtualization*
Free And Open-Source Software: *https://en.wikipedia.org/wiki/Free_and_open-source_software*
Hosted Desktop: *https://en.wikipedia.org/wiki/Hosted_desktop*
Hosted Virtual Desktop: *http://whatis.techtarget.com/definition/hosted-virtual-desktop-HVD*
Internet: *https://en.wikipedia.org/wiki/Internet*
Local Area Network: *https://en.wikipedia.org/wiki/Local_area_network*
Operating System: *https://en.wikipedia.org/wiki/Operating_system*
RFB Protocol: *https://en.wikipedia.org/wiki/RFB_protocol*
Server (Computing): *https://en.wikipedia.org/wiki/Server_%28computing%29*
Wide Area Network: *https://en.wikipedia.org/wiki/Wide_area_network*

# 3.1.54   HYPERTEXT MARKUP LANGUAGE VERSION 5

a)   **WHAT IS IT?** HyperText Markup Language Version 5 (HTML5) is the fifth version of the HyperText Markup Language (HTML), which is a markup language used to structure and present content on the *Web*. HTML5 is not yet fully complete, and is expected to be fully finalised sometime after 2014, although many aspects of it are considered mature and are already in use today. HTML5 is designed to be backwards compatible with older versions of HTML. One of the many new features included in HTML5 is direct support for *Web*-based video; meaning that a HTML5-compliant *Web Browser* can play video without the need for a special software-based video plug-in. HTML5 video is supposed to be open-source and royalty free. Three, competing, video formats have been proposed for inclusion into HTML5; *H.264*, *Theora*, and *VP8*, of which, *VP8* seems to be the leading contender, as it is open-source, royalty free and well supported by its owner, Google, Inc. HTML5 is designed to work in conjunction with a number of other *Web*-oriented programmatic and presentational technologies, such as JavaScript, Cascading Style Sheets version 3 and Synchronised Multimedia Integration Language.

b) **HOW COULD IT HELP?** Before dedicated Stream Tone Access Devices (STADs) are created it is most likely that Stream Tone Transfer Protocol-based services will be accessed using software that emulates a STAD, running on an existing personal computing device. HTML5 could be used to create, in conjunction with other *Web*-oriented programmatic and presentational technologies, a *Web Browser*-based Stream Tone Access Device Emulator. HTML5-supported video might be a good candidate for the real-time video aspect of the STTP.

c) **FURTHER READING**
Backward Compatibility: *https://en.wikipedia.org/wiki/Backward_compatibility*
Cascading Style Sheets: *https://en.wikipedia.org/wiki/Cascading_Style_Sheets*
Emulator: *https://en.wikipedia.org/wiki/Emulator*
H.264/MPEG-4 AVC: *https://en.wikipedia.org/wiki/H.264/MPEG-4_AVC*
HTML: *https://en.wikipedia.org/wiki/Html*
HTML5: *https://en.wikipedia.org/wiki/HTML5*
Internet: *https://en.wikipedia.org/wiki/Internet*
JavaScript: *https://en.wikipedia.org/wiki/JavaScript*
Synchronized Multimedia Integration Language:
*http://en.wikipedia.org/wiki/Synchronized_Multimedia_Integration_Language*
Theora: *https://en.wikipedia.org/wiki/Theora*
VP8: *https://en.wikipedia.org/wiki/VP8*
Web Browser: *https://en.wikipedia.org/wiki/Web_browser*
World Wide Web: *https://en.wikipedia.org/wiki/World_Wide_Web*

# 3.1.55 HYPERTEXT TRANSFER PROTOCOL 2.0

a) **WHAT IS IT?** The HyperText Transfer Protocol (HTTP) 2.0 is the latest revision of HTTP, which is an application-level protocol for collaborative distributed hypermedia information transfer over an *Internet Protocol*-based computer network. HTTP is a key enabling technology of the *Web*. HTTP 2.0 is being developed by the *Internet Engineering Task Force*. HTTP 2.0 will be backwards compatible with previous versions of HTTP. One of the key objectives of HTTP 2.0 is to reduce communications latencies. HTTP 2.0 will be based on the SPDY protocol, which supports multiplexed requests, prioritised requests, compressed headers, and server pushed data streams. It is expected that HTTP 2.0 will greatly benefit many modern *Web-based Services*, especially those that operate in real-time.

b) **HOW COULD IT HELP?** Many Stream Tone Transfer Protocol-based services will be highly interactive, and will therefore need to operate in real-time, and will require a low communications latency. Advanced communications technologies, such as HTTP 2.0, could help the Stream Tone to operate with the level of performance required to support the delivery of real-time interactive digital services.

c) **FURTHER READING**
Backward Compatibility: *https://en.wikipedia.org/wiki/Backward_compatibility*
Computer Network: *https://en.wikipedia.org/wiki/Computer_network*
HTTP 2.0: *https://en.wikipedia.org/wiki/Http2*

HyperText Transfer Protocol: *https://en.wikipedia.org/wiki/Hypertext_Transfer_Protocol*
Internet: *https://en.wikipedia.org/wiki/Internet*
Internet Engineering Task Force:
*https://en.wikipedia.org/wiki/Internet_Engineering_Task_Force*
Internet Protocol: *https://en.wikipedia.org/wiki/Internet_Protocol*
Server (Computing): *https://en.wikipedia.org/wiki/Server_%28computing%29*
SPDY: *http://www.chromium.org/spdy*
SPDY: *https://en.wikipedia.org/wiki/SPDY*
World Wide Web: *https://en.wikipedia.org/wiki/World_Wide_Web*

# 3.1.56 HYPERTEXT TRANSFER PROTOCOL SECURE

a) **WHAT IS IT?** HyperText Transfer Protocol Secure (HTTPS) is a secure, bidirectional, communications protocol used to provide encrypted communications over a computer network. It is widely deployed on the *Internet*. HTTPS is comprised of the *HyperText Transfer Protocol* layered on top of the Transport Layer Security protocol.

b) **HOW COULD IT HELP?** The Stream Tone Transfer Protocol (STTP) will be used to securely communicate digital content and services via the *Internet* from the *Web* to a Stream Tone Access Device. Using HTTPS could provide the STTP with a ready-made, mature, and widely-accepted approach for achieving secure communications over the *Internet*.

c) **FURTHER READING**
Computer Network: *https://en.wikipedia.org/wiki/Computer_network*
HTTP Secure: *https://en.wikipedia.org/wiki/HTTP_Secure*
HyperText Transfer Protocol: *https://en.wikipedia.org/wiki/Hypertext_Transfer_Protocol*
Internet: *https://en.wikipedia.org/wiki/Internet*
Transport Layer Security: *https://en.wikipedia.org/wiki/Transport_Layer_Security*

# 3.1.57 IMAGE SENSOR

a) **WHAT IS IT?** An image sensor is an electronic component designed to convert a light-based image into electrical data. Image sensors are generally based on two key technologies; charge-coupled devices (CCDs) and complementary metal-oxide semiconductor (CMOS) active pixel sensors. CMOS-based image sensors are generally considered to be of a lower cost and use less power than comparable CCD-based image sensors. The quality of images captured by CMOS and CCD are considered to be comparable. The image sensor is the key enabling technology of the modern digital camera and digital video camera. Digital imaging functionality is now included in many modern electronic devices, such as laptop computers, *Smart-Phones* and *Tablet Computers*. The majority of modern electronic devices that include a digital camera are now based on CMOS active pixel sensor technology. Image sensors permit photographic images and video to be captured, which can then be shared via the *Internet*. Image sensors can also be used to capture QR Codes, a type of two-dimensional barcode that has become popular for linking the real-world to the digital world. Image sensors also can be used for *Visible Light Communication*.

b) **HOW COULD IT HELP?** Digital imaging technology, based on CCD and CMOS active pixel sensors, is mature and well understood. Stream Tone Access Devices are intended to be direct replacements for all current personal computing devices, including **Smart-Phones** and **Tablet Computers**, and will therefore need to include image sensor technologies, such as CCD and CMOS active pixel sensors, in order to be able to deliver functionality comparable to current personal computing devices.

c) **FURTHER READING**
Barcode: *https://en.wikipedia.org/wiki/Barcode*
Charge-Coupled Device: *https://en.wikipedia.org/wiki/Charge-coupled_device*
CMOS: *https://en.wikipedia.org/wiki/CMOS*
Digital Camera: *https://en.wikipedia.org/wiki/Digital_camera*
Image Sensor: *https://en.wikipedia.org/wiki/Image_sensor*
Internet: *https://en.wikipedia.org/wiki/Internet*
QR Code: *https://en.wikipedia.org/wiki/QR_code*
Video Camera: *https://en.wikipedia.org/wiki/Video_camera*
Visible Light Communication: *https://en.wikipedia.org/wiki/Visible_light_communication*

# 3.1.58 INDIUM GALLIUM ZINC OXIDE BACKPLANE

a) **WHAT IS IT?** Indium Gallium Zinc Oxide (IGZO) is a metal oxide that can be used to build high-performance energy-efficient active-matrix thin-film transistor backplanes for use in flat-screen visual displays. A backplane is an array of electronic elements, such as transistors, that are used to control the pixels of a flat-screen, or flat-panel, display. IGZO-based backplanes can be used as a component in liquid-crystal displays (LCDs) and **Organic Light-Emitting Diode** (OLED) displays. IGZO has greater electron mobility than amorphous silicon, which is traditionally used for the backplanes of LCDs. Having high electron mobility allows the transistors made from IGZO to switch very quickly; a characteristic that is required to support the very-high refresh-rates expected from modern display screens. The high electron mobility of IGZO also allows the transistors that drive each pixel to be much smaller. Smaller transistors permit smaller pixels, which increases pixel density; allowing high-resolution display screens to be created. IGZO-based display screens exhibit very fast response times, which permits faster screen refresh-rates than comparable LCDs with amorphous silicon-based backplanes. IGZO-based screens use much less power than comparable displays with amorphous silicon-based backplanes because the transistors on an IGZO-based backplane operate very efficiently. IGZO-based backplanes are more transparent than comparable amorphous silicon-based backplanes, permitting more light from a backlight to pass through the backplane to illuminate the screen display; a characteristic that allows the use of less a powerful backlight which further helps to reduce power consumption. As with all active-matrix display screens, the pixels on an IGZO-based display screen do not need to be continuously powered, only when they change; a behaviour that can help to reduce power consumption and can also reduce unwanted electrical noise, thereby improving the sensitivity and accuracy of **Capacitive Sensing** overlays used to create touch-sensitive display screens. IGZO-based backplanes can be manufactured using similar production facilities to those used for traditional amorphous silicon-based backplanes. IGZO-based backplanes currently have high manufacturing yields and low manufacturing costs, which are comparable to those of traditional amorphous silicon-based backplanes. IGZO-based display screens can help to reduce the power consumption of many battery-powered portable personal computing devices, such as laptop computers, **Smart-Phones**, and **Tablet Computers**, allowing them to work for extended time periods, before their batteries need to be recharged.

b) **HOW COULD IT HELP?** Whilst some Stream Tone Access Devices (STADs) will be powered by a direct connection to mains electricity, most will be portable devices that rely on battery power. Energy efficient display technologies, such as IGZO-based backplanes, that are suitable for inclusion into mobile devices could help to reduce power consumption, and extend the battery life of a STAD.

c) **FURTHER READING**
Active Matrix: *https://en.wikipedia.org/wiki/Active_matrix*
Capacitive Sensing: *https://en.wikipedia.org/wiki/Capacitive_sensing*
Flat Panel Display: *https://en.wikipedia.org/wiki/Flat_panel_display*
IGZO: *http://www.sharpusa.com/ForHome/HomeEntertainment/LCDTV/igzo.aspx*
Indium Gallium Zinc Oxide: *https://en.wikipedia.org/wiki/Indium_gallium_zinc_oxide*
Liquid-Crystal Display: *https://en.wikipedia.org/wiki/Liquid-crystal_display*
OLED: *https://en.wikipedia.org/wiki/OLED*
Thin-Film-Transistor Liquid-Crystal Display: *https://en.wikipedia.org/wiki/Thin-film-transistor_liquid-crystal_display*

# 3.1.59   INSTANT MESSAGING

a) **WHAT IS IT?** Instant Messaging (IM) is a real-time text-based communication method designed to work over a computer network, such as the **Internet**. Both the message sender and the message receiver use a client application to send or receive messages. Most IM services use a **Web-based Service** to help connect a message sender with a message receiver, something that would be quite difficult to achieve without a third-party intermediary. Some IM services can store messages until the intended recipient becomes available, in a manner similar to email. IM functionally is very similar to telephony-based text messaging, which uses the Short Message Service (SMS) to send text-based messages via a mobile telephony system. IM is rapidly replacing SMS-based text messaging, primarily because it does not incur a per message fee. SMS-based messages are limited to 160 characters per message, whereas IM messages can be much bigger, generally permitting many thousands of characters per message. IM is available on a wide range of portable personal computing devices, including **Smart-Phones** and **Tablet Computers**.

b) **HOW COULD IT HELP?** IM can provide text-based communications far more cheaply than traditional SMS-based text messaging services. The Stream Tone Access Device is intended to be a very-simple hardware-based device that will not include specific support for legacy telephony-based services, such as SMS, but will be able provide access to Stream Tone Transfer Protocol-based IM services.

c) **FURTHER READING**
Computer Network: *https://en.wikipedia.org/wiki/Computer_network*
Instant Messaging: *https://en.wikipedia.org/wiki/Instant_messaging*
Internet: *https://en.wikipedia.org/wiki/Internet*
Short Message Service: *https://en.wikipedia.org/wiki/Short_Message_Service*

# 3.1.60    INTERNET

a)  **WHAT IS IT?** The Internet is a worldwide network of networks, that permits the global sharing of all types of digital information, and which has become an integral part of both the business and personal life of a significant proportion of the world's population, particularly in more-developed countries. The Internet originated out of research conducted in the 1960s into how to build distributed, fault-tolerant, and robust computer networks. The Internet now provides access to a wide range of digital content and services, including the inter-linked documents of the *Web* and the global email system. The Internet is built from millions of academic, business, governmental, private, and public networks that are interconnected using a wide range of telecommunication technologies. The Internet communicates using the *Internet Protocol* Suite.

b)  **HOW COULD IT HELP?** Stream Tone Transfer Protocol (STTP)-based services will be delivered globally using Stream Tone Telecommunications Infrastructures, which are conceptually subsets of the Internet. Many of those services will not be new but will be pre-existing *Web-based Services* that are simply being communicated in a new way, using the STTP.

c)  **FURTHER READING**
Computer Network: *https://en.wikipedia.org/wiki/Computer_network*
Internet: *https://en.wikipedia.org/wiki/Internet*
Internet Protocol Suite: *https://en.wikipedia.org/wiki/Internet_protocol_suite*
What is the Internet?: *http://www.internetsociety.org/Internet/what-Internet*
World Wide Web: *https://en.wikipedia.org/wiki/World_Wide_Web*

# 3.1.61    INTERNET ENGINEERING TASK FORCE

a)  **WHAT IS IT?** The **Internet** Engineering Task Force (IETF) is the principal body engaged in the development of new *Internet* standards. It is run by a group of loosely self-organised people who wish to contribute to the evolution and engineering of some of the many technologies that make up the *Internet*. The IETF is not a corporation, and it has no board of directors, no members, and no dues; it is generally described as a collection of informal happenings. Nevertheless, regardless of its informality, the IETF is considered to be highly influential. Its mission is to identify and propose solutions to pressing technical and operational problems in the *Internet*, specify the usage or development of protocols and near-term architecture to solve technical problems related to the *Internet*, make recommendations regarding the standardisation of protocols and protocol usage in the *Internet*, facilitate technology transfer to the wider *Internet* community, and provide a forum for the exchange of information between all interested parties. The work of the IETF, conducted primarily through short-lived working groups, is open, and based on rough consensus. It works in areas in which it has technical competence, or where it can develop the level of competence required. The IETF is dependent on volunteers. The IETF is part of the *Internet* Society (ISOC), which provides financial and legal support to the IETF and its sister bodies. The ISOC is an international non-profit educational organisation that promotes the open development, evolution, and use of the *Internet* for the benefit of all people throughout the world. The IETF is responsible for the *Web Real-Time Communication* protocol, amongst many other things.

b) **HOW COULD IT HELP?** Ideally, the Stream Tone Transfer Protocol (STTP) will not be a wholly new protocol but will be based on one or more pre-existing communications protocols. If the STTP is to become a widely-accepted mechanism for communicating digital content and services over the *Internet* then it will most likely need the approval and input of influential and knowledgeable bodies, such as the IETF.

c) **FURTHER READING**
Internet: *https://en.wikipedia.org/wiki/Internet*
Internet Engineering Task Force:
*https://en.wikipedia.org/wiki/Internet_Engineering_Task_Force*
Internet Society: *http://www.internetsociety.org/*
Internet Society: *https://en.wikipedia.org/wiki/Internet_Society*
Standardization: *https://en.wikipedia.org/wiki/Standardization*
The Internet Engineering Task Force: *http://www.ietf.org/*
WebRTC: *https://en.wikipedia.org/wiki/WebRTC*

# 3.1.62    INTERNET MEDIA TYPE

a) **WHAT IS IT?** An **Internet** Media Type (IMT) is used to identify different formats of data transmitted over the *Internet*. Originally known as multi-purpose *Internet* mail extensions (MIME), one objective of which was to support non-textual email content. IMTs help modern *Web Browsers* handle non-*HyperText Markup Language* (HTML) data appropriately. Definitions of the different IMTs are maintained by the *Internet* Assigned Numbers Authority.

b) **HOW COULD IT HELP?** IMTs can help to identify the different types of data that will be communicated using the Stream Tone Transfer Protocol.

c) **FURTHER READING**
Email: *https://en.wikipedia.org/wiki/Email*
HTML: *https://en.wikipedia.org/wiki/HTML*
Internet: *https://en.wikipedia.org/wiki/Internet*
Internet Assigned Numbers Authority:
*https://en.wikipedia.org/wiki/Internet_Assigned_Numbers_Authority*
Internet Media Type: *https://en.wikipedia.org/wiki/Internet_media_type*
MIME: *https://en.wikipedia.org/wiki/MIME*

# 3.1.63    INTERNET PROTOCOL VERSION 6

a) **WHAT IS IT?** The *Internet* Protocol (IP) is a connectionless communications protocol for use on packet-switched link layer networks; it is currently the dominant protocol of the *Internet*. The IP works in conjunction with the Transmission Control Protocol to permit the reliable transfer of information between networked computing devices, each identified with its own unique IP address. *Internet* Protocol version 4 (IPv4) supports a maximum of 4,294,967,296 ($2^{32}$) or about 4.3 billion, unique addresses. Given that the current world population is already close to 7 billion there are not enough addresses available in this version of the *Internet* Protocol to be able to give each person on the planet one of their own. Also, it is expected that in the future many different pieces of technology will each need a unique IP address. Techniques such as classful network design, classless inter-domain routing, and network address translation have helped to delay the impact of this problem but the continued growth of networked devices has almost exhausted this important but limited resource. If everyone on the planet, and all their many electronic devices, are to each have a unique IP address then a new addressing mechanism is going to be needed. *Internet* Protocol Version 6 (IPv6) supports a maximum of 340,282,366,920,938,463,463,374,607,431,768,211,456 ($2^{128}$), or about 340 undecillion, unique addresses.

b) **HOW COULD IT HELP?** Stream Tone Access Devices (STADs) are going to be the principle device for accessing all personal computing services in the future, they are intended to be of a fixed design, and they will be, most likely, manufactured by the billion. By supporting IPv6 right from their inception, instead of IPv4, there will be one less reason to upgrade the STAD in the future. Fewer upgrades will improve reliability and reduce inconvenience.

c) **FURTHER READING**
Classful Network: *https://en.wikipedia.org/wiki/Classful_network*
Classless Inter-Domain Routing: *https://en.wikipedia.org/wiki/Classless_Inter-Domain_Routing*
Computer Network: *https://en.wikipedia.org/wiki/Computer_network*
Internet: *https://en.wikipedia.org/wiki/Internet*
Internet Protocol: *https://en.wikipedia.org/wiki/Internet_Protocol*
IPv4: *https://en.wikipedia.org/wiki/IPv4*
IPv6: *https://en.wikipedia.org/wiki/IPv6*
Network Address Translation: *https://en.wikipedia.org/wiki/Network_address_translation*
Transmission Control Protocol: *https://en.wikipedia.org/wiki/Transmission_Control_Protocol*

# 3.1.64    INTERNET TELEVISION SERVICE

a) **WHAT IS IT?** An *Internet* television service is able to stream, on-demand, television shows and other audio-visual content from the *Web* over the *Internet*. Content is typically viewed using either a dedicated software application or a *Web Browser* running on a traditional personal computing device. Some newer *Internet*-enabled televisions are also able to view *Internet* television services. An *Internet* television service is a type of *Streaming Media* service.

b) **HOW COULD IT HELP?** *Internet* television services demonstrate the viability of delivering audio-visual content as a streamed service from the *Web* over the *Internet*. The Stream Tone Transfer Protocol will be used to communicate a wide range of digital content and services over the *Internet*, including television shows and other video-based content.

c) **FURTHER READING**
Internet: *https://en.wikipedia.org/wiki/Internet*

Internet Television: *https://en.wikipedia.org/wiki/Internet_television*
Streaming Media: *https://en.wikipedia.org/wiki/Streaming_media*
Television: *https://en.wikipedia.org/wiki/Television*
Web Browser: *https://en.wikipedia.org/wiki/Web_browser*
World Wide Web: *https://en.wikipedia.org/wiki/World_Wide_Web*

# 3.1.65   KA BAND

a)   **WHAT IS IT?** The Ka band covers the 26.5 gigahertz (GHz) to 40 GHz frequency range of the electromagnetic spectrum. The Ka band is part of the microwave spectrum, which includes frequencies from 1 GHz to 100 GHz. The Ka band is often used for radar, and *Communications Satellite* (COMSAT)-based communications. When used for COMSAT-based communications, the Ka band permits high-bandwidth data communications. Ka band communications are susceptible to the problem of rain-induced signal fade, although this can be overcome by boosting transponder power or by focusing communications on relatively dry geographies, such as sub-Saharan Africa. COMSATS that use the Ka band are capable of bringing cost-effective, fast, bi-directional, *Internet* access to remote geographies that are typically unreachable using traditional terrestrially-based telecommunications infrastructures.

b)   **HOW COULD IT HELP?** The Stream Tone needs both wired and wireless telecommunications that are highly affordable, high bandwidth, low latency, highly reliable, and ubiquitously available. High-bandwidth telecommunications based on Ka band frequencies could help to cost-effectively deliver Stream Tone Transfer Protocol-based services to geographies that may never be supported by traditional terrestrially-based telecommunications infrastructures.

c)   **FURTHER READING**
Communications Satellite: *https://en.wikipedia.org/wiki/Communications_satellite*
Electromagnetic Spectrum: *https://en.wikipedia.org/wiki/Electromagnetic_spectrum*
Internet: *https://en.wikipedia.org/wiki/Internet*
Ka Band: *https://en.wikipedia.org/wiki/Ka_band*
Radar: *https://en.wikipedia.org/wiki/Radar*

# 3.1.66   LIFESTREAMS

a)   **WHAT IS IT?** Lifestreams are a different way to experience digital life. The lifestream concept was invented by David Gelernter, a professor of computer science at Yale University, United States of America, and Eric Freeman, a computer scientist and author. Currently, digital life is typically experienced using a desktop metaphor of files and folders that are subjectively-ordered spatially by their owner. A lifestream orders digital experiences and data based on the time of creation, an approach that can potentially provide a complete history of a digital life. A lifestream is conceptually similar to a diary; opening the diary at a particular page will show events or data created at a particular date and time. Events and data created before or after that time or date can also be easily discerned, as they are located chronologically nearby. A lifestream can be searched, with the results ordered chronologically. It is believed that searching through chronologically ordered personal data is more efficient than searching through spatially ordered personal data, because people can use mental search hints based on their recollections of what they were doing digitally at the time when they created that data. Lifestream entries can be created by an individual or other entity, such as a *Web* site or *Web*-based news service. A lifestream is conceptually in continuous chronological motion, with entries continually flowing, or streaming, from the present into the past. Activities such as creating a word-processing document, submitting a micro-blog entry, sending an email, or viewing a *Web* page, all add a new entry to a lifestream in the present, which will then flow, with the passing of time, into the past. Lifestream entries can also be created for the future, such as upcoming meeting reminders, or lists of things to do. Multiple lifestreams can be combined based on user-definable criteria. Combining all possible lifestreams together creates the worldstream. The worldstream contains everything that is happening on the *Web*. The worldstream turns the *Web* from a collection of disparate data sources into a single continuous stream of always up to date information. Searching the worldstream, using a stream-based browser, for a particular subject would, by definition, search all possible sources. Using a traditional *Web Browser*, an equivalent search would require that all pertinent *Web* sites be continually searched for the latest information. Lifestreams are not yet in common use but some of the first lifestream-oriented software applications are now starting to appear.

b) **HOW COULD IT HELP?** Lifestreams are a new and different way to experience digital life, one that is based on the chronological ordering of information. If lifestreaming becomes popular, at some point in the future, then it might be well suited to delivery using the data streaming technology of the Stream Tone. A societal shift towards a lifestream-based digital life could help to accelerate the adoption of the Stream Tone.

c) **FURTHER READING**
Lifestreaming: *https://en.wikipedia.org/wiki/Lifestreaming*
Lifestreams: *http://www.cs.yale.edu/homes/freeman/lifestreams.html*
World Wide Web: *https://en.wikipedia.org/wiki/World_Wide_Web*

# 3.1.67   LINUX

a) **WHAT IS IT?** Linux is a successful, free, open-source, reliable, secure, UNIX-like operating system. Linux is commonly used on servers, mainframes, and supercomputers, where it is dominant. Linux can also be used on desktop computers and laptop computers. Linux is suitable for use in a wide range of embedded systems, such as digital video recorders, mobile-phones, music synthesisers, network firewalls and routers, portable music players, *Smart-Phones*, *Tablet Computers*, televisions, and video game consoles. Linux is available in hundreds of different variants, each tailored in some way towards a specific use. Most recently, a Linux variant known as Android has become the dominant operating system for *Smart-Phones* and *Tablet Computers*. The full and proper name of Linux is *GNU/Linux*.

b) **HOW COULD IT HELP?** Linux is a mature and well understood operating system that is suitable for use in a wide range of personal computing devices. Stream Tone Access Devices (STADs) are intended to be purely hardware-based, but should that not be possible, and an operating system is required, then one based on Linux would probably be a good choice. Before dedicated STADs are created it is most likely that Stream Tone Transfer Protocol-based services will be accessed using application software that emulates a STAD, running on a traditional personal computing device. Linux could be used to build a Stream Tone Access Device Emulator that could then be booted directly, from a *Live CD* or memory card, or run within a *Virtual Machine* manager or hypervisor, on a traditional personal computing device.

c) **FURTHER READING**
Android (Operating System):
*https://en.wikipedia.org/wiki/Android_%28operating_system%29*
Emulator: *https://en.wikipedia.org/wiki/Emulator*
Hypervisor: *https://en.wikipedia.org/wiki/Hypervisor*
Linux: *https://en.wikipedia.org/wiki/Linux*
Linux Foundation: *http://www.linuxfoundation.org/*
Live CD: *https://en.wikipedia.org/wiki/Live_cd*
Operating System: *https://en.wikipedia.org/wiki/Operating_system*
Unix: *https://en.wikipedia.org/wiki/Unix*
Unix-like: *https://en.wikipedia.org/wiki/Unix-like*

# 3.1.68    LITHIUM-ION BATTERY

a) **WHAT IS IT?** A Lithium-Ion Battery (LIB) is a type of rechargeable battery that is based on the movement of lithium ions from a negative electrode to a positive electrode when discharging, and from a positive electrode to a negative electrode when recharging. LIBs can be based on a number of different lithium-based chemistries that each has its own strengths and weaknesses, making some types of LIB more suitable for certain applications than others. LIBs are commonly used in many types of consumer electronics, including portable personal computing devices. The LIBs used in consumer electronics typically have a negative electrode made from graphite, and a positive electrode made from lithium cobalt oxide. Lithium ions move between the electrodes by means of a non-aqueous electrolyte made from lithium salts held in an organic solvent. Compared to other types of rechargeable battery, such as those based on nickel-cadmium (NiCd) chemistry, LIBs have a higher energy density, are smaller, lighter, have comparable, or better, self-discharge rates, work over a wider temperature range, and exhibit no memory of partial discharge. There is one aspect, however, where LIBs are currently unable to better NiCd batteries, and that is with regards to cost, as LIBs are more expensive than comparable NiCd batteries. LIBs are not perfect but they do represent a sensible trade-off between benefits and cost, and have helped to make many electronic devices compact, reliable, and portable.

b) **HOW COULD IT HELP?** Whilst some Stream Tone Access Devices (STADs) will be powered by a direct connection to mains electricity, most will be portable devices that rely on battery power. LIB technology is a mature and well understood rechargeable power source that is suitable for use in many portable electronic devices, and which could help to efficiently and effectively power a STAD.

c) **FURTHER READING**
Lithium-Ion Battery: *https://en.wikipedia.org/wiki/Lithium-ion_battery*
Nickel-Cadmium Battery:
*https://en.wikipedia.org/wiki/Nickel%E2%80%93cadmium_battery*

# 3.1.69 LIVE CD

a) **WHAT IS IT?** A Live CD is a CD-ROM containing a complete computer operating system that can be directly booted by a compatible personal computing device, and which will then run that operating system in memory without requiring a permanent installation onto an off-line storage device, such as a *Hard Disk Drive* or *Solid-State Drive*. A Live CD image can also be supplied on a DVD, or a memory card. Live CDs have become a popular method for testing a new operating system on a personal computing device that may already have an operating system installed. Live CD images can also be booted by a *Virtual Machine* manager or hypervisor.

b) **HOW COULD IT HELP?** Before dedicated Stream Tone Access Devices (STADs) are created it is most likely that Stream Tone Transfer Protocol-based services will be accessed using software that emulates a STAD. A Live CD could be used to distribute a fully-functional Stream Tone Access Device Emulator that can either be booted directly, or run by a *Virtual Machine* manager, on a traditional personal computing device.

c) **FURTHER READING**
Emulator: *https://en.wikipedia.org/wiki/Emulator*
Hypervisor: *https://en.wikipedia.org/wiki/Hypervisor*
Live CD: *https://en.wikipedia.org/wiki/Live_CD*
Operating System: *https://en.wikipedia.org/wiki/Operating_system*
Virtual Machine: *https://en.wikipedia.org/wiki/Virtual_machine*

# 3.1.70 MAGNETOMETER

a) **WHAT IS IT?** A magnetometer is a device for measuring the strength and/or direction of a magnet field. Many modern portable personal computing devices, such as *Smart-Phones* and *Tablet Computers*, contain a magnetometer. In such devices the magnetometer primarily functions as a compass, and works in cooperation with other built-in technologies, such as an *Accelerometer*, *Barometer*, and *Global Positioning System*, to provide enhanced navigational services.

b) **HOW COULD IT HELP?** Magnetometer technology, suitable for inclusion into portable electronic devices, is well understood and mature. Stream Tone Access Devices are intended to be direct replacements for all current personal computing devices, including *Smart-Phones* and *Tablet Computers*, and will therefore need to include navigational technologies, such as magnetometers, in order to be able to deliver functionality comparable to current personal computing devices.

c) **FURTHER READING**
Accelerometer: *https://en.wikipedia.org/wiki/Accelerometer*
Barometer: *https://en.wikipedia.org/wiki/Barometer*
Global Positioning System: *https://en.wikipedia.org/wiki/Global_Positioning_System*
Magnetometer: *https://en.wikipedia.org/wiki/Magnetometer*

# 3.1.71 MASSIVELY MULTI-PLAYER ON-LINE GAME

a) **WHAT IS IT?** A Massively Multi-player On-line Game (MMOG) is a video game technology capable of simultaneously supporting thousands of players, who share a persistent game environment, and can, if they wish, engage in cooperative play. The game environments are run on multiple computer servers that can each handle several thousand simultaneous players. MMOGs are played over computer networks, such as the *Internet*, and can be accessed from a wide variety of personal computing devices. Games are usually accessed using a dedicated software application, although some newer games only require the use of a *Web Browser*. Each player's progress through a game is shared in near real-time with all the other players. Many different types of MMOG are supported, including collectible card games, dance games, first-person shooters, puzzle games, racing, real-time strategy, rhythm games, role-playing, simulations, and sports games.

b) **HOW COULD IT HELP?** MMOGs, in all their various forms, demonstrate the viability of *Web*-based gaming services that are shared by many thousands of users, and which are totally dependent on a continuous *Internet* connection in order to function. The Stream Tone Transfer Protocol will be used to communicate a wide range of digital content and services, including MMOGs.

c) **FURTHER READING**
Application Software: *https://en.wikipedia.org/wiki/Application_software*
Internet: *https://en.wikipedia.org/wiki/Internet*
Massively Multiplayer Online Game:
*https://en.wikipedia.org/wiki/Massively_multiplayer_online_game*
Server (Computing): *https://en.wikipedia.org/wiki/Server_%28computing%29*
Video Game: *https://en.wikipedia.org/wiki/Video_game*

# 3.1.72 MESH NETWORK

a) **WHAT IS IT?** A mesh network is a type of computer network topology in which each network node connects to all other nodes, known as a full mesh network, or just to a subset of nodes, such as its closest neighbours, known as a partial mesh network. In a mesh network every node is connected to at least one other node. Each node is able to communicate with any other node by routing data from a source node to a destination node via other intermediary nodes. The movement of data from one node to another is known as a hop. Sophisticated routing algorithms are used to minimise the number hops required to send data from a source node to a destination node. Mesh networking can be used for both wired and wireless communications, although it is most commonly used for wireless communications in environments where traditional terrestrially-based telecommunications infrastructures are not practical. Typically, a wireless mesh network is built using a number of wireless network routers, although any suitable wireless network-enabled device can be used, including desktop computers and laptop computers. Mesh networks, as a whole, are fault tolerant because there is usually more than one way that data can be routed from a source node to a destination node, such that if any node fails an alternative route can usually be found easily and quickly. If a single node in a mesh network has access to an external service, such as the *Internet*, then that service can be shared between all the other network nodes. Optimised mesh networks can deliver high-bandwidth communications with relatively low latencies, such that it can be used for a wide range of interactive services, including *Voice over Internet Protocol*-based telephony. Wireless mesh networks are able to cost-effectively bring the *Web* to remote and challenging geographic environments, such as sub-Saharan Africa. The Institute of Electrical and Electronics Engineers (IEEE) 802.11s standard defines how wireless devices can be easily interconnected using standard IEEE 802.11a/b/g/n *Wi-Fi* technologies to create a wireless local area network (LAN). By default, IEEE 802.11s uses the Hybrid Wireless Mesh Protocol as its main routing protocol, but other routing protocols can be used, if required. IEEE 802.11s creates a secure communication channel between peer nodes. A network device that supports IEEE 802.11s is labelled a 'Mesh Station'.

b) **HOW COULD IT HELP?** The Stream Tone needs both wired and wireless telecommunications that are highly affordable, high bandwidth, low latency, highly reliable, and ubiquitously available. Mesh networking technologies, such as IEEE 802.11s, can help ensure that Stream Tone Transfer Protocol-based services will be available in even the most remote and challenging geographies, with sufficient bandwidth, low latency, and at an affordable price.

c) **FURTHER READING**
Computer Network: *https://en.wikipedia.org/wiki/Computer_network*
Hybrid Wireless Mesh Protocol:
*https://en.wikipedia.org/wiki/Hybrid_Wireless_Mesh_Protocol*
IEEE 802.11s: *https://en.wikipedia.org/wiki/IEEE_802.11s*
Internet: *https://en.wikipedia.org/wiki/Internet*
Mesh Networking: *https://en.wikipedia.org/wiki/Mesh_networking*
Network Topology: *https://en.wikipedia.org/wiki/Network_topology*
Voice Over IP: *https://en.wikipedia.org/wiki/Voice_over_IP*
Wireless LAN: *https://en.wikipedia.org/wiki/Wireless_LAN*
Wireless Mesh Network: *https://en.wikipedia.org/wiki/Wireless_mesh_network*
World Wide Web: *https://en.wikipedia.org/wiki/World_Wide_Web*

# 3.1.73    MODULAR DESIGN

a) **WHAT IS IT?** Modular Design (MD) is a design approach that subdivides a system into smaller functional parts, known as modules. MD effectively combines the benefits of standardisation, such as lower manufacturing costs due to high volume production, with those of customisation, which allow a system to be tailored to a specific use. Systems that use MD may have a lower performance compared to a functionally similar system that uses a non-modular or monolithic design approach, because module-to-module interfaces can be inefficient, adding an extra overhead to system operations. Systems built from highly-integrated components are less modular, as functionality is grouped more tightly together, and specific functionality cannot be easily isolated. Modules are designed so that they are able to connect to other modules that collectively make up a complete system, using a module-to-module interface. Module interfaces are often standardised. Modules often have generic applicability and can be combined with other modules that have compatible interfaces that were originally designed for use in completely different systems, to build new unique systems. Many modern systems are based on MD, including cars, offices, and computers, to name but a few. Many competing manufacturers now produce functionally-equivalent modules that can be used, interchangeably, within such systems. This permits, for example, a battery from one manufacturer to fit, and work correctly, in a car made by another manufacturer. Personal desktop computers are modular systems that contain many different types of standardised components, such as a computer monitor, **Hard Disk Drive**, keyboard, microprocessor, motherboard, mouse, network interface, optical disk drive, power supply, random-access memory, **Solid-State Drive**, and video graphics. Modular systems are considered to be environmentally friendly because they are typically much easier and cheaper to repair or upgrade compared to monolithic systems, which need to be completely replaced when they no longer work or meet requirements.

b) **HOW COULD IT HELP?** The Stream Tone Access Device (STAD) will be highly-integrated and most of its functionality will be provided by a single **System on a Chip**, in order to improve reliability, maximise performance, and reduce manufacturing costs. However, given that STADs could potentially be manufactured by the billion, it would make good sense that they are also easily repairable and upgradeable. Therefore, STADs should, where feasible, be based on a MD that allows for easy repair and upgrade; something that can greatly extend their working life, make the best use of limited raw materials, greatly reduce unnecessary waste, and keep environmentally unfriendly emissions associated with their manufacture and disposal to a minimum.

c) **FURTHER READING**
Modular Design: *https://en.wikipedia.org/wiki/Modular_design*
Product Design: *https://en.wikipedia.org/wiki/Product_design*
System On A Chip: *https://en.wikipedia.org/wiki/System_on_a_chip*

# 3.1.74 MP3

a) **WHAT IS IT?** MP3, also known as MPEG-2 Audio Layer III, is a patented, lossy, data **Compression** standard designed for compressing digital audio. The MP3 encoding algorithm uses a perceptual coding approach, based on the science of auditory masking, which uses psychoacoustic models designed to reduce the precision of, or to completely discard, audio components that are less well perceived by human hearing. MP3 supports various discrete bit and sampling rates, but most commonly audio is encoded at a bit-rate of 128 kilobits per second and a sampling rate of 44.1 kilohertz, which gives an 11:1 **Compression** ratio when compared to typical Compact Disc-based audio. MP3 has become a de facto standard for compressed audio used on many portable entertainment devices, and is a commonly used format for audio files that are shared or streamed via the **Internet**. Most modern personal computing devices also support MP3-based audio.

b) **HOW COULD IT HELP?** The Stream Tone Transfer Protocol (STTP) will be used to communicate audio-visual content and services over the **Internet** from the **Web** to a Stream Tone Access Device, and to send user-input back. MP3 is a mature and popular audio **Compression** algorithm that could potentially form a fundamental part of the STTP; providing the technology to encode and decode Stream Tone audio data. However, the fact that MP3 is currently a patented technology makes it less attractive when compared to other audio **Compression** technologies that are clearly unencumbered by patents.

c) **FURTHER READING**
Compact Disc: *https://en.wikipedia.org/wiki/Compact_disc*
Lossy Compression: *https://en.wikipedia.org/wiki/Lossy_compression*

MP3: *https://en.wikipedia.org/wiki/Mp3*
Patent: *https://en.wikipedia.org/wiki/Patent*
World Wide Web: *https://en.wikipedia.org/wiki/World_Wide_Web*

# 3.1.75  MULTI-FACTOR AUTHENTICATION

a) **WHAT IS IT?** Multi-Factor Authentication (MFA) is an identity and access management (IAM) approach based on the use of more than one form of verification to prove, or confirm, a user's identity with a high degree of certainty so that appropriate access to a secure system may then be granted. MFA verification factors include a knowledge factor, a possession factor, and an inherence factor. The more of these factors that are used to verify a user's identity the greater the level of certainty that a user is genuine. A knowledge factor is something the user knows, and verification typically relies on the entry of information, such as a personal identification number (PIN), password, or pattern. A possession factor is something the user has, and verification typically relies on the use of a token that provides verification information, such as a X.509 security certificate. Tokens generally fall into two classes; connected and disconnected. A disconnected token may be a small battery powered device with a display that is used to present challenge, sequence, or time-based verification information, which can then be viewed and manually entered into the verification device. Sometimes a device such as a mobile-phone, running appropriate software, can be used as a disconnected token. Connected tokens can directly interface to a verifying device using the audio port, parallel port, serial port, USB interface, wireless communications interface, or some other type of connection. Magnetic stripe cards can also be used as a connected token. A personal computing device can be used to provide possession factor-based verification information, such as a user's *Internet Protocol* address, geographic location, or computer configuration, although such information is not considered to be highly reliable, it can still provide useful information to help support the verification process. An inherence factor is something the user is, and verification typically relies on the capture of a user's biometric data, such as a face scan, fingerprint scan, iris scan, retina scan, or voiceprint. The different MFA verification factors have varying degrees of cost, practicality, reliability, and user acceptance that directly affects their deployment. Some of the most reliable and secure implementations of MFA are reserved for governmental and military use due to the high cost and complexity of the technologies involved. MFA is increasingly used in low-cost personal computing devices, such as *Smart-Phones* and *Tablet Computers*, which are now able to provide cost-effective security based on face scans, geographic locations, IP addresses, passwords, patterns, PINs, and voice prints. MFA is expected to become widely deployed in the future as a primary mechanism for protecting access to digital content and services. MFA is often used in conjunction with other security and access management technologies, such as *Encryption* and *Single Sign-On*.

b) **HOW COULD IT HELP?** MFA helps to increase the certainty that the user of a digital service is genuine, thereby ensuring that any data provided by that service can only be accessed by users that are authorised to do so. Stream Tone Access Devices (STADs) will be used to provide secure access to Stream Tone Transfer Protocol-based content and services, including data processing resources and personal data. IAM-oriented technologies, such as MFA, can be used to restrict access to STTP-based content and services to authorised users only.

c) **FURTHER READING**

Access Control: *https://en.wikipedia.org/wiki/Access_control*
Identity Management: *https://en.wikipedia.org/wiki/Identity_management*
Internet Protocol: *https://en.wikipedia.org/wiki/Internet_Protocol*
Multi-Factor Authentication: *https://en.wikipedia.org/wiki/Multi-factor_authentication*
Personal Identification Number:
*https://en.wikipedia.org/wiki/Personal_identification_number*
Single Sign-On: *https://en.wikipedia.org/wiki/Single_sign-on*
X.509: *https://en.wikipedia.org/wiki/X.509*

# 3.1.76    NEAR-FIELD COMMUNICATION

a)  **WHAT IS IT?** Near-Field Communication (NFC) is a set of wireless communication technologies designed to work over a very short range. Whilst NFC can work at distances of up to 20 cm, its optimal operating distance is generally less than 4 cm. NFC is based on radio-frequency identification standards. NFC is designed for close proximity applications such as contactless data exchange, contactless transactions, and as an initiator for more complex communications, such as **Wi-Fi**. The use of NFC for contactless transactions, such as electronic payments, is expected to form the basis of a digital wallet. NFC officially supports data transmission rates of 106 kilobits per second (Kbps), 212 Kbps, and 424 Kbps. NFC is built into many modern portable personal computing devices, such as **Smart-Phones**.

b)  **HOW COULD IT HELP?** Close proximity communications technology, suitable for inclusion in mobile personal computing devices, is well understood and mature. Stream Tone Access Devices are intended to be direct replacements for all current personal computing devices, including **Smart-Phones** and **Tablet Computers**, and will therefore need to include close proximity communications technologies, such as NFC, in order to be able to deliver functionality comparable to today's mobile personal computing devices.

c)  **FURTHER READING**
Digital Wallet: *https://en.wikipedia.org/wiki/Digital_wallet*
ISO/IEC 18092/2013 - Information technology - Telecommunications and information exchange between systems - Near Field Communication - Interface and Protocol (NFCIP-1):
*http://standards.iso.org/ittf/PubliclyAvailableStandards/c056692_ISO_IEC_18092_2013.zip*
Near Field Communication: *https://en.wikipedia.org/wiki/Near_field_communication*
Radio-Frequency Identification: *https://en.wikipedia.org/wiki/Radio-frequency_identification*
Wi-Fi: *https://en.wikipedia.org/wiki/Wi-Fi*

# 3.1.77    NETWORKED PERIPHERAL

a)  **WHAT IS IT?** A networked peripheral is an electronic device that provides complementary functionality to a personal computing device, and which can be accessed via a computer network, such as a local area network, wide area network, or the **Internet**. A typical example of a networked peripheral would be an all-in-one device that provides a colour printer, document scanner, fax machine, and memory card reader, which can be accessed via a wired or wireless network connection. Many older peripherals, such as printers and scanners, are not able to connect to a network and need to be directly connected to a single personal computing device in order to be used or shared with others. Networked peripherals can generally be accessed by any personal computing device that has access to the computer network to which the peripheral is connected, although each accessing device still needs to be able to communicate with the peripheral using the particular communications protocol used by that peripheral. Many modern personal computing devices, such as **Smart-Phones** and **Tablet Computers**, are only able to access peripherals via a wireless network connection. Some networked peripherals can be accessed from anywhere in the world, via the **Internet**.

b)　**HOW COULD IT HELP?** Stream Tone Access Devices (STADs) are intended to be direct replacements for all current personal computing devices. However, it is unlikely that a STAD will support all the interfaces required to connect to older peripherals, and will rely on standard wired and wireless networking connections instead. Most STAD peripherals will probably be controlled via **Web-based Services** and accessed using a variety of new and existing communications protocols. Some STAD peripherals may also directly support the Stream Tone Transfer Protocol.

c)　**FURTHER READING**
Computer Network: *https://en.wikipedia.org/wiki/Computer_network*
Internet: *https://en.wikipedia.org/wiki/Internet*
Peripheral: *https://en.wikipedia.org/wiki/Peripheral*

# 3.1.78　OPEN-SOURCE HARDWARE

a)　**WHAT IS IT?** Open-Source Hardware (OSHW) is hardware that may be constructed from freely-available designs and then used without requiring the payment of royalty fees. The design specifications for OSHW are made available under a licensing model similar to that used for **Free and Open-Source Software** (FOSS), which permits OSHW to be freely changed, copied, distributed, improved, run, and studied. OSHW licenses are largely based on FOSS licenses, which have been adapted to address issues specific to hardware-based designs. OSHW can be created by any individual, group, or entity; all that is required is that the hardware design be distributed with an OSHW-compliant license agreement. Many OSHW projects rely on communities of unpaid volunteer contributors for their development, but some are created by commercial entities. The creation of OSHW is driven by the need to solve a particular problem, and a desire to make the world a better place for everyone, rather than for commercial reasons. The OSHW approach is able to remove many of the financial and legal barriers that might otherwise prevent a particular piece of hardware becoming widely adopted. OSHW can be applied to a very wide range of hardware, both electrical and non-electrical. One area where OSHW is considered particularly useful is in the design of electronic components, such as **System on a Chip** (SOC), which are built using **Application-Specific Integrated Circuit** and **Field-Programmable Gate Array** components. SOCs are typically built from a number of semiconductor intellectual property (IP) cores, which can be based on OSHW designs, described using a hardware description language. OpenCores is an OSHW community which is dedicated to eliminating redundant design work and reducing development costs of IP cores.

b)　**HOW COULD IT HELP?** Creating the Stream Tone will undoubtedly be a challenging, complex, and multi-faceted undertaking, and it will be critically important to ensure that barriers to its development and deployment are minimised wherever possible. OSHW-based approaches can help to develop the many technologies of the Stream Tone in a manner that is collaborative, cost-effective, innovative, non-bureaucratic, participative, royalty-free, transparent, and understandable. The Stream Tone is intended to benefit everyone, everywhere, and an OSHW-based approach will help to ensure that the adoption of the Stream Tone will not be limited by its affordability, availability, or usefulness. The Stream Tone Access Device (STAD) is intended to be a hardware-based ***Thin Client*** that will be built using a low-cost energy-efficient SOC. An OSHW-based SOC will also help to reduce STAD development and manufacturing costs, which will help to ensure that the STAD will be very affordable.

c) **FURTHER READING**
Application-Specific Integrated Circuit: *https://en.wikipedia.org/wiki/Application-specific_integrated_circuit*
Field-Programmable Gate Array: *https://en.wikipedia.org/wiki/Field-programmable_gate_array*
Free And Open-Source Software: *https://en.wikipedia.org/wiki/Free_and_open-source_software*
Hardware Description Language:
*https://en.wikipedia.org/wiki/Hardware_description_language*
Open-Source Hardware: *https://en.wikipedia.org/wiki/Open-source_hardware*
OpenCores: *http://opencores.org/*
OpenCores: *https://en.wikipedia.org/wiki/OpenCores*
Royalties: *https://en.wikipedia.org/wiki/Royalties*
Semiconductor Intellectual Property Core:
*https://en.wikipedia.org/wiki/Semiconductor_intellectual_property_core*
System On A Chip: *https://en.wikipedia.org/wiki/System_on_a_chip*

# 3.1.79   OPENCORES

a) **WHAT IS IT?** OpenCores is an ***Open-Source Hardware*** (OSHW) community dedicated to eliminating redundant design work and reducing development costs of semiconductor intellectual property (IP) cores. IP cores are the functional building blocks of ***Application-Specific Integrated Circuits*** and ***Field-Programmable Gate Arrays***. IP cores are defined using a software-based hardware description language. OpenCores is committed to the concept of freely available, usable, and re-usable OSHW. The main objective of OpenCores is to design and publish core designs under a hardware license based on the GNU Lesser General Public License for software. OpenCores develops standards for open-source cores and platforms, creates tools and methods for developing open-source cores and platforms, develops open-source cores and platforms, and provides documentation for developed cores and platforms. OpenCores maintains an expanding library of IP core designs covering areas such as arithmetic, communications, co-processing, cryptography, digital signal processing, error-correction, memory control, microprocessors, peripheral control, ***System on a Chip*** (SOC), and video. OpenCores' IP cores are designed to use a non-proprietary OSHW system bus, known as Wishbone.

b) **HOW COULD IT HELP?** The Stream Tone Access Device (STAD) will be a hardware-based ***Thin Client*** for accessing Stream Tone Transfer Protocol-based services, and which will be built using a low-cost energy-efficient OSHW-based SOC. A STAD will need to support a wide range of user-oriented functionalities, including *Accelerometers*, *Ambient Light Sensors*, *Barometers*, *Capacitive Sensing* display screens, *Global Positioning Systems*, *Gyroscopes*, *Image Sensors*, loudspeakers, keyboards, *Magnetometers*, memory cards, mice, microphones, *Proximity Sensors*, and a wide range of wireless communications technologies, such as *Bluetooth*, *Fifth-Generation Mobile Communications*, *Fourth-Generation Mobile Communications*, infrared, *Near-Field Communication*, *Visible Light Communication*, and *Wi-Fi*. The STAD SOC could use pre-existing IP cores from the OpenCores library to reduce development and manufacturing costs involved in supporting such functionalities, thereby helping to ensure that the client hardware of the Stream Tone will be highly affordable. The OpenCores community could, theoretically, also help to design any new elements that will be required for the STAD SOC.

c) **FURTHER READING**

Application-Specific Integrated Circuit: *https://en.wikipedia.org/wiki/Application-specific_integrated_circuit*
Field-Programmable Gate Array: *https://en.wikipedia.org/wiki/Field-programmable_gate_array*
GNU Lesser General Public License:
*https://en.wikipedia.org/wiki/GNU_Lesser_General_Public_License*
Hardware Description Language:
*https://en.wikipedia.org/wiki/Hardware_description_language*
Open-Source Hardware: *https://en.wikipedia.org/wiki/Open-source_hardware*
OpenCores: *http://opencores.org/*
OpenCores: *https://en.wikipedia.org/wiki/OpenCores*
Semiconductor Intellectual Property Core:
*https://en.wikipedia.org/wiki/Semiconductor_intellectual_property_core*
System On A Chip: *https://en.wikipedia.org/wiki/System_on_a_chip*

# 3.1.80 OPENFLOW

a) **WHAT IS IT?** OpenFlow is a secure communications protocol for remotely controlling the data forwarding plane of network switches and routers within a *Data Centre*. OpenFlow is licensed on *Fair, Reasonable and Non-Discriminatory Licensing* terms, without royalty, by the Open Networking Foundation (ONF). The OpenFlow protocol is a key enabling technology of *Software-Defined Networking* (SDN). Network switches and routers supporting the OpenFlow protocol contain a programmable data flow table that is used to route network data packets based on the packet's header data. The flow tables, within all the OpenFlow-enabled network devices within a particular network, are typically controlled, or programmed, by a single, separate computer server running an OpenFlow Controller application. The OpenFlow protocol is supported by a number of network device vendors. Because the data forwarding aspect of network devices that support the OpenFlow protocol can be quickly and easily reprogrammed, OpenFlow-enabled networks are able to adapt to dynamic network environments, such as those found in modern *Cloud Computing*-based *Data Centres* which deploy resources, such as *Virtual Machines*, elastically on demand, and can have highly variable data traffic flows. The OpenFlow protocol can be used to create one or more virtual local area networks (VLANs), using a physical network infrastructure of network switches and routers. A VLAN can be used to insulate applications and services, in a process known as abstraction, from the physical network infrastructure. In a wireless network environment, the OpenFlow protocol can be used to implement seamless roaming by dynamically altering the network data destinations and data flow as a mobile user moves from one wireless node to another. The OpenFlow protocol can also be used to implement quality of service functionality by optimising the flow of certain types of data packets or flows over specific routes. Logically associated *Virtual Machines*, grouped based on ownership or purpose, can be quickly and easily linked together using a VLAN defined using the OpenFlow protocol. OpenFlow created VLANs can also be used to segregate data traffic in multi-tenancy environments. Using OpenFlow-based network technology, very large networks, such as those found in the *Data Centre*, educational campus, or enterprise, can be optimally configured quickly and easily, often achieving in hours what would have taken days or weeks to achieve manually. OpenFlow-based technology brings a standard, vendor-independent, interface to the network that can help to simplify and accelerate network operations management. Organisations that implement SDN, using tools such as the OpenFlow protocol, are able to reduce costs and improve control of network infrastructure.

b) **HOW COULD IT HELP?** *Cloud Computing*-based Stream Tone Service Infrastructures will, in the future, be responsible for generating all Stream Tone Transfer Protocol (STTP)-based services. Technology standardisation initiatives, such as OpenFlow, can help mature key aspects of the *Cloud Computing* industry and ensure that STTP-based services will be practical, and affordable by all.

c) **FURTHER READING**
Computer Network: *https://en.wikipedia.org/wiki/Computer_network*
Data Center: *https://en.wikipedia.org/wiki/Data_center*
Network Management: *https://en.wikipedia.org/wiki/Network_management*
Network Switch: *https://en.wikipedia.org/wiki/Network_switch*
Open Networking Foundation:
*https://en.wikipedia.org/wiki/Open_Networking_Foundation*
OpenFlow: *https://en.wikipedia.org/wiki/OpenFlow*
Quality Of Service: *https://en.wikipedia.org/wiki/Quality_of_service*
Reasonable And Non-Discriminatory Licensing:
*https://en.wikipedia.org/wiki/Reasonable_and_non-discriminatory_licensing*
Router (Computing): *https://en.wikipedia.org/wiki/Router_%28computing%29*
Software-Defined Networking: *https://en.wikipedia.org/wiki/Software-defined_networking*
Virtual LAN: *https://en.wikipedia.org/wiki/Virtual_LAN*

# 3.1.81 OPENSTACK

a) **WHAT IS IT?** OpenStack is a *Free and Open-Source Software*-based infrastructure-as-a-service (IAAS) initiative for controlling the compute, networking, and storage resources of *Cloud Computing*-based infrastructure services. OpenStack is an attempt to standardise the *Cloud Computing* industry, and, by so doing, introduce a level of compatibility and consistency that has not, thus far, existed between the various proprietary *Cloud Computing* service providers. OpenStack is developed by the OpenStack Foundation, which has a membership of thousands of individuals and hundreds of organisations, from all around the world. As platform-as-a-service and software-as-a-service services can both be built from IAAS, OpenStack is able to support all *Cloud Computing* types. OpenStack is a *Cloud Computing* operating system that controls the compute, networking, and storage resources in a ***Data Centre***. OpenStack resources are managed through the ***Web***-based OpenStack Dashboard. OpenStack Compute allows enterprises and service providers to deliver computing resources on-demand by dynamically provisioning and managing networks of ***Virtual Machines***. OpenStack Storage provides block and object storage for use with applications and servers. Block storage provides compute instances with expanded storage, better performance, and enterprise storage platform integration. Object Storage provides cost-effective scale-out storage that can be integrated directly into applications or used for backup, archiving, or data retention. OpenStack Networking provides a system for network creation, management, and traffic control. OpenStack Shared Services provides identity management, ***Virtual Machine*** image management, and a ***Web*** interface that integrates all the OpenStack components with each other as well as with external systems. OpenStack is helping to mature the ***Cloud Computing*** services industry, bringing a level of consistency and interchangeability between providers that did not exist before, and which will consequently increase competition and drive down costs. OpenStack can even be run on top of OpenStack, allowing OpenStack to be more cost-effectively and easily used, modified, and updated. OpenStack on OpenStack, also known as TripleO, is now supported by the TripleO project.

b) **HOW COULD IT HELP?** *Cloud Computing*-based Stream Tone Service Infrastructures will, in the future, be responsible for generating all Stream Tone Transfer Protocol (STTP)-based services. Technology standardisation initiatives, such as OpenStack, can help mature key aspects of the ***Cloud Computing*** industry and ensure that STTP-based services will be practical, and affordable by all.

c) **FURTHER READING**
Cloud Computing: *https://en.wikipedia.org/wiki/Cloud_computing*
Computer Data Storage: *https://en.wikipedia.org/wiki/Computer_data_storage*
Computer Network: *https://en.wikipedia.org/wiki/Computer_network*
Computing: *https://en.wikipedia.org/wiki/Computing*
Free And Open-Source Software: *https://en.wikipedia.org/wiki/Free_and_open-source_software*
OpenStack: *https://en.wikipedia.org/wiki/Openstack*
OpenStack Foundation: *http://www.openstack.org/foundation/*
TripleO: *https://wiki.openstack.org/wiki/TripleO*
Virtual Machine: *https://en.wikipedia.org/wiki/Virtual_machine*
Welcome to the Mind-Bending World of Cloud-on-Cloud Computing: *http://www.wired.com/wiredenterprise/2013/04/rackspace-openstack-openstack/*
World Wide Web: *https://en.wikipedia.org/wiki/World_Wide_Web*

# 3.1.82 OPERATING SYSTEM-LEVEL VIRTUALISATION

a) **WHAT IS IT?** Operating System-Level Virtualisation (OSLV) is a computer virtualisation technology in which a single operating system kernel supports the use of multiple isolated user-space instances. Such instances are often referred to as containers, jails, virtual private servers, or virtualisation engines. OSLV solutions are currently only available for Unix-like operating systems, such as ***Linux***. OSLV does not support the execution of multiple operating systems, only the execution of multiple software applications that have been specifically designed to run on the operating system of the OSLV host. OSLV shares the resources of its host operating system between the containers, and the allocation of those resources can be finely controlled. Containers are isolated such that the operation of software executed within one container cannot affect the operation of software executed within another container. OSLV differs from other types of virtualisation technology, such as type 1 or type 2 *Virtual Machine* monitors or hypervisors that are used to run *Virtual Machines*, in that it does not need to emulate the hardware environment of a personal computing device within which a distinct operating system can then be executed. Consequently, the resource overhead of hosting multiple containers is much less than would be incurred for hosting multiple operating systems. Also, containers can be started and stopped much quicker than a typical *Virtual Machine* because they are much simpler and smaller. For certain types of workload, OSLV allows operating system resources to be used far more efficiently and effectively than other virtualisation technologies. OSLV allows more instances of a particular software application to be simultaneously hosted on a single computer, and allows such instances to be executed with greater performance. Being able to host more instances simultaneously and for such instances to be executed with greater performance means that OSLV can significantly reduce operating costs. OSLV technology is rapidly being adopted by the *Cloud Computing* industry, and for certain types of workloads may completely replace the use of *Virtual Machines* in the very near future.

b)   **HOW COULD IT HELP?** The digital content and services that will be communicated by the Stream Tone Transfer Protocol need to be highly affordable, high bandwidth, low latency, highly reliable, and ubiquitously available. Virtualisation technologies, such as OSLV, could allow Stream Tone Service Infrastructures to cost-effectively provide such content and services.

c)   **FURTHER READING**
Cloud Computing: *https://en.wikipedia.org/wiki/Cloud_computing*
Linux: *https://en.wikipedia.org/wiki/Linux*
LXC: *https://en.wikipedia.org/wiki/LXC*
Operating System-Level Virtualization:
*https://en.wikipedia.org/wiki/Operating_system%E2%80%93level_virtualization*
Virtual Machine: *https://en.wikipedia.org/wiki/Virtual_machine*

# 3.1.83   OPTICAL FIBRE

a)   **WHAT IS IT?** Optical fibre is a transparent, flexible, fibre made from glass, designed to transmit light between its two end-points. Optical fibre is constructed of an inner of core with a relatively high refractive index, and an outer cladding with a lower refractive index. Light entering an optical fibre is propagated along that fibre due to total internal reflection, allowing light-based data to be transmitted over very long distances with very little signal loss. In comparison, metal-based communications cables, such as those made out of copper, have a tendency to loose signal strength, especially over longer distances. Also, metal cables can be affected by electromagnetic interference, something that optical fibre is immune to. Light travelling through the glass-based medium of an optical fibre moves at approximately two-thirds the speed of light in a vacuum. Optical fibre cables can cost-effectively transmit data at many terabits per second over thousands of miles, far faster, and far further than other comparable communications technologies. Optical fibre is now used to carry the bulk of the world's telecommunications traffic. Optical fibre is a key part of the long distance communications infrastructure of the *Internet*. Traditionally, optical fibre has been used for national telecommunications backbones, as well as for international communications via *Submarine Communication Cables*, but it is now starting to connect local telecommunications service, over the last mile, to the home and office. Using optical fibre for the last mile can deliver data at up to 2 gigabits per second into the home, far faster and cheaper than any other current home-oriented communications technology. Such high-bandwidth communications links to the home will lead to the development of many new data-based technologies for both play and work. Looking to the future, recently announced research shows that a new design of optical fibre, in which the traditional glass core is replaced with air, is able to transmit light at almost full speed. Transmitting data faster can help to reduce communications latency, which is a problem, or rather a characteristic, of all types of digital communication. It should be noted that, compared to most other types of data communication technology, optical fibre is already considered to be very-low latency. Being able to improve upon this particular characteristic would make an already good technology even better. Currently, the air-filled optical fibres are really only suitable for relatively short distance communications, due to signal loss over longer distances, but may still find a future role within the *Data Centre* as very high-bandwidth server to server interconnections.

b) **HOW COULD IT HELP?** The Stream Tone needs both wired and wireless telecommunications that are highly affordable, high bandwidth, low latency, highly reliable, and ubiquitously available. Most Stream Tone Access Device users will be mobile and will therefore need to rely on wireless communications technologies in order to connect to Stream Tone Transfer Protocol (STTP)-based services. However, a significant number of users will be static and will be able to take full advantage of optical fibre-based telecommunications. A Stream Tone Telecommunications Infrastructure that included optical fibre-based communications would be able to provide *Internet* connectivity that was highly affordable, high bandwidth, low latency, and highly reliable. Optical fibre-based communications can also be used to bring STTP-based services into centralised locations, such as places of work, from where such services can then be distributed by high-bandwidth short-distance wireless telecommunications technologies, such as *Wi-Fi*.

c) **FURTHER READING**
Data Center: *https://en.wikipedia.org/wiki/Data_center*
Fiber To The X: *https://en.wikipedia.org/wiki/Fiber_to_the_x*
Internet: *https://en.wikipedia.org/wiki/Internet*
Internet Backbone: *https://en.wikipedia.org/wiki/Internet_backbone*
Optical Fiber: *https://en.wikipedia.org/wiki/Optical_fiber*
Server (Computing): *https://en.wikipedia.org/wiki/Server_%28computing%29*
Submarine Communications Cable:
*https://en.wikipedia.org/wiki/Submarine_communications_cable*

# 3.1.84 OPTICAL ORTHOGONAL FREQUENCY-DIVISION MULTIPLEXING

a) **WHAT IS IT?** Optical Orthogonal Frequency-Division Multiplexing (OOFDM) is a modulation technique for high-bandwidth **Optical Fibre**-based telecommunications. OOFDM-based telecommunications can provide a much higher data carrying capacity than many other optical transmission technologies currently in use. Some implementations are able to support data rates of up to 100 gigabits per second over a single **Optical Fibre**. OOFDM is an optical version of orthogonal frequency division multiplexing (OFDM), which is used to boost the data carrying capacity of many modern wireless communications technologies, including the Institute of Electrical and Electronic Engineers (IEEE) 802.11a/g/n/ac versions of **Wi-Fi**. OFDM simultaneously transmits small chunks of digital data using many narrow-band frequencies, known as subcarriers. The subcarrier channels are orthogonal, and, as such, do not interfere with each other. OFDM is a spectrally efficient data transmission technique that is able to maximise the number of data bits transmitted over a given bandwidth. In fact, the spectral efficiency of OFDM can approach the Shannon limit, which defines the theoretical maximum rate at which data can be sent without error over a carrier channel of specified bandwidth in the presence of noise. Current OOFDM-based solutions are primarily aimed at the network backbones of long distance telecommunications carriers, where an OOFDM-based approach could potentially increase data capacity by up to ten times. Low-cost OOFDM that could possibly be used to bring multi-gigabit per second data rates into the home, over the last mile, is still be researched, but it is hoped that it will become commercially viable in the near future. An OOFDM-based solution designed to cost-effectively bring **Optical Fibre** to the home could theoretically provide **Symmetrical Broadband** up to two thousand times faster than most currently deployed last-mile connection technologies. OOFDM technology can be retrofitted to existing telecommunications infrastructures, allowing telecommunications providers to cost-effectively increase capacity of their existing **Optical Fibre**-based networks.

b) **HOW COULD IT HELP?** The Stream Tone needs both wired and wireless telecommunications that are highly affordable, high bandwidth, low latency, highly reliable, and ubiquitously available. It is hoped that new modulation techniques, such as OOFDM, will be able to make more effective use of existing **Optical Fibre**-based telecommunications infrastructures to deliver more cost-effective and higher-bandwidth **Internet** connectivity. OOFDM-based telecommunications technologies could help to ensure that Stream Tone Transfer Protocol-based services will be ubiquitously available, with sufficient bandwidth, at an affordable price.

c) **FURTHER READING**
Fiber To The X: *https://en.wikipedia.org/wiki/Fiber_to_the_x*
IEEE 802.11: *https://en.wikipedia.org/wiki/802.11*
Noisy-Channel Coding Theorem: *https://en.wikipedia.org/wiki/Noisy-channel_coding_theorem*
OOFDM for Cost Effective Access Networks:
*http://ocean.bangor.ac.uk/description.php.en*
Optical Fiber: *https://en.wikipedia.org/wiki/Optical_fiber*
Orthogonal Frequency-Division Multiplexing:
*https://en.wikipedia.org/wiki/Orthogonal_frequency-division_multiplexing*
Shannon-Hartley Theorem:
*https://en.wikipedia.org/wiki/Shannon%E2%80%93Hartley_theorem*

# 3.1.85   OPUS

a) **WHAT IS IT?** Opus is an open, royalty free, lossy, audio *Compression* format designed for the interactive transmission of both narrow-band and full-band audio over the *Internet*. It supports a wide range of variable and constant bit-rates from 6 kilobits per second (Kbps) up to 510 Kbps, and sampling rates from 8 kilohertz (KHz) up to 48 KHz. Opus can be used for both speech and general audio, such as music. Its low-latency operation also makes it ideally suited to interactive audio applications such as *Internet* telephony and video-conferencing. Some parts of the OPUS algorithm are subject to software patents which the patent holder has promised to make royalty free.

b) **HOW COULD IT HELP?** The Stream Tone Transfer Protocol (STTP) will be used to communicate audio-visual content and services over the *Internet* from the *Web* to a Stream Tone Access Device, and to send user-input back. Opus is a low-latency audio *Compression* algorithm optimised for interactive operation that could potentially form a fundamental part of the STTP; providing the technology to encode and decode Stream Tone audio data.

c) **FURTHER READING**
Internet: *https://en.wikipedia.org/wiki/Internet*
Lossy Compression: *https://en.wikipedia.org/wiki/Lossy_compression*
Opus (Audio Codec): *https://en.wikipedia.org/wiki/Opus_%28audio_codec%29*
Patent: *https://en.wikipedia.org/wiki/Patent*
Royalties: *https://en.wikipedia.org/wiki/Royalties*
World Wide Web: *https://en.wikipedia.org/wiki/World_Wide_Web*

# 3.1.86   ORBX.JS

a) **WHAT IS IT?** ORBX.js is a software-based high definition (HD) media decoder that is written in JavaScript, and which was collaboratively developed by Mozilla and Otoy Incorporated. The Mozilla software community is the developer of the Firefox *Web Browser*, amongst many other things. Otoy is a leading supplier of products and services for creating photorealistic visual content. ORBX.js is based on proprietary media streaming technology from Otoy. JavaScript is an interpreted programming language supported by most modern *Web Browsers*. ORBX.js is designed to run in any *HyperText Markup Language Version 5* (HTML5)-enabled *Web Browser*, including Chrome, Firefox, *Internet* Explorer 10, Opera, and Safari, without the need to install additional software. In comparison, many other media decoders are only supported on specific *Web Browsers*, and require the use of decoder-specific hardware. ORBX.js can make use of the *Web* Graphics Library (WebGL), where available. WebGL is a JavaScript *Application Programming Interface* for rendering two-dimensional and three-dimensional (3D) visual content. WebGL-based functionality is provided by either a graphics processing unit (GPU) that supports WebGL or by a software implementation of WebGL designed to run on a general-purpose central processing unit. ORBX.js is optimised for parallel computing environments, such as those provided by modern multi-core GPUs. On an optimally configured personal computing device with a high-bandwidth broadband *Internet* connection, ORBX.js can display HD video, with a resolution of 1920 pixels by 1080 pixels at up to 60 frames per second. ORBX.js can allow a relatively low-performance personal computing device to remotely access a wide range of interactive

***Web-based Services***, such as 3D modelling, computer-aided design, computer gaming, photorealistic rendering, remote software application access, video streaming, and ***Hosted Desktops***. The ORBX.js decoder is believed to be unencumbered by patents, and can therefore be freely used on a wide range of modern personal computing devices, including desktop computers, laptop computers, ***Smart-Phones***, and ***Tablet Computers***. The ORBX.js decoder is designed to receive a data stream that has been generated by an encoder. The encoder that feeds the ORBX.js decoder was developed by Otoy, and is a proprietary, ***Cloud Computing***-based, low-latency, adaptive bit-rate, real-time, ***Streaming Media*** technology. The encoder can be used to apply an individualised watermark to streamed digital content, such as video, potentially providing a viable alternative for ***Digital Rights Management***. When applied to video content, the encoder can offer a better ***Compression*** ratio than comparable quality ***H.264*** encoded video. The encoder may be subject to third-party patents. Being a purely software-based media decoder, albeit one that can leverage the parallel data processing hardware commonly found within a modern personal computing device, ORBX.js can potentially evolve more easily and faster than it if were wholly implemented in hardware. Otoy has stated that it plans to add a range of new functionalities to ORBX.js in the future. Affordable ORBX.js-based services are now commercially available from Amazon ***Web*** Services.

b) **HOW COULD IT HELP?** The Stream Tone Transfer Protocol (STTP) will be used to communicate digital content and services over the ***Internet*** from the ***Web*** to a Stream Tone Access Device (STAD), and to send user-input back. The STAD will be a purely hardware-based device. Before the STAD becomes available a software-based Stream Tone Access Device Emulator (STADE) will be required. The ORBX.js decoder demonstrates the feasibility and benefits of developing a media decoder in software. Such an approach could also be applied to the development of the STADE, which will be required until the STTP has been finalised and can then be implemented in hardware. Certain technologies associated with the ORBX.js decoder could, theoretically, also form the basis of, or inspire, aspects of the STTP.

c) **FURTHER READING**
Application Programming Interface:
*https://en.wikipedia.org/wiki/Application_programming_interface*
Cloud Computing: *https://en.wikipedia.org/wiki/Cloud_computing*
Desktop Virtualization: *https://en.wikipedia.org/wiki/Desktop_virtualization*
Digital Rights Management: *https://en.wikipedia.org/wiki/Digital_rights_management*
Digital Watermarking: *https://en.wikipedia.org/wiki/Digital_watermarking*
H.264/MPEG-4 AVC: *https://en.wikipedia.org/wiki/H.264/MPEG-4_AVC*
HTML5: *https://en.wikipedia.org/wiki/Html5*
Internet: *https://en.wikipedia.org/wiki/Internet*
JavaScript: *https://en.wikipedia.org/wiki/JavaScript*
Mozilla: *https://en.wikipedia.org/wiki/Mozilla*
Mozilla - Look Ma, No Plug-In For Video, Apps: *http://news.cnet.com/8301-17939_109-57582743-2/mozillalook-ma-no-plug-in-for-video-apps/*
Mozilla And OTOY Deliver The Power Of Native PC Applications To The Web, Unveil Next Generation JavaScript Video Codec For Movies And Cloud Gaming:
*http://www.otoy.com/130501_OTOY_release_FINAL.pdf*
ORBX.js: *https://en.wikipedia.org/wiki/ORBX.js*
OTOY: *http://render.otoy.com/*
OTOY: *https://en.wikipedia.org/wiki/OTOY*
Patent: *https://en.wikipedia.org/wiki/Patent*

Streaming Media: *https://en.wikipedia.org/wiki/Streaming_media*
Today I Saw The Future: *https://brendaneich.com/2013/05/today-i-saw-the-future/*
WebGL: *https://en.wikipedia.org/wiki/Webgl*

# 3.1.87 ORGANIC LIGHT-EMITTING DIODE DISPLAY SCREEN

a) **WHAT IS IT?** An Organic Light-Emitting Diode (OLED) display screen is an energy-efficient flat-panel display screen technology based on an organic compound that emits light in response to an electric current. OLED-based display screens are built from a layer of organic material sandwiched between an array of negative and positive electrodes. Screens based on OLED technology can be found in a wide variety of electronic devices, including many portable personal computing devices. A number of different types of OLED-based display technologies exist, but the type most commonly found in portable personal computing devices, such as **Smart-Phones**, uses a version of OLED known as active-matrix organic light-emitting diode (AMOLED), which currently uses a low temperature polycrystalline silicon thin-film transistor backplane to control each screen pixel. A new backplane technology based on **Indium Gallium Zinc Oxide** can also be used with OLED-based screen displays. OLED-based screen displays do not require a backlight, as each pixel is capable of emitting its own light, so when an OLED-based pixel is turned off it uses no power. In comparison, a liquid-crystal display (LCD) screen uses a constantly operating backlight which illuminates all pixels, and has a roughly constant power consumption, regardless of whether its pixels are active or not. It is for this reason that OLED-based displays exhibit much blacker blacks than a comparable LCD display, because a small amount of light will always escape from a LCD pixel even when it is supposed to be completely black. OLED-based display technology also exhibits a very high contrast ratio, light versus dark, primarily because its blacks are so dark. In general, an OLED-based display will use less power than a comparable LCD-based one, especially when displaying a darkly coloured image, however if the displayed image is predominantly white then an OLED-based display will be far less efficient, and can use several times more power. OLED-based displays can be created by a relatively cheap printing process, but currently require the use of an expensive backplane, which, overall, makes them much more expensive than a comparable LCD display. OLED-based displays are lightweight and can be built on flexible backplanes. OLED-based displays offer wide viewing angles, and display refresh rates that are far faster than any comparable LCD display. OLED-based display technology is not perfect, having a variety of issues to do with lifespan, colour balance, susceptibility to water damage, and poor performance under outdoor lighting conditions. However, practical solutions to all these problems have already been found, making OLED-based display technology an ideal, if somewhat expensive solution, for many modern portable devices.

b) **HOW COULD IT HELP?** Whilst some Stream Tone Access Devices (STADs) will be powered by a direct connection to mains electricity, most will be portable devices that rely on battery power. Energy efficient display technologies, such as OLED-based screens, suitable for inclusion into mobile devices are well understood and mature. OLED-based display screens could help to reduce power consumption, and extend the battery life of a STAD.

c) **FURTHER READING**

AMOLED: *https://en.wikipedia.org/wiki/AMOLED*
Backlight: *https://en.wikipedia.org/wiki/Backlight*
Flat Panel Display: *https://en.wikipedia.org/wiki/Flat_panel_display*
Indium Gallium Zinc Oxide: *https://en.wikipedia.org/wiki/Indium_gallium_zinc_oxide*
Liquid-Crystal Display: *https://en.wikipedia.org/wiki/Liquid-crystal_display*
OLED: *https://en.wikipedia.org/wiki/OLED*
Polycrystalline Silicon: *https://en.wikipedia.org/wiki/Polycrystalline_silicon*
Thin-Film Transistor: *https://en.wikipedia.org/wiki/Thin-film_transistor*

# 3.1.88 PHASE-CONJUGATED TWIN WAVES

a) **WHAT IS IT?** Phase-Conjugated Twin Waves (PCTW) is a spectrally-inefficient telecommunications technique that can be used to send data over very long distance *Optical Fibre*-based communications links, such as those used for international *Submarine Communications Cables*. Typically, the light signals sent over long distance *Optical Fibre*-based communications links suffer from non-linear distortions that limit transmission performance. The PCTW technique works by sending a single communications signal as a pair of mutually phase-conjugated twin waves, which are then coherently superimposed at the receiver to greatly reduce, or eliminate, the impact of any non-linear distortions. Laboratory tests of the PCTW technique demonstrated that it was possible to communicate at a bandwidth of up to 406.6 gigabits per second (Gbps) over a distance of 12,800 kilometres (km) in a TrueWave reduced slope (TWRS) *Optical Fibre* link using eight quadrature phase-shift keying (QPSK) signals, each with its twin wave modulated at the same wavelength but on the orthogonal polarisation. In another test, based on the use of Nyquist wavelength-division multiplexed (Nyquist-WDM) PCTW, 1,024 Gbps was communicated over a distance of 4,000 km in a TWRS *Optical Fibre* link using eight polarising-division multiplexed (PDM)-QPSK signals. In contrast, many current techniques for sending data over long distance *Optical Fibre*-based communications links can only achieve bandwidths of up to 100 Gbps over distances of approximately 4,000 km. In order to support the PCTW technique, telecommunications infrastructures will only need to change the transmitter and receiver end-points but not the *Optical Fibre* cabling that connects them. The PCTW technique should allow the telecommunications industry to cost-effectively offer greatly increased performance and capacity, particularly over *Submarine Communications Cables* that are used to provide international *Internet* connectivity. It is hoped that PCTW technology will be commercialised in the very near future.

b) **HOW COULD IT HELP?** The Stream Tone needs both wired and wireless telecommunications that are highly affordable, high bandwidth, low latency, highly reliable, and ubiquitously available. Advanced telecommunications techniques, such as PCTW, could allow Stream Tone Telecommunications Infrastructures to deliver Stream Tone Transfer Protocol-based services over *Optical Fibre*-based communications links that are highly affordable, high bandwidth, low latency, highly reliable, and ubiquitously available.

c) **FURTHER READING**
Generation Of 1.024-Tb/s Nyquist-WDM Phase-Conjugated Twin Vector Waves By A Polarization-Insensitive Optical Parametric Amplifier For Fiber-Nonlinearity-Tolerant

Transmission: *http://orbit.dtu.dk/fedora/objects/orbit:130289/datastreams/file_83448d64-1ea5-47d5-ab02-0edd5b735d0f/content*
Internet: *https://en.wikipedia.org/wiki/Internet*
Nonlinear Distortion: *https://en.wikipedia.org/wiki/Nonlinear_distortion*
Optical Fiber: *https://en.wikipedia.org/wiki/Optical_fiber*
Phase Conjugation: *https://en.wikipedia.org/wiki/Phase_conjugation*
Phase-Conjugated Twin Waves For Communication Beyond The Kerr Nonlinearity Limit:
*http://www.cnd.mcgill.ca/~ivan/Phase-conjugated-twin-waves-for-beating-Kerr-nonlinearity-nphoton.2013.109.pdf*
Submarine Communications Cable:
*https://en.wikipedia.org/wiki/Submarine_communications_cable*

# 3.1.89   PHOTOVOLTAICS

a)   **WHAT IS IT?** A photovoltaic is a semiconductor-based device for converting sunlight into electricity. A photovoltaic device works on the principle of the photovoltaic effect, where photons of light excite electrons within a photovoltaic material into a higher energy state, permitting those electrons to act as charge carriers for an electric current. Commonly used photovoltaic materials include amorphous silicon, cadmium telluride, copper indium gallium selenide, copper indium gallium sulfide, monocrystalline silicon, and polycrystalline silicon. Other photovoltaic materials that could become commercially viable in the future include titanium dioxide and calcium titanate. Photovoltaic devices generate direct current (DC) electricity, and an electrical-power inverter can be used to convert the DC power to alternating current, if required. The efficiency of most photovoltaic devices is still quite low compared to what is considered to be theoretically possible. However, improvements in manufacturing techniques have reduced production costs sufficiently so that solar power is now considered a viable alternative to traditional forms of power generation, in certain situations. Photovoltaic technology is still evolving, with research into increasing its efficiency and lowering its production costs on-going. Photovoltaic devices are also known as solar cells, and arrays of multiple solar cells are referred to as solar panels. Photovoltaic technology is considered to be ecologically friendly, as its generation of electricity does not create harmful greenhouse gas emissions. Nevertheless, embodied emissions from the manufacture and distribution of solar cells still exist. One of the earliest applications of photovoltaic technology was in powering spacecraft and *Communications Satellites*. Today, large scale installations of solar panels, known as solar parks, are used to help power national electrical grids, which deliver electricity to homes and businesses. Solar cells are often used to power electrical equipment in remote locations where a connection to the national electrical grid cannot be justified. Photovoltaic generated electricity can also be used to directly power a wide range of electrical equipment, and to recharge rechargeable batteries, such as the *Lithium-Ion Batteries* used in many modern portable electronic devices.

b)   **HOW COULD IT HELP?** The Stream Tone needs both wired and wireless telecommunications that are highly affordable, high bandwidth, low latency, highly reliable, and ubiquitously available. Photovoltaic technology is a viable and cost-effective technology for generating electricity in sunny locations that are not connected to the national electricity grid. Photovoltaic generated electricity can be used to power wireless telecommunications infrastructure in remote locations, such as rural wireless *Mesh Networks*, helping to ensure that Stream Tone Transfer Protocol-based services will be ubiquitously available, with sufficient bandwidth, and at an affordable price. Whilst some

Stream Tone Access Devices (STADs) will be powered by a direct connection to mains electricity, most will be portable devices that rely on battery power. Photovoltaic generated electricity can be used to recharge a STAD's rechargeable batteries, an approach that might be very useful in geographies where the electricity distribution infrastructure is underdeveloped.

c) **FURTHER READING**
Lithium-Ion Battery: *https://en.wikipedia.org/wiki/Lithium-ion_battery*
Photovoltaics: *https://en.wikipedia.org/wiki/Photovoltaics*
Power Inverter: *https://en.wikipedia.org/wiki/Power_inverter*
Semiconductor: *https://en.wikipedia.org/wiki/Semiconductor*
Solar Cell: *https://en.wikipedia.org/wiki/Solar_cell*
Wireless Mesh Network: *https://en.wikipedia.org/wiki/Wireless_mesh_network*

# 3.1.90  PHYSICAL TO VIRTUAL

a) **WHAT IS IT?** Physical to Virtual (P2V) is the process of completely or partially migrating a working computing environment from a physical computing device to a *Virtual Machine* that is hosted in a remotely-located virtualised computing environment. P2V can be used to move, or migrate, an operating system, software applications, and user-data from a physical computing device to a *Virtual Machine*. The *Virtual Machine* can be configured to closely resemble the original computing environment ensuring that very few changes, if any, will need to be made to the migrated operating system, software applications, or user-data. A P2V migration can be manual, semi-automated, or fully-automated. *Virtual Machines* are typically able to make much more efficient use of a shared pool of computing resources compared to localised computing resources, which are often underutilised and dedicated to a single user. Access to a remotely-located *Virtual Machine* generally requires only a basic, low-performance networked personal computing device, such as a *Thin Client*.

b) **HOW COULD IT HELP?** The Stream Tone will allow local personal computing functionality to be moved onto Stream Tone Transfer Protocol (STTP)-based services that will be provided by a *Cloud Computing*-based Stream Tone Service Infrastructure (STSI). Fully-automated P2V migration technology can be used to quickly and easily move a user's existing personal computing environment onto a *Virtual Machine* within a STSI with minimal inconvenience and disruption. Once moved to a STTP-based service, a typical user will notice little change and should be able to work as normal. An effective and efficient P2V solution could be a key enabling technology of the Stream Tone.

c) **FURTHER READING**
Cloud Computing: *https://en.wikipedia.org/wiki/Cloud_computing*
Computer Network: *https://en.wikipedia.org/wiki/Computer_network*
Data Center: *https://en.wikipedia.org/wiki/Data_center*
Operating System: *https://en.wikipedia.org/wiki/Operating_system*
Physical-To-Virtual: *https://en.wikipedia.org/wiki/Physical-to-Virtual*
Thin Client: *https://en.wikipedia.org/wiki/Thin_client*
Virtual Machine: *https://en.wikipedia.org/wiki/Virtual_machine*
Virtualization: *https://en.wikipedia.org/wiki/Virtualization*

# 3.1.91   POWER OVER ETHERNET

a)   **WHAT IS IT?** Power over Ethernet (POE) is a technique for providing direct current (DC) electrical power to an electronic networked device via an Ethernet communications cable. A key benefit of POE is that within a wired networking environment less cabling is required, as both communications and power are carried over a single multi-core cable. In general, network cabling is far simpler and far cheaper to install than standard electrical-power cabling. POE is available in both standard and proprietary forms. Using a category 5 (CAT5) Ethernet cable, the Institute of Electrical and Electronics Engineers (IEEE) 802.3af-2003 POE standard supports up to 15.4 Watts of DC electrical power, and the IEEE 802.3at-2009 POE standard supports up to 25.5 Watts of DC electrical power. Power is typically supplied via a network switch that supports one or both of the POE standards. In situations where a POE-enabled network switch is not available, power can also be added mid-span using a POE injector device. POE can be used to power a wide range of low-power networked devices, including clocks, computers, entry systems, industrial controllers, meters and sensors, intercoms, lighting controllers, network routers, point of sale terminals, public address systems, security cameras, telephones, webcams, and wireless access points. POE is often used to power *Thin Client* computer terminals, which have low power requirements.

b)   **HOW COULD IT HELP?** In situations where a Stream Tone Access Device uses a wired network connection, the use of POE can help to simplify cabling requirements. Less wiring reduces cost, and can help make the process of accessing Stream Tone Transfer Protocol-based services far more affordable. In rich Western nations this might be considered a small convenience, but in developing nations such a feature could represent a way to avoid potentially unaffordable infrastructure costs associated with the installation of standard electrical-power cabling, fuse boxes, and outlet sockets.

c)   **FURTHER READING**
Category 5 Cable: *https://en.wikipedia.org/wiki/Category_5_cable*
Computer Network: *https://en.wikipedia.org/wiki/Computer_network*
Ethernet: *https://en.wikipedia.org/wiki/Ethernet*
Power Over Ethernet: *https://en.wikipedia.org/wiki/Power_over_Ethernet*

# 3.1.92   PROXIMITY SENSOR

a)   **WHAT IS IT?** A proximity sensor is a device that can detect when an object is nearby. Proximity sensors are often included in mobile personal computing devices, such as *Smart-Phones*, to detect when a user's ear is near the screen during a telephone call, so that touch-based user-input can be temporarily disabled. Proximity sensors can also be used to detect that a device is no longer in use and should therefore enter a low-power state. Proximity sensors used in such devices are often based on infrared technology.

b)   **HOW COULD IT HELP?** Power-saving technologies, such as proximity sensors, that are suitable for inclusion into mobile devices are well understood and mature. Stream Tone Access Devices are intended to be direct replacements for all current personal computing devices, including *Smart-Phones* and *Tablet Computers*, and will therefore need to include a wide range of ease of use and power-saving technologies, including proximity sensors, in order to be able to deliver functionality comparable to today's mobile personal computing devices.

c) **FURTHER READING**
Proximity Sensor: *https://en.wikipedia.org/wiki/Proximity_sensor*

# 3.1.93    RADIO OVER FIBRE

a) **WHAT IS IT?** Radio over Fibre (ROF) is a radio frequency (RF) wireless communications technology in which the radio antenna and its control system can be geographically distant from each other, connected by an ***Optical Fibre***-based communications link. Light is transmitted through the ***Optical Fibre***, which has been directly modulated by the wireless signal that is to be broadcast, or has been received, by the antenna. Equipment located at the antenna to modulate and demodulate the light signal is relatively simple and cheap. Equipment located at the control system is typically complex and expensive, as the control system needs to do more than just modulate or demodulate light signals, such as interface to the larger telecommunications infrastructure of which it is an integral part. In the past, a single antenna site, known as a base-station or cell site, would contain all necessary control equipment, making each base station complex, and expensive to install and maintain. ROF can greatly reduce the cost of deploying and maintaining wireless communications infrastructure as a single centralised control system can be shared with many antenna installations. Mobile communications standards evolve over time and traditional base-stations often require the installation of new hardware, or software upgrades, in order to support a new standard. Using ROF, new standards can be supported by simply changing the hardware and software used by a centralised control system. ROF can be used to cost-effectively distribute wireless communications to locations that cannot be reliably reached by current infrastructure, such as in heavily built-up urban environments where wireless signal transmission is not optimal and expected usage may not be sufficient to justify the installation of a traditional base-station to solve the problem. ROF can also be used to create cost-effective telecommunications infrastructure over very large rural geographies.

b) **HOW COULD IT HELP?** The Stream Tone needs both wired and wireless telecommunications that are highly affordable, high bandwidth, low latency, highly reliable, and ubiquitously available. ROF can allow wireless telecommunications to be cost-effectively installed in many situations that were previously not considered to be feasible, due to remote location, lack of local support infrastructure, or relatively low expected usage. ROF can help to make Stream Tone Transfer Protocol (STTP)-based services ubiquitously available and affordable. Also, the relative simplicity of the ROF antenna installation can help ensure that STTP-based services will be highly reliable.

c) **FURTHER READING**
Antenna (Radio): *https://en.wikipedia.org/wiki/Antenna_%28radio%29*
Base Station: *https://en.wikipedia.org/wiki/Base_station*
Cell Site: *https://en.wikipedia.org/wiki/Cell_site*
Optical Fiber: *https://en.wikipedia.org/wiki/Optical_fiber*
Radio Frequency: *https://en.wikipedia.org/wiki/Radio_frequency*
Radio Over Fiber: *https://en.wikipedia.org/wiki/Radio_over_Fiber*

# 3.1.94 REAL-TIME STREAMING PROTOCOL

a) **WHAT IS IT?** The Real-Time Streaming Protocol (RTSP) is a communications protocol designed to control *Streaming Media*-servers in real-time. The protocol is used to establish and control sessions between a media-server client and a media-server. A media-server is typically used to transmit media files containing audio and video over a computer network, such as the *Internet*. Using the RTSP the media-server client can issue commands, such as play or pause, to the media-server to control its operation. The media data streamed from a media-server is not under the control of the RTSP, as media stream delivery is more generally handled by the *Real Time Transport Protocol* and the RTP Control Protocol.

b) **HOW COULD IT HELP?** The RTSP could provide the Stream Tone Transfer Protocol with a ready-made, mature, and widely-accepted approach for controlling real-time digital content and service communications over the *Internet*.

c) **FURTHER READING**
Client-Server Model: *https://en.wikipedia.org/wiki/Client%E2%80%93server_model*
Internet: *https://en.wikipedia.org/wiki/Internet*
Real Time Streaming Protocol:
*https://en.wikipedia.org/wiki/Real_Time_Streaming_Protocol*
Real-Time Transport Protocol: *https://en.wikipedia.org/wiki/Real-time_Transport_Protocol*
RTP Control Protocol: *https://en.wikipedia.org/wiki/RTP_Control_Protocol*
Streaming Media: *https://en.wikipedia.org/wiki/Streaming_media*

# 3.1.95 REAL-TIME TRANSPORT PROTOCOL

a) **WHAT IS IT?** The Real-time Transport Protocol (RTP) is an extensible communications protocol designed to transfer streamed audio and video data over *Internet Protocol* networks, such as the *Internet*. The RTP is well suited to a wide range of real-time communication and entertainment applications, including telephony, television services, and video-conferencing. The RTP is typically used together with the RTP Control Protocol, which monitors transmission statistics and quality of service. The RTP supports a wide range of multimedia formats, including *H.264* video. RTP profiles, and associated payload format specifications, are used to support new features and multimedia formats. The Secure Real-time Transport Protocol (SRTP) defines an RTP profile that supports real-time *Encryption*-based communications.

b) **HOW COULD IT HELP?** Using the SRTP, a security-oriented RTP profile, could provide the Stream Tone Transfer Protocol with a ready-made, mature, and widely-accepted approach for achieving secure, real-time, communications over the *Internet*.

c) **FURTHER READING**
Computer Network: *https://en.wikipedia.org/wiki/Computer_network*
Encryption: *https://en.wikipedia.org/wiki/Encryption*

H.264/MPEG-4 AVC: *https://en.wikipedia.org/wiki/H.264/MPEG-4_AVC*
Internet: *https://en.wikipedia.org/wiki/Internet*
Internet Protocol: *https://en.wikipedia.org/wiki/Internet_Protocol*
Real-Time Transport Protocol: *https://en.wikipedia.org/wiki/Real-time_Transport_Protocol*
RTP Control Protocol: *https://en.wikipedia.org/wiki/RTP_Control_Protocol*
Secure Real-Time Transport Protocol: *https://en.wikipedia.org/wiki/Secure_Real-time_Transport_Protocol*

# 3.1.96   REDUCED INSTRUCTION SET COMPUTING

a) **WHAT IS IT?** Reduced Instruction Set Computing (RISC) is a central processing unit, or microprocessor, design approach in which the work of each instruction is reduced; hence its name. The opposite of RISC is complex instruction set computing (CISC) which is based on the use of much more complex instructions that can achieve far greater amounts of work in the same period of time. RISC instructions complete their work quickly, within one data memory cycle, because they are computationally relatively simple. Another aspect of the simplified approach that underpins modern RISC architectures is that external memory is only accessible through the load and store instructions; all other instructions are restricted to accessing internal registers. RISC-based microprocessors are physically smaller, and therefore cheaper, than functionally comparable CISC-based ones; primarily because RISC-based microprocessors have far fewer transistors dedicated to their core logic functions. RISC-based microprocessors are often a key element of a **System on a Chip** (SOC), and can be fabricated using **Application-Specific Integrated Circuit** or **Field-Programmable Gate Array** technology. RISC-based microprocessors are commonly used to power a wide range of computing devices, including **Smart-Phones**, **Tablet Computers**, and even supercomputers.

b) **HOW COULD IT HELP?** The relatively small physical size and therefore limited use of construction materials, such as silicon substrate, of a typical SOC featuring a RISC-based microprocessor might help to reduce costs, and would support a predominantly hardware-based Stream Tone Access Device design.

c) **FURTHER READING**
Application-Specific Integrated Circuit: *https://en.wikipedia.org/wiki/Application-specific_integrated_circuit*
Central Processing Unit: *https://en.wikipedia.org/wiki/Central_processing_unit*
Complex Instruction Set Computing: *https://en.wikipedia.org/wiki/Complex_instruction_set_computing*
Field-Programmable Gate Array: *https://en.wikipedia.org/wiki/Field-programmable_gate_array*
Microprocessor: *https://en.wikipedia.org/wiki/Microprocessor*
Reduced Instruction Set Computing: *https://en.wikipedia.org/wiki/Reduced_instruction_set_computing*
System On A Chip: *https://en.wikipedia.org/wiki/System_on_a_chip*

# 3.1.97 REDUCING INTERNET TRANSPORT LATENCY

a) **WHAT IS IT?** The Reducing *Internet* Transport Latency (RITE) project, funded by the European Commission (EC), aims to reduce or remove unwanted transmission time delays from *Internet*-based data communications. Project members include: Simula Research Laboratory AS, Norway; British Telecommunications Ltd, United Kingdom; Alcatel-Lucent BELL NV, Belgium; Universitetet i Oslo, Norway; Karlstads Universitet, Sweden; Institut Mines-Telecom/Télécom Bretagne, France; and The University Court of the University of Aberdeen, United Kingdom. A time delay is measured as the time between a request for data being sent and the requested data being received, also known as latency. A certain amount of latency is unavoidable due to the physics of transmitting data over large distances at finite speeds. However, some latency is caused by inefficiencies within the hardware and software of the *Internet*, which to date has generally been more optimised towards high-bandwidth throughput than towards responsive low-latency communications. Some of these inefficiencies include the temporary buffering of data by the many network devices that comprise the *Internet*, poorly written networking software on end-points, such as computer servers, personal computing devices, and network routers, and the way that lost data is handled by some of the *Internet*'s data transmission protocols. Each small time delay, intentionally or unintentionally, added by the various network devices along the route of data communication can add up to a substantial period of time. A time delay of hundreds or thousands of milliseconds might be trivial in isolation but when applied to each portion of a large quantity of communicated data the impact can be significant, particularly if such delays occur persistently. Many modern *Web-based Services* now depend on low-latency communications in order to work as designed, especially highly-interactive services, such as computer gaming, telephony, and video conferencing. Even some non-interactive services, such as static *Web* pages that feature a lot of small data objects, can benefit from low-latency communications. The RITE project will attempt to determine the root causes of *Internet* communications latencies, and will then make recommendations on how those latencies can best be reduced or removed. Recommendations from the RITE project will also be brought to the attention of influential standardisation bodies, such as the *Internet Engineering Task Force*. One of the first activities that will be undertaken by the project will be to investigate the behaviour of the Retransmission TimeOut function of the Transmission Control Protocol and the Stream Control Transmission Protocol. The RITE project should eventually lead to far more responsive real-time communications over the *Internet*.

b) **HOW COULD IT HELP?** The Stream Tone needs both wired and wireless telecommunications that are highly affordable, high bandwidth, low latency, highly reliable, and ubiquitously available. The RITE project may be able to reduce the latency of *Internet*-based communications, which will then be able to better support the communication of highly-interactive Stream Tone Transfer Protocol-based content and services.

c) **FURTHER READING**
Computer Network: *https://en.wikipedia.org/wiki/Computer_network*
Internet: *https://en.wikipedia.org/wiki/Internet*
Internet Engineering Task Force:
*https://en.wikipedia.org/wiki/Internet_Engineering_Task_Force*

Latency (Engineering): *https://en.wikipedia.org/wiki/Latency_%28engineering%29*
Reducing Internet Transport Latency: *http://riteproject.eu/*
Server (Computing): *https://en.wikipedia.org/wiki/Server_%28computing%29*
Stream Control Transmission Protocol:
*https://en.wikipedia.org/wiki/Stream_Control_Transmission_Protocol*
The Internet Engineering Task Force: *http://www.ietf.org/*
Transmission Control Protocol:
*https://en.wikipedia.org/wiki/Transmission_Control_Protocol*

# 3.1.98   REGULATION

a) **WHAT IS IT?** Regulation is a set of rules that determine what individuals and organisational entities can do, must do, or cannot do. A regulation can allocate a responsibility, create or limit a duty, or create, limit, or constrain a right. Some regulation is designed to facilitate outcomes that might not occur under normal circumstances. Some regulation is formal, being a type of law, and some is informal. Formal regulation is often referred to as subordinate legislation that defines the application and enforcement of legislation. Legislation is the written law, which is enacted by the legislative arm of government. Written laws are typically embodied in acts or statutes. The legal authority that enables a regulation is an act. Regulations are enacted by the delegated body enabled by the act. In the modern world, regulation has a huge impact on the lives of everyone, everywhere. In particular fields, such as telecommunications, it controls aspects such as the use of radio spectrum, communications infrastructure installation, electronic device use on aeroplanes, financial transactions made by wireless devices, and the affordability of essential telecommunications services that are now integral to the lives of millions of people. Organisations such as the Bundesnetzagentur in Germany, the Federal Communications Commission in the United States of America, the Infocomm Development Authority of Singapore, and the Office of Communications (Ofcom) in the United Kingdom are charged with the efficient and effective management of their respective nation's radio spectrum. Regulations issued by such organisations control and shape how radio spectrum can be used, now and in the future, for a very wide range of applications, including *Internet* access.

b) **HOW COULD IT HELP?** The Stream Tone needs both wired and wireless telecommunications that are highly affordable, high bandwidth, low latency, highly reliable, and ubiquitously available. In order to meet the many requirements of the Stream Tone new regulations may be needed to permit radio spectrum to be used more efficiently or differently, for the installation of extensive telecommunications infrastructures, and to allow electronic devices to be used in situations where they are currently restricted, such as during the take-off and landing of aeroplanes. Regulation may also be required to help ensure that the Stream Tone, an essential service, is fit for purpose and able to provide access to Stream Tone Transfer Protocol-based services that is highly affordable, high bandwidth, low latency, highly reliable, and ubiquitously available.

c) **FURTHER READING**
Federal Communications Commission:
*https://en.wikipedia.org/wiki/Federal_Communications_Commission*
Federal Network Agency (Bundesnetzagentur):
*https://en.wikipedia.org/wiki/Federal_Network_Agency*
Infocomm Development Authority Of Singapore:

*https://en.wikipedia.org/wiki/Infocomm_Development_Authority_of_Singapore*
Internet: *https://en.wikipedia.org/wiki/Internet*
Ofcom: *https://en.wikipedia.org/wiki/Ofcom*
Regulation: *https://en.wikipedia.org/wiki/Regulation*
Spectrum Management: *https://en.wikipedia.org/wiki/Spectrum_management*

# 3.1.99    REMOTE FRAMEBUFFER

a)  **WHAT IS IT?** Remote FrameBuffer (RFB) is a *Free and Open-Source Software*-based communications protocol for displaying and controlling the graphical user-interface (GUI) of a remote computer system. The RFB protocol is a client-server technology where a server sends GUI data over a computer network, such as a local area network, wide area network, or even the *Internet*, to a remote client where it can be displayed. The client is able to control the operation of the GUI by sending keyboard and multi-button pointing device data to the distant server. The RFB protocol is compatible with a wide range of display technologies due to the fact that it obtains GUI data from a framebuffer, which is a common component of nearly all video display subsystems. A framebuffer is a video data memory buffer containing a single complete frame of video data that is used to generate the video output required drive a video display. Upon initial connection, the server uses the RFB protocol to send a baseline copy of the complete GUI to the remote client for display, after which any change to the GUI is sent as a small rectangle of pixel data containing just that particular change. Sending rectangles of pixel data is not a particularly efficient method for displaying the GUI of a remote computer system but it is very simple and compatible with a very wide range of different desktop operating systems, computing hardware, and software applications. The pixel data, sent via the RFB protocol, can be encoded in different ways, permitting various *Compression* algorithms to be applied, which can greatly improve the performance and responsiveness of any remote desktop display and control service built using the protocol. The RFB protocol can be used to access *Hosted Desktop* services.

b)  **HOW COULD IT HELP?** The Stream Tone Transfer Protocol (STTP) will be used to communicate digital content and services over the *Internet* from the *Web* to a Stream Tone Access Device (STAD), and to send user-input back. Remote desktop display and control technologies, such as the RFB protocol, could potentially form a fundamental part of the STTP; providing the technology to display and control remote desktop operating systems. The simplistic nature of the RFB protocol, based on rectangles of compressed pixel data, makes it ideally suited to a hardware-based implementation, as would be required by the STAD.

c)  **FURTHER READING**
Client-Server Model: *https://en.wikipedia.org/wiki/Client%E2%80%93server_model*
Computer Network: *https://en.wikipedia.org/wiki/Computer_network*
Data Compression: *https://en.wikipedia.org/wiki/Data_compression*
Graphical User Interface: *https://en.wikipedia.org/wiki/Graphical_user_interface*
Internet: *https://en.wikipedia.org/wiki/Internet*
Operating System: *https://en.wikipedia.org/wiki/Operating_system*
RFB Protocol: *https://en.wikipedia.org/wiki/RFB_protocol*
Server (Computing): *https://en.wikipedia.org/wiki/Server_%28computing%29*
The Remote Framebuffer Protocol (RFC 6143): *https://tools.ietf.org/html/rfc6143*
The RFB Protocol v3.8: *http://www.realvnc.com/docs/rfbproto.pdf*

# 3.1.100 ROAMING AGREEMENT

a) **WHAT IS IT?** A roaming agreement is a commercial contract between two telecommunications service providers (TSPs), such that a customer of one TSP is allowed to use the services of the other. Roaming agreements are usually reciprocal, in that the customer of one TSP may roam in the territory of another TSP, and vice versa. The two TSPs may reside within the same geography or different geographies. Services accessible under a roaming agreement typically include mobile data, text messaging, and voice calling. The existence of a roaming agreement confirms that the typical telecommunications devices belonging to the customers of one TSP are compatible with the telecommunications infrastructure of the other TSP. A roaming agreement will also describe the authentication, authorisation, and billing procedures that will be applied to a roaming customer. The cost of services obtained by a customer when roaming, especially when travelling to a different country, are nearly always more expensive than when that customer is not roaming. Some of the higher charges for services obtained whilst roaming between providers located within the same city, region, or country are now starting to be reduced or removed through government *Regulation*. Roaming agreements now exist between most TSPs, allowing customers to travel globally without having to worry about whether or not they will be able to use their telecommunications devices at their chosen destination. Roaming agreements provide the legal infrastructure that allows many millions of international travellers to use their feature-phones, mobile-phones, laptop computers, *Smart-Phones*, and *Tablet Computers* wherever they go. Without roaming agreements, access to mobile data, text-messaging, and voice calling whilst travelling would be far more complicated and much less convenient than it is today. New roaming agreements for the latest generation of mobile communications services are regularly announced.

b) **HOW COULD IT HELP?** The Stream Tone needs both wired and wireless telecommunications that are highly affordable, high bandwidth, low latency, highly reliable, and ubiquitously available. Legal arrangements, such as roaming agreements, can help to ensure that Stream Tone Transfer Protocol-based services will be available to everyone, everywhere; without the need for a travelling user to sign-up with a new TSP for each visited-geography.

c) **FURTHER READING**
Roaming: *https://en.wikipedia.org/wiki/Roaming*
Roaming Agreement: *https://wiki.cdg.org/wiki/Roaming_Agreement*
Telecommunications Service Provider:
*https://en.wikipedia.org/wiki/Telecommunications_service_provider*

# 3.1.101 SINGLE SIGN-ON

a) **WHAT IS IT?** Single sign-on (SSO) is an identity and access management (IAM) technique whereby a user is able to gain access to multiple secure systems by only providing their authentication and validation credentials once. Some *Web-based Services* are built from other *Web-based Services*, and normally a user would be required to logon to each one separately before those services could be used collectively to provide an aggregated service. SSO is able to greatly simplify this logon process, reducing it to a single logon event. The actual mechanics of logging on to all the other systems is automated under SSO, and hidden from the user. Typically, a secure centralised database is used to store the user credentials for all the systems for which access is required. A user then logs onto the centralised database, which in turn logs onto all the required systems on behalf of the user. Once SSO is complete, a user is then able to make full use of all the different services, as required, and is also able to share user-data between those services. SSO allows new types of **Web-based Service** to be built from multiple existing **Web-based Services**.

b) **HOW COULD IT HELP?** The SSO approach can allow multiple secure digital services to be seamlessly used in aggregate. The Stream Tone Access Device (STAD) has no built-in data processing abilities; it is totally reliant on data processing provided by digital services. Many of the digital services that will be accessed by a STAD will be aggregates of other digital services that have been made accessible through the use of IAM techniques, such as SSO. SSO can help to move local personal computing onto Stream Tone Transfer Protocol-based personal computing services.

c) **FURTHER READING**
Access Control: *https://en.wikipedia.org/wiki/Access_control*
Identity Management: *https://en.wikipedia.org/wiki/Identity_management*
Login: *https://en.wikipedia.org/wiki/Login*
Single Sign-On: *https://en.wikipedia.org/wiki/Single_sign-on*

# 3.1.102   SITE-SPECIFIC BROWSER

a) **WHAT IS IT?** A Site-Specific Browser (SSB) is a **Web Browser** designed to provide direct and immediate access to a single **Web**-based resource, such as a **Web** site, without the need to enter the site's uniform resource identifier (URI) address. The SSB approach provides easy access to the many **Web-based Services** that are now starting to replace locally stored and executed software applications. SSBs present **Web** sites in a simple display window that excludes the menus, toolbars and other on-screen constructs commonly included by more typical **Web Browser**s. SSB display windows are designed to look the same as local software applications, helping to create a seamless visual experience when both local and **Web**-based applications are used together. Some operating systems have fully-integrated SSB technology into their desktop-based graphical user-interfaces, so that **Web-based Services** can be launched using the same interactions as those used to launch local software applications, such as by double-clicking on a desktop icon, or by selecting an option from a drop-down menu.

b) **HOW COULD IT HELP?** SSB technology is an important intermediate step that helps to bridge the old world of personal computing, which largely relied on locally stored and executed software applications, and the new world, which will rely on **Web-based Services**. Replacing local applications with their **Web**-based equivalents is now both popular and viable, and intermediate technologies, such as SSBs, can help to address some of the short-term practicalities of such a change.

c) **FURTHER READING**
Bridging Desktop And Web Applications - A Look At Mozilla Prism:
*http://techcrunch.com/2008/03/22/bridging-desktop-and-web-applications-a-look-at-*

*mozilla-prism/*
Operating System: *https://en.wikipedia.org/wiki/Operating_system*
Site Specific Browser: *http://sitespecificbrowser.com/*
Site-Specific Browser: *https://en.wikipedia.org/wiki/Site-specific_browser*
Uniform Resource Identifier: *https://en.wikipedia.org/wiki/Uniform_resource_identifier*
Web Browser: *https://en.wikipedia.org/wiki/Web_browser*

# 3.1.103   SMALL CELL

a) **WHAT IS IT?** A small cell is a wireless communications access node that is accessible over a relatively short range. Small cells can operate in both licensed and unlicensed radio spectrum. Small cells that use licensed spectrum can be integrated into larger telecommunications infrastructures, allowing their use to be more effectively managed. Small cells use low-power transceivers that are designed specifically for short-range use. The effective range of a small cell transceiver is dependent on the operating environment; indoors it may have a range of as little as 10 metres, whilst outdoors, in an unobstructed rural environment, its range may extend to as much as 2 kilometres. *Wi-Fi* is a small cell technology that uses unlicensed radio spectrum, and which is used to provide wireless *Internet* access in the home, office, or at public venues, such as shopping malls. The small cell term is a generic, or umbrella, term that encompasses a wide range of conceptually similar technologies including class 3 femto, enterprise femtocell, femtocell, greater femto, metrocell, metro femtocell, microcell, picocell, public access femtocell, and super femto. To a small cell technology vendor the different terminology is undoubtedly important, but from a generic perspective the term simply indicates a wireless communications technology that is far less powerful, and with a far shorter range, than a typical mobile telecommunications base-station, cell site, or macrocell. Small cells can be used to provide high-bandwidth low-latency wireless *Internet* access in highly-populated built-up urban environments. In such environments, a traditional macrocell, designed to serve a relatively large geographic area, can easily reach its capacity limits, and would consequently have to restrict bandwidth, increase latency, or limit the number of active users. Of course, a small cell has similar capacity limitations, but as a small cell would typically only serve a very small geographic area containing a small number of users its limitations are much less likely to be experienced. By deploying a large number of small cells across a particular geographic area, such as a city centre, all wireless users in that area will be able to access the *Internet* without restriction. A small cell access node could be built using *Radio over Fibre* technology, which would allow the small cell hardware to be greatly simplified, requiring only a transceiver antenna assembly and an *Optical Fibre*-based communications link to a remotely-located centralised control system. Small cell technology is expected to play an important enabling role in the deployment of true *Fourth Generation Mobile Communications* (4G) networks, which will be able to deliver data at speeds of up to 1 gigabit per second. Small cell deployments are expected to increase substantially over the coming years.

b) **HOW COULD IT HELP?** The Stream Tone needs both wired and wireless telecommunications that are highly affordable, high bandwidth, low latency, highly reliable, and ubiquitously available. Small cell technology could help to deliver Stream Tone Transfer Protocol-based content and services, particularly in highly-populated built-up urban environments. Small cell technology appears to be able to support all of the Stream Tone's wireless telecommunications needs.

c) **FURTHER READING**
4G: *https://en.wikipedia.org/wiki/4G*
Antenna (Radio): *https://en.wikipedia.org/wiki/Antenna_%28radio%29*
Base Station: *https://en.wikipedia.org/wiki/Base_station*
Cell Site: *https://en.wikipedia.org/wiki/Cell_site*
Femtocell: *https://en.wikipedia.org/wiki/Femtocell*
Internet: *https://en.wikipedia.org/wiki/Internet*
Macrocell: *https://en.wikipedia.org/wiki/Macrocell*
Optical Fiber: *https://en.wikipedia.org/wiki/Optical_fiber*
Radio Over Fiber: *https://en.wikipedia.org/wiki/Radio_over_Fiber*
Radio Spectrum: *https://en.wikipedia.org/wiki/Radio_spectrum*
Small Cell: *https://en.wikipedia.org/wiki/Small_cell*
Spectrum Management: *https://en.wikipedia.org/wiki/Spectrum_management*
Wi-Fi: *https://en.wikipedia.org/wiki/Wi-Fi*

# 3.1.104  SMART ANTENNA

a) **WHAT IS IT?** A smart antenna is a part of a radio frequency wireless telecommunications system. A smart antenna is designed to efficiently and effectively send and receive wireless signals by dynamically adjusting its operation based on its current signal environment. A smart antenna permits a single signal channel to be shared between multiple spatially-distinct wireless users. A smart antenna consists of multiple antenna elements, and an analysis system that is capable of understanding, to some degree, the signal environment. The analysis system is able to track the directional position of a wireless user and then use the multiple antenna elements to control the pattern of signal radiation when transmitting, and the pattern of signal sensitivity when receiving. A smart antenna boosts signal radiation in the direction of a signal recipient and signal sensitivity in the direction of a signal sender. Signal radiation in directions that are away from a signal recipient, or which may cause interference, can be reduced. Signal sensitivity is actively reduced in directions of signal interference. A smart antenna is typically categorised based on it's transmit strategy, of which there are three main types; adaptive, dynamically-phased array, and switched beam. Adaptive smart antennas are the most advanced and are able to determine the impact of interference, multipath-fading, and noise on a required signal, and then dynamically adjust the use of the antenna elements in order to reduce those effects. Currently, the most advanced type of adaptive smart antenna technology is known as multiple-input and multiple-output (MIMO), which is based on the concept of spatial multiplexing. Compared to non-smart omnidirectional antenna-based systems, smart antenna-based communications systems have greater bandwidth, range, and security, are better able to reduce the impact of interference, and can generate directional information that can be used for new location-based services. Smart antenna-based systems are easy to integrate within existing telecommunications infrastructures because they do not require changes, such as new communications protocols. Whilst expensive to install, smart antenna-based solutions can be cost-effective to operate, as each installation has a large signal range, which can serve a larger area than comparable non-smart antenna-based solutions. Smart antenna-based solutions also make better use of available wireless spectrum through the sharing of signal channels, permitting an installation to support more simultaneous users than non-smart antenna-based solutions. Smart antennas are not yet widely used in portable communication devices, although this is expected to change in the future. Smart antenna-based solutions are a key enabling technology for true ***Fourth-Generation Mobile Communications*** (4G) networks.

b) **HOW COULD IT HELP?** The Stream Tone needs both wired and wireless telecommunications that are highly affordable, high bandwidth, low latency, highly reliable, and ubiquitously available. Smart antenna-based systems are able to dynamically adapt their behaviour to the local signal environment, cost-effectively delivering increased range, higher bandwidth, and a better overall use of the available wireless spectrum. Smart antenna-based technologies can help to ensure that Stream Tone Transfer Protocol-based services will be ubiquitously available, with sufficient bandwidth, at an affordable price.

c) **FURTHER READING**
4G: *https://en.wikipedia.org/wiki/4G*
Antenna (Radio): *https://en.wikipedia.org/wiki/Antenna_%28radio%29*
Communications Protocol: *https://en.wikipedia.org/wiki/Communications_protocol*
MIMO: *https://en.wikipedia.org/wiki/MIMO*
Radio Frequency: *https://en.wikipedia.org/wiki/Radio_frequency*
Smart Antenna: *https://en.wikipedia.org/wiki/Smart_antenna*
Spectrum Management: *https://en.wikipedia.org/wiki/Spectrum_management*

# 3.1.105 SMART-PHONE

a) **WHAT IS IT?** A smart-phone is a highly-versatile portable personal computing device, capable of mobile telephony and wireless *Internet* access. A typical smart-phone features a touch-sensitive colour flat-screen display of between 3.5 inches and 6.4 inches on the diagonal. The screen display will typically be based on either liquid-crystal display or *Organic Light-Emitting Diode* (OLED) technology. A modern smart-phone will typically support a wide range of hardware, including an *Accelerometer*, *Ambient Light Sensor*, *Barometer*, *Capacitive Sensing* display screen, *Global Positioning System*, *Gyroscope*, HDMI, *Image Sensor*, loudspeaker, *Magnetometer*, memory card reader, microphone, *Proximity Sensor*, and USB interface. Smart-phones typically support a wide range of wireless telecommunications interfaces, including *Bluetooth*, *Fourth-Generation Mobile Communications* (4G), infrared, *Near-Field Communication*, third-generation mobile communications (3G), and *Wi-Fi*. Smart-phones typically use *Reduced Instruction Set Computing*-based microprocessors, such as those designed by ARM Holdings plc, although complex instruction set computing-based x86 microprocessors manufactured by Intel Corporation, are now starting to appear. Smart-phones run operating systems that are optimised for mobile operation, such as Google Android OS and Apple iOS. The functionality of a *Smart-Phone* can be upgraded via over-the-air operating system updates, and through the installation of software applications provided by *Application Stores*. Being a portable device, the smart-phone is battery powered, usually by a *Lithium-Ion Battery*. Lacking a physical keyboard or mouse, and possessing only a relatively small display screen, smart-phones are primarily used for content consumption, rather than content creation. A smart-phone will usually include at least one software-based *Web Browser* application that permits interactive access to *Web*-based content and services. Smart-phones have become the principle device for mobile *Internet* access for many people.

b) **HOW COULD IT HELP?** Stream Tone Access Devices (STADs) are intended to be direct replacements for all current personal computing devices. Some STADs will have a smart-phone form factor that is highly portable and already familiar to most users.

c) **FURTHER READING**
3G: *https://en.wikipedia.org/wiki/3G*
4G: *https://en.wikipedia.org/wiki/4G*
Accelerometer: *https://en.wikipedia.org/wiki/Accelerometer*
Android (Operating System):
*https://en.wikipedia.org/wiki/Android_%28operating_system%29*
Application Software: *https://en.wikipedia.org/wiki/Application_software*
Application Store: *https://en.wikipedia.org/wiki/Application_store*
ARM Holdings: *https://en.wikipedia.org/wiki/ARM_Holdings*
Bluetooth: *https://en.wikipedia.org/wiki/Bluetooth*
Capacitive Sensing: *https://en.wikipedia.org/wiki/Capacitive_sensing*
Complex Instruction Set Computing:
*https://en.wikipedia.org/wiki/Complex_instruction_set_computing*
Global Positioning System: *https://en.wikipedia.org/wiki/Global_Positioning_System*
Gyroscope: *https://en.wikipedia.org/wiki/Gyroscope*
HDMI: *https://en.wikipedia.org/wiki/HDMI*
Image Sensor: *https://en.wikipedia.org/wiki/Image_sensor*
Intel: *https://en.wikipedia.org/wiki/Intel*
iOS: *https://en.wikipedia.org/wiki/IOS*
Liquid-Crystal Display: *https://en.wikipedia.org/wiki/Liquid-crystal_display*
Lithium-Ion Battery: *https://en.wikipedia.org/wiki/Lithium-ion_battery*
Magnetometer: *https://en.wikipedia.org/wiki/Magnetometer*
Near-Field Communication: *https://en.wikipedia.org/wiki/Near_field_communication*
OLED: *https://en.wikipedia.org/wiki/OLED*
Operating System: *https://en.wikipedia.org/wiki/Operating_system*
Proximity Sensor: *https://en.wikipedia.org/wiki/Proximity_sensor*
Reduced Instruction Set Computing:
*https://en.wikipedia.org/wiki/Reduced_instruction_set_computing*
Smartphone: *https://en.wikipedia.org/wiki/Smartphone*
USB: *https://en.wikipedia.org/wiki/USB*
Web Browser: *https://en.wikipedia.org/wiki/Web_browser*
Wi-Fi: *https://en.wikipedia.org/wiki/Wi-Fi*
World Wide Web: *https://en.wikipedia.org/wiki/World_Wide_Web*

# 3.1.106 SOFTWARE-DEFINED RADIO

a) **WHAT IS IT?** Software-Defined Radio (SDR) is a communications technology in which many of the traditional hardware components of radio communications have been implemented in software running on a microprocessor. Of course, some hardware is still required, such as an antenna, analogue to digital converter, digital to analogue converter, and digital signal processor. SDR is capable of sending and receiving a wide range of radio communication protocols that are defined in software, and which would previously have required the use of specific hardware elements. SDR is a future-proofing technology that allows a communications device containing a SDR to be re-purposed simply by installing new software. SDR is an enabling technology of *Cognitive Radio*. SDR may become a key part of *Fifth-Generation Mobile Communications* (5G) technology.

b) **HOW COULD IT HELP?** The Stream Tone needs both wired and wireless telecommunications that are highly affordable, high bandwidth, low latency, highly reliable, and ubiquitously available. It is likely that wireless communications will continue to evolve in the future, becoming cheaper, faster, and more ubiquitous. SDR technology can give existing Stream Tone Access Devices immediate access to the very latest wireless protocols, through the installation of a simple software update, instantly improving the Stream Tone Transfer Protocol-based service experience, and avoiding the need to purchase yet another new device.

c) **FURTHER READING**
5G: *https://en.wikipedia.org/wiki/5g*
Analog-To-Digital Converter: *https://en.wikipedia.org/wiki/Analogue-to-digital_converter*
Antenna (Radio): *https://en.wikipedia.org/wiki/Antenna_%28radio%29*
Cognitive Radio: *https://en.wikipedia.org/wiki/Cognitive_radio*
Digital Signal Processor: *https://en.wikipedia.org/wiki/Digital_signal_processor*
Digital-To-Analog Converter: *https://en.wikipedia.org/wiki/Digital-to-analog_converter*
Software-Defined Radio: *https://en.wikipedia.org/wiki/Software-defined_radio*

# 3.1.107   SOLID-STATE DRIVE

a) **WHAT IS IT?** A Solid-State Drive (SSD) is a persistent data storage device constructed from integrated circuit (IC) assemblies. SSDs have no moving parts, unlike the electromechanical *Hard Disk Drives* (HDDs) that they replace, and are therefore much more durable and reliable. A number of different approaches to building persistent, solid-state, data storage solutions exist, but SSDs are most commonly built using either battery-backed dynamic random-access memory (DRAM) or negated-and (NAND) flash memory. DRAM-based solutions are typically much faster than NAND flash memory-based solutions. DRAM is a volatile storage technology, meaning that it will loose its data unless continuously powered. NAND flash memory is non-volatile, and can retain data without continuous power. The SSDs used in most consumer electronics are based on NAND flash memory. NAND flash memory is a digital data storage technology that can be electrically programmed and erased. NAND flash memory gets its name from the structure of the interconnections between its memory cells, which are connected in series and resemble the connection of transistors in a complementary metal-oxide semiconductor (CMOS) NAND gate. NAND flash memory has a relatively short lifespan; the number of times that it can be erased and rewritten before it starts to become unreliable. The effect of this limitation is greatly reduced by the use of a wear-levelling memory controller. However, a newly developed approach that applies high heat to rejuvenate worn out NAND flash memory may soon be able to completely overcome this limitation, and greatly increase its useful lifespan. A NAND flash memory-based SSD is able to read and write data much faster, and use much less power doing so, than a comparable HDD. A typical HDD might be able to read or write data at 1,000 megabits per second (Mbps), whereas a comparable SSD might be able to reach speeds of 5,000 Mbps, or more. HDDs generally have data seek times of between 3 milliseconds (ms) and 12 ms, whereas a typical SSD can find and access its data in approximately 0.1 ms. SSDs are therefore well suited to applications requiring high data throughput, and low latencies, such as big-data processing, high-performance computing, and real-time interactive services. Recently a new method for writing data to NAND flash memory was proposed. The new method uses a middleware layer known as a logical block address scrambler, which allows new data to be written to partially used, or fragmented, memory pages within a memory block scheduled for erasure. In certain simulated scenarios, the newly proposed method can significantly increase memory write speed, reduce power consumption, and reduce the number of memory block erasures. SSDs are available in a wide range of form factors, from units designed to directly replace existing HDDs, down to tiny surface-mountable IC assemblies. SSDs are often found in **Data Centre**-based computer servers, where they help to efficiently and effectively power the **Cloud Computing**-based services of the **Web**, and also in many personal computing devices, such as desktop computers, laptop computers, **Smart-Phones**, and **Tablet Computers**, where they help to reduce power requirements, size, and weight. SSDs can be used to build personal computing devices that start up very quickly; known as instant-on.

b) **HOW COULD IT HELP?** Many Stream Tone Transfer Protocol (STTP)-based services will be highly interactive, and will therefore need to operate in real-time, which will require the use of low-latency telecommunications. The performance and cost-effectiveness of many aspects of the Stream Tone Technology Ecosystem could be enhanced through the use of advanced data storage technologies, such as SSDs. Stream Tone Access Devices (STADs) may also need a persistent data storage capability in order to retain certain required information, such as configuration settings, that could be based on SSD technology. Some STADs will be powered by a direct connection to mains electricity, but most will be portable devices, that rely on battery power. SSD technology is well understood, mature, and can provide the STAD with a power-efficient, high-performance, non-volatile data storage solution. A SSD-based STAD would also be highly reliable, as SSDs have no moving parts.

c) **FURTHER READING**
Cloud Computing: *https://en.wikipedia.org/wiki/Cloud_computing*
CMOS: *https://en.wikipedia.org/wiki/CMOS*
Data Center: *https://en.wikipedia.org/wiki/Data_center*
Dynamic Random-Access Memory: *https://en.wikipedia.org/wiki/Dynamic_random-access_memory*
Exploiting Heat-Accelerated Flash Memory Wear-Out Recovery to Enable Self-Healing SSDs: *https://www.usenix.org/legacy/event/hotstorage11/tech/final_files/Wu.pdf*
Flash Memory: *https://en.wikipedia.org/wiki/Flash_memory*
Hard Disk Drive: *https://en.wikipedia.org/wiki/Hard_disk_drive*
Integrated Circuit: *https://en.wikipedia.org/wiki/Integrated_circuit*
NAND Gate: *https://en.wikipedia.org/wiki/NAND_gate*
New Middleware Technology Quadruples SSD Speed:
*http://techon.nikkeibp.co.jp/english/NEWS_EN/20140522/353388/*
Non-Volatile Memory: *https://en.wikipedia.org/wiki/Non-volatile_memory*
Server (Computing): *https://en.wikipedia.org/wiki/Server_%28computing%29*
Solid-State Drive: *https://en.wikipedia.org/wiki/Solid-state_drive*
World Wide Web: *https://en.wikipedia.org/wiki/World_Wide_Web*

# 3.1.108   SPEEX

a) **WHAT IS IT?** Speex is a patent-free, royalty-free, lossy, stereo audio **Compression** format that is available under a **Free and Open-Source Software** (FOSS) license. Unlike most FOSS, the Speex license is not copyleft, permitting Speex to be included into proprietary software applications without having to freely release the application's source code. Speex is based on the code-excited linear prediction encoding-technique. Speex is optimised for speech-based audio, and is suitable for use with **Voice over Internet**

*Protocol* (VOIP) systems. Speex uses packet loss concealment techniques to mask the loss of audio packets transmitted via VOIP. Speex supports samples rates of 8 kilohertz (KHz), 16 KHz, and 32 KHz, and bit-rates from 2 kilobits per second (Kbps) up to 44 Kbps. Speex supports variable bit-rate and dynamic bit-rate switching. Speex is used by a wide range of audio-enabled applications, including audio processing, computer gaming, voice-based *Internet* search engines, and VOIP-based telephony.

b) **HOW COULD IT HELP?** The Stream Tone Transfer Protocol (STTP) will be used to communicate digital audio and video over the *Internet* from the *Web* to a Stream Tone Access Device, and to send user-input back. The STTP could be used to create a telephony service. The Speex audio *Compression* format is optimised for speech-based audio, and could potentially form a fundamental part of the STTP; providing the technology to encode and decode Stream Tone speech data.

c) **FURTHER READING**
Code-Excited Linear Prediction: *https://en.wikipedia.org/wiki/Code-excited_linear_prediction*
Copyleft: *https://en.wikipedia.org/wiki/Copyleft*
Data Compression: *https://en.wikipedia.org/wiki/Data_compression*
Free And Open-Source Software: *https://en.wikipedia.org/wiki/Free_and_open-source_software*
Packet Loss Concealment: *https://en.wikipedia.org/wiki/Packet_loss_concealment*
Source Code: *https://en.wikipedia.org/wiki/Source_code*
Speex: *http://www.speex.org/*
Speex: *https://en.wikipedia.org/wiki/Speex*
Variable Bit-Rate: *https://en.wikipedia.org/wiki/Variable_bit-rate*
Voice Over IP: *https://en.wikipedia.org/wiki/Voice_over_IP*

# 3.1.109   STREAMED SERVICES

a) **WHAT IS IT?** Streamed services are digital functionalities that are executed on a remotely-located computer server, the results from which are then communicated in real-time to an end-user client computer, via a computer network, such as the *Internet*. Streamed services are often generated by *Cloud Computing*-based *Data Centres*. Streamed services are a type of client-server computing in which the interaction between the client and server occurs in real-time. Streamed services are a variant of *Streaming Media* services, where, instead of just delivering multimedia content in real-time, potentially complex digital services are controlled, and the products of those services are communicated, in real-time. Streamed services are generally highly interactive, with input from a user being immediately sent from the client computer to the server computer, and the result of processing such inputs being immediately sent back to the user. Streamed services communicate by sending data, one small piece at a time, as soon as it is ready for transmission. Streamed services are often delivered using communications protocols such as the *Real-time Transport Protocol*, *Real-Time Streaming Protocol*, and RTP Control Protocol. Some streaming technologies require that consecutive pieces of a service stream be collected and briefly stored prior to presentation, in order to minimise disruptions caused by the variable nature of public computer networks, such as the *Internet*, or to firstly assemble sufficient data to decode a transmission unit. Even when a transmission requires such temporary storage, known as buffering, it is still considered to be a streamed transmission. Client computers may require the installation of specific application software in order to access streamed services; however, most streamed services can be accessed using a **Web Browser**. Most of the functional work required to deliver a streamed service is done by the remotely-located computer server, with the local client computer usually doing little more than presenting the results, and sending user-input to the server. A huge amount of functionality that was previously provided by software applications, which were installed and executed on local personal computing devices, is now available via streamed services. **File Hosting Services**, **Hosted Desktops**, **Massively Multi-player On-line Games**, and **Web Desktops** are some examples of streamed services. A key benefit of streamed services is that they are typically accessible using a wide range of client computing devices, from anywhere in the world, via the **Internet**.

b) **HOW COULD IT HELP?** Streamed service solutions demonstrate the viability of delivering a wide range of interactive digital business and leisure functionalities via the **Internet**. The Stream Tone Transfer Protocol (STTP) will be used to communicate digital content and services over the **Internet** from the **Web** to a Stream Tone Access Device, and to send user-input back. Use of the STTP will not affect the functionality provided by current digital services; it will simply deliver those services in a different way, using the STTP.

c) **FURTHER READING**
Application Software: *https://en.wikipedia.org/wiki/Application_software*
Client-Server Model: *https://en.wikipedia.org/wiki/Client%E2%80%93server_model*
Cloud Computing: *https://en.wikipedia.org/wiki/Cloud_computing*
Computer Network: *https://en.wikipedia.org/wiki/Computer_network*
Data Center: *https://en.wikipedia.org/wiki/Data_center*
File Hosting Service: *https://en.wikipedia.org/wiki/File_hosting_service*
Hosted Desktop: *https://en.wikipedia.org/wiki/Hosted_desktop*
Internet: *https://en.wikipedia.org/wiki/Internet*
Internet Television: *https://en.wikipedia.org/wiki/Internet_television*
Massively Multiplayer Online Game:
*https://en.wikipedia.org/wiki/Massively_multiplayer_online_game*
Real Time Streaming Protocol:
*https://en.wikipedia.org/wiki/Real_Time_Streaming_Protocol*
Real-Time Transport Protocol: *https://en.wikipedia.org/wiki/Real-time_Transport_Protocol*
RTP Control Protocol: *https://en.wikipedia.org/wiki/RTP_Control_Protocol*
Server (Computing): *https://en.wikipedia.org/wiki/Server_%28computing%29*
Streaming Media: *https://en.wikipedia.org/wiki/Streaming_media*
Web Browser: *https://en.wikipedia.org/wiki/Web_browser*
Web Desktop: *https://en.wikipedia.org/wiki/Web_desktop*

# 3.1.110 STREAMING MEDIA

a) **WHAT IS IT?** Streaming media is multimedia content that is continuously transmitted to an end-user client device from a remotely-located computer server, one small portion at a time, in such a way that the end-user can start to consume the content before the transmission, as a whole, has completed. Analogue radio and analogue television were some of the earliest examples of streaming media, where a performance was sent, piece by piece, to a receiving device that immediately processed and presented it to an end-user.

Modern streaming media sends digital content, such as movies, music, and television shows, one bit at a time over computer networks, such as the ***Internet***. The alternative to streaming media is data file-based media, where a complete performance is transferred to the end-user before it is consumed. File-based solutions require that sufficient end-user storage is available to hold the whole performance, which can often be a substantial size even when compressed, and for this reason is often based on physical storage media, such as optical disks. With streaming media, storage requirements are minimal, as only a very small portion of a performance needs to be stored prior to presentation, such as one frame of video or one second of music. Some streaming technologies require that consecutive pieces of a media stream be collected and briefly stored prior to presentation, in order to minimise disruptions caused by the variable nature of public computer networks such as the ***Internet*** or to firstly assemble sufficient data to decode a transmission unit. Even when transmission requires such temporary storage, known as buffering, it is still considered to be a streaming media transmission. The source of streaming media is either a live performance, or a performance recorded into a data file, which is then sent, bit by bit, to an end-user using communications protocols such as the ***Real-time Transport Protocol***, ***Real-Time Streaming Protocol***, and RTP Control Protocol. Streaming media is then received by a client, such as a personal computing device, where it is decoded and presented to the end-user. The decoding of streaming media can either be done in software or using dedicated hardware. Streaming media can support the on-demand delivery of stored content, which permits an end-user to consume such content in a manner that is most convenient. ***Internet Television Services*** are a type of streaming media service.

b) **HOW COULD IT HELP?** Streaming media solutions demonstrate the viability of delivering multimedia content via the ***Internet***. The Stream Tone Transfer Protocol (STTP) will be used to communicate digital content and services over the ***Internet*** from the ***Web*** to a Stream Tone Access Device, and to send user-input back. Use of the STTP will not affect the multimedia content that is currently available; it will simply deliver that content in a different way, using the STTP.

c) **FURTHER READING**
Client-Server Model: *https://en.wikipedia.org/wiki/Client%E2%80%93server_model*
Computer Network: *https://en.wikipedia.org/wiki/Computer_network*
Data Compression: *https://en.wikipedia.org/wiki/Data_compression*
Internet: *https://en.wikipedia.org/wiki/Internet*
Multimedia: *https://en.wikipedia.org/wiki/Multimedia*
Optical Disk: *https://en.wikipedia.org/wiki/Optical_disk*
Real Time Streaming Protocol:
*https://en.wikipedia.org/wiki/Real_Time_Streaming_Protocol*
Real-Time Transport Protocol: *https://en.wikipedia.org/wiki/Real-time_Transport_Protocol*
RTP Control Protocol: *https://en.wikipedia.org/wiki/RTP_Control_Protocol*
Streaming Media: *https://en.wikipedia.org/wiki/Streaming_media*

# 3.1.111 SUBMARINE COMMUNICATIONS CABLE

a) **WHAT IS IT?** A submarine communications cable is used to link two geographically distant land-based points, using an ***Optical Fibre***-based telecommunications cable laid on the sea bed. All the world's continents are now linked via such cables, except Antarctica. Submarine communications cables are used for a wide variety of international telecommunications including ***Internet*** access, telephony, and video-conferencing services. It is estimated that approximately 99 percent of all international ***Internet*** traffic is carried by submarine communications cables at some point on the traffic's route. Submarine communications cables are needed to globally share the incredibly-high volumes of data generated each day by billions of ***Internet*** users. Any nation not having cost-effective high-bandwidth access to the ***Internet*** can be economically and socially disadvantaged. Many new submarine communications cables are planned, which will give many nations high-bandwidth low-latency access to their geographic neighbours as well to the United States of America, which is the primary source of many of the most popular ***Web-based Services*** that now underpin the modern world. Global ***Internet*** access can also be provided by ***Communications Satellites*** (COMSATs). However, as current COMSAT-based ***Internet*** access services either have much higher communications latencies or much lower bandwidths than submarine communications cables they are largely unsuitable for most highly-interactive applications.

b) **HOW COULD IT HELP?** The Stream Tone needs both wired and wireless telecommunications that are highly affordable, high bandwidth, low latency, highly reliable, and ubiquitously available. Submarine communications cables can reliably deliver affordable, high-bandwidth, low-latency Stream Tone Transfer Protocol (STTP)-based services internationally, ensuring that STTP-based services will eventually be available to everyone, everywhere, at a reasonable cost.

c) **FURTHER READING**
Communications Satellite: *https://en.wikipedia.org/wiki/Communications_satellite*
Internet: *https://en.wikipedia.org/wiki/Internet*
Optical Fiber: *https://en.wikipedia.org/wiki/Optical_fiber*
Submarine Communications Cable:
*https://en.wikipedia.org/wiki/Submarine_communications_cable*
World Wide Web: *https://en.wikipedia.org/wiki/World_Wide_Web*

# 3.1.112  SYMMETRICAL BROADBAND

a) **WHAT IS IT?** Symmetrical broadband is a type of ***Internet*** access service in which the upstream bandwidth and downstream bandwidth are equal. Many current broadband services are asymmetrical, having a downstream bandwidth, which carries data from the ***Internet*** to a user that is much higher than the upstream bandwidth, which carries data from a user to the ***Internet***. Asymmetrical broadband services are most suitable for the consumption of digital content, whereas symmetrical broadband services are suitable for both content consumption and creation. The level of asymmetry between downstream bandwidths and upstream bandwidths can often be extreme, with the downstream bandwidth sometimes being as much as 25 times greater than the upstream bandwidth. It is expected that the next generations of wired and wireless telecommunications infrastructures will be able to reduce the level of bandwidth asymmetry, and eventually achieve bandwidth symmetry. Some new ***Optical Fibre***-based broadband services now provide symmetrical ***Internet*** connectivity.

b) **HOW COULD IT HELP?** Some Stream Tone Access Device (STAD) form factors, such as those that are the equivalent of **Smart-Phones** and **Tablet Computers**, could be considered to be more oriented towards content consumption than content creation, suggesting that asymmetric broadband would be sufficient for their use. However, many Stream Tone Transfer Protocol (STTP)-based services, such as high definition video telephony, will be capable of generating significant volumes of upstream data traffic that will require far more bandwidth than is typically provided by asymmetric broadband services in order to work effectively. STADs can also be used for content creation by accessing STTP-based content-creation services, and the efficiency and effectiveness of the Stream Tone Service Infrastructures that will be used to provide such services will, most probably, depend on the availability of high-bandwidth symmetrical broadband.

c) **FURTHER READING**
Broadband: *https://en.wikipedia.org/wiki/Broadband*
High-Definition Video: *https://en.wikipedia.org/wiki/High-definition_video*
Internet: *https://en.wikipedia.org/wiki/Internet*
Internet Access: *https://en.wikipedia.org/wiki/Internet_access*
Optical Fiber: *https://en.wikipedia.org/wiki/Optical_fiber*

# 3.1.113   SYSTEM ON A CHIP

a) **WHAT IS IT?** A System on a Chip (SOC) is an integrated circuit that combines most of the key components necessary to build a computer, or other electronic system, into a single electronic component. SOCs can be used to implement a very wide range of functionality, including arithmetic, communications, co-processing, cryptography, digital signal processing, error detection and correction, memory control, multimedia encoding and decoding, and peripheral control. SOCs can also contain a microprocessor that can be based on a **Reduced Instruction Set Computing** architecture. SOCs are built from one or more functional building-blocks, known as semiconductor intellectual property cores. A SOC is normally designed to meet highly-specific functional requirements. Generally speaking, solutions that are built using a SOC use less power and have greater performance than solutions built from multiple discrete components. **Application-Specific Integrated Circuit** and **Field-Programmable Gate Array** technologies can be used to fabricate a SOC.

b) **HOW COULD IT HELP?** A Stream Tone Access Device (STAD) needs to deliver specific functionality and performance at a minimal cost. Basing a STAD on a custom-designed SOC should help to ensure that the STAD will have just enough features and performance to do its intended job, at a price point that is affordable by all.

c) **FURTHER READING**
Application Specific Integrated Circuit: *https://en.wikipedia.org/wiki/Application-specific_integrated_circuit*
Coprocessor: *https://en.wikipedia.org/wiki/Coprocessor*
Cryptography: *https://en.wikipedia.org/wiki/Cryptography*
Digital Signal Processing: *https://en.wikipedia.org/wiki/Digital_signal_processing*
Error Detection And Correction:
*https://en.wikipedia.org/wiki/Error_detection_and_correction*
Field-Programmable Gate Array: *https://en.wikipedia.org/wiki/Field-programmable_gate_array*
Integrated Circuit: *https://en.wikipedia.org/wiki/Integrated_circuit*

Memory Controller: *https://en.wikipedia.org/wiki/Memory_controller*
Microprocessor: *https://en.wikipedia.org/wiki/Microprocessor*
Multimedia: *https://en.wikipedia.org/wiki/Multimedia*
Peripheral: *https://en.wikipedia.org/wiki/Peripheral*
Reduced Instruction Set Computing:
*https://en.wikipedia.org/wiki/Reduced_instruction_set_computing*
Semiconductor Intellectual Property Core:
*https://en.wikipedia.org/wiki/Semiconductor_intellectual_property_core*
System On A Chip: *https://en.wikipedia.org/wiki/System_on_a_chip*

# 3.1.114   TABLET COMPUTER

a)  **WHAT IS IT?** A tablet computer is a highly versatile, portable, personal computing device that is capable of wireless *Internet* access. The key feature that marks a personal computing device as a tablet computer is that it predominantly consists of a single large display screen, with its electronics mounted behind. A tablet computer does not include a physical keyboard, relying instead on a virtual or on-screen keyboard. User-input is therefore primarily achieved using a touch-sensitive screen-based user-interface. Some tablet computers support mobile telephony, like their smaller *Smart-Phone* brethren. A typical tablet computer features a touch-sensitive colour flat-screen display of between 7 inches and 13 inches on the diagonal. The screen display will typically be based on either liquid-crystal display or *Organic Light-Emitting Diode* (OLED) technology. A modern tablet computer will typically support a wide range of hardware, including an *Accelerometer*, *Ambient Light Sensor*, *Barometer*, *Capacitive Sensing* display screen, *Global Positioning System*, *Gyroscope*, HDMI, *Image Sensor*, loudspeaker, *Magnetometer*, memory card reader, microphone, and USB interface. Tablet computers typically support a wide range of wireless telecommunications interfaces, including *Bluetooth*, *Fourth-Generation Mobile Communications* (4G), infrared, *Near-Field Communication*, third-generation mobile communications (3G), and *Wi-Fi*. Tablet computers use both *Reduced Instruction Set Computing*-based microprocessors, such as those designed by ARM Holdings plc, and complex instruction set computing-based x86 microprocessors, from Intel Corporation. Tablet computers generally run operating systems optimised for mobile operation, such as Google Android OS or Apple iOS. Some tablet computers are able to run traditional desktop operating systems, such as Microsoft Windows or one of the many variants of *Linux*. The functionality of a tablet computer can be upgraded via over-the-air operating system updates, and through the installation of software applications provided by curated, *Web*-based, *Application Stores*. Being a portable device, the tablet computer is battery powered, usually by a *Lithium-Ion Battery*. Lacking a physical keyboard, or mouse, tablet computers are primarily used for content consumption, rather than content creation. A tablet computer will usually include at least one software-based *Web Browser* application that permits interactive access to *Web*-based content and services. In many ways, a typical tablet computer is just a *Smart-Phone* with a very large screen, although tablet computers often include many interface ports not usually found on the much smaller *Smart-Phones*. Tablet computers are becoming increasingly popular for mobile *Web* access.

b)  **HOW COULD IT HELP?** Stream Tone Access Devices (STADs) are intended to be direct replacements for all current personal computing devices. Some STADs will have a tablet computer form factor that is highly portable and already familiar to most users.

c) **FURTHER READING**

3G: *https://en.wikipedia.org/wiki/3G*
4G: *https://en.wikipedia.org/wiki/4G*
Accelerometer: *https://en.wikipedia.org/wiki/Accelerometer*
Android (Operating System):
*https://en.wikipedia.org/wiki/Android_%28operating_system%29*
Application Software: *https://en.wikipedia.org/wiki/Application_software*
Application Store: *https://en.wikipedia.org/wiki/Application_store*
ARM Holdings: *https://en.wikipedia.org/wiki/ARM_Holdings*
Bluetooth: *https://en.wikipedia.org/wiki/Bluetooth*
Capacitive Sensing: *https://en.wikipedia.org/wiki/Capacitive_sensing*
Complex Instruction Set Computing:
*https://en.wikipedia.org/wiki/Complex_instruction_set_computing*
Global Positioning System: *https://en.wikipedia.org/wiki/Global_Positioning_System*
Gyroscope: *https://en.wikipedia.org/wiki/Gyroscope*
Image Sensor: *https://en.wikipedia.org/wiki/Image_sensor*
Intel: *https://en.wikipedia.org/wiki/Intel*
iOS: *https://en.wikipedia.org/wiki/IOS*
Linux: *https://en.wikipedia.org/wiki/Linux*
Liquid-Crystal Display: *https://en.wikipedia.org/wiki/Liquid-crystal_display*
Lithium-Ion Battery: *https://en.wikipedia.org/wiki/Lithium-ion_battery*
Magnetometer: *https://en.wikipedia.org/wiki/Magnetometer*
Microsoft Windows: *https://en.wikipedia.org/wiki/Microsoft_Windows*
Near-Field Communication: *https://en.wikipedia.org/wiki/Near_field_communication*
OLED: *https://en.wikipedia.org/wiki/OLED*
Operating System: *https://en.wikipedia.org/wiki/Operating_system*
Reduced Instruction Set Computing:
*https://en.wikipedia.org/wiki/Reduced_instruction_set_computing*
Smartphone: *https://en.wikipedia.org/wiki/Smartphone*
Tablet Computer: *https://en.wikipedia.org/wiki/Tablet_computer*
USB: *https://en.wikipedia.org/wiki/USB*
Web Browser: *https://en.wikipedia.org/wiki/Web_browser*
Wi-Fi: *https://en.wikipedia.org/wiki/Wi-Fi*
World Wide Web: *https://en.wikipedia.org/wiki/World_Wide_Web*

# 3.1.115   THEORA

a) **WHAT IS IT?** Theora is a lossy, variable bit-rate, high definition video *Compression* algorithm. The latest version of Theora is generally considered to be roughly comparable in terms of bit-rate efficiency, design, encoding performance, and image quality to *H.264*, whilst being functionally far less sophisticated. However, unlike *H.264*, Theora has not yet been implemented in hardware and, therefore, currently relies on software for encoding and decoding. Designs for a hardware-based solution are reported to be in development. Theora compressed video can be streamed over computer networks, such as the *Internet*. Originally intended as an open, and royalty free, video *Compression* algorithm, there are concerns that it may still be subject to unknown patents.

b) **HOW COULD IT HELP?** The Stream Tone Transfer Protocol (STTP) will be used to communicate audio and video over the *Internet* from the *Web* to a Stream Tone Access Device (STAD), and to send user-input back. Theora is a video *Compression* technology that could potentially form a fundamental part of the STTP; providing the ability to encode and decode Stream Tone video data. However, the fact that it may possibly be subject to unknown patents makes it less attractive when compared to other video *Compression* technologies that are clearly unencumbered by patents. Additionally, given that a STAD does not contain a powerful built-in microprocessor, the real-time encoding and decoding of video using a purely software-based implementation of Theora is unlikely to be practical. In order for the STAD to support high-performance power-efficient video *Compression*, it will need to have a purely hardware-based video subsystem.

c) **FURTHER READING**
Computer Network: *https://en.wikipedia.org/wiki/Computer_network*
Data Compression: *https://en.wikipedia.org/wiki/Data_compression*
Free And Open-Source Software: *https://en.wikipedia.org/wiki/Free_and_open-source_software*
H.264/MPEG-4 AVC: *https://en.wikipedia.org/wiki/H.264/MPEG-4_AVC*
High-Definition Video: *https://en.wikipedia.org/wiki/High-definition_video*
Internet: *https://en.wikipedia.org/wiki/Internet*
Lossy Compression: *https://en.wikipedia.org/wiki/Lossy_compression*
Patent: *https://en.wikipedia.org/wiki/Patent*
Royalties: *https://en.wikipedia.org/wiki/Royalties*
Theora: *https://en.wikipedia.org/wiki/Theora*
Variable Bit-Rate: *https://en.wikipedia.org/wiki/Variable_bit-rate*
World Wide Web: *https://en.wikipedia.org/wiki/World_Wide_Web*

# 3.1.116   THIN CLIENT

a) **WHAT IS IT?** A thin client is a low-performance computer terminal specifically designed for a single purpose; accessing a remotely-located, generally high-performance, computer server, over a computer network, such as a local area network, wide area network, or the *Internet*. The amount of processing that takes place on the client terminal, compared to on the server, can vary, dependent on the client-server implementation, but in general terms, a thin client can do little more than present the output of its associated server and send user-input back. Modern server output can include both audio and video data, whilst server input, sent from the thin client, can include data from keyboards, multi-button pointing devices, and even third-party computer peripherals connected via USB interface. Thin clients communicate with their associated servers using real-time communications protocols, of which there are many; both *Free and Open-Source Software*-based and proprietary. The thin client user-experience can be identical to a purely localised personal computing solution, with desktop operating systems and software applications visually presented as if executed on a local personal computing device, and user interaction, via devices such as keyboard and mouse, remaining unchanged. The use of thin clients greatly simplifies operational activity by consolidating systems maintenance and systems security onto the server, instead of across multiple personal computing devices. One of the earliest thin clients was the video, or dumb, terminal that was used to access mainframe computer-based services using serial communications. The video terminal was a very simple personal computing device that was designed to receive and display alphanumeric data sent from the mainframe computer, and to send keyboard-input back. Its hardware was sufficient to do its simple job and no more. The video terminal did not have any off-line storage, or an operating system, and was therefore unable to directly run any software applications. All applications needed to be run on the mainframe computer, which was controlled via commands typed on the keyboard of the video terminal. Most modern thin clients are still simple, low-performance, personal computing devices, but unlike their video terminal forefathers, they often run a basic operating system, and are able to execute simple, manufacturer-supplied, software applications that are primarily designed for accessing their associated server over a computer network. The simple hardware and software needed to build a thin client ensures that it is affordable, power-efficient, and reliable, when compared to a more traditional personal computing device, such as desktop computer or laptop computer. Attempts to make thin clients more affordable, power-efficient, and reliable has seen the creation of ultra-thin clients and zero clients, which are more like the old-fashioned video terminals, in that they have no operating system, and all their functionally has been implemented in hardware, generally via a *System on a Chip* built using *Application-Specific Integrated Circuit* or *Field-Programmable Gate Array* technology. Without access to a server, a thin client is largely useless, and for this reason the thin client servers are designed to be highly reliable in order to minimise any unwanted downtime, something that could adversely impact a large number of users. Thin client functionality can also be implemented in software, permitting server access from a traditional personal computing device.

b) **HOW COULD IT HELP?** Thin client technology demonstrates the viability of accessing remotely-located digital services, via a computer network connection, using a very simple, single purpose, personal computing device. The Stream Tone Access Device (STAD) will be a simple, single purpose, personal computing device that is designed for accessing Stream Tone Transfer Protocol-based content and services via the *Internet*. The initial version of the STAD will be a thin client, and the final, fully hardware-based, version of the STAD will be a zero client. Many of the design and development approaches that have historically been used to create affordable, power-efficient, and reliable thin clients may also be applicable to the STAD.

c) **FURTHER READING**
Application Software: https://en.wikipedia.org/wiki/Application_software
Application-Specific Integrated Circuit: *https://en.wikipedia.org/wiki/Application-specific_integrated_circuit*
Client-Server Model: *https://en.wikipedia.org/wiki/Client%E2%80%93server_model*
Communications Protocol: *https://en.wikipedia.org/wiki/Communications_protocol*
Computer Network: *https://en.wikipedia.org/wiki/Computer_network*
Computer Terminal: *https://en.wikipedia.org/wiki/Computer_terminal*
Field-Programmable Gate Array: *https://en.wikipedia.org/wiki/Field-programmable_gate_array*
Local Area Network: *https://en.wikipedia.org/wiki/Local_area_network*
Mainframe Computer: *https://en.wikipedia.org/wiki/Mainframe_computer*
Operating System: *https://en.wikipedia.org/wiki/Operating_system*
Server (Computing): *https://en.wikipedia.org/wiki/Server_%28computing%29*
System On A Chip: *https://en.wikipedia.org/wiki/System_on_a_chip*
Thin Client: *https://en.wikipedia.org/wiki/Thin_client*
USB: *https://en.wikipedia.org/wiki/USB*
Wide Area Network: *https://en.wikipedia.org/wiki/Wide_area_network*

# 3.1.117 TRANSFLECTIVE LIQUID-CRYSTAL DISPLAY

a) **WHAT IS IT?** A transflective liquid-crystal display (LCD) is a flat panel display technology that combines light transmitting and light reflecting technologies. The name of this technology is a portmanteau of the words transmissive and reflective. Traditional LCDs are based on a transmissive approach, in which a backlight continuously transmits light through the display, illuminating pixels from behind. Traditional LCDs can often be difficult to read when ambient light levels are high, such as outdoors on a sunny day, and are generally better suited to use in environments with lower light levels, such as indoors. In comparison, transflective LCDs are readable both indoors and out. Under high ambient lighting conditions the reflective elements within a transflective display reflect ambient light back out of the display making it more easily readable. Under low ambient lighting conditions, when there is insufficient light available for the display to work by reflected light alone, a traditional backlight is used to illuminate the display. An ***Ambient Light Sensor*** is often used to detect current lighting conditions and turn on the display backlight when light levels are low, and turn off the backlight when light levels are high. When used in brightly lit environments transflective displays use much less power than a traditional backlit LCD. There are a number of different design approaches available for creating a transflective LCD, some designs support colour output in both transmissive and reflective modes, and some which only support black and white, or greyscale, when used in reflective mode.

b) **HOW COULD IT HELP?** Out of all the components typically found in a modern portable personal computing device, the power consumed by the screen display is often the highest. Whilst some Stream Tone Access Devices (STADs) will be powered by a direct connection to mains electricity, most will be portable devices that rely on battery power. Transflective LCD technology is well understood, mature, and can be used to reduce the power consumed by a STAD. Also, the ability to easily view a transflective LCD-based screen display under bright lighting conditions will permit STADs to be regularly used outdoors; something that might be particularly important for users in developing nations.

c) **FURTHER READING**
Backlight: *https://en.wikipedia.org/wiki/Backlight*
Flat Panel Display: *https://en.wikipedia.org/wiki/Flat_panel_display*
Liquid-Crystal Display: *https://en.wikipedia.org/wiki/Liquid-crystal_display*
Pixel Qi: *http://www.pixelqi.com/*
Transflective Liquid-Crystal Display: *https://en.wikipedia.org/wiki/Transflective_liquid-crystal_display*

# 3.1.118 UNIVERSAL SERVICE OBLIGATION

a) **WHAT IS IT?** The Universal Service Obligation (USO) is a business, economic, and legal term, most usually applied to government-regulated industries, that generally refers to the equal provision of a particular service to all citizens of a country. The requirements of a USO are usually enforced through legislation. A universal service is typically a service that is needed by a majority of people in order to live a modern life, and without which they could be disadvantaged. A universal service can help ensure that, regardless of circumstance, a minority can have access to the same types of service enjoyed by the majority, and at comparable prices. A universal service can also benefit businesses. In simple terms, a universal service must meet minimum quality standards and be charged at a consistent price to all users regardless of the cost of providing that service. The most familiar USO is the postal service which will deliver a standard letter, within national borders, for a standardised fee, regardless of the delivery distance. The concept of universal service is generally accepted to have originated in the United Kingdom with the adoption of the Uniform Penny Post service that commenced operation in 1840, and which offered a fixed postal rate of one penny for the delivery of a letter anywhere within the country. Universal service is now applied to many different types of service, not just the postal service, and has been adopted by many countries, both developed and developing, around the world. Today, universal service can apply to electricity supply, gas supply, healthcare, postal service, sewerage, telecommunications, transportation by land, sea, and air, and water supply. Each country generally defines its own unique set of universal services. Any shortfall between what a customer is charged for a service and what a particular service costs to deliver to that customer is made up using a Universal Service Fund (USF) or Universal Service Obligation Fund (USOF), which is generally funded from taxes levied against that particular service industry. General taxation, including income tax, can also be used to fund a USF or USOF. In the case of a typical telecommunications industry, a USO for a telephony service would ensure that everyone can be connected to the telephone network for a standard installation fee regardless of their geographic location, that telephone calls can be made at nationally standardised rates, that telephone calls will meet minimum quality standards, that telephone call boxes will be widely available, that the emergency services can be contacted free-of-charge, and that, where appropriate, maritime telecommunications will be made available. Without a USO for telephony, customers located in remote geographies, with low population densities, might be charged high installation and usage fees, and receive lower call quality compared to customers located within highly-populated urban centres. The USO ensures that everyone is treated equally. Some countries, such as Finland, Switzerland, and Taiwan, have, relatively recently, introduced a USO for *Internet* access, commonly referred to as Broadband Universal Service (BUS) or Universal Broadband Service (UBS). Many other countries are also considering adding *Internet* access as a USO. A USO for broadband would ensure that everyone could obtain access to the *Internet*, at speeds faster than was previously provided via telephone-based dial-up access, regardless of their geographic location or other circumstance. Typically, under a broadband USO, a wired *Internet* connection would be obtainable for a reasonable installation fee, and the *Internet* access service would provide acceptable data bandwidth at an affordable price. A USO-compliant broadband service would also, most likely, ensure that if data download limitations, known as data caps or download quotas, were imposed, that they would be at such a level that the average user would not be excessively restricted and that the overall *Internet* access experience would be acceptable. A USO for broadband could also be applied to wireless *Internet* access, in geographies where a wired solution was not practical, such as in rural environments. One of the key objectives for a USO for broadband would be to remove, or greatly reduce, the digital divide, which is the gap between people that benefit from having *Internet* access and those that do not have access, due to their personal circumstances, but want or need it. A USO for broadband could greatly reduce this gap, and consequently deliver benefit in a number of key areas, including economic, education, health, and social.

b) **HOW COULD IT HELP?** The Stream Tone needs both wired and wireless telecommunications that are highly affordable, high bandwidth, low latency, highly reliable, and ubiquitously available. A USO for broadband can help to ensure that Stream Tone Transfer Protocol (STTP)-based services will be available to everyone, everywhere, regardless of their individual circumstances. A USO for broadband would ensure that bandwidth, latency, and reliability were sufficient for STTP-based services to be useful and useable. A USO for broadband could help to ensure that any data cap did not adversely impact a typical user. A USO for broadband would also ensure that *Internet* access obtained using a Stream Tone Telecommunications Infrastructure was affordable by everyone that wanted or needed it.

c) **FURTHER READING**
Bandwidth Cap: *https://en.wikipedia.org/wiki/Bandwidth_cap*
Broadband: *https://en.wikipedia.org/wiki/Broadband*
Broadband Universal Service: *https://en.wikipedia.org/wiki/Broadband_universal_service*
Digital Divide: *https://en.wikipedia.org/wiki/Digital_divide*
Directive 2002/22/EC Of The European Parliament And Of The Council Of 7 March 2002 On Universal Service And Users' Rights Relating To Electronic Communications Networks And Services (Universal Service Directive): *http://ec.europa.eu/digital-agenda/sites/digital-agenda/files/136univserv_0.pdf*
Internet: *https://en.wikipedia.org/wiki/Internet*
Legislation: *https://en.wikipedia.org/wiki/Legislation*
Uniform Penny Post: *https://en.wikipedia.org/wiki/Uniform_Penny_Post*
Universal Service: *https://en.wikipedia.org/wiki/Universal_service*
Universal Service Fund: *https://en.wikipedia.org/wiki/Universal_Service_Fund*

# 3.1.119   UNLIMITED DATA PLAN

a) **WHAT IS IT?** An unlimited data plan is a type of *Internet* access service contract that does not limit the amount of digital data that a user may download or upload each month. Many *Internet* service providers (ISPs) limit, or cap, the amount of data that can be downloaded or uploaded in order to better manage their finite network resources, at a time when average data consumption is growing rapidly. Download and upload limits are sometimes applied to wired contracts, but are most commonly applied to wireless contracts. Wired contracts often have an unlimited data option available, particularly in mature markets. The cost of a particular wired contract typically varies based on download and upload speed, not on the quantity of data downloaded, such that the higher the speed, the higher the cost of the contract. Many ISPs provide an unlimited wireless data plan as their premium service offering, which is usually quite expensive, and consequently cannot be afforded by everyone. However, as telecommunications infrastructures continue to evolve and mature, it is expected that network capacity will greatly increase, and many of the current limitations will eventually ease, permitting unlimited data plans to become both more common and much more affordable.

b) **HOW COULD IT HELP?** The Stream Tone needs both wired and wireless telecommunications that are highly affordable, high bandwidth, low latency, highly reliable, and ubiquitously available. Low-cost, unlimited, data plans, for both wired and wireless *Internet* connectivity, will be required in order to ensure that sufficient data download and upload capacity is available for accessing all required Stream Tone Transfer Protocol-based content and services.

c) **FURTHER READING**

Bandwidth Cap: *https://en.wikipedia.org/wiki/Bandwidth_cap*
Computer Network: *https://en.wikipedia.org/wiki/Computer_network*
Internet: *https://en.wikipedia.org/wiki/Internet*
Internet Access: *https://en.wikipedia.org/wiki/Internet_access*
Internet Service Provider: *https://en.wikipedia.org/wiki/Internet_service_provider*
Telecommunication: *https://en.wikipedia.org/wiki/Telecommunication*

# 3.1.120 VIRTUAL MACHINE

a) **WHAT IS IT?** A virtual machine is an isolated operating system that runs within a simulation of the functional environment of a physical computer. The simulation of the physical computer is provided by a virtual machine manager. Virtual machine managers are more correctly known as virtual machine monitors or hypervisors. The virtual machine manager either runs directly on the hardware of a physical computer or as a separate software application within an operating system that is running on a physical computer. A virtual machine manager that runs directly on the hardware of a physical computer is known as a type 1, or bare metal, hypervisor. A virtual machine manager that runs as a separate software application within an operating system that is running on a physical computer is known as a type 2, or hosted, hypervisor. The virtual machine is commonly referred to as a guest operating system or simply the guest, and the virtual machine manager or the physical computer that runs the virtual machine manager, is commonly referred to as a host; such that a guest runs on a host or a guest is hosted on a particular virtual machine manager or physical computer. A guest operating system can, if required, be of a completely different type to the operating system that runs the virtual machine manager or host environment. A virtual machine manager can permit multiple guest operating systems to execute simultaneously within a single host. Virtual machines have a lower performance compared to running their guest operating system directly on the host's physical computing hardware due to the overhead of simulating the guest's required computer environment. Many modern central processing units, or microprocessors, include specific support for virtual machines, which can greatly increase their performance. Virtual machine technology can be used to consolidate multiple physical computers onto a single host. Individual physical computers are often underutilised, and by combining the workloads of several such computers onto a single host, using virtual machine technology, much better utilisation can be achieved. Virtual machines are an enabling technology for many *Cloud Computing*-based services, which are able to dynamically provision and deploy virtual machines based on real-time demand. Virtual machine technology is often used to test a new operating system on a computer that already has an operating system installed using a bootable guest operating system image, called a *Live CD*.

b) **HOW COULD IT HELP?** Before dedicated Stream Tone Access Devices (STADs) are created it is most likely that Stream Tone Transfer Protocol-based services will be accessed using application software that emulates a STAD. Virtual machine technology could be used to run a Stream Tone Access Device Emulator, supplied as a bootable guest operating system image, on a personal computing device that already has an operating system installed. Virtual machine technology will also be used in the *Cloud Computing*-based Stream Tone Service Infrastructures that will be used to provide STTP-based services.

c) **FURTHER READING**

Central Processing Unit: *https://en.wikipedia.org/wiki/Central_processing_unit*
Cloud Computing: *https://en.wikipedia.org/wiki/Cloud_computing*
Emulator: *https://en.wikipedia.org/wiki/Emulator*
Hypervisor: *https://en.wikipedia.org/wiki/Hypervisor*
Live CD: *https://en.wikipedia.org/wiki/Live_CD*
Operating System: *https://en.wikipedia.org/wiki/Operating_system*
Virtual Machine: *https://en.wikipedia.org/wiki/Virtual_machine*
Virtualisation: *https://en.wikipedia.org/wiki/Virtualization*

# 3.1.121   VISIBLE LIGHT COMMUNICATION

a)  **WHAT IS IT?** Visible Light Communication (VLC) is an unlicensed short-range high-bandwidth optical wireless communications technology, which uses electromagnetic waves that are discernible by the human eye. VLC uses light with a wavelength of between 780 nanometres (nm) and 375 nm, which corresponds to a frequency range of 385 terahertz (THz) to 800 THz in the electromagnetic spectrum. A typical human eye can detect a range of wavelengths of light from approximately 700 nm to 400 nm, which are perceived by the human brain as the colours of the rainbow ranging from red to violet. There is thousands of times more data carrying capacity available within the visible portion of the electromagnetic spectrum than within the whole of the radio frequency (RF) portion of the spectrum, which extends from 3 kilohertz up to 300 gigahertz. VLC works by modulating the output of a light source, such as a ceiling lamp, which is then detected by a photosensor, such as a charge-coupled device, *Image Sensor*, photodiode, photoresistor, or phototransistor, on a receiving device. The modulations are at a very-high frequency and are not discernible by the human eye. Any type of lamp can theoretically be used for VLC, but light-emitting diode (LED)-based lighting is currently considered to be one of the best for this type of application, as its output can be rapidly modulated, which make it highly suitable for use in low-cost high-bandwidth communications. Bidirectional VLC is possible when two devices both have VLC light sources and photosensors. A VLC light source can be connected to a computer network using standard network cabling or by using power-line communication (PLC) technology. PLC technology is particularly well suited to VLC deployments because it can cost-effectively exploit the existing infrastructure used to provide electrical power to all the lighting sources found throughout a typical home or office. VLC light transmissions are unable to penetrate opaque obstacles, such as building walls, foliage, or trees, unlike many types of mobile communications that use RF. VLC transmissions are limited to line of sight, meaning that if the photosensor on a receiving device cannot detect the light emitted from a VLC source then no communication will be possible. Of course light is often reflected off of the many different surfaces present within a home or office, with the result that VLC can often work, albeit at very much slower speeds, even when a VLC source is not directly visible to a receiving device. Whilst, some types of VLC, known as fee-space optical communication, can use lasers to communicate over distances of several kilometres, LED-based VLC generally has a maximum range of approximately 20 metres (m). The data bandwidth of VLC reduces with distance, with up to 10,000 megabits per second (Mbps) currently possible over distances of a few metres, and 100 Mbps over distances of 20 m. In order to achieve the highest communications bandwidth multiple coloured-LEDs are used in parallel. When used outdoors, bright sunlight can mask communication signals reducing the effective range of VLC. Nevertheless, VLC is expected to become widely deployed, indoors and outdoors, in the future. VLC is considered to be far more secure than RF communications because indoor data transmissions are restricted to a physically bounded area, such as the room of a house, and cannot leak out through the walls, as is the case with most RF-based communications solutions. VLC is considered to be a communications technology that can complement existing RF communications technologies. VLC-based communications are suitable for use in situations where RF-based communications are not practical due to RF waveband congestion, or less desirable, such as within hospitals or aircraft cabins. There are two main operational configurations for VLC deployments; fixed-infrastructure-to-device, and mobile-to-mobile. The fixed-infrastructure-to-device configuration provides VLC via a non-moveable lighting assembly to a receiving device that could itself be non-moveable, such as desktop computer, or to a mobile device such as a laptop computer, **Smart-Phone**, or **Tablet Computer**. The mobile-to-mobile configuration provides VLC between multiple devices that are portable, such as laptop computers, **Smart-Phones**, and **Tablet Computers**. In addition to providing high-bandwidth **Internet** access to a wide range of personal computing devices, VLC can also be used for shop-signage-to-shopper communication, public information broadcasts, as a replacement for electrical wiring, street furniture-based communications, and vehicle-to-vehicle communications. Vehicle-to-vehicle communications using VLC could be used for collision avoidance and traffic congestion avoidance. Street furniture, such as street lights or traffic lights, could use VLC to communicate local area maps to pedestrians, or traffic congestion updates to drivers. Shop signage could be used to advise nearby shoppers of special offers and shop opening times. Used within a sports venue, VLC could be used as a public broadcast mechanism to communicate sports information to spectators. Another possible use for VLC is to replace heavy and expensive copper wiring, used for data and control exchange, in motor vehicles and aeroplanes, where weight is a factor in fuel efficiency. One of the first uses of VLC is expected to be within conference rooms, to provide the largely stationary meeting participants with access to high-bandwidth communications services. Today, the only widely available devices that could potentially be used to access VLC-based services are **Smart-Phones** and **Tablet Computers**, which typically contain photosensors, in the form of **Image Sensors** and **Ambient Light Sensor**s. It has been suggested that, for aesthetic reasons, portable communications devices, such as laptop computers, **Smart-Phones**, or **Tablet Computers** featuring VLC could use infrared LEDs or RF-based communications for their **Internet** uplinks and VLC for their downlinks, in order to avoid having a bright light constantly emanating from the device whilst it is in use. VLC has not yet hit mainstream use, but as RF spectrum is likely to become more and more congested in the future, it is likely to become much more common. VLC is still a relatively new technology, with much research and development work still on-going. VLC is being standardised by the Institute of Electrical and Electronics Engineers (IEEE) 802.15 Wireless Personal Area Networks Task Group 7. VLC is also known as Li-Fi, which is promoted by the Li-Fi Consortium, an international non-profit association with the goal of raising the market awareness of optical wireless technologies. Several VLC solutions are now commercially available.

b) **HOW COULD IT HELP?** The Stream Tone will need both wired and wireless telecommunications that are highly affordable, high bandwidth, low latency, highly reliable, and ubiquitously available. Wireless communications technologies, such as VLC, can help to ensure that Stream Tone Transfer Protocol-based services will be available even in situations where RF-based communications are not possible and wired communications solutions are not convenient. VLC technology is expected to be affordable, and is compatible with many existing networking technologies, such as PLC.

c) **FURTHER READING**

Charge-Coupled Device: *https://en.wikipedia.org/wiki/Charge-coupled_device*
Computer Network: *https://en.wikipedia.org/wiki/Computer_network*
Electromagnetic Spectrum: *https://en.wikipedia.org/wiki/Electromagnetic_spectrum*
Free-Space Optical Communication: *https://en.wikipedia.org/wiki/Free-space_optical_communication*
IEEE 802.15: *https://en.wikipedia.org/wiki/IEEE_802.15*
Image Sensor: *https://en.wikipedia.org/wiki/Image_sensor*
Infrared: *https://en.wikipedia.org/wiki/Infrared*
Internet: *https://en.wikipedia.org/wiki/Internet*
Li-Fi Consortium: *http://www.lificonsortium.org/*
Light-Emitting Diode: *https://en.wikipedia.org/wiki/Light-emitting_diode*
Photodiode: *https://en.wikipedia.org/wiki/Photodiode*
Photoresistor: *https://en.wikipedia.org/wiki/Photoresistor*
Power Line Communication: *https://en.wikipedia.org/wiki/Power_line_communication*
Radio Frequency: *https://en.wikipedia.org/wiki/Radio_frequency*
Smartphone: *https://en.wikipedia.org/wiki/Smartphone*
Tablet Computer: *https://en.wikipedia.org/wiki/Tablet_computer*
Visible Light Communication: *https://en.wikipedia.org/wiki/Visible_light_communication*

# 3.1.122   VOICE OVER INTERNET PROTOCOL

a)   **WHAT IS IT?** Voice over *Internet Protocol* (VOIP) is a telephonic communications technology optimised for the real-time streaming of audio data over packet-switched computer networks, such as the *Internet*. The traditional public switched telephone network (PSTN) carries audio data, such as voice, over circuit-switched networks, which establish a dedicated point to point communications channel, or circuit, that can provide a guaranteed quality of service. In contrast, all communications sessions over a packet-switched network divide their data into small packets of digitised voice data that are then communicated over a common communications channel. Each communications session is in competition for the finite resources of the communications channel, which is therefore unable to offer the same quality of service guarantees available from circuit-switched networks. However, regardless of the inherent quality issues of VOIP technology, it has become a very popular alternative to traditional telephony solutions, primarily because it permits low-cost voice calling over both short and long distances. VOIP telephone calls between two users, each of which must be running compatible VOIP application software, can generally communicate free-of-charge regardless of distance. VOIP-based telephone calls to a traditional PSTN-based telephone user typically incur a charge. Many people use VOIP, particularly for international calling, to·save money. Some countries have therefore banned, or restricted, the use of free VOIP calling as it can financially undermine state-owned telephone service businesses. Traditional, wired telephone service providers, based on PSTN technology, provide their own power to each user's telephone equipment, ensuring that calls can be made even when there is a local power outage. Wired VOIP systems are sensitive to local area power failures, because VOIP equipment is powered locally, not by the telephone service provider. Wireless VOIP systems found in many mobile personal computing devices, such as *Smart-Phones* and *Tablet Computers*, rely on battery power, without which they will not function, the same as for any comparable PSTN-based mobile-phone. Unless a VOIP-based telephone call has been established using a highly-secure communications mechanism, such as via a virtual private network-based connection, a VOIP-based call is generally considered to be less secure than a comparable PSTN-based one. PSTN-based telephone calls to emergency services normally identify the actual location of the caller, but VOIP telephone calls currently do not. Being able to accurately identify an emergency caller's location is likely to be solved using location-based technologies, such as *Global Positioning Systems*, that are now commonly found on many modern portable personal computing devices. Most modern telephone service businesses already use packet-switched telecommunications to some degree, such as for interconnects between their switching centres, and external connections to other service providers. VOIP-based telephony is already popular and is likely to largely replace PSTN-based telephony at some point in the future.

b) **HOW COULD IT HELP?** VOIP-based telephony demonstrates the viability of a packet-switched alternative to PSTN-based telephony. The Stream Tone Access Device (STAD) will not include dedicated hardware for PSTN-based telephony. However, the STAD will support a wide range of Stream Tone Transfer Protocol-based VOIP-like telephony solutions. Excluding support for legacy technologies, such as PSTN-based telephony, from the STAD hardware design will help to keep this device affordable, reliable, and simple.

c) **FURTHER READING**
Circuit Switching: *https://en.wikipedia.org/wiki/Circuit_switching*
Computer Network: *https://en.wikipedia.org/wiki/Computer_network*
Global Positioning System: *https://en.wikipedia.org/wiki/Global_Positioning_System*
Internet: *https://en.wikipedia.org/wiki/Internet*
Internet Protocol: *https://en.wikipedia.org/wiki/Internet_Protocol*
Packet Switching: *https://en.wikipedia.org/wiki/Packet_switching*
Public Switched Telephone Network:
*https://en.wikipedia.org/wiki/Public_switched_telephone_network*
Quality Of Service: *https://en.wikipedia.org/wiki/Quality_of_service*
Streaming Media: *https://en.wikipedia.org/wiki/Streaming_media*
Virtual Private Network: *https://en.wikipedia.org/wiki/Virtual_private_network*
Voice Over IP: *https://en.wikipedia.org/wiki/Voice_over_IP*

# 3.1.123   VORBIS

a) **WHAT IS IT?** Vorbis is a variable bit-rate, lossy, audio *Compression* algorithm that was designed to be more efficient than *MP3*. It supports sample rates from 8 kilohertz (KHz) up to 192 KHz, and bit-rates from 45 kilobits per second (Kbps) up to 500 Kbps. At equivalent bit-rates, Vorbis is considered to have better audio quality than *MP3*. Vorbis can be used for streaming audio services. The quality of Vorbis encoded audio is said to degrade at very low bit-rates. Vorbis was intended, from its inception, to be patent-free, open-source, and royalty free. However, some doubts remain that it is still encumbered by patents. Nevertheless, Vorbis is well supported by both audio hardware and software. A number *HyperText Markup Language Version 5* (HTML5)-compliant *Web Browsers* natively support it.

b) **HOW COULD IT HELP?** The Stream Tone Transfer Protocol (STTP) will be used to communicate audio and video over the *Internet* from the *Web* to a Stream Tone Access Device, and to send user-input back. Vorbis is a mature and popular audio *Compression* algorithm that could potentially form a fundamental part of the STTP; providing the technology to encode and decode Stream Tone audio data. However, the fact that Vorbis might contain patented technology makes it less attractive when compared to other audio **Compression** technologies that are clearly unencumbered by patents.

c) **FURTHER READING**
Data Compression: *https://en.wikipedia.org/wiki/Data_compression*
Free And Open-Source Software: *https://en.wikipedia.org/wiki/Free_and_open-source_software*
HTML5: *https://en.wikipedia.org/wiki/HTML5*
Lossy Compression: *https://en.wikipedia.org/wiki/Lossy_compression*
MP3: *https://en.wikipedia.org/wiki/MP3*
Patent: *https://en.wikipedia.org/wiki/Patent*
Royalties: *https://en.wikipedia.org/wiki/Royalties*
Streaming Media: *https://en.wikipedia.org/wiki/Streaming_media*
Variable Bit-Rate: *https://en.wikipedia.org/wiki/Variable_bit-rate*
Vorbis: *https://en.wikipedia.org/wiki/Vorbis*
Web Browser: *https://en.wikipedia.org/wiki/Web_browser*

# 3.1.124   VORTEX RADIO

a) **WHAT IS IT?** Vortex radio is a term used to describe radio frequency (RF) waves that have been twisted by manipulating their orbital angular momentum (OAM). Current radio communications, such as **Wi-Fi**, use spin angular momentum (SAM). Vortex radio uses both SAM and OAM together. It is theorised that by manipulating the OAM of RF waves that a single communications channel, or band, can be used to simultaneously carry an almost infinite number of communications channels. Vortex radio could permit very high bandwidth telecommunications, something which would be particularly useful for wireless **Internet** access in densely populated urban areas. Vortex radio is still being researched, and has not yet been commercialised. However, based on initial reports from its inventors, vortex radio appears to be a breakthrough technology that has the potential to solve the emerging shortage of usable RF spectrum in densely populated geographies.

b) **HOW COULD IT HELP?** The Stream Tone needs both wired and wireless telecommunications that are highly affordable, high bandwidth, low latency, highly reliable, and ubiquitously available. It is hoped that vortex radio will be able to make highly effective use of the available RF spectrum, in any given locale, to deliver cost-effective, high-bandwidth, telecommunications. Vortex radio technologies could help to ensure that Stream Tone Transfer Protocol-based services will be ubiquitously available, with sufficient bandwidth, at an affordable price.

c) **FURTHER READING**
Encoding Many Channels On The Same Frequency Through Radio Vorticity - First Experimental Test: *http://iopscience.iop.org/1367-2630/14/3/033001/article*
Internet: *https://en.wikipedia.org/wiki/Internet*
Orbital Angular Momentum Of Light:
*https://en.wikipedia.org/wiki/Orbital_angular_momentum_of_light*
Radio Spectrum: *https://en.wikipedia.org/wiki/Radio_spectrum*
Spin Angular Momentum Of Light:
*https://en.wikipedia.org/wiki/Spin_angular_momentum_of_light*
Wi-Fi: *https://en.wikipedia.org/wiki/Wi-Fi*

# 3.1.125   VP8

a) **WHAT IS IT?** VP8 is a lossy high-definition video *Compression* algorithm. VP8 video quality is considered to be comparable to that of *H.264*. Designs for a hardware-based encoder and decoder are available. VP8 was originally a proprietary technology but was made open-source and royalty free by its current owner, Google, Inc.

b) **HOW COULD IT HELP?** The Stream Tone Transfer Protocol (STTP) will be used to communicate audio and video over the *Internet* from the *Web* to a Stream Tone Access Device, and to send user-input back. VP8 is an open-source, royalty free, video *Compression* technology that could potentially form a fundamental part of the STTP; providing the technology to encode and decode Stream Tone video data.

c) **FURTHER READING**
Data Compression: *https://en.wikipedia.org/wiki/Data_compression*
Free And Open-Source Software: *https://en.wikipedia.org/wiki/Free_and_open-source_software*
H.264/MPEG-4 AVC: *https://en.wikipedia.org/wiki/H.264/MPEG-4_AVC*
High-Definition Video: *https://en.wikipedia.org/wiki/High-definition_video*
Lossy Compression: *https://en.wikipedia.org/wiki/Lossy_compression*
Royalties: *https://en.wikipedia.org/wiki/Royalties*
VP8: *https://en.wikipedia.org/wiki/VP8*
World Wide Web: *https://en.wikipedia.org/wiki/World_Wide_Web*

# 3.1.126   VP9

a) **WHAT IS IT?** VP9 is the successor to the *VP8* lossy video *Compression* standard. VP9 video *Compression* is twice as efficient as that of *VP8*, whilst providing comparable video quality. One of the stated objectives for VP9 is to offer better *Compression* efficiency than the High Efficiency Video Coding standard, which is also known as *H.265*. VP9 is intended to be an open and royalty free video standard. VP9 supports ultra high definition video.

b) **HOW COULD IT HELP?** The Stream Tone Transfer Protocol (STTP) will be used to communicate audio and video over the *Internet* from the *Web* to a Stream Tone Access Device, and to send user-input back. VP9 is a new, open-source, royalty-free, highly-efficient, video *Compression* technology that could potentially form a fundamental part of the STTP; providing the technology to encode and decode Stream Tone video data.

c) **FURTHER READING**
Data Compression: *https://en.wikipedia.org/wiki/Data_compression*
Free And Open-Source Software: *https://en.wikipedia.org/wiki/Free_and_open-source_software*
High-Definition Video: *https://en.wikipedia.org/wiki/High-definition_video*
High Efficiency Video Coding:
*https://en.wikipedia.org/wiki/High_Efficiency_Video_Coding*
Lossy Compression: *https://en.wikipedia.org/wiki/Lossy_compression*

Royalties: *https://en.wikipedia.org/wiki/Royalties*
VP8: *https://en.wikipedia.org/wiki/VP8*
VP9: *https://en.wikipedia.org/wiki/VP9*
World Wide Web: *https://en.wikipedia.org/wiki/World_Wide_Web*

# 3.1.127   WEB

a)   **WHAT IS IT?** The Web is the informal name for the World Wide Web, which is the system of interlinked content and services communicated over the physical infrastructure of the **Internet**. Each piece of Web-based content, and each **Web-based Service**, is assigned a unique identifier called a uniform resource identifier (URI). Web-based content includes data in a wide variety of formats, such as audio, image, multimedia, text, video, and many others. **Web-based Services** use the communications infrastructure of the **Internet** and the interlinked content of the Web to deliver a wide range of functionality that can be used for business and leisure. Web-based content and services are accessed using a **Web Browser**, which can navigate the Web using URI-based hyperlinks.

b)   **HOW COULD IT HELP?** Stream Tone Transfer Protocol (STTP)-based services will be delivered, globally, via the physical infrastructure of the **Internet**. Many of those services will not be new but will be pre-existing **Web-based Services** that are simply being communicated in a new way, using the STTP.

c)   **FURTHER READING**
Hyperlink: *https://en.wikipedia.org/wiki/Hyperlink*
Internet: *https://en.wikipedia.org/wiki/Internet*
Uniform Resource Identifier: *https://en.wikipedia.org/wiki/Uniform_resource_identifier*
Web Browser: *https://en.wikipedia.org/wiki/Web_browser*
World Wide Web: *https://en.wikipedia.org/wiki/World_Wide_Web*

# 3.1.128   WEB-BASED SERVICES

a)   **WHAT IS IT?** **Web**-based services use the computer network infrastructure of the **Internet** and the interlinked content of the **Web** to deliver a wide range of functionalities that can be used for business and leisure. A significant amount of functionality that was previously provided by software applications that were installed and executed on a local personal computing device is now provided by **Web**-based services. It is expected that most digital business and leisure activity will move onto the **Web** in the future. **Web**-based services are typically accessed using a **Web Browser**, and for most users that is the only software application that they need to install on a local personal computing device in order to interact with such services. Many **Web**-based services are provided by **Cloud Computing**-based **Data Centres**.

b)   **HOW COULD IT HELP?** **Web**-based services demonstrate the viability of delivering business and leisure functionality from remotely-located digital sources over the **Internet**. The Stream Tone Transfer Protocol (STTP) will be used to communicate a wide range of **Web**-based services over the **Internet**. Use of the STTP will not affect current **Web**-based services; it will simply deliver them in a new way, using the STTP.

c) **FURTHER READING**
Application Software: *https://en.wikipedia.org/wiki/Application_software*
Cloud Computing: *https://en.wikipedia.org/wiki/Cloud_computing*
Computer Network: *https://en.wikipedia.org/wiki/Computer_network*
Internet: *https://en.wikipedia.org/wiki/Internet*
Online Service Provider: *https://en.wikipedia.org/wiki/Online_service_provider*
Personal Computer: *https://en.wikipedia.org/wiki/Personal_computer*
Web Browser: *https://en.wikipedia.org/wiki/Web_browser*
World Wide Web: *https://en.wikipedia.org/wiki/World_Wide_Web*

# 3.1.129   WEB BROWSER

a)   **WHAT IS IT?** A *Web* browser is a software application that permits interactive access to a wide range of digital content stored on the *Web*. A *Web* browser is able to navigate through *Web*-based content using hyperlinks, or uniform resource identifiers, that are embedded within that content, and which point to the location of other content. A *Web* browser will request that the content stored at a particular location be sent to it, and, upon receipt, will appropriately present it using a screen display or through a sound system. A *Web* browser can also be used to access an increasingly wide range of *Web-based Services*. A *Web* browser can be thought of as a software-based *Thin Client* that accesses a remotely-located computer server, which provides it with required content and services. A modern *Web* browser is a highly capable and sophisticated piece of application software, but it is largely unusable without a working connection to the *Internet*. A *Web* browser communicates with *Web*-based content and service providers using standardised communications protocols, such as the *HyperText Transfer Protocol*, and content is formatted using the *HyperText Markup Language*. *Web* browsers are a key enabling technology of the *Web*, and have become an essential part of modern digital life. Content that was previously stored locally, on a personal computing device, is now just as likely to be stored on the *Web* and accessed via a *Web* browser. Many different software applications that were previously installed and executed locally are now available as *Web-based Services* that are accessed from a *Web* browser. Increasingly, the one and only software application that a modern computer user needs is a *Web* browser.

b)   **HOW COULD IT HELP?** *Web* browsers demonstrate the viability and practicality of using the *Internet* to access a wide variety of *Web*-based content and services. All of the Stream Tone Transfer Protocol (STTP)-based content and services, which will be provided by a Stream Tone Service Infrastructure and delivered using a Stream Tone Telecommunications Infrastructure to a Stream Tone Access Device (STAD), will originate on the *Web*. Conceptually, a STAD can be thought of as a hardware-based *Web* browser for accessing STTP-based content and services.

c)   **FURTHER READING**
Application Software: *https://en.wikipedia.org/wiki/Application_software*
Client-Server Model: *https://en.wikipedia.org/wiki/Client%E2%80%93server_model*
HyperText Markup Language:
*https://en.wikipedia.org/wiki/HyperText_Markup_Language*
HyperText Transfer Protocol: *https://en.wikipedia.org/wiki/Hypertext_Transfer_Protocol*
Internet: *https://en.wikipedia.org/wiki/Internet*
Server (Computing): *https://en.wikipedia.org/wiki/Server_%28computing%29*
Thin Client: *https://en.wikipedia.org/wiki/Thin_client*

Uniform Resource Identifier: *https://en.wikipedia.org/wiki/Uniform_resource_identifier*
Web Browser: *https://en.wikipedia.org/wiki/Web_browser*
World Wide Web: *https://en.wikipedia.org/wiki/World_Wide_Web*

# 3.1.130   WEB DESKTOP

a)   **WHAT IS IT?** A *Web* desktop is a personal computing experience that is stylistically based on the desktop operating system metaphor, which is delivered as a *Web-based Service* via the *Internet*. Access to a *Web* desktop requires the use of relatively simple and low-performance client, such as a *Thin Client* or *Web Browser*. A *Web* desktop typically offers a familiar windows, icons, menus, and pointer (WIMP)-style experience, and is designed to provide many of the features and functionalities commonly found on a locally installed desktop operating system. *Web* desktops are often hosted on *Cloud Computing*-based infrastructure. All computing resources, including data storage, reside within the *Web* desktop service. *Web* desktops do not usually support the arbitrary installation of third-party application software.

b)   **HOW COULD IT HELP?** *Web* desktops demonstrate the viability of delivering a complete, desktop operating system-like, personal computing experience as a *Web-based Service*, via the *Internet*. The Stream Tone Transfer Protocol will be used to communicate a wide range of digital content and services over the *Internet*, including *Web* desktops.

c)   **FURTHER READING**
Application Software: *https://en.wikipedia.org/wiki/Application_software*
Cloud Computing: *https://en.wikipedia.org/wiki/Cloud_computing*
Internet: *https://en.wikipedia.org/wiki/Internet*
Operating System: *https://en.wikipedia.org/wiki/Operating_system*
Personal Computer: *https://en.wikipedia.org/wiki/Personal_computer*
Server (Computing): *https://en.wikipedia.org/wiki/Server_%28computing%29*
Web Desktop: *https://en.wikipedia.org/wiki/Web_desktop*
WIMP (Computing): *https://en.wikipedia.org/wiki/WIMP_%28computing%29*

# 3.1.131   WEB REAL-TIME COMMUNICATION

a)   **WHAT IS IT?** *Web* Real-Time Communication (WebRTC) is an evolving, open-source, royalty-free standard for real-time audio and video communications over a computer network, such as the *Internet*. The principle purpose of WebRTC is to enable native support for *Web Browser* to *Web Browser* communications, such as voice calling and video conferencing, without the need to install extra software or *Web Browser*-based plug-ins. WebRTC is designed for use within *HyperText Markup Language Version 5* (HTML5)-compliant *Web Browsers*. The WebRTC project is a collaborative effort between the *Internet Engineering Task Force* (IETF) and the *World Wide Web Consortium* (W3C). The IETF is providing WebRTC with a communications protocol specification based on the Secure Real-time Protocol and W3C is providing a JavaScript *Application Programming Interface* specification.

b)   **HOW COULD IT HELP?** Using WebRTC could provide the Stream Tone Transfer Protocol with a ready-made approach for achieving secure, real-time, communications over the *Internet*.

c) **FURTHER READING**
Application Programming Interface:
*https://en.wikipedia.org/wiki/Application_programming_interface*
Computer Network: *https://en.wikipedia.org/wiki/Computer_network*
Free And Open-Source Software: *https://en.wikipedia.org/wiki/Free_and_open-source_software*
HTML5: *https://en.wikipedia.org/wiki/HTML5*
HyperText Markup Language:
*https://en.wikipedia.org/wiki/HyperText_Markup_Language*
Internet: *https://en.wikipedia.org/wiki/Internet*
Internet Engineering Task Force:
*https://en.wikipedia.org/wiki/Internet_Engineering_Task_Force*
JavaScript: *https://en.wikipedia.org/wiki/JavaScript*
Royalties: *https://en.wikipedia.org/wiki/Royalties*
Secure Real-Time Transport Protocol: *https://en.wikipedia.org/wiki/Secure_Real-time_Transport_Protocol*
Web Browser: *https://en.wikipedia.org/wiki/Web_browser*
WebRTC: *https://en.wikipedia.org/wiki/WebRTC*
World Wide Web Consortium:
*https://en.wikipedia.org/wiki/World_Wide_Web_Consortium*

# 3.1.132   WEBP

a) **WHAT IS IT?** WebP is a free-of-charge, open-source, image *Compression* algorithm, which was developed by Google, Inc. WebP is based on aspects of the *VP8* video *Compression* algorithm. WebP supports both the lossy and lossless *Compression* of colour images up to 16,383 pixels by 16,383 pixels in size. The WebP image *Compression* algorithm is able to compress an image more efficiently than other comparable algorithms, such as Joint Photographic Experts Group (JPEG) or Portable Network Graphics. WebP is supported by an increasingly large range of modern programming languages, operating systems, software applications, *Web Browsers*, and *Web* sites.

b) **HOW COULD IT HELP?** The Stream Tone Transfer Protocol (STTP) will be used to communicate a wide range of digital content and services, including digital images, over the *Internet*. Image *Compression* technologies, such as WebP, could provide the STTP with an efficient image encoding algorithm.

c) **FURTHER READING**
Application Software: *https://en.wikipedia.org/wiki/Application_software*
Data Compression: *https://en.wikipedia.org/wiki/Data_compression*
Digital Image: *https://en.wikipedia.org/wiki/Digital_image*
Free And Open-Source Software: *https://en.wikipedia.org/wiki/Free_and_open-source_software*
JPEG: *https://en.wikipedia.org/wiki/JPEG*
Lossless Compression: *https://en.wikipedia.org/wiki/Lossless_Compression*
Lossy Compression: *https://en.wikipedia.org/wiki/Lossy_compression*
Operating System: *https://en.wikipedia.org/wiki/Operating_system*

Portable Network Graphics: *https://en.wikipedia.org/wiki/Portable_Network_Graphics*
Programming Language: *https://en.wikipedia.org/wiki/Programming_language*
VP8: *https://en.wikipedia.org/wiki/VP8*
Web Browser: *https://en.wikipedia.org/wiki/Web_browser*
Web Site: *https://en.wikipedia.org/wiki/Web_site*
WebP: *https://en.wikipedia.org/wiki/WebP*

# 3.1.133   WI-FI

a)   **WHAT IS IT?** Wi-Fi is the generic name for a range of wireless networking technologies based on the Institute of Electrical and Electronics Engineers (IEEE) 802.11 standards. IEEE 802.11 is an evolving set of wireless, local-area, computer networking standards that currently use the 2.4 gigahertz (GHz), 3.6 GHz, and 5 GHz radio frequency (RF) bands. Many current Wi-Fi enabled devices support IEEE 802.11n, which has a data bandwidth of up to 600 megabits per second (Mbps). The next version of Wi-Fi, IEEE 802.11ac, will support data rates of more than 1,000 Mbps. After that, IEEE 802.11ad, will use the 60 GHz RF band to deliver data rates of up to 7,000 Mbps. Wi-Fi can be used for device to device connectivity, personal area networking, wide area networking, and wireless local area networking. Wi-Fi coverage is relatively short-range, and can extend from a few rooms when using typically available equipment to several square miles, when using more powerful specialised equipment. Wi-Fi supports secure communications using a number of different wireless *Encryption* standards. Wi-Fi is used in many electronic devices, including closed-circuit television cameras, desktop computers, digital cameras, game consoles, laptop computers, network routers, printers, *Smart-Phones*, speakers, *Tablet Computers*, televisions, and video players, to name but a few. Wi-Fi can be used as a replacement for network cabling, and it can also be used where cabling may not be practical, such as outdoors. Wi-Fi is often used to redistribute a wired *Internet* connection throughout a building, such as a home, office, or coffee shop. Some Wi-Fi implementations are able to provide *Internet* connectivity across a whole city. Wi-Fi can also be used to connect a personal computing device, such as a *Smart-Phone* or *Tablet Computer*, to a nearby *Networked Peripheral*, such as a wireless document scanner or printer. Wi-Fi supports data streaming, and can therefore be used for many real-time, interactive, multimedia-based applications, such as computer gaming, telephony, and video conferencing.

b)   **HOW COULD IT HELP?** Many current personal computing devices are able to connect with a wide range of *Web-based Services* and *Networked Peripherals* using wireless communications technologies, such as Wi-Fi. Stream Tone Access Devices (STADs) are intended to be direct replacements for all current personal computing devices, including *Smart-Phones* and *Tablet Computers*, and will therefore need to include wireless communication technologies, such as Wi-Fi, in order to be able to deliver functionality comparable to current personal computing devices. Wi-Fi will allow a STAD to connect to a wide range of Stream Tone Transfer Protocol-based services, *Networked Peripherals*, as well as other STADs. Wi-Fi technology will also permit a STAD to access Stream Tone Transfer Protocol-based services that have been wirelessly redistributed from a network router with a wired connection to the *Internet*.

c)   **FURTHER READING**
Computer Network: *https://en.wikipedia.org/wiki/Computer_network*
Encryption: *https://en.wikipedia.org/wiki/Encryption*

IEEE 802.11: *https://en.wikipedia.org/wiki/IEEE_802.11*
Internet: *https://en.wikipedia.org/wiki/Internet*
Peripheral: *https://en.wikipedia.org/wiki/Peripheral*
Personal Area Network: *https://en.wikipedia.org/wiki/Personal_area_network*
Personal Computer: *https://en.wikipedia.org/wiki/Personal_computer*
Radio Frequency: *https://en.wikipedia.org/wiki/Radio_frequency*
Streaming Media: *https://en.wikipedia.org/wiki/Streaming_media*
Wi-Fi: *https://en.wikipedia.org/wiki/Wi-Fi*
Wide Area Network: *https://en.wikipedia.org/wiki/Wide_area_network*
Wireless LAN: *https://en.wikipedia.org/wiki/Wireless_LAN*

# 3.1.134   WIFOX

a) **WHAT IS IT?** WiFox is a software-based algorithm designed to reduce traffic congestion in intensely shared *Wi-Fi*-based computer networks. Intensely shared *Wi-Fi*-based computer networks can be found in many public venues, such as airports, coffee shops, convention centres, offices, and shopping malls. Network traffic congestion can greatly reduce the throughput and responsiveness of *Wi-Fi*-based networks shared by large numbers of simultaneous users. When a single wireless network, based on the Institute of Electrical and Electronic Engineers (IEEE) 802.11 wireless networking standard, generically known as *Wi-Fi*, is simultaneously used by a large number of users, traffic asymmetry can easily develop; with the number of data requests sent to a *Wi-Fi* access point (AP) by end-user devices surpassing the ability of the AP to respond with the requested data. The WiFox algorithm effectively addresses a weakness of the distributed coordination function of *Wi-Fi*-based networks, in which all users equally share the finite resources of a single communications channel, and if there are too many simultaneous users the network will suffer a congestive collapse. The WiFox algorithm detects when a backlog of data packets starts to accumulate at an AP and will then temporarily increase the transmission priority of queued data so that the backlog is quickly cleared. One of the key features of the WiFox algorithm, that makes it so effective, is that it is applied dynamically, as and when required, and when not required the AP functions as per normal. The WiFox algorithm can significantly improve data throughput and reduce communications latencies, and becomes more effective as the number of network users increases. Whilst WiFox is still being researched, it is hoped that it will be commercialised in the near future. The WiFox algorithm is purely software-based and should therefore be relatively easy to deploy as an upgrade to existing APs. A corresponding change is not required in end-user devices accessing upgraded APs.

b) **HOW COULD IT HELP?** The Stream Tone needs both wired and wireless telecommunications that are highly affordable, high bandwidth, low latency, highly reliable, and ubiquitously available. Modern telecommunications technologies, such as WiFox, will allow Stream Tone Transfer Protocol-based services to be ubiquitously available, with sufficient bandwidth, at an affordable price.

c) **FURTHER READING**
Computer Network: *https://en.wikipedia.org/wiki/Computer_network*
Distributed Coordination Function:
*https://en.wikipedia.org/wiki/Distributed_coordination_function*
IEEE 802.11: *https://en.wikipedia.org/wiki/IEEE_802.11*
Internet: *https://en.wikipedia.org/wiki/Internet*

Packet Switching: *https://en.wikipedia.org/wiki/Packet_switching*
Researchers Find Way to Boost WiFi Performance 400-700 Percent:
*http://news.ncsu.edu/releases/wms-gupta-wifi/*
Wi-Fi: *https://en.wikipedia.org/wiki/Wi-Fi*
WiFox - Scaling WiFi Performance for Large Audience Environments:
*http://conferences.sigcomm.org/co-next/2012/eproceedings/conext/p217.pdf*

# 3.1.135   WORLD WIDE WEB CONSORTIUM

a)  **WHAT IS IT?** The World Wide *Web* Consortium (W3C) is an international standards organisation for the *Web*. The W3C's principle activity is developing royalty-free, vendor neutral, protocols and guidelines to support the on-going growth of the *Web*, thereby ensuring that, over time, the *Web* achieves its full potential. The standards developed by the W3C help to define how many key parts of the *Web* work. The W3C is comprised of its own full-time staff, member organisations, and public contributors that work together to develop *Web* standards. In addition to the development of standards, the W3C is also involved in education, open discussion, outreach, and software development relating to the *Web*. The W3C's principles are based on a *Web* for all, and a *Web* on everything. Its vision for the *Web* involves the sharing of knowledge, full participation, and the development of global trust. The W3C is a key contributor to the *Web Real-Time Communication* standard, amongst many other things.

b)  **HOW COULD IT HELP?** Ideally, the Stream Tone Transfer Protocol (STTP) will not be a wholly new protocol but will be based on one or more pre-existing protocols. If the STTP is to become a widely-accepted mechanism for communicating digital content and services over the *Internet* then it will most likely need the approval and input of influential and knowledgeable bodies, such as the W3C.

c)  **FURTHER READING**
Communications Protocol: *https://en.wikipedia.org/wiki/Communications_protocol*
Royalties: *https://en.wikipedia.org/wiki/Royalties*
Standards Organization: *https://en.wikipedia.org/wiki/Standards_organization*
WebRTC: *https://en.wikipedia.org/wiki/WebRTC*
World Wide Web Consortium: *http://www.w3.org/*
World Wide Web Consortium:
*https://en.wikipedia.org/wiki/World_Wide_Web_Consortium*

# 3.1.136   X264

a)  **WHAT IS IT?** X264 (x264) is a *Free and Open-Source Software* (FOSS)-based video encoder capable of generating *H.264* compliant video. *H.264* is an advanced lossy video *Compression* standard commonly used for the recording, *Compression*, and distribution of high definition video. Over recent years, *H.264* has become commonly used for streaming video from the *Internet*, and is supported by many *Web Browsers*, running on many different operating systems. The x264 video encoder is commonly included in a number of popular video capture and editing applications. Video encoded by the x264 software is considered to be of good visual quality, and is suitable for streamed transmission over computer networks, such as the *Internet*. The x264 video encoder is intended to be patent free, but may contain an algorithm that was patented by a commercial third-party in controversial circumstances.

b) **HOW COULD IT HELP?** The Stream Tone Transfer Protocol (STTP) will be used to communicate digital audio and video over the *Internet* from the *Web* to a Stream Tone Access Device, and to send user-input back. The FOSS-based x264 video encoder is a widely-used and mature video *Compression* technology that is capable of generating *H.264* compliant video streams, and which could potentially form a fundamental part of the STTP; providing the technology to encode Stream Tone video data. However, the fact that x264 may contain patented technologies makes it less attractive when compared to other video *Compression* technologies that are clearly unencumbered by patents.

c) **FURTHER READING**
Computer Network: *https://en.wikipedia.org/wiki/Computer_network*
Data Compression: *https://en.wikipedia.org/wiki/Data_compression*
Free And Open-Source Software: *https://en.wikipedia.org/wiki/Free_and_open-source_software*
H.264/MPEG-4 AVC: *https://en.wikipedia.org/wiki/H.264/MPEG-4_AVC*
High-Definition Video: *https://en.wikipedia.org/wiki/High-definition_video*
Internet: *https://en.wikipedia.org/wiki/Internet*
Lossy Compression: *https://en.wikipedia.org/wiki/Lossy_compression*
Operating System: *https://en.wikipedia.org/wiki/Operating_system*
Patent: *https://en.wikipedia.org/wiki/Patent*
Streaming Media: *https://en.wikipedia.org/wiki/Streaming_media*
Web Browser: *https://en.wikipedia.org/wiki/Web_Browser*
X264: *https://www.videolan.org/developers/x264.html*
X264: *https://en.wikipedia.org/wiki/X264*

# 3.1.137   X265

a) **WHAT IS IT?** X265 (x265) is a *Free and Open-Source Software*-based lossy video encoder, capable of generating *H.265*-compliant video data that is currently under development. *H.265*, also known as High Efficiency Video Coding, is the successor to the *H.264* video standard. *H.265* has been designed to offer twice the *Compression* efficiency of *H.264*, halving the data bit-rate of *H.264* whilst delivering comparable picture quality. *H.265* also supports ultra high definition video, with resolutions up to 8192 pixels by 4320 pixels.

b) **HOW COULD IT HELP?** The Stream Tone Transfer Protocol (STTP) will be used to communicate digital audio and video over the *Internet* from the *Web* to a Stream Tone Access Device, and to send user-input back. The x265 video encoder could potentially form a fundamental part of the STTP; providing the technology to efficiently encode Stream Tone video data. It is hoped that such an encoder would be clearly unencumbered by patents.

c) **FURTHER READING**
Data Compression: *https://en.wikipedia.org/wiki/Data_compression*
Free And Open-Source Software: *https://en.wikipedia.org/wiki/Free_and_open-source_software*
H.264/MPEG-4 AVC: *https://en.wikipedia.org/wiki/H.264/MPEG-4_AVC*

High-Definition Video: *https://en.wikipedia.org/wiki/High-definition_video*
High Efficiency Video Coding:
*https://en.wikipedia.org/wiki/High_Efficiency_Video_Coding*
Internet: *https://en.wikipedia.org/wiki/Internet*
Lossy Compression: *https://en.wikipedia.org/wiki/Lossy_compression*
Operating System: *https://en.wikipedia.org/wiki/Operating_system*
Patent: *https://en.wikipedia.org/wiki/Patent*
Streaming Media: *https://en.wikipedia.org/wiki/Streaming_media*
X264: *https://en.wikipedia.org/wiki/X264*
X265: *https://en.wikipedia.org/wiki/X265*

# 3.1.138   ZOPFLI

a) **WHAT IS IT?** Zopfli is an efficient, asymmetric, zlib-compatible, lossless data *Compression* algorithm that was developed by Google, Inc., and which is available under a *Free and Open-Source Software* license. Zopfli typically achieves approximately 5 percent better data *Compression* than zlib, another *Compression* algorithm with which Zopfli compressed data is compatible. Compared to the speed of zlib-based *Compression*, Zopfli is very much slower, in fact, it can be as much as 100 times slower. Zopfli is considered to be best suited for compressing mainly static data that will then be accessed over a computer network, such as the *Internet*, and decompressed many times. Zopfli is a *Compression*-only algorithm that requires the use of a zlib-compatible decompression algorithm in order to decompress Zopfli compressed data. The speed of decompressing zopfli compressed data is comparable to normal zlib-based decompression.

b) **HOW COULD IT HELP?** The Stream Tone Transfer Protocol (STTP) will be used to communicate digital content and services over the *Internet* from the *Web* to a Stream Tone Access Device, and to send user-input back. The efficiency with which the STTP will be able to communicate such content and services will, in part, depend on the use of lossy and lossless data *Compression* algorithms that are optimised for compressing the different types of data that comprise such content and services. Some types of static data that will be communicated using the STTP might be suitable for *Compression* using Zopfli.

c) **FURTHER READING**
Computer Network: *https://en.wikipedia.org/wiki/Computer_network*
Data Compression: *https://en.wikipedia.org/wiki/Data_compression*
Free And Open-Source Software: *https://en.wikipedia.org/wiki/Free_and_open-source_software*
Lossless Compression: *https://en.wikipedia.org/wiki/Lossless_Compression*
Lossy Compression: *https://en.wikipedia.org/wiki/Lossy_compression*
Zlib: *https://en.wikipedia.org/wiki/Zlib*
Zopfli: *https://code.google.com/p/zopfli/*
Zopfli: *https://en.wikipedia.org/wiki/Zopfli*

# 3.2    PRECURSORS

*A glimpse of tomorrow*

a)    A precursor is defined as something that announces, indicates, leads to, precedes, or suggests that which follows or succeeds it. A precursor can be something tangible, such as a component, device, technology, or tool, which could be used in some way to construct or inspire a successor. A precursor can also be something intangible, such as a concept, feeling, idea, sentiment, theory, or thought, which could form the emotional or intellectual basis for a successor.

b)    The precursors of the Stream Tone suggest that a technology ecosystem like the Stream Tone could actually be created in the future, and give the Stream Tone a set of believable conceptual and technological foundations that are derived from current realities. The existence of relevant Stream Tone precursors also suggests that the effort required to create the Stream Tone may not be quite as great as initially imagined because a substantial amount of groundwork has already been successfully completed. The Stream Tone precursors are, conceptually and metaphorically speaking, the giants upon whose shoulders the Stream Tone will eventually stand. The Stream Tone precursors are effectively the real-world foundations of the Stream Tone. When viewed individually, no precursor can be exactly like the Stream Tone, because it would then be the Stream Tone, and universe is just not that helpful. An individual precursor will, at best, only be able to exhibit a limited number of aspects, characteristics, or qualities of the Stream Tone, as currently envisioned. However, when viewed collectively, the precursors exhibit nearly all of the aspects, characteristics, and qualities currently envisioned for the Stream Tone. Of course that does not mean that the Stream Tone can simply be built by combining the precursors together, only that many of the aspects, characteristics, and qualities currently envisioned for the Stream Tone already exist in the real-world, and that, at some level, creating something like the Stream Tone really is possible.

c)    Successfully understanding precursor trends can give a degree of confidence that even though a particular Stream Tone building block may not be available today that it will most probably become available at some point in the future because it is also needed to support the evolution of a Stream Tone precursor. For example, today's battery-powered portable personal computing devices, such as **Smart-Phones** and **Tablet Computers**, are likely to be the precursors of the Stream Tone Access Device (STAD). The power-efficiency of these devices is continually being improved so that they can be used for longer before requiring a battery recharge. The STAD should ideally be able to operate for many days, or even a week, on a single charge of its **Lithium-Ion Battery**. Is this possible today? No. Will it be possible at some point in the future? Most probably. How do we know this? By looking at the power-efficiency trends of the Stream Tone precursors.

d)    Another way to think about the Stream Tone precursors is that they are the regulatory, societal, and technological stepping stones that lead to the eventual emergence of the Stream Tone. Regulatory precursors set foundational legal precedent that could be of critical importance to the Stream Tone, or grant legal permissions that enable the deployment of technologies that could eventually be used to construct the Stream Tone. For example, **Regulations** that grant permission to use currently restricted parts of a national radio spectrum could eventually provide the Stream Tone with wireless telecommunications that are highly affordable, high bandwidth, low latency, highly reliable, and ubiquitously available. Societal precursors help prepare society for the emotional and intellectual transition from local personal computing to Stream Tone-based Comprehensive Remote Personal Computing (CRPC). For example, a current **File Hosting Service** that reliably and securely stores personal data on the **Web** could help to build trust and understanding of CRPC-like services. So, as the adoption of Stream Tone-based CRPC starts to accelerate there should be much less resistance to this particular change simply because it will be seen by society as just the next logical step in a process that has already been under way for quite some time. Technological precursors confirm the existence and viability of technology from which the Stream Tone could eventually be built. For example, the widespread availability of **Smart-Phones** and **Tablet Computers** clearly demonstrates that some of the physical technologies that could be used to build a STAD are already available, mature, and in common use.

e)   Of course, the degree and manner in which any precursor demonstrates an aspect, characteristic, or quality of the Stream Tone greatly varies. For some precursors it is very obvious, whilst for others it is much more subjective or even tenuous. Comparing things that exist today, such as the Stream Tone precursors, against something that does not yet exist, such as the Stream Tone, is always going to yield results that are open to a wide range of interpretations. Nevertheless, even at this very early stage in its life, some definite ideas about the Stream Tone already exist, and which can be compared to certain aspects of the real world. The results of such comparisons can, in many cases, be highly insightful, and can help to better define what the Stream Tone should ultimately become.

f)   The precursors listed below are an eclectic mix that is mainly comprised of fully-working **Web-based Services** and currently-available physical technologies. Not all the Stream Tone precursors are the obvious choice, since the primary criterion for their inclusion in this particular section was not commercial success, popularity, or having been the first to market. Many of the precursors were selected because they appeared to exhibit a Stream Tone-like aspect, characteristic, or quality. Some of the precursors were selected because they appeared to demonstrate a real-world use of a Stream Tone building block. Some of the precursors were included because they were enabled by **Regulations** that permitted the use of previously restricted resources that may also benefit the Stream Tone at some point in the future. Whilst others were selected because they demonstrated an obvious societal acceptance of **Web-based Services** that wholly rely on continuous **Internet** connectivity in order to function; just like the Stream Tone will do.

g)   The list of Stream Tone precursors should not be considered to be definitive or exhaustive, simply representative. They are a limited range of examples that are, in some way, suggestive of an aspect, characteristic, or quality of the Stream Tone, as currently envisioned. They have primarily been included in order to give the reader an opportunity to better understand the Stream Tone from the perspective of things that exist today; things that a reader of this book may even use on a regular basis. It should be noted that the Stream Tone precursors listed in this book represent a snapshot of things, such as **Web-based Services** and technologies, that existed when this book was written, and which may not exist as described in the future.

h)   The description of each precursor concludes with one of two possible questions; how is it like the Stream Tone or how could it enable the Stream Tone. The first question is asking what aspects, characteristics, or qualities of the precursor are similar to envisioned Stream Tone-related technologies or to digital services that are expected to be communicated using the Stream Tone Transfer Protocol (STTP). This question is generally applied to precursors that are ***Web-based Services***, or to technologies that are used to access ***Web-based Services***. The second question is asking how the precursor could help to support the development or deployment of the Stream Tone Technology Ecosystem (STTE). This question is generally applied to precursors that are service or telecommunications infrastructures, which could be used, in their current or future forms, to provide or deliver digital content and services using the STTP. This second question is also applied to ***Regulations*** which appear to support the development or use of Stream Tone-like products or services. Each question is subjectively answered using a range of assessment criteria, which are explained below.

i)   The following criteria were used to assess a precursor in terms of how is it like the Stream Tone:

- **Replaces local functionality with Web-based services:** The precursor successfully moves functionality that would traditionally have been provided as a local service to remotely-located ***Web-based Services***. *This is pertinent because the Stream Tone requires that all required functionality will be available from the **Web**.*

- **Demonstrates the viability and user acceptance of Web-based services:** The precursor demonstrates that delivering a service via the ***Internet*** is a viable approach and the fact that the precursor has a non-trivial user-base indicates that its users have actively embraced this type of delivery method. *This is pertinent because the Stream Tone only supports **Web-based Services***; *a fact that all end-users will need to accept if it is going to be successful.*

- **Reliant on an active Internet connection:** The precursor is dependent on a continuously active ***Internet*** connection in order to provide a service. *This is pertinent because the Stream Tone will rely on a continuously active connection to the **Internet** in order to deliver a service.*

- **Provides access to all types of content and services:** The precursor provides access to all the different types of digital content and services available on the ***Web***, rather than to just a few or one. *This is pertinent because the Stream Tone will be able to provide access to all types of content and services available on the **Web**.*

- **Streams all data; audio, visual, and other:** The precursor uses data streaming technology to send and receive all types of digital data in real-time. *This is pertinent because the Stream Tone will only use data streaming communications.*

- **Uses secure communications:** The precursor uses secure, **Encryption**-based, communications to protect user-data. *This is pertinent because the Stream Tone will protect all of its communications using **Encryption**.*

- **Supports real-time interactivity:** The precursor technology permits real-time user interaction with ***Web-based Services***. *This is pertinent because the Stream Tone will support interactive **Web-based Services**.*

- **Uses a low-cost thin client:** The precursor uses a simple and affordable client technology, such as a ***Thin Client*** or ***Web Browser***, for accessing ***Web-based Services***. *This is pertinent because the Stream Tone will require the use of a low-cost, simple, hardware-based, client device for accessing **Web-based Services**.*

- **Reliant on remote computing resources:** The precursor relies on remotely-located computing resources for its operation. *This is pertinent because the Stream Tone will rely on remotely-located computing resources for its operation.*

- **Based on free and open-source principles:** The precursor design is available under *Free and Open-Source Software* or *Open-Source Hardware* licensing. *This is pertinent because the Stream Tone will be based on free and open-source technologies.*

j)  The following criteria were used to assess a precursor in terms of how could it enable the Stream Tone:

- **Provides technology on free and open-source terms:** The precursor makes its technology designs available on a *Free and Open-Source Software* or *Open-Source Hardware* licensing basis. *This is pertinent because the Stream Tone will be based on free and open-source technologies.*

- **Expands Internet availability:** The precursor expands *Internet* access into geographies, locations, or situations in which the *Internet* was not previously available. *This is pertinent because the Stream Tone needs to be ubiquitously available.*

- **Improves the quality of Internet connectivity:** The precursor improves the quality of an *Internet* connection, by providing, for example, consistent bandwidth, durable connectivity, or low communications latencies across a wide range of usage situations. *This is pertinent because the Stream Tone needs to be reliable.*

- **Increases communications bandwidth:** The precursor increases the useful bandwidth of an *Internet* connection, from an end-user's perspective. *This is pertinent because the Stream Tone needs high-bandwidth communications.*

- **Reduces Internet access costs:** The precursor enables *Internet* access to be provided at a reduced cost. *This is pertinent because using the Stream Tone needs to be affordable.*

- **Enables Web-based service provision:** The precursor makes providing *Web-based Services* practical or cost effective. *This is pertinent because services accessed by the Stream Tone must be practical, and, where necessary, commercially viable.*

- **Improves the quality of Web-based service delivery:** The precursor improves *Web-based Service* usability by reducing delivery time, or by improving availability, reliability, or responsiveness. *This is pertinent because services accessed by the Stream Tone need to be usable.*

- **Improves the power efficiency of mobile computing devices:** The precursor reduces the amount of power required by portable personal computing devices or increases the capacity of the power storage technology used by portable personal computing devices. *This is pertinent because the Stream Tone will be accessed using portable personal computing devices.*

- **Enables technology deployment:** The precursor permits technology to be deployed in new locations or situations, or used for new applications. *This is pertinent because the Stream Tone may need to use technologies in ways that are currently restricted or* *impossible.*

# 3.2.1    ACER C710-2055

a) **WHAT IS IT?** The C710-2055 (C7) is an affordable laptop computer, manufactured by Acer, Inc., which is designed to run the Chrome Operating System (Chrome OS). Laptop computers that are designed to specifically run the Chrome OS are generically known as Chromebooks. The C7 has an 11.6-inch colour display screen with a resolution of 1,366 pixels by 768 pixels. It uses a duel-core Intel Celeron microprocessor, running at 1.1 gigahertz. The C7 has 4 gigabytes (GB) of random-access memory, and a 320 GB *Hard Disk Drive*. A further 100 GB of *Web*-based data storage is also available on a free-of-charge basis, for up to 2 years, from Google, Inc. The C7 supports the Institute of Electrical and Electronics Engineers (IEEE) 802.11a/b/g/n versions of *Wi-Fi*, as well as 10 megabits per second (Mbps), 100 Mbps, and 1,000 Mbps Ethernet networking. A high definition video camera is also built-in. Peripherals can be connected to the C7 using the included USB interface, HDMI, and VGA ports. The C7 also includes a reader that accepts a range of different memory cards. The C7 has a 6-cell *Lithium-Ion Battery* that can power the laptop for up to 4 hours. Using the Chrome OS the C7 is able to boot very quickly. The Chrome OS is a lightweight *Web*-centric operating system developed by Google, Inc., which is based on a vanilla version of the *Linux* operating system. Chrome OS is designed to run just one main application, the Chrome *Web Browser*, which is also made by Google. Chrome OS is based on the assumption that nearly all personal computing activities can be completed using only *Web-based Services*. The Chrome OS supports a wide range of functionality, including Adobe Flash-based multimedia, music, printing, video, and *Web* browsing. Chrome OS also has built-in support for viewing files created by the Microsoft Office application suite. A wide range of *Cloud Computing*-based productivity and social networking services, many provided by Google, are currently available for use with the Chrome OS. Additional functionality may be added to the Chrome OS by installing software-based Chrome extensions, such as the Remote Desktop extension, which allows a wide range of desktop computers to be remotely accessed and controlled. Most of the functionality provided by the Chrome OS requires a continuous connection to the *Internet* in order to work, however, a small subset will also work off-line. In some ways, the Chrome OS looks visually similar to many other modern windows, icons, menus, and pointer-style desktop operating systems, although its graphical user-interface and method of operation are largely unique, having been specifically designed to deliver an effective, intuitive, and simple *Web*-based personal computing experience. Updates for the Chrome OS are automatically installed.

b) **IS THERE ANYTHING ELSE THAT IS SIMILAR?** Yes, a number of other laptop computers designed to run the Chrome OS are also available, including the Chromebook Pixel by Google, HP Pavilion Chromebook by Hewlett Packard, Chromebook and Chromebook 550 by Samsung, and ThinkPad X131e Chromebook by Lenovo. Samsung also manufactures a small form-factor computer designed to run the Chrome OS, called the Chromebox. Many other manufacturers are expected to produce Chromebooks and Chromeboxes in the future.

c) **WHY WAS IT SELECTED?** The C7, manufactured by Acer, was selected as a Stream Tone precursor because it clearly demonstrates that personal computing devices dedicated to accessing *Web*-based content and services are now commercially available. The very existence of such devices also demonstrates that *Web-based Services*, as a whole, are now able to successfully provide a wide range of functionality that was previously only available locally. The availability of **Web**-centric personal computing devices, such as the C7, suggests that a significant societal shift, away from local personal computing and towards **Web**-based personal computing services is in progress. The C7 is conceptually similar to the Stream Tone Access Device, which is envisioned as a simple, hardware-based, device for accessing the digital content and services that will be communicated using the Stream Tone Transfer Protocol.

d) **HOW IS IT LIKE THE STREAM TONE?** ✔ Replaces local functionality with Web-based services. ✔ Demonstrates the viability and user acceptance of Web-based services. ✔ Reliant on an active Internet connection. ✔ Provides access to all types of content and services. ✘ Streams all data; audio, visual, and other. ✘ Uses secure communications. ✔ Supports real-time interactivity. ✔ Uses a low-cost thin client. ✔ Reliant on remote computing resources. ✘ Based on free and open-source principles.

e) **FURTHER READING**
Acer C7 Chromebook: *http://www.google.com/intl/en/chrome/devices/acer-c7-chromebook.html#specs*
Acer C7 Chromebook (C710-2055):
*http://www.pcmag.com/article2/0,2817,2419670,00.asp*
Chromebook: *https://en.wikipedia.org/wiki/Chromebook*
Chromebox: *http://www.google.com/intl/en/chrome/devices/chromebox.html*

# 3.2.2 AFRICAN COAST TO EUROPE SUBMARINE COMMUNICATIONS CABLE

a) **WHAT IS IT?** The African Coast to Europe (ACE) *Submarine Communications Cable* is an *Optical Fibre*-based communications link between Western Europe and West Africa. The ACE cable connects the following countries (or territories); France, Portugal, Spain (Canary Islands), Mauritania, Senegal, Republic of the Gambia, Guinea, Sierra Leone, Liberia, Côte d'Ivoire, Ghana, Benin, Nigeria, São Tomé and Príncipe, Cameroon, Equatorial Guinea, Gabon, Democratic Republic of Congo, Angola, Namibia, and South Africa. Terrestrial links from the ACE cable will also be connected to the landlocked countries of Mali and Niger. The ACE cable was constructed in four segments; the first segment is from France to Senegal, the second is from Senegal to Coté d'Ivoire, the third is from Coté d'Ivoire to São Tomé and Príncipe, and the fourth is from São Tomé and Príncipe to South Africa. The first three segments became available for use in December 2012, although not all connected countries were immediately ready to make use of it. The fourth and final segment is expected to be completed at a later date, possibly during 2015, at which point all connected countries are expected to be active. When complete, the ACE cable will be approximately 17,000 kilometres in length. The ACE cable will also be connected to other *Submarine Communications Cables* in order to provide more direct connectivity with other parts of the world, such as Asia. The ACE cable uses wavelength-division multiplexing technology with a potential data carrying capacity of up to 5.12 terabits per second (Tbps), although initially it will only support data rates of approximately 1.92 Tbps. The ACE cable is estimated to have cost over 700 million US dollars, and was built by a consortium of European and African telecommunications companies. The ACE cable brings a substantial boost in *Internet* communications capacity to many West African countries that previously had very little, or were reliant on more expensive alternatives. The increase in capacity is expected to greatly reduce the cost of *Internet* service provision, which to date had been relatively high compared to average incomes. It is also expected to bring significant economic and social benefit to a rapidly developing region of the world. A region that is home to hundreds of millions of people that will start to lead increasingly urban lifestyles, and who will consequently come to depend on modern technologies, such as the *Internet* and the *Web*, for their education, entertainment, and livelihood, just like the rest of the world.

b) **IS THERE ANYTHING ELSE THAT IS SIMILAR?** Yes, many *Submarine Communications Cables* are deployed around the world each year. For example, in 2012 the following cables were activated: Alternativa Bolivariana para los Pueblos de nuestra América, America Movil-1, Asia-Submarine-cable Express, CanaLink, Lower Indian Ocean Network 2, Loukkos, Pishgaman Oman Iran, Seychelles East Africa System, Tamares Telecom, and West Africa Cable System.

c) **WHY WAS IT SELECTED?** The ACE *Submarine Communications Cable* was selected as a Stream Tone precursor because it demonstrates that the advanced telecommunications infrastructures needed to bring *Internet* access to all parts of the world are actively being deployed on an on-going basis. The Stream Tone needs both wired and wireless telecommunications that are highly affordable, high bandwidth, low latency, highly reliable, and ubiquitously available, and telecommunications infrastructure deployments, such as the new ACE *Submarine Communications Cable*, can help to make that a reality.

d) **HOW COULD IT ENABLE THE STREAM TONE?** ✗ Provides technology on free and open-source terms. ✔ Expands Internet availability. ✔ Improves the quality of Internet connectivity. ✔ Increases communications bandwidth. ✔ Reduces Internet access costs. ✔ Enables Web-based service provision. ✗ Improves the quality of Web-based service delivery. ✗ Improves the power efficiency of mobile computing devices. ✔ Enables technology deployment.

e) **FURTHER READING**
ACE - Africa Coast To Europe: *http://www.ace-submarinecable.com/ace/default/EN/all/ace_en/*
ACE (Cable System): *https://en.wikipedia.org/wiki/ACE_%28cable_system%29*
The African Coast to Europe (ACE) Submarine Communications Cable: *http://acecable.blogspot.sg/*
Wavelength-Division Multiplexing: *https://en.wikipedia.org/wiki/Wavelength-division_multiplexing*

# 3.2.3 ALCATEL-LUCENT 400G PHOTONIC SERVICE ENGINE

a) **WHAT IS IT?** The 400G Photonic Service Engine (PSE) is an electro-optical processor for use in coherent *Optical Fibre* networking that is manufactured by Alcatel-Lucent S.A., and which was based on research and development conducted by their subsidiary, Bell Laboratories. The 400G PSE is a next generation *Optical Fibre* networking solution that is capable of data transmission speeds of up to 400 gigabits per second (Gbps) per wavelength. Most current **Optical Fibre** network implementations are based on 10 Gbps or 40 Gbps technology. Some telecommunications services are just starting to transition their networks to next generation technologies that can support transmission speeds of up to 100 Gbps as they prepare for the significant growth in **Web-based Services** accessed over the **Internet** that is expected to occur in the near future. It will take several years for the use of 100 Gbps **Optical Fibre** networking to become commonplace, and the widespread adoption of 400 Gbps **Optical Fibre** networking will most likely take several years after that. The 400G PSE is a complementary metal oxide semiconductor **Application-Specific Integrated Circuit** that was built specifically for use in the Alcatel-Lucent 1830 Photonic Service Switch (1830 PSS) platform. The 400G PSE supports per wavelength data rates of 40 Gbps, 100 Gbps, and 400 Gbps, and is backwards compatible with most of the **Optical Fibre** cables that have already been deployed around the world. The 400G PSE allows compatible **Optical Fibre** cables that are currently running at lower data transmission rates to be easily and cost-effectively upgraded to higher rates. The 400G PSE uses less electrical power and can send data over 3000 kilometres without the need for signal regeneration. Also, it can better handle **Optical Fibre** impairments, and is spectrally more efficient than previous generations of **Optical Fibre** networking solutions from Alcatel-Lucent. The 400G PSE is suitable for use in metropolitan, regional, long haul, and ultra-long haul **Optical Fibre** networks. The 400G PSE can be used to provide a photonic line capacity of up to 23,000 Gbps, over a single **Optical Fibre** pair. Whilst there are much faster solutions in development in research laboratories around the world; the 1830 PSS, featuring the 400G PSE, is one of the fastest **Optical Fibre** networking solutions commercially available today. Comparable solutions are expected to become available from other **Optical Fibre** networking vendors in the future. The first, real-world, deployment of Alcatel-Lucent's 400 Gbps **Optical Fibre** networking technology took place in France, in early 2013. It is being used by RENATER, the public interest group that manages the telecommunications network for technology, teaching, and research institutions in France, to transport the bulk of France's scientific data between Paris and Lyon. It is expected that the lessons learned from deployments of high-bandwidth **Optical Fibre** networking technologies, such as the 400G PSE from Alcatel-Lucent, will eventually lead to solutions that are capable of transmitting data at 1,000 Gbps, or more, per wavelength.

b) **IS THERE ANYTHING ELSE THAT IS SIMILAR?** Yes, there are a number of other companies that offer complete solutions or equipment for next-generation high-bandwidth **Optical Fibre** networking, including Altera, Centellax, Ciena, Ekinops, Fujitsu, GigOptix, Infinera, Inphi Corporation, Ericsson, Glimmerglass, Huawei, Nokia, and ZTE.

c) **WHY WAS IT SELECTED?** The 400G PSE from Alcatel-Lucent was selected as a Stream Tone precursor because it clearly demonstrates that the next generations of **Optical Fibre** networking solutions are actively being designed, developed, and deployed. The Stream Tone Transfer Protocol (STTP) will be used to communicate all types of digital content and services, and will require consistently high bandwidth. **Optical Fibre** networking technologies, such as the 400G PSE, could help to provide the bandwidth necessary to make STTP-based services affordable and practical. Most telecommunications service providers are not yet ready to upgrade their networks to 400 Gbps technology, but when they are, a wide range of solutions, including those from Alcatel-Lucent, will be ready and waiting for them.

d) **HOW COULD IT ENABLE THE STREAM TONE?** ✘ Provides technology on free and open-source terms. ✘ Expands Internet availability. ✘ Improves the quality of Internet connectivity. ✔ Increases communications bandwidth. ✔ Reduces Internet access costs. ✔ Enables Web-based service provision. ✔ Improves the quality of Web-based service delivery. ✘ Improves the power efficiency of mobile computing devices. ✔ Enables technology deployment.

e) **FURTHER READING**
400G Photonic Service Engine: *http://www3.alcatel-lucent.com/400g-pse/*
Alcatel-Lucent 1830 Photonic Service Switch: *http://www3.alcatel-lucent.com/wps/portal/products/detail?LMSG_CABINET=Solution_Product_Catalog&L MSG_CONTENT_FILE=Products/Product_Detail_000486.xml*
France Telecom-Orange And Alcatel-Lucent Deploy World's First Live 400 Gbps-Per-Wavelength Optical Link: *http://www3.alcatel-lucent.com/wps/portal/!ut/p/kcxml/04_Sj9SPykssy0xPLMnMz0vM0Y_QjzKLd4x3tXDUL8 h2VAQAURh_Yw!!?LMSG_CABINET=Docs_and_Resource_Ctr&LMSG_CONTENT_FI LE=News_Releases_2013/News_Article_002786.xml*
Paving the Way the World's First Commercial 400G Solution: *http://www3.alcatel-lucent.com/400g-pse/media/introducing-alcatel-Lucent-400g-pse.html*
The 400G Photonic Service Engine: *http://www2.alcatel-lucent.com/techzine/the-400g-photonic-service-engine/*
The 400G Photonic Service Engine - Leaping Toward A Future Of Faster Speeds And Higher Capacity: *http://webform.alcatel-lucent.com/res/alu/survey/alu2CustomForm.jsp?cw=alu2CorpDocDownload&LMSG_C ABINET=TheStore&LMSG_CONTENT_FILE=156691*

# 3.2.4　BBC IPLAYER RADIO

a) **WHAT IS IT?** iPlayer Radio, formerly Radioplayer, is a software-based audio player for accessing hundreds of live, on-demand, and podcast United Kingdom (UK)-only **Web**-based radio services that are broadcast over the **Internet**, and which was developed by the British Broadcasting Corporation (BBC). The BBC is a semi-autonomous, impartial, public service broadcaster that operates in the UK, the Channel Islands, and the Isle of Man. The BBC also provides a wide range of broadcasting services outside the UK through the BBC World Service. The iPlayer Radio service is an example of a **Streaming Media** service. The iPlayer Radio service is accessed using a dedicated software application or a standard **Web Browser**. The iPlayer Radio is available on a wide range of **Internet**-enabled devices, including desktop computers, laptop computers, **Smart-Phones**, and **Tablet Computers**. The iPlayer Radio service is the recommended way to access the **Web**-based radio broadcasts of the BBC.

b) **IS THERE ANYTHING ELSE THAT IS SIMILAR?** Yes, there are a many other radio player software applications currently available, including Amarok, Banshee, Clementine, Fstream, Guayadeque, iTunes, Last.fm, Nexus Radio, PCRadio, Rad.io, RadioSure, Radium, RadioMaximus, RadioTochki, RhythmBox, Screamer Radio, Snowtape 2.0, Spider Player, TapinRadio, TuneIn, UltraPlayer, UMPlayer, Winamp, and Windows Media Player, to name but a few. Globally, there are tens of thousands of freely-available digital radio services, most of which can be accessed using a standard **Web Browser**. Many of these free services are simply the retransmission of traditional radio broadcasts over the **Internet**, whilst others are pure **Web-based Services**. There are also a number of popular **Web**-based radio services with commercial offerings, including 8tracks, Aupeo! Personal Radio, Last.fm, Live365, Pandora Radio, Rdio, Slacker, Spotify, and WE7.

There are also many other music download or music streaming services available.

c) **WHY WAS IT SELECTED?** The iPlayer Radio service was selected as a Stream Tone precursor because it is a successful *Web*-based *Streaming Media* service. The existence of the iPlayer Radio service demonstrates that *Streaming Media* services are viable and widely accepted by society. The iPlayer Radio service uses data streaming communications to send audio data to end-users, which is conceptually similar to the expected operation of Stream Tone Transfer Protocol (STTP)-based audio entertainment services. The iPlayer Radio service would most probably be well suited to delivery using the STTP.

d) **HOW IS IT LIKE THE STREAM TONE?** ✔ Replaces local functionality with Web-based services. ✔ Demonstrates the viability and user acceptance of Web-based services. ✔ Reliant on an active Internet connection. ✘ Provides access to all types of content and services. ✔ Streams all data; audio, visual, and other. ✘ Uses secure communications. ✔ Supports real-time interactivity. ✔ Uses a low-cost thin client. ✔ Reliant on remote computing resources. ✘ Based on free and open-source principles.

e) **FURTHER READING**
iPlayer Radio: *http://www.bbc.co.uk/radio/*
What Is BBC iPlayer Radio?:
*http://iplayerhelp.external.bbc.co.uk/help/playing_radio_progs/what_is_iplayerradio*

# 3.2.5     CITRIX HIGH-DEFINITION USER EXPERIENCE SYSTEM ON A CHIP

a) **WHAT IS IT?** The High-Definition User Experience (HDX) from Citrix Systems, Inc., is a set of remote-computer access technologies built around a *System on a Chip* (SOC) architecture. The HDX SOC can be used to build low-cost *Thin Client* computers with standardised features. HDX is also intended to be a global marketing brand that *Thin Client* vendors can participate in, by offering HDX Ready solutions. The user of a typical HDX SOC-based *Thin Client* would experience a fully-interactive high-resolution computer desktop or software application, as if the desktop or application were running on a local personal computing device, even though it would actually be running on a computer server located in a distant *Cloud Computing*-based *Data Centre*. Citrix provides a wide range of solutions for accessing virtual desktop infrastructure using its Independent Computer Architecture (ICA) technology, which is a proprietary, platform-independent, client-server communications protocol. The ICA communications protocol is not considered to be secure although it can provide lightweight *Encryption*, if required. More heavyweight security for ICA-based communications is available for certain supported software environments through the use of additional Citrix products. ICA allows any supported operating system, or software application, with a graphical user-interface to be run on a remotely-located computer server, that is then accessed via a computer network connection using a relatively low-performance personal computing device or a *Thin Client* terminal. ICA communicates audio, graphics and video from the server to the client, and user-input and peripheral data from the client to the server. ICA-based communications can work over a local area network, wide area network, and the *Internet*. The HDX SOC allows a simple access terminal, known as a *Thin Client*, to be built at a cost that is far lower than most traditional personal computing devices, because nearly all the required hardware for such a device is built inside the HDX SOC. The HDX SOC architecture integrates a number of semiconductor intellectual property (IP) cores, including a **Reduced Instruction Set Computing**-based microprocessor and a digital signal processor (DSP), as well as IP cores for managing audio, memory, multimedia encode/decode, networking, video, and the USB interface. In fact, the only components not included into the SOC are random-access memory and external storage, which will be provided by the **Thin Client's** original equipment manufacturer (OEM). **Thin Clients** based on a HDX SOC host a **Linux**-based operating system, which is used to run remote-access software, such as Citrix Receiver, which supports ICA-based communications. The operating system and remote-access software can be updated, ensuring that the **Thin Client** will be able to support new features and functionality in the future, if required. **Thin Clients** based on the HDX SOC are also able to support remote-access protocols from other vendors. The performance of the remote-access software can optionally be accelerated by using the hardware features of the HDX SOC, such as the DSP, which can greatly improve the performance and efficiency of encoding and decoding audio, graphics, and video in real-time. The HDX SOC also includes support for USB-based peripherals which can be connected to the **Thin Client** but which are actually supported by driver software running on the remotely-located server. The HDX SOC supports the encoding and decoding of a number of **Free and Open-Source Software**-based multimedia formats, such as **Speex** and **Vorbis** for audio, and **Theora** for video. The HDX SOC has been adopted by a number of OEMs that have been able to use it to create some of the lowest-priced **Thin Clients** on the market today.

b) **IS THERE ANYTHING ELSE THAT IS SIMILAR?** Citrix HDX appears to be the only initiative attempting to create an industry-standard SOC-based architecture for **Thin Clients**. Other vendors have created their own SOC-based **Thin Clients**, which have been built using off-the-shelf components that are not specifically tailored for **Thin Client** applications, or based on proprietary SOC designs.

c) **WHY WAS IT SELECTED?** The Stream Tone Access Device (STAD) will be based on a custom-designed SOC. The features and functionality of the HDX SOC are very similar to those that will likely be required by a STAD. The existence of the HDX SOC demonstrates the feasibility of developing custom hardware for accessing digital services. Whilst early versions of the STAD will likely use technology very similar to a HDX SOC-based **Thin Client** it is expected that eventually the STAD will become a pure hardware-based device; a true zero-client that uses no software at all.

d) **HOW IS IT LIKE THE STREAM TONE?** ✔ Replaces local functionality with Web-based services. ✔ Demonstrates the viability and user acceptance of Web-based services. ✔ Reliant on an active Internet connection. ✔ Provides access to all types of content and services. ✔ Streams all data; audio, visual, and other. ✘ Uses secure communications. ✔ Supports real-time interactivity. ✔ Uses a low-cost thin client. ✔ Reliant on remote computing resources. ✘ Based on free and open-source principles.

e) **FURTHER READING**
Citrix Unveils HDX Ready System-On-Chip Initiative:
*https://www.citrix.com/news/announcements/oct-2011/citrix-unveils-hdx-ready-system-on-chip-initiative.html*
What Do You Need To Know About HDX Ready System on a Chip (SOC)?:
*http://blogs.citrix.com/2011/11/01/what-do-you-need-to-know-about-hdx-ready-system-on-a-chip-soc/*

# 3.2.6    DROPBOX

a)  **WHAT IS IT?** Dropbox is a *Web*-based *File Hosting Service*, provided by Dropbox, Inc., that can be used to store any type of digital information, including applications, database dumps, ebooks, engineering drawings, music, photos, presentations, source code, spreadsheets, text files, video, *Web* sites, and word-processing documents. Files hosted on Dropbox can be accessed from anywhere using any supported personal computing device with *Internet* connectivity, including desktop computers, laptop computers, *Smart-Phones*, and *Tablet Computers*. Files hosted on Dropbox can be globally shared with business associates, customers, family, and friends regardless of whether they have a Dropbox account or not. Files are uploaded and downloaded to and from Dropbox using a software-based client application, or through a standard *Web Browser*. Extra functionality, such as being able to upload very large files and file synchronisation, is only available when using Dropbox's software-based client. Dropbox uses *Encryption* to ensure that all hosted files are protected when in transit and at rest. Security can be further enhanced by using two-step verification, based on the time-based one-time password protocol, when accessing a Dropbox account. Dropbox also keeps multiple copies of each hosted file in multiple physical locations to protect against accidental loss. Dropbox supports multi-user version control, which keeps a history of all deleted and previous file versions for a fixed period of time. The Dropbox file synchronisation functionality ensures that any files added to a designated directory on a local personal computing device will be automatically uploaded to Dropbox. The file synchronisation feature works across multiple devices, and changing a file on any one device will cause that change to be automatically propagated to all other devices. The basic Dropbox service is available for free. Paid versions of Dropbox are also available, which have enhanced features, such as aggregated file storage space, consolidated account billing, event reporting, extra storage, file-level access control, multi-user version control, and telephone support. The Dropbox *Application Programming Interface* allows third-party developers to integrate Dropbox functionality into their own *Web-based Services*. Providing access to files stored within Dropbox is a common feature of many modern *Web-based Services*. Being able to share files between different *Web-based Service* providers is a critically important technology for enabling true *Cloud Computing*-based personal computing. Dropbox has millions of active customers that upload hundred of millions of files each day. Dropbox may introduce a *Streaming Media* service at some point in the future.

b)  **IS THERE ANYTHING ELSE THAT IS SIMILAR?** Yes, there are a number of other *File Hosting Services* currently available, each with its own unique functionality and target market, including ADrive, Amazon Cloud Drive, Amazon Simple Storage Service, Apple iCloud, ASUS WebStorage, Box, CloudMe, CloudSafe, Cortado Workplace, DocYouShare, FileJungle, FileServe, Filesplat, Google Drive, Hotfile, MediaFire, Mega, Microsoft OneDrive, RapidShare, Sharefiles, SpiderOak, SugarSync, SyncBlaze, Twindocs, Uploadstation, Wuala, and ZeroPC, to name but a few.

c)  **WHY WAS IT SELECTED?** Dropbox was selected as a Stream Tone precursor because it demonstrates the viability of moving local functionality, namely the storage of personal digital data files that were previously held on a local personal computing device, onto a *Cloud Computing*-based *File Hosting Service*. This is the type of *Web-based Service* that will help to build society's trust in remote personal computing and reduce the need for local data storage. Also, being able to share data easily and seamlessly between various

*Web-based Services* will probably be a key enabler for the move from local personal computing to Comprehensive Remote Personal Computing. *File Hosting Services*, such as Dropbox, could provide data sharing between the many *Web-based Services* that will be communicated using the Stream Tone Transfer Protocol.

d) **HOW IS IT LIKE THE STREAM TONE?** ✔ Replaces local functionality with Web-based services. ✔ Demonstrates the viability and user acceptance of Web-based services. ✔ Reliant on an active Internet connection. ✘ Provides access to all types of content and services. ✘ Streams all data; audio, visual, and other. ✔ Uses secure communications. ✔ Supports real-time interactivity. ✔ Uses a low-cost thin client. ✔ Reliant on remote computing resources. ✘ Based on free and open-source principles.

e) **FURTHER READING**
Dropbox: *https://www.dropbox.com/*
Dropbox (Service): *https://en.wikipedia.org/wiki/Dropbox_%28service%29*

# 3.2.7    FREE ZONE

a) **WHAT IS IT?** Free Zone is an *Internet* access service, provided by Google, Inc., that is based on the *Freemium* business model. The service currently provides access to Google's email, social networking, and *Internet* search engine services, free-of-charge, to users of *Internet*-enabled mobile-phones, located in Indonesia, Philippines, and South Africa. Free Zone services are accessed using the default *Web Browser* installed on the user's mobile-phone. *Web* pages directly accessed from *Internet* search results are displayed without charge. However, a *Web* page accessed via a link on another *Web* page is chargeable, as is the viewing of email attachments. Before a user is charged they are asked if they would like to sign up for a standard *Internet* service package. When used within the constraints of the service there are no charges, and no data download or usage limitations. Free Zone is an attempt to introduce the benefits of the *Internet* to people that might not naturally subscribe to such a service without having firsthand experience of it. Free Zone provides a cost-effective way for such people to become familiar with this new and important technology. Free Zone is one of the ways that the next billion people will be encouraged to adopt an *Internet* and *Web*-based lifestyle.

b) **IS THERE ANYTHING ELSE THAT IS SIMILAR?** Yes, there are other initiatives, such as *Internet*.org, which has the aims of making *Internet* access more affordable, using data more efficiently, and helping businesses drive *Internet* access. *Internet*.org is supported by Facebook, Inc., MediaTek, Inc., Nokia Oyj, Opera Software ASA, Qualcomm Inc., Samsung Group, and Telefonaktiebolaget L. M. Ericsson. There is also an initiative from Facebook that provides free-of-charge access to its social networking services to users in certain countries. O3b Networks Ltd. is building a constellation of *Communications Satellites* that will eventually be used to bring *Internet* connectivity to the other 3 billion (O3b) people on the planet that currently do not have it. Google, Inc., may also develop a *Communications Satellite*-based *Internet* access service, with similar aims, at some point in the future. Some governments provide free-of-charge dial-up access to the *Internet* and some provide free-of-charge *Internet* access at rural post offices, using *Communications Satellite*-based telecommunications. Many libraries, particularly in developed countries, provide free-of-charge *Internet* access. Most free-of-charge wireless *Internet* services are limited to a particular locale, such as an airport, hotel, shopping mall, coffee shop, or library.

c) **WHY WAS IT SELECTED?** Free Zone was selected as a Stream Tone precursor because it demonstrates that the reach of the *Internet* is not yet complete, and that just building the telecommunications infrastructures needed to provide basic *Internet* access within a given geography is not enough. The Free Zone service recognises that people must be allowed to decide for themselves whether they want the *Internet* and the *Web* in their lives. Services, such as Free Zone, can help people to better understand what the *Internet* and *Web* are, and how these two important modern technologies can benefit them, as well their communities, society, and nation. The Free Zone service will help to grow demand in geographies that have not yet heavily adopted the *Internet* and the *Web*. Once there is increased demand for such technologies then local telecommunications infrastructures can be expected to be further developed, and will eventually be sufficient to deliver *Web*-based content and services using the Stream Tone Transfer Protocol.

d) **HOW COULD IT ENABLE THE STREAM TONE?** ✘ Provides technology on free and open-source terms. ✘ Expands Internet availability. ✘ Improves the quality of Internet connectivity. ✘ Increases communications bandwidth. ✘ Reduces Internet access costs. ✔ Enables Web-based service provision. ✔ Improves the quality of Web-based service delivery. ✘ Improves the power efficiency of mobile computing devices. ✘ Enables technology deployment.

e) **FURTHER READING**
Free Zone: *http://www.google.com.ph/intl/en/mobile/landing/freezone/*

# 3.2.8 GAIKAI

a) **WHAT IS IT?** Gaikai, a subsidiary of Sony Corporation, is a *Web*-based computer gaming platform, also known as a cloud-gaming platform. Gaikai permits computer games, which usually require the use of high-performance personal computing devices in order to perform optimally, to be accessed as a *Web-based Service* from low-performance personal computing devices, via a computer network, such as the *Internet*. In simple terms, what the Gaikai platform provides is conceptually similar to an interactive television service in which each channel is an individualised computer game. Gaikai provides its platform to third-party computer gaming services, which are then able to brand and customise the user-experience to meet the specific needs of their target market. Computer games that are delivered from Gaikai are streamed, in real-time, to a user's personal computing device from remotely-located *Cloud Computing*-based *Data Centres*, which use computer servers fitted with high-performance graphics processing units to generate the visual elements of each game. Gaikai uses a standard *Web Browser* as its game client. The Gaikai computer servers convert high-quality game graphics into a compressed video stream, using a *H.264* video encoder, which is then sent to a user's *Web Browser* for decompression and display. User-input is sent from the user's *Web Browser* to the Gaikai servers in order to facilitate the interactive element of a typical computer game. Interactive *Web*-based gaming requires low-latency high-bandwidth *Internet* connectivity. So whilst Gaikai can provide games to almost anyone that has an *Internet* connection, the user-experience can, on occasion, vary based on the quality of that connection, and the physical distance of the user from a game server. In order to minimise the impact of network quality issues, the Gaikai platform will attempt to dynamically adapt to the prevailing networking conditions. Also, to help minimise performance issues that are due to a user's physical distance from a game server, Gaikai provides multiple

*Data Centre*-based game servers, which are located throughout supported geographies. The Gaikai gaming service is currently accessible from *Internet*-enabled desktop computers and laptop computers, with a wide range of other *Internet*-enabled devices, such as computer games consoles, *Smart-Phones*, *Tablet Computers*, and televisions, expected to be supported in the near future. Starting in 2014, Sony will use Gaikai to power its PlayStation Now service, which will stream a wide range of games originally designed for use on the PlayStation 3 games console to PlayStation 3, PlayStation 4, PlayStation TV, and PlayStation Vita gaming devices.

b)  **IS THERE ANYTHING ELSE THAT IS SIMILAR?** Yes; there are a number of other *Web*-based computer gaming services available, including CloudUnion, Core Online, G Cloud, GFACE, OnLive, Orange France, Shinra Technologies, and SFR. Platforms for building *Web*-based computer gaming services are available from Agawi, Approxy, CiiNOW, G-Cluster, Otoy, Playcast, and Ubitus GameCloud. Many new *Web*-based computer gaming platforms and services are expected to emerge over the coming years as the *Web*-based computer gaming industry develops, matures, and substantially expands.

c)  **WHY WAS IT SELECTED?** Gaikai was selected as a Stream Tone precursor because it demonstrates the viability of moving data processing-intensive functionality, such as computer gaming, which was previously executed on high-performance local personal computing devices, onto *Web-based Services*. This is the type of *Web-based Service* that will help to build society's trust and acceptance of remote personal computing. The Stream Tone Transfer Protocol will be used to communicate a wide range of digital content and services, including computationally-demanding photorealistic computer games, over the *Internet* from the *Web* to a Stream Tone Access Device (STAD), and send user-input back. The Gaikai platform is conceptually similar to certain aspects of the Stream Tone Technology Ecosystem. The role of the *Web Browser* used to access Gaikai services is conceptually similar to that of a STAD.

d)  **HOW IS IT LIKE THE STREAM TONE?** ✔ Replaces local functionality with Web-based services. ✔ Demonstrates the viability and user acceptance of Web-based services. ✔ Reliant on an active Internet connection. ✘ Provides access to all types of content and services. ✔ Streams all data; audio, visual, and other. ✔ Uses secure communications. ✔ Supports real-time interactivity. ✔ Uses a low-cost thin client. ✔ Reliant on remote computing resources. ✘ Based on free and open-source principles.

e)  **FURTHER READING**
Gaikai: *http://www.gaikai.com/*
Gaikai: *https://en.wikipedia.org/wiki/Gaikai*

# 3.2.9     GOOGLE DATA CENTRE, QUILICURA

a)  **WHAT IS IT?** The Google, Inc., *Data Centre* located in the municipality of Quilicura, near Santiago in Chile, is Google's first South American *Data Centre*, and which became operational at the end of 2013. Google is expanding its worldwide operations, in a programme that will also see new *Data Centres* constructed in Hong Kong, Singapore, and Taiwan. Google has invested approximately 150 million US dollars in its Quilicura operation, which is expected to be energy efficient and environmentally friendly. Many

Google services, including the video sharing service YouTube, are popular in South American countries, such as Brazil, Chile, Columbia, and Venezuela. The new Quilicura **Data Centre** will provide millions of South American users with high-bandwidth, low-latency, reliable access to Google services.

b) **IS THERE ANYTHING ELSE THAT IS SIMILAR?** Yes, many different companies operate **Data Centres** all over the world. New **Data Centres** are regularly opened in order to meet the ever growing demand for hosted services. For example, in 2012, new **Data Centres** were opened by Airtel Nigeria in Lagos, Nigeria; Amazon in Sydney, Australia; BSNL in various locations across India; Centrilogic in Hong Kong, China; Codero in Ashburn, United States of America; Embratel in São Paulo, Brazil; Green in Zurich, Switzerland; Hanoi Department of Information and Communications in Hanoi, Vietnam; HostGee in Jeddah, Saudi Arabia; IBM in Barrie, Canada; **Internet** Solutions in Randburg, South Africa; iS2 in Shanghai, China; iXcellerate in Moscow, Russia; KIO Network in Panama; Linxdatacenter in Warsaw, Poland; Meeza in Doha, Qatar; Mentor Graphics Corporation in Shannon, Ireland; MTN Ghana in Accra, Ghana; Neo Telecoms in Besançon, France; NTT Communications in Serangoon, Singapore; Philippine Long Distance Telephone in Cebu, Philippines; Revera in Upper Hutt, New Zealand; Saavis in London, United Kingdom; ServInt in Amsterdam, Holland; Stratogen in Kuala Lumpur, Malaysia; TCC Technology in Amata Nakorn, Thailand; Telehouse in Frankfurt, Germany; Tenue in Martinlaakso, Finland. The different **Data Centres** were designed to meet the needs of many different types of customer, with some being focused on consumer-oriented services and some on business-oriented services. Many other existing **Data Centres** were also upgraded or expanded in order to provide improved bandwidth, communications latency, power efficiency, redundancy, security, and server capacity.

c) **WHY WAS IT SELECTED?** The Google **Data Centre** in Quilicura, was selected as a Stream Tone precursor because it demonstrates that the physical infrastructure needed to host **Web-based Services** continues to be constructed in new geographies. Locating a **Data Centre** in close geographic proximity to its users can greatly improve their **Web-based Service** experience. Reducing the need for services to be delivered from international sources will greatly improve the practicality and responsiveness of many different types of **Web-based Service**. Local **Data Centres** are particularly beneficial when used to deliver **Web-based Services** that require high bandwidths or real-time interactivity. **Web-based Services** will only be adopted if they are usable, something that the construction of new **Data Centres** will definitely help to improve. **Data Centres**, such as the one belonging to Google at Quilicura, could most probably be used to deliver **Web**-based content and services using the Stream Tone Transfer Protocol.

d) **HOW COULD IT ENABLE THE STREAM TONE?** ✗ Provides technology on free and open-source terms. ✗ Expands Internet availability. ✗ Improves the quality of Internet connectivity. ✗ Increases communications bandwidth. ✗ Reduces Internet access costs. ✔ Enables Web-based service provision. ✔ Improves the quality of Web-based service delivery. ✗ Improves the power efficiency of mobile computing devices. ✗ Enables technology deployment.

e) **FURTHER READING**
Google: *https://en.wikipedia.org/wiki/Google*
Google - Data Centers: *https://www.google.com/about/datacenters/*
Google - Data Centers - Quilicura, Chile:
*https://www.google.com/about/datacenters/inside/locations/quilicura/*

# 3.2.10 HEWLETT-PACKARD PHOTOSMART 7520 E-ALL-IN-ONE PRINTER

a) **WHAT IS IT?** The Photosmart 7520 e-All-in-One (Photosmart 7520) is an affordable, multifunction, *Internet*-enabled device, manufactured by Hewlett-Packard Company (HP), that includes an inkjet printer, document scanner, photocopier, and fax machine. The printer is capable of borderless and two-sided printing, and the document scanner has an automatic document feeder. The Photosmart 7520 can print up to 14 pages per minute (ppm) in black and white, and up to 10 ppm in colour. The document scanner can scan, in colour, at optical resolutions of up to 1200 dots per inch. The Photosmart 7520 uses 5 individually-replaceable ink cartridges; black, cyan, magenta, photo, and yellow. The Photosmart 7520 is primarily designed to be accessed using wireless networking, but also supports USB connectivity. The printer is able to connect to existing wireless networks using the Institute of Electrical and Electronics Engineers (IEEE) 802.11/b/g/n versions of *Wi-Fi*. It also supports HP Direct Wireless, for use in situations where an established wireless network is not available. The Photosmart 7520 can be accessed from a wide range of personal computing devices, including desktop computers, laptop computers, *Smart-Phones*, and *Tablet Computers*. The Photosmart 7520 can provide access to a wide range of *Web-based Services*, including HP ePrint, and Google Cloud Print. HP ePrint is a free-of-charge *Cloud Computing*-based printing service that allows certain types of document to be sent to HP ePrint-enabled printers from any *Internet*-enabled personal computing device that supports email, located anywhere in the world. A unique email address is assigned to each printer registered with the HP ePrint service. Documents to be printed can then be emailed, as attachments, to a particular printer using its assigned email address. The documents to be printed are not sent directly to the printer, but to the HP ePrint service, where they are converted to a data format that can be understood by the printer. The converted documents are then forwarded to the printer for printing. The HP ePrint service supports a number of commonly used document data formats, including *HyperText Markup Language*, Microsoft Excel, Microsoft PowerPoint, Microsoft Word, Portable Document Format, and text. A number of image formats are also supported, including Bitmap, Graphics Interchange Format, Joint Photographic Experts Group, Portable Network Graphics, and Tagged Image File Format. Printer-specific software does not need to be installed on any device submitting a print job via the HP ePrint service. The Photosmart 7520 supports Google Cloud Print (GCP), which is a free-of-charge, secure *Cloud Computing*-based printing service provided by Google, Inc. The GCP service allows supported personal computing devices with *Internet* connectivity to print a wide range of graphics, image, and text-based digital content, from anywhere in the world, on printers that have been registered with the GCP service. The GCP service converts digital content into a data format that can be understood by all registered printers. The GCP service then forwards the converted content to a user-selected printer for printing. GCP is designed to work with both Google Cloud Print Ready (GCPR) printers, such as the Photosmart 7520, and non-GCPR printers. Non-GCPR printers must be paired with a personal computing device running GCP Connector application software. GCPR printers are available from a wide range of manufacturers, not only HP. The GCP service is typically accessed either through a software application that includes specific support for the GCP service or by using a dedicated GCP software application. Printer-specific software does not need to be installed on any personal computing device using the GCP service. The Photosmart 7520 also supports Apple AirPrint, which allows personal computing devices manufactured by Apple, Inc., to wirelessly print a wide range of graphics, image, and text-based digital content, over a local wireless computer network, without the need to install printer-specific application software. AirPrint enabled printers are available from a wide range of manufacturers, not only HP. The Photosmart 7520 can be accessed using software applications designed to run on portable personal computing devices, such as **Smart-Phones** and **Tablet Computers**. The HP ePrint application allows documents, in supported formats, to be printed from a portable personal computing device on HP printers that support HP ePrint or HP Direct Wireless. The HP Printer Control application allows the status of the Photosmart 7520 to be checked and for scanned documents to be sent directly to a portable personal computing device, over a local wireless network. The Photosmart 7520 is also able to provide a wide range of functionality without the need for a controlling personal computing device. Photographs can be printed directly from memory cards, documents can be sent and received by fax, and documents can be photocopied, through the printer control panel. The Photosmart 7520 is able to download and run a wide range of **Web**-enabled software applications, some of which are able to share scanned documents by email, send scanned documents to a **File Hosting Service**, or print out the local weather report at a scheduled time each day. The downloadable software applications are accessed using a colour, touch-sensitive, display screen. HP manufactures a wide range of popular print-oriented devices, which are used by both individuals and businesses, located all around the world.

b) **IS THERE ANYTHING ELSE THAT IS SIMILAR?** Yes, in addition to the Photosmart 7520, HP manufactures a wide range of wireless, **Internet**-enabled, printers that also support technologies such as Apple AirPrint, Google Cloud Print, HP Direct Wireless, and HP ePrint. Many other manufacturers also produce a wide range of printers with similar functionality, including Brother, Canon, Dell, Epson, Kodak, and Samsung. It is estimated that, between these manufacturers, there are several hundred different models of **Internet**-enabled printing device currently available. Cortado, a **Cloud Computing**-based **File Hosting Service** and **Web Desktop** service, also offers a **Web**-based printing service, called ThinPrint, which is designed to work with any make of printer, and is accessible from a wide range of personal computing devices, including **Smart-Phones** and **Tablet Computers**.

c) **WHY WAS IT SELECTED?** The Photosmart 7520 manufactured by HP was selected as a Stream Tone precursor because it clearly demonstrates that the next generation of computing peripherals is actively being designed, developed, and deployed. **Internet**-enabled multifunction devices, such as the Photosmart 7520, allow documents to be printed and scanned from anywhere in the world, without the need for device-specific application software. Whilst the Stream Tone Transfer Protocol (STTP) will allow local personal computing functionality to be moved onto **Web**-based personal computing services, users will still need to access local personal computing peripherals, such as document printers and scanners. Wireless and **Web**-based printing technologies, such as Apple AirPrint, Google Cloud Print, HP Direct Wireless, and HP ePrint, can enable the use of computing peripherals from portable personal computing devices, such as **Smart-Phones** and **Tablet Computers**. Such technologies can complement technologies built around the STTP, and could even be added into the STTP. Conceptually, multifunction **Internet**-enabled devices, such as the Photosmart 7520, can, from a certain perspective, be considered to be similar to the Stream Tone Access Device.

d) **HOW IS IT LIKE THE STREAM TONE?** ✔ Replaces local functionality with Web-based services. ✔ Demonstrates the viability and user acceptance of Web-based services.

✔ Reliant on an active Internet connection. ✘ Provides access to all types of content and services. ✘ Streams all data; audio, visual, and other. ✔ Uses secure communications. ✘ Supports real-time interactivity. ✔ Uses a low-cost thin client. ✔ Reliant on remote computing resources. ✘ Based on free and open-source principles.

e) **FURTHER READING**
AirPrint: *https://en.wikipedia.org/wiki/AirPrint*
AirPrint Basics: *http://support.apple.com/kb/ht4356*
Google Cloud Print: *http://www.google.com/cloudprint/learn/*
Google Cloud Print: *https://en.wikipedia.org/wiki/Google_Cloud_Print*
HP ePrint: *https://en.wikipedia.org/wiki/HP_ePrint*
HP ePrint Center: *https://h30495.www3.hp.com/c/46403/US/en/*
HP Photosmart 7520 e-All-In-One Printer: *http://www.shopping.hp.com/en_US/home-office/-/products/Printers/HP-Photosmart/CZ045A*

# 3.2.11   HYLAS 2

a) **WHAT IS IT?** Hylas 2 is a commercial *Communications Satellite* (COMSAT) that was launched into a geosynchronous earth orbit (GEO) at 31 degrees east, on 2nd August 2012, using an Ariane 5 launch vehicle from Guyana Space Centre at Kourou, French Guyana. Hylas 2 is owned by Avanti Communications plc, a United Kingdom-based telecommunications company, and was built by Orbital Sciences Corporation, a developer and manufacturer of space and launch systems, based in the United States of America. Hylas 2 is based on the GEOStar-2 platform. Hylas 2 is the second in a series of COMSATs owned by Avanti, and is named after an Argonaut that was apprenticed to the mythic Greek demigod Hercules. Hylas 2 has 24 active transponders that communicate in the *Ka Band* of the radio spectrum; between 26.5 gigahertz (GHz) and 40 GHz. Hylas 2 uses high-power transponders to overcome rain-induced signal fade, an inherent problem of *Ka Band*-based telecommunications, ensuring 99.9 percent service availability regardless of the weather. Hylas 2 is designed to bring fast bi-directional data communications to eastern and southern Africa, the Middle East, the Caucasus, and Europe. In particular, Hylas 2 will help to bring affordable *Internet* access to millions of people located in some of the remotest parts of Africa. It is estimated that up to 40 percent of sub-Saharan Africa will probably never be reached by conventional terrestrially-based telecommunications infrastructure, such as *Optical Fibre*, and will need to employ alternative technologies, such as COMSATs, in order to cost-effectively bring *Internet* connectivity to such a geographically challenging region. COMSAT-based telecommunications are designed to be highly reliable, and once commissioned will normally operate without incidence for the whole of their expected operational life. Based on its initial fuel load, it is expected that Hylas 2 will have a fifteen-year operational life. Avanti's next space-based venture, Hylas 3, will be a telecommunications payload hosted on the European Data Relay Satellite C, that is expected to launch in 2015 and will provide further cost-effective *Ka Band*-based telecommunications capacity to the Middle East, and Africa.

b) **IS THERE ANYTHING ELSE THAT IS SIMILAR?** Yes, there are many other COMSATs in GEO that currently use *Ka Band* radio frequencies, including ABS 7, Amazonas 3, AMC 15, AMC 16, Amos 3, Anik F3, Anik F2, Arabsat 5C, Asiasat 7, Astra 1L, Astra 2F, Astra 3B, Astra 4A, Badr 5, COMS 1, DirecTV 7S, DirecTV 8, DirecTV 9S, DirecTV 10, DirecTV 11, DirecTV 12, Echostar 17, Echostar G1, Eutelsat 7A, Eutelsat

16A, Eutelsat Hot Bird 13A, Eutelsat KA-SAT 9A, Hylas 1, Intelsat 20, Galaxy 23, Galaxy 28, Kizuna, Koreasat 5, Nilesat 201, Nimiq 2, Nimiq 4, Optus B3, Optus C1, Spaceway 1, Spaceway 2, Spaceway 3, Superbird B2, Thaicom 4, ViaSat 1, Venesat 1, Wildblue 1, XTAR-LANT, Yahlive, and Yahsat 1B. Not all of these COMSATS use their **Ka Band** transponders to provide **Internet** access services, although many do. Many more **Ka Band**-based COMSATs are planned for the future.

c) **WHY WAS IT SELECTED?** Hylas 2 was selected as a Stream Tone precursor because it demonstrates that the physical infrastructure needed to provide **Internet** connectivity to new geographies continues to be designed, developed, and deployed. Many regions of the world will never be served by traditional terrestrially-based telecommunications infrastructures because they are just too remote or poorly populated to make that feasible, and will need to rely on alternative technologies, such as COMSATs for **Internet** access. COMSATs, such as Hylas 2, can help to provide cost-effective and reliable **Internet** connectivity to some of the most remote places on Earth, which could significantly improve the lives of the people that live there. Hylas 2 could most probably be used to communicate digital content and services using the Stream Tone Transfer Protocol.

d) **HOW COULD IT ENABLE THE STREAM TONE?** ✘ Provides technology on free and open-source terms. ✔ Expands Internet availability. ✔ Improves the quality of Internet connectivity. ✔ Increases communications bandwidth. ✔ Reduces Internet access costs. ✘ Enables Web-based service provision. ✘ Improves the quality of Web-based service delivery. ✘ Improves the power efficiency of mobile computing devices. ✔ Enables technology deployment.

e) **FURTHER READING**
HYLAS 2: *http://www.avantiplc.com/hylas2/#where-we-cover*
HYLAS 2: *https://en.wikipedia.org/wiki/HYLAS_2*
HYLAS 2 - Fact Sheet: *http://www.orbital.com/newsinfo/publications/HYLAS2_Fact.pdf*

# 3.2.12 JOLIDRIVE

a) **WHAT IS IT?** Jolidrive is a free-of-charge **Web Desktop** service that is able to provide unified access to third-party **Web**-based content and services, and which was developed by Jolicloud. The Jolidrive service is based on the belief that all commonly needed digital content and services can be accessed from the **Web**. The Jolicloud service provides a windows, icons, menus, and pointer-style graphical user-interface that is based on the desktop metaphor, and which includes a **Web**-application launcher, **Web**-application library, and a file browser that is capable of searching for content stored on multiple third-party **File Hosting Services**. Unlike a traditional desktop operating system, new application software cannot be installed by the user, however, new bookmarks to **Web**-based content and services can be added to the Jolidrive **Web Desktop**, which can also be customised with different wallpapers. Jolidrive is a client-server technology that uses a standard **Web Browser** as its client. Communications between the Jolidrive client and the Jolidrive **Cloud Computing**-based servers are based on standard **Web** technologies, such as **HyperText Markup Language Version 5**, secured using Transport Layer Security. Jolidrive requires a continuous **Internet** connection in order to deliver its full range of functionality. Jolidrive can be accessed from any **Internet**-enabled location, using a wide range of personal computing devices, including desktop computers, laptop computers, **Smart-Phones**, and **Tablet Computers**. The capabilities of the Jolidrive service can be greatly enhanced when accessed through the Joli Operating System (Joli OS), which is a *Linux*-based operating system. Joli OS seamlessly integrates with Jolidrive, augmenting its *Web*-based functionalities with locally installed software applications, and local data storage. Joli OS has been designed to run on a very wide range of personal computing devices with Intel x86-compatible microprocessors, even those that are a number of years old.

b)  **IS THERE ANYTHING ELSE THAT IS SIMILAR?** Yes, there are a number of other *Web Desktop* services currently available, including eyeOS, SkyDesktop, and ZeroPC.

c)  **WHY WAS IT SELECTED?** Jolidrive was selected as a Stream Tone precursor because it demonstrates the viability of moving local functionality, namely desktop computing, that was previously executed on a local personal computing device, onto *Web-based Services*. This is the type of *Web-based Service* that will help to build society's trust in remote personal computing, and reduce the need for powerful local personal computing devices. The Jolidrive service would most probably be well suited to delivery using the Stream Tone Transfer Protocol.

d)  **HOW IS IT LIKE THE STREAM TONE?** ✔ Replaces local functionality with Web-based services. ✔ Demonstrates the viability and user acceptance of Web-based services. ✔ Reliant on an active Internet connection. ✔ Provides access to all types of content and services. ✘ Streams all data; audio, visual, and other. ✔ Uses secure communications. ✔ Supports real-time interactivity. ✔ Uses a low-cost thin client. ✔ Reliant on remote computing resources. ✘ Based on free and open-source principles.

e)  **FURTHER READING**
Joli OS: *https://en.wikipedia.org/wiki/Joli_OS*
Jolidrive: *http://www.jolicloud.com/*

# 3.2.13   LAGOA

a)  **WHAT IS IT?** Lagoa is a *Web*-based, proprietary, unbiased, physically-based, photorealistic, three-dimensional (3D) model collaboration and rendering service that is provided by TeamUp Technologies, Inc. Lagoa also enables the efficient and effective refinement, finishing, and approval of 3D models. Models are created locally, using commonly available computer-aided design and 3D modelling applications, and then uploaded to Lagoa for refinement and rendering. Lagoa supports a wide range of standard 3D modelling formats. Once a model has been uploaded, objects within that model can then be changed in a variety of ways, including by colour, lighting, material, opacity, orientation, placement, size, texture, and visibility, to name but a few. Changes made to a model are then photorealistically rendered on *Cloud Computing*-based servers so that all collaborators can immediately view the results of the latest changes. Lagoa uses *Encryption* to secure all communications, and all model data, held on Lagoa servers, is regularly backed-up. The Lagoa rendering process is significantly faster than what a typical desktop computer, even one equipped with a powerful graphics processing unit (GPU), could achieve. Collaborators, who can be located anywhere in the world, are able to exchange messages about the current state of a model. Access to Lagoa requires only a relatively low-performance personal computing device with an *Internet* connection, and a *Web Browser* and GPU that both support the *Web* Graphics Library (WebGL). WebGL is also available in a software-only version on certain operating systems. WebGL is based on the Open Graphics Library for Embedded Systems. A **Web Browser** that provides WebGL support is able to natively render two-dimensional and 3D graphics without needing any third-party rendering software to be installed. Lagoa uses WebGL to display its application interface, which is used for editing a model and for collaboration, but not for photorealistic rendering. The Lagoa rendering system, called MultiOptics, accurately simulates the optical properties of real-world materials, and the way light interacts between such materials. Lagoa offers both free-of-charge (FOC) and paid service options. Publicly visible projects can be created with a FOC account, whilst private projects can only be created with a paid account. Paid accounts also provide much more rendering time than FOC accounts. Lagoa can help make the collaborative 3D modelling process cheaper and faster. More efficient and effective collaboration increases the probability that a model will ultimately meet requirements. Lagoa removes the need to repeatedly distribute updated model datasets to each collaborator, as only rendered images need to be sent when a model is changed. **Cloud Computing**-based rendering removes the need for all collaborators to purchase and maintain an expensive high-performance personal computing device that is capable of photorealistically rendering complex 3D models in a timely fashion. Lagoa is a new service that is growing in popularity.

b)   **IS THERE ANYTHING ELSE THAT IS SIMILAR?** Yes, there are a number of other **Web**-based 3D-model collaboration services currently available, including GrabCAD, GTeam, MyCadBox, Sunglass.io, and Verold Studio. There are also many other **Cloud Computing**-based rendering services such as Autodesk 360, BlenderCloud, FELIX, Fox RenderFarm, GarageFarm.NET, GreenButton, Limitless Computing, Octane Render Cloud Edition, Ranch Computing, Rebus Farm, Render Nation, Render Rocket, Render Street, RenderCore, RenderEvi, Renderfarm.es, Renderfarm.fi, RenderFarm.ie, Renderfarm.pl, RenderFlow, RenderMan On Demand, RenderMonk, RenderNow, RenderSolve, RenderTITAN, RevUp Render, Stratus Farm, Summus, UltraRender, XLRender, and ZYNC.

c)   **WHY WAS IT SELECTED?** Lagoa was selected as a Stream Tone precursor because it demonstrates that computationally demanding functionality, such as the photorealistic rendering of 3D models, which was previously executed on high-performance local personal computing devices, can be successfully moved onto **Web-based Services**. The collaborative process required to refine, finish, and approve 3D models can also be moved onto **Web-based Services**, yielding enhanced convenience, cost savings, and productivity. **Cloud Computing**-based Stream Tone Service Infrastructures will be used to provide a wide range of Stream Tone Transfer Protocol-based content and services, including rendering and collaboration services.

d)   **HOW IS IT LIKE THE STREAM TONE?** ✔ Replaces local functionality with Web-based services. ✔ Demonstrates the viability and user acceptance of Web-based services. ✔ Reliant on an active Internet connection. ✘ Provides access to all types of content and services. ✔ Streams all data; audio, visual, and other. ✔ Uses secure communications. ✔ Supports real-time interactivity. ✔ Uses a low-cost thin client. ✔ Reliant on remote computing resources. ✘ Based on free and open-source principles.

e)   **FURTHER READING**
Lagoa: *http://home.lagoa.com/*

# 3.2.14    LG 55G2

a) **WHAT IS IT?** The 55G2 is an *Energy Star*-qualified 55-inch *Internet*-enabled flat-screen television manufactured by LG Corporation. *Internet*-enabled televisions are also known as Smart TVs. The 55G2 has a liquid-crystal display screen with light-emitting diode-based edge lighting. The screen has a resolution of 1920 pixels by 1080 pixels, a refresh rate of 120 Hertz, and a dynamic contrast ratio of 6 million to 1. The 55G2 supports a comprehensive range of audio-visual connectors, as well as USB, Ethernet, and *Wi-Fi* interfaces. The 55G2 is able to display three-dimensional visual content. A wireless remote control incorporates a keyboard, microphone, and motion sensor. The 55G2 also contains a duel-core *Reduced Instruction Set Computing*-based microprocessor which is used to provide access to *Web*-based content and services. The 55G2 integrates Google TV technology from Google, Inc. Google TV includes the Google Chrome *Web Browser*, Google Voice Search, and Google Play Store. The Google Chrome *Web Browser* can be used for surfing the *Web*. Google Voice Search can be used for finding information stored on the *Web*, and for controlling many TV-based activities, using voice commands. The Google Play Store is a popular *Application Store* that provides access to a wide range of installable software applications. Google TV also makes available a wide range of professionally produced audio-visual content. The *OnLive* streaming-game service is available through Google TV. *Internet*-enabled televisions are a relatively recent invention, which are becoming increasingly popular. Google TV was superseded by Android TV in 2014.

b) **IS THERE ANYTHING ELSE THAT IS SIMILAR?** Yes, there are a number of other *Internet*-enabled televisions currently available, including Panasonic TX-L55WT50B, Phillips 55PFL8007T/12, Samsung UE75ES9000U, Sharp LC-60LE847U, Sony KDL-55HX853, Toshiba 55ZL2, and Vizio M3D550KDE, to name but a few. However, the LG 55G2 is currently one of only a few devices that use Google TV technology. Some of the other devices that also use Google TV technology include the Asus Cube, the Sony NSZ-GS7, and the Vizio Co-Star, which are all set-top boxes (STBs). Many more *Internet*-enabled televisions and STBs are expected to become available in the future.

c) **WHY WAS IT SELECTED?** The 55G2 from LG was selected as a Stream Tone precursor because it clearly demonstrates that personal computing, in the form of surfing the *Web* and running software applications, has successfully entered the living room. For many people an *Internet*-enabled television will be able to meet most of their home-based personal computing needs, certainly in terms of computer gaming and multimedia consumption. In the future, it is expected that *Internet*-enabled televisions will become a viable alternative to a traditional personal computing device, such as a desktop computer or laptop computer, for many simple tasks. Much of the content presented on an *Internet*-enabled television is delivered using data streaming communications. The Stream Tone Transfer Protocol will be used to communicate a wide range of digital content and services over the *Internet* from the *Web* to a Stream Tone Access Device, and send user-input back. The 55G2 is also notable for being the very first *Internet*-enabled television to provide access to the *OnLive* streaming-game service.

d) **HOW IS IT LIKE THE STREAM TONE?** ✔ Replaces local functionality with Web-based services. ✔ Demonstrates the viability and user acceptance of Web-based services. ✔ Reliant on an active Internet connection. ✔ Provides access to all types of content and services. ✔ Streams all data; audio, visual, and other. ✘ Uses secure communications. ✔ Supports real-time interactivity. ✔ Uses a low-cost thin client. ✔ Reliant on remote computing resources. ✘ Based on free and open-source principles.

e) **FURTHER READING**
Google TV: *http://www.google.com/tv/*
Google TV: *https://en.wikipedia.org/wiki/Google_TV*
LG 55G2: *http://www.lg.com/us/tvs/lg-55G2-led-tv*
OnLive: *http://www.onlive.com/*
OnLive: *https://en.wikipedia.org/wiki/OnLive*

# 3.2.15  MOLTEN DESKTOP-AS-A-SERVICE

a) **WHAT IS IT?** Molten Desktop-as-a-Service (Molten DAAS) is a commercial, *Web*-based *Hosted Desktop* service provided by Molten Technologies Ltd, part of Molten Group Ltd. Molten DAAS uses a client-server architecture in which a virtualised desktop operating system is hosted in a remotely-located *Cloud Computing*-based *Data Centre* and accessed over a computer network, such as the *Internet*, using a *Thin Client* device or software application. Dedicated *Thin Client* hardware uses less power than a typical desktop computer, and is easier to maintain. Existing desktop computers and laptop computers can also be re-purposed as *Thin Clients*, if required. The complex infrastructure required to host the virtual desktop is provided and maintained by Molten Technologies. Molten DAAS allows a customer to switch their budgets from capital expenditure, which would have been spent purchasing desktop infrastructure, to operational expenditure, for the leasing of *Hosted Desktops*. *Hosted Desktops* are often more secure and more reliable than many other in-house desktop-based personal computing solutions. Molten DAAS is built using a desktop-as-a-service (DAAS) platform from Desktone Inc.; a pioneer of multi-tenanted DAAS technologies. Desktone is a subsidiary of VMware, Inc. The Desktone DAAS platform allows *Cloud Computing*-based service providers to quickly and easily deploy highly-scalable *Hosted Desktop* solutions. The Desktone DAAS platform is also able to provide access to software applications. Molten DAAS is able to host a wide range of modern desktop-based and server-based operating systems. Molten DAAS supports a number of proprietary display protocols, including Microsoft Remote Display Protocol, Hewlett-Packard Remote Graphics Software, and Citrix Receiver. The *Hosted Desktop* offering from Molten Technologies is suitable for deployments ranging from hundreds of desktops to many thousands.

b) **IS THERE ANYTHING ELSE THAT IS SIMILAR?** Yes, there are a number of other *Hosted Desktop* providers that use the Desktone DAAS platform, including Champion Solutions Group, Cirrus Dynamics, Dell, Dimension Data, Fujitsu, GMO Cloud America, iDEA Consulting, Kumo, Marubeni Information Systems, NaviSite, Netelligent, O4IT, Quest, Single Path, tuCloud, and Xtium. There are also a number of other *Hosted Desktop* providers that use other DAAS platforms, including Applications2U, AT&T, CloudMyOffice, dinCloud, ICC Global Hosting, iland, mindSHIFT Technologies, nGenx, nivio, OnLive, Prolinx, RapidScale, SCC, Vesk, Virtuon, and ZettaGrid, to name but a few.

c) **WHY WAS IT SELECTED?** Molten DAAS was selected as a Stream Tone precursor because it clearly demonstrates the viability and practicality of moving the functionalities of local desktop computers onto *Web-based Services*. The technology required for building, running, and accessing *Hosted Desktops* already exists and is rapidly maturing.

Many millions of users are already using ***Hosted Desktops***. The Stream Tone Transfer Protocol will be used to communicate a wide range of ***Web***-based content and services, over the ***Internet***, including ***Hosted Desktops***.

d) **HOW IS IT LIKE THE STREAM TONE?** ✔ Replaces local functionality with Web-based services. ✔ Demonstrates the viability and user acceptance of Web-based services. ✔ Reliant on an active Internet connection. ✔ Provides access to all types of content and services. ✔ Streams all data; audio, visual, and other. ✔ Uses secure communications. ✔ Supports real-time interactivity. ✔ Uses a low-cost thin client. ✔ Reliant on remote computing resources. ✘ Based on free and open-source principles.

e) **FURTHER READING**
Desktone: *http://www.desktone.com/*
Molten Technologies: *http://www.moltentechnologies.com/*

# 3.2.16   NETFLIX

a) **WHAT IS IT?** Netflix is a postal-based DVD rental service, and a ***Web***-based video on demand (VOD) service, that streams films and television shows over the ***Internet***, and which is provided by Netflix, Inc. Netflix is an example of an ***Internet Television Service***. Netflix's postal-based service is only available in the United States of America. Netflix's streaming video service continues to expand and is now available in a number of geographies, including most of the Americas, and some parts of Europe. Netflix has a library of thousands of films and television shows. Netflix uses ***Digital Rights Management*** (DRM) to secure its streamed content. Under operating systems supporting approved DRM, streamed content can be viewed using a standard ***Web Browser***, or a dedicated software-based client application. Netflix streamed content can be viewed using a wide range of ***Internet***-enabled devices, including desktop computers, digital video recorders, disk players, games consoles, laptop computers, media players, set-top boxes, ***Smart-Phones***, ***Tablet Computers***, and televisions. Netflix makes extensive use of ***Content Delivery Networks***, which are able to cache content in close geographic proximity to its viewers, which helps to greatly reduce communications latency and pressure on the ***Internet*** as a whole. Netflix uses an adaptive bit-rate streaming mechanism that tailors its data streams to the current network environment, ensuring that videos continue to play even though quality may be temporarily reduced. Netflix uses the VC-1 video format to encode its content. The VC-1 video format provides high image quality and high ***Compression*** efficiency, characteristics that make it well suited to use in video streaming applications. The VC-1 video format is considered, in many respects, to be comparable to the ***H.264*** video format. Encoding and decoding video to and from VC-1 is computationally demanding and generally requires hardware-based acceleration. VC-1 is actually the informal name for the Society of Motion Picture and Television Engineers 421M video codec. VC-1 is based on a number of patented technologies, and its use may be subject to the payment of licensing fees. Netflix is a popular service that has tens of millions of subscribers, some of which have ceased to use other entertainment sources in favour of Netflix.

b) **IS THERE ANYTHING ELSE THAT IS SIMILAR?** Yes, there are a number of other VOD services available, including Amazon Prime, Hulu, and VuDu.

c) **WHY WAS IT SELECTED?** Netflix was selected as a Stream Tone precursor because it demonstrates the viability of moving visual entertainment functionality, previously delivered using physical media, onto **Web-based Services**. This is the type of digital service that will help to build society's acceptance and trust of **Web**-based entertainment services and reduce the need for physical entertainment media. The Netflix service could be considered to be conceptually similar to audio-visual entertainment services that will be communicated using the Stream Tone Transfer Protocol.

d) **HOW IS IT LIKE THE STREAM TONE?** ✔ Replaces local functionality with Web-based services. ✔ Demonstrates the viability and user acceptance of Web-based services. ✔ Reliant on an active Internet connection. ✘ Provides access to all types of content and services. ✔ Streams all data; audio, visual, and other. ✔ Uses secure communications. ✔ Supports real-time interactivity. ✔ Uses a low-cost thin client. ✔ Reliant on remote computing resources. ✘ Based on free and open-source principles.

e) **FURTHER READING**
Netflix: *https://signup.netflix.com/global*
Netflix: *https://en.wikipedia.org/wiki/Netflix*

# 3.2.17 NVIDIA VGX-K1

a) **WHAT IS IT?** The VGX-K1 is a hardware-based graphics card, with four entry-level Kepler-class graphics processing units (GPUs) that is designed for use in large-scale, centralised, virtualisation environments, and which is manufactured by Nvidia Corporation. The VGX-K1 supports both two-dimensional and three-dimensional (3D) graphics. The VGX-K1 supports the Microsoft DirectX, Nvidia Compute Unified Device Architecture, and Open Graphics Language **Application Programming Interface** standards. Each GPU on the VGX-K1 contains 192 processing cores that are able to execute in parallel. The VGX-K1 supports real-time **H.264** video encoding. The VGX-K1 has 16 gigabytes of random-access memory, and is capable of supporting the basic graphics processing needs of up to 100 simultaneous users. The VGX-K1 is optimised for low-latency remote display applications that are delivered over a local area network, wide area network, or even the **Internet**. The VGX-K1 is compatible with a number of different virtual desktop infrastructure (VDI) technologies, including **Citrix High-Definition User Experience**. Depending on how it is deployed, the video output from a VGX-K1, communicated as a real-time data stream, can be accessed using a **Thin Client** computer, a software-based client application, or a standard **Web Browser**. The VGX-K1 is a component of the Nvidia GRID, which is an elastic, demand-based, **Cloud Computing** platform that supports a wide range of uses, including the generation of graphical user-interfaces for **Hosted Desktops**, remotely-executed software applications, and **Web Desktops.** The VGX-K1 can also be used for **Web**-based computer gaming, and the photorealistic rendering of 3D models in real-time. The VGX-K1 represents a cost-effective means of remotely generating graphically rich content for use by a large numbers of users.

b) **IS THERE ANYTHING ELSE THAT IS SIMILAR?** Yes, the Advanced Micro Devices FirePro S10000 graphics card is capable of providing both remote graphics solutions and VDI solutions to multiple users. Also, the graphics cards typically found in desktop computers can also be deployed in **Cloud Computing**-based **Data Centres** although they are not generally able to support large numbers of simultaneous users.

184

c) **WHY WAS IT SELECTED?** The VGX-K1 was selected as a Stream Tone precursor because it demonstrates that the physical infrastructure needed to provide useful and cost-effective *Web-based Services* is actively being designed, developed, and deployed. The digital content and services that will be communicated using the Stream Tone Transfer Protocol will be provided by *Cloud Computing*-based Stream Tone Service Infrastructures (STSIs). Advanced graphics processing technologies, such as the VGX-K1, can support the data processing needs of many remote users, and could become a key element of STSIs.

d) **HOW COULD IT ENABLE THE STREAM TONE?** ✘ Provides technology on free and open-source terms. ✘ Expands Internet availability. ✘ Improves the quality of Internet connectivity. ✘ Increases communications bandwidth. ✘ Reduces Internet access costs. ✔ Enables Web-based service provision. ✔ Improves the quality of Web-based service delivery. ✔ Improves the power efficiency of mobile computing devices. ✘ Enables technology deployment.

e) **FURTHER READING**
Nvidia GRID: *http://www.nvidia.com/object/enterprise-virtualization.html*
Nvidia GRID K1 Graphics Board:
*http://www.nvidia.com/content/grid/pdf/GRID_K1_BD-06633-001_v02.pdf*

# 3.2.18   ONLIVE

a) **WHAT IS IT?** OnLive is a *Web*-based computer game and *Hosted Desktop* streaming service that can be accessed via the *Internet*, and which is provided by OL2, Inc. The OnLive service is an example of a *Cloud Computing*-based computer gaming service, also known as a cloud-gaming service. Hundreds of top-tier computer games are available to play via a monthly subscription to the PlayPack service. OnLive has also partnered with Steam, a digital computer game distribution service owned by Valve Corporation, to offer the CloudLift subscription service that provides streamed access to a number computer games that are also available for purchase and download from Steam. The OnLive Go service is a hosting platform for use by *Massively Multi-Player On-line Game* and virtual world providers that can be used to test games that are still in development or to simplify access to existing games. The first virtual world hosted by the OnLive Go service was Second Life, which was developed by Linden Research, Inc. The OnLive gaming service permits short videos of game play, known as Brag Clips, to be recorded and shared with other users. The OnLive Arena allows games currently in progress to be viewed by spectators. The OnLive service can be accessed from any supported personal computing device that has good *Internet*-based connectivity to an OnLive *Data Centre*, even if the personal computing device used for such access is not powerful enough to directly run a top-tier computer game or *Hosted Desktop* environment. The computer games and *Hosted Desktops* provided by OnLive are executed on custom *Cloud Computing*-based servers. OnLive's servers also convert the game and *Hosted Desktop* graphics into *H.264* video streams, ready for transmission to remotely-located users via the *Internet*. OnLive has *Data Centres*, which house its servers, located in a number of geographies in order to minimise communications latencies. OnLive recommends that users should be physically located within 1,000 miles of an OnLive *Data Centre* in order to experience a responsive interactive service. At a minimum, users should have a 2 megabit per second (Mbps) *Internet* connection for accessing the OnLive computer gaming service; although OnLive recommends a 5 Mbps connection in order to obtain an optimal gameplay experience. At a minimum, users should have a 1 Mbps *Internet* connection for accessing the OnLive Desktop service; although OnLive recommends a 2 Mbps connection in order to obtain an optimal *Hosted Desktop* experience. OnLive services are accessed using a software-based client, or a hardware-based micro-console that runs a *Linux*-based operating system. Dependent on the operating system being used, the software client is either a dedicated software application or a *Web Browser* plug-in. The OnLive service supports access from a number of popular operating systems and a wide variety of *Internet*-enabled devices, including games consoles, desktop computers, laptop computers, *Smart-Phones*, *Tablet Computers*, and televisions. Both the software client and the micro-console support the use of peripherals, such as game controllers, keyboards, and mice. Game controllers typically connect to the micro-console using wireless communications, and keyboards and mice typically connect via the USB interface. The micro-console also includes connections for audio, network, and video. Computer games and *Hosted Desktops* provided by the OnLive service are displayed in high resolution; 1,280 pixels by 720 pixels. OnLive computer games are often run with high quality settings enabled, which ensures that visual effects, such as lighting, particles, reflections, shadows, and textures, are realistically portrayed. Video quality can be very good, similar to using a locally installed and executed computer game, but can sometimes be reduced due to the variable nature of *Internet*-based communications. The OnLive Desktop service provides access to an individualised *Hosted Desktop* environment based on the Microsoft Windows Server operating system, which has the Microsoft Office applications of Excel, PowerPoint, and Word pre-installed. The Adobe Reader software application is also available. The OnLive Desktop service includes a *File Hosting Service* to store data files created within the *Hosted Desktop* environment. The basic version of the OnLive Desktop service is available free-of-charge (FOC). Versions of the OnLive Desktop service with more features, such as more file storage, are available for a monthly fee. New applications cannot be installed into the FOC version of the OnLive Desktop service. The most expensive version of the OnLive Desktop service allows the installation of a limited range of pre-approved third-party software applications. Most configuration settings for the operating system and desktop environment of an OnLive Desktop are disabled, having been pre-set by OnLive in order to deliver an optimal user-experience. The subscription-based versions of the OnLive Desktop service include *Web Browser*-based access to the *Web* via a high-bandwidth *Internet* connection.

b) **IS THERE ANYTHING ELSE THAT IS SIMILAR?** Yes; *Web*-based computer gaming services are available from CloudUnion, Core Online, G Cloud, GFACE, Orange France, Shinra Technologies, and SFR. Platforms for building *Web*-based computer gaming services are available from Agawi, Approxy, CiiNOW, G-Cluster, Gaikai, Otoy, Playcast, and Ubitus GameCloud. Many new *Web*-based computer gaming platforms and services are expected to emerge over the coming years as the *Web*-based computer gaming industry develops, matures, and substantially expands.

c) **WHY WAS IT SELECTED?** OnLive was selected as a Stream Tone precursor because it demonstrates the viability of moving local functionality, such as computer gaming and desktop computing, that was previously executed on a local personal computing device, onto *Web-based Services*. These are the types of *Web-based Services* that will help to build society's trust in remote personal computing, and reduce the need for powerful personal computing devices. The OnLive service could be considered to be conceptually similar to Stream Tone Transfer Protocol-based computer gaming services. The OnLive micro-console could be considered to be conceptually similar to a Stream Tone Access

Device.

d) **HOW IS IT LIKE THE STREAM TONE?** ✔ Replaces local functionality with Web-based services. ✔ Demonstrates the viability and user acceptance of Web-based services. ✔ Reliant on an active Internet connection. ✗ Provides access to all types of content and services. ✔ Streams all data; audio, visual, and other. ✗ Uses secure communications. ✔ Supports real-time interactivity. ✔ Uses a low-cost thin client. ✔ Reliant on remote computing resources. ✗ Based on free and open-source principles.

e) **FURTHER READING**
OnLive: *http://www.onlive.com/*
OnLive: *https://en.wikipedia.org/wiki/OnLive*

# 3.2.19    OPERA

a) **WHAT IS IT?** Opera is a free, highly capable, modern, *Web Browser* that supports *HyperText Markup Language Version 5*, and which is provided by Opera Software ASA. The Opera *Web Browser* supports the delivery of *Web*-based content and services, via the *Internet*, including *Cloud Computing* services, *File Hosting Services*, *Hosted Desktops*, *Instant Messaging* services, *Internet Television Services*, *Massively Multi-player On-line Games*, *Streamed Services*, *Streaming Media*, and *Web Desktops*. The Opera *Web Browser* is available for use on a wide range of operating systems, such as FreeBSD, *Linux*, OS X, Solaris, and Windows. The Opera *Web Browser* is suitable for use on different types of personal computing device, including desktop computers, laptop computers, *Smart-Phones*, and *Tablet Computers*. One particularly notable feature of the Opera *Web Browser* is that it has a special mode of operation, known as Turbo Mode, which supports compressed *Web* page data. *Web* page *Compression* is handled by Opera computer servers, which provide an intermediary, or proxy, service to the Opera *Web Browser*. A *Web* page request, made by a user using an Opera *Web Browser* is firstly sent to an Opera computer server, which then downloads the *Web* page and compresses it, before forwarding the compressed data to the Opera *Web Browser* for decompression and display. Compressed *Web* page data is quantitatively smaller than the original, uncompressed, *Web* page data and can, consequently, be transmitted much more quickly over computer networks, such as the *Internet*. Turbo Mode is particularly useful when used with low-bandwidth communications services. The Opera *Web Browser* is expected to add video *Compression* functionality in the future. Opera is a popular *Web Browser* that is often installed on portable personal computing devices, and which is used by hundreds of millions of people, all around the world.

b) **IS THERE ANYTHING ELSE THAT IS SIMILAR?** Yes, there are a number of other *Web Browser*s currently available, including Amazon Silk, Chrome, Dolphin Browser, Firefox, *Internet* Explorer, and Safari. Opera also makes two *Web Browsers* for use on *Smart-Phones* and *Tablet Computers*; Opera Mini, and Opera Mobile, both of which support *Compression*-based *Internet* access.

c) **WHY WAS IT SELECTED?** The Opera *Web Browser* was selected as a Stream Tone precursor because it is a free-of-charge software-based *Thin Client*, designed for accessing *Web*-based content and services that could be considered conceptually similar to a Stream Tone Access Device. The Opera *Web Browser's* Turbo Mode is also an example of a *Web-based Service* that repackages *Web*-based content and services that could be considered conceptually similar to certain envisioned operational aspects of the Stream Tone.

d) **HOW IS IT LIKE THE STREAM TONE?** ✘ Replaces local functionality with Web-based services. ✔ Demonstrates the viability and user acceptance of Web-based services. ✔ Reliant on an active Internet connection. ✔ Provides access to all types of content and services. ✘ Streams all data; audio, visual, and other. ✔ Uses secure communications. ✔ Supports real-time interactivity. ✔ Uses a low-cost thin client. ✔ Reliant on remote computing resources. ✘ Based on free and open-source principles.

e) **FURTHER READING**
Opera: *http://www.opera.com/*
Opera (Web Browser): *https://en.wikipedia.org/wiki/Opera_%28web_browser%29*

# 3.2.20  PEPPERMINT

a) **WHAT IS IT?** Peppermint is a *Web*-oriented *Linux*-based desktop operating system, which was developed by Peppermint LLC. Peppermint is available under a *Free and Open-Source Software* license. The Peppermint operating system is designed to support the on-going transition of local personal computing to *Web*-based personal computing. Peppermint is built on the assumption that most commonly needed digital content and services can increasingly be obtained from the *Web*. Unlike many other *Linux* distributions, the Peppermint operating system only provides a minimal set of pre-installed software applications. Any functionality that is not yet available from the *Web* can be installed and run locally, if required. New links to *Web*-based content and services can be easily added to the Peppermint menu and desktop. As with most local desktop operating systems, the desktop environment can be heavily customised. Links to *Web*-based content and services activate a *Site-Specific Browser* that displays that content or services in a simplified *Web Browser* display window.

b) **IS THERE ANYTHING ELSE THAT IS SIMILAR?** Yes, there are a number of other *Web*-oriented operating systems available, including, Baidu Cloud Smart, BrowserLinux, Chrome OS, Firefox OS, Joli OS, and Yun OS.

c) **WHY WAS IT SELECTED?** The Peppermint operating system was selected as a Stream Tone precursor because it is a technology that supports both local and *Web*-based personal computing. As more and more digital content and services are moved onto the *Web*, desktop operating systems, such as Peppermint, can help to seamlessly support a mixed environment of local and *Web-based Services* whilst providing a consistent user-experience. The existence of the Peppermint operating system clearly indicates that the transition from local personal computing to Comprehensive Remote Personal Computing is well under way.

d) **HOW IS IT LIKE THE STREAM TONE?** ✔ Replaces local functionality with Web-based services. ✔ Demonstrates the viability and user acceptance of Web-based services. ✔ Reliant on an active Internet connection. ✔ Provides access to all types of content and services. ✘ Streams all data; audio, visual, and other. ✔ Uses secure communications. ✔ Supports real-time interactivity. ✔ Uses a low-cost thin client. ✔ Reliant on remote computing resources. ✔ Based on free and open-source principles.

e) **FURTHER READING**
Peppermint: *http://peppermintos.com/*
Peppermint Linux OS: *https://en.wikipedia.org/wiki/Peppermint_Linux_OS*

# 3.2.21   QUALCOMM MDM9625

a) **WHAT IS IT?** The Mobile Data Modem 9625 (MDM9625) is a thin form-factor *Application Specific Integrated Circuit* that provides wireless mobile communications functionality, and which was developed by Qualcomm, Inc., using a 28 nanometre fabrication process. The MDM9625 is part of the *Fourth-Generation Mobile Communications* (4G) Long-Term Evolution-Advanced (LTE-Advanced) range of Qualcomm Gobi Modems. The MDM9625 has a higher performance and uses power more efficiently than previous generations of this product range. The MDM9625 supports a wide range of second, third, and fourth generation mobile communications standards. The MDM9625 includes Global Navigation Satellite System support for enhanced location-based services. The MDM9625 includes a power-efficient *Reduced Instruction Set Computing*-based microprocessor, as well as support for USB version 2.0, and *Wi-Fi*. The MDM9625 is designed for use in a wide range of wireless devices, including laptop computers, mobile hotspots, network routers, portable game systems, power-line network adaptors, smart meters, *Smart-Phones*, speakers, *Tablet Computers*, and USB dongles. The MDM9625 supports data download speeds of up to 150 megabits per second (Mbps) and upload speeds of up to 50 Mbps on 4G networks based on the LTE-Advanced standard. The MDM9625 can be used in conjunction with the *Qualcomm RF360 Front End Solution* to build a 4G device that supports high-bandwidth communications and which will work anywhere in the world. The technology behind the MDM9625 is expected to become incorporated into many other mobile communications components in the future.

b) **IS THERE ANYTHING ELSE THAT IS SIMILAR?** Yes, there are a number of other wireless modems available that support data transfer speeds of up to 150 Mbps, including Broadcom BCM21892, HiSilicon Technologies Balong 710, Marvell Technologies PXA1801 and PXA1802, Qualcomm MDM9225, Renesas Mobile SP2532, and Sequans SQN3110, SQN3120, and SQN5120. The NVIDIA Tegra 4i *System on a Chip*, which includes a LTE-Advanced and an Evolved High Speed Packet Access baseband processor, can also support mobile communications bandwidths of up to 150 Mbps.

c) **WHY WAS IT SELECTED?** The MDM9625 was selected as a Stream Tone precursor because it clearly demonstrates that the technology needed to support next generation mobile communications standards is actively being designed, developed, and deployed. The high bandwidth supported by the latest generations of wireless modems, such as the MDM9625, will be sufficient for communicating a wide range of content and services using the Stream Tone Transfer Protocol.

d) **HOW COULD IT ENABLE THE STREAM TONE?** ✘ Provides technology on free and open-source terms. ✘ Expands Internet availability. ✔ Improves the quality of Internet connectivity. ✔ Increases communications bandwidth. ✘ Reduces Internet access costs. ✔ Enables Web-based service provision. ✔ Improves the quality of Web-based service delivery. ✔ Improves the power efficiency of mobile computing devices. ✔ Enables technology deployment.

e) **FURTHER READING**
Gobi Product Specs: *http://www.qualcomm.com/media/documents/gobi-product-specs*
Qualcomm Gobi Modems: *http://www.qualcomm.com/chipsets/gobi*
Qualcomm Third Generation LTE Chipsets Are First To Support HSPA+ Release 10, LTE Advanced With LTE Carrier Aggregation:
*http://www.qualcomm.com/media/releases/2012/02/27/qualcomm-third-generation-lte-chipsets-are-first-support-hspa-release-10*

# 3.2.22 QUALCOMM RF360 FRONT END SOLUTION

a) **WHAT IS IT?** The RF360 Front End Solution (RF360 FES), launched in 2013, is a family of small form factor *Application-Specific Integrated Circuits*, developed by Qualcomm, Inc., which can be used to create a single design for a mobile communications subsystem that is capable of supporting all mobile communications standards currently in worldwide use. In simple terms, a front end solution handles the transmission and receipt of analogue radio signals, providing an interface between the antenna and the digital processing systems of a typical wireless communications device. In marketing terms, there are currently three generations of digital mobile communications standards in active use worldwide. Each generation supports a number of different communications technologies. Second-generation mobile communications (2G) uses Global System for Mobile Communications and Code Division Multiple Access. Third-generation mobile communications (3G) uses Enhanced Voice-Data Optimised/Only, Universal Mobile Telecommunications System, and High-Speed Packet Access. *Fourth-Generation Mobile Communications* (4G) uses Long-Term Evolution and Long-Term Evolution-Advanced. Mobile communications implementations within specific geographic regions typically support some but not all of these technologies. Additionally, different geographies allocate different parts of the radio spectrum for use with each mobile communications technology. Devices designed for use in one geographic region will not work in another geographic region that uses different radio frequencies, different mobile communications technologies, or both. The inconsistent use of mobile communications technologies and radio frequencies is known as fragmentation, and currently there are approximately 40 different mobile communications implementations in use worldwide. In an attempt to overcome this fragmentation, and to be able to support multiple geographic regions, mobile communications device manufacturers developed products that contained multiple mobile communications subsystems; one for each supported geographic region. This was, however, an imperfect approach as only a few geographic regions could realistically be supported due to the limited space available within many portable communications devices, such as *Smart-Phones* and *Tablet Computers*. Therefore, in order to support all the different mobile communications implementations in global use, a large number of distinct communications devices still had to be designed, developed, and deployed; an expensive and time consuming process. The RF360 FES now allows mobile device manufacturers to design a single version of their product that will work with all mobile communications technologies and radio frequencies currently in worldwide use; effectively solving the fragmentation problem. The RF360 FES should help manufacturers to reduce their design, development, and deployment costs, which should lead to more affordable mobile communications devices in the future. The RF360 FES includes a number of components: QFE15xx, a dynamic antenna matching tuner; QFE11xx, an envelope power tracker;

QFE23xx, an integrated power amplifier and antenna switch; and QFE27xx, a multi-mode multi-band power amplifier and antenna switch combined with the associated filters and duplexers required to support 2G, 3G, and 4G radio frequencies. The RF360 FES can be used in conjunction with the **Qualcomm MDM9625** to build devices that support high-bandwidth communications and which will work anywhere in the world. The technology behind the RF360 FES is expected to become incorporated into many other mobile communications components in the future.

b) **IS THERE ANYTHING ELSE THAT IS SIMILAR?** No, when the RF360 FES from Qualcomm was launched it was the only compact solution, suitable for practical inclusion into portable devices, and which provided worldwide support for all currently deployed 2G, 3G, and 4G standards. A number of other companies, such as Avago, Broadcom, EPCOS, Fujitsu, Huawei, Innofidei, Intel, IQE, Lime Microsystems, NetLogic, Nujira, Peregrine Semiconductor, RF Micro Devices, Skyworks Solutions, Texas Instruments, and TriQuint, also make front end solutions or components for mobile communications, although not all are aimed at the portable device market.

c) **WHY WAS IT SELECTED?** The RF360 FES was selected as a Stream Tone precursor because it clearly demonstrates that the technology needed to support ubiquitous access to next generation mobile communications systems is actively being designed, developed, and deployed. The RF360 FES allows mobile communications devices to be used anywhere in the world without the need to tailor such devices to geographic region-specific mobile communications technologies or radio frequencies. The Stream Tone needs both wired and wireless telecommunications that are highly affordable, high bandwidth, low latency, highly reliable, and ubiquitously available. Mobile communications component technologies, such as the RF360 FES, could be used to develop an affordable and power-efficient Stream Tone Access Device that will be usable anywhere in the world.

d) **HOW COULD IT ENABLE THE STREAM TONE?** ✘ Provides technology on free and open-source terms. ✔ Expands Internet availability. ✔ Improves the quality of Internet connectivity. ✔ Increases communications bandwidth. ✔ Reduces Internet access costs. ✔ Enables Web-based service provision. ✔ Improves the quality of Web-based service delivery. ✔ Improves the power efficiency of mobile computing devices. ✔ Enables technology deployment.

e) **FURTHER READING**
Qualcomm RF360 Front End Solution: *http://www.qualcomm.com/chipsets/gobi/rf-solutions/qualcomm-rf360-front-end*
Qualcomm RF360 Front End Solution Enables Single, Global LTE Design for Next-Generation Mobile Devices:
*http://www.qualcomm.com/media/releases/2013/02/21/qualcomm-rf360-front-end-solution-enables-single-global-lte-design-next*
Qualcomm RF360 Front End Solution Product Brief:
*http://www.qualcomm.com/media/documents/qualcommr-rf360-front-end-solution-product-brief*

# 3.2.23   SHARP AQUOS ZETA SH-02E

a) **WHAT IS IT?** The Aquos Zeta SH-02E (SH-02E) is a **Smart-Phone** manufactured by

Sharp Corporation. The SH-02E is powered by a quad-core **Reduced Instruction Set Computing**-based microprocessor that runs at 1.5 gigahertz. The SH-02E has 4.9-inch thin-film transistor liquid-crystal display screen with an **Indium Gallium Zinc Oxide** (IGZO) backplane. The IGZO-based display is more power efficient than traditional display designs, and can allow the SH-02E to run for almost two days, under normal usage conditions, before its battery requires recharging. Previous **Smart-Phone** designs, used similarly, required daily charging.

b) **IS THERE ANYTHING ELSE THAT IS SIMILAR?** Yes, there are many other **Smart-Phones** currently available, including the Acer Liquid E1, Alcatel One Touch Scribe X, Apple iPhone 5, Asus PadFone 2, Blackberry Z10, BLU Vivo 4.65, Celkon A225, Gigabyte Maya M1, Huawei Ascend P2, HTC One, Icemobile Galaxy Prime Plus, Karbonn S5 Titanium, Kyocera Torque, Lenovo IdeaPhone K860, LG Optimus G Pro, Micromax A116 Canvas HD, Meizu MX2, Motorola Droid RAZR HD, NIU NiuTek 3G 4.0, Nokia Lumia 920, Panasonic ELUGA Power, Pantech Vega Iron, Plum Might, Samsumg Galaxy S IV, Sony Xperia Z, Spice Stellar Pinnacle Mi-530, Toshiba Regza T-02D, verykool S758, Xiaomi MI-2, Yezz Andy 3G 4.0, and ZTE Grand Memo, to name but a few. However, the Sharp Aquos Zeta SH-02E is one of only a relatively few devices that currently use an IGZO-based display screen, some of the others are the Asus PadPhone 2, Dell XPS 15, Sharp Aquos Pad SHT21, Sharp Aquos Phone EX SH-02F, Sharp Aquos Phone Zeta SH-01F, Sharp Mebius Pad, Sharp PN-K321, and Sharp RW-16G. More devices featuring IGZO-based display screens are expected to become available in the future.

c) **WHY WAS IT SELECTED?** The SH-02E was selected as a Stream Tone precursor because it clearly demonstrates that the highly power-efficient electronic components needed to build the next generation of portable electronic devices are actively being designed, developed, and deployed. The Stream Tone Access Device (STAD) will need to be based on highly power-efficient components, such as display screens with IGZO backplanes, in order to ensure that it can actively function for extended periods of time before its batteries require recharging. By reducing the power consumed by STAD subsystems, such as the display screen, more power can be made available for use by the wireless communications subsystem, which will be required to operate continuously.

d) **HOW COULD IT ENABLE THE STREAM TONE?** ✘ Provides technology on free and open-source terms. ✘ Expands Internet availability. ✘ Improves the quality of Internet connectivity. ✘ Increases communications bandwidth. ✘ Reduces Internet access costs. ✘ Enables Web-based service provision. ✘ Improves the quality of Web-based service delivery. ✔ Improves the power efficiency of mobile computing devices. ✘ Enables technology deployment.

e) **FURTHER READING**
Aquos Phone Zeta SH-02 (Translated From Japanese Into English):
*http://translate.google.com/translate?hl=en&sl=ja&u=http://www.sharp.co.jp/products/s h02e/&prev=/search%3Fq%3DSHARP%2BAQUOS%2BZETA%2BSH-02E%26hl%3Den%26biw%3D1640%26bih%3D933*

# 3.2.24 SINGAPORE THIRD-GENERATION MOBILE QUALITY OF SERVICE FRAMEWORK

a) **WHAT IS IT?** The Singapore Third-Generation Mobile Quality of Service Framework (3G Mobile QOS Framework) is a consumer protection measure that was put in place by the Infocomm Development Authority of Singapore (IDA), and which came into effect in April 2012, with the objective of raising the minimum quality of service (QOS) standards for third-generation mobile communications (3G) services across the island of Singapore. The 3G Mobile QOS Framework set minimum standards in a number of areas, including peak hour call success rates, call drop rates, barring of premium rate services, limiting of data roaming charges, and the publication of typically available broadband speeds. Mobile telecommunications service providers (TSPs) were also required to provide mobile telecommunications services with 99 percent coverage, or better, to all outdoor areas, 99 percent coverage, or better, within each new road and mass rapid transit (MRT) tunnel, and 95 percent coverage, or better, within each existing road and MRT tunnel. Coverage within all buildings was to be increased to at least 85 percent, by April 2013. Many people in Singapore regularly travel by public transport. In fact, Singapore is one of the few countries in the world where is practical to not own a car because its public transport system is so affordable and effective. It is, therefore, of both economic and social importance that all travellers are able to access a full range of mobile telecommunications services throughout all parts of a public transport journey. *Regulations*, such as the 3G Mobile QOS Framework, can help to ensure that, regardless of whether a passenger is waiting at a station or travelling by bus, taxi, or train, either above or below ground, reliable 3G services are almost certain to be available. *Fourth-Generation Mobile Communications* services are also now available in Singapore, and are expected to become just as accessible and just as reliable as the current 3G services within a very short period of time.

b) **IS THERE ANYTHING ELSE THAT IS SIMILAR?** Yes, mobile telecommunications services are also available, to some degree, within the stations and tunnels of many other rail networks around the world, including Beijing Subway in China, Berlin U-Bahn in Germany, Budapest Subway in Hungary, Dubai Metro in the United Arab Emirates, Glasgow Subway in the United Kingdom, Moscow Metro in Russia, New York Subway in the United States of America, Paris Metro in France, Prague Metro in the Czech Republic, São Paulo Metro in Brazil, Soul Metropolitan Subway in South Korea, Sydney CityRail in Australia, and Tokyo Metro in Japan. In all cases, it is reasonable to assume that some form of *Regulation* was issued by the various government departments responsible for the use of radio spectrum and/or transport facilities in order to make such services available.

c) **WHY WAS IT SELECTED?** The Singapore 3G Mobile QOS Framework was selected as a Stream Tone precursor because it clearly demonstrates that ubiquitously available mobile telecommunications services can rely just as much upon effective government *Regulation* as upon the deployment of physical telecommunications infrastructure. *Regulation*, such as the Singapore 3G Mobile QOS Framework, requires incumbent mobile TSPs to provide a consistent QOS across a whole geographic region, and not just to the most commercially profitable areas within that region. The Stream Tone needs both wired and wireless telecommunications that are highly affordable, high bandwidth, low latency, highly reliable, and ubiquitously available. *Regulation*, such as the Singapore 3G

Mobile QOS Framework, can help to ensure that the digital content and services that will be communicated using the Stream Tone Transfer Protocol will be available from every location and situation required.

d) **HOW COULD IT ENABLE THE STREAM TONE?** ✔ Provides technology on free and open-source terms. ✔ Expands Internet availability. ✔ Improves the quality of Internet connectivity. ✗ Increases communications bandwidth. ✗ Reduces Internet access costs. ✔ Enables Web-based service provision. ✔ Improves the quality of Web-based service delivery. ✗ Improves the power efficiency of mobile computing devices. ✔ Enables technology deployment.

e) **FURTHER READING**
IDA Raises Quality of Service Standards for 3G Mobile Services to Improve Consumer Experience: *https://www.ida.gov.sg/About-Us/Newsroom/Media-Releases/2012/IDA-Raises-Quality-of-Service-Standards-for-3G-Mobile-Services-to-Improve-Consumer-Experience.aspx*

# 3.2.25   SIRI

a) **WHAT IS IT?** Siri is a natural speech-based intelligent personal assistant and knowledge navigator made by Apple, Inc. Siri uses a voice-independent speech recognition system that works without user-specific training. Siri automatically refines its speech recognition system, and its accuracy improves with use. Siri is integrated into Apple's iOS version 5, and above, operating system, which is designed for use on Apple mobile personal computing devices, such as **Smart-Phones** and **Tablet Computers**. Siri requires an active **Internet** connection in order to work. Siri simultaneously converts speech into text-based instructions using both the local device, as well as on powerful, remotely-located, **Cloud Computing**-based servers. Server-based conversion is more accurate but it is not always needed if the spoken instructions are simple and easily translated. If the instructions can be handled directly on the mobile device then further remote data processing is not required. If the instructions are more complex or spoken less intelligibly then they will be executed on remote servers, with results sent back to the local device, often within a couple of seconds. Siri works with a wide range of iOS software applications and services, including alarms, application launch, calendar, contacts, Facebook, Facetime, Find My Friends, local search, mail, maps, messages, movies, music, notes, phone, reminders, sports, stocks, timer, Twitter, weather, **Web** search, Wikipedia, Wolfram|Alpha, and world clock. The speech-to-text functionality used by Siri is also available to any software application that uses the virtual keyboard; allowing text-based content to be easily dictated. Siri supports a number of different languages, including Chinese (Cantonese and Mandarin), English, French, German, Italian, Japanese, Korean, and Spanish. Country specific accents and dialects are also supported for Australia, Canada, China, France, Germany, Hong Kong, Italy, Japan, Korea, Mexico, Spain, Switzerland, Taiwan, United Kingdom, and United States of America. The speech-to-text functionality provided within iOS is suitable for use by both the visually impaired and unimpaired. iOS also provides text-to-speech functionality which when combined with Siri forms the basis of a complete speech-based personal computing solution. The speech-to-text translation system used by Siri is capable of understanding natural speech, and is able to remember context between sentences. Siri permits some fairly sophisticated verbal exchanges, such as "Is it going to be chilly in Boston this weekend?" to which Siri might reply "Not too cold, maybe down to 59 degrees in Boston". Responding to this answer with a further question of "What about New York?" might then yield the response "Doesn't seem like it". Siri is location aware and can tailor its responses to the user's current location or to pre-configured locations, permitting instructions such as "What's the traffic like around here?". Contacts can be defined based on their relationship to the user, permitting instructions such as "Text my mother I'm going to be thirty minutes late". The use of voice-controlled personal assistants and knowledge navigators is becoming increasingly popular, and, like the keyboards and mice that preceded them, are expected to become a standard method for interfacing with personal computing devices in the future.

b) **IS THERE ANYTHING ELSE THAT IS SIMILAR?** Yes, there are a number of other voice-controlled software applications available for use on mobile personal computing devices, including AIVC by YourApp24, Angie by xBrainSoft, Assistant by Speaktoit, Dragon Go! by Nuance, EVA Intern by BulletProof, Evi by True Knowledge, Iris by dexetra, Jeannie by Pannous, Maluuba International by Maluuba, Now by Google, S Voice by Samsung, Sherpa Virtual Assistant by Sherpa, Skyvi by BlueTornado, Speech Recognition by Microsoft, utter! by brandall, Voice Command by Vlingo, Voice Control by Blackberry, and Voice Search by Google.

c) **WHY WAS IT SELECTED?** Siri was selected as a Stream Tone precursor because it is a *Web-based Service* that relies on a continuous connection to the *Internet* in order to work with high accuracy. The Stream Tone Access Device will be used to access Stream Tone Transfer Protocol-based content and services, and will rely on a continuous connection to the *Internet* in order to work. The popularity of *Web-based Services*, such as Siri, demonstrates that society now understands and accepts the need for continuous connectivity to the *Internet* in order to be able to use such services.

d) **HOW IS IT LIKE THE STREAM TONE?** ✔ Replaces local functionality with Web-based services. ✔ Demonstrates the viability and user acceptance of Web-based services. ✔ Reliant on an active Internet connection. ✔ Provides access to all types of content and services. ✘ Streams all data; audio, visual, and other. ✘ Uses secure communications. ✔ Supports real-time interactivity. ✔ Uses a low-cost thin client. ✔ Reliant on remote computing resources. ✘ Based on free and open-source principles.

e) **FURTHER READING**
Siri: *https://www.apple.com/ios/siri/*
Siri: *https://en.wikipedia.org/wiki/Siri*

# 3.2.26   SKYPE

a) **WHAT IS IT?** Skype is a commercial *Voice over Internet Protocol* (VOIP) telephony service, owned by Microsoft Corporation. The service allows users to communicate internationally, free-of-charge, by *Instant Messaging*, voice, and video, over the *Internet*. Skype also supports voice and video conference calling. Voice calls to landline-based telephones and mobile-phones are chargeable. Skype users are also able to receive incoming calls from landline-based telephone and mobile-phones, as well as other Skype users. The Skype service has also been used for educational purposes, such as distance learning, particularly of foreign languages where multiple students and a native-language-speaking teacher are able to interact via voice and video conference calls. As VOIP services, such as Skype, provide users with a low-cost alternative to more expensive local telephone service providers, those local providers consequently loose revenue, with the result that some VOIP services have been restricted or banned in a number of geographies. Skype services are accessed using a software-based client application that is available for all popular operating systems. Users also need a microphone for voice input, speakers or earphones for voice output, a keyboard for text input, and a display screen for viewing text and video content. The Skype service can be accessed from a wide range of *Internet*-enabled devices, including desktop computers, disk players, games consoles, laptop computers, set-top boxes, Skype phones, *Smart-Phones*, *Tablet Computers*, and televisions. The Skype service is based on a peer-to-peer network architecture in which users directly communicate with each other. Skype provides user validation via its login servers. Skype's user directory is decentralised; being distributed among all the user clients. Some user clients, known as supernodes, that have high communications bandwidth and are not restricted, by a firewall or subject to network address translation, are co-opted to provide intermediary connection services. Skype uses a proprietary data streaming communications protocol. Skype has stated that its communication services are secure; it is believed that the RC4 stream cipher is used for signalling and the Advanced *Encryption* Standard is used for voice data. Skype uses the SILK audio *Compression* format, which was subsequently used as the basis for the *Free and Open-Source Software*-based *Opus* audio *Compression* format. Skype uses the *VP8* video *Compression* format for standard definition video and the *H.264* video *Compression* format for high definition video. Skype is a popular service that has over half a billion registered users, and regularly supports tens of millions of simultaneous connections. Each year, Skype carries hundreds of billions of minutes of voice and video calls, and more than a hundred million text messages.

b) **IS THERE ANYTHING ELSE THAT IS SIMILAR?** Yes, there are many other VOIP-based communications solutions available; some of the more popular examples include iCall, FriendCaller, Fring, Libon, LINE, Nimbuzz, ooVoo, Tango, Truphone, Viber, and Vonage.

c) **WHY WAS IT SELECTED?** Skype was selected as a Stream Tone precursor because it provides a free-of-charge *Internet*-based telephony service that uses secure, streamed data communications. The Stream Tone Transfer Protocol will be a secure data streaming communications protocol that will most likely be used to provide *Web*-based telephony services. Viable *Web*-based alternatives for many traditionally off-line, or non-*Web*-based, services are now starting to emerge, and, if the popularity of Skype is any indication, could start to completely supplant them in the relatively near future.

d) **HOW IS IT LIKE THE STREAM TONE?** ✔ Replaces local functionality with Web-based services. ✔ Demonstrates the viability and user acceptance of Web-based services. ✔ Reliant on an active Internet connection. ✘ Provides access to all types of content and services. ✔ Streams all data; audio, visual, and other. ✔ Uses secure communications. ✔ Supports real-time interactivity. ✔ Uses a low-cost thin client. ✔ Reliant on remote computing resources. ✘ Based on free and open-source principles.

e) **FURTHER READING**
Skype: *http://www.skype.com/en/*
Skype: *https://en.wikipedia.org/wiki/Skype*

# 3.2.27    SO-NET NURO LIGHT

a)  **WHAT IS IT?** NURO Light is a high-bandwidth *Optical Fibre*-based *Internet* access service that is available in Japan. *Internet* access services are also known as broadband services. NURO Light is provided by So-net Entertainment Corporation, an *Internet* service provider (ISP), which is a subsidiary of Sony Corporation. NURO Light is a fibre-to-the-home broadband service that is available to both homes and businesses in Chiba, Gunma, Ibaraki, Kanagawa, Saitama, Tochigi, and Tokyo, that was launched in April 2013. NURO Light is based on gigabit-capable passive optical networks technology. NURO Light provides an asymmetrical broadband service with 2 gigabits per second (Gbps) of downstream bandwidth and 1 Gbps of upstream bandwidth. When NURO Light was launched it was the highest bandwidth residentially-available broadband service in the world.

b)  **IS THERE ANYTHING ELSE THAT IS SIMILAR?** Yes, there are a number of other ISPs that offer high-bandwidth *Optical Fibre*-based broadband services, including: Free which provides an asymmetrical broadband service with 1 Gbps downstream and 0.2 Gbps upstream in Paris, France; Google Fiber which provides a 1 Gbps *Symmetrical Broadband* service in Kansas City, United States of America; Hong Kong Broadband Network which provides a 1 Gbps *Symmetrical Broadband* service in Hong Kong, China; HyperOptic which provides a 1 Gbps *Symmetrical Broadband* service in London, United Kingdom; KORNET which provides a 1 Gbps *Symmetrical Broadband* service in Seoul, South Korea; StarHub which provides an asymmetrical broadband service with 1 Gbps downstream and 0.5 Gbps upstream throughout Singapore; Swisscom which provides an asymmetrical broadband service with 1 Gbps downstream and 0.1 Gbps upstream in Switzerland. *Optical Fibre*-based *Internet* access services providing bandwidths of 1 Gbps, or more, are expected to become more widely available in the near future.

c)  **WHY WAS IT SELECTED?** The NURO Light service was selected as a Stream Tone precursor because it demonstrates that the next generation of high-bandwidth *Internet* access services are actively being designed, developed, and deployed. High-bandwidth *Internet* access services will be required to deliver content and services using the Stream Tone Transfer Protocol.

d)  **HOW COULD IT ENABLE THE STREAM TONE?** ✘ Provides technology on free and open-source terms. ✘ Expands Internet availability. ✘ Improves the quality of Internet connectivity. ✔ Increases communications bandwidth. ✔ Reduces Internet access costs. ✔ Enables Web-based service provision. ✔ Improves the quality of Web-based service delivery. ✘ Improves the power efficiency of mobile computing devices. ✔ Enables technology deployment.

e)  **FURTHER READING**
NURO Light (Translated From Japanese Into English):
*http://translate.google.com/translate?hl=en&sl=ja&u=http://www.so-net.ne.jp/access/hikari/nuro_hikari/&prev=/search%3Fq%3DSO-NET%2BNURO%2BLIGHT%26hl%3Den*
Sony-Backed ISP Unveils 2Gbps Internet Service In Japan:
*http://www.pcmag.com/article2/0,2817,2417845,00.asp*

# 3.2.28   SOUNDHOUND

a)   **WHAT IS IT?** SoundHound is a *Web*-based music search service that is able to recognise currently playing music, or music that is hummed or sung by a user. SoundHound was developed by SoundHound, Inc. SoundHound uses a proprietary technology to quickly and efficiently identify music, within seconds, even in relatively noisy environments. SoundHound supports a number of entertainment devices that typically include a microphone and *Internet* connectivity, including *Smart-Phones* and *Tablet Computers*. SoundHound functionality is accessed using a software-based client application. SoundHound's search results include information about the music and its performer, music samples, song lyrics that are synchronised to the playing song, links to *Web*-based stores that sell the music, links to related *Web*-based videos, and links to *Web*-based radio services that may feature the music or music that is similar. SoundHound also provides the ability to share search results on a number of popular social networking sites. SoundHound is available free-of-charge, and is funded by advertising presented within its client application. An advertising free version, known as SoundHound Infinity, is also available to purchase from various *Application Stores*. SoundHound has over a hundred million users that make millions of searches every day.

b)   **IS THERE ANYTHING ELSE THAT IS SIMILAR?** Yes; Shazam.

c)   **WHY WAS IT SELECTED?** SoundHound was selected as a Stream Tone precursor because it provides a new type of *Web-based Service*, for which there is really no practical local equivalent. The real-time identification of playing-music is a service that has only been made possible by the *Internet* and the *Web*. Its users have accepted that their use of the SoundHound service relies on a continuous connection to the *Internet*. The SoundHound client sends music captured by microphone across the *Internet* for identification by SoundHound's *Cloud Computing*-based servers. The SoundHound service is fully reliant on remote data processing. The Stream Tone Transfer Protocol (STTP) will be used to stream data from a Stream Tone Access Device to a Stream Tone Service Infrastructure for data processing and storage. The SoundHound service would most probably be well suited to being communicated using the STTP.

d)   **HOW IS IT LIKE THE STREAM TONE?** ✘ Replaces local functionality with Web-based services. ✔ Demonstrates the viability and user acceptance of Web-based services. ✔ Reliant on an active Internet connection. ✘ Provides access to all types of content and services. ✘ Streams all data; audio, visual, and other. ✘ Uses secure communications. ✘ Supports real-time interactivity. ✔ Uses a low-cost thin client. ✔ Reliant on remote computing resources. ✘ Based on free and open-source principles.

e)   **FURTHER READING**
SoundHound: *http://www.soundhound.com/*
SoundHound: *https://en.wikipedia.org/wiki/SoundHound*

# 3.2.29   TELSTRA MOBILE BROADBAND

a)   **WHAT IS IT?** Mobile Broadband is a high-bandwidth mobile communications service provided by Telstra Corporation Ltd that is available in most Australian cities. The Mobile Broadband service from Telstra is marketed as a *Fourth-Generation Mobile*

*Communications* service, and is based on the Long-Term Evolution-Advanced (LTE-Advanced) mobile communications standard. The LTE-Advanced mobile communications standard is a pure packet-switched, *Internet Protocol* (IP), technology, that replaces the circuit-switched technologies used by earlier generations of mobile communications. The LTE-Advanced mobile communication standard supports theoretical downstream bandwidths of up to 1,000 megabits per second (Mbps). The Mobile Broadband service from Telstra currently supports real-world downstream bandwidths of between 2 Mbps and 40 Mbps, with bandwidths of between 150 Mbps and 300 Mbps expected in the near future. LTE-Advanced mobile communications technology supports communications with end-users that are in high-speed motion, such as travellers in aeroplanes, buses, cars, or trains. LTE-Advanced supports both *Small Cell* and large cell deployments. There are two main variants of LTE-Advanced; frequency-division duplex LTE-Advanced, as used by the Mobile Broadband service from Telstra, and time-division duplex LTE-Advanced. Currently, the Mobile Broadband service from Telstra has over one million connected mobile communications devices.

b) **IS THERE ANYTHING ELSE THAT IS SIMILAR?** Yes, high-bandwidth mobile communications services that are based on either the Long-Term Evolution (LTE) or the LTE-Advanced mobile communications standard are also available from a number of other Australian mobile communications service providers, including Optus, Next Broadband Network, and Vodaphone. Internationally, high-bandwidth mobile communications services that are based on either the LTE or the LTE-Advanced mobile communications standard are also available in Angola, Armenia, Austria, Azerbaijan, Bahrain, Belgium, Bolivia, Brazil, Canada, Chile, Columbia, Croatia, Czech Republic, Denmark, Dominican Republic, Estonia, Finland, France, Germany, Greece, Hong Kong, Hungary, India, Italy, Japan, Kazakhstan, Kuwait, Kyrgyzstan, Latvia, Lebanon, Lithuania, Luxembourg, Malaysia, Mauritius, Mexico, Namibia, Netherlands, New Zealand, Norway, Oman, Paraguay, Philippines, Poland, Portugal, Puerto Rico, Qatar, Romania, Russia, Saudi Arabia, Singapore, Slovakia, South Africa, South Korea, Spain, Sri Lanka, Sweden, Switzerland, Thailand, United Arab Emirates, United Kingdom, United States, Uzbekistan, and Venezuela. Many LTE and LTE-Advanced deployments have been enabled by the digital switch-over from analogue terrestrial television to digital terrestrial television that made extra radio spectrum available for use by next generation mobile communications services.

c) **WHY WAS IT SELECTED?** The Mobile Broadband service from Telstra was selected as a Stream Tone precursor because it demonstrates that the physical infrastructure needed to deliver high-bandwidth mobile communications is actively being designed, developed, and deployed on national scales. Advanced telecommunications technologies, such as LTE and its successors, will form the basis of many Stream Tone Telecommunications Infrastructures.

d) **HOW COULD IT ENABLE THE STREAM TONE?** ✘ Provides technology on free and open-source terms. ✔ Expands Internet availability. ✔ Improves the quality of Internet connectivity. ✔ Increases communications bandwidth. ✔ Reduces Internet access costs. ✔ Enables Web-based service provision. ✔ Improves the quality of Web-based service delivery. ✘ Improves the power efficiency of mobile computing devices. ✔ Enables technology deployment.

e) **FURTHER READING**
4G Australia: *https://en.wikipedia.org/wiki/4G_Australia*

Telstra: *http://www.telstra.com.au/*
Telstra: *https://en.wikipedia.org/wiki/Telstra*
Telstra 4G: *http://www.telstra.com.au/broadband/mobile-broadband/coverage-networks/networks/#tab-telstra-4g*

# 3.2.30    TIGHTVNC

a)    **WHAT IS IT?** TightVNC is a *Free and Open-Source Software* (FOSS)-based remote desktop computer display and control software application that is based on the pixel-streaming *Remote FrameBuffer* (RFB) communications protocol. The TightVNC software application can also be used to provide access to *Hosted Desktops*. TightVNC is developed by Glavsoft LLC. TightVNC works well even over relatively low-bandwidth computer networks. TightVNC is available free-of-charge for both private and commercial use. TightVNC is available as a Java-based software application, allowing it to be run on any platform or any operating system that supports Java. TightVNC is also available for the desktop and server versions of the Microsoft Windows operating system. TightVNC is a client-server application. TightVNC allows a remote desktop computer, running the TightVNC server, to communicate over a local area network, wide area network, or even the *Internet*, with another computer, running the TightVNC client. The screen display of the desktop computer is sent by the server across the network to the client for display, and user-input, from the keyboard and mouse, is sent from the client back to the server. The client device can be a low-performance desktop computer, laptop computer, *Smart-Phone*, or *Tablet Computer*, and can even be running a different type of operating system compared to that of the remote desktop computer. TightVNC is compatible with a wide range of third-party remote desktop computer display and control solutions that are also based on the RFB communications protocol. This compatibility allows a TightVNC server to communicate with a third-party developed client, and a third-party developed server to communicate with a TightVNC client. The RFB communications protocol is not secure, and needs to be sent over a computer network connection that has been secured using an *Encryption* algorithm if security is required. The latest versions of the TightVNC software application allow a secure computer network connection to be easily configured. TightVNC reduces the quantity of image data that needs to be exchanged between the server and the client by only sending image rectangles containing the data that has changed. The quantity of changed image data can be further reduced by using a wide range of supported image *Compression* algorithms, prior to transmission. TightVNC also provides optimised support for the transmission of desktop video, which some other RFB-based products do not do. The visual quality and interactive responsiveness of a desktop environment that is displayed and controlled using TightVNC is largely dependent on the bandwidth and latency characteristics of the computer network connection used to access that environment. The better the quality of the connection, the better the display and control experience will be. The processing power of the server, which is used to compress the remote desktop computer image data, is also a factor, although to a much lesser extent. The source code of TightVNC, which is available under a FOSS license, has been used as the basis for many other remote desktop computer display and control solutions. For example, TurboVNC, which is based on TightVNC, is optimised towards the remote control of three dimensional graphics applications and video. TightVNC is a popular remote desktop computer display and control software application that is in widespread use.

b)    **IS THERE ANYTHING ELSE THAT IS SIMILAR?** Yes, there are many other remote desktop computer display and control solutions that make use of the RFB communications protocol, including akRDC, Apple Remote Desktop, Cendio ThinLinc, Chicken, ChunkVNC, CrossLoop, Dameware Mini Remote Control, EchoVNC, Fog Creek Copilot, FreeNX, Goverlan Remote Control, iTALC, iTap mobile VNC, JollysFastVNC, KRDC, Mac HelpMate, N-central, noVNC, OnlineVNC, RealVNC, Remote Desktop Manager, Remoter VNC, Remotix, TigerVNC, TurboVNC, UltraVNC, Win2VNC, and x11vnc. There are also many other remote desktop computer display and control solutions that use other communications protocols, including AetherPal, Anyplace Control, AnywhereTS, Bomgar, Chrome Remote Desktop, Citrix XenApp, CoRD, Dameware Mini Remote Control, DeskRoll, Ericom PowerTerm WebConnect, FreeNX, FreeRDP, GO-Global, GoSupportNow, GoToMyPC, Goverlan Remote Control, HOB RD VPN blue edition, IBM Director Remote Control, iRAPP, ISL Light, iTap mobile RDP, KRDC, LogMeIn, Mikogo, N-central, Ncomputing, Netop Remote Control, NetSupport Manager, Netviewer, OnLive Desktop, OpenText Exceed onDemand, Oracle Secure Global Desktop, Proxy Networks, QVD, Radmin, rdesktop, Remote Desktop Manager, Remote Desktop Services, Remote Graphics Software, Remote Utilities, Remotix RDP, RHUB TurboMeeting, Rsupport RemoteView, ScreenConnect, SimpleHelp, Splashtop, Supremo, Symantec pcAnywhere, TeamViewer, Techinline, Teradici, Thinc, Timbuktu Enterprise, Ulteo Open Virtual Desktop, WebEx, X2go, XDMCP, and XP/VS Server. Not all the remote desktop computer display and control solutions are available free-of-charge, or based on FOSS, in fact many are proprietary products that use proprietary communications protocols, and are only available commercially.

c) **WHY WAS IT SELECTED?** TightVNC was selected as a Stream Tone precursor because it clearly demonstrates that the technology needed to display and control remote desktop computers over computer networks, such as the *Internet*, already exists and is in widespread use. The Stream Tone Transfer Protocol (STTP) will be used to communicate a wide range of digital content and services over the *Internet*, including *Hosted Desktops* and *Web Desktops*. Key aspects of the STTP could be based on existing remote desktop computer display and control technologies, such as TightVNC and the RFB protocol, in order to allow existing local desktop computer environments to be moved onto *Web-based Services*.

d) **HOW IS IT LIKE THE STREAM TONE?** ✔ Replaces local functionality with Web-based services. ✔ Demonstrates the viability and user acceptance of Web-based services. ✔ Reliant on an active Internet connection. ✔ Provides access to all types of content and services. ✔ Streams all data; audio, visual, and other. ✔ Uses secure communications. ✔ Supports real-time interactivity. ✔ Uses a low-cost thin client. ✔ Reliant on remote computing resources. ✔ Based on free and open-source principles.

e) **FURTHER READING**
TightVNC: *http://tightvnc.com/*
TightVNC: *https://en.wikipedia.org/wiki/TightVNC*

# 3.2.31   TWITCH

a) **WHAT IS IT?** Twitch is a *Web*-based video streaming service for sharing live and recorded personal computer gaming sessions with a wider audience via the *Internet*, and which is operated by Twitch Interactive, Inc.[16] The Twitch service has partnered with a number of computer gaming leagues and regularly broadcasts computer gaming tournaments. Some gaming sessions include live commentary and may also include additional video feeds of the game players or commentators. Viewers are often able to communicate via *Instant Messaging* with game players during live games. The Twitch service can be used to learn new game play strategies. The Twitch service is also used to broadcast computer gaming-related talk shows. Gamers typically use a commercially available third-party software application to capture game video, convert it into an Adobe Flash-compatible format, and send it to Twitch's *Cloud Computing*-based servers. Adobe Flash supports the following multimedia formats: VP6, *x264*, AAC-LC, and *Speex*. Computer gaming hardware generally needs to be quite powerful in order to not only play a game at a high resolution and high frame refresh rate, but also to simultaneously encode and broadcast the video stream to Twitch via the *Internet*. The Twitch service then re-broadcasts the video to viewers, over the *Internet*. Viewers can access a Twitch video stream using a standard *Web Browser* that supports Adobe Flash-based video. The Twitch service can be accessed from a wide range of *Internet*-enabled personal computing devices, including desktop computers, laptop computers, *Smart-Phones*, and *Tablet Computers*. Each game broadcaster, whether amateur or professional, has their own channel. Some channels broadcast high-resolution video. Many channels are available free-of-charge; however, some channels require a paid subscription in order to view content in high resolution. Some channels include commercial advertising. Twitch is a popular service that has been experiencing steadily increasing viewer numbers, and can now regularly attract over one million viewers per day.

b)  **IS THERE ANYTHING ELSE THAT IS SIMILAR?** Yes, there are a number of other live video streaming services currently available, including BlogTV, LiveStream, Ustream, Veetle, and YouTube, although not all are oriented towards the real-time viewing of computer gaming sessions.

c)  **WHY WAS IT SELECTED?** Twitch was selected as a Stream Tone precursor because it provides a new type of *Web-based Service* for which there is really no practical local equivalent. The real-time viewing of other people's computer gameplay is a service that has only been made possible by the existence of the *Internet* and the *Web*. Twitch users have accepted that their consumption of the service relies on a continuous connection to the *Internet*. The Twitch service streams audio and video data from a game player's personal computing device across the *Internet* to multiple viewers. The Stream Tone Transfer Protocol will be used to stream real-time digital content and services across the *Internet*, including live computer gameplay.

d)  **HOW IS IT LIKE THE STREAM TONE?** ✘ Replaces local functionality with Web-based services. ✔ Demonstrates the viability and user acceptance of Web-based services. ✔ Reliant on an active Internet connection. ✘ Provides access to all types of content and services. ✔ Streams all data; audio, visual, and other. ✘ Uses secure communications. ✔ Supports real-time interactivity. ✔ Uses a low-cost thin client. ✔ Reliant on remote computing resources. ✘ Based on free and open-source principles.

e)  **FURTHER READING**

---

[16] At the time of writing, Amazon.com, Inc., had announced its intention to purchase Twitch Interactive, Inc.

Twitch: *http://www.twitch.tv/*
Twitch (Website): *https://en.wikipedia.org/wiki/Twitch_%28website%29*

# 3.2.32    UBISLATE 7C+

a) **WHAT IS IT?** The UbiSlate 7C+ is a low-cost *Tablet Computer*, with a 7-inch *Capacitive Sensing*-based multi-touch display screen, that is capable of accessing *Web*-based content and services. The UbiSlate 7C+ was created by Datawind Ltd. It also works as a mobile-phone. The UbiSlate 7C+ is a commercially available version of the Aakash 2 *Tablet Computer* that was designed to be an affordable personal computing device for students in India. The UbiSlate 7C+ is built using a low-cost *System on a Chip* that features a *Reduced Instruction Set Computing*-based microprocessor. The UbiSlate 7C+ runs the Google Android operating system, which is a *Linux*-based operating system. The UbiSlate 7C+ comes with a range of pre-installed software applications, including email, games, music, office, social networking, and video. Additional software applications can be obtained from an *Application Store*. The UbiSlate 7C+ supports *Wi-Fi*. The UbiSlate 7C+ uses older-generation mobile communications technologies, which have relatively slow data communication speeds. Datawind provides mobile *Internet* access, for users of their products, through its own *Cloud Computing*-based servers, which compress *Web* data before sending it to the UbiSlate 7C+; an approach that can greatly minimise the impact of slower communications technologies. Large numbers of UbiSlate and Aakash *Tablet Computers* have been sold, particularly in India, providing many people with their very first experience of the *Internet*, personal computing, and *Web*.

b) **IS THERE ANYTHING ELSE THAT IS SIMILAR?** Yes, there many other *Tablet Computers* of a similar size that are currently available, including the Acer A110-07g08u, Ainol Novo 7 Flame, Alcatel One Touch EV07, Amazon Kindle Fire HD 7, Apple iPad Mini, Archos 70 Titanium, Asus Nexus 7, Blackberry PlayBook, Chuwi V70, Coby MID7065, Creative ZiiO 7, HCL ME Tablet Y3, HP Slate 7, Huawei MediaPad, Hyundai T7, JXD S7300, Lenovo A2107, Micromax Funbook P600, NATPC M009S, Panasonic ToughPad JT-B1, Samsung Galaxy Tab 2 7.0, Sharp Aquos Pad SHT 21, Toshiba Excite 7.7, Viewsonic ViewPad N710, Videocon VT71, Zeepad 7.0, ZTE Light Tab, and Zync Pad Z990, to name but a few. There are also a very large number of *Tablet Computers* that have screens larger than 7 inches. Most *Tablet Computers* are manufactured in China by large-scale original equipment manufacturers which are rapidly evolving their offerings to meet the diverse needs of both local and international markets. The *Tablet Computer* market space is highly dynamic, with new devices being launched almost daily.

c) **WHY WAS IT SELECTED?** The UbiSlate 7C+ was selected as a Stream Tone precursor because it demonstrates that a useable and useful *Internet*-enabled personal computing device can be manufactured at a very low cost, and that limitations due to the use of low-performance hardware or older generation mobile communications can be mitigated through the use of *Cloud Computing*-based services. The Stream Tone Access Device will be a low-cost low-performance device that will be totally reliant on Stream Tone Transfer Protocol-based services that will be provided by *Cloud Computing*-based Stream Tone Service Infrastructures.

d) **HOW COULD IT ENABLE THE STREAM TONE?** ✘ Provides technology on free and open-source terms. ✔ Expands Internet availability. ✘ Improves the quality of

Internet connectivity. ✔ Increases communications bandwidth. ✔ Reduces Internet access costs. ✘ Enables Web-based service provision. ✘ Improves the quality of Web-based service delivery. ✔ Improves the power efficiency of mobile computing devices. ✘ Enables technology deployment.

e) **FURTHER READING**
Aakash: *http://www.datawind.com/aakash/index.html*
Aakash (Tablet): *https://en.wikipedia.org/wiki/Aakash_%28tablet%29*
UbiSlate: *http://www.datawind.com/ubislate/*

# 3.2.33 UNITED KINGDOM DIGITAL DIVIDEND

a) **WHAT IS IT?** The Digital Dividend (DD) is the benefit derived from the *Regulation* that required a switch-over from analogue terrestrial television (ATT) to digital terrestrial television (DTT) within the United Kingdom (UK). The UK officially completed its digital switch-over (DSO) on 24th October 2012. The DSO freed up the radio spectrum that was previously used to broadcast five national television channels, and a few other smaller localised television channels, within the UK. The bulk of the freed radio spectrum was then reused for nationally available DTT, digital radio broadcasts, and digital interactive services. The remaining unused portion of the freed radio spectrum then formed the basis of the DD. Television channels broadcast using DTT technology make much better use of the radio spectrum, which allows multiple digital channels to be broadcast using the spectrum previously used by a single analogue television channel. Exactly how many DTT channels can fit in the spectrum freed up by the DSO is dependent on the whether the DTT transmission is in a standard definition (SD) format or high definition (HD) format. Currently, there are approximately sixty SD channels being broadcast using DTT, most of which are nationally available 24-hours per day. A small number of channels are only available at specific times of the day or within particular geographic regions. There are also four HD channels and more than two dozen radio services. Many of the new DTT channels are available free-of-charge, but a small number are only available on a subscription or pay-per-view basis. A portion of the freed radio spectrum, at around 800 megahertz (MHz), known as the DD has now been auctioned off to a number of mobile telecommunications service providers. Profits from this auction then went into the UK public purse. The bulk of the DD will be used to provide expanded mobile data services, which are then expected to bring a wide range of direct and indirect benefits to UK citizens. Mobile data communications are primarily used to access *Web*-based content and services over the *Internet*. The 800 MHz waveband is particularly well suited to mobile data communications because radio signals sent over this waveband are able to travel long distances without significant degradation and are able to easily penetrate the walls of buildings. It is expected that the DD will help to greatly expand both the bandwidth and coverage of nationally available mobile data services. In particular, many rural communities, which traditionally have not been well served by high-bandwidth copper or *Optical Fibre*-based telecommunications services, are expected to benefit from the new and improved mobile telecommunications services derived from the DD.

b) **IS THERE ANYTHING ELSE THAT IS SIMILAR?** Yes, many other countries have already completed a DSO and created their own DD, including Andorra, Austria,

Belgium, Canada, Croatia, Cyprus, Czech Republic, Denmark, Estonia, Finland, France, Germany, Gibraltar, Guernsey, Ireland, Isle of Man, Israel, Italy, Japan, Jersey, Kenya, Latvia, Lithuania, Luxembourg, Malta, Monaco, Netherlands, Norway, Oman, Portugal, Qatar, San Marino, Saudi Arabia, Serbia, Slovakia, Slovenia, South Korea, Spain, Sweden, Switzerland, Taiwan, United Arab Emirates, United Kingdom, and United States of America. Other countries expected to complete a DSO within the coming years include Algeria, Argentina, Australia, Azerbaijan, Bolivia, Brazil, Brunei, Bulgaria, Chile, Colombia, Costa Rica, Cuba, El Salvador, Hong Kong, Hungary, Iceland, India, Indonesia, Iran, Libya, Macedonia, Malaysia, Mauritania, Mauritius, Mexico, Moldova, Morocco, Namibia, Nigeria, New Zealand, Panama, Peru, Philippines, Poland, Romania, Russia, Rwanda, Singapore, South Africa, Thailand, Tunisia, Turkey, Ukraine, Uruguay, Venezuela, Vietnam, Western Sahara, and Zimbabwe. The global DSO, for participating countries, is expected to be fully complete by 2024.

c) **WHY WAS IT SELECTED?** The UK DD was selected as a Stream Tone precursor because it demonstrates that some of the radio spectrum needed to expand the bandwidth and coverage of mobile telecommunications can be obtained from *Regulation* that requires a DSO from ATT to DTT. Most of the digital content and services that will be communicated over the *Internet* using the Stream Tone Transfer Protocol will require the use of a mobile telecommunications infrastructure that is able to ubiquitously provide high-bandwidth data communications, such as those now being developed in the UK based on its recent DD.

d) **HOW COULD IT ENABLE THE STREAM TONE?** ✘ Provides technology on free and open-source terms. ✔ Expands Internet availability. ✔ Improves the quality of Internet connectivity. ✔ Increases communications bandwidth. ✔ Reduces Internet access costs. ✔ Enables Web-based service provision. ✔ Improves the quality of Web-based service delivery. ✔ Improves the power efficiency of mobile computing devices. ✔ Enables technology deployment.

e) **FURTHER READING**
Digital Dividend After Digital Television Transition:
*https://en.wikipedia.org/wiki/Digital_dividend_after_digital_television_transition*
Digital Dividend Review - A Statement On Our Approach To Awarding The Digital Dividend:
*http://stakeholders.ofcom.org.uk/binaries/consultations/ddr/statement/statement.pdf*
Digital Dividend Review - A Statement On Our Approach To Awarding The Digital Dividend - Annexes:
*http://stakeholders.ofcom.org.uk/binaries/consultations/ddr/statement/ddrannex.pdf*
Digital Television Transition: *https://en.wikipedia.org/wiki/Digital_television_transition*
Digital Terrestrial Television In The United Kingdom:
*https://en.wikipedia.org/wiki/Digital_terrestrial_television_in_the_United_Kingdom*

# 3.2.34   VIASAT EXEDE INTERNET

a) **WHAT IS IT?** Exede *Internet* (Exede) is a high-bandwidth in-flight *Internet*-connectivity solution offered by ViaSat, Inc. The Exede service is capable of delivering up to 12 megabits per second of downstream bandwidth to each passenger on a commercial airline, via on-board *Wi-Fi*. The Exede service is delivered by the ViaSat-1 *Communications Satellite* (COMSAT) owned by ViaSat. ViaSat-1 is a model LS-1300

COMSAT that was designed and manufactured by Space Systems Lorel. ViaSat-1 was launched using a Proton-M rocket on 19th October 2011 from Baikonur Cosmodrome, Kazakhstan. ViaSat-1 currently holds geosynchronous earth orbit at 115 degrees west, and has a life expectancy of 12 years. ViaSat-1 has 56 *Ka Band* transponders that are configured to serve the major population centres of North America. ViaSat-1 has a total communications capacity of 134 gigabits per second, which was more than the combined capacity of all existing North American COMSATs at the time of its launch. The very high communications capacity of ViaSat-1 is considered to be an economic game changer that will significantly reduce the cost of COMSAT-based *Internet*-connectivity services to users located in the air, on the ground, or at sea. ViaSat-1 is expected to be able to effectively service up to one million users. The ground systems supporting ViaSat-1 have been optimised to minimise communications latency, a common problem when sending data over the very large distances involved in COMSAT-based telecommunications. During 2013, JetBlue Airways, a low-cost commercial airline serving many destinations across North America, became one of the very first airlines to use the ViaSat Exede service.

b) **IS THERE ANYTHING ELSE THAT IS SIMILAR?** Yes, there are a number of other companies that also provide in-flight *Internet*-connectivity services for commercial airlines, including AeroMobile Communications, Gogo, OnAir, Panasonic Avionics Corporation, and Row 44. Not all of these in-flight *Internet*-connectivity providers use COMSATs to deliver their services; some use ground to air mobile communications.

c) **WHY WAS IT SELECTED?** The ViaSat Exede service was selected as a Stream Tone precursor because it demonstrates that the technology necessary to deliver *Internet*-connectivity in the air is actively being designed, developed, and deployed. The digital content and services that will be communicated over the *Internet* using the Stream Tone Transfer Protocol will need to be ubiquitously available, from air, land, and sea. COMSAT-based telecommunications services, such as the ViaSat Exede service, can help to cost-effectively extend *Internet* access to all required usage locations.

d) **HOW COULD IT ENABLE THE STREAM TONE?** ✘ Provides technology on free and open-source terms. ✔ Expands Internet availability. ✔ Improves the quality of Internet connectivity. ✔ Increases communications bandwidth. ✔ Reduces Internet access costs. ✔ Enables Web-based service provision. ✔ Improves the quality of Web-based service delivery. ✘ Improves the power efficiency of mobile computing devices. ✔ Enables technology deployment.

e) **FURTHER READING**
Exede In-Flight Connectivity For Commercial Airlines: *http://www.viasat.com/exede-in-the-air*
Exede Internet: *http://www.exede.com/*

# 3.2.35   WEB 2.0 CALC

a) **WHAT IS IT?** *Web* 2.0 Calc is a *Web*-based scientific calculator service operated by britnex. The *Web* 2.0 Calc service is a client-server application that requires a constant connection to the *Internet* in order to work. The *Web* 2.0 Calc client application runs within a standard *Web Browser*.

b) **IS THERE ANYTHING ELSE THAT IS SIMILAR?** Yes, there are many other *Web*-based mathematical calculators that are currently available, including Calculate for Free, Calculator Tab, eCalc, and Math Open Reference.

c) **WHY WAS IT SELECTED?** *Web* 2.0 Calc was selected as a Stream Tone precursor because it demonstrates the viability of moving local functionality, namely a calculator utility that would have previously been installed and executed on a local personal computing device, onto a *Web-based Service*. This is the type of *Web-based Service* that will help to build society's trust in remote personal computing and reduce the need for locally-based functionality. Calculator utilities, such as *Web* 2.0 Calc, are the type of service that could easily be communicated using the Stream Tone Transfer Protocol.

d) **HOW IS IT LIKE THE STREAM TONE?** ✔ Replaces local functionality with Web-based services. ✔ Demonstrates the viability and user acceptance of Web-based services. ✔ Reliant on an active Internet connection. ✘ Provides access to all types of content and services. ✘ Streams all data; audio, visual, and other. ✘ Uses secure communications. ✔ Supports real-time interactivity. ✔ Uses a low-cost thin client. ✔ Reliant on remote computing resources. ✘ Based on free and open-source principles.

e) **FURTHER READING**
Web2.0calc: *http://web2.0calc.com/*

# 3.2.36    WHATSAPP MESSENGER

a) **WHAT IS IT?** WhatsApp Messenger is a proprietary cross-platform *Instant Messaging* service for *Smart-Phones* that is provided by WhatsApp, Inc.[17] The software-based WhatsApp Messenger client application is available for a number of different *Smart-Phone* operating systems. WhatsApp Messenger is believed to use secure communications on some supported operating systems. WhatsApp Messenger can also be used to send multimedia data files, including audio, images, and video. WhatsApp Messenger essentially provides a free-of-charge replacement for the chargeable Short Message Service available on most mobile-phones. Dependent on the brand of *Smart-Phone* used, the WhatsApp Messenger client application is either available for purchase at a low price, or for a low-priced annual subscription after one year of free service. WhatsApp Messenger is a popular service that has hundreds of millions of global users, which send billions of messages each day.

b) **IS THERE ANYTHING ELSE THAT IS SIMILAR?** Yes, there are many other software-based *Instant Messaging* applications that are available for *Smart-Phones*, including AIM, BeejiveIM, BlackBerry Messenger, ChatON, Chikka Text Messenger, eBuddy Messenger, Facebook Messenger, Google Talk, Hall, iCall, ICQ, IM+, iMessage, imo messenger, KakaoTalk, Kik Messenger, LINE, LinPhone Video, LiveProfile, Mercury Messenger, MyPeople Messenger, Nimbuzz, Palringo Group Messenger, Skype, TigerText, Touch, Trillian, VeeChat, Verbs, Viber, WeChat, and Wickr, and Yahoo Messenger.

---

[17] *At the time of writing, Facebook, Inc., had announced its intention to purchase WhatsApp, Inc.*

c) **WHY WAS IT SELECTED?** WhatsApp Messenger was selected as a Stream Tone precursor because it allows *Smart-Phone* users to communicate via *Instant Messaging* over the *Internet*. The Stream Tone Transfer Protocol will be used to communicate over the *Internet*, and will support the use of *Instant Messaging* services.

d) **HOW IS IT LIKE THE STREAM TONE?** ✔ Replaces local functionality with Web-based services. ✔ Demonstrates the viability and user acceptance of Web-based services. ✔ Reliant on an active Internet connection. ✘ Provides access to all types of content and services. ✘ Streams all data; audio, visual, and other. ✔ Uses secure communications. ✘ Supports real-time interactivity. ✔ Uses a low-cost thin client. ✔ Reliant on remote computing resources. ✘ Based on free and open-source principles.

e) **FURTHER READING**
WhatsApp: *http://www.whatsapp.com/*
WhatsApp: *https://en.wikipedia.org/wiki/WhatsApp*

# 3.2.37 WILMINGTON TELEVISION WHITE SPACES BROADBAND NETWORK

a) **WHAT IS IT?** The first, commercially deployed, television white spaces (TVWS) broadband network in the United States of America (USA), approved by the Federal Communications Commission (FCC), was officially activated on 26th January 2012 in Wilmington, New Hanover County, North Carolina. Wilmington is a port city, located on the east coast of the USA that has a population of approximately 100,000. Previously, on 8th September 2008, Wilmington was the first city in the USA to complete the digital switch-over (DSO) from analogue terrestrial television (ATT) to digital terrestrial television (DTT). The rest of the USA completed the DSO on 12th June 2009, with the exception of certain low-power ATT channels which were allowed to operate until 1st September 2015. It is the DSO that made TVWS-based communications possible. The TVWS broadband network in Wilmington has been used to cost-effectively provide a free-of-charge *Internet* access service in the city's parks, as well as a range of traffic and security solutions for use by the Wilmington Police Department. TVWS broadband is sometimes referred to as Super *Wi-Fi*, because it is a wireless communications technology with a much greater broadcast range than traditional *Wi-Fi*, although it is not actually based on *Wi-Fi* technology, and is therefore a misnomer. It is, however, like *Wi-Fi*, an unlicensed wireless communications technology. TVWS communications technology was approved, by a FCC *Regulation*, for national use on 1st March 2013. The technology behind the TVWS broadband network utilises unused portions of the licensed radio spectrum reserved for DTT. The radio spectrum available for use by TVWS-based communications extends from 54 megahertz (MHz) up to 698 MHz; television channels 2 to 51, with a few exceptions. Channels 3, 4, and 37 are not available, as they have been reserved for other uses. Dependent on location, there is approximately 200 MHz of spectrum available that can potentially be used for TVWS-based communications in the USA. More TVWS spectrum is generally available in rural locations, which have fewer DTT transmissions, compared to more densely-populated areas, such as cities, which typically have more DTT transmissions and less available TVWS spectrum. The radio spectrum used for TVWS-based communications is particularly well suited to the task because radio signals in this waveband are able to travel long distances without significant degradation and are able penetrate building walls, foliage, and trees. A device for accessing TVWS-based communications is known as a TV band device (TVBD). There are two types of TVBD; portable and fixed. Portable devices are only allowed to use channels 21 to 51, and must transmit at a maximum of 100 milliwatts (mW) effective isotropic radiated power (EIRP). Fixed devices are allowed to use channels, 2, 5 to 36, and 38 to 51, and may transmit at up to 4,000 mW EIRP. The antennas of fixed devices are generally located outdoors, at no higher than 30 metres (m) above ground level and no higher than 220m above average terrain height. Under favourable conditions, fixed TVBDs can have a useable range of up to 10 miles. Before a TVBD is allowed to operate it must consult a national TVWS database that contains details of all DTT channels that are in use within the locality of the TVBD. The TVWS system is designed to transmit at a very low power and only on channels that are not used by a nearby DTT broadcast station. TVWS systems are also designed to reduce their transmit power to the minimum required to maintain communications. Such behaviours help to ensure that TVWS systems are very unlikely to interfere with any nearby DTT broadcasts. The TVWS broadband network in Wilmington uses a TVWS database maintained by Spectrum Bridge Incorporated, and the fixed TVBDs were provided by KTS Wireless, the supplier of the Agility White Space Radio, the first commercially available TVWS radio certified by the FCC. TVWS-based communications technology is still very much in its infancy, and the rules and *Regulations* governing its use will most likely be subject to on-going change and refinement based on feedback from real-world deployments. Within the USA, the amount of spectrum potentially available for use by TVWS-based communications systems, particularly in rural areas, is highly significant. TVWS-based communications technology is able to bring *Internet* connectivity to many locations that to date have been underserved or unserved with such connectivity. Many rural communities, that are collectively the home of millions of people, which previously had to rely on either slow telephone-based dial-up or expensive *Communications Satellite* (COMSAT)-based *Internet* connectivity solutions are likely to be some of the first beneficiaries of this new technology. In the future, TVWS may also be used by the *Internet* of Things and for machine-to-machine communications.

b)   **IS THERE ANYTHING ELSE THAT IS SIMILAR?** Yes, since the use of TVWS-based communications was approved by the FCC many more deployments are being planned all across the USA. COMSATs, such as ViaSat-1, are another technology that is able to cost-effectively bring *Internet* connectivity to many rural locations. However, COMSAT-based communications tend to have much higher communications latencies than terrestrially-based wireless communications solutions, which can make COMSAT-based communications less suitable for certain types of *Web-based Service*. In addition to Spectrum Bridge Incorporated, there are a number of other USA-based TVWS database providers, including Airity Incorporated, Comsearch, Frequency Finder Incorporated, Google Incorporated, LS Telcom AG, Key Bridge Global LLC, Microsoft Corporation, Neustar Incorporated, and Telcordia Technologies. TVWS database providers are licensed by the FCC for a five-year period, after which their licenses must be renewed. TVWS-based communications solutions are actively being deployed, investigated, or piloted in a number of other countries around the world, including Australia, Belgium, Brazil, Canada, Cyprus, Finland, France, Germany, Greece, Ireland, Japan, Kenya, New Zealand, Philippines, Poland, Portugal, Singapore, Slovakia, South Africa, South Korea, Spain, Sweden, United Kingdom, and Uruguay, to name but a few. It is expected that many countries will adopt TVWS technology once they have completed their own DSOs.

c)   **WHY WAS IT SELECTED?** The TVWS broadband network deployed in Wilmington was selected as a Stream Tone precursor because it clearly demonstrates that the telecommunications technologies needed to provide ubiquitous ***Internet*** access are actively being designed, developed, and deployed. The Stream Tone needs both wired and wireless telecommunications that are highly affordable, high bandwidth, low latency, highly reliable, and ubiquitously available. Communications technologies, such as TVWS broadband networking, can help to make the digital content and services communicated over the ***Internet*** using the Stream Tone Transfer Protocol available from everywhere.

d) **HOW COULD IT ENABLE THE STREAM TONE?** ✘ Provides technology on free and open-source terms. ✔ Expands Internet availability. ✔ Improves the quality of Internet connectivity. ✔ Increases communications bandwidth. ✔ Reduces Internet access costs. ✔ Enables Web-based service provision. ✔ Improves the quality of Web-based service delivery. ✘ Improves the power efficiency of mobile computing devices. ✔ Enables technology deployment.

e) **FURTHER READING**
Agility White Space Radio (AWR): *http://www.ktswireless.com/agility-white-space-radio-awr/*
Office Of Engineering And Technology Announces The Approval Of Spectrum Bridge, Inc's TV Bands Database System For Operation:
*http://hraunfoss.fcc.gov/edocs_public/attachmatch/DA-11-2043A1.pdf*
TV White Spaces Powering Smart City Services - The First Database Driven TV White Spaces "Smart City":
*http://www.spectrumbridge.com/ProductsServices/WhiteSpacesSolutions/success-stories/wilmington.aspx*
White Spaces (Radio): *https://en.wikipedia.org/wiki/White_spaces_%28radio%29*

# 3.2.38  WORLD OF WARCRAFT

a) **WHAT IS IT?** World of Warcraft (WOW) is a massively multi-player on-line role-playing game (MMORPG), in which a player controls an avatar, or character, within a vast, persistent, game world, known as a realm. WOW was created by Blizzard Entertainment, Inc., a leading developer of ***Massively Multi-player On-line Games*** (MMOGs). Blizzard Entertainment, Inc., is a subsidiary of Activision Blizzard, Inc. A WOW realm contains a wide variety of visual and conceptual elements, drawn from fantasy, science fiction, and steampunk. Players are likely to encounter hundreds of different mythical creatures within each realm, such as dragons, dwarves, elementals, elves, ghosts, ghouls, giants, goblins, golems, gryphons, harpies, imps, orcs, satyrs, succubi, trolls, werewolves, wraiths, and zombies. Players are able to explore a realm, undertake quests, fight monsters, join guilds, buy and sell virtual goods, and interact with other players, both virtual and real. The simple objective of the game is to develop your game character by acquiring new skills and abilities; a process that can often take many months of dedicated play. One of the principle ways in which to develop a game character is to undertake quests, which may involve such things as defeating monsters, gathering resources, interacting with virtual players, visiting certain locations, interacting with objects, or transporting an object from one place to another. The game world can be viewed from either a first-person or third-person perspective. Multiple players may combine their efforts to participate in cooperative activities. Game play within WOW involves two opposing factions; the Horde, and the Alliance. Players will create an avatar by choosing a faction, a character type or race, a class, and a gender. Blood Elves, Goblins, Orcs, Tauren, Trolls, and Undead are races belonging to the Horde, and Draenei,

Dwarves, Gnomes, Humans, Night Elves, and Worgen are races belonging to the Alliance. Pandaren are a neutral race, which are aligned to neither the Alliance nor the Horde. Avatar classes are Death Knight, Druid, Hunter, Mage, Monk, Paladin, Priest, Rogue, Shaman, Warlock, and Warrior. Race is essentially an in-game social choice, whilst class determines what a character can and cannot do within the game. WOW uses a client-server systems architecture to provide its gaming services. The software-based WOW client application, which runs on an ***Internet***-enabled personal computing device, such as a desktop computer or laptop computer, handles the visual display of the game and sends user-input to WOW's ***Cloud Computing***-based servers. The WOW client locally caches as much information as possible about the game world, in order to minimise on-going communications traffic with the WOW servers. Communications between the WOW client and WOW servers are based on a proprietary communications protocol that is secured using ***Encryption***. The WOW server tracks the activities of all the players, and any changes to the game world, which it then selectively streams, as real-time updates, to all affected WOW clients. Data sent from the WOW servers to the WOW clients can be substantial, and the game ideally requires a high-bandwidth ***Internet*** connection with low communications latencies in order to achieve the best game experience. The WOW client software application can be updated, permitting new game realms, known as expansion packs, to be made available. WOW is not available free-of-charge, as game time must be purchased. WOW has millions of subscribers, some of which play for up to a hundred hours each month.

b) **IS THERE ANYTHING ELSE THAT IS SIMILAR?** Yes, there are many, many other MMORPGs currently available, including 4Story, The 4th Coming, 9Dragons, Ace Online, AdventureQuest Worlds, Aerrevan, AfterWorld, Age of Conan: Unchained, Age of Titans, Age of Wulin, Aion, AIKA Online, Alganon, Allods Online, Ancients of Fasaria, Anarchy Online, Angels Online, ArcheAge, ArchLord, ARGO Online, Asda 2, Asheron's Call, Atlantica Online, Avalon Heroes, Battlestar Galactica Online, Blade & Soul, Blazing Throne, Blood Wars, Broken Realm, Cabal Online, Cartoon Network Universe: FusionFall, Champions Online, City of Steam, Clan Lord, Club Penguin, Conquer Online, Continent of the Ninth Seal, Cronous, Crowns of Power, Crystal Saga, Dark Age of Camelot, Dark Ages, DarkEden, Dawn of Darkness, Dawntide, Dead Frontier, DC Universe Online, Doctor Who: Worlds in Time, Dofus, Drackensang Online, Dragon's Call, Digimon Masters Online, Dragon Ball Online, Dragon Eternity, Dragon Nest, Dragon Knights Online, Dragon Oath 2, Dragon Quest X, Dragon Saga, Dragonica, DragonRealms, Dungeons & Dragons Online: Stormreach, Dynasty Warriors Online, Eden Eternal, The Elder Scrolls Online, Emil Chronical Online, Empire & State, Entropia Universe, Eternal Blade, Eternal Lands, EVE Online, EverQuest, EverQuest II, Fantage, Face of Mankind, Fallen Earth, Fantasy Westward Journey, Fiesta Online, Final Fantasy XI, Final Fantasy XIV, Florensia, Flyff, Free Realms, Furcadia, Gekkeiju Online, GodsWar Online, Gods & Heroes: Rome Rising, Grand Fantasia, Granado Espada, Guild Wars, Guild Wars 2, Helbreath, Hello Kitty Online, Hero Online, Heroes of Gaia, The Hooded Gunman, Hundred Years' War, Istaria: Chronicles of the Gifted, Jade Dynasty, Kal Online, King of Kings 3, Knight Online, La Tale, Land of Chaos Online, Last Chaos, League of Legends, The Legend of Mir 2, Lime Odyssey, Lineage, Lineage II, Loong, The Lord of the Rings Online, Love, Lunia: Record of Lunia War, Mabinogi, Maestia: Rise of Keledus, Magical Land, Maple Story, Meridian 59, Metin 2, Minions of Mirth, Moonlight Online, Mortal Online, Mu Online, A Mystical Land, Myth War II Online, Mythos, Nadirim, Neocron 2, Neverwinter, Nexus: The Kingdom of the Winds, NosTale, Odin Quest, Omerta, Overkings, Pardus, Parallel Kingdom, Perfect World International, Perpetuum, Phantasy Star Online 2, Pirates of the Burning Sea, Pirates of the Caribbean

Online, Pirate101, PlaneShift, Planetarion, Priston Tale, Priston Tale 2, Poptropica, Puppet Guardian, Puzzle Pirates, Ragnarok Online, Ragnarok Online 2, RAN Online, RaiderZ, Rappelz, Realm of the Mad God, The Realm Online, Regnum Online, Remnant Knights, Requiem: Memento Mori, RF Online, Rift, R.O.H.A.N.: Blood Feud, Rosh Online, Runes of Magic, RuneScape, Rusty Hearts, Ryzom, Salem, Scarlet Blade, Seal Online, The Secret World, Sentou Gakuen, Sevencore, Scions of Fate, Shin Megami Tensei: Imagine, Shaiya, Shot Online, Silkroad Online, Soul of the Ultimate Nation, Spiral Knights, Star Trek Online, Star Wars: The Old Republic, Starlight Story, StarQuest Online, Supreme Destiny, A Tale in the Desert, Tales of Pirates, Talisman Online, Tamer Saga, Tantra Online, TERA, Terra: Battle for the Outlands, Tibia, Toontown Online, Transformers Universe, Traveller AR, Trickster, Twelve Sky 2, Ultima Online, Uncharted Waters Online, Urban Dead, Vanguard: Saga of Heroes, Vindictus, Voyage Century Online, Vendetta Online, Wakfu, War of the Immortals, Warhammer Online: Age of Reckoning, Warhammer Online: Wrath of Heroes, Waren Story, Wartune, WildStar, With Your Destiny, Wizard101, Wonderland Online, World of Tanks, Wurm Online, Xiah Rebirth, Xsyon: Prelude, Zheng Tu, and Zu Online. There are also many other MMOGs belonging to other genres. Whilst many MMOGs may only have a few hundred regular players, some have millions, with the result that, collectively, hundreds of millions of people now play MMOGs, of one form or another, on a regular basis.

c) **WHY WAS IT SELECTED?** WOW was selected as a Stream Tone precursor because it successfully demonstrates that in order to create the exciting and challenging multi-player experiences that many gamers now seek that computer gaming has moved onto the *Web*. The ever-growing popularity of MMOGs, such as WOW, demonstrates that *Web*-based gaming is now accepted by society, technically viable, and well established. Many MMOGs still rely on powerful personal computing devices to generate the game graphics but this is likely to change in the future as more game functionality is moved onto the *Web*, and *Cloud Computing*-based streamed gaming services become more prevalent. The Stream Tone Transfer Protocol will be used to communicate a wide range of digital content and services over the *Internet*, including MMOGs.

d) **HOW IS IT LIKE THE STREAM TONE?** ✔ Replaces local functionality with Web-based services. ✔ Demonstrates the viability and user acceptance of Web-based services. ✔ Reliant on an active Internet connection. ✘ Provides access to all types of content and services. ✔ Streams all data; audio, visual, and other. ✔ Uses secure communications. ✔ Supports real-time interactivity. ✔ Uses a low-cost thin client. ✔ Reliant on remote computing resources. ✘ Based on free and open-source principles.

e) **FURTHER READING**
World Of Warcraft: *https://en.wikipedia.org/wiki/World_of_Warcraft*
World Of Warcraft - Official Site: *http://us.battle.net/wow/en/?-*
Wowhead: *http://www.wowhead.com/*
WoWWiki: *http://www.wowwiki.com/Portal:Main*

# 3.2.39   YOUTUBE

a) **WHAT IS IT?** YouTube is a *Web*-based video streaming service that allows amateur and professional quality video to be uploaded, viewed, and shared, and which is owned by Google, Inc. Videos are delivered on-demand over the *Internet*. Unregistered users can view videos free-of-charge, whilst registered users are also able to upload videos. In some geographic regions video-based content is available to rent from YouTube's rental library, which contains thousands of movies and television shows. YouTube is a for-profit business and its principle revenue source is advertising. Most registered users are only allowed to upload relatively short video clips, but a small group of approved users are allowed to upload long videos. YouTube videos are streamed from a number of globally-dispersed **Cloud Computing**-based **Data Centres** that are often located in places that can provide low-cost electricity from renewable sources or are in close geographic proximity to cold water sources that can be used for cost-effective cooling. YouTube videos can be viewed using a wide range of **Internet**-enabled devices, including, desktop computers, digital video recorders, disk players, games consoles, laptop computers, set-top boxes, **Smart-Phones**, **Tablet Computers**, and televisions. YouTube videos are viewed using a software-based client application or through a standard **Web Browser**. YouTube client software is available for all popular operating systems. YouTube uses the H.263, **H.264**, MPEG-4, **VP8**, and **VP9** video formats, and the AAC, **MP3**, and **Vorbis** audio formats. YouTube supports a wide range of video resolutions, from 144p up to 3072p, although most videos are less than 1080p. Most video is sent to the viewer's client device and watched immediately, however, some videos may be downloaded and viewed offline. YouTube video is generally sent using the **HyperText Transfer Protocol**. Video sent to certain types of mobile device can also be sent using the **Real-time Transport Protocol**. YouTube is one of the most visited destinations on the **Web**. Thousands of new videos are uploaded to YouTube each day, and hundreds of millions of users play billions of videos each month.

b) **IS THERE ANYTHING ELSE THAT IS SIMILAR?** Yes, there are a number of other video hosting services currently available, including 56.com, Blip, blogTV, Break.com, Dailymotion, EngageMedia, EXPO, Funny or Die, Flickr, GodTube, Lafango, LiveLeak, Mail.ru, Myspace, MyVideo, Nico Nico Douga, OpenFilm, Photobucket, Rutube, SchoolTube, ScienceStage, Sevenload, SmugMug, Tout, Trilulilu, Tudou, VBOX7, Veoh, Viddler, Viddy, Videojug, Videolog, Vimeo, Vine, vzaar, wildscreen.tv, Yahoo! Screen, and Youku, to name but a few. There are also innumerable video hosting services providing adult-oriented content.

c) **WHY WAS IT SELECTED?** YouTube was selected as a Stream Tone precursor because it provides a new type of **Web-based Service**, for which there is really no practical local equivalent. Consumption of the YouTube service relies on a continuous connection to the **Internet**. The Stream Tone Access Device will rely on a continuous connection to the **Internet** in order to access digital content and services that will be communicated using the Stream Tone Transfer Protocol (STTP). The YouTube service transmits audio and video data across the **Internet**. The STTP will be used to communicate audio-visual data over the **Internet**.

d) **HOW IS IT LIKE THE STREAM TONE?** ✘ Replaces local functionality with Web-based services. ✔ Demonstrates the viability and user acceptance of Web-based services. ✔ Reliant on an active Internet connection. ✘ Provides access to all types of content and services. ✘ Streams all data; audio, visual, and other. ✘ Uses secure communications. ✔ Supports real-time interactivity. ✔ Uses a low-cost thin client. ✔ Reliant on remote computing resources. ✘ Based on free and open-source principles.

e) **FURTHER READING**
YouTube: *https://www.youtube.com/*
YouTube: *https://en.wikipedia.org/wiki/YouTube*

# 3.2.40   ZEROPC

a) **WHAT IS IT?** ZeroPC is a *Cloud Computing*-based, persistent, *Web Desktop* service that supports a wide range of functionality, including audio playback, email, image viewing and editing, *Instant Messaging*, microblogging, text editing, video playback, and *Web* browsing. ZeroPC also provides a *File Hosting Service*. ZeroPC is owned and operated by ZeroDesktop Inc. ZeroPC is a client-server technology. The ZeroPC client is a software-based *Web* application that is designed to run inside a standard *Web Browser*. The ZeroPC client needs continuous *Internet*-based access to the ZeroPC servers in order to fully function. Communications between the ZeroPC client and the remote ZeroPC servers are secured using the *Encryption* capabilities of the Transport Layer Security protocol. ZeroPC is built using standard *Web* technologies, such as Asynchronous JavaScript and Extensible Markup Language, Cascading Style Sheets, *HyperText Markup Language* and JavaScript. User files stored within a ZeroPC account can be can be uploaded, downloaded, or shared. Audio and video content stored within a ZeroPC account can be streamed to the *Web* client application for instant playback. The ZeroPC *Web Desktop* has a traditional windows, icons, menus, and pointer-style graphical user-interface based on the desktop metaphor. Each user's *Web Desktop* can be customised using visual themes and wallpapers. Some visual themes and wallpapers can be used to mimic the graphical elements of familiar desktop operating systems. A key feature of the ZeroPC service is that it is able to interact with a number of other *Web-based Services*, such as *File Hosting Services*, permitting content stored on those services to be accessed, managed, searched, and shared from within the ZeroPC *Web Desktop* environment. Unlike a traditional desktop operating system, new application software cannot be installed by a user onto a ZeroPC *Web Desktop*; however, links to other *Web*-based content and services can be added to the desktop environment of the ZeroPC *Web Desktop*. The ZeroPC service can be accessed from any *Internet*-enabled location, using a wide range of personal computing devices including desktop computers, laptop computers, *Smart-Phones*, and *Tablet Computers*. ZeroPC has both free-of-charge and paid service options. The paid service options offer more data storage space, larger file upload sizes, increased monthly communications bandwidth, and extra functionality, such as *Web*-based data backup services.

b) **IS THERE ANYTHING ELSE THAT IS SIMILAR?** Yes, there are a number of other *Web Desktop* services currently available, including eyeOS, Jolidrive, and SkyDesktop.

c) **WHY WAS IT SELECTED?** ZeroPC was selected as a Stream Tone precursor because it demonstrates the viability of moving personal computing functionality that was previously executed on a local personal computing device onto *Web-based Services*. This is the type of *Web-based Service* that will help to build society's trust in remote personal computing, and reduce the need for powerful personal computing devices. The Stream Tone Transfer Protocol (STTP) will be used to communicate a wide range of digital content and services over the *Internet*, including *Web Desktops*. The ZeroPC service would most probably be well suited to delivery using the STTP. The ability of the ZeroPC service to access and manipulate data stored within other *Web-based Services* is exactly the sort of enabling-technology that will be required to build the many STTP-based personal computing services that will be used to replace all local personal computing functionality.

d) **HOW IS IT LIKE THE STREAM TONE?** ✔ Replaces local functionality with Web-based services. ✔ Demonstrates the viability and user acceptance of Web-based services. ✔ Reliant on an active Internet connection. ✘ Provides access to all types of content and services. ✘ Streams all data; audio, visual, and other. ✔ Uses secure communications. ✔ Supports real-time interactivity. ✔ Uses a low-cost thin client. ✔ Reliant on remote computing resources. ✘ Based on free and open-source principles.

e) **FURTHER READING**
ZeroPC: *http://www.zeropc.com/*
ZeroPC: *https://en.wikipedia.org/wiki/ZeroPC*

# 3.2.41 ZOHO.COM

a) **WHAT IS IT?** Zoho.com (Zoho) provides a comprehensive suite of *Web*-based business, collaboration, and productivity applications. Zoho.com is a division of Zoho Corporation Pvt. Ltd. Services, such as Zoho, are also known as *Web*-based office suites. Zoho is a software-as-a-service provider. Zoho allows individuals and businesses to transition from locally installed and executed software applications to *Web-based Services*, which are provided by Zoho's *Cloud Computing*-based *Data Centres*. The Zoho applications are accessible from any *Internet*-enabled personal computing device, located anywhere in the world, using a standard *Web Browser*. The Zoho business applications include the following: Assist, a remote support solution; Books, small business accounting solution; BugTracker, a bug tracking system; Campaigns, an email-based marketing solution; ContactManager, a business contact information capture and sharing solution; Creator, a business application development platform; CRM, a customer relationship management solution; Invoice, a customer invoicing solution; LiveDesk, a real-time customer support solution; Marketplace, a discovery service for Zoho-enabled business applications; People, a human resources management solution; Recruit, an applicant tracking and recruitment solution; Reports, a reporting and business intelligence solution; Site24x7, a *Web* site monitoring service; Sites, a *Web* site creation tool; Support, a multi-channel help desk solution; Survey, an online survey solution; Vault, secure storage service for passwords and other sensitive information. The Zoho collaboration applications include the following: Chat, an instant messaging solution; Discussions, a community-based discussion forum solution; Docs, a document management solution; Mail, an email client; Meeting, a remote-desktop sharing solution; Projects, a project management solution; Pulse, a social networking solution; Wiki, a knowledge-base solution. The Zoho productivity applications include the following: Calendar, a group-oriented event scheduling solution; Notebook, a shareable note-taking tool; Sheet, a spreadsheet tool; Show, a slide presentation tool; Writer, a word processing tool. Zoho offers both free-of-charge and subscription-based services. Subscription-based offerings, which provide more capacity or functionality, are available on a per-application basis, allowing service levels to be tailored to individual needs. Zoho is a popular service with millions of individual and business users.

b) **IS THERE ANYTHING ELSE THAT IS SIMILAR?** Yes, there are a number of other services that provide *Web*-based office suites, including CloudOn, Docs.com, Google Docs, Live Documents, Microsoft Office *Web* Apps, and ThinkFree Online Office. There are also a number of other services that provide a different mix of business, collaboration, and/or productivity functionality, including Apptivo, CentralDesktop, ContactOffice, Feng Office, and HyperOffice.

c) **WHY WAS IT SELECTED?** Zoho.com was selected as a Stream Tone precursor because it clearly demonstrates that a very wide range of business, collaboration, and productivity functionality that was previously provided by locally installed and executed software applications has now been successfully moved onto **Web-based Services**. The Stream Tone Transfer Protocol will be used to communicate a wide range of **Web**-based content and services over the **Internet**, including business, collaboration, and productivity applications.

d) **HOW IS IT LIKE THE STREAM TONE?** ✔ Replaces local functionality with Web-based services. ✔ Demonstrates the viability and user acceptance of Web-based services. ✔ Reliant on an active Internet connection. ✘ Provides access to all types of content and services. ✔ Streams all data; audio, visual, and other. ✔ Uses secure communications. ✔ Supports real-time interactivity. ✔ Uses a low-cost thin client. ✔ Reliant on remote computing resources. ✘ Based on free and open-source principles.

e) **FURTHER READING**
Zoho: *https://www.zoho.com/*
Zoho Office Suite: *https://en.wikipedia.org/wiki/Zoho_Office_Suite*

# 3.2.42 ADDITIONAL REGULATORY PRECURSORS

a) Many other **Regulation**-based Stream Tone precursors also exist, some of which are briefly described below. Collectively, these additional precursors will help to create a regulatory environment that is able to better support the design, development, and deployment of a wide range of new technologies, including the Stream Tone.

## 3.2.42.1 A REPORT FROM THE PORTABLE ELECTRONIC DEVICES AVIATION RULEMAKING COMMITTEE TO THE FEDERAL AVIATION ADMINISTRATION: RECOMMENDATIONS ON EXPANDING THE USE OF PORTABLE ELECTRONIC DEVICES DURING FLIGHT

a) At the end of September 2013 the Portable Electronic Devices (PED) Aviation Rulemaking Committee (ARC) published a report, supporting a Federal Aviation Administration (FAA) **Regulation**, titled "A Report from the Portable Electronic Devices Aviation Rulemaking Committee to the Federal Aviation Administration: Recommendations on Expanding the Use of Portable Electronic Devices During Flight". A supporting fact sheet issued by the FAA summarised the report's conclusions and contained the following statements: *"Most commercial airplanes can tolerate radio interference signals from PEDs; the FAA should provide airlines with new procedures to assess if their airplanes can tolerate radio interference from PEDs; once an airline verifies their fleet is PED tolerant, it may allow passengers to use handheld, lightweight* *electronic devices – such as tablets, e-readers, and smartphones, at all altitudes; in some instances of severe weather with low-visibility, the crew should continue to instruct passengers to turn off their devices during landing; heavier devices, such as standard laptops, should be safely stowed under seats* [or] *in overhead bins during takeoff and landing; items that do not meet the operator's size criteria for use during takeoff and landing must be stowed in accordance with the aircraft operator's approved carry-on baggage program; all loose items should be held or put in the seat back pocket prior to takeoff and landing; the ARC did recommend that the FAA consult with the Federal Communications Commission (FCC) to review their current rules".*

b)　In simple terms, the findings of this report will lead to a ***Regulation*** that will allow the use of PEDs in situations that were previously prohibited, namely during the take-off, landing, and taxiing of a commercial airplane. Previously PEDs were not allowed to be used until a commercial airplane had reached a height of at least 10,000 feet. The findings of the PED ARC supports the use of most types of PED below 10,000 feet, which will allow approved devices to be used continuously from the moment that a passenger enters an airplane at the departure gate until that passenger then leaves the airplane at the arrival gate.

## 3.2.42.2　AMENDMENT OF THE COMMISSION'S RULES WITH REGARD TO COMMERCIAL OPERATIONS IN THE 1695-1710 MHz, 1755-1780 MHz, AND 2155-2180 BANDS

a)　On the 31st March 2014 the Federal Communications Commission (FCC) adopted a Report and Order (R&O), a type of ***Regulation***, with the title "Amendment of the Commission's Rules with Regard to Commercial Operations in the 1695-1710 MHz [megahertz], 1755-1780 MHz, and 2155-2180 MHz Bands". Section 1 of the R&O included the following statements: *"Today we adopt rules governing use of spectrum in the 1695-1710 MHz, 1755-1780 MHz, and 2155-2180 MHz bands that will make available significantly more commercial spectrum for Advanced Wireless Services (AWS). We refer to these bands as AWS-3. 1 This additional 65 megahertz of spectrum for commercial use will help ensure that the speed, capacity, and ubiquity of the nation's wireless networks keeps pace with industry demands for wireless service".* Section 2 of the R&O included the following statements: *"We will license the AWS-3 spectrum in two sub-bands. We will pair the 2155-2180 MHz band for downlink/base station operations with the 1755-1780 MHz band for uplink/mobile operations. The 2155-2180 MHz band is already currently allocated for non-Federal, commercial use. The 1755-1780 MHz band is being made available on a shared basis with a limited number of Federal incumbents indefinitely, while many of the Federal systems will over time relocate out of the band. We also adopt rules to allocate and license the 1695-1710 MHz band for uplink/mobile operations on an unpaired shared basis with incumbent Federal meteorological-satellite (MetSat) data users. We will assign AWS-3 licenses by competitive bidding, offering 5 megahertz and 10 megahertz blocks that can be aggregated using Economic Areas (EAs) as the area for geographic licensing, except for 1755-1760/2155-2160 MHz, which will be licensed by Cellular Market Areas (CMAs)".*

b)　In simple terms, this ***Regulation*** authorises the FCC to sell a total of 65 MHz of radio spectrum in an upcoming auction. A total of 40 MHz of this auctioned radio spectrum will be made available for commercial uses, such as for **Fourth-Generation Mobile Communications** services.

## 3.2.42.3 BROADBAND DELIVERY UK

a) Broadband Delivery UK (BDUK) is a programme of the government of the United Kingdom (UK) that aims to support economic growth in the UK, including in rural areas, to ensure that the UK has the best super-fast broadband in Europe by the end of the UK Parliamentary year 2015, to ensure delivery of standard broadband to virtually all communities in the UK by the end of the UK Parliamentary year 2015, and to ensure the efficient use of funding to deliver super-fast broadband and standard broadband to assist other government initiatives which are dependent upon customers ability to access broadband-based services. A stated ambition of the BDUK programme is to provide super-fast broadband to at least ninety percent of premises in the UK and to provide universal access to standard broadband with a speed of at least 2 megabits per second (Mbps). The Office of Communications (Ofcom), the independent regulator and competition authority for the UK communications industries, has recommended that the minimum download speed for standard broadband provided by the BDUK programme should be 8 Mbps.

b) In simple terms, the BDUK programme will help to ensure, through the application of various rules and **Regulations**, that every UK citizen is able to access the **Internet**, if they want to, even if they are currently prevented from doing so due to financial circumstances or geographic location. The concept of universal access to standard broadband within the UK can be considered to be a precursor to a formal **Universal Service Obligation** for broadband in the UK.

## 3.2.42.4 EXPANDING THE ECONOMIC AND INNOVATION OPPORTUNITIES OF SPECTRUM THROUGH INCENTIVE AUCTIONS

a) On the 28th September 2012, the Federal Communications Commission (FCC) adopted a Notice of Proposed Rulemaking (NPRM), a type of **Regulation**, titled "Expanding the Economic and Innovation Opportunities of Spectrum Through Incentive Auctions". Section 3 of the NPRM contained the following statements: *"The 2010 National Broadband Plan introduced the idea of incentive auctions as a tool to help meet the Nation's spectrum needs. Incentive auctions are a voluntary, market-based means of repurposing spectrum by encouraging licensees to voluntarily relinquish spectrum usage rights in exchange for a share of the proceeds from an auction of new licenses to use the repurposed spectrum. The incentive auction idea is the latest in a series of world-leading spectrum policies pioneered in the U.S., including unlicensed spectrum uses such as WiFi, Bluetooth, near field communication, and other innovations and the original FCC spectrum auctions in the 1990s. On February 22, 2012, Congress authorized the Commission to conduct incentive auctions, and directed that we use this innovative tool for an incentive auction of broadcast television spectrum"*. Section 4 of the NPRM contained the following statements: *"The purpose of this Notice is to develop a* *rulemaking record that will enable us to meet the challenges presented by the Spectrum Act's unique grant of authority to the Commission. The broadcast television spectrum incentive auction will be the first such auction ever attempted worldwide. It will be a groundbreaking event for the broadcast television, mobile wireless, and technology sectors of our economy. It presents a significant financial opportunity for broadcasters who remain on the air and continue providing the public with diverse, local, free over-the-air television service. At the same time, the spectrum reclaimed through the incentive auction will promote economic growth and enhance America's global competitiveness, increase the speed, capacity and ubiquity of mobile broadband service, such as 4G* [Fourth-Generation Mobile Communications] *LTE* [Long-Term Evolution] *and Wi-Fi like networks, and accelerate the smartphone- and tablet-led mobile revolution, benefitting consumers and businesses throughout the country. This proceeding is an important component of the Commission's unprecedented commitment and efforts to make additional licensed and unlicensed spectrum available for broadband".*

b)  In simple terms, the FAA plans, through the use of **Regulation**, to invite television broadcasters that currently own licensed radio spectrum in the 600 megahertz (MHz) waveband to voluntarily give up some of their radio spectrum so that it can be sold at auction. Television broadcasters will then receive a share of the proceeds from the sale of their licensed radio spectrum. The auctioned radio spectrum will then be re-assigned, primarily for use with **Fourth-Generation Mobile Communications** services. This incentive auction, in the 600 MHz waveband, is considered to be a rare event that is unlikely to be repeated for many years, if ever. Originally planned for June 2014, the auction has been delayed due to its complex nature, and is now expected to be held sometime during 2015.

# 3.2.42.5    P7_TA(2014)0281: EUROPEAN SINGLE MARKET FOR ELECTRONIC COMMUNICATIONS

a)  On the 3rd April 2014, Members of the European Parliament voted overwhelmingly to approve a proposed **Regulation** titled "P7_TA(2014)0281: European Single Market for Electronic Communications. European Parliament legislative resolution of 3 April 2014 on the proposal for a Regulation of the European Parliament and of the Council laying down measures concerning the European single market for electronic communications and to achieve a Connected Continent, and amending Directives 2002/20/EC, 2002/21/EC, 2002/22/EC, and Regulations (EC) No 1211/2009 and (EU) No 531/2012 (COM(2013)0627 – C7-0267/2013 – 2013/0309(COD))". Within the resolution, **Regulation** (EU) No 531/2012 Article 6a contained the following statements: *"With effect from 15 December 2015, roaming providers shall not levy any surcharge in comparison to the charges for mobile communications services at domestic level on roaming customers in any Member States for any regulated roaming call made or received, for any regulated roaming SMS* [Short Message Service]/*MMS* [Multimedia Messaging Service] *message sent and for any regulated data roaming services used, nor any general charge to enable the terminal equipment or service to be used abroad".* Within the resolution, **Regulation** (EU) No 531/2012 Article 13 - paragraph 2 contained the following statements: *"With effect from 1 July 2012, the retail charge (excluding VAT) of a euro-data tariff which a roaming provider may levy on its roaming customer for the provision of a regulated data roaming service shall not exceed EUR 0,70 per megabyte used. The* *maximum retail charge for data used shall decrease to EUR 0,45 per megabyte used on 1 July 2013 and to EUR 0,20 per megabyte used on 1 July 2014. The maximum charges applicable as of 1 July 2014 shall expire 16 December 2015 save for regulated data roaming services in excess of any fair use limit applied in accordance with Article 6b."*

b) In simple terms, this **Regulation** will end mobile data roaming fees within the European Union as of 15th December 2015. This **Regulation** will also end Multimedia Messaging Service, Short Message Service, and voice-calling roaming fees by the same date. Currently, roaming fees are charged when a customer of a mobile communications service provider located in one European Member State uses the services of a mobile communications service provider located in another European Member State. After 15th December 2015, the fees for all such services are expected to become the same as the fees that are charged when a customer is using a mobile communications service within his/her own European Member State.

## 3.2.42.6   MARCO CIVIL DA INTERNET

a) The Marco Civil da **Internet** has been described as the constitution of the **Internet** in Brazil. The Marco Civil da **Internet** provides protection for net neutrality, open government, privacy rights, and safe harbours for **Internet** service providers and online service providers, and established that **Internet** access is a requisite for exercising civic rights. The Marco Civil da **Internet** was approved, and signed into law on the 22nd April 2014. The Marco Civil da **Internet** is a type of **Regulation**.

b) In simple terms, this **Regulation** will help to build confidence and trust in use of the **Internet** within Brazil.

## 3.2.42.7   PRESIDENTIAL MEMORANDUM: UNLEASHING THE WIRELESS BROADBAND REVOLUTION

a) On the 28th June 2010, the President of the United States of America, Barack Obama, issued a presidential memorandum, a type of **Regulation**, titled "Unleashing the Wireless Broadband Revolution". Section 1 of this document contained the following statements: *"The Secretary of Commerce, working through the National Telecommunications and Information Administration (NTIA), shall (a) collaborate with the Federal Communications Commission (FCC) to make available a total of 500 MHz [megahertz] of Federal and non-federal spectrum over the next 10 years, suitable for both mobile and fixed wireless broadband use. The spectrum must be available to be licensed by the FCC for exclusive use or made available for shared access by commercial and Government users in order to enable licensed or unlicensed wireless broadband technologies to be deployed".*

b) In simple terms, this **Regulation** will lead to more radio spectrum being made available for both licensed and unlicensed wireless communications in the near future.

## 3.2.42.8 PRESIDENTIAL MEMORANDUM: EXPANDING AMERICA'S LEADERSHIP IN WIRELESS INNOVATION

a)  On the 14<sup>th</sup> June 2013, the President of the United States of America, Barack Obama, issued a presidential memorandum, a type of **Regulation**, titled "Expanding America's Leadership in Wireless Innovation". The first paragraph of this document contained the following statements: *"Expanding the availability of spectrum for innovative and flexible commercial uses, including for broadband services, will further promote our Nation's economic development by providing citizens and businesses with greater speed and availability of coverage, encourage further development of cutting-edge wireless technologies, applications, and services, and help reduce usage charges for households and businesses. We must continue to make additional spectrum available as promptly as possible for the benefit of consumers and businesses. At the same time, we must ensure that Federal, State, local, tribal, and territorial governments are able to maintain mission critical capabilities that depend on spectrum today, as well as effectively and efficiently meet future requirements".* The second paragraph of this document contained the following statements: *"One means of doing so is by allowing and encouraging shared access to spectrum that is currently allocated exclusively for Federal use".* Section 1 of this document contained the following statements: *"The Spectrum Policy Team shall monitor and support advances in spectrum sharing policies and technologies. Within 1 year of the date of this memorandum, the Spectrum Policy Team shall publish a report describing how NTIA* [National Telecommunications and Information Administration] *and FCC* [Federal Communications Commission] *are incorporating spectrum sharing into their spectrum management practices".*

b)  In simple terms, this **Regulation** will lead to more radio spectrum that is currently designated for Federal-only use being made available for both licensed and unlicensed non-Federal wireless communications in the near future.

## 3.2.42.9 REVISION OF PART 15 OF THE COMMISSION'S RULES TO PERMIT UNLICENSED NATIONAL INFORMATION INFRASTRUCTURE (U-NII) DEVICES IN THE 5 GHZ BAND

a)  On the 31<sup>st</sup> March 2014 the Federal Communications Commission (FCC) adopted a Report and Order (R&O), a type of **Regulation**, titled "Revision of Part 15 of the Commission's Rules to Permit Unlicensed National Information Infrastructure (U-NII) Devices in the 5 GHz [gigahertz] Band". Section 1 of this R&O contained the following statements *"In this First Report and Order (First R&O), we increase the utility of the 5 GHz band where U-NII devices are currently permitted to operate, and modify certain U-NII rules and testing procedures to ensure that U-NII devices do not cause harmful interference to authorized users of these bands. Specifically: For U-NII devices in the 5.15-5.25 GHz band, we remove the indoor-only restriction and increase the permitted power, thus increasing the utility of spectrum and accommodating the next generation of Wi-Fi technology. We extend the upper edge of the 5.725-5.825 GHz band to 5.85 GHz and consolidate the Part 15 rules applicable to all digitally modulated devices operating* *across this 125 megahertz of spectrum to ensure that all such devices comply with U-NII requirements intended to protect authorized users from harmful interference. We require that all U-NII device software be secured to prevent its modification to ensure that the devices will operate as authorized by the Commission, thus reducing the potential for harmful interference to authorized users. To protect Terminal Doppler Weather Radar (TDWR) systems and other radar systems operating in the 5.250-5.350 GHz and 5.470-5.725 GHz bands from harmful interference, we modify certain technical rules and compliance measurement procedures for U-NII devices operating in these bands."*

b)  In simple terms, what this means is that through this **Regulation** the FCC has removed some of the restrictions on the use of parts of the national radio spectrum of the United States of America that are currently used for certain types of **Communications Satellite**-based communications services in the 5 GHz waveband. The principle benefit of lifting these restrictions is that wireless communications that currently make use of the 100 MHz of radio spectrum in the 5.15-5.25 GHz range, such as **Wi-Fi**, will now be able to operate outdoors and at much greater transmit power. Such changes will greatly enhance the usefulness of such wireless communications technologies.

# 3.2.42.10 STATEMENT ON THE REQUESTS FOR VARIATION OF 900 MHZ, 1800 MHZ, AND 2100 MHZ MOBILE LICENSES

a)  On the 9th July 2013, the Office of Communications (Ofcom), the independent regulator and competition authority for the United Kingdom (UK) communications industries, published a document supporting a change of **Regulations** titled "Statement on the Requests for Variation of 900 MHz [megahertz], 1800 MHz and 2100 MHz Mobile Licences". The summary section of this document contained the following statements: *"For the reasons set out in this Statement, we have decided to proceed with the variations that permit the use of 4G [Fourth-Generation Mobile Communications] technology in each of the 900 MHz, 1800 MHz and 2100 MHz licences and to increase the maximum permitted power in the 900 MHz licences by 3 dB [decibels]. At the same time we will update a number of terms and conditions in these licences in order to align them more closely with the equivalent terms and conditions in the recently awarded 800 MHz and 2.6 GHz [gigahertz] licences. This decision delivers a long standing objective to liberalise all mobile licences so as to remove the regulatory barriers to deployment of the latest available mobile technology. Even though operators may not seek to deploy 4G services in the newly liberalised bands in the immediate future, the interests of consumers will be served by the fact that these bands have been liberalised now, ahead of a market led transition to their use for 4G technology in future. As a result, operators can plan and implement a transition to 4G technology in these bands without having to engage in a further regulatory process".*

b)  In simple terms, Ofcom has, through revised **Regulations**, simplified the process by which radio spectrum that was previously used with less efficient and now outdated mobile telecommunications technologies, such as second-generation mobile communications, can be reassigned for use with newer mobile telecommunications technologies, such as **Fourth-Generation Mobile Communications**. This liberalisation of mobile communications licenses is expected to lead to the development of a much more capable and modern telecommunications environment with the UK.

# 3.2.43 ADDITIONAL SOCIETAL PRECURSORS

a)  Many other service-oriented Stream Tone precursors also exist, a wide variety of which are briefly described below. In contrast to the precursors described in the main section on precursors, these particular precursors have primarily been included because of their commercial success or popularity. Factors that strongly suggest that society may now be ready to accept the transition to Comprehensive Remote Personal Computing that the Stream Tone will bring. Collectively, these additional precursors provide a highly diverse range of functionalities.

## 3.2.43.1 ABCNEWS.COM

a)  ABCNews.com is a *Web*-based news service provided by American Broadcasting Companies, Inc., a subsidiary of The Walt Disney Company, Inc. ABCNews.com offers a wide range of *Web-based Services*, including a *Streaming Media* service.

## 3.2.43.2 ALIBABA.COM

a)  Alibaba.com is a *Web*-based e-commerce service provided by Alibaba Group. Alibaba.com is an example of a *Cloud Computing*-based service.

## 3.2.43.3 AMAZON.COM

a)  Amazon.com is a *Web*-based shopping and digital content distribution service provided by Amazon.com, Inc. Amazon.com offers a wide range of *Web-based Services*, including a *Streaming Media* service. Amazon.com is an example of a *Cloud Computing*-based service.

## 3.2.43.4 AMAZON WEB SERVICES

a)  Amazon *Web* Services (AWS) is a comprehensive remote computing service provided by Amazon.com, Inc. AWS is an example of a *Cloud Computing*-based service that can be used to build a wide range of *Web-based Services*, including *Streaming Media* services and *Streamed Services*.

## 3.2.43.5 APPLE APP STORE

a)  The App Store is a *Web*-based software application distribution platform, also known as an *Application Store*, which is provided by Apple Inc. The App Store is an example of a *Cloud Computing*-based service.

# 3.2.43.6    BAIDU.COM

a)    Baidu.com is a *Web*-based *Web* search engine provided by Baidu, Inc. Baidu.com is an example of a *Cloud Computing*-based service.

# 3.2.43.7    BBC.CO.UK

a)    BBC.co.uk is a *Web*-based news and entertainment service that is provided by the British Broadcasting Corporation (BBC). BBC.co.uk offers a wide range of *Web-based Services*, including a *Streaming Media* service. BBC.co.uk is an example of a *Cloud Computing*-based service.

# 3.2.43.8    BITCOIN

a)    Bitcoin is a digital, peer-to-peer, *Encryption*-based currency that was invented by pseudonymous developer Satoshi Nakamoto. Bitcoin can be used to purchase a wide range of digital and analogue products and services.

# 3.2.43.9    BT INFINITY 300

a)    The BT Infinity 300 is a residential *Optical Fibre*-based communications service that offers bandwidths of up to 300 megabits per second, which is provided by British Telecommunications (BT), the trading name of BT Group plc. The BT Infinity 300 service can be used to access a wide range of *Internet* and *Web-based Services*, including *Cloud Computing*-based services, *Streaming Media* services, and *Streamed Services*.

# 3.2.43.10    CHASE.COM

a)    Chase.com is a *Web*-based banking service that is provided by JPMorgan Chase & Co. Chase.com is an example of a *Cloud Computing*-based service.

# 3.2.43.11    CISCO SYSTEMS WEBEX

a)    WebEx is a *Web*-based multimedia collaboration platform that is provided by Cisco Systems, Inc. WebEx is an example of a *Cloud Computing*-based service and a *Streaming Media* service.

# 3.2.43.12    CLOUD9 IDE

a)    Cloud9 IDE is a *Web*-based integrated development environment service that is provided by Cloud9 IDE, Inc. Cloud9 IDE is an example of a *Cloud Computing*-based service that can be used to develop a wide range of *Web-based Services*, including *Streaming Media* services and *Streamed Services*.

## 3.2.43.13     CNN.COM

a)   CNN.com is a *Web*-based news service that is provided by Turner Broadcasting System, Inc., a subsidiary of Time Warner, Inc. CNN.com offers a wide range of *Web-based Services*, including a *Streaming Media* service. CNN.com is an example of a *Cloud Computing*-based service.

## 3.2.43.14     CODEANYWHERE

a)   CodeAnywhere is a *Web*-based integrated development environment service provided by Ademptio LLC. CodeAnywhere is an example of a *Cloud Computing*-based service that can be used to develop a wide range of *Web-based Services*, including *Streaming Media* services and *Streamed Services*.

## 3.2.43.15     COMIXOLOGY

a)   Comixology is a *Web*-based digital comic book distribution service that is provided by Iconology, Inc., a subsidiary of Amazon.com, Inc. Comixology is an example of a *Cloud Computing*-based service.

## 3.2.43.16     COURSERA

a)   Coursera is a *Web*-based massive open on-line course service that offers a wide range of educational courses and which is provided by Coursera, Inc. Coursera is an example of a *Cloud Computing*-based service and a *Streaming Media* service.

## 3.2.43.17     CRAIGSLIST

a)   Craigslist is a *Web*-based classified advertising service that is provided by Craigslist, Inc.

## 3.2.43.18     EBAY

a)   Ebay is a *Web*-based consumer-to-consumer marketplace and auction service that is provided by eBay, Inc. Ebay is an example of a *Cloud Computing*-based service.

## 3.2.43.19     ENGINE YARD

a)   Engine Yard is a *Web*-based platform-as-a-service that is provided by Engine Yard, Inc. Engine Yard is an example of a *Cloud Computing*-based service that can be used to build a wide range of *Web-based Services*, including *Streaming Media* services and *Streamed*

*Services*.

## 3.2.43.20    EXPEDIA

a)    Expedia is a *Web*-based travel and accommodation booking service that is provided by Expedia, Inc. Expedia is an example of a *Cloud Computing*-based service.

## 3.2.43.21    FACEBOOK

a)    Facebook is a *Web*-based social networking service that is provided by Facebook, Inc. Facebook is an example of a *Cloud Computing*-based service.

## 3.2.43.22    FLICKR

a)    Flickr is a *Web*-based image and video hosting service that is provided by Yahoo! Inc. Flickr is an example of a *Cloud Computing*-based service.

## 3.2.43.23    GITHUB

a)    GitHub is a *Web*-based collaborative software development platform that is provided by GitHub, Inc. GitHub is an example of a *Cloud Computing*-based service that can be used to support the development of a wide range of *Web-based Services*, including *Streaming Media* services and *Streamed Services*.

## 3.2.43.24    GO DADDY

a)    Go Daddy is a *Web*-based *Internet* domain registrar and *Web* site hosting service that is provided by GoDaddy.com LLC. Go Daddy is an example of a *Cloud Computing*-based service.

## 3.2.43.25    GOOGLE ADWORDS

a)    AdWords is a *Web*-based advertising service that is provided by Google, Inc. AdWords is an example of a *Cloud Computing*-based service.

## 3.2.43.26    GOOGLE APP ENGINE

a)    App Engine is a *Web*-based platform-as-a-service that is provided by Google, Inc. App Engine is an example of a *Cloud Computing*-based service that can be used to build a wide range of *Web-based Services*, including *Streaming Media* services and *Streamed Services*.

## 3.2.43.27    GOOGLE EARTH

a)  Earth is a *Web*-based geographical information service that is provided by Google, Inc. Earth is an example of a *Cloud Computing*-based service, and a *Streaming Media* service.

## 3.2.43.28    GOOGLE FIBER

a)  Fiber is an affordable 1 gigabit per second *Optical Fibre*-based *Internet* service that is provided by Google, Inc. The Fiber service can be used to access a wide range of *Internet* and *Web-based Services*, including *Cloud Computing*-based services, *Streaming Media* services, and *Streamed Services*.

## 3.2.43.29    GOOGLE GMAIL

a)  Gmail is a *Web*-based email service that is provided by Google, Inc. Gmail is an example of a *Cloud Computing*-based service.

## 3.2.43.30    GOOGLE MAPS

a)  Maps is a *Web*-based map service that is provided by Google. Maps is an example of a *Cloud Computing*-based service and a *Streaming Media* service.

## 3.2.43.31    GOOGLE MAPS NAVIGATION

a)  Maps Navigation is a *Web*-based navigation service that is provided by Google, Inc. Maps Navigation is an example of a *Cloud Computing*-based service and a *Streaming Media* service.

## 3.2.43.32    GOOGLE PLAY

a)  Play is a *Web*-based digital software application distribution service, also known as an *Application Store*, which is provided by Google, Inc. Play is an example of a *Cloud Computing*-based service and a *Streaming Media* service.

## 3.2.43.33    GOOGLE SEARCH

a)  Search is a *Web*-based *Web* search engine that is provided by Google, Inc. Search is an example of a *Cloud Computing*-based service.

## 3.2.43.34    GOOGLE STREET VIEW

a)   Street View is a *Web*-based geographical information service that is provided by Google, Inc. Street View is an example of a *Cloud Computing*-based service and a *Streaming Media* service.

## 3.2.43.35    GOOGLE TRANSLATE

a)   Translate is a *Web*-based language translation service that is provided by Google, Inc. Translate is an example of a *Cloud Computing*-based service.

## 3.2.43.36    HM GOVERNMENT G-CLOUD

a)   G-Cloud is the *Web*-based procurement framework of the United Kingdom government. G-Cloud is an example of a *Cloud Computing*-based service.

## 3.2.43.37    HM GOVERNMENT GOV.UK

a)   Gov.uk is the *Web*-based information service of the United Kingdom government. Gov.uk is an example of a *Cloud Computing*-based service.

## 3.2.43.38    HOUSE OF CARDS

a)   House of Cards is a critically acclaimed television drama series that was developed by *Netflix*, Inc. House of Cards premiered on the *Web*-based *Netflix* entertainment service in February 2013. *Netflix* is a *Streaming Media* service.

## 3.2.43.39    INSTAGRAM

a)   Instagram is a *Web*-based image hosting, editing, sharing, and social networking service that is provided by Instagram LLC, a subsidiary of Facebook, Inc. Instagram is an example of a *Cloud Computing*-based service.

## 3.2.43.40    INTERNATIONAL BUSINESS MACHINES SMARTCLOUD

a)   SmartCloud is a comprehensive *Web-based Service* solution that includes infrastructure-as-a-service, platform-as-a-service, and software-as-a-service that is provided by International Business Machines Corporation. SmartCloud is an example of a *Cloud Computing*-based service that can be used to build a wide range of *Web-based Services*, including *Streaming Media* services and *Streamed Services*.

## 3.2.43.41    INTERNET MOVIE DATABASE

a)    The Internet Movie Database (IMDb) is a *Web*-based database of films, television shows, and video games that is provided by Imdb.com, Inc., a subsidiary of Amazon.com, Inc. IMDb is an example of a *Cloud Computing*-based service.

## 3.2.43.42    KOBO

a)    Kobo is a *Web*-based e-book retail service that is provided by Kobo, Inc., a subsidiary of Rakuten, Inc. Kobo is an example of a *Cloud Computing*-based service.

## 3.2.43.43    LASTMINUTE.COM

a)    Lastminute.com is a *Web*-based travel, accommodation, and entertainment booking service that is provided by Last Minute Network Ltd, a subsidiary of Sabre Holdings Corporation. Lastminute.com is an example of a *Cloud Computing*-based service.

## 3.2.43.44    LAUNCHPAD

a)    LaunchPad is a *Web*-based collaborative software development platform provided by Canonical Ltd. LaunchPad is an example of a *Cloud Computing*-based service that can be used to develop a wide range of *Web-based Services*, including *Streaming Media* services and *Streamed Services*.

## 3.2.43.45    LINKEDIN

a)    LinkedIn is a *Web*-based social networking service for business professionals that is provided by LinkedIn Corporation. LinkedIn is an example of a *Cloud Computing*-based service.

## 3.2.43.46    LOGMEIN

a)    LogMeIn is a *Web*-based a remote connectivity, collaboration, and support service that is provided by LogMeIn, Inc. LogMeIn is an example of a *Cloud Computing*-based service and a *Streaming Media* service.

## 3.2.43.47    LULU

a)    Lulu is a *Web*-based self-publishing book service that is provided by Lulu Enterprises, Inc. Lulu is an example of a *Cloud Computing*-based service.

# 3.2.43.48    MAIL ONLINE

a)    The Mail Online is a *Web*-based news service provided by DMG Media Ltd., a subsidiary of Daily Mail and General Trust plc. The Mail Online offers a wide range of *Web-based Services*, including a *Streaming Media* service. The Mail Online is an example of a *Cloud Computing*-based service.

# 3.2.43.49    MASHERY

a)    Mashery is a *Web-based Service* platform for *Application Programming Interface* management that is provided by Mashery, Inc., a subsidiary of Intel Corporation. Mashery is an example of a *Cloud Computing*-based service that can be used to support the development of a wide range of *Web-based Services*, including *Streaming Media* services and *Streamed Services*.

# 3.2.43.50    MICROSOFT AZURE

a)    Azure is a *Web*-based platform-as-a-service and an infrastructure-as-a-service that is provided by Microsoft Corporation. Azure is an example of a *Cloud Computing*-based service that can be used to build a wide range of *Web-based Services*, including *Streaming Media* services and *Streamed Services*.

# 3.2.43.51    MICROSOFT BING

a)    Bing is a *Web*-based *Web* search engine that is provided by Microsoft Corporation. Bing is an example of a *Cloud Computing*-based service.

# 3.2.43.52    MICROSOFT OUTLOOK.COM

a)    Outlook.com is a *Web*-based email service that is provided by Microsoft Corporation. Outlook.com is an example of a *Cloud Computing*-based service.

# 3.2.43.53    NETSUITE

a)    Netsuite is a *Web*-based enterprise-oriented software-as-a-service that is provided by Netsuite, Inc. Netsuite is an example of a *Cloud Computing*-based service.

# 3.2.43.54    PAYPAL

a)    PayPal is a *Web*-based payment service that is provided by PayPal, Inc., a subsidiary of eBay, Inc. PayPal is an example of a *Cloud Computing*-based service.

## 3.2.43.55    PICASA

a)    Picasa is a *Web*-based image editing, storage, and viewing service that is provided by Google, Inc. Picasa is an example of a *Cloud Computing*-based service.

## 3.2.43.56    PINTEREST

a)    Pinterest is a *Web*-based image sharing service that is provided by Pinterest, Inc. Pinterest is an example of a *Cloud Computing*-based service.

## 3.2.43.57    PRIVATE INTERNET ACCESS

a)    Private Internet Access is a *Web*-based virtual private networking service that is provided by London Trust Media, Inc. Private Internet Access provides a secure, *Encryption*-based mechanism for accessing a wide range of *Internet* and *Web-based Services*, including *Cloud Computing*-based services, *Streaming Media* services, and *Streamed Services*.

## 3.2.43.58    PROGRAMMABLEWEB

a)    ProgrammableWeb is a *Web*-based directory service for *Application Programming Interfaces* that can be used to access *Web-based Services* that is provided by ProgrammableWeb.com. ProgrammableWeb is an example of a *Cloud Computing*-based service.

## 3.2.43.59    PUREVPN

a)    PureVPN is a *Web*-based virtual private networking service that is provided by GZ Systems Ltd. PureVPN provides a secure, *Encryption*-based mechanism for accessing a wide range of *Internet* and *Web-based Services*, including *Cloud Computing*-based services, *Streaming Media* services, and *Streamed Services*.

## 3.2.43.60    REDDIT

a)    Reddit is a *Web*-based social news and entertainment service that is provided by Reddit, Inc. Reddit is an example of a *Cloud Computing*-based service.

## 3.2.43.61    SALESFORCE.COM

a)    Salesforce.com is a *Web*-based enterprise-oriented software-as-a-service that is provided by Saleforce.com, Inc. Salesforce.com is an example of a *Cloud Computing*-based service and a *Streamed Service*.

# 3.2.43.62   SCRIBD

a) Scribd is a **Web**-based document hosting and sharing service that is provided by Scribd, Inc. Scribd is an example of a **Cloud Computing**-based service.

# 3.2.43.63   SHUTTERSTOCK

a) Shutterstock is a **Web**-based stock photography service that is provided by Shutterstock, Inc. Shutterstock is an example of a **Cloud Computing**-based service.

# 3.2.43.64   SINGTEL PRESTIGE 150

a) The SingTel Prestige 150 is a mobile broadband service that offers a bandwidth of up to 150 megabits per second bandwidth, which is provided by Singapore Telecommunications Ltd (SingTel). The SingTel Prestige 150 service can be used to access a wide range of **Internet** and **Web-based Services**, including **Cloud Computing**-based services, **Streaming Media** services, and **Streamed Services**.

# 3.2.43.65   SKY GO

a) Sky Go is an **Internet Television Service** that is provided by British Sky Broadcasting Group plc (Sky). Sky Go is an example of a **Cloud Computing**-based service and a **Streaming Media** service.

# 3.2.43.66   SOUNDCLOUD

a) SoundCloud is a **Web**-based audio hosting, distribution, and collaboration service that is provided by SoundCloud Ltd. SoundCloud is an example of a **Cloud Computing**-based service and a **Streaming Media** service.

# 3.2.43.67   SQUARE

a) Square is a **Web**-based point of sale service for merchants that is provided by Square, Inc. Square is an example of a **Cloud Computing**-based service.

# 3.2.43.68   STEAM

a) Steam is a **Web**-based digital content distribution service that is provided by Valve Corporation. Steam is an example of a **Cloud Computing**-based service that provides access to a wide range of computer games, including **Massively Multi-player On-line Games**.

## 3.2.43.69   STUMBLEUPON

a)   StumbleUpon is a *Web*-based digital content discovery service that is provided by StumbleUpon, Inc. StumbleUpon is an example of a *Cloud Computing*-based service.

## 3.2.43.70   SURVEYMONKEY

a)   SurveyMonkey is a *Web*-based survey service that is provided by SurveyMonkey, Inc. SurveyMonkey is an example of a *Cloud Computing*-based service.

## 3.2.43.71   TENCENT WEIYUN

a)   Weiyun is a free-of-charge *File Hosting Service* that is provided by Tencent Holdings Limited. Weiyun offers up to 10 terabytes of digital data storage per user. Weiyun is an example of a *Cloud Computing* service.

## 3.2.43.72   TUMBLR

a)   Tumblr is a *Web*-based social network and blogging service that is provided by Yahoo! Inc. Tumblr is an example of a *Cloud Computing*-based service.

## 3.2.43.73   TWITTER

a)   Twitter is a *Web*-based social networking and microblogging service that is provided by Twitter, Inc. Twitter is an example of a *Cloud Computing*-based service.

## 3.2.43.74   UDACITY

a)   Udacity is a *Web*-based massive open on-line course service that offers a wide range of educational courses and which is provided by Udacity, Inc. Udacity is an example of a *Cloud Computing*-based service and a *Streaming Media* service.

## 3.2.43.75   UDEMY

a)   Udemy is a *Web*-based massive open on-line course service that offers a wide range of educational courses and which is provided by Udemy, Inc. is an example of a *Cloud Computing*-based service and a *Streaming Media* service.

## 3.2.43.76   VIRGIN TV ANYWHERE

a)   TV Anywhere is an *Internet Television Service* that is provided by Virgin Media, Inc. TV Anywhere is an example of a *Cloud Computing*-based service and a *Streaming Media* service.

## 3.2.43.77   WEEBLY

a)   Weebly is a **Web**-based **Web** site builder and hosting service that is provided by Weebly, Inc. Weebly is an example of a **Cloud Computing**-based service and a **Streaming Media** service.

## 3.2.43.78   WIKIPEDIA

a)   Wikipedia is a **Web**-based encyclopaedia service that is provided by the non-profit Wikimedia Foundation, Inc. Wikipedia is an example of a **Cloud Computing**-based service.

## 3.2.43.79   WOLFRAMALPHA

a)   WolframAlpha is a **Web**-based computational knowledge service that is provided by Wolfram Alpha LLC. WolframAlpha is an example of a **Cloud Computing**-based service.

## 3.2.43.80   YAHOO! MAIL

a)   Mail is a **Web**-based email service that is provided by Yahoo! Inc. Yahoo! Mail is an example of a **Cloud Computing**-based service.

## 3.2.43.81   YAHOO! SEARCH

a)   Search is a **Web**-based **Web** search engine service that is provided by Yahoo! Inc. Search is an example of a **Cloud Computing**-based service.

## 3.2.43.82   ZAPPOS.COM

a)   Zappos.com is a **Web**-based shopping service that is provided by Zappos.com, Inc., a subsidiary of Amazon.com, Inc. Zappos.com is an example of a **Cloud Computing**-based service.

## 3.2.43.83   ZINIO

a)   Zinio is a **Web**-based digital magazine distribution service that is provided by Gilvest LP. Zinio is an example of a **Cloud Computing**-based service.

# 3.2.44 ADDITIONAL TECHNOLOGY PRECURSORS

a) Many other technology-oriented Stream Tone precursors also exist, a wide variety of which are briefly described below. In general, these precursors demonstrate the use of technologies that may be helpful in the construction of the Stream Tone Technology Ecosystem.

## 3.2.44.1 ADVANCED MICRO DEVICES OPTERON A1100

a) The Opteron A1100 is a cost-effective power-efficient multi-core microprocessor that is manufactured by Applied Micro Devices, Inc. Opteron A1100 microprocessors provide a *System on a Chip* that is based on *ARMv8*, which is a 64-bit *Reduced Instruction Set Computing* architecture. The intended use of the Opteron A1100 microprocessor is within *Data Centre*-based computer servers. The Opteron A1100 microprocessor could be used in *Cloud Computing*-based *Data Centres* to cost-effectively provide a wide range of *Internet* and *Web-based Services*.

## 3.2.44.2 ALCATEL ONE TOUCH FIRE

a) The One Touch Fire is a low-cost *Smart-Phone* that runs the *Web*-oriented Firefox OS operating system, and which is manufactured by Alcatel Mobile Phones, a joint manufacturing venture between Alcatel-Lucent S.A. and TCL Communication Technology Holdings, Ltd, a subsidiary of TCL Corporation. The One Touch Fire can be used to access a wide range of *Internet* and *Web-based Services*, including *Cloud Computing*-based services, *Streaming Media* services, and *Streamed Services*. The One Touch Fire demonstrates that practical personal computing devices can be manufactured at affordable price points.

## 3.2.44.3 AMAZON KINDLE PAPERWHITE

a) The Kindle Paperwhite is an e-reader with a power-efficient *Electronic Paper*-based display screen that is manufactured by Amazon.com, Inc. Some versions of the Stream Tone Access Device may include an *Electronic Paper*-based display screen.

## 3.2.44.4 APPLE IPAD

a) The iPad is a *Tablet Computer* that is manufactured by Apple, Inc. The iPad can be used to access a wide range of *Internet* and *Web-based Services*, including *Cloud Computing*-based services, *Streaming Media* services, and *Streamed Services*.

# 3.2.44.5 APPLIED MICRO CIRCUITS X-GENE

a) The X-Gene is a cost-effective, power-efficient multi-core microprocessor that is manufactured by Applied Micro Circuits Corporation. The X-Gene microprocessors provide a **System on a Chip** that is based on **ARMv8**, which is a 64-bit **Reduced Instruction Set Computing** architecture. The intended use of the X-Gene microprocessor is within **Data Centre**-based computer servers. The X-Gene microprocessor could be used in **Cloud Computing**-based **Data Centres** to cost-effectively provide a wide range of **Internet** and **Web-based Services**.

# 3.2.44.6 ARTEMIS PCELL

a) pCell is a **Distributed-Input-Distributed-Output**-based communications technology that was developed by Artemis Networks LLC. pCell can be used to access a wide range of **Internet** and **Web-based Services**, including **Cloud Computing**-based services, **Streaming Media** services, and **Streamed Services**.

# 3.2.44.7 ASPERA FAST AND SECURE PROTOCOL

a) The Fast and Secure Protocol (FASP) is a connectionless, fast, low-latency, network-adaptive, proprietary, patented, secure communications protocol for use on computer networks, such as the **Internet**, and which was developed by Aspera, Inc., a subsidiary of International Business Machines Corporation. FASP is able to transfer data over the **Internet** significantly faster than other communication protocols; often achieving in minutes what other protocols take hours to achieve. FASP can be used to enable a wide range of **Internet** and **Web-based Services**, including **Streaming Media** services and **Streamed Services**.

# 3.2.44.8 CAVIUM PROJECT THUNDER

a) Project Thunder is a scalable range of cost-effective, power-efficient multi-core microprocessors that is manufactured by Cavium, Inc. Project Thunder microprocessors provide a **System on a Chip** that is based on **ARMv8**, which is a 64-bit **Reduced Instruction Set Computing** architecture. The intended use of the X-Gene microprocessor is within **Data Centre**-based computer servers. Project Thunder microprocessor could be used in **Cloud Computing**-based **Data Centres** to cost-effectively provide a wide range of **Internet** and **Web-based Services**.

# 3.2.44.9 CISCO SYSTEMS 3G SMALL CELL

a) The 3G **Small Cell** is a **Small Cell** mobile telecommunications technology manufactured by Cisco Systems, Inc. 3G **Small Cell** can be used to access a wide range of **Internet** and **Web-based Services**, including **Cloud Computing**-based services, **Streaming Media** services, and **Streamed Services**.

## 3.2.44.10    DELL CLOUD CONNECT

a)   Cloud Connect, previously known as Project Ophelia, is a low-cost *Thin Client* device designed for remote personal computing that is manufactured by Wyse Technology, Inc., a subsidiary of Dell, Inc. Cloud Connect can be used to access a wide range of *Internet* and *Web-based Services*, including *Cloud Computing*-based services, *Streaming Media* services, and *Streamed Services*.

## 3.2.44.11    DELL WIRELESS DOCK D5000

a)   The Wireless Dock D5000 is *Wi-Fi*-enabled docking station for use with Dell Latitude 6430u, and similar, laptop computers, that is manufactured by Dell, Inc. The Wireless Dock D5000 uses the Institute of Electrical and Electronic Engineers (IEEE) 802.11ad version of *Wi-Fi*. The Wireless Dock D5000 can be used to access a wide range of computer peripherals, including document scanners, fax machines, keyboards, mice, and printers.

## 3.2.44.12    DELL WYSE ZENITH PRO 2

a)   The Zenith Pro 2 is a power-efficient zero-client, a type of *Thin Client*, for remote personal computing that is manufactured by Wyse Technology, Inc., a subsidiary of Dell, Inc. The Zenith Pro 2 can be used to access a wide range of *Internet* and *Web-based Services*, including *Cloud Computing*-based services, *Streaming Media* services, and *Streamed Services*.

## 3.2.44.13    DEVON IT CEPTOR

a)   The Ceptor is a low-cost *Thin Client* device for remote personal computing that is manufactured by Devon IT, Inc. The Ceptor can be used to access a wide range of *Internet* and *Web-based Services*, including *Cloud Computing*-based services, *Streaming Media* services, and *Streamed Services*.

## 3.2.44.14    DOCKER

a)   Docker is a container-based software application distribution technology that was developed by the *Free and Open-Source Software*-based Docker project. Docker is an *Operating System-Level Virtualisation* solution. Docker can be used to build cost-effective *Cloud Computing*-based service infrastructures that provide *Streaming Media* services and *Streamed Services*.

## 3.2.44.15    DOLBY VISION

a)   Vision is a screen display technology that provides increased brightness, colour gamut, and contrast, which was developed by Dolby Laboratories, Inc. Vision can be used to create visual display devices, such as computer monitors, laptop computers, *Smart-Phones*, *Tablet Computers*, and televisions, that can display highly life-like visual imagery.

## 3.2.44.16    ENERGY SCIENCES NETWORK

a)   The Energy Sciences Network (ESnet) is high-bandwidth private computer network that is managed by the Lawrence Berkeley National Laboratory, United States of America (USA). ESnet is used to connect United States Department of Energy scientists, and their collaborators. In 2013, ESnet demonstrated a data transfer rate of 91 gigabits per second over more than 1,500 miles, between Denver, USA and Greenbelt, USA. ESnet could be used to access a wide range of *Internet* and *Web-based Services*, including *Cloud Computing*-based services, *Streaming Media* services, and *Streamed Services*.

## 3.2.44.17    EUCLIDEON UNLIMITED DETAIL

a)   Unlimited Detail is a software-based three-dimensional image rendering technology developed by Euclideon Pty Ltd. Unlimited Detail can cost-effectively achieve in software what was previously only possible using expensive and sophisticated graphics-oriented hardware. Unlimited Detail could be used to significantly reduce the data processing load and operational costs of a wide range of *Web-based Services*, including *Cloud Computing*-based services, *Streaming Media* services, and *Streamed Services*.

## 3.2.44.18    FACEBOOK WEDGE

a)   The Wedge is an Open Compute Switch that was developed by Facebook, Inc., as part of the Open Compute Project. The Wedge uses a power-efficient *System on a Chip* that is based on *ARMv8*, which is a 64-bit *Reduced Instruction Set Computing* architecture. The Wedge can be used in *Cloud Computing*-based *Data Centres* to help provide a wide range of *Web-based Services*, including *Streaming Media* services and *Streamed Services*.

## 3.2.44.19    FAIRPHONE

a)   The Fairphone is an ethical *Smart-Phone* developed by Fairphone B.V. The Fairphone is manufactured using only conflict-free materials and acceptable labour practices. The Fairphone demonstrates that it is possible to manufacture a modern personal computing device without causing harm to people or the planet. The Fairphone can be used to access a wide range of *Internet* and *Web-based Services*, including *Cloud Computing*-based services, *Streaming Media* services, and *Streamed Services*.

## 3.2.44.20   GOOGLE GLASS

a)   Glass is a compact personal computer system with a retina-based display that is manufactured by Google, Inc. Glass can be used to access a wide range of *Internet* and *Web-based Services*, including *Cloud Computing*-based services, *Streaming Media* services, and *Streamed Services*.

## 3.2.44.21   GUIFI.NET

a)   GUIFI.net is a free, neutral, and open *Mesh Network* located in Catalonia and the Valencian Community of Spain, which is believed to be the largest wireless *Mesh Network* in the world. GUIFI.net is collectively owned by its user community. GUIFI.net can be used to access a wide range of *Internet* and *Web-based Services*, including *Cloud Computing*-based services, *Streaming Media* services, and *Streamed Services*.

## 3.2.44.22   HEWLETT-PACKARD APOLLO 8000

a)   The Apollo 8000 is a high-performance computing system with power-efficient water cooling that is manufactured by Hewlett-Packard Company. The Apollo 8000 can be used to support a wide range of *Internet* and *Web-based Services*, including *Cloud Computing*-based services, *Streaming Media* services, and *Streamed Services*.

## 3.2.44.23   HEWLETT-PACKARD PROLIANT MOONSHOT SERVER

a)   The ProLiant Moonshot Server is a power-efficient computer server array that is manufactured by Hewlett-Packard Company. The ProLiant Moonshot Server can be used to cost-effectively host a wide range of *Web-based Services*, including *Cloud Computing*-based services, *Streaming Media* services, and *Streamed Services*.

## 3.2.44.24   ICEOTOPE

a)   Iceotope is a power-efficient full-immersion-based cooling system for computer servers that is manufactured by Iceotope Ltd. Iceotope-based technology can be used to cost-effectively cool *Cloud Computing*-based *Data Centres*.

## 3.2.44.25   INTERNATIONAL BUSINESS MACHINES AQUASAR

a)   Aquasar is a large-scale computer system with power-efficient hot water cooling that is manufactured by International Business Machines Corporation. Aquasar-based technology can be used to cost-effectively cool *Cloud Computing*-based *Data Centres*.

## 3.2.44.26    JUNIPER NETWORKS WLA632

a)   The WLA632 is a *Small Cell* mobile telecommunications technology that is manufactured by Juniper Networks, Inc. The WLA632 can be used to access a wide range of *Internet* and *Web-based Services*, including *Cloud Computing*-based services, *Streaming Media* services, and *Streamed Services*.

## 3.2.44.27    MOZILLA FIREFOX OS

a)   Firefox OS is a *Web*-oriented *Web Browser*-based operating system for mobile personal computing devices, such as *Smart-Phones* and *Tablet Computers*, which was developed by Mozilla Corporation, a subsidiary of Mozilla Foundation. Firefox OS can be used to access a wide range of *Internet* and *Web-based Services*, including *Cloud Computing*-based services, *Streaming Media* services, and *Streamed Services*.

## 3.2.44.28    NOKIA LIQUID NET

a)   Liquid Net is a mobile communications optimisation technology developed by the Networks business division of Nokia Corporation. Liquid Net can be used to access a wide range of *Internet* and *Web-based Services*, including *Cloud Computing*-based services, *Streaming Media* services, and *Streamed Services*.

## 3.2.44.29    NOVENA

a)   Novena is an *Open-Source Hardware*-based personal computing platform that is offered by Sutajio Ko-usagi Pte Ltd (Kosagi). Novena uses a *Free and Open-Source Software*-based *Linux* operating system. Novena includes a *Field-Programmable Gate Array*, *Reduced Instruction Set Computing*-based microprocessor, and *Software-Defined Radio*. Novena can be used to access and develop a wide range of *Internet* and *Web-based Services*, including *Cloud Computing*-based services, *Streaming Media* services, and *Streamed Services*.

## 3.2.44.30    ONE LAPTOP PER CHILD XO-4

a)   The XO-4 is a low-cost rugged educational laptop for children developed by the One Laptop Per Child Association and One Laptop Per Child Foundation. The XO-4 runs a *Linux*-based operating system, has a daylight-readable *Transflective Liquid-Crystal Display*, and supports *Mesh Networking*. The XO-4 can be used to access a wide range of *Internet* and *Web-based Services*, including *Cloud Computing*-based services, *Streaming Media* services, and *Streamed Services*.

## 3.2.44.31    PANDORA

a)   Pandora is a handheld games console that was developed by the OpenPandora Project.

Pandora is based on *Free and Open-Source Software*, such as *Linux*, and *Open-Source Hardware*.

## 3.2.44.32   PROJECT ARA

a)   Project Ara is a *Smart-Phone* and *Tablet Computer* architecture based on a *Modular Design* approach, developed by Google, Inc., in collaboration with PhoneBloks, a group of *Modular Design*-oriented *Smart-Phone* designers. Project Ara was started by Motorola Mobility LLC, a subsidiary of Google, Inc.[18]

## 3.2.44.33   PROJECT LOON

a)   Project Loon is an *Aerial Platform Network* technology based on high-altitude balloons that was developed by Google, Inc., which can be used to bring *Internet* connectivity to remote geographies. Project Loon can be used to access a wide range of *Internet* and *Web-based Services*, including *Cloud Computing*-based services, *Streaming Media* services, and *Streamed Services*.

## 3.2.44.34   QUALCOMM TOQ

a)   The Toq is a smart-watch with an always-on Mirasol-based daylight-readable display screen that is manufactured by Qualcomm, Inc. Mirasol is a power-efficient interferometric modulator-based display screen technology developed by Qualcomm, Inc.

## 3.2.44.35   QUANTENNA COMMUNICATIONS QSR1000

a)   The QSR1000 is a quad-stream Institute of Electrical and Electronics Engineers (IEEE) 802.11ac *Wi-Fi* chipset that is manufactured by Quantenna Communications, Inc. The QSR1000 can be used to build communications devices that can be used to access a wide range of *Internet* and *Web-based Services*, including *Cloud Computing*-based services, *Streaming Media* services, and *Streamed Services*.

## 3.2.44.36   RANGE NETWORKS OPENCELL 5150

a)   The OpenCell 5150 is a radio access network node with integrated radio resource control that is manufactured by Range Networks, Inc. The OpenCell 5150 can be used in conjunction with the *Free and Open-Source Software*-based Open Base Transceiver Station software application to build second-generation mobile communications (2G) base stations for a fraction of the cost of a traditional 2G base-station. The OpenCell 5150 can be used to access a wide range of *Internet* and *Web-based Services*, including *Cloud*

---

[18] At the time of writing, Lenovo Group Ltd. had announced its intention to purchase Motorola Mobility LLC.

*Computing*-based services, ***Streaming Media*** services, and ***Streamed Services***.

## 3.2.44.37  SAMSUNG GALAXY NOTE 4

a) The Galaxy Note 4 is a power-efficient ***Smart-Phone*** with a 5.7 inch high-resolution active matrix ***Organic Light-Emitting Diode Display Screen*** that is manufactured by Samsung Electronics Company Ltd., a subsidiary of Samsung Group. The Galaxy Note 4 display screen offers enhanced brightness, colour gamut, and contrast compared to the previous generations of Samsung ***Smart-Phones***. The Galaxy Note 4 can be used to access a wide range of ***Internet*** and ***Web-based Services***, including ***Cloud Computing***-based services, ***Streaming Media*** services, and ***Streamed Services***.

## 3.2.44.38  SEAMICRO SM15000-OP

a) The SM15000-OP is a power-efficient computer server array that is manufactured by SeaMicro, Inc., a subsidiary of Advanced Micro Devices, Inc. The SM15000-OP can be used to cost-effectively host a wide range of ***Web-based Services***, including ***Cloud Computing***-based services, ***Streaming Media*** services, and ***Streamed Services***.

## 3.2.44.39  SONY XPERIA Z

a) The Xperia Z is a water-resistant and dust resistant ***Smart-Phone*** with a high-resolution display screen, and which is manufactured by Sony Corporation. The Xperia Z can be used to access a wide range of ***Internet*** and ***Web-based Services***, including ***Cloud Computing***-based services, ***Streaming Media*** services, and ***Streamed Services***.

## 3.2.44.40  TRIMBLE YUMA 2

a) The Yuma 2 is a ***Tablet Computer*** with a power-efficient ***Transflective Liquid-Crystal Display*** that is manufactured by Trimble Navigation Ltd. The Yuma 2 can be used to access a wide range of ***Internet*** and ***Web-based Services***, including ***Cloud Computing***-based services, ***Streaming Media*** services, and ***Streamed Services***.

## 3.2.44.41  VIEWSONIC SD-A245

a) The SD-A245 is a ***Citrix High-Definition User Experience***-compatible ***Thin Client*** device that is manufactured by Viewsonic Corporation. The SD-A245 can be used to access ***Hosted Desktop*** and ***Web Desktop*** services.

## 3.2.44.42  XG TECHNOLOGY XMAX

a) The xMax is a ***Cognitive Radio***-based data communications solution manufactured by xG Technology, Inc. xMax can be used to access a wide range of ***Web-based Services***, including *Cloud Computing*-based services, *Streaming Media* services, and *Streamed Services*.

# 3.2.44.43    XI3 X7A MODULAR COMPUTER

a)    The X7A Modular Computer is a personal computing device with a *Modular Design* that can be easily upgraded by a user, and which is manufactured by Xi3 Corporation. The X7A Modular Computer can be used to access a wide range of *Internet* and *Web-based Services*, including *Cloud Computing*-based services, *Streaming Media* services, and *Streamed Services*.

# 3.2.44.44    XLX SYS VP8 DECODER

a)    The VP8 Decoder is a semiconductor intellectual property (IP) core that can be used build a *VP8* decoder using *Application-Specific Integrated Circuit*-based technologies, and which is manufactured by XLX SYS. The VP8 Decoder IP core can be used to cost-effectively build a *System on a Chip* for use in *Smart-Phones* and *Tablet Computers*.

# 3.2.44.45    YUN OS

a)    Yun OS, also known as Aliyun OS, is a *Web*-oriented operating system for mobile personal computing devices, such as *Smart-Phones* and *Tablet Computers*, which was developed by Alibaba Group. Yun OS can be used to access a wide range of *Internet* and *Web-based Services*, including *Cloud Computing*-based services, *Streaming Media* services, and *Streamed Services*.

# 3.2.44.46    ZTE ECO-MOBIUS

a)    The Eco-Mobius is a *Smart-Phone* concept that is based on a *Modular Design* approach developed by ZTE Corporation. The Eco-Mobius *Smart-Phone* should be easy to repair and upgrade.

# 3.2.44.47    ZTE OPEN

a)    The Open is a low-cost *Smart-Phone* that runs the Firefox OS, a *Web*-oriented operating system, and which is manufactured by ZTE Corporation. The Open can be used to access a wide range of *Internet* and *Web-based Services*, including *Cloud Computing*-based services, *Streaming Media* services, and *Streamed Services*. The Open demonstrates that practical personal computing devices can be manufactured at affordable price points.

# 3.3 LESSONS OF THE PRESENT

*Contemporary enlightenment*

a) To quote Aristotle, the famous Greek philosopher and scientist; *"One swallow does not a summer make, nor one fine day; similarly one day or brief time of happiness does not make a person entirely happy".*[19] So, even though there may exist many potential building blocks from which to construct the Stream Tone, and many precursors that suggest that aspects of the Stream Tone are already in widespread and socially-accepted use, the Stream Tone still lies very far from reality.

b) Being able to draw any useful conclusions from this chapter is dependent upon two key assumptions. The first is that the identified building blocks could actually be used to create the Stream Tone, as currently envisioned. The second is that the identified precursors are, in some way, the actual predecessors of the Stream Tone, and therefore indicative of what may be achievable by the development of the Stream Tone in the future. If both of these assumptions are valid, which they most probably are, then there are a number of useful lessons that can be learnt from these building blocks and precursors.

c) In brief, the Stream Tone building blocks suggest that a very wide range of technologies, from which to build the Stream Tone, already exist, having been independently developed for use in other applications. Any aspect that is wholly unique to the Stream Tone, and which must therefore be specifically developed, can assuredly rely upon an experienced workforce that is skilled in the development of many similar technological components. Being able to leverage many existing technologies and mature workforce skills in the construction of the Stream Tone should help to greatly reduce its development time and cost.

d) In brief, the Stream Tone precursors suggest that there are many existing services and technologies that exhibit aspects, characteristics, or qualities that are similar to aspects, characteristics, or qualities of the currently envisioned Stream Tone. In fact, one or two of the precursors could even be considered to be early Stream Tone prototypes, such is their similarity. Collectively, the precursors suggest that nearly all required Stream Tone functionality already exists, and that the development of the Stream Tone may, in fact, already be half complete. All that is now required is that a number of disparate technological threads be tied together. The precursors also suggest that many of the technologies that will underpin the Stream Tone are not unique, but are in fact commonly used within many other **Internet** and **Web**-oriented service and telecommunications solutions. The precursors help to show that the Stream Tone is not a technology that is new from the ground up, but simply a technology that will use existing technologies in different ways. The precursors also help to suggest that the Stream Tone is both reasonable in terms of its concept and practical in terms of its eventual implementation.

---

[19] *One of the many translations that are available for the "One swallow does not a summer make..." adage found within Aristotle's Nicomachean Ethics.*

# 4    THE FUTURE

*Like today, but better*

a)    This chapter considers, at a high level: how some of the Stream Tone building blocks, identified in the previous chapter, could be used to construct the Stream Tone; some possible use cases for the Stream Tone; ways that the Stream Tone could be commercialised; a possible timeline for the development and deployment of the Stream Tone; and some of the lessons that should be considered before the Stream Tone starts to be developed.

b)    The contents of this chapter are highly speculative, and have been included in order to provide a small insight into what the future may hold in terms of the development and deployment of the Stream Tone.

## 4.1    STREAM TONE TECHNOLOGY ECOSYSTEM

*Interacting and interconnecting*

a)    In the same way that the modern **Internet** and the **Web** are a mosaic of many different technologies, all working seamlessly together, the Stream Tone will also be a system of many cooperative parts. Some of those parts will be new, invented specifically for use in the Stream Tone Technology Ecosystem (STTE), whilst many others will be based on already existing parts of today's **Internet** and **Web**.

b)    The STTE will be comprised of a communications protocol, access device, service infrastructure, and telecommunications infrastructure. In simple terms, the STTE will function in the following way: the communications protocol will be used to communicate digital content and services to an access device, the access device will be used to present that digital content and those digital services to a user for interaction and consumption, the service infrastructure will be used to provide that digital content and those digital services, and the telecommunications infrastructure will be used to deliver that digital content and those digital services to the access device.

c)    Certain aspects of the STTE will be governed and overseen by the Stream Tone **Foundation** (STF).

d)    The STTE will be created and maintained by the Stream Tone Community (STC).

e)    The following high-level descriptions represent a first attempt at guessing some the behaviours, building blocks, capabilities, characteristics, components, dependencies, nomenclatures, operations, and structures of the STTE. These descriptions are highly speculative, and unrefined, but should, nevertheless, still provide a very useful starting point for understanding the STTE.

f)    The following high-level descriptions will probably be just as useful for identifying things that could or should be excluded from the STTE as they are for identifying things that

245

could or should be included.

g)  The following high-level descriptions should not be considered definitive or exhaustive, simply representative of some of the elements that may be required in order to develop and deploy the STTE.

# 4.1.1    STREAM TONE FOUNDATION

a)  Even though the Stream Tone will be an initiative that is largely driven by the ***Free and Open-Source Software*** (FOSS) and ***Open-Source Hardware*** (OSHW) communities, a number of administrative, fiduciary, governance, legal, and promotional aspects are expected to require the support of a more formally structured organisation. The Stream Tone ***Foundation*** (STF) will be a non-profit organisation that is responsible for supporting, and governing a limited number of aspects, of the Stream Tone Technology Ecosystem (STTE).

b)  It is expected that the STF will have a small number of full-time staff that are supported by a larger number of unpaid individual volunteers and volunteer organisations, collectively known as the Stream Tone Community (STC). The STF will have a flat organisational structure. The STF will have a single public-facing leader, known as the Chief Executive Officer (CEO) or similar. In order to help minimise staffing requirements, the STF will augment its capabilities through the purchase of specialist third-party products and services, as and when required.

c)  The ethos of the STF will be technical excellence and fiscal frugality, because the Stream Tone must be the best it can be from a technical perspective but it must also be highly affordable at the point of use by everyone, everywhere. The existence of the STF should have a zero or reductive impact on the end-user pricing of STTP-based services.

d)  The STF will be responsible for managing the third-party development of various Stream Tone deliverables, including the Stream Tone Access Device Emulator, Stream Tone Graphics Interface, Stream Tone Software Development Kit, Stream Tone Service Portal, Stream Tone Security Service (STSS), and Stream Tone Transfer Protocol (STTP). The STF will also be responsible for managing the third-party development of the reference-design for the Stream Tone Access Device (STAD).

e)  The STF will be responsible for publishing the product designs of the many hardware and software-based components that will comprise the STTE under FOSS and OSHW licenses.

f)  The STF may delegate certain responsibilities to the STC or other trusted and responsible third parties, as and when required.

g)  The STF will offer guidance to the telecommunications and service industries on how those industries can best meet the affordability, availability, bandwidth, latency, and reliability requirements of the Stream Tone.

h)  The STF will provide oversight and governance for the creation, and third-party provision, of the STSS.

i) The STF will liaise with international standards organisations, such as the ***Internet Engineering Task Force*** (IETF) and ***World Wide Web Consortium*** (W3C). It will be important that the Stream Tone complements the existing technologies of the ***Internet*** and the ***Web***, and in this respect such organisations are expected to be invaluable development partners. It is hoped that representatives of such organisations will also fulfil a number of key roles within the STF.

j) The use of any patent encumbered technologies within the STTE, even those available under ***Fair, Reasonable and Non-Discriminatory Licensing*** terms, will be subject to written approval by the STF. The STF will not permit any patent encumbered technologies to be included into the STTP. It is recognised that the actual ability of the STF to influence the use of patent encumbered technologies within the service and telecommunications infrastructures that will be used to provide and deliver the digital content and services that will be communicated using the STTP is likely to be very limited.

k) The STF will be funded through charitable donations, consulting services offered to industry, and through fees levied for administrative services relating to the use of the Stream Tone ***Certification Mark*** (STCM). Other sources of income may be identified in the future.

l) The STF will own and control the use of the STCM. The STCM will be used by original equipment manufacturers (OEMs) to indicate that their products correctly support the STTP and other important aspects, characteristics, or qualities of the Stream Tone. OEMs will be required to comply with terms and conditions published by the STF in order to include the STCM on their products. The STCM may be based on the Stream Tone Logo, as shown in Figure 2:

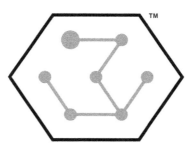

*Figure 2: The Stream Tone Logo*

m) In addition to funding its day to day operations, the STF will use its income to promote the use and widespread adoption of the Stream Tone, and to support the on-going development of the STTE. The STF will also fund the STSS, if possible.

n) The STF will protect the free and open-source nature of the Stream Tone.

o) The STF will audit the STTE to ensure that the aspects of the STTE, such as the STTP, that are meant to be available free-of-charge are not being exploited for profit.

p) The STF will be an equal partner with the STC, not its supervisor. The STF and STC may be two separate and distinct bodies but they will function as a single cohesive unit. Most, if not all, members of the STF will also be members of the STC, and some members of the STC will also be members of the STF. The STF and STC will treat each other with utmost respect at all times. The STF and the STC will be required to maintain highly effective channels of communication between each other and will seek to work constructively together. The STF and STC will vigorously avoid situations where one party does not know what the other party is doing, and also where one party makes public announcements without the knowledge and support of the other party. In simple terms, the STF and STC will be required to play nice with each other at all times and under all circumstances!

q)  When required, the STF will help to broker connections between the different parts of the STC, and between the STC and any interested third parties.

r)  The STF will maintain a big picture view of the STTE that will allow it to offer guidance and direction on the evolution of the STTE to the STC and any other interested parties. It is not expected that the STF will be able to maintain a knowledge and understanding of every small part of the STTE because the STTE will probably be very large and complex, and ultimately such things will be the responsibility of the individual contributors working under peer review of the STC. Nevertheless, the STF will maintain a clear understanding and opinion on the nature and direction of the STTE. The STC will use an exception reporting approach to bring important matters to the timely attention of the STF. The STF will not be an information or decision-making bottleneck as it is expected that most information and decisions relating to the STTE will arise from within the STC or international standards organisations such as the IETF or W3C.

s)  The STF will provide a *Web*-based discussion forum, known as the Stream Tone Community Forum (STCF), for use by any and all parties that are interested in constructively supporting the creation and further development of the STTE. Use of the STCF will be strictly moderated.

t)  Decision-making within the STF will be based on the consensus view of a rough majority of active and respected STF members. The CEO of the STF will not be able to override the consensus view. STF decision-making will also consider the consensus view of the STC.

# 4.1.2    STREAM TONE COMMUNITY

a)  The Stream Tone will be created and maintained by the Stream Tone Community (STC), which will predominantly be comprised of members of the *Free and Open-Source Software* (FOSS) and *Open-Source Hardware* (OSHW) communities. Members of the STC can be either individuals or organisations.

b)  The STC will be responsible for creating and maintaining the Stream Tone Technology Ecosystem (STTE) under free and open-source principles. In particular, the Stream Tone Transfer Protocol (STTP), a key part of the STTE, will be developed as a non-profit free-of-charge technology by the STC.

c)  The STC will ensure that all constituent parts of the STTE are able to meet required levels of affordability, availability, bandwidth, latency, and reliability.

d)  The STC will be an inclusive organisation, to which all are welcome. Contributors to the STC can come from a wide variety of backgrounds; non-profit as well as for-profit. Most members of the STC will be unpaid volunteers, as is the norm for FOSS and OSHW projects. Some members of the STC may be commercial organisations that wish to help shape the Stream Tone; a technology that they will probably seek to profit from in the future through the provision of Stream Tone-related products or services.

e)  The STC will cultivate and maintain strong working links with international standards organisations, such as the **Internet Engineering Task Force** (IETF) and the **World Wide Web Consortium** (W3C). It will be important that the Stream Tone complements the existing technologies of the **Internet** and the **Web**, and in this respect such organisations are expected to be invaluable development partners. It is hoped that members of such organisations will also become active members within the STC.

f)  The STC will make extensive use of the **Web**-based discussion forum provided by the Stream Tone **Foundation** (STF), known as the Stream Tone Community Forum (STCF). Use of the STCF will be subject to strict moderation.

g)  The STC will make extensive use of a wide range of community-oriented **Web**-based collaborative development services. Some of the development services used by the STC may be funded by the STF.

h)  The STC will work under the assumption that nearly all of the technologies that will be required to build and operate the STTE are already in existence. The STC will, wherever possible, re-use or re-purpose existing technologies in the construction of the STTE. Accordingly, it is hoped that the bulk of the effort provided by the STC will therefore be directed towards the task of integrating those technologies into what will eventually become the STTE. In essence, the STC will create the glue that binds those technologies together.

i)  The STC will be an equal partner of the STF, not a subordinate. The STF and STC may be two separate and distinct bodies but they will function as a single cohesive unit. Some members of the STC will also be members of the STF, and most, if not all, members of the STF will also be members of the STC. The STC and STF will treat each other with utmost respect at all times. The STC and the STF will be required to maintain highly effective channels of communication between each other and will seek to work constructively together. The STC and STF will vigorously avoid situations where one party does not know what the other party is doing, and also where one party makes public announcements without the knowledge and support of the other party. In simple terms, the STC and STF will be required to play nice with each other at all times and under all circumstances!

j)  When required, the STC will seek guidance and direction from the STF, which will maintain a big picture view of the STTE on behalf of the STC for just such a purpose. It is not expected that the STF will be able to maintain a knowledge and understanding of every small part of the STTE because the STTE will probably be very large and complex, and ultimately such things will be the responsibility of the individual STC contributors working under peer review of the STC. The STC will use an exception reporting approach to bring important matters to the timely attention of the STF. Most information and decisions relating to the STTE are expected to arise from within the STC or international standards organisations such as the IETF or W3C.

k) The STC will be responsible for the development of various Stream Tone deliverables, including the Stream Tone Access Device Emulator, Stream Tone Graphics Interface, Stream Tone Software Development Kit, Stream Tone Service Portal, Stream Tone Security Service, and STTP. The STC will also be responsible for developing the reference-design of the Stream Tone Access Device.

l) The STC will not make use of any patent encumbered technologies within the STTE, even when those technologies are available under **Fair, Reasonable and Non-Discriminatory Licensing** terms, without the express written approval of the STF. The STC will not include any patent encumbered technologies within the STTP.

m) Decision-making within the STC will be based on the consensus view of a rough majority of active and respected STC members. STC decision-making will also consider the consensus view of the STF.

# 4.1.3 STREAM TONE TRANSFER PROTOCOL

## 4.1.3.1 OVERVIEW

a) The Stream Tone Transfer Protocol (STTP) will form the basis of an affordable and ubiquitous technology ecosystem that will support the comprehensive replacement of local personal computing with remote personal computing.

b) The STTP will be an adaptive, bi-directional, evolvable, intelligent, low-latency, real-time, secure, data streaming technology designed to support the use of Comprehensive Remote Personal Computing services delivered over packet-switched computer networks, such as the **Internet**. In simple terms, the STTP will be a pixel-streaming, or bit-streaming, communications protocol that is designed to send digital data from a remotely-located computer server to a Stream Tone Access Device (STAD) for presentation to a user. The STTP will also be used to send user-input from a STAD to a computer server.

c) The STTP will be used to connect a STAD to a Stream Tone Service Infrastructure (STSI)-based computer server, or to another STAD.

d) The STTP will be used to communicate all types of digital data, both structured and unstructured. Three main classes of digital data will be supported; audio data, visual data, and non-audio-visual data.

e) The STTP will be used to transmit digital data generated by user-oriented functionalities present in, or connected to, a STAD, such as an **Accelerometer**, **Ambient Light Sensor**, **Barometer**, **Capacitive Sensing** display screen, **Image Sensor**, **Global Positioning System**, **Gyroscope**, keyboard, **Magnetometer**, mouse, microphone, **Networked Peripheral**, or **Proximity Sensor**. Data from such functionalities will be passed to remote computing systems for data processing and storage; as such data will not be directly processed on the STAD.

f) The STTP will be intelligent, in that it will be able to detect changing network conditions, and then dynamically adapt to those conditions, ensuring that, for example, interactive STTP-based services remain useable even when communications bandwidth becomes significantly reduced. When bandwidth becomes unexpectedly reduced, STTP-based content and services will degrade in acceptable and predictable ways.

g) The STTP will be based on the assumption that all communicated audio-visual data is transitory in nature, and that the moderate loss of such data during transmission will be a common but largely unimportant occurrence; as is the case with a lost frame of visual data from a television broadcast. The STTP will also be based on the assumption that non-audio-visual data is not transitory and that the loss of such data during transmission is unacceptable and will need to be fully recovered should it occur, ensuring that all non-audio-visual data will always be reliably delivered.

h) The STTP will support four sub-classes of visual data: fast-changing visual imagery, such as video; graphical cursors, such as the text entry cursor within a word processing application or a desktop mouse pointer; slow-to-change visual imagery, such as the graphical user-interfaces of desktop operating systems; and static visual imagery, such as photographs.

i) The STTP will allow multiple graphical cursors to be defined so that the display of such cursors can be locally handled by a STAD. In order to minimise network bandwidth only basic movement and action data, relating to a cursor, will be sent over the network to a remote server for data processing. Graphical-cursor definitions will support animated or slow-to-change, as well as static, visual imagery.

j) The STTP will allow fast-changing visual imagery to be transmitted with an acceptable loss of visual detail, and at a frame rate that maintains human persistence of vision.

k) The STTP will allow static, and slow-to-change, visual imagery to be progressively transmitted with little or no loss of visual detail. Such imagery may initially lack detail but will become progressively clearer over a very short period of time. For slow-to-change visual data, only the smallest visual region practical that encloses the change will be transmitted.

l) The STTP will support the display of irregularly-shaped non-rectangular visual imagery. The STTP will also support ordered layers of visual imagery and visual imagery with transparent elements, such that one layer can overlay and partially obscure another.

m) The STTP will use both lossless and lossy data *Compression* and data caching in order to minimise the use of communications bandwidth and data transmission times.

n) The STTP will be designed to minimise communications latency.

o) The STTP will seamlessly and intelligently support remote personal computing environments that simultaneously combine audio, fast-changing visual imagery, graphical cursors, slow-to-change visual imagery, static visual imagery, and non-audio-visual data.

p) All digital data transmitted using the STTP will be timestamped, allowing data transmission times to be monitored in real-time. Data transmission parameters, such as data *Compression* ratios and screen refresh rates, will then be modified in order to minimise transmission delays. Timestamps will also be used to synchronise the delivery of data that has been split into multiple separate data streams, such as audio and video.

q) The practical operation of the STTP will be reliant on a telecommunications infrastructure that is able to meet a range of criteria, including affordability, availability, bandwidth, latency, and reliability.

r) Development of the STTP will draw upon the guidance of third-party organisations, such as the *Internet Engineering Task Force* and the *World Wide Web Consortium*, where appropriate.

s) The STTP will be published under a *Free and Open-Source Software* license.

# 4.1.3.2     DESIGN

a) The Stream Tone Transfer Protocol (STTP) will be an application layer communications protocol that relies upon other application-layer protocols and lower level transport-layer protocols of the *Internet Protocol* Suite for its operation.

b) The STTP will only support *Internet Protocol Version 6* addressing, or its successors.

c) The STTP could be based on one or more existing remote personal computing protocols. Many existing protocols are proprietary and may not be able to support all the different features, functionalities, and use cases envisioned for the STTP. Basing the STTP on a new design will ensure that it is able to natively support all required features, functionalities, and use cases without compromise, and for development to be based on *Free and Open-Source Software* (FOSS) principles. The STTP will therefore be based on one or more existing real-time communications technologies that are available under a FOSS license, and which can be engineered to support all required features, functionalities and use cases envisioned for the STTP.

d) Potential building blocks for constructing, or inspiring, the STTP will include technologies such as *Anamorphic Stretch Transform*, *ChaCha20-Poly1305*, *Daala*, *Dynamic Adaptive Streaming over HTTP*, *H.264*, *H.265*, *HyperText Markup Language Version 5*, *MP3*, *Opus*, *ORBX.js*, *Real-Time Streaming Protocol*, *Real-time Transport Protocol*, *Remote FrameBuffer*, *Speex*, *Theora*, *Voice over Internet Protocol*, *Vorbis*, *VP8*, *VP9*, *Web Real-Time Communication*, *WebP*, *x264*, *x265*, and *Zopfli*, to name but a few. The use of some of these technologies is mutually exclusive. Some of these technologies are encumbered by patents but are, nevertheless, in widespread use, and are, consequently, industry standards.

e) Different types of digital data transmitted using the STTP will be identified by *Internet Media Type* or an equivalent classification system.

f) To protect all digital data the STTP will use one or more strong *Encryption*-algorithm implementations that are available under a FOSS license, such as one of the various implementations of the Advanced *Encryption* Standard (AES) algorithm. It is assumed that the data *Encryption* approach selected for use in the STTP will be sufficiently flexible to allow new data *Encryption* algorithms to be adopted, as and when required, in the future. This is one of the ways that the STTP will be able to evolve, if required, in the future. All *Encryption* technologies selected for use in the STTP will support hardware-only implementation. The actual ***Encryption*** algorithm that will be used by the STTP will most probably be determined by the selection of the secure communications protocol that will be the basis for the STTP.

g) To support digital audio data the STTP will use one or more audio encoding formats that are available under a FOSS license, such as ***Opus***. It is assumed that the audio encoding approach selected for use in the STTP will be sufficiently flexible to allow new audio encoding formats to be adopted, as and when required, in the future. This is one of the ways that the STTP will be able to evolve, if required, in the future. All audio encoding technologies selected for use in the STTP will support hardware-only implementation.

h) To support digital video data the STTP will use one or more video encoding formats that are available under a FOSS license, such as ***VP9*** or ***Daala***. It is assumed that the video encoding approach selected for use in the STTP will be sufficiently flexible to allow new video encoding formats to be adopted, as and when required, in the future. This is one of the ways that the STTP will be able to evolve, if required, in the future. All video encoding technologies selected for use in the STTP will support hardware-only implementation.

i) To support digital graphical-cursor image definitions the STTP will use one or more image encoding formats that are available under a FOSS license, such as ***WebP***. It is assumed that the image encoding approach selected for use in the STTP will be sufficiently flexible to allow new image encoding formats to be adopted, as and when required, in the future. This is one of the ways that the STTP will be able to evolve, if required, in the future. All image encoding technologies selected for use in the STTP will support hardware-only implementation.

j) To support slow-to-change digital image data the STTP will use one or more change-oriented remote desktop display and control protocols that are available under a FOSS license, such as ***Remote FrameBuffer***. It is assumed that the remote desktop display and control approach selected for use in the STTP will be sufficiently flexible to allow new remote desktop display and control protocols to be adopted, as and when required, in the future. This is one of the ways that the STTP will be able to evolve, if required, in the future. All remote desktop display and control technologies selected for use in the STTP will support hardware-only implementation. The initial starting point for the display of a remote desktop will be a complete static digital image of that desktop, therefore the remote desktop display and control technologies used by the STTP will need to work in conjunction and be compatible with the image encoding technologies used by the STTP, see below.

k) To support static digital image data the STTP will use one or more image encoding formats that are available under a FOSS license, such as ***WebP***. It is assumed that the image encoding approach selected for use in the STTP will be sufficiently flexible to allow new image encoding formats to be adopted, as and when required, in the future. This is one of the ways that the STTP will be able to evolve, if required, in the future. All image encoding technologies selected for use in the STTP will support hardware-only implementation. The transmission of static digital image data, using the STTP, will be progressive, such that a static digital image will initially appear as a low-quality, low-resolution, image that will quickly be incrementally refined and improved over a very short period of time. The initial starting point for the display of a remote desktop will be a complete static digital image of that desktop, therefore the static digital image encoding technologies used by the STTP will need to work in conjunction and be compatible with the remote desktop display and control technologies used by the STTP, see above.

l)  To support non-audio-visual digital data the STTP will use one or more lossless data *Compression* formats that are available under a FOSS license, such as *Zopfli*. It is assumed that the non-audio-visual data *Compression* approach selected for use in the STTP will be sufficiently flexible to allow new non-audio-visual data *Compression* formats to be adopted, as and when required, in the future. This is one of the ways that the STTP will be able to evolve, if required, in the future. All non-audio-visual data *Compression* technologies selected for use in the STTP will support hardware-only implementation. It is expected that all user-input, except audio and video, will be communicated as non-audio-visual data using the STTP. The quality of non-audio-visual data will always be preserved, it is not permissible for it to become degraded in any way, and it will only be compressed using lossless data *Compression* technologies. This is in contrast to standard STTP-based audio and video data which will be compressed, to vary degrees, using lossy data *Compression* technologies that result in a permanent reduction of quality. It will be necessary for the user to indicate, through the use of an appropriate STTP-based service, when audio or video can be handled as a standard transitory or lossy data stream and when it must be handled as a non-transitory or lossless data stream. Some user-input data may be discarded if it is determined to have become outdated, but only after it has been successfully communicated.

m)  To communicate all the different types of digital data supported by the STTP, a real-time communications protocol, such as the *Web Real-Time Communication* (WebRTC) protocol will be used, and which is available under a FOSS license. To ensure data security the WebRTC protocol uses the *HyperText Transfer Protocol Secure* and the Secure Real-Time Protocol (SRTP). The SRTP is a secure profile of the *Real-time Transport Protocol* that uses the AES algorithm. The WebRTC protocol supports the *Opus* audio encoding format and the *VP8* video encoding format. The WebRTC protocol can also support the transmission of non-audio-visual data. The WebRTC protocol is expected to support *VP9*, the successor to the *VP8* video encoding format, at some point in the future. Alternatively, the STTP could be based on another communications protocol, such as the *Real-Time Streaming Protocol*, if required.

n)  The STTP will be published under a *Free and Open-Source Software* license.

# 4.1.3.3    STREAM TONE TRANSFER PROTOCOL CODEC

a)  The Stream Tone Transfer Protocol Codec (STTP-CODEC) is comprised of the encoding and decoding algorithms of the Stream Tone Transfer Protocol (STTP). An encoder and decoder pair is known as a codec. The STTP-CODEC is normally referred to as the Stream Tone Transfer Protocol or STTP.

b)  The STTP-CODEC will comprise of the Stream Tone Transfer Protocol Encoder (STTPE) and the Stream Tone Transfer Protocol Decoder (STTPD), both of which are described below.

c)  The STTP-CODEC will be published under a *Free and Open-Source Software* license.

## 4.1.3.3.1        STREAM TONE TRANSFER PROTOCOL ENCODER

a) The Stream Tone Transfer Protocol Encoder (STTPE) will be an implementation of the algorithm that is used to convert a stream of digital data into a format that is suitable for transmission over a packet-switched computer network, such as the *Internet*, using the Stream Tone Transfer Protocol (STTP), to a Stream Tone Transfer Protocol Decoder (STTPD).

b) The STTPE is part of the Stream Tone Transfer Protocol Codec (STTP-CODEC).

c) The design of the STTPE algorithm will be optimised for real-time low-latency operation on computer systems that support hardware-based parallel-processing.

d) The STTPE will support three classes of digital data; audio data, visual data, and non-audio-visual data. The STTPE will support four sub-classes of visual data; fast-changing visual imagery, graphical cursors, slow-to-change visual imagery, and static visual imagery. Different classes or sub-classes of data will be encoded into separate data streams.

e) Audio data will be converted to the most appropriate audio data *Compression* format supported by the STTP, such as *Opus*. Determination of what is the most appropriate audio data *Compression* format will be based on the type of audio data that is to be communicated by the STTP. The level of data *Compression* that will be applied to the audio data will be dynamically varied in order to meet a data bit-rate transmission target that has been calculated based on the content and nature of the audio data, user preference, and prevailing network conditions.

f) Fast-changing visual imagery will be converted to the most appropriate video data *Compression* format supported by the STTP, such as *VP9* or *Daala*. Determination of what is the most appropriate video data *Compression* format will be based on the type of video data that is to be communicated by the STTP. The level of data *Compression* that will be applied to the video data will be dynamically varied in order to meet a data bit-rate transmission target that has been calculated based on the content and nature of the video data, user preference, and prevailing network conditions.

g) Graphical cursors will be converted to the most appropriate image data *Compression* format supported by the STTP, such as *WebP*. Determination of what is the most appropriate image data *Compression* format will be based on the type of graphical cursor image data that is to be communicated by the STTP. As the overall quantity of graphical-cursor image data is expected to be relatively small the level of data *Compression* that will be applied to such data will primarily be based on user preference and not a dynamically varied-data bit-rate transmission target as is used for fast-changing, slow-to-change, and static visual imagery.

h) Slow-to-change visual imagery will be converted into the most appropriate change-oriented desktop display and control data format supported by the STTP, such as *Remote FrameBuffer*. Determination of what is the most appropriate desktop display and control format will be based on the type of slow-to-change image data that is to be communicated by the STTP. The level of data *Compression* that will be applied to the slow-to-change image data will be dynamically varied in order to meet a data bit-rate transmission target that has been calculated based on the content and nature of the desktop display and control data, user preference, and prevailing network conditions.

i) Static visual imagery will be converted to the most appropriate image data *Compression* format supported by the STTP, such as *WebP*. Determination of what is the most appropriate image data *Compression* format will be based on the type of static image data that is to be communicated by the STTP. The level of data *Compression* that will be applied to the static image data will be dynamically varied in order to meet a data transmission bit-rate target that has been calculated based on the content and nature of the image data, user preference, and prevailing network conditions.

j) Non-audio-visual data will be compressed using the most appropriate data *Compression* algorithm supported by the STTP, such as *Zopfli*. It should be noted that *Zopfli* is a very slow but highly efficient *Compression* algorithm that may require the use of a hardware-based data *Compression* accelerator, particularly if used on a STAD. Determination of what is the most appropriate data *Compression* algorithm will be based on the type of non-audio-visual data that is to be communicated by the STTP. As most non-audio-visual data cannot be degraded in any way during data transmission, it will require the use of a lossless data *Compression* algorithm. Non-audio-visual data does not need to meet a data transmission bit-rate target.

k) All encoded data will be timestamped. The clock used by the STTPE to timestamp encoded data will be synchronised with the clock used by the STTPD to decode that data.

l) All encoded data will be strongly encrypted using the most appropriate *Encryption* algorithm supported by the STTP.

m) The level and nature of *Compression* that can be applied to digital data by the STTPE will be variable, ranging from lossless to lossy. In general, the level and nature of the *Compression* that will be applied to STTP-encoded data will be dynamically varied in order to meet a data transmission bit-rate target that has been calculated based on the content and nature of the data to be communicated, user preference, and prevailing network conditions.

n) The STTPE will be able to send a reference to visual data held within the Stream Tone Image Cache (STIC) to a STTPD. When a STTPD receives such a reference it will obtain the referenced visual data from the STIC and cause that data to be appropriately presented on the display screen of the Stream Tone Access Device.

o) The STTPE will be published under a *Free and Open-Source Software* license.

## 4.1.3.3.2 STREAM TONE TRANSFER PROTOCOL DECODER

a) The Stream Tone Transfer Protocol Decoder (STTPD) will be an implementation of the algorithm used to convert a Stream Tone Transfer Protocol-compliant data stream, sent from a Stream Tone Transfer Protocol Encoder (STTPE), which contains audio, visual, or non-audio-visual data, into a format suitable for use by a receiving device, such as a Stream Tone Access Device.

b)   The STTPD is part of the Stream Tone transfer Protocol Codec (STTP-CODEC).

c)   The design of the STTPD algorithm will be optimised for real-time low-latency operation on computer systems that support hardware-based parallel-processing.

d)   The STTPD will be able to receive a reference to visual data held within the Stream Tone Image Cache (STIC) from a STTPE. When a STTPD receives such a reference it will obtain the referenced visual data from the STIC and cause that data to be appropriately presented on the display screen of the Stream Tone Access Device

e)   Decoded STTP-based data will be associated with its corresponding STTP timestamp. The clock used by the STTPD to decode timestamped data will be synchronised with the clock used by the STTPE to encode that data.

f)   The STTPD will be published under a *Free and Open-Source Software* license.

# 4.1.3.4    STREAM TONE SOFTWARE DEVELOPMENT KIT

a)   The Stream Tone Software Development Kit (STSDK) will contain the software-based tools for developing software applications that are able to communicate using the Stream Tone Transfer Protocol.

b)   The STSDK will be comprised of the Stream Tone *Application Programming Interface* and Stream Tone Function Library, both of which are described below.

c)   The STSDK will be available free-of-charge.

d)   The STSDK will be published under a *Free and Open-Source Software* license.

## 4.1.3.4.1    STREAM TONE APPLICATION PROGRAMMING INTERFACE

a)   The Stream Tone *Application Programming Interface* (STAPI) will provide a standardised range of programming language-specific software interfaces to the Stream Tone Function Library.

b)   The STAPI is part of the Stream Tone Software Development Kit (STSDK).

c)   Versions of the STAPI will be available for all commonly-used programming languages.

d)   The STAPI will be published under a *Free and Open-Source Software* license.

## 4.1.3.4.2    STREAM TONE FUNCTION LIBRARY

a)   The Stream Tone Function Library (STFL) will provide a software-based implementation of the Stream Tone Codec (STTP-CODEC), as well as high-level interfaces to the audio, graphical user-interface, network, and video subsystems of end-point devices. The STFL will also provide an interface to the Stream Tone Security Service (STSS).

b) The STFL is part of the Stream Tone Software Development Kit (STSDK).

c) The STFL will be designed primarily for use on data-source devices, such as the remotely-located Stream Tone Service Infrastructure-based computer servers that will be used to generate the digital content and services that will then be communicated as Stream Tone Transfer Protocol (STTP)-compliant data streams to a Stream Tone Access Device (STAD) for presentation. The STAD will contain a hardware-based equivalent of the STFL.

d) In simple terms, the STFL will provide all necessary functionality to obtain audio-visual data from a data source, to then encode that data into an STTP-compliant data stream, and send it via a computer network, such as the *Internet*, to a recipient device, known as a STAD, for presentation. The STFL will also be able to do the opposite; receive STTP-compliant data from a computer network, decode it and then send it to an audio-visual subsystem for presentation.

e) The STFL will also provide functionality for accessing, building, and maintaining the Stream Tone Image Cache (STIC). The STFL will provide functionality for storing new and previously unseen visual data in the STIC, for extracting a copy of stored visual data from the STIC so that it can be displayed, and for deleting specific visual data, ranges of visual data, or all visual data from the STIC.

f) The STFL will provide functionality for monitoring available network bandwidth, so that data *Compression* levels and data communications bit-rate targets can be appropriately adjusted in real-time.

g) The STFL will also contain functionality that is able to recognise data streams that are already encoded into the STTP data format, so that they can be passed on, or forwarded, with unchanged content, to their intended recipients, but with appropriate administrative changes applied. As STTP-based data streams are encrypted for security, the data forwarding feature will need to take this into account and will be able to handle already encrypted elements that it is not able to decrypt itself because it is not the intended recipient of such data.

h) The STFL will provide access to the STSS, which provides *Multi-Factor Authentication* and *Single Sign-On* functionality.

i) The STFL will not be a fully-automated system; it will be a library of software-based routines that requires external programmatic control. The capabilities provided by the STFL will be accessed and controlled via the Stream Tone *Application Programming Interface*.

j) The STFL will be available for a range of microprocessor instruction set architectures and operating systems.

k) The STFL will be able to accelerate its operation by using, where available, parallel-processing hardware such as that provided by general-purpose graphics processing units, or by application-specific semiconductor intellectual property cores within a ***System on a Chip***.

l)    The STFL will be able to request that a STAD report its functional capabilities. This is needed to ensure that audio-visual data sent to a STAD will be compatible with the STAD's particular hardware. For example, STADs of different form factors will typically have display screens of different resolutions, and understanding the functional capabilities of a particular STAD will allow video data with a resolution that exactly matches that of the STAD's display screen to be sent.

m)   The STFL will be published under a ***Free and Open-Source Software*** license.

# 4.1.3.5    STREAM TONE IMAGE CACHE

a)    The Stream Tone Image Cache (STIC) will be a database of visual data that can be used to reduce the communications bandwidth required to retransmit certain types of visual data over an active communications channel, between a Stream Tone Transfer Protocol Encoder (STTPE) and a Stream Tone Transfer Protocol Decoder (STTPD). The STIC is expected to be of particular benefit when the graphical user interfaces of desktop operating systems, software applications, and ***Web Browser***s are communicated using the Stream Tone Transfer Protocol (STTP). Functionality equivalent to the STIC may be a standard feature of the remote desktop display and control technology that is adopted by the STTP, or it may need to be a custom development. The description contained within this section assumes a custom development.

b)    The STIC will be built and maintained at both the STTPE end-point and at the STTPD end-point. Contents of the STIC at each end-point will be identical. Operations applied to the STIC at one end-point, such as visual data additions or deletions, will be duplicated in the STIC at the other end-point.

c)    The STIC will be dynamically built by storing a copy of visual data, such as graphical-cursor data, the visual-change data from slow-to-change visual imagery, and static visual data, when such visual data is first sent from the STTPE end-point to the STTPD end-point. The STIC will not be used to store video data, which is considered to be transitory in nature. Before a STTPE sends any visual data to a STTPD it will first need to determine if that visual data has already been seen and is currently held within the STIC. The data processing required to determine if visual data is already held within the STIC may be highly demanding and may, consequently, require the support of application-specific hardware.

d)    Each piece of visual data stored within the STIC will be assigned a unique reference, or identifier, known as a Stream Tone Image Cache Identifier (STIC-ID). Each piece of visual data stored within the STIC will also be classified by ***Internet Media Type*** or an equivalent classification system.

e)    The STTPE will be able to cause the display of required visual data on a Stream Tone Access Device by simply sending the STIC-ID of the required visual data to the STTPD, which will then obtain a copy of that data from its local copy of the STIC. Obtaining the required visual data from a local copy of the STIC removes the need to resend that data over the computer network connection between STTPE and the STTPD, which will help to reduce communications bandwidth usage.

f)   It is assumed that under normal circumstances the **Compression** of visual data stored within the STIC will not be necessary as the STIC will be of a sufficient size to hold all required visual data in an uncompressed format. The use of uncompressed visual data avoids the data processing overhead incurred when decompressing compressed visual data each time it needs to be displayed. If visual data does need to be compressed, for example to save space in the STIC, then a fast-operating and energy-efficient lossless **Compression** algorithm will be used.

g)   Visual data held within the STIC will be held on an end-point to end-point connection basis, from a STTPE to a STTPD, and when such a connection is explicitly or implicitly terminated then all such visual data will be securely deleted.

h)   The STIC will be able to support a number of simple data-oriented operations, such as store, read, and delete. The store operation adds new visual data, of a specific type, into the STIC. Duplicate visual data will be discarded. Stored visual data will automatically be assigned a unique STIC-ID. Visual data stored within the STIC can be irregularly shaped or non-rectangular. The read operation will obtain a copy of stored visual data identified by its STIC-ID. The delete operation will remove specific visual data, a range of visual data, or all visual data from the STIC. In the instance where required visual data is no longer in the STIC then that visual data will be re-requested from the original source.

i)   Individual visual-change data for slow-to-change visual imagery may need to be periodically consolidated into a single static image in order to manage the cumulative quantity of visual-change data held within the STIC. The individual visual-change data will then be deleted, whilst the newly constructed static image will be retained. Without the use of consolidation the STIC may regularly become full and require time-consuming housekeeping. Consideration should be given as to whether the consolidation of visual-change data needs to be a continuous process.

j)   Functionality to create, access, and maintain the STIC will be provided by the Stream Tone Software Development Kit (STSDK).

k)   It is assumed that the storage space available for the STIC will be finite and that a deletion algorithm based on the principle of first-in-first-out will need to be applied in order to remove the oldest visual data and make room for the storage of new visual data, when free space within the STIC drops to near zero. Visual-change data can also be consolidated in order to free up storage space within the STIC.

l)   The STIC database will have a fast operation, and a simple data structure that is optimised for low-latency operation.

m)   The STIC will be published under a **Free and Open-Source Software** license.

# 4.1.4    STREAM TONE ACCESS DEVICE

## 4.1.4.1    OVERVIEW

a)   The Stream Tone Access Device (STAD) will be a single-purpose computer that can only be used to access remotely-served digital content and services that are communicated using the Stream Tone Transfer Protocol (STTP). The STAD is a type of ***Thin Client***, also known as a zero-client or dumb terminal. The digital content and services that will be accessed by a STAD will originate predominately on the ***Web*** and be delivered over the ***Internet***.

b) The STAD will wholly rely on remotely-sourced services in order to provide user-oriented functionalities, as it will not possess any significant data processing capability of its own; it will have just enough data processing capability to fulfil its allotted job of audio-visual presentation and no more. The STAD will be a pure audio-visual presentation device. In simple terms, the STAD will effectively be an interactive television and the streams of digital content and services that are presented on it will be conceptually similar to television broadcast channels.

c) The STAD will support a wide range of built-in features and functionalities that are common, familiar, and expected by users of today's personal computing devices. Data generated by such built-in functionalities will be sent to remotely-located computer servers for appropriate processing and storage. A generic mechanism will be adopted for adding new functionalities that may be required by the STAD in the future.

d) A key characteristic of the STAD is that it will be a hardware-based device that will not require an operating system or any application software; ensuring that it is essentially maintenance free. Should an operating system or application software be required, due to real-world practicalities, then it will be very simple in nature, and specifically designed to require little or no maintenance.

e) The STAD will be an instant-on, always-on, device. Once a STAD is turned on it will be fully operational with a few seconds, and will then automatically establish a highly-reliable computer network connection to at least one STTP-based service a few seconds later. Once a STAD has been turned on, it will stay turned on, and will maintain a constant connection to one or more STTP-based services.

f) A number of physically different STAD form factors will be available.

g) The STAD control electronics will be standardised and applicable to all STAD form factors.

h) The STAD will have a highly durable and easily repairable ***Modular Design***, with a working life expectancy, in a wide range of environments, of at least 10 years. Many STAD form factors, particularly those that are designed to be portable, will be drop, dust, and water resistant.

i) The STAD is intended to be affordable by everyone, everywhere, not just by rich people living in highly-developed countries. A STAD, regardless of its form factor, will cost much less than a non-STTP-based equivalent. The fact that a STAD will have a long working life will also contribute to its perceived affordability because most other types of personal computing devices have a working life of just a few years. The STAD's expected 10-year minimum working life will significantly change the value proposition for personal computing devices.

j) The STAD will be designed to be highly power-efficient, as portable battery-powered versions are expected to be common and popular.

k)  Any third-party technologies that are required to build the STAD will be obtained under either an *Open-Source Hardware* (OSHW) licence or a *Free and Open-Source Software* (FOSS) license. In the worst case scenario, that patent encumbered technologies are unavoidably required to build a STAD then such technologies must be obtained on *Fair, Reasonable, and Non-Discriminatory Licensing* terms that have been approved in writing by the Stream Tone *Foundation*.

l)  The reference design for the STAD hardware will be published under an OSHW licence. STAD software will be published under a FOSS license. The STAD hardware license may not require copyleft.[20] The STAD software license will require copyleft.

## 4.1.4.2     DESIGN

a)  The Stream Tone Access Device (STAD) reference design will be developed by the Stream Tone Community (STC).

b)  Where possible, the development of the STAD will make extensive use of *Free and Open-Source Software* (FOSS) and *Open-Source Hardware* (OSHW) building blocks, such as those provided by the *OpenCores* community. Should third-party technology that is encumbered with patents be unavoidably required in the development of the STAD then such technology will be obtained on a *Fair, Reasonable, and Non-Discriminatory Licensing* basis and will require the written approval of the Stream Tone Foundation.

c)  The STAD will contain a hardware-based equivalent of the Stream Tone Function Library.

d)  The STAD hardware will comply with environmental standards, such as the *Electronic Product Environmental Assessment Tool* and the *Energy Star* initiative.

e)  The STAD hardware will be based on a *Modular Design* that permits the efficient and effective repair of individual components. A *Modular Design* will also permit the easy and cost-effective upgrading of individual components, such as display screens, case enclosures, and other more sophisticated components. The STAD hardware design will adopt a *Backward Incompatibility* approach that primarily focuses on current and future needs rather than attempting to support a full range of legacy interfaces and technologies. For example, the STAD will use the *Internet Protocol Version 6*-based addressing standard and not the older *Internet Protocol* version 4 standard. The STAD will only support *Fourth-Generation Mobile Communications*, or better, and not third-generation mobile communications. Modular components will use a standardised interface that will allow components from different manufacturers to be used interchangeably.

f)  The evolution of the STAD will be supported through the use of a forward compatibility design approach. For example, the inclusion of a *Software-Defined Radio* subsystem will allow the STAD to use new mobile telecommunications standards, simply by installing a software update. A *Modular Design* approach will be able to accommodate the inclusion

---

[20] TBD: A non-copyleft hardware license will allow Stream Tone Access Device original equipment manufacturers to innovate.

of new hardware-based functionalities in the future.

g) Some of the telecommunications technologies that the STAD will likely support, include **Bluetooth**, **Cognitive Radio**, infrared, **Fourth-Generation Mobile Communications**, infrared, **Near-Field Communication**, **Smart Antennas**, **Software-Defined Radio**, standard wired networking, **Visible Light Communication**, and **Wi-Fi**. In the future, the STAD will also support **Fifth-Generation Mobile Communications**, when it becomes available.

h) Using both wired and wireless communications, the STAD will support a wide range of **Networked Peripherals**, including computer monitors, digital cameras, document scanners, fax machines, game controllers, keyboards, mice, microphones, printers, projectors, speakers, televisions, video cameras, virtual-reality headsets, and wristwatches.

i) The STAD will be built using power-efficient electronic components, such as radio frequency power amplifiers based on **Asymmetric Multilevel Outphasing** technology, microprocessors based on **Reduced Instruction Set Computing** architectures, and display screens based on **Electronic Paper**, **Indium Gallium Zinc Oxide Backplanes**, **Organic Light-Emitting Diodes**, and **Transflective Liquid-Crystal**.

j) The STAD will support the use of multi-point touch-enabled display screens based on **Capacitive Sensing** technology. The STAD will support the use of **Autostereoscopic Display Technology** in order to more accurately represent three-dimensional imagery. Other technologies that will also likely be included in the STAD include an **Accelerometer**, **Ambient Light Sensor**, **Barometer**, **Global Positioning System**, **Gyroscope**, **Image Sensor**, loudspeakers, **Magnetometer**, memory card reader, microphone, and **Proximity Sensor**. Certain STAD form factors may also support the HDMI and USB interface, or their successors.

k) The STAD will have at least 1 gigabyte of high-speed random-access memory (RAM) that will mainly be used to hold communications data buffers and the Stream Tone Image Cache. In order to minimise malfunctions, the STAD RAM will use **Error Correcting Code Memory**. The STAD will contain a small **Solid-State Drive** that will be used to hold STAD configuration data. Microcode, or other types of embedded software, will be held in read-only memory.

l) Portable STAD form factors will be powered by a **Lithium-Ion Battery**, or similar. Some portable STADs will contain an integral battery charger based on **Photovoltaic** technology. Most STAD form factors will be able to obtain electrical power from a variety of sources, such as an external power supply unit or a **Power over Ethernet**-based network connection.

m) The operational heart of the STAD will be a **System on a Chip** (SOC) that contains a wide range of power-efficient application-specific semiconductor intellectual property (IP) cores, such as an audio controller, data **Compression**/decompression engine, digital signal processor, **Encryption**/decryption security engine, global navigation controller, memory controller, mobile communications controller, multi-core general-purpose microprocessor based on a **Reduced Instruction Set Computing** architecture, multi-core graphics processing unit with general-purpose computing capabilities, multi-point touch-screen controller, network interface controller, sensor controller, Stream Tone Transfer Protocol

Codec, USB controller, video display controller, and wireless communications controller. The STAD SOC will be built using a **Field-Programmable Gate Array, Application-Specific Integrated Circuit**, or perhaps a combination of the two. Each independent IP-core within a STAD SOC will operate at a clock speed that is just fast enough to get the job done. IP core clock speeds will be dependent on their current workload, with a greater workload requiring a faster clock speed. Some tasks, such as STTP encoding and decoding, will be handled by multiple IP cores working in parallel. The STAD SOC will be a standardised component, regardless of STAD form factor. For example, the same SOC component will be able to support a portable STAD with a high definition display screen with a resolution of 1920 pixels by 1080 pixels or a television with an ultra high definition (UHD) display screen with a resolution of 7680 pixels by 4320 pixels. In order to support the extra processing that is required to drive an UHD screen, the relevant processing cores within the STAD SOC will either be run at a faster clock speed or multiple processing cores will be used in parallel. Active, or mechanical, cooling of the SOC may be required for a very limited number of STAD form factors that offer very high performance operations, such as STADs with very high display screen resolutions. However, in general, STADs will make use of passive, non-mechanical, cooling technologies. All cooling technologies used for the STAD will be highly durable and low maintenance. Passive cooling technologies will be favoured over active cooling technologies because passive technologies are simpler in design, have no moving parts, do not require regular maintenance, and are, therefore, much less prone to failure. Any active cooling technology that is used, such as a cooling fan, will be very easy and cost effective for a STAD owner to replace should it inadvertently fail.

n)  The STAD will be a hardware-based device that does not need an operating system. However, if the STAD should require the use of an operating system then a FOSS-based operating system, such as **Linux**, will be selected. Such an operating system will need to be optimised for highly-reliable, low-latency, low-maintenance, real-time operation.

o)  Once the functional design of the Stream Tone Transfer Protocol has been finalised the functional design of the STAD will be frozen. The functionality of a STAD will become fixed and unchanging, but how the STAD provides that functionality will not. The implementation of the STAD design can continue to be refined and improved with the objectives of making the STAD more affordable, durable, power-efficient, reliable, and repairable.

p)  The reference design for the STAD hardware will be published under an OSHW licence. STAD software will be published under a FOSS license. The STAD hardware license may not require copyleft.[21] The STAD software license will require copyleft.

## 4.1.4.3    FORM FACTORS

a)  The Stream Tone Access Device (STAD) will be available in a wide range of form factors, including computer monitors, desktop computers, games consoles, laptop computers, **Smart-Phones**, **Tablet Computers**, and televisions.

---

[21] *TBD: A non-copyleft hardware license will allow Stream Tone Access Device original equipment manufacturers to innovate.*

b)  In the future, STADs with radically different form factors, such as contact lenses, cookers, eyeglasses, microwave ovens, neural implants, refrigerators, washing machines, and wristwatches, are expected to become available.

c)  The first STADs are expected to use the popular **Smart-Phone** and **Tablet Computer** form factors.

d)  STAD control electronics will be standardised, ensuring that the control electronics of all STAD form factors will be identical. Different STAD form factors may feature a wide range of built-in functionalities or peripherals, such as display screens with various resolutions, fingerprint scanners, keyboards, or mice, but they will not have different control electronics.

e)  STADs, in a wide variety of forms factors will be built, on a commercial basis, by original equipment manufacturers.

f)  The initial cost of manufacturing a STAD, regardless of form factor, is not expected to be significantly less than for a comparable non-Stream Tone Transfer Protocol-based device. However, given that a STAD will be technically simpler than a comparable non-STTP-based device, in that it does not need to contain large amounts of non-volatile storage, large amounts of random-access memory, a high-performance central processing unit, or a sophisticated three-dimensional graphics processing unit, technologies that typically add appreciable cost to such devices, therefore as volume production and the standardisation of components, across all form factors, ramps up, manufacturing costs are expected to reduce substantially.

# 4.1.4.4    FUNCTIONALITY

a)  The Stream Tone Access Device (STAD) will be an instant-on device. What this means in practical terms is that the STAD will become fully operational a few seconds after it has been turned on. It will then automatically establish a connection to a Stream Tone Transfer Protocol (STTP)-based service a few seconds later.

b)  The STAD will deactivate its display screen if user interaction is not detected within a user-defined period of time. The STAD will reactivate its display screen when the user next interacts with the device.

c)  The STAD will feature a status indicator light, known as the Stream Tone Indicator (STI). The STI will provide a simple, easily understandable, language-independent, mechanism for communicating the current operational status of a STAD. When a STAD is turned on the STI will be illuminated by a sequence of coloured lights; red, orange, and green. Each light will be illuminated for approximately one second, after which the STAD will have fully powered up and started to automatically connect with its default STTP-based service, usually a Stream Tone Service Portal (STSP). If a STAD is turned on and this light sequence is not seen then the STAD power source is disconnected, the STAD's **Lithium-Ion Battery** is empty, or the STAD is suffering from a very serious malfunction. Once the STAD has successfully been turned on the STI will then start to indicate the STAD's operational status. If the STAD is connected to a STTP-based service and that connection meets minimum quality of service (QOS) standards and no minor or major hardware fault on the STAD is detected then the STI will be illuminated with a steady green light. If the STAD display screen then becomes deactivated, after the STAD has not been used for a period of time, the STI will be illuminated with a flashing green light. A minor hardware fault is defined as the failure of a non-critical subsystem that does not prevent the STAD from connecting with a STTP-based service or the basic use of a connected STTP-based service. A major hardware fault is defined as the failure of a critical subsystem that prevents the STAD from connecting with a STTP-based service or the basic use of a connected STTP-based service. If the STAD is connected to a STTP-based service and that connection does not meet minimum QOS standards then the STI will be illuminated with a steady orange light. The STI will be illuminated with a flashing orange light if a minor hardware fault on the STAD is detected. If the STAD becomes disconnected from all STTP-based services, or is unable to initially connect with a default STTP-based service, then the STI will be illuminated with a steady red light. The STI will be illuminated with a flashing red light if a major hardware fault on the STAD is detected. Other STI colours and STI blink codes may also be supported in the future.

d) The STAD will be able to securely log onto one or more STTP-based services at the same time. The credentials of the user of the STAD will be validated using **Multi-Factor Authentication** (MFA). Most Stream Tone-based services will support **Single Sign-On** (SSO) that will use the credentials obtained from MFA. MFA and SSO functionality will be provided by the Stream Tone Security Service.

e) The STAD will maintain a constant connection to at least one STTP-based service, typically the user's default STSP. The computer server providing the STTP-based service will determine that a STAD is connected based on the regular receipt of data sent from the STAD. Such data will be generated by user-input, built-in functionalities, **Networked Peripherals**, or a watchdog data pulse that is sent when other types of data are absent. When a server does not receive any type of data for a user-configurable period of time then the link between the STAD and the server will be considered to be disconnected. Conversely, if a STAD does not receive any type of data from a server for a user-configurable period of time then the link between server and the STAD will be considered to be disconnected.

f) If a STAD becomes disconnected from a STTP-based service then that service will continue, pause, or terminate. Disconnection behaviour will be user-configurable on a per service basis through the STSP Service Launcher.

g) The STAD will be able to play audio that has been sent from a STTP-based service. The presentation of audio data will occur immediately upon receipt of an atomic block of decodable audio data. Audio data will be synchronised with any associated visual data, as appropriate. Received audio data will be discarded once it has been presented, or superseded by new data. It should be noted that STAD networking services may need to buffer a small amount of audio data sufficient to handle variable network conditions, and that such buffering will introduce small but necessary latencies into the audio presentation pipeline. The STAD will be able to capture audio data and send it to a STTP-based service for subsequent processing and storage using the STTP.

h) The STAD will be able to display visual data that has been sent from a STTP-based service. The presentation of visual data will occur immediately upon receipt of an atomic block of decodable visual data. Visual data will be synchronised with any associated audio data, as appropriate. Received visual data will be discarded once it has been presented, or superseded by new data. It should be noted that STAD networking services may need to buffer a small amount of visual data sufficient to handle variable network conditions, and that such buffering will introduce small but necessary latencies into the visual presentation pipeline. The STAD will be able to capture visual data and send it to a STTP-based service for subsequent processing and storage.

i) The STAD will be able to capture user-input data, obtained from a keyboard, mouse, multi-point touch-enabled screen display, or other human interface device, and send it to a STTP-based service, for subsequent processing and storage. User-input will be able to alter an on-going the audio-visual presentation in real-time, enabling the delivery of highly-responsive interactive services.

j) The STAD will be able send data generated by functionalities built directly into a STAD, or from **Networked Peripherals** connected to a STAD, to a STTP-based service for processing and storage. If such data is non-transitory and should not be lost, then when such data is sent to a STTP-based service, a copy of that data will be retained on the STAD within random-access memory (RAM), until the STTP-based service has confirmed safe receipt of that data, at which point it will then be deleted. The sending of further data will be suspended until safe receipt of previously sent data has occurred.

k) The STAD will be able to receive non-audio-visual data, which will then be stored on a removable memory card, or forwarded to other functionalities built into the STAD or to **Networked Peripherals** for processing and storage. The non-audio-visual data transfer mechanism will also support the transmission of audio and video data files.

l) The STAD will obtain graphical cursors, slow-to-change visual data, and static visual data from the Stream Tone Image Cache; a reserved portion of RAM that contains a store of previously received visual data, which can be used to minimise network traffic when that visual data needs to be redisplayed.

m) When displaying local video data that has been captured by a STAD **Image Sensor**, the display of that video data will be processed locally, directly on the STAD, and will not be handled by STTP-based services. If the video data is also to be stored, or processed in some way, then it will be sent to a STTP-based service that provides such functionality.

n) The STAD hardware will be configurable, and will store configuration data in non-volatile data storage. STAD configuration settings will allow user preferences to be set, user authentication criteria to be defined, whether built-in functionalities or **Networked Peripherals** are enabled or disabled, and the behaviour of built-in functionalities or **Networked Peripherals** to be controlled. The STAD will provide a visually simple graphical user-interface (GUI) to support basic STAD configuration. A visually sophisticated GUI that supports more advanced STAD configurations will be provided by STTP-based services.

o) The STAD will support a diagnostic mode of operation that will, typically, display raw data generated by all functionalities built directly into the STAD in a highly comprehensive single screen of information. As a simple aid to understanding, if the data generated by a given built-in functionality or setting is within an acceptable range it will be displayed in green, and if it falls outside of the acceptable range then it will be displayed in red. Functionalities that are currently deactivated will be displayed in orange. Some of the data fields on the diagnostic screen will be interactive, allowing STAD configuration settings to be changed by the user. Diagnostic mode will be activated based upon a simple user interaction, such as by a gesture detected by a touch-enabled display screen. On STADs, that do not include a built-in touch-enabled display screen, a dedicated diagnostic mode button may be provided. Alternatively, a long press on the STAD's power button may be used to activate diagnostic mode. Some examples of the type of diagnostic data that will be displayed are: *Accelerometer* readings as measured in metres per second squared, *Ambient Light Sensor* readings as measured in millivolts, audio system status indicator expressed as good or bad, *Barometer* readings as measured in millibars, *Bluetooth* signal strength as measured in decibels above one milliwatt, built-in functionality user-enabled or user-disabled status, central processing unit load expressed as a percentage, clock reading as measured in hours:minutes:seconds, date reading as measured in year:month:day, default STSP *Internet Protocol* (IP) address expressed in standard *Internet Protocol Version 6* (IPv6) format, display screen brightness expressed on a scale of 0-10, display screen contrast expressed on a scale of 0-10, display screen timeout expressed in minutes:seconds, *Global Positioning System* readings as measured in degrees of latitude and longitude, *Gyroscope* readings as measured in degrees, *Image Sensor* video preview mode status indicator, language of the diagnostic mode, *Lithium-Ion Battery* charge level expressed as a percentage, *Lithium-Ion Battery* charging indicator expressed as on or off, loudspeaker or headphone volume expressed on a scale of 0-10, *Magnetometer* readings as measured in tesla, memory card reader contents as measured in gigabytes, microphone input expressed in decibels and as a dynamic waveform display, mobile telecommunications signal strength measured in decibels above one milliwatt, network communications latency as measured in milliseconds, network data download total as measured in bytes, network data download speed as measured in megabits per second, network data transmission error count as measured in data packets, network data upload total as measured in bytes, *Networked Peripheral* list, network upload speed as measured in megabits per second, *Proximity Sensor* reading as measured in millivolts, random-access memory usage expressed as a percentage, STAD IP address expressed in standard IPv6 format, STAD manufacturer details, STAD serial number, Stream Tone Indicator status long-form explanation, user contact details, *Wi-Fi* signal strength as measured in decibels above one milliwatt. Other diagnostic information will be included based upon the final features and functionality of the STAD.

# 4.1.4.5     STREAM TONE ACCESS DEVICE EMULATOR

a)    Before physical, hardware-based, Stream Tone Access Devices (STADs) become widely available, digital content and services communicated using the Stream Tone Transfer Protocol (STTP) will be accessed using a software-based Stream Tone Access Device Emulator (STADE). The STADE will provide nearly all of the functionality provided by a physical STAD. The exact functional capabilities of a STADE will be dependent on the capabilities of the physical hardware that it is run on.

b)    The STADE will be developed by the Stream Tone Community.

c)    The STADE will be able to run on pre-existing personal computing hardware, either directly as a native software application or indirectly as a *Virtual Machine* within a *Virtual Machine* manager or hypervisor. The *Virtual Machine* image will use a lightly-modified version of a mature and stable *Linux*-based operating system, such as Debian, Mint, or Ubuntu. The *Virtual Machine* image will also form the basis of a STADE *Live*

*CD*.

d)  It is expected that nearly all currently available personal computing devices, such as desktop computers, games consoles, *Internet*-enabled televisions, laptop computers, set-top boxes, *Smart-Phones*, and *Tablet Computers*, will be able to run some form of the STADE software.

e)  The STADE software application will be developed using a wide range of development technologies, such as *HyperText Markup Language Version 5* and *Linux*.

f)  The STADE software will be provided as a *Live CD* so that it can be easily used on existing personal computing devices without being permanently installed.

g)  Installable versions of the STADE software will be available from *Application Stores*.

h)  The STADE will be built using the Stream Tone Software Development Kit.

i)  The STADE will be published under a *Free and Open-Source Software* license.

# 4.1.5    STREAM TONE SERVICE INFRASTRUCTURE

## 4.1.5.1    OVERVIEW

a)  The digital content and services that will be communicated using the Stream Tone Transfer Protocol (STTP) will be provided by Stream Tone Service Infrastructures (STSIs). The STSIs will be able to provide content and services that are highly affordable, high bandwidth, low latency, highly reliable, and ubiquitously available.

b)  STSI can be used as a generic term to describe all the service infrastructures used to provide STTP-based content and services. STSI can also be used to describe a specific service infrastructure that is used to provide STTP-based content or services.

c)  In simple terms, a STSI will comprise of one or more service infrastructures, or parts thereof, that are used, on a particular occasion, to provide the digital content or services that will then be communicated using the STTP. STSI encompasses such technologies as *Data Centres*, *Cloud Computing*, operating systems, software applications, and *Virtual Machines*.

d)  It should be noted that just because a particular service infrastructure, or part thereof, is used by the Stream Tone, and therefore referred to as a STSI, does not mean that such an infrastructure inherently meets the full affordability, availability, bandwidth, latency, and reliability requirements of the Stream Tone. In fact, the exact nature, and therefore the capabilities and performance, of any particular STSI is expected to vary by circumstance, location, market, and time.

e)  It is not envisioned that the STSI will require the specific development of any new service infrastructure technologies, but the STSI is expected to directly benefit from improvements to the affordability, availability, bandwidth, latency, and reliability of such infrastructures that are continually in progress.

f) It should be noted that, the various service infrastructures, or parts thereof, that will comprise any given STSI will continue to independently evolve and mature based on drivers that are unique to the digital services industry. Therefore, the influence that the Stream Tone will actually have over any aspect of the STSI will most probably be limited to the issuance of advice and recommendations on how such infrastructures can be optimised for providing STTP-based content and services. Realistically, whether or not the digital services industry will heed such advice will ultimately depend on the success of the Stream Tone concept within the market.

g) The Stream Tone is, essentially, a communications protocol, and the digital content and services that it will be used to communicate will need to be provided by a wide range of third-party service providers. Some of these services will be pre-existing and will simply be accessed in a new way using the STTP, and some will be brand new services that have been developed specifically for use with the STTP. Existing services will need to be re-engineered if they are to be directly accessed using the STTP. Some existing services will not need to be re-engineered as they will be indirectly accessed through intermediaries that will convert the audio-visual inputs and outputs of those services into STTP-based data streams. The Stream Tone does not need new services to be specifically developed for it, although its audio-visual communications capabilities will undoubtedly be a catalyst for the creation of many new and exciting services, some of which were not previously feasible. The use of the STTP will not limit the type or nature of digital content or services that can be accessed or provided.

h) Some STTP-based services will be available free-of-charge and some will be chargeable, just like some types of **Web-based Service** are today. Some services will be funded through advertising and others through philanthropy. Some types of service, such as those requiring the persistent use of dedicated hardware or substantial data processing resources, are likely to be very expensive, particularly in the short term.

i) All STTP-based services will be provided by a STSI and will then be delivered using a Stream Tone Telecommunications Infrastructure. STTP-based services will be provided using the technology of **Cloud Computing**, which is based on the efficient and effective use of **Data Centre** resources, such as **Virtual Machines**, on massive scales. The physical scale and quantity of the **Data Centres** that will be needed to support Comprehensive Remote Personal Computing will be substantial, and a programme of **Data Centre** construction and upgrading will need to be undertaken in all geographies in order to meet that need. **Data Centres** will need to be located within close geographic proximity of users in order to minimise telecommunications latencies.

j) STSIs will need to be able to provide highly affordable, high bandwidth, low latency, highly reliable, and ubiquitously available STTP-based services. STSIs capable of supporting such characteristics will largely be achieved through the adoption of a wide range of new service-oriented technologies that have been specifically optimised for use on efficient and effective **Cloud Computing**-based infrastructures. The adoption of such technologies is expected to occur naturally and not because they are specifically required to support the provision of STTP-based content and services.

## 4.1.5.2     DEVELOPMENT

a)   The process for developing the Stream Tone Transfer Protocol (STTP)-based services that will be provided using the Stream Tone Service Infrastructure (STSI) will essentially remain the same as for current non-STTP-based service development, but with two important differences; one, that the services will need to support bi-directional STTP-based communications, and, two, that all development will be server-side only, centred on the **Data Centre**, with none on the user access device or client-side. The development model for STTP-based services can still be based on the classic client-server architecture model that has been successfully used for most current **Web-based Services**. However, under the Stream Tone, the classic client is functionally and logically split between a dumb user-client and an intelligent **Data Centre**-client. The dumb user-client is known as the Stream Tone Access Device (STAD), which is a simple hardware-based audio-visual presentation device. The intelligent **Data Centre**-client embodies the software-based functionality that would have previously been used to access remotely-located services from a user's local personal computing device. In simple terms, the STAD remotely controls the **Data Centre**-client, which in turn requests data from a remote server that is located elsewhere on the **Internet**. The remote server then returns the requested data to the **Data Centre**-client, which then converts that data into an audio-visual representation that is suitable for presentation on the STAD. Topologically, the architectural role of the **Data Centre**-client is context-dependent; when it is communicating with a STAD it can be thought of as a server, and when it is communicating with another server it is a client. Alternatively, the **Data Centre**-client can just be thought of as **Data Centre**-based middleware or an interface to a remote server. Some STTP-based service providers may decide, for simplicity and/or efficiency, to combine the **Data Centre**-client and the remote server into a single operational unit. Such a combination would give developers complete control over all aspects of a STTP-based service, thereby potentially enabling many beneficial optimisations.

b)   Digital services will need to leverage the Stream Tone Software Development Kit (STSDK) and the Stream Tone Graphics Interface in order to support STTP-based communications.

c)   STTP-based services can continue to use existing programming languages and integrated development environments (IDEs). Stream Tone-specific programming languages and IDEs will not be required. The STSDK will be available for all popular programming languages. In simple terms, it will be possible to build STTP-based services for any operating system or hardware platform that supports **Internet** connectivity. STTP-based services can be built using portable, platform-agnostic technologies or non-portable, platform-specific, technologies, as per the preferences of the developer.

d)   Some STTP-based services will need to support the Stream Tone Security Service (STSS). The STSS will provide **Multi-Factor Authentication** (MFA) and **Single Sign-On** (SSO) functionality. MFA functionality will be used to validate users of STTP-based services with a high degree of confidence, based on what the user knows, has, and is. SSO functionality will then allow a validated user to access other STTP-based services that also support the STSS, without the need to explicitly log onto those services.

e)   STTP-based services will need to secure all user-data, whether in transit, at rest, or in use, using strong **Encryption** whenever such data is within its sphere of control. The STAD will primarily be a presentation device that does not need to retain any audio-visual data

271

that is sent to it after that data has been briefly buffered and then presented. The STTP will be a secure communications protocol, so using the STTP will protect user-data while it is in transit, but in all other situations it will be the responsibility of the STTP-based service provider and the various STSIs to develop and maintain suitable mechanisms for the strong protection of user-data.

f)   STTP-based services will need to be optimised for operation within resource constrained **Cloud Computing**-based environments that may have restrictive data processing, memory, network, power, and storage budgets. Such environments will also be characterised by the use of dynamic resource allocation and deallocation, multi-tenancy, resource pooling, **Virtual Machines**, and virtual networking.

g)   STTP-based services will need to be able to leverage the efficiencies of hardware-based application-specific accelerators, such as those offered by general-purpose graphics processing units or application-specific semiconductor intellectual property cores within a **System on a Chip**, where available.

h)   Some STTP-based services will need to be able to exchange data with other **Web-based Services**, either directly or indirectly through the use of third-party intermediaries such as **File Hosting Services** (FHSs). STTP-based services will need to be able store user-data, either within a user-specific account offered by that service or in a user-specific account of another service, such as a FHS. STTP-based services that read data from, or store data on, a FHS will need to ensure that the FHS is only accessed when absolutely necessary, in order to minimise communications bandwidth between the STTP-based service and the FHS. STTP-based services that need to communicate with other **Web-based Services** are at liberty to use whatever communications protocol is deemed most appropriate for the exchange of user-data, and not necessarily the STTP, as long as user-data is always securely handled and protected from loss, damage, and interference.

i)   The STSI will need to be optimised in terms of affordability, availability, bandwidth, latency, and reliability. STSI operational costs will need to be kept low so that STTP-based services will be affordable. STTP-based services will be ubiquitously available due to their accessibility from any **Internet** connection point. STTP-based services will use the absolute minimum amount of communications bandwidth required to deliver an acceptable user-experience. STTP-based services will operate with minimal latency in order to support highly-responsive user-oriented interactivity. STTP-based services will be engineered for reliable operation to ensure that such services will always perform as expected when required.

j)   Many STTP-based services will very likely be chargeable, and in order to keep costs to an absolute minimum such services will need to use all available data processing resources highly efficiently and highly effectively, something that has not really been commonplace since the very earliest days of personal computing when personal computing devices contained only tiny amounts of random-access memory and microprocessor capabilities were only a small fraction of what they are today.

k)   Some STTP-based services will need to integrate advertising into their service offerings in order to reduce costs. It should be noted that advertising that is embedded within an STTP-based service cannot be easily blocked, certainly not using a STAD. STTP-based services that use an advertising-based business model should ensure that such advertising is not overly annoying or intrusive.

l)   Some STTP-based services will be built from other services; STTP-based, non-STTP-based, or a combination of the two.

m)   STTP-based services will need to be aware of the hardware-based capabilities of the STAD or Stream Tone Access Device Emulator (STADE) that they are serving. For example, different devices will, most likely, have display screens of different resolutions, and STTP-based services will need to be aware of the required resolution before visual data can be sent. It should, however, be noted that, apart from some relatively minor variations in capabilities, that all STADs are essentially identical from a service development perspective. So, unless a STTP-based service requires the presence of a particularly unusual hardware-based capability, all STTP-based services should work with all STADs, regardless of form factor.

# 4.1.5.3    SERVICE HARDWARE

a)   The Stream Tone Service Infrastructures (STSIs) that will be used to provide Stream Tone Transfer Protocol (STTP)-based services will be based on generic **Cloud Computing** hardware that is optimised for **Data Centre** use. In simple terms, the STSIs will not require the use of any STTP-specific or specialised hardware in order to operate. Of course, if specialised hardware is available, such as for accelerated video **Compression** or accelerated data **Encryption**, then the STSI will naturally make use of such hardware in order to increase operational efficiency and effectiveness.

b)   STSI hardware will need to provide STTP-based services with sufficient communications bandwidth, both internally within a **Data Centre**, and externally to and from the **Internet**. In simple terms, this means that STSI hardware must be capable of supporting very-high communications bandwidths, such as those offered by the latest generations of **Optical Fibre**-based telecommunications.

c)   STSI hardware will need to allow interactive STTP-based services to respond to user-input almost instantly. In simple terms, this means that STSI hardware must be capable of supporting low-latency operations, primarily through the provision of high-performance data processing and computer networking resources.

d)   STSI hardware will need to be highly reliable so that STTP-based services will, in turn, be highly reliable. In simple terms, this means that STSI hardware must be designed and built for continuous and consistent operation. The STSI hardware will need to be fault tolerant and able to instantly recover from any unexpected interruption. Ideally, users should never become aware that any interruption, regardless of its duration, has occurred.

e)   STSI hardware will need to provide STTP-based services with sufficient **Internet** connectivity so that such services will be ubiquitously available.

f)   STSI hardware will typically be provided on an indirect, virtualised, basis through the use of **Virtual Machines** which will be dynamically allocated on-demand, although some types of STTP-based services will require the use of dedicated, persistent, non-virtualised, resources.

g)   The electrical power used by a typical **Data Centre** is often a significant operational cost.

**Data Centres** have therefore evolved a number of strategies for using power in a highly effective and highly efficient manner. Also, because of the very large scale of most **Data Centre** operations, resources, such as application software, data processing, cooling, electrical power, and **Internet** bandwidth, can be sourced very cost effectively. As a result, the cost of providing **Data Centre**-based digital services will generally be much less, all things considered, than if those services were provided using a local personal computing device, such as a desktop computer or laptop computer. The cost effectiveness of **Data Centre** operations has been steadily improving over the years, and is expected to continue to do so in the future, with the result that most STTP-based services will soon be affordable by everyone, everywhere.

h)   STSI hardware will very likely vary from **Data Centre** to **Data Centre**, and geography to geography, until a standardised hardware configuration, that is generically suitable for use by a wide range of STTP-based services, is adopted by the digital services industry. Some examples of the hardware-based technologies that could potentially be used by the STSI include: **Error Correcting Code Memory**, which allows memory errors to be detected and corrected in real-time, thereby greatly improving the reliability of **Data Centre**-based computer servers built with such technology; **Hard-Disk Drives**, which are mechanical non-volatile data storage systems that continue to offer very cost-effective and reliable data storage and retrieval solutions within the **Data Centre**; **Heterogeneous Computing**, which is the complementary use of different computing architectures that can be used to highly efficiently and highly effectively solve data processing problems within the **Data Centre**; **Open-Source Hardware**, which is based on freely-available hardware designs that can be used to cost-effectively build many of the physical systems used within a **Data Centre**; **Optical Fibre**, which is a light-based communications technology that can be used to provide very-high bandwidth communications inside the **Data Centre**, and from the **Data Centre** to the **Internet**; **Reduced Instruction Set Computing** (RISC), which is a type of microprocessor architecture that offers good computing performance for the electrical power it consumes, and which may be ideally suited to running many types of STTP-based services in the **Data Centre**. A new RISC-based instruction set architecture known as **ARM v8** that supports 64-bit memory addressing will allow STTP-based services to access very large amounts of random-access memory; **Solid-State Drives**, which are non-mechanical non-volatile data storage systems that can provide high-performance data storage and retrieval solutions for use within the **Data Centre**.

# 4.1.5.4   SERVICE SOFTWARE

a)   Stream Tone Service Infrastructure (STSI) software can be divided into two main types; software that is used to provide Stream Tone Transfer Protocol (STTP)-based services and software that is used to create an operational environment, or platform, for those services.

b)   All STSI software will need to be highly affordable, high bandwidth, low latency, highly reliable, and ubiquitously available in order to be able to provide STTP-based services that exhibit the exact same characteristics.

c)   The Stream Tone Graphics Interface (STGI) will be a Stream Tone Transfer Protocol (STTP)-based remote display and control solution for use on desktop operating systems. The STGI will be a key enabling technology of the Stream Tone as it will allow STTP-based access to existing operating systems and software applications. Existing **Web-based Services** will be available through any **Web Browser** that is run on a STGI-enabled operating system.

d)  The Stream Tone Security Service (STSS) will provide *Multi-Factor Authentication* and *Single Sign-On* functionality for use by Stream Tone Service Portals (STSPs) and STTP-based services. User-access to a STSP will require the mandatory use of the STSS. Use of the STSS by STTP-based services is optional. Some STTP-based services, because of their nature, will not require the use of an access and identity management solution, such as the STSS.

e)  The software-based STSP application will be a user-oriented STTP-based service platform that allows the user of a Stream Tone Access Device (STAD) to find and access STTP-based services. Use of a STSP is optional as a STTP-based service can also be accessed by entering its *Internet Protocol Version 6* address, or uniform resource identifier, directly into a STAD.

f)  All STTP-based services must be designed to communicate with a STAD using the STTP. Some existing *Web-based Services* will be modified to use the STTP using tools provided by the Stream Tone Software Development Kit, and some will be accessed using a STTP-based front-end, such as that provided by the STGI.

g)  STTP-based services will, in general, be the product of custom software development activities. Some STTP-based services will be built using other digital services; STTP-based, non-STTP-based, or a combination of the two.

h)  Most of the operational environments that will be used to provide STTP-based services will be typical *Cloud Computing*-based *Data Centre* environments. *Virtual Machine* manager software, also known as a hypervisor, will be used to create the virtualised operational environments required to support the provision of most STTP-based services. Many of these operational environments will be built using *Free and Open-Source Software* (FOSS), such as *Linux* and *OpenStack*.

i)  Communications within STSI-based *Data Centres* will utilise FOSS-based *Software-Defined Networking* technologies, such as *OpenFlow*.

j)  Some STTP-based services will be created by migrating application software, operating systems, and user-data from a local personal computing device onto a *Virtual Machine* located in a STSI-based *Data Centre* using *Physical to Virtual* functionality.

## 4.1.5.4.1    STREAM TONE GRAPHICS INTERFACE

a)  The Stream Tone Graphics Interface (STGI) will be a Stream Tone Transfer Protocol (STTP)-based remote display and control solution for use on desktop operating systems. The STGI can be used to build STTP-based services.

b)  The STGI is a technology that is primarily designed for use on *Data Centre*-based computer servers, although it could also be used to remotely display and control a traditional desktop computer or laptop computer using a Stream Tone Access Device (STAD).

c)  The STGI will be available for all commonly used desktop operating systems, hypervisors, and microprocessor instruction set architectures.

d) Development of the STGI will be phased, and will start with a version of the STGI for use on *Linux*-based operating systems running on Intel x86-compatible hardware. Other versions will become available shortly thereafter. The STGI will be developed by the Stream Tone Community.

e) The STGI will support most video graphics hardware, including hardware that features general-purpose graphics processing units.

f) The STGI will be built using the Stream Tone Software Development Kit, plus additional operating system-specific or hypervisor-specific code.

g) The STGI will support *Multi-Factor Authentication* and *Single Sign-On* functionality provided by the Stream Tone Security Service.

h) The STGI will support display screen panning and scaling, which can be used when a remote desktop display screen has a different resolution to the display screen on the STAD that is used to access it. The STGI will support multiple remote display screens.

i) The STGI will be able to suspend the operation of a remote desktop if the STAD that is used to access it becomes disconnected from its computer network or becomes unexpectedly unresponsive.

j) The STGI will be able to indirectly provide access to *Web*-based content and services that are normally only accessible using *Internet Protocol* version 4 (IPv4) addressing, and will be able to make them available to a STAD, which only supports *Internet Protocol Version 6* (IPv6) addressing. This will be achieved by running an IPv4-compatible *Web Browser* on a remote desktop operating system that is then accessed by the STGI, which will then send, using the STTP, a representation of the audio-visual output from that *Web Browser* to a STAD using IPv6 addressing.

k) The STGI will be a key technology for enabling the rapid adoption of the Stream Tone, as it will allow a significant amount of local personal computing functionality to be migrated onto remote *Web-based Services*. Once a STGI has been added to a desktop operating system, the graphical user-interface of that operating system, and all software applications and user-data hosted on that operating system, will be available from a STAD.

l) The STGI will be published under a *Free and Open-Source Software* license.

## 4.1.5.4.2    STREAM TONE SECURITY SERVICE

a) The Stream Tone Security Service (STSS) is a *Web*-based identity and access management (IAM) solution that will provide *Multi-Factor Authentication* (MFA) and *Single Sign-On* (SSO) functionality via the *Internet* for use with Stream Tone Transfer Protocol (STTP)-based services. The STSS will be an important part of the Stream Tone's security strategy. The STSS will be globally available.

b) The STSS will be an integral part of the Stream Tone Service Infrastructure.

c) Use of the STSS by a STTP-based service is optional. Some STTP-based services, because of their nature, will not need to validate their users, and will therefore not need to make use of an IAM solution, such as that provided by the STSS. STTP-based services can also, if they wish, use alternative IAM solutions, although such services will probably not be able to support the seamless hand-off from a Stream Tone Service Portal (STSP) to such a service.

d) Use of the STSS is mandated for initial user-access to a STSP.

e) MFA functionality will be used to validate the credentials of STTP-based service users with a high degree of confidence, based on what the user knows, has, and is. A range of different authentication factors will be supported. The range of authentication factors supported by the STSS is expected to increase over time.

f) SSO functionality will allow a user that has been validated by MFA to access other STTP-based services that also support the STSS, without the need to explicitly log onto each of those services.

g) The first STTP-based service that a user will normally access when activating a STAD will be the user's default STSP, which is a service that provides access to all of a user's preferred STTP-based services. Once a user has been validated using MFA functionality, SSO functionality will then allow unrestricted access to all other STTP-based services that also support the STSS, and which are available from the user's STSP.

h) Programmatic access to the STSS will be provided by the Stream Tone Software Development Kit.

i) Given that the STSS will only be accessed by either a STSP or a STTP-based service, and not directly by a STAD, the STSS will probably not need to use the STTP for communications. Therefore, unless compelling reasons are determined that the STSS should use the STTP the STSS will use other existing communications protocols that are commonly used for the safe and secure transmission of IAM data over the ***Internet***.

j) The creation and operation of the STSS will be under the oversight and governance of the Stream Tone ***Foundation*** (STF).

k) The provision of the STSS will be on a non-profit basis in order to keep the costs of using this service as low as possible. The main users of this service will be STSP operators and STTP-based service providers. The STF may be able to fund the operation of the STSS, in which case the cost to STSS users will be nil. However, if the STF is unable to fully fund the operating costs of the STSS then any shortfall will need to be recovered in other ways. One possible method of recovery would be by directly charging STSS users for their use of the service. Of course, any charges that are levied in such a circumstance will need to be kept to an absolute minimum, and offered on flexible payment terms that are compatible with businesses of all sizes and shapes, ranging from a small one-person start-up to a multi-national corporation.

l) Ideally, the STSS will be provided by a single third party that is an established and experienced provider of globally-accessible IAM solutions.

m) The STSS may be based on a proprietary or Stream Tone-specific development. If any part of the STSS is based on a Stream Tone-specific development then that development will be the responsibility of the Stream Tone Community and all products of that development will be published under a *Free and Open-Source Software* license.

## 4.1.5.4.3 STREAM TONE SERVICE PORTAL

a) Most Stream Tone Transfer Protocol (STTP)-based services will be accessed via a Stream Tone Service Portal (STSP), which will be the principle user-oriented mechanism for accessing such services. The STSPs will be gateways into the world of STTP-based services, and it will be through such gateways that all the digital content and services that the *Internet* and *Web* have to offer will be accessed.

b) There will be multiple STSPs that will be provided by a wide range of for-profit and non-profit operators. Competition between STSP operators is expected to be highly creative and vigorous. It is expected that continuous competition between STSP operators will help to ensure that STTP-based services become increasingly affordable.

c) Individually, and collectively, the STSPs will form an integral part of a Stream Tone Service Infrastructure (STSI).

d) Each STSP will be created using STSP application software that is designed to run on STSI-based *Cloud Computing* hardware. The STSP application software will be developed by the Stream Tone Community. The STSP application software will be published under a *Free and Open-Source Software* license.

e) STSP operators will be able to configure the STSP application software to support their own branding and to offer unique user experiences. Many *Internet* service providers are expected to offer a STSP as a new type of value-added-service to their customers. The STSP will support a number of business models, including advertising-based, commission-based, fee-based, and free-of-charge-based, or a mixture of different types.

f) Each STSP, regardless of operator or geography of provision, will be globally accessible from any *Internet*-enabled location.

g) The STSP will be responsible for initiating, or brokering, a connection between a Stream Tone Access Device (STAD) and a STTP-based service, on behalf of a user.

h) STTP-based services that are initially accessed through a STSP will not have their bi-directional data streams routed through that STSP, as all such streams will be sent directly from the service to the STAD and from the STAD to the service.

i) Use of a STSP, when accessing STTP-based services, will not be mandatory, as STTP-based services will also be accessible by entering the *Internet Protocol Version 6* address, or uniform resource identifier, for the service directly into a STAD.

j) Each user will have their own STSP account that will be used to store links to their preferred STTP-based services. When a user activates their personal STAD they will be automatically connected to their default STSP and after successfully completing user-validation will be logged onto their individual STSP account.

k) The STSP will communicate with a STAD using the STTP. The STSP will natively support the STTP because it will be built using the Stream Tone Software Development Kit.

l) The STSP will use the Stream Tone Security Service (STSS) to verify the identity and access permissions of a STAD user. The STSS will provide **Multi-Factor Authentication** and **Single Sign-On** (SSO) functionality. The SSO functionality will allow the STSP to provide seamless and fully-automated access to other STTP-based services that also support the STSS without the need to for the user to explicitly log onto each of those services. Use of the STSS is mandatory for initial user-access to a STSP.

m) A STSP will comprise of two key functionalities; a STSP Service Launcher, and a STSP Service Store.

n) The STSP Service Launcher will have a user-configurable graphical user-interface (GUI) that can display available services in a wide variety of visual formats. The GUI of the STSP Service Launcher will indicate which services are currently available, paused, running, or unavailable. It will be possible to display each service within a small window or on the whole STAD display screen. Each running service will update the display in real-time. The GUI of the STSP Service Launcher will be sent as a distinct STTP-based data stream that will be combined on the STAD with other STTP-based data streams, such as those from STTP-based services, as and when required. The GUI of the STSP Service Launcher will be simple, ergonomic, multi-lingual, and highly intuitive.

o) It will be possible to run multiple different STTP-based services at the same time. Some services will permit multiple instances of the same service to be run at the same time. Multiple services will be able to share the STAD display screen. Some services may have conflicting STAD resource requirements and will not be able to run at the same time, or may run with reduced functionality. When multiple STTP-services are run at the same time, only one service will hold operational focus at a time. A service that holds operational focus will have access to all required STAD functionality. For example, a service that holds operational focus, and which requires the use of the STAD's audio system would be able to play music, whilst another service with the same requirement but without operational focus would be muted. Operational focus will be applied to, or removed from, a service by a simple user interaction. The behaviour of individual STTP-based services that were running when they lost operational focus will be user-configurable, through the STSP Service Launcher. A running service that looses operational focus can be set to continue, pause, or terminate. The same user-configurable behaviours will also be applied to running services when the communications link between a STAD and those services is unexpectedly lost. It will be possible to configure a STTP-based service to be uninterruptible, which will prevent that service from loosing operational focus when it is running, unless operational focus is manually removed by the user.

p) It will be possible to configure some STTP-based services to automatically run in the background whenever a STAD is active. Background services, like all STTP-based services, are always run on STSI-based servers, and not on the STAD that is used to access them. By default such background services will not hold operational focus, but will be able to temporarily capture operational focus and notify the user when certain events occur, such as when an alarm activates or a personal message is received. If another service held the operational focus when such an event occurs then that service will loose operational focus and will continue, pause or terminate, as per its usual behaviour in such a circumstance. After the event has finished, operational focus will be returned to the service that held the focus before the event occurred, assuming that it was not configured to automatically terminate when it lost operational focus. There will be no technical limit on the number of background services that can be configured. There may, however, be other limiting factors, such as cost or telecommunications bandwidth. The behaviour of background services will be configurable using the STSP Service Launcher. Background services will need to either support the STSS, or not require any user authentication at all. It is expected that a typical user will have many background services configured.

q)  STTP-based services will be added to a user's STSP Service Launcher using the functionality of the STSP Service Store. The STSP Service Store provides functionality similar to an **Application Store**, except that instead of providing a mechanism for finding and managing software applications it finds and manages STTP-based services. The STSP Service Store will offer a very wide range of STTP-based services that can be added to a user's list of preferred services. Once an available service has been selected it will appear on the user's STSP Service Launcher, and after it has been appropriately configured will be available for immediate use. Like the GUI of the STSP Service Launcher, the GUI of the STSP Service Store will also be simple, ergonomic, multi-lingual, and highly intuitive. The GUI of the STSP Service Launcher and the GUI of the STSP Service Store will be visually and operationally similar in order to provide a consistent user-experience.

r)  The use of some STTP-based services, including some background services, will be chargeable, and the STSP Service Launcher will allow a user's payment details to be configured so that such services will be immediately available when required, and the user will not be required to make a manual payment each time a chargeable service is used.

s)  The cost of operating a STSP will be borne by each STSP operator. The STSP operator may consequently seek to recover operating costs from its customers. Operation of a STSP will require the use of the STSS, which may or may not be made available free-of-charge to the STSP operator.

# 4.1.6    STREAM TONE TELECOMMUNICATIONS INFRASTRUCTURE

## 4.1.6.1    OVERVIEW

a)  The digital content and services that will be communicated using the Stream Tone Transfer Protocol (STTP), and provided by a Stream Tone Service Infrastructure, will be delivered by a Stream Tone Telecommunications Infrastructure (STTI). STTIs will provide both wired and wireless telecommunications that are highly affordable, high bandwidth, low latency, highly reliable, and ubiquitously available.

b)  Security will be a significant requirement for the Stream Tone but that will not be provided by a STTI as it will primarily be handled through the use of the strong

***Encryption*** technologies built into the STTP. Nevertheless, a STTI will endeavour to restrict any form of unauthorised access to even encrypted STTP-based data streams.

c) STTI can be used as a generic term to describe all the telecommunications infrastructures used to carry STTP-based content and services. STTI can also be used to describe a specific telecommunications infrastructure that is used to carry STTP-based content and services.

d) In simple terms, a STTI will comprise of one or more telecommunications infrastructures, or parts thereof, including the many interlinked telecommunications networks that comprise the ***Internet***, that are used, on a particular occasion, to deliver digital content and services using the STTP. A STTI will also include the various telecommunications technologies that will be used to connect a Stream Tone Access Device to the ***Internet***, over the last mile, via an ***Internet*** service provider.

e) It should be noted that just because a particular telecommunications infrastructure, or part thereof, is used by the Stream Tone, and therefore referred to as a STTI, does not mean that such an infrastructure inherently meets the full affordability, availability, bandwidth, latency, and reliability requirements of the Stream Tone. In fact, the exact nature, and therefore the capabilities and performance, of any particular STTI is expected to vary by circumstance, location, market, and time.

f) It is not envisioned that STTIs will require the specific development of any new telecommunications infrastructure technologies, but all STTIs are expected to directly benefit from improvements, to the affordability, availability, bandwidth, latency, and reliability of such infrastructures, that are continually in progress.

g) It should be noted that, the various telecommunications infrastructures, or parts thereof, that will comprise any given STTI will continue to independently evolve and mature based on drivers that are unique to the telecommunications industry. Therefore, the influence that the Stream Tone will actually have over any aspect of a STTI will most probably be limited to the issuance of advice and recommendations on how such infrastructures can be optimised for carrying STTP-based traffic. Realistically, whether or not the telecommunications industry will heed such advice will ultimately depend on the success of the Stream Tone concept within the market. In general, it is more likely that it will be the Stream Tone that will need to adapt to changes in telecommunications infrastructures, rather than the other way round. However, regardless of whether the telecommunications industry changes to support the Stream Tone, or the Stream Tone changes to support the telecommunications industry, the end result should be the same; modern telecommunications infrastructures that are compatible with the Stream Tone and a Stream Tone that is compatible with modern telecommunications infrastructures.

h) STTIs that are able to fully meet the affordability, availability, bandwidth, latency, and reliability requirements of the Stream Tone are likely to emerge gradually over a number of years, in parallel with the adoption and maturation of the Stream Tone. In some geographic regions, STTIs will undoubtedly take longer to meet these requirements than in others. Developed nations may lead the way or it may be that developing nations are able to leap ahead of developed nations on this occasion, should they decide to skip intermediate technologies and directly adopt the Stream Tone instead. It should be noted that the Stream Tone will be adaptable to telecommunications infrastructures that have less capability or performance than those that might be considered more ideal, and will also be able to comfortably coexist with current non-Stream Tone-based technologies. So, just because a given telecommunications infrastructure does not perfectly meet all the requirements does not mean that the Stream Tone cannot be used, it just means that certain types of STTP-based content and services may not be fully supported.

i)    The STTP only supports *Internet Protocol Version 6* (IPv6), therefore STTIs will only need to support IPv6.

j)    Some examples of the technologies that could potentially be used by STTIs to help meet the Stream Tone's affordability, availability, bandwidth, latency, and reliability requirements are: *Asymmetric Multilevel Outphasing* which can be used to greatly reduce the power and cooling requirements of the radio frequency power amplifiers that are used within mobile communications base-stations, and which is expected to be particularly helpful in bringing mobile communications to rural geographies; *Coded Transmission Control Protocol*, which is a data packet encoding approach for mitigating the effects of data packet loss during wireless communications, allowing more data to be carried by current telecommunications infrastructures; *Cognitive Radio*, which is a dynamic mobile communications approach that can more efficiently and more effectively use available radio spectrum; *Communications Satellites*, especially those with *Electrically Powered Spacecraft Propulsion* and which communicate in the high-bandwidth *Ka Band*, which can be used to cost-effectively bring *Internet* access to remote rural geographies; *Content Delivery Network*s, which can cache digital content in close geographic proximity to users, thereby reducing expensive long-haul bandwidth usage and lowering communications costs and latencies; *Distributed-Input-Distributed-Output*, which can be used to deliver consistently high signal-strength, full-bandwidth mobile communications services over large geographic areas that have high population densities; *Dynamic Adaptive Streaming over HTTP*, which is an approach for mitigating some of the effects of variable network transmission quality on the streaming of audio-visual data; *Fourth-Generation Mobile Communications* (4G), which is the next generation of mobile communications after third-generation mobile communications, that is capable of providing communications with greatly improved affordability, availability, bandwidth, latency and reliability; *G993.5*, which is a crosstalk cancellation technology designed for use on copper wire-based telecommunications infrastructures, that is able to cost-effectively increase data bandwidth; *Mesh Networking*, which can be used to build dynamic telecommunications networks based on a mesh topology, that can be used to cost-effectively bring *Internet* access to rural geographies; *Optical Orthogonal Frequency-Division Multiplexing*, which is used to increase the data carrying capacity of *Optical Fibre*-based communications links; *Phase-Conjugated Twin Waves*, which are able to greatly extend the range of *Optical Fibre*-based communications links; *Radio over Fibre*, which can be used to simplify and centralise the control electronics of mobile communications base-stations; *Reduced Internet Transport Latency*, which is an initiative with the aim of reducing or moving unwanted time delays or latencies from *Internet*-based communications; *Roaming Agreements*, that allow the users of one commercial telecommunications network to legally and transparently use the services of another network; *Small Cells*, which can be used to cost-effectively provide high-bandwidth wireless *Internet* connectivity, using 4G and *Wi-Fi*, over limited geographic areas; *Smart Antennas*, which are able to more efficiently and more effectively transmit data over wireless communications networks; *Submarine Communications Cables*, which are used to provide international *Internet* connectivity over *Optical Fibres*; *Symmetrical Broadband*, which is a type of *Internet* access service in which the upstream and downstream bandwidths are equal, that can be used to enable a wide range of cost-effective digital content-creation services; ***Unlimited Data Plans***, which offer unmetered access to the ***Internet*** and which are becoming increasingly common; ***Universal Service Obligation*** for broadband service, which defines ***Internet*** access as a basic human right, that is under consideration or has actually been implemented in a number of countries; ***Visible Light Communication***, which can be used to provide cost-effective high-bandwidth ***Internet*** access based on short-range optical-wireless communications technology; ***Vortex Radio***, which is an approach for substantially increasing the data carrying capacity of wireless communications systems that is currently being researched; ***Wi-Fi***, which is a generic wireless networking technology that can be used to provide cost-effective high-bandwidth ***Internet*** access; ***WiFox***, which is a technique for mitigating the impact of congestion within wireless communications networks.

## 4.1.6.2      AFFORDABILITY

a)    The ***Internet***-connectivity services used by Stream Tone Telecommunications Infrastructures to deliver Stream Tone Transfer Protocol (STTP)-based content and services will need to be affordable by everyone, everywhere, not just by rich people living in highly-developed countries but also by poor people living in developing countries that are just starting to make use of the ***Internet***, personal computing devices, and ***Web***. What this should mean in practice is that the annual cost of ***Internet***-connectivity that will be used for accessing STTP-based content and services will be in no way prohibitive, approximating to, for example, no more than 1 percent of the average annual income for a given geography.[22]

b)    The affordability of accessing STTP-based content and services will be dependent on affordable ***Internet***-connectivity services being made available by ***Internet*** service providers. The affordability of both wired and wireless ***Internet*** connectivity will largely be achieved through the adoption of a wide range of new telecommunications infrastructure technologies that will be able to provide ***Internet*** connectivity with all the required characteristics at increasingly low price points. The adoption of such technologies is expected to occur naturally and not because it is specifically required to support the use of STTP-based content and services.

c)    Historically, the cost of ***Internet*** connectivity, as measured in gigabytes of downloaded data per unit of cost, has steadily reduced, year on year, and is expected to continue to do so in the future, ensuring that in the very near future that the delivery of STTP-based content and services will be highly affordable by everyone, everywhere.

## 4.1.6.3      AVAILABILITY

a)    Stream Tone Telecommunications Infrastructures will rely on telecommunications infrastructures that are able to provide both wired and wireless broadband ***Internet*** connectivity that is ubiquitously available. What this means in practice is that it will be

---

[22] *A subjectively determined estimate of the level of financial impact that most people in the world should be able to easily absorb without it negatively impacting their everyday lives.*

possible to access Stream Tone Transfer Protocol (STTP)-based content and services from any location, on land, whether above or below ground, at sea, or in the air, and in any circumstance whether in motion within an aeroplane, bus, car, or train, or from any stationary location whether inside a building or outside on a street. Connectivity will be continuous and uninterrupted.[23]

b) The ubiquitously available *Internet* connectivity that will be required to support the delivery of STTP-based content and services will largely be achieved through the adoption of a wide range of new telecommunications infrastructure technologies that are able to provide *Internet* connectivity under all circumstances to all locations. The adoption of such technologies is expected to occur naturally and not because they are specifically required to support the use of STTP-based content and services.

c) Historically, the availability of *Internet* connectivity has been steadily growing, and what was once only available from fixed locations, such as homes or offices, is now available from almost anywhere, particularly in urban environments with high population densities, using a wide range of modern telecommunications technologies. The availability of *Internet* connectivity is expected to continuing growing in the future, and will eventually achieve one hundred percent coverage across many geographic regions, urban and rural alike, ensuring that STTP-based content and services will be available from everywhere that it is required.

# 4.1.6.4   BANDWIDTH

a) Stream Tone Telecommunications Infrastructures (STTIs) will rely on telecommunications infrastructures that are able to provide both wired and wireless *Internet* connectivity with adequate data bandwidth. What this means in practice is that enough data bandwidth will be available for accessing all the different types of Stream Tone Transfer Protocol (STTP)-based content and services that will be required by a typical Comprehensive Remote Personal Computing (CRPC) user.[24] Additionally, the total quantity of data that can be uploaded or downloaded within a given period of time will be more than sufficient for continuously accessing all such content and services. Available bandwidth will most likely vary based on circumstance, location, market, or time; for example, stationary users will probably obtain a higher bandwidth than users that are in rapid motion within an aeroplane, bus, car, or train.

b) Wired and wireless *Internet* connectivity with sufficient data bandwidth will largely be achieved through the adoption of a wide range of new telecommunications infrastructure technologies that are able to provide multi-megabyte per second communications. The adoption of such technologies is expected to occur naturally and not because they are specifically required to support the use of STTP-based content and services.

c) Historically, the bandwidth provided by a typical *Internet* connection has been steadily growing. In fact, wired *Internet* connections are already able to provide more bandwidth than a typical user can effectively make use of, whilst wireless *Internet* connections are

---

[23] *A subjectively determined estimate of the availability criteria that a Stream Tone Telecommunications Infrastructure would need to meet before most people would be willing to fully switch from local personal computing devices to STTP-based services.*
[24] *Largely dependent on the resolution and refresh rate of the Stream Tone Access Device display screen.*

rapidly catching up. Wired and wireless bandwidth is expected to continue growing in the future, and will eventually achieve levels sufficient for nearly all types of use, ensuring that STTP-based content and services will not be limited by the data bandwidth of the *Internet* connection used to access them.

d) Ideally, the telecommunications infrastructures used by a STTI to access STTP-based content and services will be able to support **Symmetrical Broadband** in which the upstream and downstream bandwidths are equal. The quantity of data that can be uploaded or downloaded within a given period of time will not be limited, or if limited then such limits will be more than sufficient for nearly all envisioned CRPC uses.

e) In simple terms, the actual data bandwidth required to support CRPC is expected to be largely dependent on the display screen resolution and display screen refresh rate of the Stream Tone Access Device (STAD), with higher resolution display screens and faster display screen refresh rates requiring more bandwidth than lower resolution display screens and slower display screen refresh rates. Of course, bandwidth requirements will also be affected by user actions and the type of STTP-based content or services being accessed. Assuming the use of a current generation **VP8**-class video encoder and a **Remote FrameBuffer**-based remote computer desktop display and control solution, typical STAD communications bandwidth requirements are expected to range from a minimum of approximately 2 megabits per second (Mbps), when accessing a **Hosted Desktop** with a resolution of 1280 pixels by 720 pixels, to a maximum of approximately 10 Mbps, when using a highly-interactive **Streamed Service** that requires almost perfect graphical precision at a resolution of 1920 pixels by 1080 pixels. Watching a video, with a resolution of 1920 pixels by 1080 pixels and a frame rate of 30 frames per second (FPS), would require a bandwidth of approximately 6 Mbps. Browsing **Web**-based content, consisting of a mixture of text, static images, and low-resolution video, will probably require a bandwidth of approximately 5 Mbps. Use of a next-generation video encoder, such as **VP9** or **Daala**, will be able to significantly reduce the maximum bandwidth requirements of STTP-encoded visual data, compared to current generation video **Compression** algorithms. The final version of the STTP, the one that will become the basis for the hardware-based STAD, will most probably be based on a **VP9**-class, or better, video encoder. A **VP9**-class video encoder should be able to deliver acceptable quality video with a resolution of 1920 pixels by 1080 pixels at 30 FPS using as little as 3 Mbps, video with a resolution of 3840 pixels by 2160 pixels at 60 FPS using 21 Mbps bandwidth, and video with a resolution of 7680 pixels by 4320 pixels at 60 FPS using 85 Mbps bandwidth. Not every STTP-based service will need to operate at a high resolution, so even though a STAD might have a display screen with a resolution of 3840 pixels by 2160 pixels, many services will be able to operate acceptably at much lower resolutions and will consequently consume much less bandwidth. Technologies, such as video and image up-scaling and video intra-frame prediction, can be used to display relatively low-resolution imagery and low-frame-rate video with a visual quality that would be more than acceptable for most uses, particularly on STADs with smaller-sized display screens, whilst consuming much less bandwidth. It should also be noted that the development of hardware-based **VP9**-class encoders is still in progress and that further improvements in video **Compression** ratios may still be possible.

f) The flipside of bandwidth is data usage, which is essentially the bandwidth consumed multiplied by the time taken to consume that bandwidth. STTP-based services will consume very large quantities of data, ideally provided by **Unlimited Data Plans** that offer high-bandwidth **Internet** access services without any data transfer constraints.

Assuming that STTP-based services are used for a continuous 24-hour period, the following quantities of data will be transferred: 21.6 gigabytes (GB) at 2 Mbps, 32.4 GB at 3 Mbps, 54.0 GB at 5 Mbps, 64.8 GB at 6 Mbps, 108.0 GB at 10 Mbps, 226.8 GB at 21 Mbps, and 918.0 GB at 85 Mbps. Over the course of a 31-day calendar month, the total data transferred would then be: 669.6 GB at 2 Mbps, 1,004.4 GB at 3 Mbps, 1,674.0 GB at 5 Mbps, 2,008.8 GB at 6 Mbps, 3,348.0 GB at 10 Mbps, 7,030.8 GB at 21 Mbps, and 28,458.0 GB at 85 Mbps. However, most users do not generally use their personal computing devices for continuous 24-hour periods. So, perhaps it may be more realistic to assume that on average STTP-based services will only be used for a total of 8 hours per day. In which case, the following amounts of data would then be transferred: 7.2 GB at 2 Mbps, 10.8 GB at 3 Mbps, 18.0 GB at 5 Mbps, 21.6 GB at 6 Mbps, 36.0 GB at 10 Mbps, 75.6 GB at 21 Mbps, and 306.0 GB at 85 Mbps. Over the course of a 31-day calendar month, the total data usage would then be: 223.2 GB at 2 Mbps, 334.8 GB at 3 Mbps, 558.0 GB at 5 Mbps, 669.6 GB at 6 Mbps, 1,116.0 GB at 10 Mbps, 2,343.6 GB at 21 Mbps, and 9,486.0 GB at 85 Mbps. Therefore, assuming that a typical user has a STAD with a screen resolution of 1920 pixels by 1080 pixels and a screen refresh rate of 30 FPS, a 10 Mbps bandwidth ***Internet*** connection should be sufficient for accessing most STTP-based services, including data-intensive services such as high definition video streaming. Data usage for such a device would be up to 36.0 GB per 8-hour period, 108.0 GB per 24-hour period, 1,116.0 GB per 31-day calendar month assuming 8 hours of use per day, and 3,348.0 GB per 31-day calendar month assuming 24 hours of use per day. Of course, less demanding usage scenarios, such as reading a ***Web***-based book or simply using the STAD for fewer hours per day, are likely to require substantially less data.

g) True ***Fourth-Generation Mobile Communications*** based on telecommunications technologies, such as Long Term Evolution-Advanced, are expected to be able to deliver mobile communications bandwidths of up to 1,000 Mbps per second. A mobile communications service that is capable of providing 1,000 Mbps bandwidth would be able to transfer up to 3,600 GB per 8-hour period, 10,800 GB per 24-hour period, and 334,800 GB over a 31-day calendar month assuming 24 hours of use per day, which should be more than enough data to support even the most demanding STTP-based services. ***Optical Fibre***-based communications are already able to provide bandwidths of 1,000 Mbps or more, but are not yet ubiquitously available, primarily due to relatively high infrastructure costs. Given that future telecommunications infrastructures are expected to offer very high bandwidth communications, both wired and wireless, a single ***Internet*** connection will be able to easily support multiple, simultaneous, STTP-based data streams, which would be sufficient to support the diverse CRPC needs of a small business or a typical family unit. For example, an ***Internet*** connection offering 1,000 Mbps bandwidth would be able to support 10 simultaneous users, each with a STAD that has a screen resolution of 7680 pixels by 4320 pixels and a screen refresh rate of 60 FPS. The use of lower resolution display screens with lower refresh rates, such as those with a resolution of 1920 pixels by 1080 pixels and a refresh rate of 30 FPS, would potentially allow as many as one hundred users to be simultaneously supported by a single ***Internet*** connection with 1,000 Mbps bandwidth.

h) Given that STTP-based communications will generally have an upper data bandwidth requirement, any STTI that is capable of transmitting data at bandwidths faster than this requirement can allow STTP-encoded data to be effectively delivered with reduced communications latency. Very high bandwidth communications will also be able to effectively provide much more time to process communicated data, such as in terms of aggressive data ***Compression*** and very strong ***Encryption***, on both the sending and receiving device.

i)  Stream Tone bandwidth requirements are based on the concept of goodput, which is application-level data throughput that excludes any communications protocol and data retransmission overheads.

j)  The STTP will be able to work well in dynamically-variable bandwidth environments due to its ability to adapt to prevalent network conditions.

k)  Long-haul bandwidth, used for the delivery of certain types of commonly accessed STTP-based content, will be greatly reduced, where appropriate, through the use of **Content Delivery Networks**, which are able to cache digital content in close geographic proximity to users.

l)  The bandwidth required to communicate STTP-based content and services can be optimised, where appropriate, through the use of adaptive communications and content preparation technologies, such as **Dynamic Adaptive Streaming over HTTP**.

# 4.1.6.5    LATENCY

a)  Stream Tone Telecommunications Infrastructures (STTIs) will rely on telecommunications infrastructures that are able to provide both wired and wireless broadband **Internet** connectivity with low communications latency. What this means in practice is that it will be possible to access Stream Tone Transfer Protocol (STTP)-based content and services with minimal communications delays that are solely and unavoidably due to a STTI. The communications delay of a typical STTI, as measured using a simple ping test, between a data request and a data response, will be no more than 25 milliseconds,[25] assuming the use of a Stream Tone Service Infrastructure-based computer server that is 1,000 miles from the user. Closer servers will offer less latency, down to an absolute unavoidable minimum, and servers that are further away than 1,000 miles will have higher latencies. It should be noted that many **Web-based Services** that do not require real-time interactivity will be able to operate acceptably with very much higher latencies; perhaps as much as ten or twenty times higher.

b)  Low-latency wired and wireless broadband **Internet** connectivity will largely be achieved through the adoption of a wide range of new telecommunications infrastructure technologies that have been specifically optimised for low-latency operation. The adoption of such technologies is expected to occur naturally and not because they are specifically required to support the use of STTP-based content and services.

c)  Historically, the telecommunications infrastructures that comprise the **Internet** have been predominantly optimised for high-bandwidth communications and not for low latency communications. It is, however, expected that in the future telecommunications infrastructures will become increasingly optimised for low-latency operation, ensuring that all types of STTP-based service can be supported, including those that require real-

---

[25] *A subjectively determined estimate based on the time it takes a photon travelling at two-thirds of the-speed-of light-in-a-vacuum to travel 1000 miles through an Optical Fibre-based communications link plus a bit extra to cover worst-case electronic processing overheads. This is a maximum value and average values would be much lower.*

time interactivity.

d) The communications latency of STTP-based content and services will be greatly reduced, where appropriate, through the use of **Content Delivery Network**s, which are able to cache commonly accessed content in close geographic proximity to users.

e) The time required for preparing digital content and services ready for communication using the STTP contributes to the latency of STTP-based communications, which can be optimised, where appropriate, through the use of adaptive communications and content preparation technologies, such as **Dynamic Adaptive Streaming over HTTP**.

# 4.1.6.6      RELIABILITY

a) Stream Tone Telecommunications Infrastructures (STTIs) will rely on telecommunications infrastructures that are able to provide both wired and wireless **Internet** connectivity that is completely reliable. What this means in practice is that it will be possible to access Stream Tone Transfer Protocol (STTP)-based content and services continuously and without any interruption, 24 hours per day, 7 days per week, and 52 weeks per year, from all locations and under all circumstances.[26] **Internet** connectivity will also be highly consistent in terms of bandwidth and latency.

b) The completely reliable **Internet** connectivity that will be required to support the delivery of STTP-based content and services will largely be achieved through the adoption of a wide range of new telecommunications infrastructure technologies that are able to provide consistent, continuous, and uninterrupted **Internet** connectivity under all circumstances to all locations. The adoption of such technologies is expected to occur naturally and not because they are specifically required to support the use of STTP-based content and services.

c) Historically, the reliability of **Internet** connectivity has been steadily improving and is expected to continue to improve in the future, and will eventually achieve almost one hundred percent reliability in many environments, urban and rural alike, ensuring that STTP-based content and services will be reliably accessible whenever and wherever they are required.

d) The STTP will be based on the assumption that all the audio-visual data that will be communicated by the STTP will be transitory in nature, and that the moderate loss of such data during transmission will be a common but largely unimportant occurrence, like the loss of one frame of video from a television broadcast. Consequently, any audio-visual data that is lost when using the STTP will be quickly replaced with subsequent data, which effectively obscures any loss, and creates the impression of reliability even when such reliability temporarily may not actually exist.

---

[26] *A subjectively determined estimate of the reliability criteria that a Stream Tone Telecommunications Infrastructure would need to meet before most people would be willing to fully switch from local personal computing devices to STTP-based services.*

# 4.2    USE CASES

*Practical examples*

a)    A small number of use cases for the Stream Tone are considered below.

b)    The use cases have been designed to demonstrate how the Stream Tone could be used to provide many familiar types of service.

c)    Some use cases describe the provision or use of more than one type of service.

d)    The use cases are intentionally presented at a high level as they are not intended to be implementation-ready blueprints, just a flavour of what might be possible when using the Stream Tone.

e)    Some of the use cases are dependent on technologies that are not yet available.

f)    The use cases demonstrate that Stream Tone Transfer Protocol (STTP)-based services can have systems architectures and operational processes that are similar to current non-STTP-based services.

g)    The operational practices and systems architectures described, or suggested, by the use cases are not intended to recommend the use of any particular operational practice or systems architecture.

h)    In general, the role of the Stream Tone within each use case is not particularly dominant; it is simply a small but important part of a greater system, as would be expected of something like a new access device or communications protocol. It can be seen that the Stream Tone has been used to enable aspects of the services described in the use cases, but those services also rely on many other critically important elements in order to function and be useful.

i)    One aspect that is not specifically emphasised within the use cases, but which is, nevertheless, important, is the fact that STTP-based services are expected to work without any notable fuss or bother, and be available when they are needed, regardless of location or circumstance, functioning reliably, and with sufficient capabilities to always get the job done.

j)    The use cases have a narrative structure that is designed to illustrate the use of STTP-based services within a real-world context.

k)    Most of the use cases describe services that are chargeable. This is because most of the entities providing those services will typically incur non-trivial capital and operational costs in the provision of those services, costs that will, in most cases, need to be passed directly onto the user. Any services that are provided free-of-charge will be funded by alternative means, such as through advertising, barter, or philanthropy. Vigorous commercial competition between providers is expected to ensure that most STTP-based services will be very affordable, and a good many others will be available free-of-charge.

l)    The use cases assume the use of a Stream Tone Access Device (STAD), but could just as easily make use of a Stream Tone Access Device Emulator (STADE) that is running on a traditional personal computing device, such as a desktop computer, laptop computer, **Smart-Phone** or **Tablet Computer**.

m) The STTP is not the only communications protocol used by the services described in the use cases. However, the STTP is the only communications protocol used to communicate with a STAD.

# 4.2.1    COMPUTER GAMING

a) In brief and simple terms, a computer gaming service (CGS) built using the Stream Tone might operate in the following manner:

b) A user, seated on a high-speed train that has just left the station on a journey through France between Paris and Nice, activates a Stream Tone Access Device (STAD). The STAD has a **Tablet Computer** form factor that is optimised for computer gaming, and which includes a large multi-point touch-enabled **Autostereoscopic** display screen with a large bezel that features physical gaming controls. The STAD is powered by a long-life **Lithium-Ion Battery**. The STAD has also been, considerately, paired with a comfortable set of **Bluetooth**-enabled headphones, so as not to disturb the other passengers on the train.

c) The STAD connects to a Stream Tone Service Portal (STSP), via the **Internet**. The user's **Internet** connection is provided by a true **Fourth-Generation Mobile Communications** (4G) service that supports **Internet** access from a wide variety of locations, including from within a moving vehicle, such as the train that the user is currently travelling on. The 4G service will also work within any railway tunnels that may be encountered along this particular route from Paris to Nice. The user's STAD connects to the **Internet** service using mobile data communications. The **Internet** service is quite expensive, as the user opted to pay a higher than normal monthly subscription in order to obtain an **Internet** service package that included an **Unlimited Data Plan**, suitable for **Web**-based computer gaming, and a free-of-charge STAD. This particular **Internet** service package is considered to offer good value for money, and is affordable by a worker earning slightly above the national average wage of France. The STAD communicates with the STSP using the Stream Tone Transfer Protocol (STTP). The user's identity is verified by the STSP using **Multi-Factor Authentication** (MFA) functionality provided by the Stream Tone Security Service (STSS). The STSP Service Launcher then presents the user with a personalised list of available services.

d) The user selects a stream offering a familiar CGS from the list. The CGS offers a very wide range of games, from casual to triple-A (AAA) titles. Many of the games offer high-fidelity photorealistic graphics, and sophisticated multi-user gameplay. The CGS offers a number of gaming packages, and the user subscribes to a mid-level package that offers unlimited access to all available games that are at least six months old, which is paid for by monthly subscription.

e) The STSP then connects the STAD to a front-end computer server located in a remote **Data Centre**, which is part of the highly-scalable **Cloud Computing**-based Stream Tone Service Infrastructure (STSI) that will be used to provide the CGS. The STAD communicates with the front-end server using the STTP. The CGS natively supports the STTP because it was built using the Stream Tone Software Development Kit and the

Stream Tone Graphics Interface (STGI). The user is automatically logged onto the CGS by the STSP. Both the STSP and the CGS support *Single Sign-On* functionality provided by the STSS, so once a user has successfully logged onto the STSP, further logins for other supported services are handled automatically and do not require any user involvement.

f) Each computer game available from the CGS requires its own unique operating system and microprocessor environment in order to operate, which is provided by the STSI used by the CGS. The STSI is based on a *Heterogeneous Computing* architecture that is comprised of *Application-Specific Integrated Circuit*-based accelerators, multi-core complex instruction set computing (CISC)-based microprocessors, multi-core general-purpose graphics processing unit-based accelerators, and multi-core *Reduced Instruction Set Computing* (RISC)-based microprocessors. The *Heterogeneous Computing* architecture allows the CGS to offer computer games that were originally designed for use on a very wide range of gaming platforms, including desktop computers, games consoles, *Smart-Phones*, *Tablet Computers*, and *Web Browsers*.

g) The front-end server sends a visual representation of the computer game selection screen to the STAD using the STTP. The user interacts with the computer game selection screen, and selects a casual game. The front-end server then connects the STAD to the gaming server that will be used to run the casual computer game. The gaming server is running a *Virtual Machine* (VM) manager, also known as a hypervisor. The casual game that the user has selected requires the use of a multi-core RISC-based microprocessor, and a *Linux*-based operating system. The hypervisor allocates the appropriate server resources that will be needed to run the selected computer game, and starts the VM. The VM will be used to run two software applications; the computer game and the STGI. A third software application is also available, which provides on-screen gaming controls for use with STADs that do not provide physical gaming controls. As the user's STAD provides physical gaming controls the software application that provides on-screen gaming controls will not be run on this occasion.

h) The selected computer game is then run, and the STGI then sends an audio-visual representation of the computer game's graphical user-interface (GUI) to the STAD using the STTP. The user interacts with the computer game's GUI using the STAD's physical gaming controls, and proceeds to play the casual game for a few minutes. The user then stops the computer game, which automatically terminates the VM and releases allocated resources. The STAD is then disconnected from the gaming server, and reconnected to the front-end server.

i) The user then selects a AAA computer game, a *Massively Multi-Player On-line Game*, from the computer game selection screen. The front-end server then connects the STAD to the gaming server that will be used to run the AAA computer game. The gaming server is running a VM manager, also known as a hypervisor. The AAA game that the user has selected requires the use of a multi-core CISC-based microprocessor, and a non-*Linux*-based proprietary operating system. The hypervisor allocates the appropriate server resources that will be needed to run the selected computer game, and starts the VM. The VM will run two software applications; the computer game and the STGI. The selected computer game is then run, and the STGI then sends an audio-visual representation of the computer game interface to the STAD using the STTP. The user has played this particular game before, and had saved progress in the game the last time it was played. When the game restarted the previous game progress was automatically restored. The user then interacts with the computer game's GUI using the STAD's physical gaming controls, and proceeds to play the game, from where was it was last saved, for a couple of hours.

j) The user then returns to the STSP in order to select a new service. The CGS was automatically paused when the user returned to the STSP. The paused CGS is clearly indicated on the STSP Service Launcher. The user then selects an email service, which is indicating that several new emails have been received, from the STSP Service Launcher, and proceeds to read the recently received emails. The user then terminates the email service and returns to the STSP. The user then selects the paused CGS. The GUI of the paused AAA game is then re-displayed. The user resumes playing the computer game. After several more hours of play, the train that the user was travelling on finally arrives in Nice. The user then saves the latest game progress and stops the computer game, which terminates the VM and releases allocated resources. The user exits the CGS, and returns to the STSP. The user then deactivates the STAD.

# 4.2.2     FOREIGN LANGUAGE TUTOR

a) In brief and simple terms, a foreign language tutor service (FLTS) built using the Stream Tone might operate in the following manner:

b) A user, located at home in the suburbs of Rio de Janeiro, Brazil, activates a Stream Tone Access Device (STAD). The STAD has a television form factor that has a large-sized display screen that supports three-dimensional (3D) visual content. The STAD has a built-in stereoscopic *Image Sensor*. The STAD has been paired with a wireless keyboard that includes a built-in touch-pad and microphone. The keyboard communicates with the STAD using *Bluetooth*. The 3D-effect of the STAD is based on *Autostereoscopic* display technology that does not require the viewer to wear special eyeglasses. The STAD is located in the main living space of the user's home, opposite the sofa.

c) The STAD connects to a Stream Tone Service Portal (STSP), via the *Internet*. The *Internet* service is delivered using coaxial cable-based television infrastructure. The user's *Internet* service package provides a high-bandwidth *Unlimited Data Plan* that includes access to a large number of Stream Tone Transfer Protocol (STTP)-based services at no extra charge. The *Internet* service package is paid by monthly subscription, and is affordable by a worker earning the national average wage of Brazil. The STAD is connected to the *Internet* service using *Wi-Fi*.

d) The STAD communicates with the STSP using the STTP. The user's identity is verified by the STSP using *Multi-Factor Authentication* functionality provided by the Stream Tone Security Service (STSS). The STSP Service Launcher then presents the user with a personalised list of available services. The user selects a stream offering a FLTS from the list. The FLTS is one of the STTP-based services that are included in the user's *Internet* service package at no extra charge. The STSP then connects the STAD to a computer server, located in a remote *Data Centre*, which is part of the highly-scalable *Cloud Computing*-based Stream Tone Service Infrastructure that will be used to provide the FLTS. The STAD communicates with the server using the STTP. The FLTS natively supports the STTP because it was built using the Stream Tone Software Development Kit (STSDK). The user is automatically logged onto the FLTS by the STSP. Both the STSP and the FLTS support *Single Sign-On* functionality provided by the STSS, so once a user has successfully logged onto the STSP further logins, for other supported services, are handled automatically and do not require any user involvement. The server sends a visual representation of the foreign-language lesson selection screen to the STAD using the STTP. The user interacts with the lesson selection screen, and selects an Italian practice lesson.

e) The FLTS is a hybrid service, also known as a mash-up, which has been built from a number of other STTP-based services. The FLTS provides the text of a foreign language phrase that the user will be asked to repeat. A second STTP-based service then converts the foreign language text into a foreign-language speech data stream. A third STTP-based service provides a computer-generated photorealistic 3D talking-head video stream that will mouth the foreign language phrase, so that the user can observe the shape of the speaker's mouth and facial expressions when a phrase is spoken. The talking-head is able to look directly at the user, regardless of where the user is situated in front of the STAD, using user-position data derived from the video data stream captured by the stereoscopic *Image Sensors* built into the STAD. The *Image Sensors* are also used to determine the perfect 3D representation of the talking-head based upon the position of the user's eyes. The stereoscopic image data captured by the STAD is sent, unprocessed, to the FLTS using the STTP. The FLTS then forwards the stereoscopic data to the talking-head service for processing in real-time. The FLTS will also capture the user's attempt to repeat the foreign language phase, using the microphone built into the keyboard that has been paired with the STAD, and compare it with the correct version of the phrase in order to determine the user's proficiency in the foreign language. The user's speech data will be sent from the microphone, built into the keyboard, to the STAD using *Bluetooth* and from the STAD to the FLTS using the STTP. When the user's pronunciation of the Italian phrase is correct, the talking head will smile and congratulate the user. When the user's pronunciation of the Italian phrase is not correct, the talking head will look serious and ask the user to try again. The foreign-language speech and talking-head video services are directly controlled by the FLTS, using an *Application Programming Interface* that each service provides. The foreign-language speech and talking-head video services are third-party commercial STTP-based services that the FLTS has purchased in order to provide the audio-visual elements of the FLTS. The foreign-language speech and talking-head video services have many other customers, in addition to the FLTS, that use these services to build many other types of service, including a 24-hour multi-language news-on-demand service that is presented by a computer-generated newsreader. The output of the foreign-language speech and talking-head video services are STTP-based data streams that are sent directly to the FLTS. The foreign-language speech and talking-head video services natively support the STTP because they were both built using the STSDK. The FLTS synchronises the foreign-language speech audio with the talking-head video by manipulating administrative elements within each of the data streams. The FLTS does not alter the foreign-language speech audio or talking-head video contained in the data streams. The foreign-language speech audio and talking-head video are only delayed for a small fraction of second when they are processed by the FLTS. The FLTS then forwards the two data streams to the user's STAD, where they are seamlessly combined into a single audio-visual presentation. The FLTS also sends informational text and graphics in a separate STTP-based data stream. The communications links between the user and the FLTS, and between the FLTS and the speech and the talking head services, are all based on high-bandwidth low-latency communications, ensuring that the overall user-experience is very smooth and highly responsive.

f) Before the Italian practice lesson starts, the user is offered a range of photorealistic 3D talking heads to choose, including ones that are male, female, young, and old. The user is also able to select a voice style. The user then uses the wireless keyboard that has been paired with the STAD to select the default talking head for this lesson, an older female with a soft voice. The Italian practice lesson then starts and the talking head instructs the user to repeat a number of Italian phrases. The user repeats each Italian phrase, speaking clearly into the microphone built into the keyboard. When the user gets the pronunciation of the Italian phrase correct the talking head will say "Buono. Ben fatto!", or similar. When the user fails to pronounce the Italian phrase correctly, the talking head will say "Prova di nuovo.", or similar. The user likes to pace about the room during the Italian practice lesson, and the talking head automatically adjusts its gaze so it is always looking directly at the user. Throughout the Italian practice lesson, the user pays close attention to the talking head as it speaks each phrase, in order to understand the correct mouth shapes that should be used for each phrase. The user continues the lesson until the end. The FLTS then displays a summary of the user's progress, indicating the phrases that were repeated correctly and those that need more work. The user then stops the FLTS and returns to the STSP to select another service.

# 4.2.3    HOSTED DESKTOP

a)   In brief and simple terms, a *Hosted Desktop* service (HDS) built using the Stream Tone might operate in the following manner:

b)   A user, located at home in the city of Tokyo, Japan, activates a Stream Tone Access Device (STAD). The STAD has a laptop computer form factor that includes a display screen, keyboard, and a separate mouse.

c)   The STAD connects to a Stream Tone Service Portal (STSP), via the *Internet*. The user's *Internet* connection is provided by an *Optical Fibre*-based communications link to the home. The user's STAD connects to the *Internet* service using category 6 (CAT6) Ethernet cabling. The user pays for *Internet* service by monthly subscription. The user's *Internet* service package is considered to be quite inexpensive even though it provides very-high bandwidth *Symmetrical Broadband* with an *Unlimited Data Plan*. The *Internet* package is easily affordable by a worker earning the national average wage of Japan.

d)   The STAD communicates with the STSP using the Stream Tone Transfer Protocol (STTP). The user's identity is verified by the STSP using *Multi-Factor Authentication* functionality provided by the Stream Tone Security Service (STSS). The STSP Service Launcher then presents the user with a personalised list of available services. The user selects a stream offering a familiar HDS from the list. The HDS is available on a time-used basis that is paid for in advance. It is an expensive service because it requires the consistent and continual use of a number of non-trivial data processing resources.

e)   The STSP then connects the STAD to a front-end computer server located in a remote *Data Centre*, which is part of the highly-scalable *Cloud Computing*-based Stream Tone Service Infrastructure that will be used to provide the HDS. The STAD communicates with the front-end server using the STTP. The HDS natively supports the STTP because it was built using the Stream Tone Software Development Kit (STSDK) and the Stream Tone Graphics Interface (STGI). The user is automatically logged onto the HDS by the STSP. Both the STSP and the HDS support *Single Sign-On* (SSO) functionality provided by the STSS, so once a user has successfully logged onto the STSP further logins, for other supported services, are handled automatically and do not require any user involvement.

f)  The front-end server sends a visual representation of the *Hosted Desktop* selection screen to the STAD using the STTP. The user interacts with the *Hosted Desktop* selection screen, and selects a desktop operating system. The front-end server then connects the STAD to the desktop server that will be used to run the selected desktop operating system. The desktop operating system that the user selected is one that previously used to run on the user's local personal computing device, a desktop computer, and which was subsequently transferred to the HDS using *Physical to Virtual* (P2V) migration technology. The P2V migration transferred not only the complete operating system, as configured by the user, but also all of the user's data files and installed software applications.

g)  The desktop server is running a *Virtual Machine* (VM) manager, also known as a hypervisor. The hypervisor allocates the appropriate server resources needed to run the user's selected desktop operating system, and then activates a new VM that will be used to host the selected desktop. The VM then runs the desktop operating system selected by the user. The selected desktop operating system is a proprietary operating system that would normally require the payment of a prorated licensing fee when it is used on a HDS. However, because the user already owns a perpetual license for this particular operating system, the licensing fee that would normally be collected by the HDS is not required. Additionally, the VM also runs the STGI. This is not the first time that the user has used this particular desktop operating system, and the configuration of the desktop environment, such as desktop wallpaper, installed software applications, and user-created data files, has been retained.

h)  The STGI sends an audio-visual representation of the desktop graphical user-interface (GUI) to the STAD using the STTP. The user interacts with the *Hosted Desktop*, which provides a classic windows, icons, menus, and pointer-style GUI. The user then runs a slide presentation editor, by clicking the mouse pointer on a desktop icon, and proceeds to create a new slide presentation. The user then saves the new slide presentation to a data storage resource provided by the HDS. The user then decides to print the slide presentation on a newly purchased network printer located in the same room as the user. The printer is connected to the *Internet* in the same manner as that of the user's STAD, using CAT6 Ethernet cabling. This is the first time that the user has attempted to use the new printer. The user then returns to the STSP and selects the free-of-charge *Cloud Computing*-based printing service, also known as a cloud print service (CPS), provided by the printer's manufacturer from the STSP Service Launcher. It is not necessary for the user to manually log onto the CPS as it supports the SSO functionality provided by the STSS. The CPS was built using the STSDK. The user adds the new printer to the CPS, and a test document is automatically printed to confirm that the new printer has been added correctly. The newly added printer is now accessible to the user from any *Internet*-enabled location via the CPS. The user then returns to the *Hosted Desktop* environment provided by the HDS and configures access to the CPS and the newly added printer. From within the slide presentation editor, the user then selects the print option, and proceeds to print the slide presentation on the new printer. The slide presentation is then sent, via email, from the HDS to the CPS where it is converted into a data format that is understood by the printer. The converted slide presentation is then sent to the printer, and printed. The user inspects the printout, and being satisfied closes the slide presentation editor. The user then runs an integrated development environment (IDE), by clicking the mouse pointer on a menu option, and proceeds to modify some software code that was previously stored on the HDS data storage resource. The user then saves the modified code to the data storage resource, and then starts a code compilation that will take several hours.

i) The user then returns to the STSP. The user's *Hosted Desktop* continues to run, along with the compilation, in the background, and the user will continue to pay for the service even though it is not being directly used by the user. The HDS, listed on the STSP Service Launcher, clearly indicates that it is still running. The user then accesses some other services that are available from the STSP, and after several hours returns to the HDS. On seeing that the code compilation has finished the user then initiates a test run of the newly compiled code. Satisfied with the result of the test run the user then exits the IDE, and proceeds to shut down the *Hosted Desktop*. The VM that was used to run the user's *Hosted Desktop* is deactivated, and allocated server resources are released. The user returns to the *Hosted Desktop* selection screen, and then exits the HDS. The user is then returned to the STSP, and selects a different service.

# 4.2.4 PERSONAL NAVIGATION

a) In brief and simple terms, a personal navigation service (PNS) built using the Stream Tone might operate in the following manner:

b) A user, located at the Tanglin Gate entrance to the Botanic Gardens in Singapore, activates a Stream Tone Access Device (STAD). The user is a tourist from Seoul, South Korea who is visiting Singapore whilst on holiday.

c) The STAD has an eyeglasses form factor that includes an *Accelerometer*, *Barometer*, *Global Positioning System* (GPS), integrated earphones, long-life *Lithium-Ion Battery*, *Magnetometer*, microphone, stereoscopic lightweight display screens, and stereoscopic *Image Sensors*. The STAD looks like a slightly oversized pair of sunglasses.

d) The STAD connects to a Stream Tone Service Portal (STSP), via the *Internet*. The user's *Internet* connection in Singapore is provided by a true *Fourth-Generation Mobile Communications* service that supports high-bandwidth *Internet* access from a wide variety of locations, including from within moving vehicles, such as cars, buses, and trains. The user's STAD connects to the *Internet*-access service using mobile data communications. The user is able to connect to the *Internet*-access service in Singapore because the user's usual mobile *Internet*-access provider, based in South Korea, has a *Roaming Agreement* with a mobile *Internet*-access provider based in Singapore. The user pays for the *Internet*-access service by monthly subscription in South Korea, and does not need to make any payment directly to the Singaporean provider. The user's home *Internet*-access service package is considered to be expensive as it provides an *Unlimited Data Plan* with a high bandwidth and global roaming. The user's home *Internet*-access service package is affordable by a worker earning slightly above the national average wage of South Korea. The STAD communicates with the STSP using the Stream Tone Transfer Protocol (STTP). The user's identity is verified by the STSP using *Multi-Factor Authentication* functionality provided by the Stream Tone Security Service (STSS). The STSP Service Launcher then presents the user with a personalised list of available services. The user selects a stream offering a PNS from the list. The user has purchased the PNS for the duration of the visit to Singapore, and has paid for this in advance. The PNS is quite inexpensive, costing less than the cost of a nice cup of coffee per week. The

PNS is a type of augmented reality system that works by overlying textual and graphical location-specific information onto a live video display of the real-world. The location information is based on the current physical location and orientation of the user's head, as determined by the *Accelerometer*, *Barometer*, *Global Positioning System*, and *Magnetometer* built into the STAD, that is currently located on the user's head in the form of eyeglasses. The location and orientation data is then sent to the PNS using the STTP. The PNS then converts the location and orientation data into location-specific information. The location-specific information updates in real-time, based on the user's current location and orientation. The live video display of the world is captured using the STAD's stereoscopic *Image Sensors*. The real-world video is not sent to the PNS, as the service does not support real-time image processing. The real-world video is simply displayed on the STAD's stereoscopic display and the location-specific information is then displayed on top of this. The PNS accepts a number of voice commands that are captured using the STAD's microphone. The voice commands allow the display of certain types of location-specific information to be activated or deactivated. Voice commands can also be used to request travel directions, which are then presented on the stereoscopic display, and any associated audio instructions are relayed to the user via the STAD's built-in earphones. Voice commands can also be used to access a wide range of features and functions provided by the PNS. The voice commands are processed by the remote servers of the PNS and not by the user's STAD. The STSP then connects the STAD to a computer server, located in a remote *Data Centre*, which is part of the highly-scalable *Cloud Computing*-based Stream Tone Service Infrastructure that will be used to provide the PNS. The STAD communicates with the server using the STTP. The PNS natively supports the STTP because it was built using the Stream Tone Software Development Kit. The user is automatically logged onto the PNS by the STSP. Both the STSP and the PNS support *Single Sign-On* functionality provided by the STSS, so once a user has successfully logged onto the STSP further logins, for other supported services, are handled automatically and do not require any user involvement. The server then activates the user's PNS. The server sends a visual representation of the PNS graphical user-interface (GUI) to the STAD using the STTP. The PNS GUI is overlaid on the user's current video-based view of the world. The user interacts with the PNS GUI, and, using voice commands, proceeds to activate the points of interest feature that will display information relating to physical structures, such as tourist attractions and shops, within the user's current field of view. The activation of this feature is confirmed by an audio message that is relayed to the user via the STAD's built-in earphones. The user then activates a map of the nearby area and proceeds to study the map, identifying a number of interesting places to visit.

e)  It is three o'clock in the afternoon and the user is currently located at the Tanglin Gate entrance of the Singapore Botanic Gardens. The user wishes to travel on foot from the Singapore Botanic Gardens to the ION shopping mall located on Orchard Road, and then go to another shopping mall called Plaza Singapura, which is also located on Orchard Road. The user then wishes to travel from Plaza Singapura, using Singapore's Mass Rapid Transport (MRT) rail system, to the City Hall MRT station. From the City Hall MRT station the user then wishes to proceed on foot to the Esplanade. From the Esplanade the user then wishes to walk to the Marina Bay Sands integrated resort, via the Helix Bridge. The user then verbally notifies the PNS of the places that need to be visited, and activates the route navigation feature. The PNS then visually and audibly indicates that the user should proceed in an easterly direction along the left-hand side of Napier Road. As the user looks around, a wide variety of information about the current location is presented in the user's native language, Korean. As the user walks along the road, navigational instructions are continuously relayed to the user. The user instructs the PNS to play some relaxing music in the background. The PNS then starts to play some Korean instrumental music at a low volume.

f) Looking to the left the user sees a visual PNS indicator explaining that the large building that the user is now looking at is the famous Gleneagles Hospital. Looking to the right, the user is informed that the buildings in the distance are the Australian High Commission, and the Embassy of the United States of America, along with their usual opening hours. The user then continues to walk along Napier Road, which merges with Tanglin Road. A short way along Tanglin Road, the user looks to the right and is informed that the row of old-fashioned shops that is now in view is called the Tudor Court Shopping Gallery, along with a list of merchandise stocked by those shops. The user continues along Tanglin Road, past the entrance for The Regent hotel, St. Regis Residencies, Tanglin Shopping Centre, and Orchard Parade Hotel. As the user looks at the various hotels, current room rates are displayed. Tanglin Road then merges with the world famous Orchard Road. Walking eastwards along Orchard Road, the user can see Delfi Orchard to the left, and the Forum Shopping Centre to the right. The user continues along Orchard Road. On the right-hand side of the road the user can see the Hilton hotel, Far East Shopping Centre, Liat Towers, and Wheelock Place. The display of the PNS indicates that the user's first destination, the ION shopping mall, is now only a short distance away on the right-hand side of the road. The user now stands at a crossroad, with the ION shopping mall diagonally opposite. The crossroad is particularly busy, too busy to cross at street level. The PNS informs the user that there is a nearby pedestrian underpass that can be used to cross the road. The underpass connects directly into the basement levels of the ION shopping mall. Upon arriving at the ION shopping mall, the user suspends operation of the PNS, and proceeds to explore the shopping mall, which is very large and upmarket. An hour later, the user exits the shopping mall and returns to Orchard Road. The user then resumes the operation of the PNS, which quickly determines the user's current location, and continues to guide the user along the user's previously specified route. The user then continues along the right-hand side of Orchard Road. On the left, the user can see the Marriott Hotel, Tang Plaza, Lucky Plaza, Tong Plaza, and Paragon. On the right Wisma Atria, and Ngee Ann City, home to the world famous Takashimaya Shopping Centre. The user then walks past the Mandarin Gallery, which is in front of the Mandarin Orchard hotel. The PNS service indicates that there are several coffee shops within the Mandarin Gallery, and the user decides to stop for a quick drink. The user selects a suitable European-style coffee shop, and is escorted, by a smartly dressed waiter, to a vacant table. The user is given a menu by the waiter. The user is not able to understand all of the options on the menu, and so instructs the PNS to translate it. A version of the menu in Korean is then displayed for the user. The user then orders a cup of house-speciality coffee, and proceeds to drink it. A short while later, feeling much refreshed, the user continues along Orchard Road. On the left the user can see many small shops and businesses, whilst on the right the user can see the 313@Somerset shopping mall. The PNS informs the user that the entrance to the Somerset MRT station is located within this mall. Further along Orchard Road, on the left, the user can see the Centrepoint shopping mall, and on the right the Orchard Gateway and Orchard Central shopping malls. The user is beginning to realise that Singapore truly is a shopper's paradise. Next the user can see the Concorde Hotel on the left and a green open space on the right, where the user looks up, admiring some fine examples of the tropical Rain Tree for which Singapore is well known. The greenery continues with Istana Park on the right and the main entrance to the Istana on the left. The user is informed by the PNS that the Istana is the official residence and working office for both the President and Prime Minster of

Singapore, and that it is open to the public for five days per year, unfortunately today is not one, and so the user continues along Orchard Road.

g) The display of the PNS indicates that the user's second destination, the Plaza Singapura shopping mall, is just ahead on the left-hand side of the road. The user crosses the road using another pedestrian underpass. The user then enters the shopping mall, which is pleasantly cool and refreshing after the humidity and heat outside. Again, the user suspends the operation of the PNS, and proceeds to have a look at the many shops and food outlets available in the mall. Then, resuming the operation of the PNS the user is guided to a basement level in order to connect with the Dhoby Ghaut MRT station which is located next to the mall. As the user enters the Dhoby Ghaut MRT station, information on how to use the MRT ticketing machines is displayed by the PNS. The user then purchases a one-way ticket to the City Hall MRT station. The user then walks a short distance to the platform, and enters the next train going to the City Hall MRT station.

h) A few minutes later the train arrives at the user's third destination, City Hall MRT station. The multi-level station is quite busy, and the PNS guides the user to the correct escalator for exiting the platform. The user then leaves the station, and, walking to the right, immediately enters the CityLink Mall, an underground shopping mall that leads to several destinations, including the Esplanade. The user then walks along the CityLink Mall. Information about the many shops and restaurants that line either side of the mall is continuously displayed by the PNS as the user looks around. The user is then instructed by the PNS to take a turning on the right which leads away from the CityLink, towards the Esplanade.

i) The user then arrives at the Esplanade, the fourth destination on the user's route plan. The PNS explains that an esplanade is a long, level, and open area, typically next to a large body of water or river, where people may promenade, and that the Esplanade is home of Theatres on the Bay, Singapore's centre for the performing arts. As the user looks towards the box office, the PNS displays information relating to upcoming concerts that will be shown in the concert hall, and plays that will be performed in the theatre. The user requests further information on an upcoming concert, and ticket prices and seat availability are displayed. The user then instructs the PNS to remind the user to look in more detail at upcoming concerts at a later time. The PNS then sends an email containing the reminder to the user's email account. The user then follows the directions of the PNS and leaves the Esplanade on foot. The user is now on the right-hand side of Raffles Avenue, and commences to walk in an easterly direction. On the left, the Marina Square shopping mall and Mandarin Oriental hotel can be seen, whilst on the right is the Marina Bay Seating Gallery that looks out onto the Marina Bay Floating Platform. The PNS informs the user that the Marina Bay Floating Platform has been a regular venue for Singapore's National Day Parade over recent years, and that Singapore's National Day is held on 9th August each year. The Singapore National Day proudly commemorates Singapore's independence from Malaysia, which took place on that date in 1965. Another regular venue for the Singapore National Day Parade was the Singapore National Stadium but since that was demolished in 2007, so that a new stadium could be built, the Marina Bay Floating Platform has been used almost exclusively. It is expected that the Singapore National Day Parade will return to the new Singapore National Stadium in 2016. Just beyond the Marina Bay Seating Gallery, on the right-hand side of the road, is the entrance to the Helix Bridge, which is a curved pedestrian footbridge that links Raffles Avenue with the Marina Bay Sands integrated resort.

j)    The Helix Bridge is the fifth destination on the user's route plan. It is now almost seven o'clock in the evening and it is starting to get dark. The footbridge is illuminated by hundreds of coloured lights. The user instructs the PNS to take a photograph of the illuminated footbridge. The photograph is automatically stored on a third-party *File Hosting Service* (FHS) that the user had previously configured the PNS to use. The FHS is the primary store for all of the user's digital media, which the user pays for by yearly subscription. The user then starts walking across the footbridge. The PNS informs the user that the Helix Bridge was officially opened on 24$^{th}$ April 2010, won the World's Best Transport Building award at the World Architecture Festival that same year, has an unusual left-handed DNA-like structure, and that a large portion of the footbridge is built out of highly durable stainless steel.

k)    The user then reaches the end of the footbridge and arrives at the sixth, and final, destination on the user's route plan, the Marina Bay Sands integrated resort. The PNS informs the user that the Marina Bay Sands integrated resort opened on 27$^{th}$ April 2010, held its official grand opening on 17$^{th}$ February 2011, and cost S\$8 billion to build. The PNS then continues to inform the user that the Marina Bay Sands integrated resort is comprised of three separate 55-story hotel towers that are interconnected by a sky terrace on the roof, which features the world's longest elevated swimming pool, and that the structures in front of the towers house an arts and science museum, convention centre, exhibition centre, ice rink, shopping mall, theatre, and a casino with 1,000 gaming tables and 1,400 slot machines. The user then explores the integrated resort, and sees many interesting displays, shops, and restaurants, and even passes by several of the entrances to the casino. The user decides to visit the sky terrace, which is called the SkyPark, and the PNS guides the user to a nearby ticketing booth. The user then purchases a ticket, and ascends by elevator to the SkyPark. Upon arrival, the PNS informs the user that the SkyPark features a large infinity swimming pool for use by hotel guests, a number of bars and restaurants, and offers spectacular views of Marina Bay and the Singapore skyline. As it is now dark, the user can see that many of the skyscrapers that line Marina Bay are attractively illuminated, as is the roof of the Esplanade, which the user visited earlier. As the user looks around, the PNS displays information about the many sights that can been seen from the SkyPark, such as the Fullerton Hotel, which is located to the west, with its neo-classical design, and which was previously the General Post Office before being converted into a five-star luxury hotel. The PNS also highlights the Marina Bay Street Circuit of the Singapore Grand Prix; an exciting Formula 1 night race that is held each year in the month of September. The user then instructs the PNS to record a video, as the user slowly pans the STAD *Image Sensors* over the view. The video is automatically stored by the PNS on the user's preferred FHS. Feeling hungry after so much walking and sightseeing the user instructs the PNS to provide a list of nearby restaurants. The user then selects a restaurant that specialises in North West Indian cuisine. The PNS then guides the user to the restaurant. The user then stops the PNS and removes the STAD. The user then enjoys a spicy meal accompanied by a refreshing drink or two.

l)    The user then realises that it is now really quite late in the day. So, having successfully explored a little bit of Singapore, and now being somewhat tired from all the walking, the user decides to return to the hotel where the user has been staying. The user's hotel is located on Beach Road, and the user decides to travel there using the MRT. The user then uses the PNS to navigate to the nearest MRT station, which is the Bayfront MRT station, located nearby, between the Marina Bay Sands integrated resort and the innovative Gardens by the Bay horticultural park. The user then travels from the Bayfront MRT station to the Promenade MRT station in order to connect with another train that will stop at the Esplanade MRT station, which is the nearest MRT station to the user's hotel. The user finally arrives at the Esplanade MRT station and then walks the short distance, in the balmy night air, from the MRT station to the colonial-style Raffles Hotel, one the world's most famous and iconic luxury hotels.

# 4.2.5 VIDEO-ON-DEMAND

a) In brief and simple terms, a video on demand service (VODS) built using the Stream Tone might operate in the following manner:

b) A user, located in the economy section of an aeroplane that is flying over the North Atlantic Ocean, between London, United Kingdom and New York, United States of America, activates a Stream Tone Access Device (STAD). The STAD has a *Tablet Computer* form factor that includes a large *Capacitive Sensing*-based multi-point touch-enabled display screen and a long-life *Lithium-Ion Battery*. The STAD display screen is larger than the display screen offered by the in-flight entertainment system that is built into the back of each economy seat. The STAD has been considerately paired with a set of wired earphones, so as not to disturb the other passengers on the aeroplane.

c) The STAD connects to a Stream Tone Service Portal (STSP), via the *Internet*. The in-flight *Internet* service is provided by a *Communications Satellite* with *Electrically Powered Spacecraft Propulsion* that transmits and receives in the *Ka Band*. The STAD connects to the *Internet* service using an optical wireless technology known as *Visible Light Communication*. The user has purchased a premium in-flight *Internet* service for the duration of the transatlantic flight, and has paid for this in advance. This premium *Internet* service provides much higher bandwidth than the standard, free-of-charge, in-flight *Internet* service, and is capable of handling the delivery of high-quality video content.

d) The STAD communicates with the STSP using the Stream Tone Transfer Protocol (STTP). The user's identity is verified by the STSP using *Multi-Factor Authentication* functionality provided by the Stream Tone Security Service (STSS). The STSP Service Launcher then presents the user with a personalised list of available services. The user selects a stream offering a VODS from the list. This particular VODS provides access to the very latest television shows, most of which are not available from the in-flight entertainment service. On this particular occasion, the VODS will be providing the user with access to the latest episode of a favourite science fiction show that aired on a terrestrial television network the day before, and which is not available from the in-flight entertainment service. The VODS that the user has selected from the STSP Service Launcher is an entertainment service that the user regularly uses at home, and pays for by monthly subscription. The VODS can be accessed by the user from any *Internet*-enabled personal computing device, located anywhere in the world. The VODS is a composite service, or mash-up, that combines three separate STTP-based data streams. Two streams provide the audio and video entertainment content and the third provides a branded video-player graphical user-interface (GUI). The three data streams are seamlessly combined on the STAD into a single audio-visual experience. The entertainment content is actually provided by a third-party television network, and the video player GUI is provided by the VODS. The reason that the VODS is structured in this way is because the television network does not wish to sell individual television shows directly to the public or provide individualised technical support. The television network also does not wish to give any third party, not even the VODS, unsecured access to its intellectual property. So the television network provides an unbranded, vanilla, video delivery service that various *Internet*-oriented commercial enterprises, like the VODS, buy in bulk and then sell on to individual members of the public. The television network is able to protect its intellectual property using the *Digital Rights Management*-like features of the STTP, which permits a uniquely encrypted data stream to be sent to each user. Additionally, once audio-visual data has been delivered to a STAD it is immediately presented to the user and then discarded, ensuring that it does not persist long enough in any easily accessible form for it to be easily stolen. When the user interacts with the video player GUI the user's input is sent from the STAD to the VODS, which then controls the audio-visual presentation using a video delivery *Application Programming Interface* provided by the television network. Both the VODS and the television network's video delivery service natively support the STTP because they were both built using the Stream Tone Software Development Kit.

e)   The STSP then connects the STAD to a computer server located in a remote *Data Centre*, which is part of the highly-scalable *Cloud Computing*-based Stream Tone Service Infrastructure (STSI) that will be used to provide the VODS. The STAD communicates with the server using the STTP. The user is automatically logged onto the VODS by the STSP. Both the STSP and the VODS support *Single Sign-On* functionality provided by the STSS, so once a user has successfully logged onto the STSP further logins, for other supported services, are handled automatically and do not require any user involvement.

f)   The server sends a visual representation of the television show selection screen to the STAD using the STTP. The user interacts with the television show selection screen, and selects the required episode of the recently aired science fiction television show. The VODS then sends the current *Internet Protocol Version 6* address of the STAD to the television network. The selected television show is then sent directly from the television network to the STAD using the STTP. The television network also employs a highly-scalable *Cloud Computing*-based STSI to run its video delivery service. In order to greatly reduce the data processing resources needed to encode audio-visual content for use at different communications bandwidths, display screen resolutions, and display screen fresh rates, the television network encodes and stores multiple different versions of all content in advance. The television network then sends the most appropriate version of the content to the STAD. If networking conditions on the *Internet* connection to the STAD subsequently change then the television network is able to dynamically select a more appropriate version of the content to send in order to keep the content flowing even if that means that visual quality is temporarily reduced. The video player GUI is also sent from the VODS to the STAD using the STTP. The three STTP-based data streams, one carrying the television show audio, one carrying the television show video, and one carrying the video player GUI, are then combined on the STAD.

g)   The user then watches the television show, making full use of the on-screen controls to pause the show when the aeroplane's flight attendant served lunch, and to rewind the show when a critical story event needed to be viewed multiple times. Once the show is over, the user then closes the VODS, and returns to the STSP in order to select a new service.

# 4.2.6   VIDEO TELEPHONY

a)   In brief and simple terms, a video telephony service (VTS) built using the Stream Tone might operate in the following manner:

b) A user, located in an office within the business district of a large mid-western American town, activates a Stream Tone Access Device (STAD). The STAD has a **Smart-Phone** form factor that includes an **Image Sensor**, microphone, and **Capacitive Sensing**-based multi-point touch-enabled **Organic Light-Emitting Diode Display Screen**.

c) The STAD connects to a Stream Tone Service Portal (STSP), via the **Internet**. The user's **Internet** connection is provided by a true **Fourth-Generation Mobile Communications** service that supports very-high bandwidth mobile communications. The user's STAD connects to the **Internet** service using mobile data communications. STAD's do not support traditional mobile telephony, only a Stream Tone Transfer Protocol (STTP)-based equivalent. The STAD communicates with the STSP using the STTP. The user's identity is verified by the STSP using **Multi-Factor Authentication** functionality provided by the Stream Tone Security Service (STSS). The STSP Service Launcher then presents the user with a personalised list of available services. The user selects a stream offering a VTS from the list. The VTS is already running because it has been configured to automatically run as a background service whenever the user's STAD is powered-on, so that incoming video telephony calls can be received.

d) The VTS is available free-of-charge as it is supported by non-intrusive advertising on the recipient selection screen. The communications bandwidth needed to carry the actual video telephone call is provided by the user's **Internet** service package, which is paid for by a monthly subscription. The user's **Internet** service package is not considered to be expensive, and is affordable by a worker earning the national average wage of the United States of America.

e) The STSP then connects the STAD to a computer server located in a remote **Data Centre**, which is part of the highly-scalable **Cloud Computing**-based Stream Tone Service Infrastructure that will be used to provide the VTS. The STAD communicates with the server using the Stream Tone Transfer Protocol (STTP). The VTS natively supports the STTP because it was built using the Stream Tone Software Development Kit. The user is automatically logged onto the VTS by the STSP. Both the STSP and the VTS support **Single Sign-On** functionality provided by the STSS, so once a user has successfully logged onto the STSP further logins, for other supported services, are handled automatically and do not require any user involvement.

f) The VTS is not directly involved in the actual video telephone call, which is simply a STTP-based peer-to-peer communication between the caller's STAD and the recipient's STAD. The VTS is only responsible for initiating, or brokering, the call, and for providing some simple on-screen controls for use during the call.

g) The server sends a visual representation of the recipient selection screen to the STAD using the STTP. The user interacts with the recipient selection screen, and selects a person to call. The intended recipient of the call then receives notification that there is an incoming call, via the VTS that is already running as a background service on their own STAD.

h) Once the recipient has accepted the incoming call, audio-visual data is then exchanged between the two STADs using the STTP. The caller and the recipient then engage in a video telephone call. The video for the call is captured using the STAD's **Image Sensor**, and audio is captured using the STAD's microphone. Simple on-screen controls for managing the call are provided by the VTS, and are sent in a separate STTP-based data stream. The data streams containing the call video and the data stream containing the on-screen controls are then combined on the STAD. Call audio is sent in a third and separate data stream, and is synchronised with the call video using timestamp data contained in each data stream. A self-view video feature, for correctly positioning the ***Image Sensor***, is provided by functionality built directly into the STAD. The VTS also supports audio-only calls, allowing the STAD to function in a manner similar to a traditional mobile-phone, if required. The VTS is able to control a video call by sending simple instructions to a STAD to enable or disable a particular data stream, which allows individual audio and video streams to be turned on or off. A terminate instruction sent by the VTS to both the caller and the recipient STADs is used to explicitly end a video call.

i)   The user then ends the video telephone call, using the on-screen controls, and returns to the STSP in order to select another service.


# 4.2.7     WEB BROWSING

a)   In brief and simple terms, a ***Web*** browsing service (WBS) built using the Stream Tone might operate in the following manner:

b)   A user, located in a small village on the rural West African coast, activates a Stream Tone Access Device (STAD). The STAD has a ***Tablet Computer*** form factor that includes a ***Capacitive Sensing***-based multi-point touch-enabled display screen and a ***Photovoltaic*** charger for its long-life ***Lithium-Ion Battery***. The display screen is based on ***Transflective Liquid-Crystal Display*** technology that is both power efficient and daylight readable. The STAD is waterproof, dust-proof, and impact resistant.

c)   The STAD connects to a Stream Tone Service Portal (STSP), via the ***Internet***. The user's ***Internet*** connection is provided by a ***Mesh Network*** that is connected to the global ***Internet*** by an ***Optical Fibre***-based ***Submarine Communications Cable*** that runs from West Europe to West Africa. The user's STAD connects to the ***Internet*** service using ***Wi-Fi***. Each STAD is a node in the **Mesh Network**. The user pays for ***Internet*** service in advance, using mobile-phone credits. The ***Internet*** service is very cheap, and well within the household budget of a typical rural West African family.

d)   The STAD communicates with the STSP using the Stream Tone Transfer Protocol (STTP). The user's identity is verified by the STSP using ***Multi-Factor Authentication*** functionality provided by the Stream Tone Security Service (STSS). The STSP Service Launcher then presents the user with a personalised list of available services. The user selects a stream offering a WBS from the list. The WBS is available free-of-charge as it is partly supported by non-intrusive advertising, and partly by the philanthropic sponsorship of a large multi-national corporation based in the United States of America.

e)   The STSP then connects the STAD to a front-end computer server located in a remote ***Data Centre***, which is part of the highly-scalable ***Cloud Computing***-based Stream Tone Service Infrastructure (STSI) that will be used to provide the WBS. The STAD communicates with the front-end server using the STTP. The WBS natively supports the STTP because it was built using the Stream Tone Software Development Kit (STSDK) and the Stream Tone Graphics Interface (STGI).

f) The user is automatically logged onto the WBS by the STSP. Both the STSP and the WBS support *Single Sign-On* (SSO) functionality provided by the STSS, so once a user has successfully logged onto the STSP further logins, for other supported services, are handled automatically and do not require any user involvement. This is not the first time that the user has used this particular WBS, and the user's *Web* browsing preferences and bookmarks have been stored from the user's last use of the service.

g) The front-end server sends a visual representation of the *Web Browser* selection screen to the STAD using the STTP. A wide range of popular *Web Browsers* are available for selection by the user. The user interacts with the *Web Browser* selection screen, and selects a familiar *Web Browser*. The front-end server then connects the STAD to the *Web Browser* server that will be used to run the selected *Web Browser*.

h) The *Web Browser* server is running a *Virtual Machine* (VM) manager, also known as a hypervisor. The hypervisor allocates the appropriate server resources that will be needed to run the *Web Browser* selected by the user. The WBS uses multi-core *Reduced Instruction Set Computing*-based microprocessors. The hypervisor activates a new VM that will provide the user's required *Web Browser*. The VM hosts a highly-simplified *Linux*-based operating system, which is used to run three main software applications; the user's selected *Web Browser*, a virtual keyboard, and the STGI. The operating system is not visible to the user, only the graphical user-interface (GUI) of the *Web Browser*, and the virtual keyboard when activated.

i) The STGI then sends an audio-visual representation of the *Web Browser* to the STAD using the STTP. The user then selects a *Web* site for viewing from a list of previously saved bookmarks. The *Web Browser* then connects to the bookmarked *Web* site using the *Data Centre*'s high-bandwidth, low-latency, *Optical Fibre*-based *Internet* connection. The *Web Browser* then obtains the *Web* site data and displays it. The user then spends a few minutes reading the *Web* site. The user then activates the virtual keyboard in order to enter some *Web* search criteria. The user is looking for some photographs of drought-resistant crop-plants for use in an upcoming school project. The search results are then returned, and presented to the user. The user then reviews the results, and saves the best crop-plant photographs to a free-of-charge *File Hosting Service*, access to which is natively supported by the WBS. The user has been collecting photographs of drought-resistant crop-plants for some time and has built up an extensive collection, which is now stored on the FHS. The WBS communicates with the FHS using an industry-standard FHS *Application Programming Interface* (API).

j) One of the user's many friends then visits. The friend also has an upcoming school project on drought-resistant crop-plants but thus far has not collected any photographs. The friend asks the user for a copy of the photographs that the user has already collected. The user agrees, and suggests, that as there are quite a lot, that the photographs should be transferred, en masse, directly from the user's FHS to the friend's FHS. The user's FHS is not the same one as the FHS used by the friend; it is supplied by a different service provider.

k) The user returns to the STSP. The WBS that the user had just been using is automatically paused. The paused WBS is clearly indicated in the user's list of preferred services on the STSP Service Launcher. The user then selects the FHS that was just used to store the crop-plant photographs from within the WBS from the STSP Service Launcher. The user is automatically logged onto the FHS by the STSP because the FHS supports SSO functionality provided by the STSS. The STSP then connects the STAD to a computer server located in a remote **Data Centre**, which is part of the highly-scalable **Cloud Computing**-based STSI that is used to provide the FHS. The STAD communicates with the server using the STTP. The FHS natively supports the STTP because it was built using the STSDK.

l)   The server sends a visual representation of the FHS GUI to the STAD using the STTP. The user interacts with the FHS GUI, and marks all the crop-plant photographs to be copied. The user then activates the FHS-to-FHS data transfer function that will be used to send the marked photographs to the friend's FHS. The uniform resource identifier (URI) of the friend's FHS will be obtained from a Quick Response Code (QR Code) that will be displayed on the screen of the friend's STAD.

m)   The friend's STAD is activated and the friend's STSP accessed. The friend selects a preferred FHS from the STSP Service Launcher. Functionality to display the QR Code of the friend's FHS account is then activated. The friend's FHS QR Code is then captured using the **Image Sensor** on the user's STAD. The captured QR Code is then automatically sent to the user's FHS, which then decodes the QR Code and obtains the URI of the friend's FHS. The user's FHS then transfers the user's crop-plant photographs to the friend's FHS using an industry-standard FHS API.

n)   The transfer only takes a few seconds, after which a message, confirming that the data transfer is complete is displayed on each of the STADs. The friend then visually verifies that copies of all the crop-plant photographs have be correctly transferred. Seeing that all the photographs have been successfully transferred, the friend then thanks the user and leaves in order to work on the school project. The user then stops the FHS and returns to the STSP.

o)   The user then selects the paused WBS from the STSP Service Launcher and continues to surf the **Web** for a few more minutes. The user then disconnects from the WBS. The VM that was used to run the service is deactivated and allocated resources are released. The user is then returned to the **Web Browser** selection screen. The user then exits the **Web Browser** selection screen and is returned to the STSP. The user then selects a different service from the STSP.

# 4.2.8   WEB DESKTOP

a)   In brief and simple terms, a **Web Desktop** service (WDS) built using the Stream Tone might operate in the following manner:

b)   A user, located at home, in suburban Germany, activates a Stream Tone Access Device (STAD). The STAD has a desktop computer form factor that is connected to a separate display screen, keyboard, and mouse.

c)   The STAD connects to a Stream Tone Service Portal (STSP), via the **Internet**. The user's **Internet** connection is provided by a local **Internet** service provider (ISP) using a combination of **Optical Fibre**-based communications and copper-wire-based communications. **Optical Fibre** is used to deliver the **Internet** to a distribution point located within a few hundred metres of the user's home, and copper-wire is then used to connect the distribution point to the user's home. The bandwidth of the copper-wire connection is boosted using a crosstalk cancellation technology known as *G993.5*. The user's STAD connects to the *Internet* service using category 5 (CAT5) Ethernet cabling. The STAD communicates with the STSP using the Stream Tone Transfer Protocol (STTP). The user's identity is verified by the STSP using *Multi-Factor Authentication* functionality provided by the Stream Tone Security Service (STSS). The STSP Service Launcher then presents the user with a personalised list of available services. The user selects a stream offering a WDS from the list.

d)   The WDS is provided as part of the user's premium *Internet* service package, which is paid for by monthly subscription. The *Internet* service package is quite expensive, but is still considered to be affordable by a worker earning the national average wage of Germany. Since the emergence of the Stream Tone, and the widespread adoption of Comprehensive Remote Personal Computing, most users have now successfully switched from using a traditional personal computing device, such as a desktop computer or laptop computer with its own operating system and software applications, to a STTP-based WDS.

e)   The WDS that the user has selected is a premium service that provides access to a wide range of best-in-class software applications that are available without any usage limitation. Each software application requires its own unique operating system and microprocessor environment in order to function, which is provided by a highly-scalable *Cloud Computing*-based Stream Tone Service Infrastructure (STSI). The STSI used to support the WDS is based on a *Heterogeneous Computing* architecture that is comprised of *Application-Specific Integrated Circuit*-based accelerators, multi-core general-purpose graphics processing unit-based accelerators, multi-core complex instruction set computing-based microprocessors, and multi-core *Reduced Instruction Set Computing*-based microprocessors. The WDS seamlessly integrates all the available software applications into a single, coherent, personal computing environment. Each software application and the *Web Desktop* graphical user-interface (GUI) are handled as separate STTP-based data streams, which are then sent to a STAD where they are combined ready for use.

f)   The STSP then connects the STAD to a computer server located in a remote *Data Centre*, which is part of the highly-scalable *Cloud Computing*-based STSI that will be used to provide the WDS. The STAD communicates with the server using the STTP. The WDS natively supports the STTP because it was built using the Stream Tone Software Development Kit and the Stream Tone Graphics Interface. The user is automatically logged onto the WDS by the STSP. Both the STSP and the WDS support *Single Sign-On* (SSO) functionality provided by the STSS, so once a user has successfully logged onto the STSP further logins, for other supported services, are handled automatically and do not require any user involvement. The server activates the user's unique *Web Desktop* instance. This is not the first time that the user has used this service, and so the previous state of the user's *Web Desktop* is restored.

g)   The server then sends an audio-visual representation of the *Web Desktop* GUI to the STAD. The user interacts with the *Web Desktop* GUI, which provides a classic windows, icons, menus, and pointer-style user-experience based on the desktop metaphor. The user then runs an industry-standard word-processing application by clicking the mouse pointer on the appropriate menu option. The user then creates a new document using keyboard input, which is then saved to a previously configured third-party *File Hosting Service*

307

(FHS). The user did not need to explicitly log onto the FHS because it also supports SSO functionality provided by the STSS.

h)   The user then decides to print the newly created document, so that it can be used by a work colleague. The printer is located in the user's normal place of work, and not at the user's home. The document is then sent, using email, from the WDS, to a third-party **Cloud Computing**-based printing service, also known as a cloud print service (CPS). The printer in the user's workplace has already been registered with the CPS. The CPS is a service that has been purchased by the user's employer. The document is then received by the CPS, which then converts it into a data format that will be understood by the printer. The converted document is then sent by the CPS to the printer so that it can be printed. The document is then printed, and read by the user's work colleague.

i)   Leaving the word-processing application still active, the user then runs a video editor. The user wishes to work on a video file that was previously uploaded to the FHS. The video file in question was previously created using another STTP-based service that is able to record high definition video that was captured by a STAD **Image Sensor**. The user opens the video file using the video editor, and proceeds to edit it as required. The user does not save the edited video file because the editing process is not yet complete.

j)   The user then returns to the STSP, and the WDS is automatically paused. The WDS, listed on the STSP Service Launcher, clearly indicates that it is now paused. The user then selects another service from the STSP Service Launcher, and proceeds to use it. The user plans to return to the WDS at a later time, at which point the user will most probably finish editing the video file, save the video file to the FHS, close the word-processor, exit the **Web Desktop**, and return once again to the STSP.

# 4.3   COMMERCIALISATION

*Opportunities for all*

a)   It is expected that the Stream Tone will be able to support a wide range of commercial activity. The following section briefly considers the commercial compatibility of the Stream Tone from the perspective of business models, economics, products, and services. The Stream Tone's ability to support commercial activity is likely to play a significant role in determining the ultimate success of the Stream Tone.

b)   The section on business models briefly considers the Stream Tone from the perspective of the different types of business model that the Stream Tone should be able to support.

c)   The section on economics briefly considers the Stream Tone from the perspective of the development, provision, delivery, and access of Stream Tone Transfer Protocol (STTP)-based services.

d)   The section on products briefly considers the Stream Tone from the perspective of a number of fictional Stream Tone Access Devices (STADs) with varying hardware form factors that have product names that are based on the Stream Tone nomenclature.

e)   The section on services briefly considers the Stream Tone from the perspective of a number of fictional STTP-based services with trading names that are based on Stream

Tone-related nomenclature. This section also considers how a particular *Internet* domain could be used to better indicate STTP-based services.

f)   The commercial compatibilities of the Stream Tone that are briefly described below should not be considered to be definitive or exhaustive, simply representative of some of the commercial compatibilities that the Stream Tone may exhibit.

# 4.3.1   BUSINESS MODELS

a)   Most business models that are currently used in association with non-Stream Tone Transfer Protocol (STTP)-based services are also likely to be applicable to STTP-based services. Additionally, wholly new business models may be developed specifically for use with STTP-based services, although what these might look like is unknown at this point in time.

b)   Whether the cost of providing a STTP-based service is high or low, and not zero, any such service must be funded in some way. Most currently-available *Web-based Services* are provided on a free-of-charge basis by individuals, and other entities, either through philanthropy or some form of corporate, product, or service marketing. Other *Web-based Services* are provided on a purely commercial basis. All such economic options will be available for use with the Stream Tone.

c)   The business models that are briefly described below should not be considered to be definitive or exhaustive, simply representative of some of the business models that the Stream Tone may be able to support.

## 4.3.1.1   ADVERTISING

a)   Some Stream Tone Transfer Protocol-based services may be made available on an ongoing free-of-charge basis, funded by third-party advertising that is directed at the user.

## 4.3.1.2   BARTER

a)   Some Stream Tone Transfer Protocol-based services may be made available on what is essentially an on-going free-of-charge basis but is actually in exchange for digital content provided by the user. The service then sells or leases the user's content in part, in full, or in aggregate with other user's content, in order to fund the operation of the service.

## 4.3.1.3   CHARITY

a)   Some Stream Tone Transfer Protocol-based services may be made available on an ongoing free-of-charge basis to specific groups of disadvantaged users, funded by charitable donations. The charitable provision of such services may become an acceptable mechanism for developed countries to help support the economic, social, and technological development of developing nations.

# 4.3.1.4 DISCRETIONARY

a) Some Stream Tone Transfer Protocol-based services may be made available on an on-going basis for a single optional upfront fee. Such discretionary payments need to be sufficient to fund the provision for the service for all users; those that pay and those that do not.

# 4.3.1.5 FREEMIUM

a) Some Stream Tone Transfer Protocol-based services may be available in two forms; standard and premium. The standard service will be available on an on-going free-of-charge basis and will be limited in some way compared to the premium version of the same service. The premium version of the service will only be available through a purchase or subscription and will not be limited in anyway. Profits obtained from the premium service will sustainably fund the provision of both the standard and premium services.

# 4.3.1.6 LOSS-LEADER

a) Some Stream Tone Transfer Protocol-based services may be made available on an on-going free-of-charge or reduced-charge basis. Loss-leader-based services are typically funded by the profits from other commercial activities undertaken by the provider of those services. A loss-leader-based service is a type of marketing that is designed to promote an organisation, product, or other service that has been associated with the loss-leader-based service.

# 4.3.1.7 MICROPAYMENTS

a) Some Stream Tone Transfer Protocol-based services may be available on a small-fee-per-use basis, also known as a micropayment. Typically, a user would maintain a pre-paid account and each use of the service, generally at a transaction level, would subtract a small fee from the account. Monthly micropayment credits could be offered as part of an *Internet* service package.

# 4.3.1.8 PURCHASE

a) Some Stream Tone Transfer Protocol-based services may be made available in perpetuity for a single mandatory upfront fee.

# 4.3.1.9 SUBSCRIPTION

a) Some Stream Tone Transfer Protocol-based services may be made available for a mandatory periodically-repeating upfront fee. Some subscription-based service packages may provide access to a number of different services, both STTP-based and non-STTP-based.

## 4.3.1.10 SUBSIDISED

a) Some Stream Tone Transfer Protocol-based services may be made available on a temporary or on-going free-of-charge or reduced-charge basis, funded by the purchase of an associated product or service, such as a STAD or *Internet* access service.

# 4.3.2 ECONOMICS

a) The Stream Tone changes the nature of how *Web-based Services* are developed, provided, delivered, and accessed; all of which will have impacts on the economics that underpin such services. Many aspects of the Stream Tone are still unknown, so any discussion of its economic characteristics is likely to be highly speculative and somewhat brief. However, even at this early stage, certain characteristics are already discernible.

b) Cost has always been a very real factor in the development, provision, delivery, and access of *Web-based Services*, and whilst the arrival of the Stream Tone may change the source of some of that cost, it will always exist to some degree. Some aspects may become more expensive and some may become less expensive, but overall the economics of the Stream Tone are expected to be comparable with those of many current generation non-Stream Tone Transfer Protocol-based *Web* services.

c) The economics of the Stream Tone that are briefly described below should not be considered to be definitive or exhaustive, simply representative of some of the economic characteristics that the Stream Tone may exhibit.

## 4.3.2.1 DEVELOPMENT

a) Traditionally, under the classic client-server architecture model that is commonly used by most *Web-based Services*, the development of a new or upgraded service often required changes at both end points; on the multiple client devices that were used to access the service and on a lesser number of remotely-located computer servers that were used to generate the service. The client devices would often use a wide range of different hardware and software, which often complicated the development process, making it both expensive and time consuming.

b) The Stream Tone will simplify the development process by requiring that all client-side development be pushed into the *Data Centre*, and onto the server. This will be necessary because the Stream Tone Access Device (STAD), which will be the client device used to access Stream Tone Transfer Protocol (STTP)-based content and services, will be a very simple audio-visual presentation device with fixed functionality that cannot be reprogrammed and does not support the direct execution of software applications. So, a client-server architecture will still be possible when using the Stream Tone but it will need to be one that is based on a client-application running on a *Data Centre* server that communicates with a server-application running on another *Data Centre* server. The client-application will then communicate with a STAD using the STTP in order to deliver a service

c)  Limiting service development to just one end point, the server, will potentially reduce development complexity, cost, and time, and allow services to evolve at a potentially accelerated rate, independently from the client access device. It should also allow new or upgraded services to be easily deployed without any involvement of the user.

d)  Additionally, the Stream Tone will not significantly impact the cost or methods of service construction, as all current development techniques and tools, as well as operating systems and programming languages, are expected to be compatible with the Stream Tone. The most notable change that the Stream Tone will bring is that all user-oriented service inputs and outputs must be converted into STTP-compatible data streams, using the Stream Tone Software Development Kit or the Stream Tone Graphics Interface.

# 4.3.2.2    PROVISION

a)  Stream Tone Transfer Protocol (STTP)-based services will completely rely on the data processing capabilities of the Stream Tone Service Infrastructures (STSIs), primarily in the form of the **Cloud Computing**-based **Data Centres** that will be used to generate those services, as the Stream Tone Access Device will only be capable of presenting audio-visual content and not programmatically generating it. On average, a STTP-based service will require far more data processing resources, primarily for encoding audio-visual data, than would be required for a comparable non-STTP-based service. Consequently, the cost of providing a STTP-based service will initially be much higher than for a comparable non-STTP-based service. It is expected that this disparity will only be short lived, as on-going advancements in the hardware and software used by the STSIs will ensure that future STTP-based services will be no more expensive than current generation non-STTP-based services.

b)  Of course, some types of STTP-based services are always likely to be expensive, such as persistent dedicated **Hosted Desktops** that require the on-going rental of dedicated computer servers and licensed computer operating systems. Today, such services incur non-trivial costs that cannot easily be absorbed by the provider, and must therefore be borne by the customer. When such services are communicated using the STTP they do not suddenly become any cheaper or free-of-charge. Local personal computing has always required an investment in computing resources. Using the STTP to deliver remote personal computing services simply changes most of that investment from a capital expense into an operational one.

c)  The fact that some STTP-based services will cost more than comparable non-STTP-based services implies that some customers will be required to pay more than they are currently used to doing, that marketing budgets will have to be expanded to cover the extra costs, or that even greater philanthropy will be required. None of these consequences are unreasonable, or unexpected, given the nature and potential benefits of STTP-based services. However, most of these consequences are unlikely to be popular with the entities that are ultimately responsible for paying for these new types of service, even if it is only likely to be for just a short period of time until STTP-based services become more affordable. STTP-based services will therefore require careful construction, packaging, and marketing until society becomes comfortable with the predominantly subscription-based model that will most likely be required to support Comprehensive Remote Personal Computing.

d)   The STSIs that will be used to provide STTP-based services will generally need to be located in close geographic proximity to the users of those services, primarily in order to minimise communications latencies. New STSIs will need to be constructed in geographies that do not currently possess suitably located infrastructures, and the construction cost will most probably have to be recovered through higher service charges.

e)   In the long term, it is expected that the STSIs will adopt many highly efficient and highly effective hardware and software technologies, such as those used for ***Cloud Computing***, which will allow operating costs to be substantially reduced. Lower STSI operating costs will allow many STTP-based services to be provided free-of-charge, or at a nominal cost, as is the case with most current ***Web-based Services***.

# 4.3.2.3   DELIVERY

a)   The quantity of communicated data, provided by a telecommunications connection to the ***Internet***, which will be required to support the operation of a Stream Tone Access Device (STAD) will, on average, be much higher than the quantity of data required to support the operation of a comparable non-Stream Tone Transfer Protocol (STTP)-based personal computing device. This is because, in simple terms, the STAD display screen must be continuously updated using data sent from remotely-located computer services in order to operate, and the quantity of data required to support such updates can be substantial. Additionally, no user-data is held on a STAD, as it is all held remotely, and a representation of that data must be regularly communicated to the STAD in order for that data to be accessed by a user. In comparison, a non-STTP-based personal computing device will, on average, only require relatively small quantities of data, if any, to be sent from remote services in order to operate, because the bulk of its operational data is already held on the device in local storage. Of course, there will always be exceptions, and a non-STTP-based personal computing device might need to communicate substantial quantities of data in order to operate as required. In such a situation, the quantity of communicated data required to support the operation of a STAD and a non-STTP-based device would probably be very similar. In some ways, the STAD uses data communications inefficiently; using a large quantity of communicated data to complete a task that a non-STTP-based personal computing device would be able to complete using much less communicated data. However, given that data communications bandwidth is expected to become significantly cheaper and more plentiful in the future,[27] such an inefficiency it is not expected to impede the design, development, or deployment of the Stream Tone. In fact, many current wired telecommunications technologies are already able to support the Stream Tone from both a bandwidth and a cost perspective. The next generation of wireless telecommunications technologies will also be able to cost-effectively support the bandwidths required by the Stream Tone as well.

b)   In simple terms, the telecommunications bandwidth required to support the operation of a STAD will have an upper limit that is primarily governed by the resolution of the STAD

---

[27] *The cost of electrons and photons is getting cheaper all the time!*

display screen and the required display screen fresh rate. It is expected that future telecommunications infrastructures, including those used by Stream Tone Telecommunications Infrastructures (STTIs), will be able to provide bandwidths far in excess of those that will be required to support the operation of a STAD, regardless of the resolution of its display screen or display screen refresh rate. Any bandwidth beyond this upper limit will be used to improve real-time interactivity through the reduction of operational latencies. The fact that the Stream Tone will not necessarily need to use the highest possible bandwidths will help to ensure that the delivery of STTP-based services will be highly affordable.

c) As the telecommunications bandwidth required to support the operation of a STAD is primarily governed by the resolution of the STAD display screen and the required display screen refresh rate, the way that a STAD, of any given form factor, consumes bandwidth will be, on the whole, consistent and predictable. In comparison, a non-STTP-based personal computing device may consume bandwidth in a highly inconsistent and unpredictable manner that is driven by the needs of the user, and the user's application software and operating system, all of which can vary enormously from one moment to the next. So, all things being equal, it is probably far easier for telecommunications infrastructures to manage consistent and predictable bandwidth demands rather than demands that are highly inconsistent and unpredictable. Therefore, it is highly likely that future telecommunications infrastructures will engineer their communications systems to specifically support the Stream Tone, ensuring that sufficient bandwidth will be continuously available and highly affordable.

d) The total quantity of communicated data, measured in bytes, consumed by a STAD is governed by the duration of STAD use multiplied by the communications bandwidth available during that use. It is expected that the total number of bytes consumed by a typical STAD over a given period of time will be quite substantial, and will, in many instances, amount to many terabytes (TB), multiples of 1,000,000,000,000s bytes, per calendar month. Such a consumption of communicated data is far beyond what is typically consumed today, even by individuals lucky enough to have high-bandwidth *Optical Fibre*-based *Internet* connections. To put this quantity of data into some sort of real-world context, a typical 90 minute high definition (HD) movie, such as might be found on a Blu-ray disk, is approximately 25,000,000,000 bytes, or 0.025 TB, in size, so one TB of data would be sufficient to communicate 40 HD movies, which would be considered by most normal standards to be a very substantial quantity of data, even if it were communicated over the period of a month. Today, cost-effectively consuming such a quantity of data on a regular basis using wired telecommunications infrastructures is already possible, but not all that common. On the other hand, using current generation wireless mobile telecommunications infrastructures to consume such quantities of data would probably be both technically challenging and prohibitively expensive. Also, many *Internet* access services, especially those that are accessed using wireless mobile telecommunications, limit the total quantity of data that can be communicated per month, and consuming data beyond the monthly limit, even if permitted, usually incurs substantial additional costs. Such data consumption limits can often be as low as 1,000,000,000 bytes or 0.001 TB, per calendar month. However, in the future it is expected that the quantity of communicated data that a STAD will be able to cost-effectively consume will increase by several orders of magnitude, primarily due to the introduction of the next generations of wired and wireless telecommunications infrastructures. Such substantial increases will ensure that the delivery of all types of STTP-based content and services will be both highly affordable and practical.

e) In the interim, before the consumption of very large quantities of wirelessly communicated data becomes both affordable and practical, the use of STADs may be limited primarily to locations with wired *Internet* connectivity, which is already able to cost-effectively support the consumption of large quantities of communicated data. However, as the quantity of wirelessly communicated data that can be cost-effectively consumed increases, so too will the use of STADs with wireless-*Internet* connectivity.

## 4.3.2.4    ACCESS

a) The Stream Tone Access Device (STAD) will be used to access Stream Tone Transfer Protocol (STTP)-based content and services. The STAD will be used to present audio-visual data that has been sent from Stream Tone Service Infrastructure-based computer servers over the *Internet*. The STAD will be a low-performance device that wholly relies on remotely-located data processing resources for its operation. The STAD will be specifically designed to be functionally good enough to do its intended job, and no more. The STAD will be designed to be highly affordable, and will cost much less than a comparable non-STTP-based personal computing device. The STAD will also be designed to require minimal maintenance and be easily repairable.

b) The STAD will be available in a number of different form factors, including desktop computer, games console, laptop computer, *Smart-Phone*, and *Tablet Computer*. All STADs, regardless of their form factor, will share standardised control electronics that are based on familiar and mature technologies. This standardisation, combined with the relative simplicity of the control electronics that are needed to drive an essentially dumb device and the economies of scale that will be possible when manufacturing STADs in very high volumes, should help to ensure that the STAD will be a very affordable technology.

c) Before the STAD hardware becomes available, a free-of-charge software-based Stream Tone Access Device Emulator (STADE) will be required to access STTP-based services. The STADE will be available for use on a wide range of non-STTP-based personal computing devices, including desktop computers, laptop computers, *Smart-Phones*, and *Tablet Computers*. The STADE will be compatible with a wide range of popular microprocessor architectures and operating systems, and will be available from all popular *Application Stores*. The STADE will also be available as a *Live CD* and *Virtual Machine* image.

d) Whilst the STADE may be available free-of-charge, and the STAD will be a highly affordable piece of hardware, both will require the use of an *Internet* access service that is not likely to be available free-of-charge. The STADE and STAD will also need access to STTP-based services, some of which will undoubtedly be available free-of-charge, and some for a fee.

## 4.3.3    PRODUCTS

a) The hardware-based product that will be used to access Stream Tone Transfer Protocol (STTP)-based services is known as a Stream Tone Access Device (STAD). The STAD is expected to be available in a wide range of different form factors, including computer monitors, desktop computers, eyeglasses, games consoles, laptop computers, **Smart-Phones**, **Tablet Computers**, televisions, and wristwatches. In the future, STADs may also become available in a number of radically new form factors, such as contact lenses and neural implants.

b) STADs will also eventually be built into a number of common household appliances, such as cookers, microwave ovens, refrigerators, and washing machines. One of the key advantages of including a STAD into a household appliance is that the STAD cannot become obsolete, as it is purely an audio-visual presentation device, like a traditional television set, that is only designed to access STTP-based content and services. So as STTP-based content and services evolve the STAD built in to a household appliance does not need to change, and will therefore remain useful throughout the whole of the long working life expected from such an appliance. STADs may even be built into automobiles.

c) A number of possible Stream Tone-based products, with the form factors mentioned above, are described below. It should be noted that the hardware-based functionalities that are built directly into the different STAD form factors have been varied because it is assumed that the inclusion of any type of hardware-based functionality incurs a cost that cannot be easily justified in devices that can never practically make use of it, such as a **Global Positioning System** that has been fitted to a refrigerator. However, it should be noted that a key tenet of the STAD is that it will contain a single standardised set of control electronics, regardless of form factor, and having any variation in the STAD hardware would go against that tenet. Still, at some level, including hardware-based functionalities that can never be used seems to be out of place, wasteful, and contradictory of the intent that all STADs will be highly affordable to everyone, everywhere. Of course, in the future it may well be simpler and far more cost effective to just include a large base-set of functionalities into all STADs, regardless of form factor, even though some of those functionalities will never be used because the cost of inclusion will actually be negligible due to the very high manufacturing volumes that are expected for the standardised STAD control electronics. A possible solution might be to make such functionalities modular, through the use of a **Modular Design** approach, such that they can be very easily added or removed as required by a particular STAD form factor.

d) Most of the functionality built directly into the STAD hardware is very similar to hardware found on current-generation personal computing devices, such as **Smart-Phones** and **Tablet Computers**. Of course, some STADs will have functionality that is a little more exotic and futuristic, and not likely to be commonly available for quite some time. However, for the most part, the STAD hardware described in this section is based on real technologies and not science fiction, which makes sense given that the Stream Tone is essentially just a new way of communicating data and not a brand new hardware paradigm.

e) The naming convention adopted for the Stream Tone-based products is very simple, and is based on a suffix that roughly describes the product, which has been appended to a common base that is comprised of the words "Stream" and "Tone". For example, using this approach, a Stream Tone-based cooker would therefore be called something along the lines of "Stream Tone Cook" or "StreamToneCook".

f) The Stream Tone-based products listed below should not be considered to be definitive or exhaustive, simply representative of the types of products that could, theoretically, be created.

## 4.3.3.1     STREAM TONE CONSOLE

a)   The StreamToneConsole will be a screen-less Stream Tone Access Device (STAD) with an entertainment-console form factor that is designed to wirelessly connect to a television or computer monitor.

b)   The StreamToneConsole will provide access to a wide range of entertainment services, such as computer games, films, music, and TV shows that will be provided by digital services that are communicated using the Stream Tone Transfer Protocol.

c)   The StreamToneConsole will be based on a standardised *System on a Chip* that will be common to all STADs, regardless of form factor. The StreamToneConsole will include a *Bluetooth* interface, *Fourth-Generation Mobile Communications* interface, memory card reader, USB interface, *Wi-Fi* interface, and wired networking interface. Some versions of the StreamToneConsole will also include an *Image Sensor* and microphone.

d)   The StreamToneConsole will support the use of human interface devices, such as game controllers.

e)   Being a predominantly stationary device, the StreamToneConsole will not include functionality, such as an *Accelerometer*, *Ambient Light Sensor*, *Barometer*, *Global Positioning System*, *Gyroscope*, *Lithium-Ion Battery*, *Magnetometer*, *Near-Field Communication* interface, or *Proximity Sensor*, that is more commonly found in more portable devices.

f)   The StreamToneConsole will be very similar to the StreamToneDesk, except that the StreamToneDesk will generally be sold in a package that includes a wireless keyboard and mouse, whereas the StreamToneConsole will generally be sold in a package that includes a pair of wireless game controllers.

g)   Being a relatively simple device, the StreamToneConsole has a very small form factor that is just sufficient to house its electronics and interfaces. The StreamToneConsole is a fraction of the size of a traditional computer games console.

h)   Some versions of the StreamToneConsole are designed to be mounted on the top of a television or computer monitor so that the *Image Sensor*, if included, can obtain an unobstructed view of the user.

i)   The StreamToneConsole is expected to be popular within the computer gaming community because it is well suited to streaming *Web*-based computer games.

## 4.3.3.2     STREAM TONE COOK

a)   The StreamToneCook will be a cooker with a built-in Stream Tone Access Device (STAD) that can be used to access Stream Tone Transfer Protocol (STTP)-based content and services, particularly those relating to cooking, food, and shopping. The STAD will also be able to present information relating to the operation of the StreamToneCook. The

317

STAD can also be used for entertainment purposes, such as watching an *Internet Television Service*.

b)   The Stream Tone-based technology within the StreamToneCook will not be used to directly control the actual cooking functions of the cooker, which will be provided by an independent control system. The independent control system of the cooker may be optionally configured to safely accept certain control instructions from a STTP-based service, if required by the user and permitted by *Regulation*.

c)   The StreamToneCook will include a display screen that supports *Capacitive Sensing*.

d)   The StreamToneCook will be based on a standardised *System on a Chip* that will be common to all STADs, regardless of form factor. The StreamToneCook will include an *Ambient Light Sensor*, *Bluetooth* interface, *Fourth-Generation Mobile Communications* interface, *Image Sensor*, memory card reader, USB interface, *Wi-Fi* interface, and wired networking interface.

e)   Being a predominantly stationary device, the StreamToneCook will not include functionality, such as an *Accelerometer*, *Barometer*, *Global Positioning System*, *Gyroscope*, *Lithium-Ion Battery*, *Magnetometer*, *Near-Field Communication* interface, or *Proximity Sensor*, that is more commonly found in more portable devices.

# 4.3.3.3    STREAM TONE COOL

a)   The StreamToneCool will be a refrigerator with a built-in Stream Tone Access Device (STAD) that can be used to access Stream Tone Transfer Protocol (STTP)-based content and services, particularly those relating to cooking, food, and shopping. The STAD will also be able to present information relating to the operation of the StreamToneCool. The STAD can also be used for entertainment purposes, such as watching an *Internet Television Service*.

b)   The Stream Tone-based technology within the StreamToneCool will not be used to directly control the actual cooling and freezing functions of the refrigerator, which will be provided by an independent control system. The independent control system of the refrigerator may be optionally configured to safely accept certain control instructions from a STTP-based service, if required by the user and permitted by *Regulation*.

c)   The StreamToneCool will include a display screen that supports *Capacitive Sensing*.

d)   The StreamToneCool will be based on a standardised *System on a Chip* that will be common to all STADs, regardless of form factor. The StreamToneCool will include an *Ambient Light Sensor*, *Bluetooth* interface, *Fourth-Generation Mobile Communications* interface, *Image Sensor*, memory card reader, USB interface, *Wi-Fi* interface, and wired networking interface.

e)   Being a predominantly stationary device, the StreamToneCool will not include functionality, such as an *Accelerometer*, *Barometer*, *Global Positioning System*, *Gyroscope*, *Lithium-Ion Battery*, *Magnetometer*, *Near-Field Communication* interface, or *Proximity Sensor*, that is more commonly found in more portable devices.

# 4.3.3.4 STREAM TONE DESK

a) The StreamToneDesk will be a screen-less Stream Tone Access Device (STAD) with a desktop computer form factor that is designed to wirelessly connect to a television or computer monitor.

b) The StreamToneDesk will provide access to a wide range of digital content and services that will be communicated using the Stream Tone Transfer Protocol.

c) The StreamToneDesk will be based on a standardised *System on a Chip* that will be common to all STADs, regardless of form factor. The StreamToneDesk will include a *Bluetooth* interface, *Fourth-Generation Mobile Communications* interface, HDMI, memory card reader, USB interface, *Wi-Fi* interface, and wired networking interface. Some versions of the StreamToneDesk will include an *Image Sensor* and microphone.

d) The StreamToneDesk will support the use of human interface devices, such as keyboards and mice.

e) Being a predominantly stationary device, the StreamToneDesk will not include functionality, such as an *Accelerometer*, *Ambient Light Sensor*, *Barometer*, *Fourth-Generation Mobile Communications* interface, *Gyroscope*, *Lithium-Ion Battery*, *Near-Field Communication* interface, *Magnetometer*, or *Proximity Sensor*, that is more commonly found in more portable devices.

f) The StreamToneDesk will be very similar to the StreamToneConsole, except that the StreamToneConsole will generally be sold in a package that includes a pair of wireless game controllers, whereas the StreamToneDesk will generally be sold in a package that includes a wireless keyboard and mouse.

g) Being a relatively simple device, the StreamToneDesk has a very small form factor that is just sufficient to house its electronics and interfaces. The StreamToneDesk is a fraction of the size of a traditional desktop computer system.

h) Some versions of the StreamToneDesk are designed to be mounted on the top of a television or computer monitor so that the *Image Sensor*, if included, can obtain an unobstructed view of the user.

i) The StreamToneDesk is expected to be popular within the business community because it is well suited to a wide range of content creation tasks.

# 4.3.3.5 STREAM TONE DIRECT

a) The StreamToneDirect will be a Stream Tone Access Device (STAD) that is directly interfaced with the human brain. The StreamToneDirect will be able to safely and securely present Stream Tone Transfer Protocol-based content and services directly into the brain structures responsible for sight, smell, sound, taste, and touch.

b) Most of the control electronics of the StreamToneDirect will be located outside of the human head, with only those elements required to stimulate the human senses being directly embedded within the human brain. The embedded elements of the StreamToneDirect will be surgically implanted within the human brain using computer-controlled robot surgeons. Implantation of a StreamToneDirect will only be possible, and legally permitted, in human adults. The StreamToneDirect will not be implanted into the brains of children and adolescents because their brains have not finished growing.

c)   The control electronics of the StreamToneDirect will communicate with the elements embedded within the human brain using wireless communications that have been secured using very strong *Encryption*.

d)   The external control electronics of the StreamToneDirect will be based on a standardised *System on a Chip* that will be common to all STADs, regardless of form factor. The StreamToneDirect will include an *Accelerometer*, *Ambient Light Sensor*, *Barometer*, *Bluetooth* interface, *Fourth-Generation Mobile Communications* interface, *Global Positioning System*, *Gyroscope*, *Image Sensor*, *Magnetometer*, memory card reader, microphone, *Near-Field Communication* interface, *Proximity Sensor*, USB interface, *Wi-Fi* interface, and wired networking interface.

e)   The external control electronics of the StreamToneDirect will either be housed in a dedicated device that will most probably be screen-less, or provided by any other available STAD.

f)   The StreamToneDirect will be able to accept input directly from the user's brain.

g)   The StreamToneDirect could theoretically support the development of technology-based human telepathy and the creation of humanity's first hive mind.

h)   The technology behind the StreamToneDirect is highly dependent on advancements in the fields of biologically-compatible materials, neural implantation, and neural physiology that may not be practical for many decades.

## 4.3.3.6   STREAM TONE DISPLAY

a)   The StreamToneDisplay will be a multi-point touch-enabled computer monitor with a built-in Stream Tone Access Device (STAD). The StreamToneDisplay will primarily be designed to be used in conjunction with non-Stream Tone Transfer Protocol (STTP)-based personal computing devices, such as a traditional desktop computer system. When the StreamToneDisplay is not required to display content from a non-STTP-based personal computing device it can be used, as a standalone STAD, to provide access to STTP-based content and services

b)   The StreamToneDisplay will be based on a standardised *System on a Chip* that will be common to all STADs, regardless of form factor. The StreamToneDisplay will include an *Ambient Light Sensor*, *Bluetooth* interface, *Capacitive Sensing*-based display screen, *Fourth-Generation Mobile Communications* interface, HDMI, loudspeaker, memory card reader, microphone, USB interface, *Wi-Fi* interface, and wired networking interface.

c)   Being a predominantly stationary device, the StreamToneDisplay will not include functionality, such as an *Accelerometer*, *Barometer*, *Global Positioning System*, *Gyroscope*, *Lithium-Ion Battery*, *Magnetometer*, *Near-Field Communication* interface, or **Proximity Sensor**, that is more commonly found in more portable devices.

d) The StreamToneDisplay will provide similar functionality to the StreamToneConsole and StreamToneDesk, in a single device. The StreamToneDisplay will also provide similar functionality to the StreamToneTV, the main difference being that the StreamToneDisplay will not be supplied with television-oriented peripherals and will be unable to receive traditional digital terrestrial television signals. It will be possible to connect a StreamToneTV to a traditional personal computing device, such as computer desktop, if required, the same as the StreamToneDisplay.

e) The StreamToneDisplay is expected to be popular within the business community because it well suited to content creation tasks that are run on more traditional personal computing devices, such as desktop computers.

# 4.3.3.7    STREAM TONE LOOK

a) The StreamToneLook will be a Stream Tone Access Device (STAD) with a contact lens form factor that has an augmented reality-based graphical user-interface, which is visually overlaid onto a direct view of the real world. The StreamToneLook will be used to access Stream Tone Transfer Protocol (STTP)-based content and services.

b) The StreamToneLook will be designed to be a fully-functional standalone personal computing device that does not need to be paired with a larger and more powerful personal computing device, such as a **Smart-Phone** or **Tablet Computer**, in order to be useful. Like all STADs, the StreamToneLook will rely on STTP-based services for its operation.

c) The StreamToneLook will be designed to be worn in either both eyes, or, if required or preferred, on just a single eye. Certain types of three-dimensional functionality will not be available if the StreamToneLook is only worn on one eye.

d) The StreamToneLook will be based on a standardised **System on a Chip** that will be common to all STADs, regardless of form factor. The StreamToneLook will include an **Accelerometer, Ambient Light Sensor, Barometer, Bluetooth** interface, **Fourth-Generation Mobile Communications** interface, **Global Positioning System, Gyroscope, Image Sensor, Lithium-Ion Battery** (LIB), **Magnetometer, Photovoltaic** battery charger, transparent display screen, and **Wi-Fi** interface.

e) Given that the StreamToneLook will have a very small form factor, it will not include functionality more commonly found on other types of STADs, such as a **Capacitive Sensing**-based display screen, HDMI, memory card readers, **Near-Field Communication** interface, **Proximity Sensor**, USB interface, or wired networking interfaces.

f) Control of the StreamToneLook will be achieved using eye blinks, hand gestures, and voice commands. Hand gestures will be detected using an **Image Sensor** built into the iris section of the STAD. Voice commands will be input using a separate microphone that has been wirelessly paired with the STAD.

g) The StreamToneLook will typically be paired with a set of wireless earphones that include a jawbone-based microphone. Audio feedback from the StreamToneLook will be sent to the wireless earphones.

h)   The StreamToneLook will be powered by a miniature LIB, that can be recharged using a *Photovoltaic* charger built into the iris section of the STAD.

i)   Given that the StreamToneLook will be a portable device that is primarily battery powered, it will need to use a display screen that is highly power-efficient, such as one based on *Indium Gallium Zinc Oxide Backplane* technology.

j)   The functionality of the StreamToneLook will be similar to that of the StreamToneView. The StreamToneView will be a less advanced version of the StreamToneLook and will be the previous generation product that the StreamToneLook evolved from.

k)   The technology behind the StreamToneLook is highly dependent on advancements in a wide range of fields, including biologically-compatible materials, electronic miniaturisation, and micro-optics, that may not be practical for many years.

## 4.3.3.8      STREAM TONE MOVE

a)   The StreamToneMove will be a Stream Tone Access Device (STAD) form factor designed for embedded use within all types of automobile. The StreamToneMove will be used to access Stream Tone Transfer Protocol (STTP)-based content and services, particularly those relating to automotive information, entertainment, and navigation.

b)   The StreamToneMove will not be used to directly control the physical operations of an automobile, which will be provided by an independent control system. The independent control system of the automobile may be optionally configured to safely accept certain control instructions from a STTP-based service, if required by the user and permitted by *Regulation*.

c)   The StreamToneMove will be based on a standardised *System on a Chip* that will be common to all STADs, regardless of form factor. The StreamToneMove will include an *Accelerometer*, *Ambient Light Sensor*, *Barometer*, *Bluetooth* interface, *Capacitive Sensing*-based display screen, *Fourth-Generation Mobile Communications* interface, *Global Positioning System*, *Gyroscope*, HDMI, *Image Sensor*, *Magnetometer*, memory card reader, microphone, *Proximity Sensor*, USB interface, *Wi-Fi* interface, and wired networking interface.

d)   In the same way that having a STAD built into a household appliance ensures that the household appliance never becomes obsolete due to its embedded personal computing device becoming outdated, the same is also true for the StreamToneMove.

## 4.3.3.9      STREAM TONE PAD

a)   The StreamTonePad will be a Stream Tone Access Device (STAD) with a *Tablet Computer* form factor. The StreamTonePad will be used to access Stream Tone Transfer Protocol (STTP)-based content and services. The StreamTonePad will be a complete and perfect replacement for a traditional, non-STTP-based, *Tablet Computer*. The StreamTonePad will provide access to STTP-based equivalents for all traditional *Tablet*

*Computer* functionality.

b) As per a traditional *Tablet Computer*, the StreamTonePad user-interface will be based on a multi-point touch-enabled display screen.

c) The StreamTonePad will be based on a standardised *System on a Chip* that will be common to all STADs, regardless of form factor. The StreamTonePad will include an *Accelerometer*, *Ambient Light Sensor*, *Barometer*, *Bluetooth* interface, *Capacitive Sensing*-based display screen, *Fourth-Generation Mobile Communications* interface, *Global Positioning System*, *Gyroscope*, HDMI, *Image Sensors*, *Lithium-Ion Battery*, loudspeaker, *Magnetometer*, memory card reader, microphone, *Near-Field Communication* interface, *Proximity Sensor*, USB interface, *Wi-Fi* interface, and wired networking interface.

d) Given that the StreamTonePad will be a portable device that is primarily battery powered, it will need to use a display screen that is highly power-efficient, such as one based on *Electronic Paper*, *Indium Gallium Zinc Oxide Backplane*, *Organic Light-Emitting Diode*, or *Transflective Liquid-Crystal Display* technology.

e) Along with the StreamTonePhone, the StreamTonePad is expected to be one of the most popular STAD form factors.

# 4.3.3.10    STREAM TONE PHONE

a) The StreamTonePhone will be a Stream Tone Access Device (STAD) with a *Smart-Phone* form factor. The StreamTonePhone will be used to access Stream Tone Transfer Protocol (STTP)-based content and services. The StreamTonePhone will be a complete and perfect replacement for a traditional, non-STTP-based, *Smart-Phone*. The StreamTonePhone will provide access to STTP-based equivalents for all traditional *Smart-Phone* functionality.

b) As per a traditional *Smart-Phone*, the StreamTonePhone user-interface will be based on a multi-point touch-enabled display screen.

c) The StreamTonePhone will not able to directly connect with traditional mobile telephony services as it only supports an STTP-based equivalent of *Voice over Internet Protocol*. The StreamTonePhone will be able to connect with traditional mobile telephony services through STTP-based intermediary services.

d) The StreamTonePhone will be based on a standardised *System on a Chip* that will be common to all STADs, regardless of form factor. The StreamTonePhone will include an *Accelerometer*, *Ambient Light Sensor*, *Barometer*, *Bluetooth* interface, *Capacitive Sensing*-based display screen, *Fourth-Generation Mobile Communications* interface, *Global Positioning System*, *Gyroscope*, HDMI, *Image Sensors*, *Lithium-Ion Battery*, loudspeaker, *Magnetometer*, memory card reader, microphone, *Near-Field Communication* interface, *Proximity Sensor*, USB interface, *Wi-Fi* interface, and wired networking interface.

e) Given that the StreamTonePhone will be a portable device that is primarily battery powered, it will need to use a display screen that is highly power-efficient, such as one based on *Electronic Paper*, *Indium Gallium Zinc Oxide Backplane*, *Organic Light-*

*Emitting Diode*, or *Transflective Liquid-Crystal Display* technology.

f)   Along with the StreamTonePad, the StreamTonePhone is expected to be one of the most popular STAD form factors.

# 4.3.3.11   STREAM TONE PORTABLE

a)   The StreamTonePortable will be a Stream Tone Access Device (STAD) with a laptop computer form factor. The StreamTonePortable will be used to access Stream Tone Transfer Protocol (STTP)-based content and services. The StreamTonePortable will be a complete and perfect replacement for a traditional, non-STTP-based, laptop computer. The StreamTonePortable will provide STTP-based equivalents for all traditional laptop computer functionality.

b)   As per a traditional laptop computer the StreamTonePortable will include a built-in multi-point touch-enabled display screen, and a keyboard.

c)   The StreamTonePortable will be based on a standardised *System on a Chip* that will be common to all STADs, regardless of form factor. The StreamTonePortable will include an *Accelerometer*, *Ambient Light Sensor*, *Barometer*, *Bluetooth* interface, *Capacitive Sensing*-based display screen, *Fourth-Generation Mobile Communications* interface, *Global Positioning System*, *Gyroscope*, HDMI, *Image Sensor*, *Lithium-Ion Battery*, loudspeaker, *Magnetometer*, memory card reader, microphone, *Proximity Sensor*, USB interface, *Wi-Fi* interface, and wired networking interface.

d)   Given that the StreamTonePortable will be a portable device that is primarily battery powered, it will need to use a display screen that is highly power-efficient, such as one based on *Electronic Paper*, *Indium Gallium Zinc Oxide Backplane*, *Organic Light-Emitting Diode*, or *Transflective Liquid-Crystal Display* technology.

e)   The StreamTonePortable is expected to be popular within the business community because it will be well suited to a wide range of content creation tasks.

# 4.3.3.12   STREAM TONE TV

a)   The StreamToneTV will be a multi-point touch-enabled television with built-in Stream Tone Access Device (STAD) functionality. In addition to providing traditional television functionality, the StreamToneTV will also be able to function as a STAD, and provide access to Stream Tone Transfer Protocol (STTP)-based content and services.

b)   The StreamToneTV will be able to receive traditional digital terrestrial television signals, as well as STTP-based television services. Traditionally delivered television shows and STTP-based television shows will be seamlessly integrated into a unified viewing experience.

c)   The StreamToneTV will be able to accept user-input by hand gestures, voice command, and wireless remote control, as well as through a wireless keyboard and wireless mouse. The StreamToneTV will also have a multi-point touch-enabled display screen that will support on-screen gestures.

d) The StreamToneTV will be based on a standardised **System on a Chip** that will be common to all STADs, regardless of form factor. The StreamToneTV will include an **Ambient Light Sensor**, **Bluetooth** interface, **Capacitive Sensing**-based display screen, **Fourth-Generation Mobile Communications** interface, HDMI, **Image Sensor**, loudspeaker, memory card reader, microphone, USB interface, **Wi-Fi** interface, and wired networking interface.

e) Being a predominantly stationary device, the StreamToneConsole will not include functionality, such as an **Accelerometer**, **Barometer**, **Global Positioning System**, **Gyroscope**, **Lithium-Ion Battery**, **Magnetometer**, **Near-Field Communication** interface, or **Proximity Sensor**, that is more commonly found in more portable devices.

f) The StreamToneTV will provide similar functionality to the StreamToneConsole and StreamToneDesk, in a single device. The StreamToneTV will also provide similar functionality to the StreamToneDisplay; the main difference being that the StreamToneTV will be supplied in a package that includes television-oriented peripherals and is able to receive traditional digital terrestrial television signals. It will be possible to connect the StreamToneTV to a traditional personal computing device, such as desktop computer if required, the same as the StreamToneDisplay.

# 4.3.3.13 STREAM TONE VIEW

a) The StreamToneView will be a Stream Tone Access Device (STAD) with an eyeglasses form factor that has an augmented reality-based graphical user-interface, which is visually overlaid onto a direct view of the real world. The StreamToneView will be used to access Stream Tone Transfer Protocol-based content and services.

b) The StreamToneView will be based on a standardised **System on a Chip** that will be common to all STADs, regardless of form factor. The StreamToneView will include an **Accelerometer**, **Ambient Light Sensor**, **Barometer**, **Bluetooth** interface, **Fourth-Generation Mobile Communications** interface, **Global Positioning System**, **Gyroscope**, **Image Sensors**, **Lithium-Ion Battery**, loudspeakers, **Magnetometer**, memory card reader, microphone, **Proximity Sensors**, transparent display screens, USB interface, **Wi-Fi** interface, and wired networking interface.

c) Given that the StreamToneView will have a very small form factor, it will not include functionality more commonly found on other types of STADs, such as a **Capacitive Sensing**-based display screen, HDMI, **Near-Field Communication** interface, or wired networking interface.

d) Control of the StreamToneView will be achieved using hand gestures and voice commands. Hand gestures will be detected using the STAD's built-in **Image Sensors**. Voice commands will be input using a microphone that is built directly into the STAD.

e) Given that the StreamToneView will be a portable device that is primarily battery powered, it will need to use a display screen that is highly power-efficient, such as one based on **Indium Gallium Zinc Oxide Backplane** technology.

f) The functionality of the StreamToneView will be similar to that of the StreamToneLook.

The StreamToneLook will be a more advanced version of the StreamToneView and will be the next generation product that the StreamToneView will eventually evolve into. Unlike the StreamToneLook, it will be possible to build the StreamToneView using current technologies.

## 4.3.3.14    STREAM TONE WASH

a)    The StreamToneWash will be a washing machine with a built-in Stream Tone Access Device (STAD) that can be used to access Stream Tone Transfer Protocol (STTP)-based content and services, particularly those relating to cleaning products and services. The STAD will also be able to present information relating to the operation of the StreamToneWash. The STAD can also be used for entertainment purposes, such as watching an *Internet Television Service*.

b)    The Stream Tone-based technology within the StreamToneWash will not be used to directly control the actual cleaning functions of the washing machine, which will be provided by an independent control system. The independent control system of the washing machine may be optionally configured to safely accept certain control instructions from a STTP-based service, if required by the user and permitted by *Regulation*.

c)    The StreamToneWash will include a display screen that supports *Capacitive Sensing*.

d)    The StreamToneWash will be based on a standardised *System on a Chip* that will be common to all STADs, regardless of form factor. The StreamToneWash will include an *Ambient Light Sensor*, *Bluetooth* interface, *Fourth-Generation Mobile Communications* interface, *Image Sensor*, memory card reader, USB interface, *Wi-Fi* interface, and wired networking interface.

e)    Being a predominantly stationary device, the StreamToneWash will not include functionality, such as an *Accelerometer*, *Barometer*, *Global Positioning System*, *Gyroscope*, *Lithium-Ion Battery*, *Magnetometer*, *Near-Field Communication* interface, or *Proximity Sensor*, that is more commonly found in more portable devices.

## 4.3.3.15    STREAM TONE WATCH

a)    The StreamToneWatch will be a Stream Tone Access Device (STAD) with a small and portable form factor that can be worn on the wrist, pinned to the chest, or hung around the neck. The StreamToneWatch will be used to access Stream Tone Transfer Protocol-based content and services.

b)    The StreamToneWatch will be based on a standardised *System on a Chip* that will be common to all STADs, regardless of form factor. The StreamToneWatch will include an *Accelerometer*, *Ambient Light Sensor*, *Barometer*, *Bluetooth* interface, *Capacitive Sensing*-based display screen, *Fourth-Generation Mobile Communications* interface, *Global Positioning System*, *Gyroscope*, *Image Sensor*, *Lithium-Ion Battery* (LIB), loudspeaker, *Magnetometer*, microphone, *Near-Field Communication* interface, *Photovoltaic* battery charger, *Proximity Sensor*, USB interface, *Wi-Fi* interface, and wired networking interface.

c) Because the StreamToneWatch will have a relatively small form factor, it will not be able to house a particularly large or long-lasting LIB. The StreamToneWatch will therefore make use of a built-in *Photovoltaic* battery charger to help recharge its LIB.

d) Given that the StreamToneWatch will be a portable device that is primarily battery powered, it will need to use a display screen that is highly power-efficient, such as one based on *Electronic Paper*, *Indium Gallium Zinc Oxide Backplane*, *Organic Light-Emitting Diode*, or *Transflective Liquid-Crystal Display* technology.

e) Control of the StreamToneWatch will be achieved using hand gestures and voice commands. Hand gestures will be detected using the STAD's multi-point touched-enabled display screen. Voice commands will be input using a microphone that is built directly into the STAD.

f) The StreamToneWatch will typically be paired with a pair of wireless earphones.

g) The StreamToneWatch will have similar functionality to the StreamTonePhone and the StreamTonePad except that it will be much smaller, and have a shorter battery life.

# 4.3.3.16    STREAM TONE WAVE

a) The StreamToneWave will be a microwave oven with a built-in Stream Tone Access Device (STAD) that can be used to access Stream Tone Transfer Protocol (STTP)-based content and services, particularly those relating to cooking and food. The STAD will also be able to present information relating to the operation of the StreamToneWave. The STAD can also be used for entertainment purposes, such as watching an *Internet Television Service*.

b) The Stream Tone-based technology within the StreamToneWave will not be used to directly control the actual cooking functions of the microwave oven, which will be provided by an independent control system. The independent control system of the microwave oven may be optionally configured to safely accept certain control instructions from a STTP-based service, if required by the user and permitted by *Regulation*.

c) The StreamToneWave will include a display screen that supports *Capacitive Sensing*.

d) The StreamToneWave will be based on a standardised *System on a Chip* that will be common to all STADs, regardless of form factor. The StreamToneWave will include an *Ambient Light Sensor*, *Bluetooth* interface, *Fourth-Generation Mobile Communications* interface, *Image Sensor*, memory card reader, USB interface, *Wi-Fi* interface, and wired networking interface.

e) Being a predominantly stationary device, the StreamToneWave will not include functionality, such as an *Accelerometer*, *Barometer*, *Global Positioning System*, *Gyroscope*, *Lithium-Ion Battery*, *Magnetometer*, *Near-Field Communication* interface, or *Proximity Sensor*, that is more commonly found in more portable devices.

# 4.3.4 SERVICES

a) Many of the digital services that will be communicated using the Stream Tone Transfer Protocol (STTP) will be pre-existing, and will continue to use their current trading names and uniform resource identifiers (URIs). However, some new STTP-based services may decide to adopt trading names that are related in some way to the Stream Tone, such as through the use of aquatic, flow, liquid, or water-related nomenclature. The URIs of STTP-based services will normally begin with "sttp://" to indicate that such services use the STTP.

b) Of course, Stream Tone-based services can use any available top-level domain name in their URI. However, many new STTP-based services may decide to adopt a URI based on the *Internet* country-code top-level domain for the Democratic Republic of São Tomé and Príncipe, which is ".st", because its two-letter code can be used to clearly indicate a digital service that will be communicated using the STTP, which is more commonly known as the Stream Tone. For example, the URI *sttp://www.football-videos.st* could be used for a football-related streaming-video service that was communicated using the STTP. The official registry for ".st" domain names is: *http://www.nic.st*

c) The Stream Tone Service Portal (STSP) is expected to be the principle mechanism for accessing STTP-based services. The STSP can be configured by STSP operators to offer uniquely branded user experiences.

d) Listed below are some possible trading names for some fictional STTP-based services that are based on the use of the ".st" *Internet* domain and Stream Tone-related nomenclature. They have been included to illustrate how the adoption of Stream Tone-based technologies could lead to the creation of some new and uniquely named services based on, or around, the Stream Tone-related nomenclature.

e) The list of STTP-based services should not be considered to be definitive or exhaustive, simply representative of the types of names that could, theoretically, be used for such services.

## 4.3.4.1 ACHERON

a) The Acheron is a river in Greece. In Greek mythology, the Acheron was known as one of the five rivers of the Greek underworld. Acheron might make a good trading name for a Stream Tone Transfer Protocol-based computer gaming service. The uniform resource identifier for such a service might be: *sttp://www.acheron-gaming.st*

## 4.3.4.2 ARROYO

a) An arroyo is a water-carved channel. Arroyo might make a good trading name for a Stream Tone Transfer Protocol-based woodcarving supplies service. The uniform resource identifier for such a service might be *sttp://www.arroyo-woodcarving.st*

# 4.3.4.3     AVALANCHE

a)    An avalanche is the rapid flow of a mass of snow and ice down a mountain. Avalanche might make a good trading name for a Stream Tone Transfer Protocol-based snowboarding and skiing supplies service. The uniform resource identifier for such a service might be *sttp://www.avalanche-outfitters.st*

# 4.3.4.4     BAYOU

a)    A bayou is a creek, secondary watercourse, or minor river. Bayous are often found in the Gulf Coast region of the southern United States of America, a region that is traditionally associated with the French-speaking Cajun culture. Bayou might make a good trading name for a Stream Tone Transfer Protocol-based Cajun-inspired cooking service. The uniform resource identifier for such a service might be *sttp://www.bayou-cooking.st*

# 4.3.4.5     BILLABONG

a)    A billabong is a seasonal streambed or backwater that is commonly associated with the Australian outback. Billabong might make a good trading name for a Stream Tone Transfer Protocol-based outdoor supplies service. The uniform resource identifier for such a service might be *sttp://www.billabong-camping.st*

# 4.3.4.6     BRIDGE

a)    A bridge is a structure that carries a path or roadway over an obstacle, such as a river. A bridge is also a part of a musical instrument. Bridge might make a good trading name for a Stream Tone Transfer Protocol-based musical instrument supplies service. The uniform resource identifier for such a service might be *sttp://www.bridge-instruments.st*

# 4.3.4.7     BROOK

a)    A brook is a natural stream of water that is smaller than a river. Brook might make a good trading name for a Stream Tone Transfer Protocol-based children's clothing supplies service. The uniform resource identifier for such a service might be *sttp://www.brook-clothing.st*

# 4.3.4.8     CANAL

a)    A canal is a navigable artificial waterway used to transport people and materials. A canal can also be a tubular anatomical passage. Canal might make a good trading name for a Stream Tone Transfer Protocol-based delivery service. The uniform resource identifier for such a service might be *sttp://www.canal-deliveries.st*

## 4.3.4.9    CHURCHILL

a)    The Churchill River is 1,609 kilometres long, and is located in Canada. Named after John Churchill, 1st Duke of Marlborough. Sir Winston Churchill was a former Prime Minister of the United Kingdom. Churchill might make a good trading name for a Stream Tone Transfer Protocol-based political news service. The uniform resource identifier for such a service might be *sttp://www.churchill-news.st*

## 4.3.4.10    CONGO

a)    The Congo River is 4,700 kilometres long, and is located in Central Africa. Large sections of the Congo River are navigable. The Congo River is of great economic importance to the many Africa countries through which it flows. Congo might make a good trading name for a Stream Tone Transfer Protocol-based import and export business service. The uniform resource identifier for such a service might be *sttp://www.congo-trading.st*

## 4.3.4.11    CROSSING

a)    A crossing is a point in the course of a river where travellers are able to easily move from one riverbank to the other. Crossing might make a good trading name for a Stream Tone Transfer Protocol-based holiday travel service. The uniform resource identifier for such a service might be *sttp://www.crossing-holidays.st*

## 4.3.4.12    DRIFT

a)    To drift, within a boat, upon an ocean or river, is the involuntary act of gently travelling at the whim of water currents. Drift might make a good trading name for a Stream Tone Transfer Protocol-based bedding and sleep supplies services. The uniform resource identifier for such a service might be *sttp://www.drift-bedding.st*

## 4.3.4.13    FLOTSAM

a)    Flotsam is miscellaneous, often natural, material afloat on the sea. Flotsam might make a good trading name for a Stream Tone Transfer Protocol-based content discovery service. The uniform resource identifier for such a service might be *sttp://www.flotsam-search.st*

## 4.3.4.14    GREEN

a)    The Green River is 1,170 kilometres long, and is located in the United States of America. The colour green is associated with nature and environmentalism. Green might make a good trading name for a Stream Tone Transfer Protocol-based environmental awareness service. The uniform resource identifier for such a service might be *sttp://www.green-awareness.st*

## 4.3.4.15 GYRE

a)   A gyre is a giant, oceanic, surface current. Gyre might make a good trading name for a Stream Tone Transfer Protocol-based social networking service. The uniform resource identifier for such a service might be *sttp://www.gyre-social.st*

## 4.3.4.16 JETSAM

a)   Jetsam are man-made materials, generally related to marine craft, that are often accidentally lost, or purposefully jettisoned, overboard from a ship, and which are now afloat upon the surface of the ocean. Jetsam might make a good trading name for a Stream Tone Transfer Protocol-based auction service. The uniform resource identifier for such a service might be *sttp://www.jetsam-auctions.st*

## 4.3.4.17 JUGULAR

a)   The jugular veins, located in the human neck, carry de-oxygenated blood from the head back to the heart. Jugular might make a good trading name for a Stream Tone Transfer Protocol-based medical drama-oriented television service. The uniform resource identifier for such a service might be *sttp://www.jugular-television.st*

## 4.3.4.18 LAVA

a)   Lava is molten rock, at a temperature of between 700 and 1,200 degrees Celsius, which is often seen flowing out of volcanoes. Lava might make a good trading name for a Stream Tone Transfer Protocol-based barbecue supplies service. The uniform resource identifier for such a service might be *sttp://www.lava-hot-sauces.st*

## 4.3.4.19 MEANDER

a)   A meander is a turn or winding of a stream or river. Meander can also refer to wandering casually or aimlessly without urgent destination. Meander might make a good trading name for a Stream Tone Transfer Protocol-based easy-listening radio service. The uniform resource identifier for such a service might be *sttp://www.meander-radio.st*

## 4.3.4.20 PIPE

a)   A pipe is a tubular or cylindrical object, part, or passage, which can be used to conduct a liquid, gas, or finely divided solid. Pipe might make a good trading name for a Stream Tone Transfer Protocol-based plumbing supplies service. The uniform resource identifier for such a service might be *sttp://www.pipe-plumbing-supplies.st*

## 4.3.4.21    POUR

a)   Pour means to cause to flow in a stream. Drinks are often poured into glasses. Pour might make a good trading name for a Stream Tone Transfer Protocol-based cocktail drink reference service. The uniform resource identifier for such a service might be *sttp://www.pour-me-a-cocktail.st*

## 4.3.4.22    RAPIDS

a)   Rapids are a part of a fast-flowing river where the surface is broken by obstructions, such as rocks. Rapids might make a good trading name for a Stream Tone Transfer Protocol-based extreme water-sports service. The uniform resource identifier for such a service might be *sttp://www.rapids-water-sports.st*

## 4.3.4.23    STYX

a)   There are a number of rivers called Styx, which are located in a various countries around the world. In Greek mythology, the Styx was known as one of the five rivers of the Greek underworld. Styx might make a good trading name for a Stream Tone Transfer Protocol-based computer gaming service. The uniform resource identifier for such a service might be *sttp://www.styx-gaming.st*

## 4.3.4.24    THAMES

a)   The River Thames flows through southern England, with its lower reaches dividing the city of London into two. Historically, the River Thames has been an enabler of trade and industry, especially within London. Thames might make a good trading name for a Stream Tone Transfer Protocol-based London-oriented news service. The uniform resource identifier for such a service might be *sttp://www.thames-news.st*

## 4.3.4.25    TRIBUTARY

a)   A tributary is a stream feeding a lake or river. A tribute is a gift marking affection, gratitude, or respect. Tributary might make a good trading name for a Stream Tone Transfer Protocol-based memorial service. The uniform resource identifier for such a service might be *sttp://www.tributary-memorials.st*

## 4.3.4.26    VIADUCT

a)   A viaduct is an elevated roadway, often over water. An aqueduct is a similar construction for conveying water over uneven terrain. Viaduct might make a good trading name for a Stream Tone Transfer Protocol-based email service. The uniform resource identifier for such a service might be *sttp://www.viaduct-email.st*

## 4.3.4.27 VOLGA

a) The Volga River is 3,692 kilometres long, and located in Russia. It connects 11 of Russia's 20 largest cities, including Moscow. Today, the Volga is an important trade and communication route. Volga might make a good trading name for a Stream Tone Transfer Protocol-based stocks and shares trading service. The uniform resource identifier for such a service might be *sttp://www.volga-brokerage.st*

## 4.3.4.28 WASH

a) A wash is a shallow body of water, often fed by the ebb and flow of sea tides. The act of washing is to cleanse by rubbing with water. Wash might make a good trading name for a Stream Tone Transfer Protocol-based bathroom supplies service. The uniform resource identifier for such a service might be *sttp://www.wash-supplies.st*

## 4.3.4.29 ZAMBEZI

a) The Zambezi River is 2,574 kilometres long and is located in Africa. The Zambezi River is of great agricultural importance. Zambezi might make a good trading name for a Stream Tone Transfer Protocol-based agricultural supplies service. The uniform resource identifier for such a service might be *sttp://www.zambezi-agriculture.st*

# 4.4 TIMELINE

*Step by step*

a) The Stream Tone Transfer Protocol (STTP) and its associated technology ecosystem, as currently envisioned, do not yet exist. The Stream Tone timeline, presented below, is a thought experiment that speculates, at a fairly-high level, on how the Stream Tone could possibly emerge, and some of the activities that may be required to create it. One of the main purposes of the timeline is to show just how quickly the Stream Tone could, in theory at least, become part of everyday life. The timeline is probably overly optimistic, given the many challenges, tasks, and unknowns that undoubtedly lie ahead of the Stream Tone. Nevertheless, such a thought experiment can still provide useful insights into what the future may hold, and may also lead to more realistic design and planning processes during the earliest stages of actual Stream Tone development.

b) The timeline is divided into two main time periods; Before Stream Tone (BST), which is the period of time before the STTP has been defined, and After Stream Tone (AST), which is the period of time after the STTP has been defined. As few new technologies make the journey from inception to maturity overnight, the timeline describes an arbitrary six-year time period; with one year allocated BST and five years allocated AST. The BST and AST time periods are then broken down into a number of sub-periods. The BST period contains two sub-periods; figuratively described as today and tomorrow. Today focuses on the launch of the Stream Tone concept. Tomorrow focuses on the initial development of the STTP. The AST period contains five sub-periods that collectively describe the development of the Stream Tone Technology Ecosystem (STTE), and the deployment of STTP-based services, year by year, over a five-year period.

c)   The entries within each timeline period are not listed in a strict chronological order, but they do reflect a logical and progressive flow from one year to the next. Many activities occur in parallel and assume the use of substantial resources.

# 4.4.1     BEFORE STREAM TONE

a)   This section describes the Before Stream Tone (BST) time period; the time period before the Stream Tone Transfer Protocol (STTP) is first published. This time period is expected to last approximately one year, although in reality it will probably last significantly longer.

## 4.4.1.1     TODAY

a)   The Stream Tone concept is announced with the publication of this book.

b)   Interest in the Stream Tone, and Comprehensive Remote Personal Computing, which is enabled by the Stream Tone, slowly increases as it starts to be discussed in the media, and on social networking sites.

c)   The Stream Tone concept is endorsed and dismissed in equal measure.

d)   The emergence of the Stream Tone concept starts to catalyse productive discussions on the future of personal computing.

e)   Many existing technologies, and digital services, are recognised as Stream Tone precursors.

f)   Many promising technologies are identified as potential Stream Tone building blocks.

## 4.4.1.2     TOMORROW

a)   Prominent technologists acknowledge the Stream Tone as the next logical step in personal computing.

b)   Speculative purchases of **Web** domain names based on the ".st" country-code top-level domain for the Democratic Republic of São Tomé and Príncipe begin.

c)   The Stream Tone Community Forum (STCF), an official, moderated, **Web**-based forum for the Stream Tone Community (STC) to discuss the technicalities of developing the Stream Tone, is set up. Membership of the STC and use of the STCF grows. STCF discussions start to identify practical and cost-effective approaches for designing, developing, and deploying the Stream Tone.

d) The Stream Tone attracts small-scale corporate and philanthropic interest.

e) Discussions are held on establishing a non-profit **Foundation**, to be known as the Stream Tone **Foundation** (STF) that will help to promote and guide development of the Stream Tone Technology Ecosystem (STTE). The STF would also be responsible for certifying Stream Tone Transfer Protocol (STTP)-compliant devices, the use of a Stream Tone **Certification Mark**, and governance of the Stream Tone Security Service (STSS) provided by approved third parties.

f) Expert input on the STTP is sought and obtained from a number of different **Internet** standards bodies, such as the **Internet Engineering Task Force** (IETF) and the **World Wide Web Consortium** (W3C). Formal development of the STTP is passed to IETF and/or W3C. STTP development is supported by the STC. Design work on the STTP is started.

g) Design work on the software-based Stream Tone Software Development Kit (STSDK) is started. Development of the STSDK is the responsibility of the STC. The STSDK will comprise of the Stream Tone **Application Programming Interface** and Stream Tone Function Library.

h) Design work on the Stream Tone Access Device (STAD) is started. Development of the STAD is the responsibility of the STC. The first STADs will be based on **Field-Programmable Gate Array** technology, which can be reprogrammed to support the rapid evolution and maturation of the STTP that is expected to occur over the first few years of its life.

i) Design work on the Stream Tone Access Device Emulator (STADE) is started. Development of the STADE is the responsibility of the STC.

j) Design work on the Stream Tone Service Portal (STSP) is started. Development of the STSP is the responsibility of the STC. The STSP will provide a simple mechanism for users to access STTP-based services.

k) Design work on the STSS is started. Development of the STSS is the responsibility of the STC. The STSS will provide identity and access management services for use by the STSP and STTP-based services.

l) The STTP is published under a **Free and Open-Source Software** licence.

# 4.4.2    AFTER STREAM TONE

a) This section describes the After Stream Tone (AST) time period; the time period after the Stream Tone Transfer Protocol (STTP) is first published. This time period is expected to last approximately five years.

## 4.4.2.1    FIRST YEAR

a) The Stream Tone Transfer Protocol (STTP) continues to evolve and mature.

335

b) Design work on the Stream Tone Software Development Kit (STSDK) is completed. Implementation work on the STSDK is started. Implementation work on the STSDK is completed. The STSDK is published under a ***Free and Open-Source Software*** (FOSS) license.

c) Design work on the Stream Tone Access Device Emulator (STADE) is completed. Implementation work on the STADE is started. Early versions of STADE runtime binaries are made available, free-of-charge, for testing, along with a simple STTP-based service that has been created for demonstration purposes. Implementation work on the STADE is completed. The STADE is published under a FOSS license.

d) Design work on the Stream Tone Access Device is expanded to include a wide range of device form factors.

e) Design work on the Stream Tone Graphics Interface (STGI) for use with a number of popular operating systems and hypervisors, is started. Development of the STGI is the responsibility of the Stream Tone Community (STC). Design work on the STGI for ***Linux***-based operating systems (STGI for ***Linux***) is completed. Implementation work on the STGI for ***Linux*** is started.

f) Design work on the Stream Tone ***Web*** Browse (STWB) platform is started. Development of the STWB platform is the responsibility of the STC. The STWB platform allows STTP-based ***Web*** browsing services to be built that are able to provide access to all existing ***Web***-based audio-visual content and services. The STWB platform is based on the STGI for ***Linux***. The STWB service uses a wide range of commonly available ***Web Browsers***, ensuring that the ***Web Browsing*** experience will be immediately familiar.

g) Design work on the Stream Tone Service Portal (STSP) is completed. Implementation work on the STSP is started.

h) Design work on the Stream Tone Security Service (STSS) is completed. Implementation work on the STSS is started.

i) The media continues to follow the on-going development of the Stream Tone Technology Ecosystem (STTE).

j) The Stream Tone Community Forum remains the focal point for discussions on the STTE.

k) The non-profit Stream Tone ***Foundation*** (STF) is formally established.

l) The Stream Tone ***Certification Mark*** is globally registered by the STF.

m) Businesses with entrenched investments in non-STTP-based technologies suggest alternatives to the STTP; the STC is largely unmoved by such suggestions.

## 4.4.2.2    SECOND YEAR

a) Implementation of the Stream Tone Graphics Interface (STGI) for ***Linux*** is completed. The STGI for ***Linux*** is published under a ***Free and Open-Source Software*** (FOSS) license.

b) Design work on the Stream Tone *Web* Browse (STWB) platform is completed. Implementation work on the STWB platform is started. Implementation work on the STWB platform is completed. The STWB platform is published under a FOSS license. Design work on a STWB service is started. Design work on a STWB service is competed. Implementation work on a STWB service is started. Implementation work on a STWB service is completed. The first STWB service is launched. Two versions of the STWB service are made available; a free-of-charge version that is funded by advertising and a subscription-based version that is advertising-free. *Internet* service providers and *Cloud Computing*-based *Data Centre* operators start to investigate the technical practicality and commercial viability of the STWB platform.

c) The launch of the first STWB service is paired with the launch of the first Stream Tone Access Device Emulator (STADE) software application. The STWB service can only be accessed using a STADE. The STADE is available, free-of-charge, from all popular *Application Stores*. Versions of the STADE are available for all commonly-used operating systems. A bootable *Live CD* version of the STADE is also made available, for use on a wide range of current personal computing devices, such as desktop computers and laptop computers. The Stream Tone *Live CD* allows the STADE to be run without the need to permanently install the STADE software application or to install a new operating system that specifically supports the STADE. The Stream Tone *Live CD* boots the Stream Tone Operating System, which is an existing *Linux*-based operating system that has simply been re-branded and configured to run a single application, namely the STADE. The STADE is also available via a downloadable *Virtual Machine* image.

d) The STWB service proves to be very popular, with the STADE being downloaded millions of times within its first week of availability.

e) Initial media reports on the STWB service cover a wide range of views, such as "the future of personal computing has arrived today", and "it obviously has great potential but is still very rough around the edges".

f) Design work on the STGI for non-*Linux*-based operating systems, and hypervisors, is started. Design work on the STGI for non-*Linux*-based operating systems, and hypervisors, is completed. Implementation work on the STGI for non-*Linux*-based operating systems, and hypervisors, is started. Implementation work on the STGI for non-*Linux*-based operating systems, and hypervisors, is completed. The STGI for non-*Linux*-based operating systems, and hypervisors, is published under a FOSS license.

g) Implementation work on the Stream Tone Security Service (STSS) is completed. The STSS is published under a FOSS license. The operation of the STSS is passed to a third party that has experience of providing globally available identity and access management solutions. The STSS is activated.

h) Implementation work on the Stream Tone Service Portal (STSP) is completed. The STSP is published under a FOSS license. Various organisations start to investigate the benefits and challenges of running a STSP. The first STSP is launched.

i) *Hosted Desktop* service providers start to investigate the STGI. The first Stream Tone Transfer Protocol (STTP)-based *Hosted Desktop* service is launched.

j)   Design work on a version of the STWB platform that is based on the STGI for non-*Linux*-based operating systems, and hypervisors, is started.

k)   A small number of existing *Web-based Services* announce that they will introduce support for the STTP. New STTP-only services are developed and deployed. The new STTP-based services are built using the Stream Tone Software Development Kit and the STGI. All STTP-based services require the use of a STADE. The first STTP-based services demonstrate that they can only be as good as the service and telecommunications infrastructures that are used to deliver them, with some services suffering from data download caps, limited bandwidth, high-latency communications, unreliable *Internet* connectivity, and high usage costs. STTP-based services, such as the advertising-free version of the STWB service, start to be included into some *Internet* service packages.

l)   Purchases of ".st"-based *Web* domain names increase; some of which are used by new STTP-based services.

m)   Some users complain that many of the new STTP-based services are unacceptably expensive, and they do not understand why. A promotional campaign is launched, which explains the many benefits that the Stream Tone brings to personal computing, such as affordability, convenience, and simplicity. The campaign also explains that whilst many STTP-based services are available free-of-charge, not all can be. Certain types of STTP-based services, for example *Hosted Desktops* that require the use of persistent dedicated hardware, incur non-trivial costs that must consequently be borne by the user.

n)   New impetus is added to discussions on the global transition from *Internet Protocol* version 4 to *Internet Protocol Version 6* (IPv6), as the Stream Tone only supports IPv6 addressing.

o)   The Stream Tone begins to be actively promoted as a viable alternative to local personal computing.

p)   The *Cloud Computing*, digital services, information technology, and telecommunications industries start to evaluate the benefits and challenges associated with the possible widespread adoption of the Stream Tone.

q)   Some businesses with entrenched investments in non-STTP-based technologies launch proprietary alternatives to STTP-based technologies. Whilst others announce that they will start to develop STTP-compliant technologies or operate a STSP. A number of original equipment manufacturers (OEMs) commit to manufacturing a Stream Tone Access Device (STAD).

r)   Design work on the *Field-Programmable Gate Array* (FPGA)-based STAD range is completed. FPGA-based STAD reference designs are published under an *Open Source Hardware* license. Software related to the FPGA-based STAD, such as microcode, is published under a FOSS license. Implementation work on the FPGA-based STAD range, by various OEMs supported by the Stream Tone *Foundation* and the Stream Tone Community, is started.

s)   Some governments start to investigate whether the Stream Tone can assist with their *Universal Service Obligation* for *Internet* access.

# 4.4.2.3    THIRD YEAR

a) The Stream Tone Access Device Emulator (STADE), Stream Tone Graphics Interface (STGI), Stream Tone Software Development Kit (STSDK), Stream Tone Service Portal (STSP), Stream Tone Security Service (STSS), and Stream Tone Transfer Protocol (STTP) continue to evolve and mature, becoming simpler, more efficient, and more reliable.

b) Design work on a version of the Stream Tone *Web* Browse (STWB) platform that is based on the STGI for non-*Linux*-based operating systems, and hypervisors, is completed. Implementation work on a version of the STWB platform that is based on the STGI for non-*Linux*-based operating systems, and hypervisors, is started. Implementation work on a version of the STWB platform that is based on the STGI for non-*Linux*-based operating systems, and hypervisors, is completed. The STWB platform for non-*Linux*-based operating systems, and hypervisors, is published under a *Free and Open-Source Software* (FOSS) license. The first third-party STWB services are launched

c) *Hosted Desktop* services start to support the STTP as standard.

d) Several new STSPs become available. Competition between STSPs is vigorous. The new STSPs have created popular new digital-hubs on the *Internet* that are creative, dynamic, entertaining, fun, and interesting, and, consequently, existing *Internet* portal providers start to see their visitor numbers reduce. Some existing portal providers start to offer STSPs of their own.

e) Users better understand, and accept, the need to pay for certain types of STTP-based services. Some chargeable STTP-based services become highly profitable.

f) STTP-based services are now regularly included in *Internet* service packages.

g) Most high-profile digital services now offer the STTP as a delivery option.

h) New STTP-based services are regularly launched, many of which are only available via the STTP.

i) Many non-STTP-based *Web* services are regularly accessed using a STWB service.

j) Most traditional personal computing devices now support the STTP through the use of STADE functionality.

k) Personal computing devices that have been optimised for use with a STADE are popular purchases because of their affordability, long battery life, and simplicity.

l) For many users, the STADE is the only application software that is directly run on their personal computing devices, all other applications are accessed through STTP-based services.

m) Some mid-range household appliances, such as cookers, refrigerators, microwave ovens, and washing machines, start to include STADE-based functionality.

n) Implementation work on the ***Field-Programmable Gate Array***-based Stream Tone Access device (STAD) range is completed. STAD firmware designs are published under a FOSS license. STAD hardware designs are published under an ***Open-Source Hardware*** license. Design work on an ***Application-Specific Integrated Circuit***-based STAD is started.

o) The first STADs to enter manufacturing are certified by the Stream Tone ***Foundation***, and use of the Stream Tone ***Certification Mark*** is authorised.

p) The first STADs are launched. Available STAD form factors include desktop computer, laptop computer, ***Smart-Phone***, and ***Tablet Computer***. All devices in the STAD range are much cheaper than comparable non-STTP-based personal computing devices.

q) Some STADs are sold in a package that includes a period of free-of-charge ***Internet*** access and STTP-based services.

r) Telecommunications infrastructures evolve and mature to better support the affordability, availability, bandwidth, latency, and reliability requirements of STTP-based services. Many telecommunications service providers (TSPs) partner with ***Cloud Computing***-based ***Data Centre*** operators that are able to provide STTP-based services in close geographic proximity to users. New ***Data Centres***, located in close geographic proximity to users are built, in order to support the low-latency communications required by many STTP-based interactive services. Power-efficient ***Data Centre*** solutions optimised for STTP-based services start to be deployed. TSPs discover that the communications bandwidth requirements of STTP-based devices are more consistent and more predictable than for many non-STTP-based devices; accordingly, ***Internet*** service charges, for users of STADs and STADEs, are reduced.

s) Progress is made on the global transition from ***Internet Protocol*** version 4 to ***Internet Protocol Version 6***.

t) The non-STTP-based technologies that were launched as competitive alternatives to STTP-based technologies are found to be largely unpopular, as public opinion now firmly supports the Stream Tone.

## 4.4.2.4　　FOURTH YEAR

a) After two years of real-world use by millions of users, and three years of development, the Stream Tone Transfer Protocol (STTP) is finalised, having successfully reached long-term stability. The STTP is now ready for ***Application-Specific Integrated Circuit*** (ASIC)-based implementation.

b) A new version of the Stream Tone Access Device Emulator (STADE) application software that supports the final version of the STTP is released free-of-charge.

c) A new version of the firmware, used by ***Field-Programmable Gate Array***-based Stream Tone Access Devices (STADs), which supports the final version of the STTP, is released free-of-charge through a wide variety of digital distribution points.

d) Design work on a STAD based on ASIC technology is completed. ASIC-based STAD reference designs are published under an ***Open Source Hardware*** license. Software related to the ASIC-based STAD, such as microcode, is published under a ***Free and Open-source Software license***. Implementation work on the ASIC-based STAD range, by various OEMs supported by the Stream Tone ***Foundation*** and the Stream Tone Community, is started.

e)   Within most developed countries, STTP-based services are accessible from nearly all urban locations; above ground, below ground, in moving vehicles, at sea within sight of land, and in the air. Within developing countries, demand for STTP-based services is driving substantial investment in modern, cost-effective, service and telecommunications infrastructures.

f)   Progress continues to be made on the global transition from ***Internet Protocol*** version 4 (IPv4) to ***Internet Protocol Version 6*** (IPv6). A number of countries launch highly publicised IPv4 to IPv6 migration initiatives. A few governments and large businesses start to sell freed IPv4 addresses for substantial profit.

g)   New ***Data Centres***, located in close geographic proximity to users, continue to be built.

h)   Many digital services now offer the STTP as a standard delivery option. Some digital services that previously supported a range of communication protocols now only support the STTP.

i)   Third-party Stream Tone ***Web*** Browse services continue to be launched.

j)   Most ***Hosted Desktop*** service providers support the STTP as a standard option.

k)   All ***Internet*** service packages include the provision of STTP-based services, and are priced accordingly.

l)   The Stream Tone Service Portal is now a familiar part of modern life.

## 4.4.2.5   FIFTH YEAR

a)   Implementation work on the ***Application-Specific Integrated Circuit*** (ASIC)-based Stream Tone Access Device (STAD) range is completed. The ASIC-based STAD range is launched. The ASIC-based STAD range is cheaper and more power-efficient than the ***Field-Programmable Gate Array*** (FPGA)-based STAD range.

b)   Production of the FPGA-based STAD range is terminated. Support for the FPGA-based STAD range continues, including in terms of spare parts and repair services.

c)   Sales of the ASIC-based STAD range rapidly increase, whilst sales of non-Stream Tone Transfer Protocol (STTP)-based personal computing devices starts to decrease.

d)   Highly affordable, high bandwidth, low latency, and highly reliable STTP-based services are now ubiquitously available. Some chargeable STTP-based services are highly profitable. The first STTP-based service successfully completes an initial product offering on the London Stock Exchange.

e)   The STTP has become the basis for nearly all personal computing.

f) All existing *Web*-based content and services are available for delivery using the STTP, either directly or via intermediate Stream Tone *Web* Browse (STWB) services.

g) The use of uniform resource identifiers (URIs) based on the ".st" *Web* domain by STTP-based services is now as common as ".com"-based URIs were just a few years earlier.

h) The STAD, in a wide variety of form factors, has become an established part of modern life. Most users do not really notice the difference between their new STTP-based personal computing experience and their old non-STTP-based personal computing experience, as all previously-used functionality continues to be available, if required.

i) STAD prices start to exhibit a steady downward trend, as the fixed technology of the STAD supports on-going materials and manufacturing cost-reductions. STAD original equipment manufacturers (OEMs) employ some of the most highly automated and efficient production lines in the world. Competition between OEMs also helps to drive STAD prices down.

j) Premium versions of the STAD start to be offered, which have cases that are constructed from expensive or highly durable materials but which contain only standard STAD electronics.

k) Many users of Stream Tone Access Device Emulator (STADE)-based personal computing devices start to replace their devices with a STAD.

l) Many users, particularly in wealthy developed nations, often own multiple STADs. Less affluent family units, which in the past might have owned a single non-STTP-based personal computing device, now own at least one STAD per family member.

m) Developed nations start to replace some foreign aid, destined for developing nations, with STADs that are supported with free-of-charge STTP-based services.

n) Many non-STTP-based devices, with built-in data processing capabilities, such as traditional desktop computers, laptop computers, *Smart-Phones*, and *Tablet Computers* are no longer available for purchase or have become very expensive. Such devices are now only used in hostile or geographically remote environments that do not have reliable *Internet* connectivity, or where one hundred percent service uptime is mandatory, such as for certain types of medical equipment and the control of nearly all electromechanical equipment.

o) Many mid-to-high-range household appliances now provide, at little extra cost, interactive, graphical user-interfaces, based on Stream Tone technology, as standard. Household appliance manufacturers use their STTP-based services as key product differentiators.

p) Many governments have built their *Universal Service Obligation* for *Internet* access around the Stream Tone. For qualifying citizens basic STTP-based services, such as STWB services, are made available at competitive rates and services levels.

q) The number of *Data Centres* has substantially increased in order to support the shift to Comprehensive Remote Personal Computing that has been enabled by the introduction of the Stream Tone. New **Data Centres**, located in close geographic proximity to users, continue to be built, particularly within developing nations. **Data Centre** use of STTP-optimised **Cloud Computing** technologies combined with hardware and software standardisation, massive economies of scale, highly efficient resource usage, and infrastructure centralisation have significantly reduced the cost of delivering STTP-based services. **Data Centres** have become the primary customer of nearly all traditional data processing hardware manufacturers, especially those that produce general-purpose microprocessors, graphics processing units, **Hard Disk Drives**, networking equipment, random-access memory, and **Solid-State Drives**. **Data Centre** operators start to influence microprocessor design. **Data Centre** operators are also starting to influence the development of more resource-efficient software applications and operating systems, which are the basis of all STTP-based services.

r)   Freed from the need to develop and update client-side software applications in parallel with server-side functionality, the development of new and improved digital services has accelerated and development costs have significantly reduced. Consequently, the cost of STTP-based services to end-users continues to drop.

s)   Significant progress is made on the global transition from **Internet Protocol** version 4 (IPv4) to **Internet Protocol Version 6** (IPv6). A number of countries have completed their transition, with many more starting or already in progress. Sales of freed IPv4 addresses continue, although at greatly reduced prices. Significant pockets of IPv4 use are expected to continue for the foreseeable future; especially since a notable quantity of IPv4 addresses are now available on the open market. Overall, the need for IPv4 addresses has greatly reduced, as most people now use STADs for all their personal computing needs, which are based solely on IPv6 addressing.

t)   Many manufacturers, that previously produced non-STTP-based devices, and which did not switch over to making STTP-based devices, have either gone out of business or have become STTP-based service providers or Stream Tone Service Portal operators, offering uniquely-styled and highly creative digital experiences in order to preserve their brands and market valuations.

u)   The huge resources that were previously directed at the continual design, development, and deployment of consumer-oriented personal computing devices have been successfully redirected towards improving the quality and diversity of STTP-based services and the affordability, availability, bandwidth, latency, and reliability of global digital service and telecommunications infrastructures.

v)   The Stream Tone has become an established but largely invisible part of the **Internet** and the **Web**. After a few more years, the Stream Tone is likely to only be a notable concern of information technologists, geeks, and esoteric history buffs. The Stream Tone has changed the world for the better, whilst ensuring that it remained comfortably familiar, which is probably the best sort of change you can have.

# 4.5   LESSONS FOR THE FUTURE

*Forewarned is forearmed*

a)   It is probably fair to say that this chapter demonstrates, reasonably well, that it is possible to describe a coherent and believable future based on the Stream Tone. Of course, a brutally honest assessment of this chapter might also conclude that much of this possible future has been described at a very high technical level and that many critically important and complex details have been glossed over or conveniently left out. This lack of detail is, however, wholly necessary given that the Stream Tone has not yet been invented, and the only aspects of it that currently do exist are those that are described in this book. So, regardless of whether or not any coherence or believability relating to the Stream Tone can be perceived from reading this chapter, a vast amount of critically important detail still needs to be defined, and as was mentioned right at the beginning of this book, in the Prologue, the Devil, that is to say, all the really important stuff, most definitely lies in that detail. Therefore, until some of those details start to materialise the Stream Tone will remain a frustratingly vague but tantalising mirage floating just out of reach on the technological horizon. An idea with huge potential that simply needs a lot more work before its true value can be clearly ascertained. Nevertheless, if this general lack of technical detail can, temporarily at least, be put to one side, this chapter does manage to successfully describe the Stream Tone from a wide range of perspectives, and that should still allow a number of useful lessons for the future to be identified.

b)   Firstly, it is encouraging that the various constituent parts of the Stream Tone have been assigned distinct names and acronyms. By defining a Stream Tone nomenclature, specific parts of the Stream Tone can be discussed and considered in isolation, whilst at the same time ensuring that their place in the greater scheme of things can be clearly discerned. Having a Stream Tone nomenclature should really help with the process of clarifying what the Stream Tone should or should not be. The fact that acronyms have also been defined ensures that subsequent references to these parts are kept concise and manageable; because things that are easy to work with have a tendency to actually get worked on. So, whether you have come to love the Stream Tone or hate it, its newly defined nomenclature will now allow you to more easily identify and communicate the parts that bring a smile to your face or a tear to your eye.

c)   In aggregate, the Stream Tone is something that is essentially new and different, but when it is broken down into its individual components it can be seen that it is largely based on, or, rather, intended to be based on, a number of existing concepts and technologies, many of which have already been field-tested and matured. The Stream Tone does not attempt to re-invent the wheel, instead it attempts to function as conceptual and technological glue that connects and supports the use of these existing concepts and technologies in a new and useful way. Such an approach seems eminently sensible as it should significantly help to speed the design, development, and deployment of the Stream Tone, and help to ensure that the cost of such activities can be kept to an absolute minimum.

d)   This chapter identified that even though the Stream Tone is at its heart just another communications protocol for use on computer networks, such as the ***Internet***, it will still need the support of an infrastructure of complementary technologies in order to fulfil its intended purpose, which is to completely move personal computing from a local mode of operation to a remote mode, known as Comprehensive Remote Personal Computing (CRPC). This support infrastructure is known as the Stream Tone Technology Ecosystem (STTE) and is comprised of the Stream Tone Access Device (STAD), Stream Tone Service Infrastructure (STSI), Stream Tone Telecommunications Infrastructure (STTI), and Stream Tone Transfer Protocol (STTP). The STTE is intended to work in the following, simplified, manner: the STSI will be used to generate digital content and services that will then be communicated using the STTP over the STTI to a STAD for user interaction and consumption. Which, from a systems architecture point of view, all seems logically reasonable and constructionally feasible, and, strangely enough, somewhat familiar. In fact, this type of architecture is nothing new, it is used by most modern digital services, which use *Cloud Computing*-based *Data Centres* to generate content and services that are then communicated using the *HyperText Transfer Protocol* over the *Internet* to a *Web Browser* for user interaction and consumption.

e) The development of the STTE will be based on free and open-source principles, and all products of that development will be published under *Free and Open-Source Software* (FOSS) and *Open-Source Hardware* (OSHW) licenses. The STTE will be created by the Stream Tone Community (STC), the membership of which will be comprised of individuals and organisations from the FOSS and OSHW communities. This FOSS and OSHW-based approach should ensure that the Stream Tone in general, and the STTP in particular, cannot be exploited or inappropriately influenced by big business in any way that might restrict access to the Stream Tone to a rich and privileged minority. The Stream Tone is intended to benefit everyone, everywhere, and the application of FOSS and OSHW principles to its development should really help to make that intent a reality.

f) The STC will be supported and partnered with the Stream Tone *Foundation* (STF), a non-profit entity, with minimal staff, that will be able to provide the Stream Tone with a range of administrative, fiduciary, governance, and legal support services. The STF will also supervise the use of the Stream Tone *Certification Mark* that will be used by original equipment manufacturers to indicate that their products correctly support the STTP. Having a distinct legal body to represent the Stream Tone should help to ensure, for example, that the STC will be protected when required and is free to focus purely on the day-to-day aspects of designing, developing, and deploying the STTE.

g) Whilst the responsibility for developing the STTP will primarily lie with the STC, supported by the STF, significant assistance and guidance from *Internet* standards bodies, such as the *Internet Engineering Task Force* and the *World Wide Web Consortium*, on how best to design, develop, and deploy a new *Internet* communications protocol that is largely based on other existing *Internet* communications protocols, will probably be required. Such bodies may even assume direct responsibility for the creation and maturation of the STTP. The *Internet* standards bodies are probably the very best organisations to help bring the STTP into existence as they have extensive experience in developing new communications protocols for use on the *Internet*. They should also be able to ensure that the STTP complies with all existing rules and *Regulations* pertaining to *Internet* communications and that the STTP does not interfere with any of the normal operations of the *Internet*. Quite frankly, not involving at least one of the *Internet* standards bodies in the creation of the STTP would be somewhat cavalier and foolish. Thankfully this does not seem to be the case, which is most sensible and encouraging.

h) The success of the Stream Tone will, to a large degree, be dependent on its adoption by third-party developers that will use it to provide STTP-based services. Encoding and decoding data to and from the STTP format will be handled by the Stream Tone Transfer Protocol Encoder (STTPE) and the Stream Tone Transfer Protocol Decoder (STTPD), respectively. Together the STTPE and the STTPD will comprise the Stream Tone Transfer Protocol Codec (STTP-CODEC). Software routines that implement the STTP-CODEC, and other STTP-related functionalities, will be provided by the Stream Tone Software Development Kit (STSDK), which will comprise of the Stream Tone *Application Programming Interface* and Stream Tone Function Library. A remote desktop display and control solution that will be known as the Stream Tone Graphics Interface will be built using the STSDK. The provision of a software development kit is the industry standard approach for supporting third-party development of new digital technologies, such as the Stream Tone. The STSDK is intended for use by developers that wish to support the STTP within their own application software and digital services. The remote desktop display and control solution provided by the STGI will ensure that most existing operating systems, and the application software that runs on those operating systems, will be accessible using the STTP without the need to alter those operating systems or that application software. Access to Stream Tone-related functionalities will be provided in a way that should be very familiar to existing digital service developers, and compatible with existing development tools, such as integrated development environments, which will ensure that adoption of the Stream Tone by the development community will be relatively painless and straightforward, and comparable in cost to developing for other digital technologies that also support a SDK-based development approach.

i) Being able to ensure the safe transmission of the user and intellectual property data that will be communicated by the STTP will be crucially important to the ultimate success of the Stream Tone. If the STTP cannot protect such data whilst it is communicating it then the Stream Tone will stand absolutely no chance of winning the trust of its potential users, and will, consequently, become a complete non-starter in the race for the future of personal computing. To succinctly address this issue, the STTP is intended to be based on one or more existing communication protocols that already support mature and field-proven data protection mechanisms, such as strong *Encryption*, which can be used to secure user and intellectual property data whilst it is being transmitted over computer networks, such as the *Internet*. By re-using existing communications protocols the STTP should be able to immediately provide secure and trustworthy data carriage, win the trust of its users, and allay any concerns that might have been otherwise raised over the STTP's suitability to safely carry such data. This seems like an eminently sensible approach for ensuring that the STTP will be able to provide a believably secure data transfer capability right from the very start.

j) The STAD is intended to be a low-cost *Thin Client* that completely relies on STTP-based services for its operation. The STAD is, for all intents and purposes, just a modern incarnation of the dumb computer terminal that was commonly used to access mainframe computer-based services in the 1970s. The STAD will not require the use of an operating system and will not be able to run user-space application software. Characteristics which should greatly help to ensure that the STAD is likely to be much more reliable and much lower maintenance than any comparable traditional personal computing device. STADs are expected to be available in a wide range of different form factors, including computer monitors, desktop computers, eyeglasses, games consoles, laptop computers, *Smart-Phones*, *Tablet Computers*, televisions, and wristwatches, to name but a few. STADs are also expected to be built into domestic appliances, such as cookers, microwave ovens, refrigerators, and washing machines, where they will help to future-proof equipment that generally has a very long working life. STADs are not intended to be a niche product but will have a broad applicability which should significantly help to drive their adoption and consequently the swift and efficient replacement of most traditional personal computing devices. All STADs, regardless of their form factor, will share standardised control electronics that are based on familiar and mature technologies. This standardisation, combined with the relative simplicity of the control electronics that are needed to drive an essentially dumb device, and the economies of scale that will be possible when manufacturing STADs in very high volumes, should help to ensure that the STAD will be a very affordable technology. The availability of STADs in a wide range of different form factors should help to ensure that there is a STAD for every occasion and taste. Additionally, the operational simplicity of the STAD, due to its essentially dumb nature, should help to lower barriers to its adoption and subsequent integration into daily life as the definitive tool for CRPC.

k) STSIs are intended to be based on current and next generation service infrastructures. The digital services industry that predominantly creates and owns those infrastructures is, on the whole, focused on the common needs of the majority of its customers and, consequently, will not readily change to support the particular needs of anything new, such as the Stream Tone, unless it is driven to do so by the bulk of those customers. The Stream Tone sensibly recognises such practical limitations and, consequently, will seek to simply advise those infrastructures on how they can be better optimised for use by STTP-based services. Although the amount of control that the Stream Tone will have over the service infrastructures that comprise the STSIs is likely to be very limited, including such infrastructures within the framework of the STTE should greatly help to ensure that the elements of those infrastructures that are likely to be important to the Stream Tone can be fully considered at the earliest stages of the STTE design, development, and deployment processes. The Stream Tone also makes a number of suggestions on how developers can use the STSDK to support the Stream Tone Transfer Protocol from within application software and digital services. A STSI is expected to include two key services; the Stream Tone Security Service (STSS) and Stream Tone Service Portal (STSP). The STSS will provide *Multi-Factor Authentication* (MFA) and *Single Sign-On* (SSO) functionality, and the STSP will provide the principle user-oriented mechanism for finding and accessing STTP-based services. The STSP is supplied in the form of application software to STSP operators that are then expected to apply their own unique branding to the STSP graphical user-interface. Use of the STSS is mandated for the STSP. Once a user has been validated by the MFA functionality, the SSO functionality will allow that user to access other STTP-based services that also support the STSS without the need to log on to each individual service. The STSS is intended to be a globally-available service that will be provided by an experienced provider of identity and access management solutions. The governance of the STSS will be a key responsibility of the STF. Overall, the Stream Tone appears to contain all the elements needed to support the provision of STTP-based services. The Stream Tone appears to place very few new or unique demands on the service infrastructures that will comprise the STSIs, a characteristic that should help to ensure that the Stream Tone will face very few barriers to adoption from within the digital services industry.

l) STTIs are intended to be based on current and next generation telecommunications infrastructures. The telecommunications industry that creates and owns those infrastructures is, on the whole, the master of its own fate, and, consequently, will not readily change to support the particular needs of anything new, such as the Stream Tone, unless it really wants or needs to do so. The Stream Tone sensibly recognises such practical limitations and, consequently, will seek to simply advise those infrastructures on how they can be better optimised for use by the Stream Tone. If that approach fails then it will most probably be the Stream Tone that has to change, if compatibility between such infrastructures and the Stream Tone is ever going to be achieved. Overall, it appears that the approach that has been identified for creating the STTIs is definitely one based on taking the path of least resistance and seeking to win the battles that can be won, whilst recognising that there will be many other battles that can probably never be won and thus best avoided. Additionally, even though the amount of control that the Stream Tone will have over the telecommunications infrastructures that comprise the STTIs is likely to be very limited, including such infrastructures within the framework of the STTE should greatly help to ensure that the elements of those infrastructures that are likely to be important to the Stream Tone can be fully considered at the earliest stages of the STTE design, development, and deployment processes. One of the key requirements that the Stream Tone will have for the STTI is that it will need to be able to provide high bandwidth communications and very large quantities of downloaded data. Wired communications bandwidths are already at the sort of levels required to support the efficient and effective operation of STTP-based services, and wireless communications bandwidths are rapidly catching up. The total quantity of very high bandwidth data that can cost-effectively be downloaded wirelessly in a given period of time, such as per month, is currently being limited by the telecommunications industry, and at this point in time it is probably several orders of magnitude too small to support practical CRPC. However, as the telecommunications infrastructures used to access the *Internet* continue to improve, it should not be too long, relatively speaking, before the data download requirements of the Stream Tone can be cost-effectively met. At first glance, the fact that the Stream Tone is based on a requirement that is not even remotely possible today, such as being able to cost-effectively wirelessly-download very large quantities of data per month, seems somewhat flawed and illogical. However, any review of the past developments in the telecommunications industry will show that there is a clearly discernible trend of continual improvement and cost reduction that strongly suggests that the Stream Tone will eventually be able to get all that it needs in terms of affordable data download quantities. In fact, the Stream Tone will most probably depend on a number of capabilities and technologies, not just in terms of affordable data download quantities, that may not become available for quite some time. Starting the creation of the Stream Tone as early as possible should help to ensure that by the time all the required capabilities and technologies do become available that the Stream Tone will definitely be ready and able to make good use of them. This is simply planning for the future, based on a belief that past trends in telecommunications will continue in the future, which is not at all flawed or illogical. It does, of course, represent a leap of faith, but not an unreasonable one, given that this is still a very early stage in the life of the Stream Tone.

m)   The use cases contained in this chapter describe a number of scenarios in which Stream Tone-based technology is used in some fairly common situations and environments to access a wide range of STTP-based content and services. Many of the scenarios appear to be quite familiar, mundane, and realistic, and not at all science fictional. In fact, the scenarios could have, with just a few small alterations, just as easily described the use of products and services that are based on current technologies, instead of the Stream Tone. The use cases help to show just how small a change the Stream Tone is actually making to the practicalities of personal computing whilst simultaneously creating a substantial foundation for a future that supports both accelerated development and technical stability. From a functional perspective the Stream Tone is not intended to turn the world upside-down, rather, it consciously encourages and supports the recreation of the types of user experiences that are currently familiar and comfortable. Of course, the Stream Tone can also allow STTP-based services to be built and operate in wholly new and exciting ways, if that is required, which it undoubtedly will be at some point. Being able to support the creation of familiar user experiences should help the Stream Tone become a ready-to-go slot-in replacement for many current local personal computing services, a characteristic that should significantly help to speed its adoption and subsequent integration into daily life as the definitive tool for CRPC. Being able to support the creation of new user experiences should also help to ensure that the Stream Tone will become a key technology platform of the future.

n)   From a commercial perspective, it is not expected that the Stream Tone will significantly change the way that businesses, such as digital service providers or product manufacturers, operate. The Stream Tone will be able to support business-as-usual, whilst providing opportunities to try something new, if desired or required. The Stream Tone is expected to be able to support the use of all commonly used business models, which suggests that it will be compatible with most types of business. In terms of economics, the Stream Tone is not some sort of technological magic bullet that makes all the costs of personal computing disappear. On the contrary, there has always been a cost associated with personal computing, even if it was not always obvious to a typical user, and there probably always will be. What the Stream Tone will do is simply reallocate most of those costs from capital to operational expenditure. So, whilst there are expected to be definite savings in terms of the cost of the device that is used to access STTP-based services, there are also likely to be some very noticeable, and largely unavoidable, cost increases due to the greater use of chargeable services. However, as the STTE matures, costs associated with the development, provision, delivery, and access of STTP-based services, should start to reduce. Initially, the cost of developing STTP-based services will probably be similar to the current cost of developing non-STTP-based services. Over time, the fact that the development of STTP-based services will be wholly focused within the **Data Centre**, and not on the user's access device, should help to ensure that many development costs will be reduced. Initially, the cost of providing most STTP-based services will probably be similar to the current cost of providing non-STTP-based services. Over time, as the service infrastructures used by a STSI to provide those services improve and become better optimised for use with the STTP, the cost of provision should reduce. Although, some types of STTP-based services, that require the use of dedicated and persistent resources, may always be quite expensive. The STSIs that will be used to provide STTP-based services will generally need to be located in close geographic proximity to the users of those services. New STSIs will need to be constructed in geographies that do not already possess suitable infrastructures, and the construction cost will most probably have to be recovered through higher service charges. Initially, the cost of delivering STTP-based services will probably be similar to the current cost of delivering non-STTP-based services. Over time, as the telecommunications infrastructures used by the STTIs to deliver those services improve and become better optimised for use with the STTP, the cost of delivery should reduce. The STADs that are used to access STTP-based services are intended to be low-cost hardware devices that contain standardised control electronics. Initially that might not be possible, but over a relatively short period of time, as the process of manufacturing a STAD becomes optimised, the manufacturing cost should reduce. New technologies can often catalyse the creation of new products and services based on, or around, those technologies. The creation of the Stream Tone is expected to stimulate the creation of many new products and services, some of which may adopt trade names based on, or related to, the Stream Tone nomenclature. Some businesses may even adopt uniform resource identifiers based on the ".st" **Internet** country-code top-level domain for the Democratic Republic of São Tomé and Príncipe. The STSP is expected to be the principle mechanism for accessing STTP-based services, and can be configured by STSP operators that want to create their own uniquely branded user experiences. Overall, the Stream Tone appears to be compatible with most aspects of modern business, and should, therefore, experience little resistance to its adoption from a commercial perspective.

o)   The timeline describing how the Stream Tone might be emerge, and become a part of normal everyday personal computing life, paints an obviously optimistic view of that process. Nevertheless, it contains some very interesting suggestions on what might happen in the years between the invention of the STTP and the subsequent worldwide adoption of STTP-based CRPC. The timeline shows that there will be many intermediate steps, and that it will not necessarily be plain sailing all the way, with many developmental, societal, and technical challenges to be overcome. There will also be some degree of resistance to the Stream Tone and all the changes that it will consequently bring. The adoption of the Stream Tone will upset the status quo and may negatively impact many established digital service providers and personal computing device manufacturers. The Stream Tone is also likely to catalyse the creation of many new businesses, products, and services. Most of the elements contained within the timeline are generally believable, once the basic premise that the Stream Tone will eventually replace the world's current personal computing paradigm has been accepted. The timeline describes the period of elapsed time that the Stream Tone will take to become established in terms of a number of years, which seems a very realistic time frame, given how long **Smart-Phones** and **Tablet Computers** recently took to become similarly established. Overall, the timeline appears to be a most useful tool for setting expectations relating to the establishment of the Stream Tone, and for identifying some of the many intermediate steps that will be required on the Stream Tone's journey from inception to maturity.

p) The lessons for the future identified in this chapter should allow the Stream Tone to be discussed in far more concrete terms. Such discussions should help to better define what the Stream Tone will actually be, and the processes by which it will be designed, developed, and deployed.

# 5 REFLECTIONS

*All things considered*

a)  The Stream Tone may well be greater than the sum of its individual parts, but it is only as strong as its weakest part or the weakest link between those parts, and like all complex technologies has advantages and disadvantages. The advantages and disadvantages presented in this section are not unique to the Stream Tone as most of them stem from the many different technologies from which the Stream Tone is expected to be built.

b)  The advantages and disadvantages described below should not be considered to be definitive or exhaustive, simply representative of some of the advantages and disadvantages that the Stream Tone may possess. The advantages and disadvantages have primarily been included in order to expand upon some of the consequences, ideas, and thinking briefly touched upon in earlier sections of this book. The advantages and disadvantages are ordered alphabetically based on their section titles.

## 5.1 ADVANTAGES

*Not too bad*

### 5.1.1 BEST PRACTICE

a)  The Stream Tone Service Infrastructures (STSIs), that will be used to provide Stream Tone Transfer Protocol (STTP)-based services, will be based on *Cloud Computing* technologies. All of the many benefits that *Cloud Computing* offers will therefore be available to a STSI, and all the STTP-based services provided by that STSI. *Cloud Computing* can be used to enhance agility, availability, collaboration, and scaling. It also offers the potential for significant cost reductions through the efficient and effective use of data processing resources. *Cloud Computing* is typically characterised by broad network access, measured service, multi-tenancy, on-demand self-service, rapid elasticity, and resource pooling. *Cloud Computing*-based infrastructure is built from a wide range of rapidly evolving technologies, such as energy-efficient microprocessors, *Free and Open-Source Software*, micro-servers, *Open-Source Hardware*, open standards, *Optical Fibre*-based communications, redundant power supplies, renewable energy supplies, *Software-Defined Networking*, standardised commodity hardware, standardised commodity software, tiered data storage, and virtualisation.

b)  The *Cloud Computing* industry is highly competitive, and, consequently, continually seeks to improve its services in order to win new customers and retain existing customers. Many of the services that the *Cloud Computing* industry offers are only possible because of the centralised nature of *Cloud Computing*, in which highly concentrated hardware and software-based infrastructures are used to simultaneously support very large numbers of customers that all have, at one level or another, very similar needs. This allows *Cloud Computing*-based service providers to not only offer a wide range of services but to offer services that support a wide range of industry best practices. Many organisations are not able to adopt best practices because they are too small, the practices are too expensive, or the practices require a level of expertise that is not available within their organisation and are therefore not practical. ***Cloud Computing***-based service providers are able to offer best practice-based services because the cost of providing those services can be shared between its many paying customers. Also, the use of some best practices is mandated in certain industries, and the ***Cloud Computing*** industry really has no option but to provide such best practice-based services in order to win business from customers that operate within such industries.

c)  ***Cloud Computing***-based services are able to support a wide range of industry best practices, particularly in the governance and operational domains. Some of the governance best practices that are supported include: compliance and audit; governance and enterprise risk management; information lifecycle management; legal and electronic discovery; portability and interoperability. Some of the operational best practices that are supported include: application security; ***Data Centre*** operations; ***Encryption*** and key management; identity and access management; incident response, notification, and remediation; traditional security, business continuity, and disaster recovery; and virtualisation. Customers that might not have been able to implement such best practices in the past are now able to easily obtain them simply by paying a usage or time-based fee.

d)  So, as the adoption of the Stream Tone increases, so too will the ability of STTP-based services to support best practices, in terms such as accessibility, audit, availability, consistency, continuity, compliance, durability, interoperability, maintainability, performance, portability, recoverability, reliability, resiliency, security, supportability, and upgradeability, as standard.

# 5.1.2    COMPATIBLE

a)  The application software and operating systems that the Stream Tone will be able to support are exactly the same as the application software and operating systems that are in common use today. The only difference is that instead of running such application software and operating systems on a local personal computing device they will be run on remotely-located ***Cloud Computing***-based Stream Tone Service Infrastructures (STSIs). With the exception of tasks that are dependent on the use of specialised hardware, everything that could previously be run on a local personal computing device will be able to run on a STSI.

b)  The way that all of this will be achieved is that the audio-visual output from a software application or operating system running on a STSI will be sent to a Stream Tone Access Device (STAD) for presentation to a user, and any input from that user will be sent to the STSI for appropriate data processing. This behaviour is very similar to the way old mainframe computers used to work in cooperation with their dumb computer terminals. It is also very similar to how modern ***Web*** surfing works. A ***Web*** page is sent from a ***Web*** server to a ***Web Browser*** for display. Any user interaction with the ***Web*** page, such as a mouse click, effectively gets sent back to the ***Web*** server for processing, causing the ***Web*** page to be updated and sent with different content to the ***Web Browser*** for display.

c)  The fact that the Stream Tone will be inherently compatible with all existing software-based personal computing technologies, will be a critically important factor as it seeks to gain mass acceptance as a replacement for most current personal computing platforms. This high degree of compatibility will help to minimise the cost and inconvenience of migrating from traditional personal computing devices to STADs and STSIs, and ensure that any associated learning curve will be shallow and short. It will also help to avoid much of the resistance that would surely have arisen had the Stream Tone required the use of completely new application software and operating systems. In fact, compared to many previous technological changes in similar fields, the move to the Stream Tone should be quite painless and straightforward.

# 5.1.3     CRIME

a)   Modern personal computing devices, such as desktop computers, laptop computers, **Smart-Phones**, and **Tablet Computers**, are available in a very wide range of constantly updated designs. Some of these devices, particularly the very latest top-of-the-range models that are considered to be the most attractive, capable, and desirable, can be very expensive to purchase, and are, therefore, beyond the fiscal reach of a significant section of society. Consequently, there has been a notable trend in crime relating to such devices, particularly theft, some of which also involves intimidation and physical violence. Some stolen devices are sold to either knowing or unsuspecting buyers and some are stripped down and sold for spare parts. Some legislatures have attempted, with variable success, to mandate that manufacturers include anti-theft technologies into such devices. Anti-theft technologies are able to remotely disable such devices after they have been stolen, which makes them much less valuable. Some active anti-theft technologies can even be used to trace the whereabouts of a stolen device, enabling law enforcement officials to arrest the criminals responsible, and return the stolen device to its rightful owner. Unfortunately, such anti-theft technologies are only installed on a relatively small proportion of devices, and actually activated on even less.

b)   The Stream Tone may be able to reduce such crime, without the use of active anti-theft technologies, by simplifying and standardising personal computing devices. The Stream Tone Access Device (STAD) will be a simple hardware-based device for accessing Stream Tone Transfer Protocol-based content and services. STADs will be available in a wide range of form factors, including desktop computer, laptop computer, **Smart-Phone**, and **Tablet Computer**. All STADs will share a common, or standardised, set of control electronics. The capabilities of a STAD, of a particular form factor, will also be standardised. Such standardisations will allow STADs to be manufactured very cost effectively, meaning that STADs will be affordable by everyone, everywhere. One STAD will be identical to another, save for perhaps small aesthetic variations that allow one STAD manufacturer to visually distinguish its offerings from those of another. Additionally, STADs will be very long-lasting, because they will be fully repairable, highly modular, and have affordable spare parts. Consequently, when there is far less variation in the capabilities, construction materials, design, repairability, and value of our personal computing devices there should, hopefully, be far less crime associated with such devices. Of course, wherever and whenever there is an opportunity to turn a quick profit at the expense of others there will always be crime, but, as a general rule, when products and services become more affordable, available, durable, maintainable, and less exclusive they become much less likely to be the targets of criminal activity. The high price and exclusivity of certain personal computing devices appears to be actively driving crime, whilst an affordable and standardised alternative, such as the STAD, should, in theory, be able to do the opposite.

# 5.1.4    DESIGN

a)    The Stream Tone Access Device (STAD) will have a fixed functional design, both in terms of hardware and software. Other technologies that have also benefited from having fixed functional designs include the electronic calculator, digital wristwatch, radio receiver, telephone handset, and television. Technologies with fixed functional designs can be optimised so that they deliver good enough performance at ever reducing price points.

b)    In the United Kingdom, the earliest telephones could not generally be purchased, only rented from a national telephone company, which maintained a tight control over what sort of devices could be connected to its wire-based telephony network. When telephones did eventually become available for sale they were quite expensive, and even to this very day still have to be approved by a national telephony regulator before they are allowed to be connected to the national telephone network. However, as the principle nature and interfaces of a typical telephone have remained largely unchanged for many years, the telephone has been able to become very affordable. The cost of a telephone was reduced little by little through a programme of iterative redesign, also known as cost-reduction exercises, in which the cost of manufacturing a new telephone was minimised whilst ensuring that the new telephone was still able to comply with the telephone approvals process required to connect a telephone to the telephony network. Similar cost-reduction exercises have also been applied to electronic calculators, digital wristwatches, and radio receivers. Some of the first portable electronic calculators became widely available in the early 1970s and cost several hundred US dollars, but today they are available for a few bucks. The capabilities of such calculators are almost identical to their predecessors. They can add, divide, multiply, and subtract. All the things that you would expect from a basic calculator. However, in marked contrast to their predecessors, if you were to open one up and look inside, you would be surprised by just how little they now contain. Part of the reason for this is the incredible miniaturisation of electronic components that has occurred over the last 50 years, which has resulted in a calculator's central processing unit becoming an almost microscopic speck embedded in a blob of cheap melted plastic. It is also due to numerous cost-reduction exercises that have optimised the calculator so that it now uses the bare minimum of constructions materials, as can now be seen by the fact that many internal connecting wires are now unsheathed to shave a bit extra off the bill of materials. The end result is a device that is just good enough for its job; even after all the cost reductions that have been applied. The same sort of cost reduction can also be seen with digital wristwatches that were similarly expensive when they were launched but which can now cost less than one US dollar. Of course, at such a price, this would be the most basic of wristwatches but it would still be able to fulfil all the requirements for a fully-functional timepiece, albeit one housed in a simple plastic enclosure. The radio receiver has a similar history; initially being very expensive, but subsequently reducing substantially in price.

c)    As the STAD will also have a fixed nature and interfaces it is expected that similar cost-reduction exercises will be able to ensure that it will eventually be possible to manufacture STADs, in a wide range of form factors, for a fraction of the cost required to manufacture traditional personal computing devices. The increasingly low price of STADs is expected to lead to a significant increase in the use of the ***Internet***, personal computing devices, and ***Web*** around the world, particularly in developing countries.

# 5.1.5   DEVELOPMENT

a)   The Stream Tone will be based on client-server technology in which a dumb client, the Stream Tone Access Device (STAD), communicates with a remotely-located Stream Tone Service Infrastructure (STSI)-based computer server. As long as the digital services that are provided by that server are always communicated using the Stream Tone Transfer Protocol (STTP) then those services can be changed in any way required. Both the hardware and software used to provide a STTP-based service can be changed without involving the STAD, or its user, with the result that after a service change has been successfully implemented all a user will see is a new and improved service. The actual act of changing the service is effectively hidden from the user.

b)   Many current **Web-based Services** that are accessed using a **Web Browser** offer similar benefits, as a typical **Web** site or **Web-based Service** can easily be changed without requiring a corresponding change to the **Web Browser**. However, **Web Browser** application software is continually evolving, and often requires regular replacement, patching, and the installation of functional enhancements. So whilst **Web** sites and **Web-based Services** might be able to evolve independently of the **Web Browser** used to access them, the **Web Browser** also needs to evolve in ways that are independent of the **Web**-based content and services that it is used to access, as it seeks, in its own right, to become a better **Web Browsing** tool. Whilst similar, the Stream Tone will not be a **Web Browser**-based technology, as the data that will be communicated between a STSI and a STAD will be much more primitive; primarily consisting of basic audio-visual and user-input data. Support for these data primitives will be inherent in the capabilities of a STAD, and there will be little reason for them to change, and, consequently, there will be little reason for a STAD to change, unlike a **Web Browser**.

c)   This means that STTP-based services will be able to change and STADs will not need to follow. A situation that creates great stability for the user, and increased flexibility and opportunities for the digital services provider. The digital services provider will be able to upgrade its services at a greatly accelerated rate as it no longer has to wait for its users to play their usual parts in the upgrade process; a most liberating circumstance that should greatly benefit both business and society as a whole.

# 5.1.6   ENERGY

a)   A typical Stream Tone Access Device (STAD) will consume very little power, perhaps an average of a few watts or even less,[28] compared to a more traditional personal computing device, such as a desktop computer, that can easily consume more than 100 watts. The principle reason for this is that all of the digital content and services that a STAD will be used to access will be provided by a Stream Tone Service Infrastructure (STSI). STSIs will be based on **Cloud Computing** technologies that are run in remotely-located **Data Centres**. A typical **Data Centre** is able to make very efficient and effective use of its data processing resources, unlike a home or office-based personal computing device, which cannot. In fact, when compared on a watt for watt basis with a traditional personal

---

[28] *A subjectively determined estimate of the power efficiency that a Stream Tone Access Device would need to support in order to be able to continuously operate at a useful level for an extended period of time, such as one week.*

computing device, a **Data Centre** is a veritable paragon of economy.

b)   Nevertheless, a typical **Data Centre** is still far from perfect because, in absolute terms, it uses a huge amount of electricity that is often generated from the burning of non-renewable energy resources, such as fossil fuels, to power its computer servers and cooling systems. The burning of fossil fuels can release greenhouse gases, such as carbon dioxide, into the atmosphere, which can potentially lead to an unwanted rise in global temperatures. Even in the best **Data Centres**, the computer servers still use electricity relatively inefficiently, causing them to get hot, and because computer servers can malfunction if they get too hot such servers need to be cooled. The cooling systems within a typical **Data Centre** can often require more electricity to cool the computer servers than is needed to operate those servers. The cooling systems can also use very large quantities of water. Given that even an average sized **Data Centre** can house many thousands of servers, the electrical and water requirements of a typical **Data Centre** can be most substantial.

c)   Increasingly, modern **Data Centres** are now being designed to use electricity and water in the most efficient of ways, and which would be impractical to reproduce in a typical home or office setting. The computer servers, used within such **Data Centres**, now contain energy efficient central processing units and storage systems, and are closely mounted together in racks that are then mounted within arrays of cabinets. The cabinets are typically supplied with electrical power in the correct format for direct use, which ensures that the servers do not need to have their own individual power supplies; something that can be quite inefficient. The high density of servers found within a typical cabinet maximises the efficacy of the centrally supplied cool air, and the segregation of air flows into warm and cold isles helps to boost efficacy even further. **Data Centres** are now often run at much higher temperatures than in the past, which also helps to reduce overall cooling requirements. Some **Data Centres** are geographically located where it is naturally cold, or where large bodies of cold water are available, in order to greatly reduce the amount of electricity used for cooling. Other **Data Centres** use electricity produced from renewable sources, such as wind power or hydro-electric schemes, to chill refrigerants overnight when electricity is both cheaper and not required for other things. **Data Centres** that use such techniques can be incredibly efficient and effective, compared to the same data processing resources being located in a number of home or office-based personal computing devices. The computer servers used within a **Data Centre** typically run virtualised operating systems that can be dynamically provisioned, activated, or deactivated based on real-time demand. Virtualisation can help to ensure that servers are always efficiently and effectively utilised, and, when demand drops, any idle or underutilised servers can be shut down, ensuring that electrical power is only used when it is really needed.

d)   Of course, the energy efficiencies of the modern **Data Centre** will not be limited to just the Stream Tone, because most modern digital services are run in the exact same way. What is different with the Stream Tone is that when a user starts using a STAD to access Stream Tone Transfer Protocol-based services, they will be replacing energy-inefficient traditional personal computing devices with an energy-efficient STAD and STSI-provided services, which will yield a net reduction in energy consumption. When aggregated over the life of millions or billions of STADs, the reduction in the consumption of non-renewable energy resources should be very significant.

# 5.1.7   ENVIRONMENTAL

a)   The process of manufacturing a personal computing device typically uses a lot of energy and consumes large quantities raw materials; an approach that is ultimately unsustainable in the long-term. Using less energy and raw materials is good for the planet. A lot of energy generated today is derived from the burning of fossil fuels, which is a finite non-renewable resource, and which emits carbon dioxide, and other greenhouse gases, into the atmosphere. A lot of plastics that are used in the construction of personal computing devices are also derived from fossil fuels such as oil. Personal computing devices also contain a number of rare elements that must be mined from the ground, which is an energy intensive activity that can also lead to greenhouse gas emissions and other environmental pollution.

b)   Stream Tone Access Devices (STADs) will be available in a wide range of physical forms, with *Smart-Phones* and *Tablet Computers* being some of the most common. The energy and raw materials required to construct a STAD is expected to be much less than for a comparable personal computing device of traditional design, because a STAD is a much simpler device. Requiring less energy and raw materials means that there will be a corresponding reduction in embodied emissions; the release of greenhouse gases associated with the extraction and transportation of raw materials, the transformation of raw materials into products, the delivery of products to customers, and the eventual disposal of those products at the end of their working life.

c)   The long life expected of a STAD may cause a shift away from the use of plastics, often used for device enclosures, towards metal, such as aluminium, which is typically more durable and also very easy to recycle. So the introduction of the Stream Tone may lead to a significant reduction in the energy and raw materials used by the personal computing device manufacturing industry, and also a shift towards the use of more durable materials that are easier to recycle.

# 5.1.8   FAMILIAR

a)   The Stream Tone changes the way that personal computing functionality is accessed. It moves personal computing away from local personal computing devices and onto Stream Tone Transfer Protocol (STTP)-based services that are provided by remotely-located Stream Tone Service Infrastructures (STSIs) and delivered by Stream Tone Telecommunications Infrastructures to Stream Tone Access Devices (STADs).

b)   Local personal computing functionality will be replaced by either a STTP-based equivalent or a virtualised version of that functionality that has been migrated onto a STSI and then communicated using the STTP. STTP-based services will be able to provide access to all existing operating systems and software applications, if required. The user-experience when accessing operating systems and software applications through a STTP-based service will be identical to accessing those operating systems and software applications on a local personal computing device, ensuring that familiar approaches to play and work will not need to be changed. The STAD will be available in a wide range of familiar form factors, including desktop computer, laptop computer, *Smart-Phone*, and *Tablet Computer*. STADs will support a wide range of familiar peripherals, including cameras, document scanners, fax machines, game controllers, keyboards, mice, and printers. The STAD will support a wide range of familiar wired and wireless communications technologies, such as **Bluetooth**, **Fourth-Generation Mobile Communications**, **Wi-Fi**, and wired networking, which will allow STTP-based services to be accessed from familiar locations and under familiar circumstances.

c)   The fact that the Stream Tone will be able to recreate a familiar personal computing experience should significantly help to minimise any resistance that may exist to the transition from local personal computing to STTP-based Comprehensive Remote Personal Computing. Of course, the Stream Tone will also support wholly different, new, and unfamiliar ways of playing and working as well.

# 5.1.9   MOORE'S LAW

a)   In 1965 Gordon E. Moore, co-founder of Intel Corporation, had a paper published in the 19th April 1965 edition of "Electronics", titled "Cramming More Components onto Integrated Circuits". The paper described the trend in the number of components, or transistors, per integrated circuit for minimum cost that had occurred between 1959 and 1964. Moore extrapolated this trend to 1975, predicting that as many as 65,000 transistors per integrated circuit for minimum cost would then be possible. The trend that Moore observed became an industry standard known as Moore's law, which stated that the number of transistors on integrated circuits doubles approximately every two years. In actuality, Moore's law is not really a law in the classic sense, but an observation or conjecture. So far, since its inception, Moore's law has roughly held true, but as the size of the integrated circuit components get ever smaller it may not be able to remain so for much longer. As the components get smaller they become both harder and more expensive to fabricate, and also more difficult to operate with the level of reliability required by digital logic. Integrated circuits are manufactured in semiconductor chip fabrication plants, and Rock's law, created by Arthur Rock, states that the cost of a semiconductor chip fabrication plant doubles every four years.

b)   Given that integrated circuits power many modern digital electronic devices, the capabilities of such devices are all directly linked to Moore's law. So, as the number of transistors on an integrated circuit increases so too does the energy efficiency, image sensor resolution, memory capacity, and processing speed of those devices. Over the years, these ever increasing capabilities, expressed in terms of faster processing speeds, greater energy efficiency, higher resolution image sensors, and more memory, have been used very effectively to market such devices to both new and repeat customers. In fact, marketing based on such increased capabilities has been a notable driving force for technological change within society, one that has not only spurred significant progress but also the premature and wasteful replacement of many modern technologies that were still useful, by creating the perception that such technologies had become obsolete due to the availability of newer and better technologies. Consumer demand for ever-greater capabilities is now unrelenting, and it is very likely that one day in the relatively near future that it will no longer be possible to cost-effectively add any more components onto an integrated circuit. At which point, the capabilities of many digital electronic devices, and the technology fields that they underpin, will start to plateau. In fact, this has already started to happen to some degree, with the result that multiple integrated circuits are now being used in parallel as a way to cost-effectively increase energy efficiency, memory capacity, and processing speeds. The use of multiple integrated circuits for image sensing has not yet entered the mainstream, although it probably will not be very long before it does.

c) The Stream Tone works in a different way. It uses a Stream Tone Access Device (STAD) to access Stream Tone Transfer Protocol (STTP)-based content and services that are provided by a remotely-located Stream Tone Service Infrastructure (STSI) and delivered using a Stream Tone Telecommunications Infrastructure. The STAD contains an integrated circuit, or microprocessor, that is just sufficient to support its audio-visual presentation responsibilities and no more. All the hard work, the intensive data processing that is needed to create such content and services, is provided by a STSI. The *Cloud Computing*-based *Data Centres* used by a STSI are not as constrained by electrical power or physical space requirements as a modern portable personal computing device. For example, a modern *Smart-Phone* must be small enough to fit into a trouser pocket or handbag and be able to run for several days on its internal *Lithium-Ion Battery*. In contrast, a typical *Data Centre* can be millions of times larger than a typical portable personal computing device and powered by a direct connection to the national electrical-power grid. Consequently, the types of integrated circuit used within a *Data Centre* can provide much more data processing than the integrated circuits used within portable personal computing devices. The data processing capabilities of integrated circuits used within the *Data Centre* can also be efficiently and effectively aggregated. When a STAD is used to access a STTP-based service the only thing that is likely to be of concern to a typical user is whether or not that service is actually able to provide the functionally and performance expected of that service. The technical capabilities, in terms of energy efficiency, memory capacity, processing speed, or any other relevant attribute, of the data processing hardware that was used to provide that service are no longer likely to be of any concern. So, whether single or multiple integrated circuits were used, or how many components were on those integrated circuits, becomes wholly irrelevant.

d) In a world based on Comprehensive Remote Personal Computing, enabled by technologies such as the Stream Tone, Moore's law could come to an end tomorrow and no one would really notice. Personal computing as we currently know it would continue pretty much unchanged. Everything that could be done before would still be possible after. In short, the end of Moore's law would not cause mankind to enter some sort of technological Dark Age because a new and better technology-architecture would have already been adopted. One that was far less sensitive to the number of transistors on an integrated circuit. Of course, Moore's law is unlikely to end for a good few more years, or maybe even decades, but when it does, it will, undoubtedly, be a significant moment. One that will mark the end of one era and the start of another. The point at which the computing industry is finally forced to look to totally different types of architecture, chemistry, and physics for the construction of its hardware. However, whilst Moore's law may eventually come to an end, the expectation that the quantity of data processing per unit of cost will double roughly every two years, which is the real-world consequence of Moore's law, will most probably not. Society has become accustomed to such advances, and will expect them to continue unabated in the future. So, Moore's law will probably be replaced with another, a corollary that effectively describes the natural consequence of the end of Moore's law and the shift to *Cloud Computing*; that the quantity of data processing per unit of cost provided by remotely-sourced digital services will double approximately every two years. No one will really care how this is achieved, and any technology that is capable of achieving it will be deemed acceptable. All that will be important is that the new law is able to hold true for a substantial period of time, and because this new law will not be based on being able to perpetually double the number of transistors on an integrated circuit for minimum cost approximately every two years, that should not be a significant problem, in fact it should be pretty darn easy.

# 5.1.10   SIMPLE

a)   Whilst the Stream Tone Access Device (STAD) might appear to be a normal personal computing device when in operation, and will be able to provide all the typical capabilities of such a device, it is not. The STAD will be a ***Thin Client*** for accessing Stream Tone Transfer Protocol (STTP)-based services that have been provided by a remotely-located Stream Tone Service Infrastructure and delivered using a Stream Tone Telecommunication Infrastructure. All the functionality that a STAD will offer will be obtained from STTP-based services, and the STAD will be fully optimised to work in this way. The STAD will be a dumb terminal that is really little different from the dumb computer terminals that were used to access mainframe computer services back in the 1970s. Of course, it will be built using the latest electronic technologies and know-how, and unlike the old dumb terminals will be available in a wide range of highly-portable and wirelessly-connected form factors.

b)   The core functionality of the STAD will not be changeable by a user, which is very different to a traditional personal computing device, the operation of which can be readily changed through the use of different operating systems and software applications. People that have grown up expecting to be able to change their personal computing device to meet their own unique needs will probably find the fixed nature of the STAD initially quite frustrating, but it will have been designed to be this way in order to provide functional stability and operational reliability. Preventing software-based changes helps to ensure that the capabilities and usefulness of the STAD will never be compromised by any type of modification during its lifetime.

c)   The software-based functionality of a STAD, what little of it there may be, will be designed to be static and only alterable by its manufacturer in exceptional circumstances. In fact, as the technology of the STAD matures it is expected to quickly become fully hardware-based with no software aspect at all; a zero client. A significant portion of the STAD's abilities will be achieved through application-specific hardware in order to deliver a highly-responsive user-experience and low power consumption. The STAD's embedded software stack, or firmware, will be designed to primarily glue the STAD's various hardware components together into a cohesive whole, and to support a simple diagnostic graphical user-interface. The STAD will be designed to be very durable, and in simple terms, if a STAD works the day it is first assembled in the factory then it should be able to work reliably after 10 years in the field.

# 5.1.11   UPGRADES

a)   In simple terms, operating systems provide the software-based functional environment within which application software is executed, or run. Operating systems also provide a standardised interface to the hardware-based functionality of a computing system. Operating systems are not only used on computer servers that are used to provide digital services, but also on traditional personal computing devices that are used by end-users to access such services.

b)   A new operating system is often obtained when a new personal computing device, containing that operating system is purchased. In such an instance, the user simply transfers any required application software and user-data onto that device and starts to use it. It is a relatively painless and straightforward process. An equally common method for obtaining a new operating system is by upgrading an existing installation of the same operating system or by replacing an existing installation of a completely different operating system; processes that are often complex, expensive, risky, and time consuming. Consequently, the upgrade or replacement of an operating system is often avoided, which can lead to a proliferation of outdated operating systems both on personal computing devices, as well as on computer servers. One of the principle hurdles that must be overcome before a new operating system can be adopted is whether the new operating system supports a seamless migration from the old operating system, such that all required application software, services, and user-data will continue to be available. If a seamless migration is not possible then there is likely to be huge resistance to changing to the new operating system. Even when a seamless migration is possible, many users still do not want to go through the inconvenience of upgrading what may well be a stable and well performing system; so users tend to wait until they need to replace their personal computing hardware, or the manufacturer forces the issue by no longer providing support for the version of the operating system currently installed. So even though a new operating system may offer many benefits, those benefits may never be realised. Some operating system developers release improvements incrementally in order to mitigate such problems, but sometimes a move to a wholly new operating system is simply the best and only solution.

c)   The Stream Tone can help to solve some of these problems. Firstly, the Stream Tone Access Device (STAD) does not contain an operating system, so a user will never be inconvenienced by the need to install an upgrade or replacement onto their personal computing device. Secondly, the Stream Tone Service Infrastructures (STSIs) that are used to provide Stream Tone Transfer Protocol (STTP)-based services are effectively under the direct control of the developers of those services, such that any new operating system that may be required can be installed at their convenience and in a manner that is wholly invisible to a typical user of those services. Thirdly, a complete personal computing environment, consisting of application software, operating system, and user-data, that has been migrated onto a STSI, in order to be accessed as a STTP-based service, will be able to use **Cloud Computing** technologies, such as **Virtual Machines**, to ease the process of upgrading or replacing the operating system portion of that environment. Being able to adopt the latest version of a currently installed operating system, or even being able to move to a radically different operating system, without significantly disrupting a STTP-based service's user community will particularly benefit businesses that previously took a much more conservative approach to such things because of the costs and risks involved. The Stream Tone will allow new operating systems to be more easily adopted, ensuring that the latest advancements in operating system technologies will be made available far quicker than was ever previously possible.

# 5.2 DISADVANTAGES

*Not all good*

## 5.2.1 ADVERTISING

a) All the Stream Tone Transfer Protocol (STTP)-based services that will be accessed using a Stream Tone Access Device will be provided by a remotely-located Stream Tone Service Infrastructure (STSI) and delivered by a Stream Tone Telecommunications Infrastructure. The data processing activity, also known as computer cycles, provided by that STSI will have a very real cost that someone will ultimately have to pay for.

b) Currently, **Web-based Service** providers employ a wide range of cost-recovery mechanisms in order to fund their digital service-provision activities, and STTP-based services will likely be no different. Some STTP-based services will be free, supported through advertising or philanthropy, and some will be chargeable.

c) A possible problem with the advertising-supported model of service provision is that advertising audio-visuals embedded within STTP-based data streams may in certain instances be highly annoying and intrusive. A STTP-based data stream is essentially unmodifiable because of the security mechanisms that the STTP uses to protect personal data and intellectual property whilst in transit. This means that any annoying or intrusive advertising cannot be blocked or circumvented, which is unlike most advertising currently delivered from the **Web** that can be blocked or circumvented fairly easily.

d) Of course, the same economic forces are at work today on the **Web**, which seems to have largely learnt how to deliver a very acceptable digital-service experience even when it is supported by advertising. However, by the time that the Stream Tone is in widespread use the data processing capabilities of the STSIs should be able to cost-effectively support the provision of most types of STTP-based service, which should help to mitigate some of the more annoying and intrusive behaviours of STTP-based advertisers. It should also be noted that in order to guarantee an acceptable and advertising-free STTP-based service experience some users may decide to subscribe to chargeable STTP-based services, in the same way that some viewers currently subscribe to cable or satellite-based television services in order to avoid advertising.

e) So whilst advertising is likely to be a key part of any Stream Tone-based future it should not, on the whole, lead to **Web-based Service** experiences that are any worse than those of today.

## 5.2.2 LICENSING

a) From a licensing perspective, running third-party software, whether it is a software application or an operating system, on a personal computing device that is physically in the possession of the software's owner is often considered to be very different to running the exact same piece software on remotely-located **Cloud Computing**-based infrastructures. Running software in circumstances that are not specifically supported by its license can be illegal. A Stream Tone Service Infrastructure is a remotely-located

*Cloud Computing*-based infrastructure that is used to provide Stream Tone Transfer Protocol (STTP)-based content and services that will then be delivered over a Stream Tone Telecommunications Infrastructure to a Stream Tone Access Device. *Cloud Computing*-related licensing issues may, therefore, adversely affect the use of third-party software applications and operating systems when they are accessed through a STTP-based service.

b)   In the past, when third-party software was licensed it was often assumed that it would be run on a single personal computing device that was located in the software owner's home or office. Running the exact same piece of software anywhere else, such as on a remotely-located *Cloud Computing*-based service, is considered to be illegal based on the terms and conditions of many current licenses. Being able to legally run third-party software on a remotely-located *Cloud Computing*-based service may, therefore, require a new license to be issued by the software's manufacturer; one that specifically supports this type of use. Unfortunately, licenses for existing third-party software may not be updated to support such a use, thereby requiring a new version of that software, which does support such a use, to be purchased. Unfortunately, purchasing new versions of third-party software may not always be practical, as suitably-licensed third-party software may not be available. Similar software with *Cloud Computing*-compatible licensing may be available from alternative sources, but such software may not always be able to provide the same level of functionality or quality of service as the original. In some instances, suitable alternative sources will simply not exist. Consequently, not being able to access certain types of commonly-used software-based functionality through remotely-located *Cloud Computing*-based services could significantly slow the adoption of the Stream Tone.

c)   New *Cloud Computing*-compatible licensing approaches are actively being developed by many application software and operating system vendors. Such approaches should ultimately benefit all software applications and operating systems that are run on remotely-located *Cloud Computing*-based infrastructures, including those of the Stream Tone.

# 5.2.3    MANUFACTURING

a)   The manufacturers of existing personal computing devices may be adversely affected by the emergence of the Stream Tone, which is a new technology platform that is expected to rapidly supplant the use of many older personal computing technologies. The manufacture of personal computing devices is a multi-billion dollar global business and some very large companies may be adversely impacted by the emergence of the Stream Tone if they do not quickly support the new personal computing paradigm that it introduces.

b)   Traditional personal computing devices will continue to have an important place in the world, but for most people, they will be increasingly seen as expensive tools for specialists, something that is no longer relevant to average folks. In mature markets, where a large portion of current personal computing device sales are due to repeat business, as people regularly upgrade to the latest model, it is expected that sales of such devices will become substantially reduced. Manufacturers that previously relied upon such sales, particularly those with markets that were limited to particular geographic regions, may need to start looking further afield, and adopt a much more global approach to their businesses. Some manufacturers that cannot effectively and efficiently compete in a global personal computing device market that is now based on Stream Tone technologies may need to radically change their business model or start to pursue completely different lines of business altogether.

c)  The Stream Tone Access Device (STAD) does not need to be regularly replaced, as it is designed to last a substantial period of time, is much simpler than a traditional personal computing device, and requires no hardware or software changes or updates, except possibly for modular repairs, throughout its life. The STAD is intended to be a low-cost device, and it is likely that it will be so affordable in certain markets that some users will own several. However, it is expected that sales into many mature markets will quickly reach saturation point. It is hoped that new markets for the STAD will rapidly emerge in developing countries, and that many of the manufacturers of traditional personal computing devices will switch over to producing STADs for such markets. Some emerging markets are expected to be substantial, as currently only a fraction of the world's 7 billion inhabitants own a personal computing device and have access to digital services. Even though all STADs are intended to be functionally identical, it is expected that manufacturers will supply them in a wide variety of styles and colours, catering to a broad range of customer tastes. A profitable after-market, selling add-ons, such as case covers, and carry pouches, is also expected to emerge, providing another possible business avenue for any manufacturer negatively impacted by the emergence of the Stream Tone.

# 5.2.4    MIGRATION

a)  Moving from a current personal computing environment to a new one has never been particularly easy, and even today often presents many costly and time-consuming challenges. The Stream Tone may suffer from similar problems, which could adversely impact the adoption of this important new technology. If the Stream Tone is to avoid such a consequence it will need to provide efficient and effective migration tools; some of which may need to be wholly new and unique in order to support the Stream Tone.

b)  However, as all current application software and operating systems are inherently supported by the Stream Tone, it is expected that, in most situations, migrating to a Stream Tone Transfer Protocol (STTP)-based personal computing solution will actually be quite painless and straightforward. In simple terms, it will only require that all user-data be copied from the old personal computing device to a STTP-based service. More complex migration scenarios may require the transfer of the entire digital image of an existing personal computing device onto a Stream Tone Service Infrastructure; such an approach would permit the creation of a fully-functional virtualised-version of the personal computing device that is indistinguishable from the original.

c)  Many of the migration challenges that the Stream Tone will face are identical to those already being faced during current migrations to **Cloud Computing**-based services, and, as the Stream Tone is also a **Cloud Computing**-based technology, many of the techniques and tools that have been created to support these current migrations will be reusable by the Stream Tone.

# 5.2.5   PROGRESS

a)   The Stream Tone Access Device (STAD) will be a hardware-based *Thin Client* for accessing Stream Tone Transfer Protocol (STTP)-based content and services provided by a remotely-located Stream Tone Service Infrastructure (STSI) and delivered by a Stream Tone Telecommunications Infrastructure (STTI). The STAD will essentially be a dumb computer terminal and, just like the dumb terminals that were used to access mainframe computers back in the 1970s, it will be designed to have a fixed and unchanging functionality. The STAD will not be programmable, and it will not require an operating system or support the execution of software applications. All of the user-oriented functionalities accessed by the STAD will be provided by STTP-based services. The STAD will have just enough data processing capability to fulfil its allotted task of presenting audio-visual data received from a STTP-based service and to send user-input back. The STAD will be designed in this way to reduce cost and increase reliability. A device that relies on STTP-based services does not need a powerful microprocessor and so will be cheaper to manufacture than a device that needs to support local data processing. A device that does not require an operating system or support the execution of software applications will be much simpler, and therefore more reliable, than a device that does.

b)   STTP-based services, the STSIs that will provide those services, the STTIs that will deliver those services, and limited aspects of the STTP, will all be able to change but the STAD that will be used to access those services will not. The potential problem with this type of design is that whilst the functionality of a STAD will not change throughout its life, the world, in which it will operate, will. New personal computing technologies are being developed all the time, and if the STAD is not able to support some, if not all, of them then it will quickly become obsolete, regardless of its initial benefits. The STAD will effectively become an immovable rock that is left behind the fast flowing river of technological progress. Of course, one of the key reasons that the Stream Tone concept was initially proposed was to stabilise the technology of personal computing devices so that such devices did not need to be replaced on a regular basis. Nevertheless, if a new or improved *Compression* or *Encryption* algorithm, display screen technology, navigational service, mobile or wireless communications standard, peripheral, or rechargeable-battery technology is developed then people will expect their STAD to be able to support it.

c)   In order to support new technologies the STAD will be based on a forward-compatible *Modular Design* approach. This approach will allow a wide range of new features and functionalities to be added to the STAD at a later date. The use of a *System on a Chip* (SOC) containing a general-purpose microprocessor will allow the STAD to use new *Compression* and *Encryption* algorithms. The use of a SOC containing application-specific semiconductor intellectual property cores will be able to accelerate a wide range of old and new data processing algorithms, including those for *Compression* and *Encryption*. All STAD built-in functionality will be based on removable single-function hardware modules, for which replacements and upgrades will be cheaply and readily available. The STAD hardware module interface will be intuitive, robust, and simple, and will allow all of the STAD's built-in functionalities to be easily repaired or upgraded, without the use of any tools, by an untrained user. For example, the installation of a new display screen would simply require that the old display screen module be manually removed and the new display screen module to be manually installed; a process that should only take a few seconds. The use of a *Software-Defined Radio* will allow the STAD to use the latest mobile and wireless communications standards simply by installing a software update. New peripherals, even those that did not exist when a STAD was manufactured, will be able to connect to a STAD using a standardised wireless peripheral interface, such as **Bluetooth** or **Wi-Fi**. The use of a removable **Lithium-Ion Battery** will allow the STAD's battery to be replaced when it is no longer functional or when a better rechargeable-battery technology becomes available. The behaviour of functionality built into a STAD will be changeable by updating microcode held on a **Solid-State Drive**.

d) Earlier in this book, it was suggested that the first STAD would contain a SOC based on relatively expensive but functionally changeable **Field-Programmable Gate Array** (FPGA) technology, which would then be superseded, when the design of the STTP was finalised, by a STAD that would contain a SOC based on less expensive but functionally unchangeable **Application-Specific Integrated Circuit** (ASIC) technology. This approach was suggested because it seemed to offer a way to significantly reduce the cost of manufacturing a STAD whilst also improving operational performance and power efficiency. However, a better approach may actually be a hybrid of the two; such that functionality that is most likely to remain stable will be implemented using a low-cost but unchangeable ASIC and functionality that is likely to change will be implemented using a more expensive but changeable FPGA. Such an approach is unlikely to reduce the cost of manufacturing a STAD but it would provide a way to retain the ability to support many new features and functionalities in the future. Having said all that, it would be strongly preferred if a purely ASIC-based approach for supporting new features and functionalities can be found because STAD manufacturing costs will need to be kept as low as possible so that the STAD will be affordable by everyone, everywhere.

e) So, even though the STAD will be a hardware-based device of fixed and unchanging functionality, it will still be possible for it to support a wide range of new technologies in the future if it is based on a forward-compatible **Modular Design** approach. Such an approach should ensure that the STAD will always be able to go with the flow of technological progress and not get left behind, like an immovable rock in a river.

# 5.2.6    RESEARCH AND DEVELOPMENT

a) The Stream Tone will not be appropriate for all usage scenarios, as there will undoubtedly be a whole host of applications that will continue to require local data processing, perhaps to control electromechanical systems or in medical fields where even the smallest possibility of an interruption to a remotely-sourced service would be considered highly unacceptable or even life threatening. The more traditional forms of personal computing that are required to support such usage scenarios will undoubtedly continue to exist long after the introduction of the Stream Tone, but the technological shift towards the Stream Tone may still have some far reaching and unexpected impacts on these older types of technology.

b) A general technological shift towards the Stream Tone may lead to a significant reduction in the research and development (R&D) activity that has historically been associated with more traditional forms of personal computing. R&D in one field often leads to benefits in another; so a reduction in R&D in the field of traditional personal computing may possibly have adverse impacts on many other fields, causing progress to slow and costs to rise in affected fields. R&D that supports the Stream Tone may not help other fields that, due to their very different natures, cannot benefit from advancements in data streaming technologies. So, the rise in popularity of the Stream Tone may have the unexpected and unwanted consequence that, for example, electromechanical control systems or medical equipment might become much more expensive.

c) Of course, such incidental problems are common when one technology replaces another, and normally such transitions occur with minimal inconvenience; the modern world is, after all, well accustomed to change in all its myriad forms.

## 5.2.7 RESILIENCE

a) The Stream Tone Access Device (STAD) is the primary mechanism for accessing Stream Tone Transfer Protocol (STTP)-based services; it is vulnerable to a single point of failure within the service and telecommunications infrastructures that are used to provide and deliver those services. As an essentially dumb-client technology, a STAD can do nothing without access to at least one fully-functional STTP-based service. If a STAD looses connectivity with a single service due to a failure of the Stream Tone Service Infrastructure (STSI) that is used to provide that service then the functionality normally provided by that service will no longer be available to the user of that STAD. If that service was supporting multiple users at the time of failure then all of those users will be adversely affected. Of course, if the Stream Tone Telecommunications Infrastructure (STTI) used to deliver that service is still functional then the STAD may be able to access alternative services. If there is a failure of the STTI that was delivering that service then access to all STTP-based services will be impossible and no useful functionality will be accessible through any connected STAD; at which point everyone using that particular STTI will have to stop work, or play. An event that could potentially affect hundreds, thousands, or even millions of people. This behaviour differs from a traditional personal computing device that supports local processing and which may be able to offer a wide range of alternative functionalities even though its connection to one particular digital service, or the *Internet* as a whole, has been lost.

b) The fact that the provision and delivery of STTP-based services is wholly dependent on a fully-functional service and telecommunications infrastructure is not unique to the Stream Tone as many other modern technologies, such as radio, telephony, television, and the *Web*, all have similar dependencies and are consequently equally susceptible to single points of failure to some degree. Ensuring that STTP-based services will not be subjected to unexpected downtime or degradation will require the use of a range of high-availability approaches, such as load-balancing, fail-over, and redundancy; approaches that are already successfully employed by many current service and telecommunications infrastructures. So whilst, unexpected downtime can never be totally prevented, it can be kept to an absolute minimum, ensuring that the Stream Tone can become a reliable part of our personal computing future.

## 5.2.8 RESOLUTION

a) The Stream Tone concept is being proposed at a time when display screen resolutions are rapidly increasing. It seems like it was really not all that long ago that high definition (HD) display screens, with a resolution of 1920 pixels by 1080 pixels (1080p), were considered to be more than good enough for most needs, particularly when used on personal computing devices, such as desktop computers, laptop computers, **Smart-Phones**, and **Tablet Computers**. Now, ultra high definition (UHD) display screens with resolutions of 3840 pixels by 2160 pixels (2160p) are starting to become the norm, and it will probably not be too long before display screens with resolutions of 7680 pixels by 4320 pixels (4320p) will also start to become more widely available.

b)  UHD display screen resolutions have, to a certain extent, been made desirable by personal computing device and television manufacturers looking for improved attributes to market. A television with a 2160p display screen has more pixels than a television with a 1080p display screen; so it must be better. Of course, there is no disputing that there are more pixels on 2160p display screen than there are on a 1080p display screen but whether the human eye can really discern the difference when watching a movie on a typically-sized television from 10 feet away is debatable. Also, when a 2160p display screen is used on a portable personal computing device,[29] such as a **Smart-Phone** or **Tablet Computer**, which have display screens that are generally no larger than 6 inches on the diagonal for a **Smart-Phone** and 13 inches on the diagonal for a **Tablet Computer**, whether the human eye can really discern any real improvement over a 1080p display screen is also debatable, because the pixels are already too small for most people to see.

c)  In simple terms, with each increase in resolution comes an increase in the amount of digital data that must be communicated in order to drive such display screens. Based on resolution alone, a 2160p display screen needs 4 times more data than a 1080p display screen and a 4320p display screen needs 16 times more data than a 1080p display screen. Additionally, in parallel with the recent increase in the resolution of display screens there has also been an increase in the use of visual content that requires higher display screen refresh rates, with both 2160p and 4320p display screens commonly being used at 60 frames per second (FPS), compared to the 30 FPS that is typically used with 1080p display screens. With the result that, in simple terms, a 2160p display screen can actually need 8 times more data than a 1080p display screen and a 4320p display screen can actually need 32 times more data than a 1080p display screen in order to optimally display the latest visual content.

d)  The amount of data communications bandwidth that will be required to make effective use of Stream Tone Transfer Protocol (STTP)-based services will be directly related to the resolution and refresh rate of the display screen used on the Stream Tone Access Device (STAD) to access those services. The higher the resolution and refresh rate of the STAD display screen the more data bandwidth that will be required to drive it, and the lower the resolution and refresh rate the less data bandwidth that will be required to drive it. The service infrastructures that the Stream Tone Service Infrastructures (STSIs) will initially use to provide STTP-based content and services have already reached a performance level that can easily support the widespread use of display screen resolutions of 1080p, but will probably require a wide range of improvements in order to support 2160p and 4320p. The telecommunications infrastructures that the Stream Tone Telecommunications Infrastructures (STTIs) will initially use to deliver the STTP-based content and services have almost reached a performance level that can support the widespread use of display screen resolutions of 1080p, but will definitely require a wide range of improvements in order to support 2160p and 4320p. If the use of UHD display screen resolutions

---

[29] *Current generation Smart-Phones and Tablet Computers support display screen resolutions of up to 1440p and 1600p, respectively. The next generations of these devices are expected to be able to support resolutions of up to 2160p.*

continues, as it seems that it will most likely do, then many STTP-based services may not be able to initially support them because many of the STSIs that will be used to provide those services and many of the STTIs that will be used to deliver those services may not be able to initially support the widespread use of such resolutions.

e)  A similar marketing-driven increase in the resolution of *Image Sensors*, such as those used in digital cameras and *Smart-Phones*, has started to slow a little, with the result that a few manufacturers have reduced the resolution of their *Image Sensors* in order to provide improved image quality, particularly in low light conditions. So perhaps the headlong rush towards higher display screen resolutions will also start to slow at some point in the future, particularly on portable personal computing devices with smaller-sized display screens, as consumers realise that resolution is not the only visual attribute that can be used to improve the display screen viewing experience. For example, three attributes that can have a very positive impact on the display screen viewing experience are brightness, colour gamut, and contrast. Individually, each of these attributes can be used to moderately improve viewing experiences, but when used together they can be used to substantially improve viewing experiences and create highly life-like imagery. Brightness, colour gamut, and contrast are all technical capabilities of the display screen hardware. Display screens that offer significantly increased brightness, colour gamut, and contrast are able to improve the viewing experience using existing image and video data sources, but for the very best results the source image and video data really needs to have an increased number of bits per pixel. This means that, for example, a pixel that was previously encoded using 24-bits per pixel (bpp) would need to use 30 bpp in order to make optimal use of significantly increased brightness, colour gamut, and contrast capabilities. In simple terms, based on screen resolution alone, this would increase the quantity of data required to display an image on a 1080p display screen from 49.8 megabits (Mb) to 62.2 Mb; a 25 percent increase, which is far less than the 400 percent increase that occurred when display screen resolutions were increased from 1080p to 2160p. Of course, a 1080p display screen, even one with significantly increased brightness, colour gamut, and contrast will always have fewer pixels than a 2160p display screen, but when used to view a movie on a typically-sized television from 10 feet away or on a *Smart-Phone* with a 6-inch display screen, will having fewer pixels really matter? Probably not enough to justify the cost of the extra data bandwidth that will be required to drive such displays, especially when the highly-noticeable benefits of increased brightness, colour gamut, and contrast are taken into account.

f)  The Stream Tone will be designed to support UHD visual data, right from its inception. For certain applications it may be both practical and highly cost-effective for STTP-based services to use HD images and video data even though it will be displayed on a STAD with a UHD display screen, particularly if that STAD is able to offer significantly increased brightness, colour gamut, and contrast. Of course, for some applications, which have been specifically designed to operate at UHD display screen resolutions, the use of HD images and video will simply not be option, and the cost of the extra data bandwidth that such applications will require in order to operate optimally cannot be avoided.

# 5.2.9  SECURITY

a)  Currently, a lot of people keep a large portion of their personal data, such as ebooks, games, photographs, music, spreadsheets, text files, videos, word-processing documents, and other digital material on their personal computing device. But given the fact that a

Stream Tone Access Device has no built-in data storage available for user-data, all such data will need to be stored on Stream Tone Transfer Protocol (STTP)-based services.

b)  The fact that nearly everyone's personal data would then be held on remotely-located **Cloud Computing**-based data storage services could lead to privacy infringements on a massive scale, if that data was accessed by unauthorised entities or even by overzealous governments. However, such a problem ought to be nearly impossible due to the policy that all data communicated using the STTP, or held within a STTP-based service, must be secured using strong **Encryption**. Nevertheless, having all personal data stored at arms length could be a worry for some people.

c)  Keeping personal data on a **File Hosting Service** or other **Web-based Service** is becoming increasingly common, and by the time the Stream Tone is in general use such behaviour is likely to be the accepted norm.

# 5.2.10  TELECOMMUNICATIONS

a)  For the Stream Tone to become a reality it needs highly affordable, high bandwidth, low latency, highly reliable, and ubiquitously available wireless telecommunications; something that may be not be possible for many years, due to the substantial upfront investments that will likely be required to build such capable and extensive telecommunications infrastructures. Without an affordable, high-performance, wireless telecommunications infrastructure available from day one, the Stream Tone will only be able to achieve its full potential in a fully-wired setting. Wired telecommunications, particularly those that use **Optical Fibre**-based connectivity, are already able to fully support Stream Tone Transfer Protocol (STTP)-based services. Wireless solutions, based on current technologies, may only permit STTP-based services to be experienced for limited periods of time or with reduced fidelity.

b)  A wired-only solution, or a limited and reduced wireless-based solution, may deter some people from adopting the Stream Tone and could possibly delay its deployment into geographies that only have less-advanced telecommunications infrastructures available. However, if such limitations do arise, they are only expected to last for a relatively short period of time as telecommunications infrastructures are continually evolving and maturing. Still, some very significant and costly improvements are going to be required before wireless telecommunications start to approach the affordability, availability, bandwidth, latency, and reliability of current wired solutions. Nevertheless, it is not expected that an initial absence of suitable wireless telecommunications infrastructures will adversely affect the creation and maturation of the Stream Tone.

# 5.2.11  VULNERABLE

a)  The Stream Tone is vulnerable to abuse. If either a Stream Tone Service Infrastructure (STSI) that is used to provide Stream Tone Transfer Protocol (STTP)-based services or a Stream Tone Telecommunications Infrastructure (STTI) that is used to deliver STTP-based services were purposefully disabled then very large numbers of people could be adversely affected. For example, hackers might interrupt the operations of a STSI or block the communications mechanisms of a STTI for criminal, ideological, or mischievous reasons. Civil unrest might be quashed by a dictatorial regime that blocks access to particular STTP-based services or to a particular STTI in order to curtail the spread of dissent. Because Stream Tone Access Devices (STADs) are useless without access to STTP-based services, removing access to such services, or even threatening to remove access to such services, could be used to exert significant influence over a populace that, as a whole, might have become highly reliant on the use of STADs and STTP-based services.

b) Of course, similar concerns could be expressed about many of life's other essential services, such as electricity, gas, postal, sewerage, telephony, or water, but which, from a global perspective, are rarely abused or persistently attacked. Sometimes, regardless of a technology's actual or theoretical vulnerabilities, society just has to move forward and focus on obtaining the immediately realisable benefits of adopting that technology. Society cannot, and should not, be paralysed by the mere possibility of a threat when genuine benefits are clearly achievable. For example, just because a communal water supply may be vulnerable to terrorist attack does not mean that such a technology should not be adopted or that everyone should have to dig their own water well. On the contrary, the communal water supply should be built so that everyone will have easy access to the potable water that they need to live, and the water supply should be appropriately protected against any reasonable possibility of attack.

c) So, even though the Stream Tone may have its own particular vulnerabilities, such as abuse by hackers or dictatorial regimes, any concerns that may exist over such vulnerabilities should not be allowed to hinder the design, development, or deployment of such an important new technology. Instead, those vulnerabilities simply need to be thoroughly understood and, where practical, fully mitigated.

# 6    CONCLUSION

*The final analysis*

a)    At the beginning of this book, it was suggested that **Data Centres** might one day grow to be mankind's equivalent of the fictional Great Machine of the Krell. That suggestion, while obviously a little far fetched and definitely tongue-in-cheek, was based on the simple notion that the capabilities and role of the modern **Data Centre** are going to continue growing, possibly at exponential rates, and that the **Data Centre** will eventually become the very best place for all types of personal computing in the future. Nearly all the personal computing that we perform today, using local personal computing devices, such as desktop computers, laptop computers, **Smart-Phones**, and **Tablet Computers**, can, if we wish, be moved into the **Data Centre** tomorrow. The consequence of such a move would be that **Data Centres** would need to grow in both capability and size, and if they grow enough then perhaps they can become our very own Great Machines. Who knows what mankind will then be able to achieve. A cure for cancer? A solution for global warming? Artificial intelligence? Dyson spheres? Faster than light travel? Flying cars? Hover boards? Immortality? Jet packs? Moon bases? Nuclear fusion energy? Personal robots? The discovery of alien life? The end of world hunger? The unification of general relativity and quantum mechanics? Whole brain emulation? World peace? Or, perhaps, personal computing that is so seamlessly and unobtrusively woven into the very fabric of our lives that it is finally indistinguishable from magic. Anything could be possible in such a future. We just won't know until we have our own Great Machines to play with.

b)    It may seem impossible that the way we perform personal computing could ever change, but the replacement of local personal computing functionalities with functionalities that are executed in remotely-located **Data Centres** is already well under way. Today, we call this new type of computing, **Cloud Computing**. However, **Cloud Computing** is just a small, but nonetheless critically important, part of what will actually be needed to completely shift society from local personal computing devices to remote personal computing services. It will require a service infrastructure that can provide all required personal computing services, a communications protocol that can communicate those services, a telecommunications infrastructure that can deliver those services, and a device that can access those services. In other words, it will need a complete technology ecosystem. This is exactly what the Stream Tone aims to provide, and why it is so much more than just **Cloud Computing** by another name. In fact, this is why it is more than all the individual technologies from which the Stream Tone will be built. The Stream Tone will be the purposeful, holistic, approach to solving the problem of how to implement Comprehensive Remote Personal Computing (CRPC) for the benefit of everyone, everywhere, not just the rich living in developed countries. The Stream Tone will bring accelerated advancement and technological stability, help to bring the **Internet**, personal computing, and **Web** to the next billion people, and change the world for the better in ways we cannot even begin to guess at today.

c)    This book has considered the Stream Tone concept from three simple perspectives; the past, the present, and the future. The chapter on the past briefly discussed some of the inspirational work of the father of Information Science, Paul Otlet, as well as briefly summarising the history of personal computing. Lessons from the past suggested that centralised information services were not only possible but could also offer some very real benefits to modern personal computing, that simpler personal computing devices could be more reliable than complex personal computing devices, and that the telecommunications technologies used to connect such services to such devices were continually improving and were almost at the point where they could support a complete and total shift to a new type of personal computing. The chapter on the present discussed some of the building blocks from which the Stream Tone could possibly be built, as well as some of the precursors to the Stream Tone that already exist today. Lessons of the present suggested that a very wide range of existing technologies are available from which the Stream Tone could be built, and that the apparent existence of many precursors to the Stream Tone suggested that certain aspects of the Stream Tone may already exist, albeit in nascent forms. The chapter on the future speculated on the technology ecosystem that will be required to support the Stream Tone, the many different ways in which the Stream Tone could potentially be used, the commercial opportunities that the Stream Tone could bring to business, and a timeline for the design, development, and deployment of the Stream Tone. Lessons for the future suggested that a realistic and believable world based on the Stream Tone could be successfully described from a number of different perspectives. Each of these chapters was able to put a small piece of speculative flesh onto the speculative bones of the Stream Tone, and by so doing has helped to create a much better understanding of just what sort of a beast the Stream Tone could potentially be. Of course, this is all still a fiction, because the Stream Tone does not exist in any way, except in the pages of this book. Nevertheless, it now feels a little more detailed. A little more tangible. A little more ready to become the foundation for the future of personal computing.

d) Whilst the Stream Tone will be, in many ways, a new technology, it is one that will be based on the client-server architectural model that has been a mainstay of the computing industry for many years. The Stream Tone will be a purposeful return to the some of the earliest days of computing, when mainframe computers were accessed through dumb computer terminals. All data processing was performed on the mainframe computer, and the computer terminal was just a simple mechanism to input data and instructions, and a medium for viewing the results of that processing. The computer terminal was a simple and relatively inexpensive device, certainly when compared to the complexity and expense of the typical mainframe computer that it was connected to via serial communications links. The Stream Tone will also use a simple and inexpensive client device to access digital content and services that are provided by remotely-located computer servers, which are the modern day successors to the old mainframe computers. The digital content and services will then be carried using a secure data streaming communications protocol that is optimised for real-time operations, and delivered using industry-standard telecommunications infrastructures. The Stream Tone will represent the point at which personal computing architectures have finally gone full circle, from centralised to distributed, and back to centralised again. The Stream Tone may be inspired by a technology from the past but it will have a thoroughly modern implementation that is more than capable of taking mankind into a new and exciting CRPC-based era.

e) One of the key technologies that the Stream Tone will be highly dependent upon, but which it may have very little direct influence over, is that of telecommunications. Today, wired telecommunications infrastructures are already able to support most of the affordability, availability, bandwidth, latency, and reliability requirements of the Stream Tone, but wireless telecommunications infrastructures are still far from ready. Significant improvements will be required before such infrastructures are able to fully support all of the Stream Tone's many requirements, and such improvements may arrive far quicker than might otherwise be expected. Over the last thirty-five years wired telecommunications bandwidths have increased more than a million fold, whilst over the last fifteen years wireless telecommunications bandwidths have increased more than a thousand fold, and there is every expectation that both types of telecommunications will only continue to improve in the future, possibly at an even greater pace than they have in the past. It will, therefore, probably not be too long before wireless telecommunications infrastructures are able to catch up with their wired brethren, and both types of infrastructure will finally be able to provide the Stream Tone with all that it requires to change the world of personal computing.

f)  The Stream Tone will be designed to benefit everyone, everywhere, primarily through its use of a low cost and long-lasting Stream Tone Access Device (STAD), and by wholly moving the development of Stream Tone Transfer Protocol (STTP)-based services away from that device and onto the Stream Tone Service Infrastructures (STSIs) that will be used to provide those services. STTP-based content and services will then be delivered using a Stream Tone Telecommunications Infrastructure (STTI). Together, the STAD, STSI, STTI, and STTP will comprise the Stream Tone Technology Ecosystem (STTE). The Stream Tone will stimulate significant improvements in terms of the affordability, availability, bandwidth, latency, and reliability of the hardware and software systems that comprise the STTE. The Stream Tone will shift capital expenditure, which was previously spent on personal computing devices, to operational expenditure, which will be spent on STTP-based services. Many STTP-based services will be made available free-of-charge, funded by advertising or philanthropy, whilst others will be chargeable. Some types of STTP-based services will be surprisingly expensive. The cost of providing and delivering all types of STTP-based services are expected to substantially reduce over time. Many new and existing businesses will find many opportunities to make both a name for themselves and a commercial profit from the changes that the Stream Tone will bring to the world. One particular way that businesses will be able to benefit from the Stream Tone is that it will allow the creation of uniquely branded user experiences that businesses are able to fully control. The Stream Tone will become an integral part of the technology ecosystem that powers the *Internet* and the *Web*. The existing *Web* will remain largely unchanged by the Stream Tone, with one notable exception, that all of its content and services will become accessible using the STTP. It is hoped that the Stream Tone will be developed based on free and open-source principles. The Stream Tone will seek to reuse and re-purpose as many existing technologies as possible. In an ideal world, the Stream Tone will be nothing more than the conceptual and technological glue that binds the Stream Tone's constituent parts together. Its global development community will be based on consensus, equality, and respect.

g)  As was noted in the chapter on reflections, the Stream Tone is not yet a completely perfect technology. Even at this early stage in its life it obviously possesses a number of disadvantages in addition to its many advantages. Fully understanding those disadvantages should allow many of them to be mitigated, and the earlier that process of understanding starts the better. It is always easier and cheaper to fix problems earlier in the life of a project, during the requirements and design phases, than later, during the implementation, testing, release, or support phases. So hopefully, the imperfect concept that the Stream Tone is today will become the much less imperfect technology that enables CRPC in the future.

h)  The next step in the life of the Stream Tone is for lots of other people to become involved. To bring their collective experience, ideas, intellects, knowledge, skills, and understanding to bear on the challenge of how to create the Stream Tone. To study this book and help to determine which bits make sense and should be kept, and which bits do not and should be discarded. If you feel that you have something useful to contribute, please do. All are welcome to join this endeavour. So, put your best thinking cap on and form an orderly line, because the future of personal computing may very well be starting right here...

# 7   EPILOGUE

*Last words*

a)   My book is now finished, or as close to being finished as it is ever likely to be. Basically, I managed to herd my technological cats into a momentary configuration that was sufficient for basic comprehension and quickly hit the save key. It was not easy; they were very naughty cats.

b)   My belief, that personal computing will transition to a wholly **Web**-based mode of operation at some point in the future, remains as strong today as it was the day I started writing this book. Currently, this transition seems to be largely uncoordinated, and subject to potentially conflicting and divisive commercial interests. Some sort of broadly-inclusive and unifying initiative, such as the Stream Tone, is clearly going to be required if an affordable and non-proprietary Comprehensive Remote Personal Computing (CRPC) solution that is suitable for use by everyone, everywhere, is ever going to be realised.

c)   It is estimated that **Fifth-Generation Mobile Communications** will start to become available around 2020, and may be able to support data bandwidths of up to 10 gigabits per second. It has been asked what type of digital content or services will need, or be able to make effective use of, such bandwidths. My answer to that question is very simple; Stream Tone-based CRPC. The mobile communications services of 2020 may provide 30 times[30] more bandwidth than the fastest services of 2014 but they are very unlikely to cost 30 times more; they are, in fact, likely to have costs that are very similar to those of 2014. So, unless ridiculously small download caps[31] are still being imposed in 2020, CRPC, as enabled by the Stream Tone, will definitely be affordable and feasible.

d)   The concept of the Stream Tone did not suddenly appear fully formed in my mind one day. It grew from the small seed of an idea, and evolved slowly over an extended period of time. It became much simpler in some ways, and far more complex in others. As a consequence, this book probably contains a number of imperfections and inconsistencies. Also, with hindsight, many subjective decisions, such as the choice of building blocks and precursors could have been better, supporting arguments could have been stronger, trivial subjects could have been more concise, important subjects could have been more detailed, and the alphabet soup of acronyms and the use of Handwavium[32] could have been reduced. Nevertheless, I hope that you, my reader, will have been able to follow the scant trail of bits and bytes left behind my technological meanderings to make sense of an idea that continues to be very important to me. I hope that it can, in some small way, also become important to you too.

---

[30] *Based on the maximum theoretical bandwidth that is commercially available in 2014 of 300 megabits per second.*
[31] *At a bandwidth of 10 gigabits per second a download cap of one gigabyte per month would be reached in 0.8 seconds.*
[32] *A hand wave is often used to gloss over a problem; suggesting that the details of the problem should be ignored, regardless of how complex or intractable the problem may actually be. Handwavium is a conveniently available, mysterious, and possibly magical element that can be used to easily solve any highly complex or intractable problem, such as the Stream Tone. Handwavium is a television trope.*

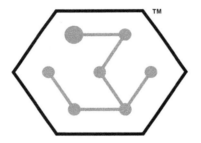

# 8    INDEX

*From A to Z*

## A

# B

# F

# G

# M

# Q

# R

# S

# T

# U

# V

# W

www.ingramcontent.com/pod-product-compliance
Lightning Source LLC
Chambersburg PA
CBHW051044050326
40690CB00006B/591